Novel Applications of Optical Sensors and Machine Learning in Agricultural Monitoring—2nd Edition

Novel Applications of Optical Sensors and Machine Learning in Agricultural Monitoring—2nd Edition

Guest Editors

Haikuan Feng
Yanjun Yang
Ning Zhang
Chengquan Zhou
Jibo Yue

MDPI

Basel • Beijing • Wuhan • Barcelona • Belgrade • Novi Sad • Cluj • Manchester

Guest Editors

Haikuan Feng
Information Technology Research Center
Beijing Academy of Agriculture and Forestry Sciences
Beijing
China

Yanjun Yang
Institute of Botany
Chinese Academy of Sciences
Beijing
China

Ning Zhang
Agricultural Information Institute
Chinese Academy of Agricultural Sciences
Beijing
China

Chengquan Zhou
Institute of Agricultural Equipment
Zhejiang Academy of Agricultural Sciences
Hangzhou
China

Jibo Yue
College of Information and Management Science
Henan Agricultural University
Zhengzhou
China

Editorial Office
MDPI AG
Grosspeteranlage 5
4052 Basel, Switzerland

This is a reprint of the Special Issue, published open access by the journal *Agriculture* (ISSN 2077-0472), freely accessible at: https://www.mdpi.com/journal/agriculture/special_issues/UGGAROVY74.

For citation purposes, cite each article independently as indicated on the article page online and as indicated below:

Lastname, A.A.; Lastname, B.B. Article Title. *Journal Name* **Year**, *Volume Number*, Page Range.

ISBN 978-3-7258-6814-8 (Hbk)
ISBN 978-3-7258-6815-5 (PDF)
https://doi.org/10.3390/books978-3-7258-6815-5

Contents

agriculture

Editorial

Novel Applications of Optical Sensors and Machine Learning in Agricultural Monitoring—2nd Edition

Haikuan Feng [1,2], Yanjun Yang [3], Ning Zhang [4], Chengquan Zhou [5] and Jibo Yue [1,*]

1 College of Information and Management Science, Henan Agricultural University, Zhengzhou 450002, China; fenghk@nercita.org.cn
2 Key Laboratory of Quantitative Remote Sensing in Agriculture of Ministry of Agriculture and Rural Affairs, Information Technology Research Center, Beijing Academy of Agriculture and Forestry Sciences, Beijing 100097, China
3 College of Agro-Grassland Science, Nanjing Agricultural University, Nanjing 210095, China; yanjunyang@njau.edu.cn
4 Agricultural Information Institute, Chinese Academy of Agricultural Sciences, Beijing 100081, China; zhangning@caas.cn
5 Institute of Agricultural Equipment, Zhejiang Academy of Agricultural Sciences, Hangzhou 310021, China; zhoucq@zaas.ac.cn
* Correspondence: yuejibo@henau.edu.cn

1. Introduction

The integration of optical sensors and machine learning (ML) technologies has revolutionized agricultural monitoring, enabling precise, real-time insights into crop health, growth dynamics, and environmental interactions [1]. As global agriculture faces mounting challenges from climate change, population growth, and resource scarcity, these tools offer scalable solutions for enhancing productivity, sustainability, and resilience [2]. Optical sensors, ranging from multispectral and hyperspectral cameras to RGB cameras, capture detailed spectral signatures that reveal subtle physiological changes in crops, such as chlorophyll content, water stress, and nutrient deficiencies [3]. When combined with ML algorithms, these data streams are transformed into actionable intelligence, supporting decisions in precision farming, yield prediction, and disease management.

The second edition of the Special Issue "Novel Applications of Optical Sensors and Machine Learning in Agricultural Monitoring" expands on the foundational work established by previous studies in the field, including related editorials that highlight the synergy between optical sensing and deep learning for smart agriculture. For instance, advancements in unmanned aerial vehicle (UAV)-based multispectral imaging and deep neural networks have demonstrated substantial improvements in production management, as evidenced by recent compilations of research emphasizing real-time detection and phenotyping. The first edition of this thematic issue highlighted early breakthroughs in applying these technologies to staple crops, whereas the present edition broadens the scope to encompass a wider range of applications across different crop types, growth stages, and environmental conditions.

Comprising 17 original research articles, this collection addresses critical gaps in current methodologies, such as handling data imbalance, enhancing model transferability, and integrating multi-sensor data for robust monitoring. The contributions in this issue span a wide array of innovations, from hyperspectral data processing for disease severity estimation to UAV-derived digital surface models for biomass prediction. They collectively underscore the evolving role of optical sensors in capturing high-resolution, multi-dimensional data, which ML models then leverage for pattern recognition and predictive analytics. Key themes include the use of radiative transfer models (RTMs) coupled with ML for parameter inversion, time-series analysis for phenological tracking, and lightweight deep learning architectures for on-field deployment [4]. These studies not only refine existing techniques but also lay the groundwork for future integrations, such as edge computing and artificial intelligence (AI)-driven automation in agricultural systems.

2. Overview of Contributions

Optical sensors can provide non-invasive, high-throughput data for monitoring crop status. Multispectral sensors, deployed on UAVs or satellites platforms such as Sentinel-2, capture reflectance across visible, near-infrared, and red-edge spectral bands, enabling the derivation of vegetation indices (VIs) such as NDRE, CIRE, and NDVI [5]. These indices are sensitive to chlorophyll, LAI, and biomass, but saturation in dense canopies remains a challenge. Hyperspectral sensors offer finer resolution (e.g., 400–1000 nm), revealing subtle biochemical signatures for disease detection and nutrient estimation, as demonstrated in studies using ASD spectrometers or UAV-mounted imagers. Using RTMs such as PROSAIL to simulate spectra, aiding parameter inversion with reduced-field measurements [6]. Moreover, integration with platforms such as UAVs has democratized access, enabling plot-scale phenotyping at high resolution [7].

ML has transformed raw sensor data into predictive insights, with deep learning dominating owing to its strong feature-extraction capabilities [8]. Convolutional neural networks (CNNs), transformers, and hybrid models can handle complex tasks such as image segmentation [9], classification [10], and regression [11]. Emerging trends integrate optical sensors with AI for opto-intelligent agriculture, including edge–cloud collaborative inference and meta-learning for improved model adaptability. In addition, multi-sensor data fusion, particularly the integration of optical and SAR observations, helps overcome weather-related limitations and has proven effective in crop parameter estimation [12].

This editorial summarizes the 17 papers by grouping them thematically and provides an in-depth analysis of the current state and emerging trends in the field, leveraging recent advancements to forecast future research directions. They can be broadly categorized into four themes (Table 1): (1) hyperspectral and multispectral data for crop parameter estimation; (2) UAV-based imagery for yield and growth monitoring; (3) disease and stress detection using spectral analysis and deep learning; and (4) phenological and structural modeling with integrated sensor data. Each paper presents novel methodologies validated through field experiments and emphasizes their practical implications for precision agriculture.

Several papers focus on leveraging hyperspectral and multispectral sensors to estimate key crop parameters like leaf area index (LAI), chlorophyll content (LCC), and nitrogen levels. In one study, researchers developed a coupled radiative transfer model integrated with UAV hyperspectral data to estimate rice canopy LAI and LCC [13]. The model outperformed the traditional PROSAIL by reducing RMSE by 0.0359 in spectral simulations, and when combined with extreme learning machine (ELM), achieved RMSE values of 0.6357 for LAI and 6.0101 $\mu g \cdot cm^{-2}$ for LCC. This approach demonstrates the value of mechanistic models in enhancing ML-driven inversions. Another contribution explored multispectral UAV imaging combined with PROSAIL and ML (random forest (RF) and partial least squares regression (PLSR)) to estimate potato LAI across growth stages [14]. The hybrid model improved R^2 by up to 263% over lookup table methods, with final R^2 = 0.87, emphasizing the role of red-edge bands in overcoming saturation issues. In a novel frequency-domain approach, hyperspectral data from rice were transformed using wavelet packet transform, first-order differentiation, and harmonic analysis, then fed into a deep neural network. This yielded $R^2 > 0.9$ for single-stage chlorophyll estimation and $R^2 = 0.971$ across periods, showcasing data compression techniques for improved stability [15]. Similarly, for winter wheat nitrogen content, multispectral features (spectral, texture, structural) were fused in ML models, with RF achieving $R^2 = 0.90$ across stages and varieties, highlighting variety-specific sensitivities [16]. Near-infrared spectroscopy was also applied for fertilizer detection, with back propagation neural networks and competitive adaptive reweighted sampling achieving 93% accuracy in identifying fertilizer types and concentrations, with RMSE values ranging from 1.0034 to 2.4947 [17].

Table 1. Summary of publications in this Special Issue.

Articles	Models	Sensors	Platforms	Authors	References
1	PROSAIL + ELM	GaiaSky-mini	UAV	Jin et al.	[13]
2	PROSAIL + RF + PLSR	RedEdge-P	UAV	Li et al.	[14]
3	WPT-FD-HA + DNN	ASD FieldSpec 4	Field	Du et al.	[15]
4	GPR + RF + PLSR + SVR	DJI Phantom 4	UAV	Shu et al.	[16]
5	BPNN + PLSR + SVR	Cary 5000 NIR	Field	Ma et al.	[17]
6	K-Shape Clustering	MCA	UAV	Li et al.	[18]
7	BPNN	K6 multispectral	UAV	Guo et al.	[19]
8	RF + PLSR	DSC-QX100	UAV	Yang et al.	[20]
9	DeepLabV3	Sentinel-2	Satellite	Maleki et al.	[21]
10	ResNeSt_E	HIS-VNIR-B1621	Field	Huang et al.	[22]
11	FOD + CNN	ASD Field Spec3	Field	Sun et al.	[23]
12	Mask R-CNN(Swin-T)	Canon IXY DIGITAL 220 IS + Samsung MV800	Field	Seo et al.	[24]
13	CCRSNet	iPhone 14 Pro	Field	Gao et al.	[25]
14	Phenofit	MODIS	Satellite	Lin et al.	[26]
15	Color Index	Canon EOS M50 Mark II	Field	Wang et al.	[27]
16	WCM	Sentinel-1	Satellite	Wang et al.	[28]
17	AFX	MODIS	Satellite	Lin et al.	[29]

UAV platforms dominate several studies for their high-resolution capabilities in yield prediction and biomass estimation. One study clustered time-series UAV RGB images and multispectral data using k-shape to predict multi-genotype rice yield, with canopy volume curves yielding $R^2 = 0.82$ and RMSE = 315.39 kg/ha, outperforming spectral features [18]. For winter wheat biomass, UAV-derived digital surface models provided plant height, integrated into a back propagation (BP) neural network via AGB/height ratio, boosting R^2 to 0.88 and reducing RMSE by 51.72% [19]. Yield estimation in winter wheat used UAV digital images to extract color indexes and texture features, fused in PLSR and RF models, with fused features at filling stage achieving $R^2 = 0.76$ [20]. Another study refined Cropland Data Layer using confidence intervals and filters, improving DL segmentation accuracy by 1.5% for major crops via Sentinel-2 composites [21].

Disease monitoring features prominently, with hyperspectral imaging and ML detecting mechanical damage in corn seeds. A ResNeSt_E network with joint dimensionality reduction (PCA + FA) achieved 99.0% accuracy [22]. For peanut southern blight, SMOTE and fractional-order differentiation enhanced 1D-CNN performance, yielding OA = 88.81% validation and 82.76% testing [23]. Peach fruit segmentation under adverse conditions used Swin Transformer in Mask R-CNN, achieving AP = 60.2 overall and 40.4 for small objects, doubling CNN-based performance [24]. Crop residue coverage was segmented using a CCRSNet deep learning model from smartphone images, with mIoU = 92.73% and RMSE = 1.05–3.56% for proportions [25].

MODIS NDVI and the phenofit package were used for Phenology tracking for post-extreme events, revealing EOS delays (e.g., 4.97 days for cropland) after 2021 rainfall in

Henan, with recovery by 2022 [26]. Anthocyanin phenotyping in purple corn employed digital cameras and color indexes, with linear models achieving NRMSE < 30% across organs [27]. Corn growth parameters were estimated by integrating optical vegetation indexes with SAR differential radar information in the Water Cloud Model, reducing nRMSE to 14.64% for height using red-edge features [28]. Phenological impacts on MODIS-derived fractional vegetation cover were analyzed, indicating that Bidirectional Reflectance Distribution Function corrections enhance accuracy during stable growth phases but not at season transitions [29]. These papers collectively advance the field by addressing data challenges, model robustness, and practical deployment, with many achieving $R^2 > 0.8$ and RMSE reductions of 20–50% over baselines.

The sector involving optical sensors and ML-driven precision farming tools is advancing rapidly, propelled by advancing technological capabilities and critical global demands arising from shifting weather patterns, workforce shortages, and the imperative to feed an anticipated 10.3 billion inhabitants by the middle of the 2080s. Optical sensing technologies, including hyperspectral imaging and near-infrared spectroscopy, are increasingly deployed via UAVs, satellites, and ground-based platforms to monitor crop traits non-destructively. Machine learning, particularly deep learning variants such as CNNs and transformers, has enabled the extraction of complex features from these data, improving accuracy in tasks such as yield estimation and stress detection. Challenges include data volume, noise, and cost, but innovations such as lightweight sensors and edge processing are mitigating these challenges. Deep-tech domains such as AI-driven robotics will enhance climate resilience. Challenges related to ethical AI and data privacy must be carefully addressed; nevertheless, the overall trajectory points to transformative impacts on global food systems. This second edition advances the application of optical sensors and ML in agricultural monitoring, with 17 papers offering innovative solutions validated in real-world settings. From hyperspectral chlorophyll estimation to UAV biomass modeling, the contributions enhance accuracy and practicality. Looking ahead, the field's status is robust, with trends toward fusion, automation, and sustainability promising to bolster food security.

Conflicts of Interest: The authors declare no conflicts of interest.

References

1. LeCun, Y.; Bengio, Y.; Hinton, G. Deep Learning. *Nature* **2015**, *521*, 436–444. [CrossRef]
2. Hultgren, A.; Carleton, T.; Delgado, M.; Gergel, D.R.; Greenstone, M.; Houser, T.; Hsiang, S.; Jina, A.; Kopp, R.E.; Malevich, S.B.; et al. Impacts of Climate Change on Global Agriculture Accounting for Adaptation. *Nature* **2025**, *642*, 644–652. [CrossRef] [PubMed]
3. Umapathi, R.; Park, B.; Sonwal, S.; Rani, G.M.; Cho, Y.; Huh, Y.S. Advances in Optical-Sensing Strategies for the on-Site Detection of Pesticides in Agricultural Foods. *Trends Food Sci. Technol.* **2022**, *119*, 69–89. [CrossRef]
4. Yu, F.; Bai, J.; Fang, J.; Guo, S.; Zhu, S.; Xu, T. Integration of a Parameter Combination Discriminator Improves the Accuracy of Chlorophyll Inversion from Spectral Imaging of Rice. *Agric. Commun.* **2024**, *2*, 100055. [CrossRef]
5. Rouse, J.W.; Haas, R.H.; Schell, J.A.; Deering, D.W. Monitoring Vegetation Systems in the Great Plains with ERTS. In *Proceedings of the Third ERTS-1 Symposium*; NASA: Washington, DC, USA, 1974; Volume 1, pp. 309–317.
6. Sun, Q.; Jiao, Q.; Chen, X.; Xing, H.; Huang, W.; Zhang, B. Machine Learning Algorithms for the Retrieval of Canopy Chlorophyll Content and Leaf Area Index of Crops Using the PROSAIL-D Model with the Adjusted Average Leaf Angle. *Remote Sens.* **2023**, *15*, 2264. [CrossRef]
7. Bongomin, O.; Lamo, J.; Guina, J.M.; Okello, C.; Ocen, G.G.; Obura, M.; Alibu, S.; Owino, C.A.; Akwero, A.; Ojok, S. UAV Image Acquisition and Processing for High-throughput Phenotyping in Agricultural Research and Breeding Programs. *Plant Phenome J.* **2024**, *7*, e20096. [CrossRef]
8. Zhu, W.; Rezaei, E.E.; Nouri, H.; Sun, Z.; Li, J.; Yu, D.; Siebert, S. UAV-Based Indicators of Crop Growth Are Robust for Distinct Water and Nutrient Management but Vary between Crop Development Phases. *Field Crops Res.* **2022**, *284*, 108582. [CrossRef]
9. Ronneberger, O.; Fischer, P.; Brox, T. U-Net: Convolutional Networks for Biomedical Image Segmentation. In *Medical Image Computing and Computer-Assisted Intervention—MICCAI 2015*; Spring: Berlin/Heidelberg, Germany, 2015; pp. 234–241.

https://doi.org/10.3390/agriculture16020271

10. Sangeetha, V.; Prasad, K.J.R. Deep Residual Learning for Image Recognition. *ChemInform* **2006**, *37*, 1951–1954. [CrossRef]
11. Yue, J.; Li, T.; Feng, H.; Fu, Y.; Liu, Y.; Tian, J.; Yang, H.; Yang, G. Enhancing Field Soil Moisture Content Monitoring Using Laboratory-Based Soil Spectral Measurements and Radiative Transfer Models. *Agric. Commun.* **2024**, *2*, 100060. [CrossRef]
12. Zhang, R.; Yang, Y.; Li, Z.; Li, P.; Wang, H. Optical and SAR Image Fusion: A Review of Theories, Methods, and Applications. *Remote Sens.* **2025**, *18*, 73. [CrossRef]
13. Jin, Z.; Liu, H.; Cao, H.; Li, S.; Yu, F.; Xu, T. Hyperspectral Remote Sensing Estimation of Rice Canopy LAI and LCC by UAV Coupled RTM and Machine Learning. *Agriculture* **2024**, *15*, 11. [CrossRef]
14. Li, S.; Lin, Y.; Zhu, P.; Jin, L.; Bian, C.; Liu, J. Combining UAV Multispectral Imaging and PROSAIL Model to Estimate LAI of Potato at Plot Scale. *Agriculture* **2024**, *14*, 2159. [CrossRef]
15. Du, L.; Luo, S. Spectral-Frequency Conversion Derived from Hyperspectral Data Combined with Deep Learning for Estimating Chlorophyll Content in Rice. *Agriculture* **2024**, *14*, 1186. [CrossRef]
16. Shu, M.; Wang, Z.; Guo, W.; Qiao, H.; Fu, Y.; Guo, Y.; Wang, L.; Ma, Y.; Gu, X. Effects of Variety and Growth Stage on UAV Multispectral Estimation of Plant Nitrogen Content of Winter Wheat. *Agriculture* **2024**, *14*, 1775. [CrossRef]
17. Ma, Y.; Wu, Z.; Cheng, Y.; Chen, S.; Li, J. Rapid Detection of Fertilizer Information Based on Near-Infrared Spectroscopy and Machine Learning and the Design of a Detection Device. *Agriculture* **2024**, *14*, 1184. [CrossRef]
18. Li, Q.; Zhao, S.; Du, L.; Luo, S. Multi-Genotype Rice Yield Prediction Based on Time-Series Remote Sensing Images and Dynamic Process Clustering. *Agriculture* **2024**, *15*, 64. [CrossRef]
19. Guo, Y.; He, J.; Zhang, H.; Shi, Z.; Wei, P.; Jing, Y.; Yang, X.; Zhang, Y.; Wang, L.; Zheng, G. Improvement of Winter Wheat Aboveground Biomass Estimation Using Digital Surface Model Information Extracted from Unmanned-Aerial-Vehicle-Based Multispectral Images. *Agriculture* **2024**, *14*, 378. [CrossRef]
20. Yang, F.; Liu, Y.; Yan, J.; Guo, L.; Tan, J.; Meng, X.; Xiao, Y.; Feng, H. Winter Wheat Yield Estimation with Color Index Fusion Texture Feature. *Agriculture* **2024**, *14*, 581. [CrossRef]
21. Maleki, R.; Wu, F.; Oubara, A.; Fathollahi, L.; Yang, G. Refinement of Cropland Data Layer with Effective Confidence Layer Interval and Image Filtering. *Agriculture* **2024**, *14*, 1285. [CrossRef]
22. Huang, H.; Liu, Y.; Zhu, S.; Feng, C.; Zhang, S.; Shi, L.; Sun, T.; Liu, C. Detection of Mechanical Damage in Corn Seeds Using Hyperspectral Imaging and the ResNeSt_E Deep Learning Network. *Agriculture* **2024**, *14*, 1780. [CrossRef]
23. Sun, H.; Zhou, L.; Shu, M.; Zhang, J.; Feng, Z.; Feng, H.; Song, X.; Yue, J.; Guo, W. Estimation of Peanut Southern Blight Severity in Hyperspectral Data Using the Synthetic Minority Oversampling Technique and Fractional-Order Differentiation. *Agriculture* **2024**, *14*, 476. [CrossRef]
24. Seo, D.; Lee, S.K.; Kim, J.G.; Oh, I.-S. High-Precision Peach Fruit Segmentation under Adverse Conditions Using Swin Transformer. *Agriculture* **2024**, *14*, 903. [CrossRef]
25. Gao, G.; Zhang, S.; Shen, J.; Hu, K.; Tian, J.; Yao, Y.; Tian, Q.; Fu, Y.; Feng, H.; Liu, Y.; et al. Segmentation and Proportion Extraction of Crop, Crop Residues, and Soil Using Digital Images and Deep Learning. *Agriculture* **2024**, *14*, 2240. [CrossRef]
26. Lin, Y.; Guo, X.; Liu, Y.; Zhou, L.; Wang, Y.; Ge, Q.; Wang, Y. Vegetation Phenology Changes and Recovery after an Extreme Rainfall Event: A Case Study in Henan Province, China. *Agriculture* **2024**, *14*, 1649. [CrossRef]
27. Wang, Z.; Liu, Y.; Wang, K.; Wang, Y.; Wang, X.; Liu, J.; Xu, C.; Song, Y. Phenotyping the Anthocyanin Content of Various Organs in Purple Corn Using a Digital Camera. *Agriculture* **2024**, *14*, 744. [CrossRef]
28. Wang, Y.; Wu, Z.; Luo, S.; Liu, X.; Liu, S.; Huang, X. Estimating Corn Growth Parameters by Integrating Optical and Synthetic Aperture Radar Features into the Water Cloud Model. *Agriculture* **2024**, *14*, 695. [CrossRef]
29. Lin, Y.; Fan, T.; Wang, D.; Cai, K.; Liu, Y.; Wang, Y.; Yu, T.; Xu, N. Influence of Vegetation Phenology on the Temporal Effect of Crop Fractional Vegetation Cover Derived from Moderate-Resolution Imaging Spectroradiometer Nadir Bidirectional Reflectance Distribution Function–Adjusted Reflectance. *Agriculture* **2024**, *14*, 1759. [CrossRef]

https://doi.org/10.3390/agriculture16020271

agriculture

MDPI

Article

Hyperspectral Remote Sensing Estimation of Rice Canopy LAI and LCC by UAV Coupled RTM and Machine Learning

Zhongyu Jin [1,2], Hongze Liu [1,2], Huini Cao [1,2], Shilong Li [1,2], Fenghua Yu [1,2,3,*] and Tongyu Xu [1,2,3]

1 School of Information and Electrical Engineering, Shenyang Agricultural University, Shenyang 110866, China; 2023200006@stu.syau.edu.cn (Z.J.); 2023220016@stu.syau.edu.cn (H.L.); 2023240083@stu.syau.edu.cn (H.C.); 2023220015@stu.syau.edu.cn (S.L.); xutongyu@syau.edu.cn (T.X.)

2 Key Laboratory of Intelligent Agriculture in Liaoning Province, Shenyang 110866, China

3 National Digital Agriculture Sub-Center of Innovation (Northeast Region), Shenyang 110866, China

* Correspondence: adan@syau.edu.cn

Abstract: Leaf chlorophyll content (LCC) and leaf area index (LAI) are crucial for rice growth and development, serving as key parameters for assessing nutritional status, growth, water management, and yield prediction. This study introduces a novel canopy radiative transfer model (RTM) by coupling the radiation transfer model for rice leaves (RPIOSL) and unified BRDF model (UBM) models, comparing its simulated canopy hyperspectra with those from the PROSAIL model. Characteristic wavelengths were extracted using Sobol sensitivity analysis and competitive adaptive reweighted sampling methods. Using these wavelengths, rice phenotype estimation models were constructed with back propagation neural network (BPNN), extreme learning machine (ELM), and broad learning system (BLS) methods. The results indicate that the RPIOSL-UBM model's hyperspectra closely match measured data in the 500–650 nm and 750–1000 nm ranges, reducing the root mean square error (RMSE) by 0.0359 compared to the PROSAIL model. The ELM-based models using the RPIOSL-UBM dataset proved most effective for estimating the LAI and LCC, with RMSE values of 0.6357 and 6.0101 $\mu g \cdot cm^{-2}$, respectively. These values show significant improvements over the PROSAIL dataset models, with RMSE reductions of 0.1076 and 6.3297 $\mu g \cdot cm^{-2}$, respectively. The findings demonstrate that the proposed model can effectively estimate rice phenotypic parameters from UAV-measured hyperspectral data, offering a new approach to assess rice nutritional status and enhance cultivation efficiency and yield. This study underscores the potential of advanced modeling techniques in precision agriculture.

Keywords: RPIOSL model; UBM model; LAI; LCC; UAV

1. Introduction

1.1. Importance of LCC and LAI

Leaf chlorophyll content(LCC) and leaf area index (LAI) are vital for rice growth and development, serving as key indicators of the crop's nutritional status [1–3]. Chlorophyll absorbs light energy and converts it into chemical energy to promote photosynthesis and absorbs different wavelengths of light and converts them into energy that can be used by plants [4]. The lack of chlorophyll affects photosynthesis, leading to a decrease in photosynthetic efficiency and affecting plant growth and development [5–7]. The LAI is a measure of the density of the plant leaf area, which reflects the plant's ability to absorb light energy [8], and a higher LAI also helps to regulate the water balance of the plant, while a lower LAI leads to a limitation of photosynthesis, affecting the plant's growth and development and, then, affecting the yield of rice [9,10]. Therefore, monitoring the LCC and LAI of rice leaves is important for understanding rice growth, water management, and yield prediction, which can help improve the efficiency and yield of rice cultivation [11–13].

1.2. Rationale for Combining Radiative Transfer and Machine Learning Models

Hyperspectral imaging technology is increasingly used in agriculture and has become an important driver of change in modern agriculture [14] . By obtaining spectral information on crops, it is possible to accurately identify crop health, detect pests and diseases, assess nutritional levels, and monitor water content [15–18]. Estimating the phenotypic traits and nutrient elements of rice using hyperspectral data for diagnosing its nutritional status has become a significant research topic for experts and scholars in the field of agricultural information technology, both domestically and internationally [19]. At present, the construction of models to estimate rice phenotypic parameters often adopts a data-driven approach, which is mainly based on machine learning techniques, by constructing a vegetation index or screening characteristic wavelengths [20–22]. Although the data-driven approach is simple and easy to implement, it is affected by multiple factors, such as test locations, varietal differences, and data collection methods, so the generalizability of the model is weak and lacks deep-level mechanistic explanations. In contrast, the crop radiative transfer model (RTM) can emulate the reflectance of the crop canopy by entering phenotypic parameters and explain the association between the spectra and thephenotypic parameters from a mechanistic perspective [23]. Estimating the phenotypic parameters of rice with the help of the RTM can help to make up for the deficiencies of the data-driven approach in terms of mechanism and improve the explanatory power and generalization ability of the estimation model.

1.3. Limitations of Current Methods

The RTM for vegetation leaves simulates the light transmission mechanisms within the foliage, accurately reflecting and transmitting light based on the dynamic changes in various components throughout plant growth [24,25]. The most typical leaf RTM of vegetation is the PROSPECT model, which consists of four phenotypic parameters, that is, structural parameters, chlorophyll, equivalent water thickness, and dry matter weight. Jiang et al. proposed that the layered structure of the leaf blade caused the difference in optical properties and proposed the FASPECT model, in which the upper and lower surfaces of the leaf blade were symmetrically treated as a four-layer structure. Yu et al. [15] adopted the same idea as that of the FASPECT model to construct the FASPECT model. The same idea as in the FASPECT model was used to construct the PIOSL model [26]. Xiang et al. [27] proposed the assumption of layered optical properties of the rice blade structure, combined the PIOSL model based on the assumption of layered optical properties with the structure of the rice blade, and proposed the RPIOSL model capable of simulating the reflectance spectra of rice blades. The model was able to simulate the reflectance spectra of rice leaves with more accuracy by entering the structural parameters of the stratification of the rice leaf, the LCC, the equivalent thickness of water, and the weight of the dry matter. The canopy RTM describes the propagation and interaction of light within the vegetation canopy based on the bidirectional reflectance properties of the vegetation. This model is grounded in the principles of physical optics and takes into account the structure of the vegetation, as well as the processes of light absorption, scattering, and reflection. One of the most well-known canopy RTMs is the SAIL model, which, when combined with the PROSAIL leaf RTM, becomes one of the most commonly used mechanistic models for describing the RT processes in vegetation canopies. However, this model is built on the assumption that the canopy is uniformly distributed, which does not accurately reflect the condition of rice canopies during the early tillering stage. To address this limitation, Xu et al. [28] developed a vegetation bidirectional reflectance distribution function (BRDF) model based on geometric optics and re-aggregation probability theory, incorporating the structural characteristics of row planting. They optimized the quantitative expression of the optical properties of the canopy in a row structure and provided results for the canopy BRDF model. Since RPIOSL optimizes the internal structure compared with the PROSPECT model, so that the model results are more in line with the measured results of rice leaves, and the UBM breaks the assumption that the vegetation canopy is uniformly distributed compared with the SAIL model, and fully takes into account the structural characteristics of the row structure of the row sown crops, the RPIOSL model coupled with the UBM model was chosen to construct the simulation data set of rice canopy reflectance for the present study. Therefore, in this study, the RPIOSL model coupled with the UBM model was chosen to construct the rice canopy reflectance simulation data set.

Due to the complex non-linear relationship between hyperspectral data and phenotypic covariates, traditional linear regression methods have some limitations in dealing with such problems [29,30]. However, neural networks have powerful nonlinear processing capabilities, and, thus, have been widely used in research related to hyperspectral estimation [31,32]. Luo et al. [33] successfully constructed a model for estimating anthocyanins in peony leaves by using hyperspectral data and employing multiple stepwise regression (MSR), partial least squares (PLS), BPNN, and random forest (RF). In addition, the broad learning system (BLS) proposed by Zhu et al. [34] used ridge regression approximation to compute the pseudo-inverse of the output weights and iteratively updated the pseudo-inverse for regression prediction. Neural networks have the advantage of multiple inputs and multiple outputs and are able to estimate multiple phenotypic covariates at the same time; therefore, in this paper, BPNN, ELM, and BLS neural networks were used for estimation to better deal with the complex nonlinear relationship between hyperspectral data and phenotypic parameters.

1.4. Aim of the Study

Compared to multispectral data and RGB images, hyperspectral data provide richer spectral information [35,36], effectively representing a wide range of plant phenotypic traits [37–39]. However, these data also contain redundancy, as the features of adjacent wavelengths tend to be similar, leading to wasted computational resources and increased model runtime, which limits the application of large-scale phenotypic parameter estimation [40]. Therefore, extracting sensitive wavelengths for chlorophyll and leaf area index (LAI) from hyperspectral data can significantly enhance the efficiency of estimation models. To achieve this goal, this study proposes to employ the competitive adaptive reweighted sampling (CARS) method combined with Sobol sensitivity analysis to extract the sensitive wavelengths for chlorophyll and LAI. The extracted sensitive wavelengths will be used to construct estimation models. The objective of this study is to develop a fast, accurate, and mechanistic estimation model for rice leaf area index (LAI) and leaf chlorophyll content (LCC) by integrating the advantages of data-driven methods with radiative transfer models.

2. Materials and Methods

2.1. Overview of the Study Area and Experimental Design

The study area is located at the Precision Agriculture Aviation Research Base in Gengzhuang Town, Anshan City, Liaoning Province, China (122°43′33″ E, 40°58′43″ N). Gengzhuang Town has flat terrain, fertile soil, and a temperate continental monsoon climate, which is characterized by four distinct seasons, the same rainy and hot seasons, concentrated precipitation, and abundant sunshine. The temperature difference is large. The average annual precipitation os 652 mm, the average annual temperature is 8.4 °C, the average annual sunshine hours is 3663 h, the annual effective cumulative temperature is 3400 °C–3500 °C, and the mean yearly frost-free duration is 165 d. The rice variety in the test area is Shennong 9816, with a fertility period of about 157 d, which is a medium-late maturing variety. The seedling leaf color is green, the leaf blade is straight, the plant shape is compact, and the tillering capacity is a medium-strong, semi-upright spike type. The experimental area was divided into 11 plots, and the management of all plots was the same, as shown in Figure 1. The experiment was carried out twice in the field at the nodulation and tasseling stages of rice, on 11 July and 15 August 2023, respectively, and representative rice holes were selected to collect canopy spectra, which were analyzed in the laboratory to determine the biochemical parameters. A total of 22 groups of samples were collected in this study, with a digital footprint of 10 GB/ha [41].

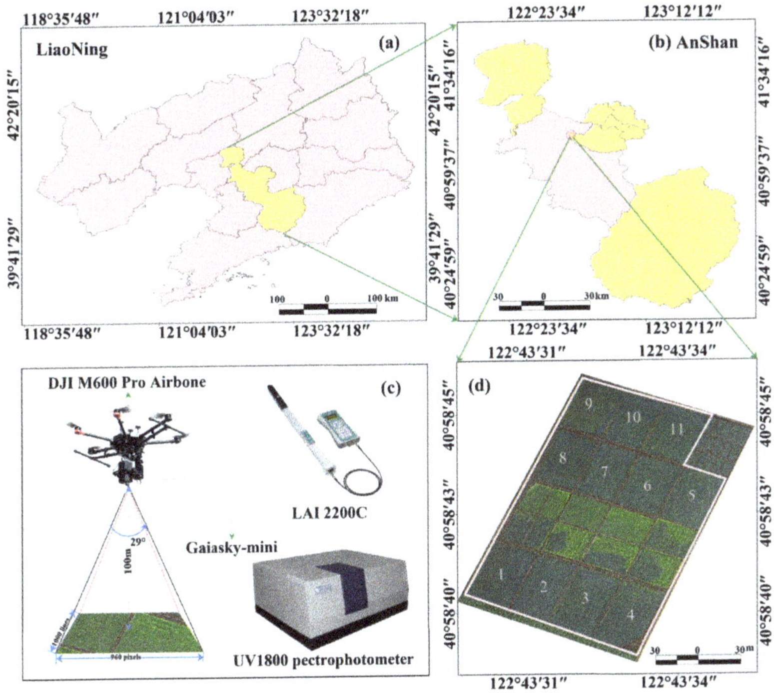

Figure 1. Overview of the study area. (**a**) Vector map of Liaoning Province, with Anshan City in the yellow area; (**b**) vector map of Anshan City, with Gengzhuang Town in the pink area; (**c**) map of instrumentation, including the UAV hyperspectral acquisition system, the LAI 2200C, and the visible-ultraviolet spectrophotometer; and (**d**) map of the experimental area, with the sampling areas labelled 1–11 in the map.

2.2. Data Acquisition

2.2.1. Acquisition of Hyperspectral Data

Canopy hyperspectral acquisition was performed using a UAV-mounted imaging hyperspectrometer (Dualix Spectral Imaging, Wuxi, China). A DJI M600 PRO rotor UAV (DJI-Innovations Inc., Shenzhen, China) was used to carry a built-in GaiaSky-mini push-scan airborne hyperspectral imaging system (Dualix Spectral Imaging, Wuxi, China), which measured the spectral range of 400–1000 nm, with a spectral resolution of 3 nm, a spectral sampling interval of 0.7 nm, and a flight altitude of 100 m. Under clear and cloudless weather conditions, with good midday light and low wind speeds, it is possible to ensure both stable light and smooth UAV flight. The lens was calibrated with a white board on the ground before measurement, and photos were taken with a standard white cloth for post-collection reflectance calibration after takeoff. After take-off, photos with standard white cloth were taken for post-collection reflectance calibration. The hyperspectral remote sensing data from the UAV platform were collected between 11:00 and 13:00, and during the measurement, the UAV flight speed was set to 2 m/s and the average flight time was 150 min/ha. In the process of data acquisition, the pilot manually controls the UAV hover; the UAV hovered above the test plot and waited for the imaging to complete. Reflectance calibrations and atmospheric corrections were made using the white cloth calibration curve by selecting the captured image with the standard white cloth in the SpectView software (Dualix Spectral Imaging, Wuxi, China). The sampling points were extracted using ENVI5.3+IDL tool software (GeoScene Information Technology Co., Beijing, China), and then, the spectra were resampled and smoothed using Gaussian smoothing method using MATLAB R2023 software with a spectral sample interval of 5 nm after resampling.

2.2.2. Measurement of Sample Data

Data on biophysical and biochemical factors determined in this study included LAI, leaf chlorophyll, equivalent water thickness, and dry matter content. The determination methods were as follows:

- LAI: The LAI was measured using the LAI-2200C canopy analyzer (Li-Cor, Inc., Lincoln, NE, USA), and three LAI values were measured in each graph and then averaged to represent the LAI of the graph; the specific formula is as in Equation (1).

$$LAI = \frac{LAI_1 + LAI_2 + LAI_3}{3}, \tag{1}$$

  Among them, LAI_1 is the first measured LAI, LAI_2 is the second measured LAI, and LAI_3 is the third measured LAI.
- LCC: A rice leaf was sampled, and its maximum length and width were measured to calculate the average leaf area.

$$A_{leaf} = a * b * 0.7746 \tag{2}$$

  where a is the maximum length of leaves, b is the maximum width of leaves, and 0.7746 is the leaf area correction coefficient of rice leaves. A weight of about 0.1 g of fresh rice leaf sample was put into a grinding container, a little quartz sand was added, and the mixture was ground into a homogeneous paste; grinding continued until the tissue became obviously white, and then, it was put on the table to stand. A piece of filter paper was placed in a funnel, the filter paper was moistened with a small amount of ethanol solution, and the extract was slowly injected into the funnel using a glass rod, filtered into a 50 mL volumetric flask. The mantle, the grinding rod, and the glass rod were rinsed with a small amount of ethanol solution, and finally, poured together into a volumetric flask. When it reached the 50 mL mark the volume was fixed at 50 mL by using a rubber burette, and was shaken well. The solution was kept in the dark for up to 24 h (to prevent chlorophyll degradation) until all the chlorophyll had been extracted and a small amount of chlorophyll extract was taken up with a rubber burette and dropped into a colorimetric cup of 1 cm diameter. As blank solution, 95% ethanol was taken and the absorbance of the liquid fraction containing chlorophyll at 665 nm and 649 nm wavelengths was quantified using uv1800pc UV-Vis spectrophotometer (Macylab Instrument Co., Shanghai, China). The concentration values of chlorophyll a and chlorophyll b were calculated using Equations (3) and (4) and then converted to $\mu g \cdot cm^{-2}$ unit [27,42].

$$C_a = 13.95 * \mathrm{A665} - 6.88 * \mathrm{A649} \tag{3}$$

$$C_b = 24.96 * \mathrm{A649} - 7.32 * \mathrm{A665} \tag{4}$$

  where A665 indicates the absorbance of the 665 nm sample and A649 indicates the absorbance of the 649 nm sample, C_a is the content of chlorophyll a, C_b is the content of chlorophyll b, and LCC is equal to the sum of chlorophyll a and chlorophyll b.
- Equivalent water thickness: A rice leaf was first weighed for its fresh weight M_{fresh}, then, placed in an oven at 105 °C for 30 min, and subsequently, dried at 70 °C until a constant weight was achieved. The dried leaves were reweighed to obtain the dry matter weight M_{dry} and the equivalent water thickness of the leaves was calculated using Equation (5).

$$C_w = \left(M_{dry} - M_{fresh}\right) / A_{leaf} \tag{5}$$

- Dry matter content: Dry matter content was calculated based on the dry matter weight M_{dry} and the average leaf area A_{leaf}.

$$C_m = M_{dry}/A_{leaf} \tag{6}$$

2.3. *Methodology*

2.3.1. The RPIOSL Model

The RPIOSL model is a sophisticated radiation transfer model tailored for rice leaves, created by refining the parameters of the PIOSL model. Leveraging the Non-dominated Sorting Genetic Algorithm-III (NSGA-III) for parameter optimization, the RPIOSL model precisely simulates the complex processes of light reflection, scattering, and transmission within rice leaves. This model is pivotal in advancing our understanding of the optical properties of rice leaves, thereby enabling the development of highly accurate hyperspectral detection methods for evaluating the physical and chemical parameters of rice. Its application is instrumental in enhancing the monitoring, management, and overall productivity of rice crops, making it a valuable tool for modern agricultural practices.

In this study, both field observations and insights from the existing literature were employed to establish the range of input parameters for the RPIOSL model. These parameters are detailed in Table 1, providing a comprehensive foundation for the model's accurate simulation of light interactions within rice leaves.

Table 1. RPIOSL parameter list.

Parameter	Symbol	Scope	Unit
Structural parameters of the first-layer blade	N_1	1–3	
Structural parameters of the second-layer blade	N_2	1–3	
Leaf chlorophyll content	Cab	0–100	$\mu g \cdot cm^{-2}$
Leaf moisture content	Cw	0.004–0.04	$\mu g \cdot cm^{-2}$
Leaf dry matter content	Cm	0.0019–0.0165	$\mu g \cdot cm^{-2}$
The leaf chlorophyll ratio between the first and second layers	Cab_{12}	0–1	
The leaf water ratio between the first and second layers	Cw_{12}	0–1	
Leaf dry matter ratio between the first and second layers	Cm_{12}	0–1	

2.3.2. Unified BRDF Model for Plants

The Unified BRDF model (UBM) gives an analytical expression of the primary and multiple scattering reflectance for different incident light conditions and vegetation types [28]. Based on geometrical optics, the foothold is shifted from the tree canopy to the vegetation elements, and the nonisotropic character of the primary scattering term is attributed to the geometrical relationship between the sun-target sensor, the multiscale cluster superposition, and the ratio of the direct sun and sky scattering to the irradiance of the target. As different vegetation types are the result of multiscale cluster superposition, the method of obtaining the four-component area ratio is re-given based on Poisson distribution, so that it is applicable to various vegetation types, and then, an approximate analytical expression for the primary scattering term is obtained. With the help of the theory of "recollision probability", the multiple scattering processes within the canopy and between the canopy and the soil are considered, the formation principle of the multiple scattering term is revealed, and the model parameters are shown in the Table 2.

Table 2. UBM parameter list.

Parameter	Symbol	Scope	Unit
Leaf area index	LAI	1–8	
Zenith angle	θ_i	0–90	°
Observational angle	θ_v	0–90	°
Plant height	H	0.1–2.5	m
Gathering index	$Clup$	0–1	
Sky-scattered light ratio	β	0–1	
G function	G	0.5	
Background reflectivity	$background\_reflectance$	0–1	

2.3.3. The PROSAIL Model

The PROSAIL RTM integrates the PROSPECT leaf optical model with the BRDF SAIL model of the vegetation canopy [43], and has been extensively utilized in recent years for estimating vegetation canopy parameters. The PROSPECT model conceptualizes the leaf structure as a multilayered flat plate with rough surfaces. It generates the reflectance and transmittance of leaves across different spectral bands through a sophisticated simulation process that requires the input of various leaf biochemical parameters, such as LCC, dry matter content, equivalent water thickness, and structural parameters.

Conversely, the SAIL model assumes a homogeneous vegetation canopy with leaves exhibiting uniform characteristics in all directions. It is grounded in the theory of RT equations. The reflectance and transmittance outputs from the PROSPECT model serve as inputs for the SAIL model, which then simulates the vegetation structure as a multilayered, rough-surfaced flat plate. This simulation process accurately reproduces the RT phenomena, including multiple reflections and scattering within the vegetation canopy. The parameters used in the model are detailed in Table 3.

Table 3. PROSAIL parameter list.

Parameter	Symbol	Scope	Unit
Leaf structure parameters	N	1–3	
Leaf chlorophyll content	Cab	0–100	$\mu g \cdot cm^{-2}$
Leaf moisture content	Cw	0.004–0.04	$g \cdot cm^{-2}$
Leaf dry matter content	Cm	0.0019–0.0165	$g \cdot cm^{-2}$
Leaf area index	LAI	1–8	
Zenith angle	tts	0–90	°
Observational angle	tto	0–90	°
Relative azimuth angle	psi	0–360	°
Type of leaf inclination angle distribution	$TypeLIDF$	1/2	
Agrotype	$rsoil$	1/2	
Hot parameter	$hspot$	0–1	

2.3.4. Extraction of Hyperspectral Characteristic Wavelengths

Competitive adaptive reweighting sampling (CARS) is a statistical method tailored for variable selection, particularly effective in high-dimensional data analysis such as chemometrics and bioinformatics involving spectral data [44]. The essence of CARS lies in its iterative and adaptive approach to reducing the number of unimportant variables through a competitive process. This enhances both the predictive performance and interpretability of models. CARS excels in handling high-dimensional datasets by minimizing redundancy and noise, thereby improving the accuracy and robustness of predictive models. Its adaptive adjustment and competitive mechanism allow CARS to dynamically customize the variable selection process based on the data's characteristics, resulting in more precise and reliable outcomes.

2.3.5. Machine Learning Methods

- Back propagation neural network: The core advantage of the BPNN algorithm lies in the process of the forward propagation of data and backward propagation of errors, and the use of gradient descent to continually adjust the connection weights and thresholds between neurons in order to bring the results of the network's output layer closer and closer to the desired value. Among many artificial intelligence or neural network algorithms, BPNNs are able to deeply mine, identify, and learn multidimensional nonlinear relationships embedded in massive data. Therefore, with the help of the BPNN's ability to learn intelligently, model highly, and predict accurately in the face of complex multidimensional nonlinear relationships, an attempt can be made to establish an intelligent prediction method, the network structure diagram is shown in Figure 2.

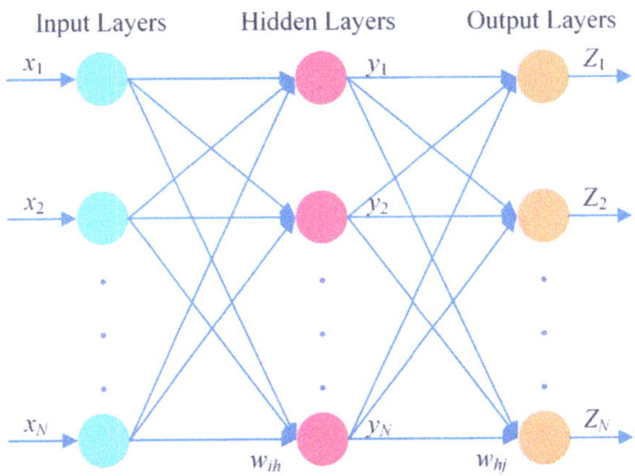

Figure 2. Schematic of BPNN, where blue is the input layer, pink is the implied layer, orange is the output layer, $x_1, x_2 \cdots x_N$ is the input variable, $y_1, y_2 \cdots y_N$ is the intermediate variable, $Z_1, Z_2 \cdots Z_N$ is the output variable, and w_{ih}, w_{hj} is the weight.

- Extreme learning machine: The extreme learning machine (ELM) is an efficient algorithm designed for the rapid training of feedforward neural networks, offering significantly faster learning speeds compared to traditional methods. It operates by randomly generating the weights and biases of the hidden layer and, then, directly computing the output layer weights using the least squares method, thereby greatly simplifying the training process. Unlike traditional neural networks, the ELM does not require iterative optimization, which avoids the local minima issues of gradient descent and significantly accelerates training [45]. Renowned for its speed, simplicity, and robust generalization capabilities, the ELM is widely utilized in a range of machine learning tasks, such as classification, regression, and feature learning, due to its efficiency and rapid training capabilities. Its efficiency in handling large-scale datasets and real-time applications makes the ELM a highly effective and practical approach to neural network training [46]. The network structure is illustrated in Figure 3.

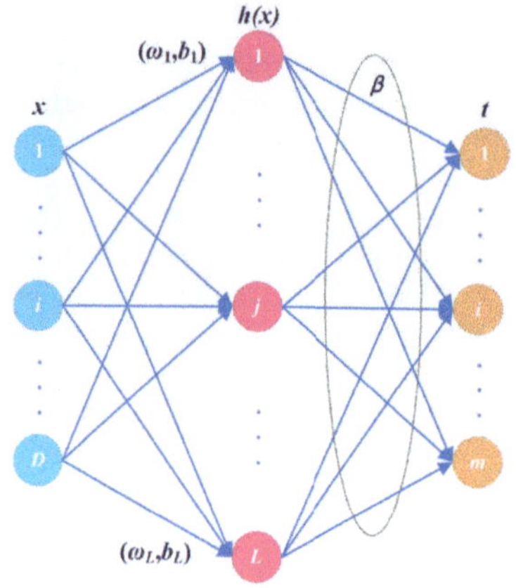

Figure 3. Schematic diagram of the ELM, where blue is the input layer, pink is the hidden layer, orange is the output layer, $1 \cdots D$ is the input variable, $1 \cdots L$ is the intermediate variable, $1 \cdots m$ is the output variable, and ω_L, b_L is the weight.

- Broad learning system: The broad learning system (BLS) is a single-layer incremental learning framework that offers rapid convergence and high accuracy, distinguishing it from traditional deep network models. Its incremental learning capability allows the network model to efficiently scale with growing datasets [34,47]. BLS employs a horizontal scaling strategy, utilizing input-mapped features as the network's feature nodes. These nodes are then expanded into augmentation nodes with randomly generated weights. Both the mapped features and augmentation nodes are directly connected to the outputs, and the corresponding output coefficients are determined using the pseudo-inverse method [48,49]. Therefore, upon the introduction of new neural nodes (including newly incorporated feature nodes), BLS circumvents the necessity for retraining from the ground up. Instead, it merely requires the recalibration of the weights corresponding to the newly added nodes, facilitating rapid incremental learning. The network structure is depicted in Figure 4.

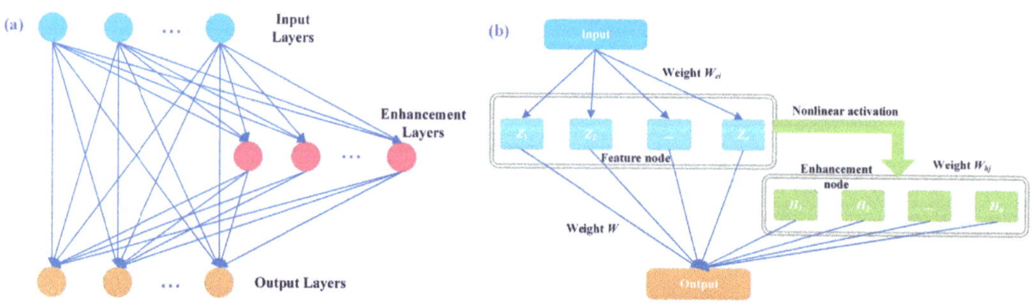

Figure 4. Schematic diagram of BLS. (**a**) Schematic diagram of a neural network connected by traditional random vector functions, where blue is the input layer, pink is the enhancement node, and orange is the output layer; and (**b**) schematic diagram of BLS, including the input layer, feature nodes, enhancement nodes, and the output layer.

2.3.6. Construction of the Model

In this study, 50,000 sets of parameters corresponding to the model were randomly generated based on the measured ranges of physical and chemical parameters based on the PROSAIL model and the RPIOSL-UBM model, respectively. Based on the measured canopy spectra and physicochemical parameter data, the unknown parameters (e.g., N1,

N2, etc.) in the RPIOSL model were optimized using the NSGA-III optimization algorithm, and the specific optimization steps are shown in Figure 5.

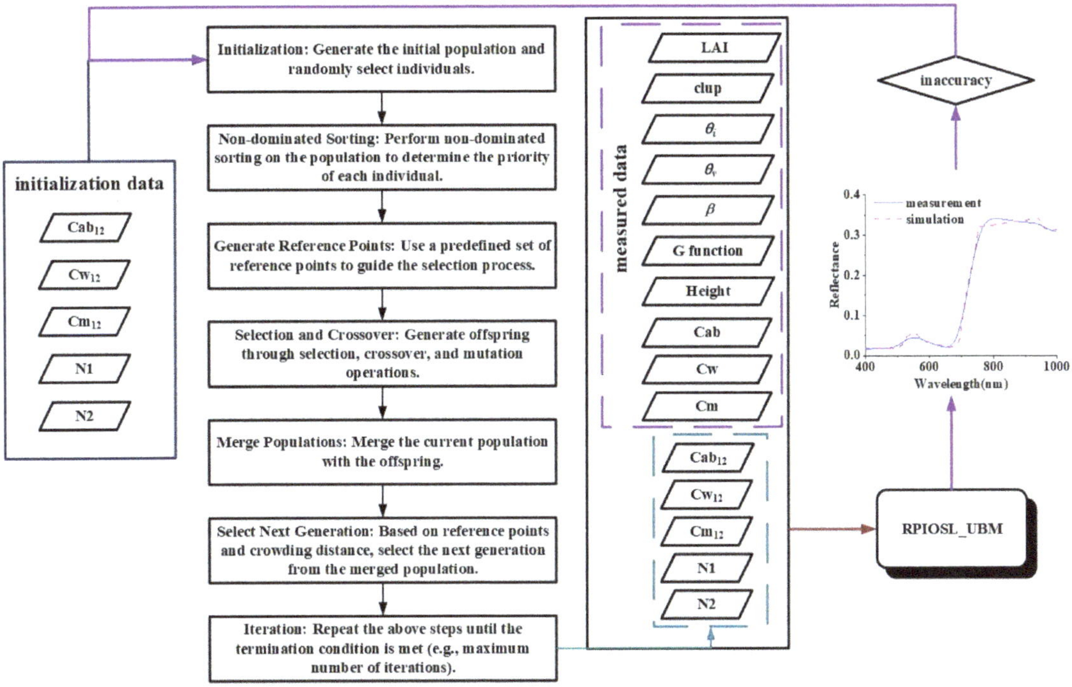

Figure 5. Parameter optimization flowchart. Based on the parameters in the measured data as well as the measured spectral data, the parameters (N1, N2, etc.) were optimized based on the NSGA-III optimization algorithm with the model output spectra and the measured spectral errors as evaluation indexes.

Based on the optimized parameters as well as the measured parameters, the dataset is screened so that the model parameters match the measured data. Sensitivity analyzes of the two RTMs were performed using the Sobol sensitivity analysis method, and the characteristic wavelengths were screened based on the competitive adaptive reweighted sampling method. After the feature wavelengths and parameters screened were randomly divided according to the 7:3 ratio for the training set, the test set, LAI, and LCC were estimated and modeled using the BP neural network, ELM, and BLS, respectively, and precision was verified and evaluated using the measured hyperspectral data from the UAV. Among them, the evaluation indexes of the estimation model are R^2 and RMSE, and the model accuracy validation index is the RMSE of the measured data.The technology roadmap is illustrated in Figure 6.

$$R^2 = 1 - \left(\sum_i (y_i - y_i')^2 / n\right) / \left(\sum_i (y_i - \bar{y})^2 / n\right) \tag{7}$$

$$RMSE = \sqrt{\sum_i (y_i - y_i')^2 / n} \tag{8}$$

where y_i and y_i' represent the measured and simulated values, respectively; $\bar{y}$ is the mean value of measurement; and n is the sample size.

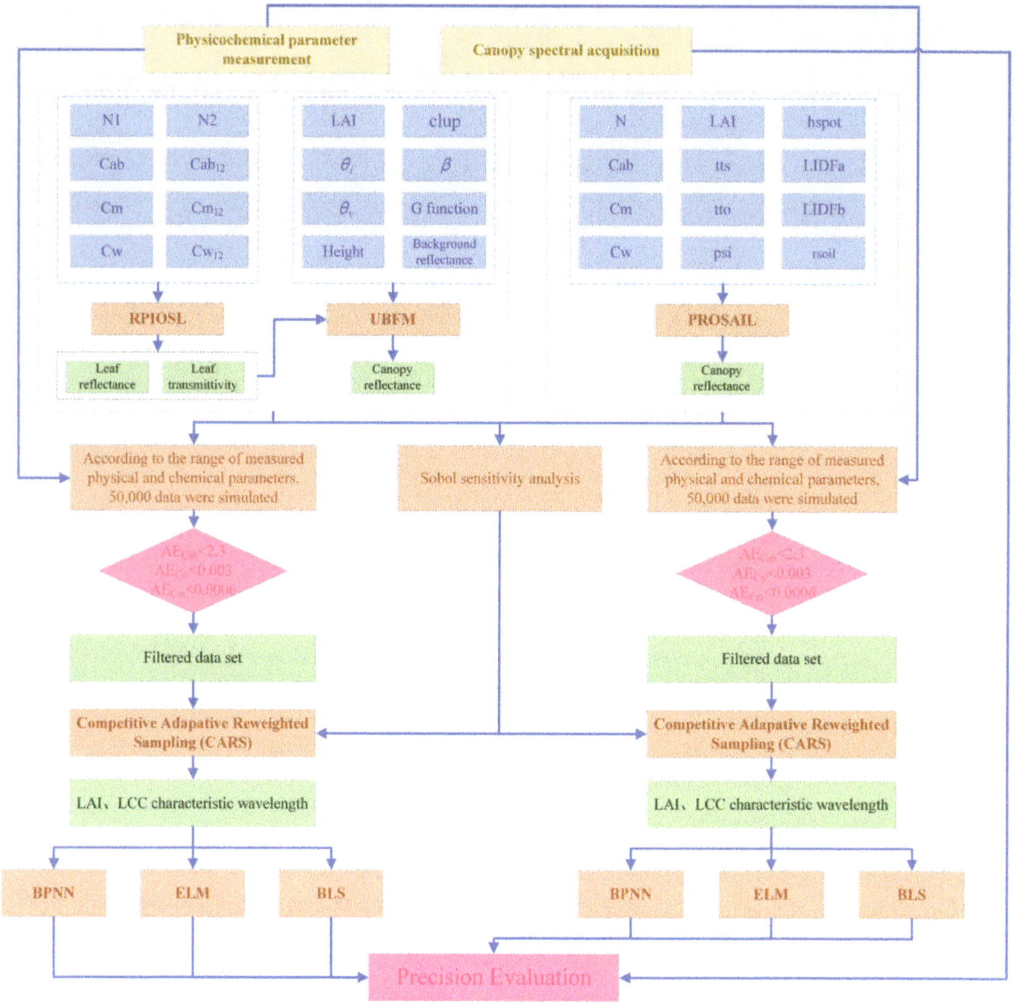

Figure 6. Technical roadmap.

3. Results

3.1. Spectral Simulation Results

In this study, the RPIOSL-UBM model and the PROSAIL model were used to simulate rice canopy spectra, respectively. In both models, the same values were used for the same input parameters (e.g., LAI, LCC, equivalent water thickness, dry matter weight). In addition, the solar zenith angle and observed azimuth angle were also consistent with the measured data. The simulation outcomes are illustrated in Figure 7, and are analyzed in comparison with the measured data. Since the SAIL model is constructed based on the assumption of a uniformly distributed vegetation canopy, the simulation results of the SAIL model in the near-infrared band range will be biased higher than those of the UBM model and the measured data, as discussed in the analysis in Section 4.1. The RMSE of the model simulation results in the critical band range is shown in Table 4.

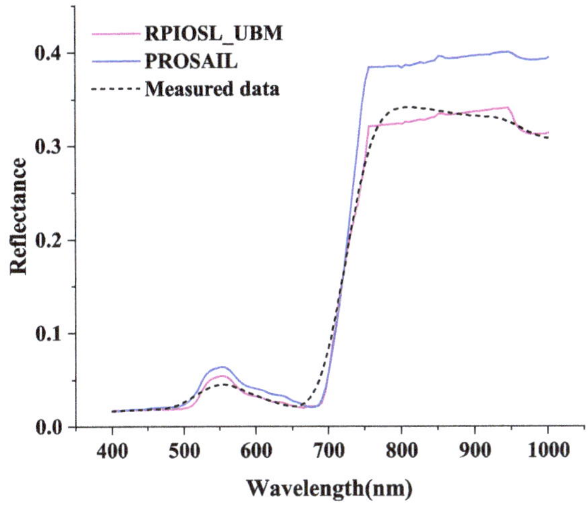

Figure 7. Spectral simulation and sensitivity analysis results.

Table 4. RMSE of model simulation results in the critical band range.

	450–700 nm	800–1000 nm
RPIOSL-UBM	0.0089	0.0082
PROSAIL	0.0115	0.0655

As illustrated in Figure 7 and Table 4, the spectral simulation performance of the RPIOSL-UBM model surpasses that of the PROSAIL model. Notably, the spectra generated by the RPIOSL-UBM model exhibit a closer alignment with the measured spectra. The RMSE of the simulation results in the range of 400–1000 nm for the RPIOSL-UBM model is 0.0086, compared to 0.0446 for the PROSAIL model. This represents a reduction in the RMSE of 0.0359 for the RPIOSL-UBM model, indicating a substantial improvement in simulation accuracy. Moreover, there is a large reduction in the RMSE in both the 450–700 nm and 800–1000 nm band ranges separately.

3.2. Feature-Wavelength Extraction Results

In this study, sensitivity analyses of the two RTMs were conducted independently using the Sobol sensitivity analysis method. The results of these analyses are presented in Figure 8. The sensitivity analyzes were mainly carried out on rice phenotypic covariates, and some of the optically related parameters were not subjected to sensitivity analyses. As depicted in Figure 8a,b, the RPIOSL-UBM model shows that chlorophyll-sensitive bands are primarily located between 400 and 750 nm, while LAI-sensitive bands span the entire range from 400 to 1000 nm, with higher sensitivity observed in the 750–1000 nm range compared to the 400–750 nm range. In contrast, the PROSAIL model indicates that chlorophyll-sensitive bands are mainly confined to the 400–750 nm range, and LAI-sensitive bands are predominantly found in the 750–1000 nm range.

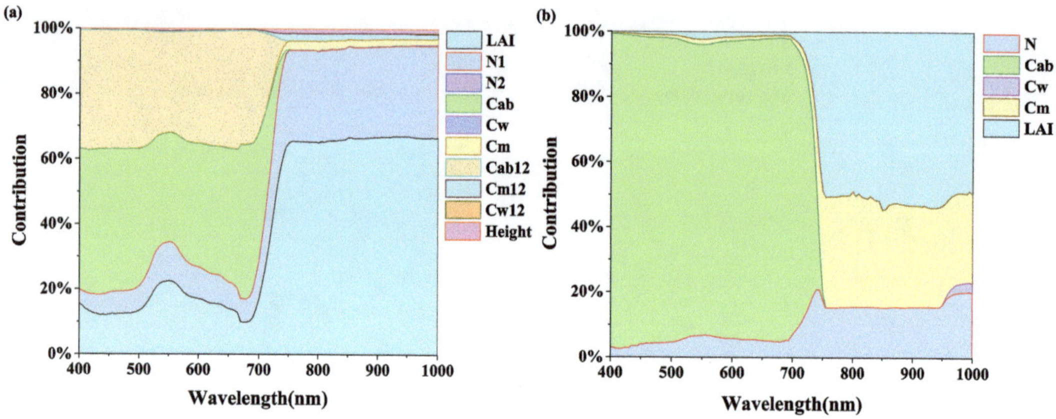

Figure 8. Graph of the sensitivity analysis results, where (**a**) shows the RPIOSL-UBM model sensitivity analysis results and (**b**) shows the PROSAIL model sensitivity analysis results.

In this study, the parameter sets simulated by the two RTMs were screened using measured data, the training and validation datasets were constructed, and the characteristic wavelengths of LAI and LCC were extracted by the competitive adaptive reweighted sampling method, respectively. The LAI and LCC and their corresponding spectral data were subjected to the CARS variable selection process 50 times, respectively, repeatedly selecting the number of generation sampling times and comparing the RMSECV values of each sampling until the optimal subset of variables contained in the smallest RMSECV value was found. The results of feature selection are shown in Figure 9, where 24 chlorophyll feature wavelengths were selected in the RPIOSL-UBM model, namely 415, 430, 435, 440, 445, 465, 470, 480, 530, 535, 540, 575, 580, 585, 590, 620, 680, 780, 820, 830, 860, and 870 nm; 15 LAI characteristic wavelengths were selected, which were 425, 440, 535, 560, 580, 645, 720, 745, 750, 765, 815, 825, 850, 855, and 865 nm. A total of 19 chlorophyll characteristic wavelengths were screened in the PROSAIL model, which were 400, 410, 415, 430, 435, 440, 445, 450, 475, 485, 490, 500, 510, 560, 615, 650, 665, 695, and 700 nm; and 13 LAI characteristic wavelengths were screened as 765, 770, 775, 790, 800, 860, 865, 870, 880, 915, 920, 940, and 945 nm. In the PROSAIL model, the results after feature wavelength extraction using CARS are consistent with the sensitivity analysis results. However, in the RPIOSL-UBM model, the extracted chlorophyll characteristic wavelengths contained wavelengths between 750 and 1000 nm, which was inconsistent with the sensitivity analysis results. Therefore, in this study, the 780 nm, 820 nm, 830 nm, 860 nm, and 870 nm data in the RPIOSL-UBM model were removed, and only the characteristic wavelengths in the wavelength range of 400–750 nm were used for modeling.

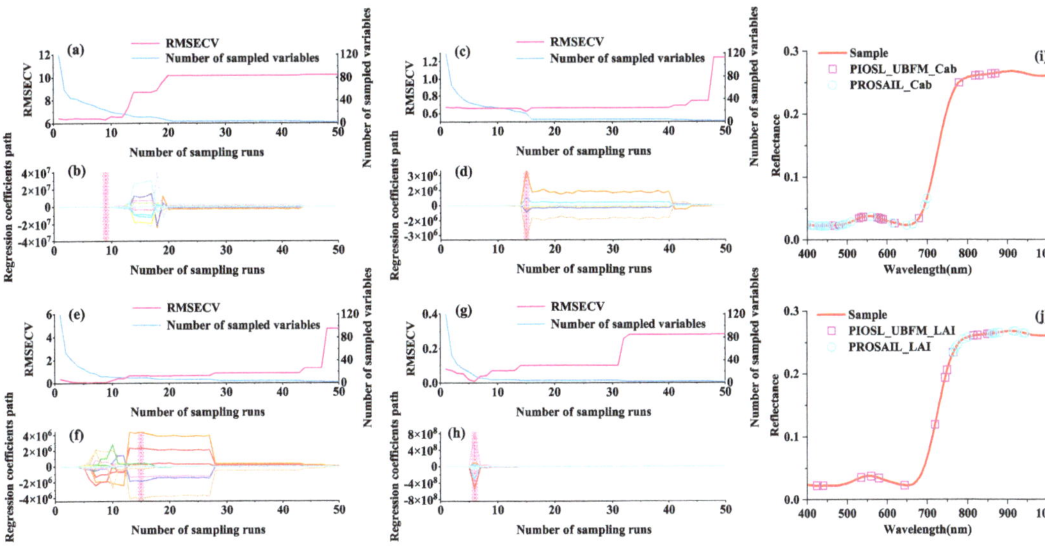

Figure 9. Graphs of feature wavelength screening results, where (**a**,**b**) are the LCC feature wavelength results based on the RPIOSL-UBM model screening; (**c**,**d**) are the LAI feature wavelength results based on the RPIOSL-UBM model screening; (**e**,**f**) are the LCC feature wavelength results based on the PROSAIL model screening; (**g**,**h**) are the PROSAIL model-based screening LAI characteristic wavelength results; (**i**) is a schematic diagram of the LCC characteristic wavelength band of the two RTMs; and (**j**) is a schematic diagram of the LAI characteristic wavelength band of the two RTMs. The pink lines in (**b**,**d**,**f**,**h**) respectively correspond to the minimum RMSECV in (**a**,**c**,**e**,**g**).

3.3. Model Results Based on BPNN Method

To develop a rice phenotypic parameter estimation model for predicting LCC and LAI, a BPNN model was employed. The dataset was divided into training and test sets in a 7:3 ratio and validated using measured data. Due to the differing mechanisms of the two RTMs, the number of neurons required in the hidden layer for the estimation models varied. For the LAI estimation models based on the RPIOSL-UBM and PROSAIL datasets, the number of hidden layer neurons ranged from one to si. For the LCC estimation models, the number of neurons in the hidden layer ranged from 10 to 60 for both datasets. The training results are illustrated in Figure 10, which presents the evaluation metrics. The primary focus of this study is on the validation results using the measured dataset, as the goal is to develop a practically applicable rice phenological parameter estimation model. The graphs reveal that the optimal LAI estimation model, derived from the RPIOSL-UBM dataset, was attained with the incorporation of four hidden layer neurons, yielding an $RMSE_{real}$ of 1.4288. For the PROSAIL dataset, the best LAI estimation model was obtained with one hidden layer neuron, resulting in an $RMSE_{real}$ of 3.5525. Regarding LCC estimation, the optimal model based on the RPIOSL-UBM dataset was achieved with 60 hidden layer neurons, with an $RMSE_{real}$ of 18.08 $\mu g{\cdot}cm^{-2}$. The best model based on the PROSAIL dataset was obtained with three hidden layer neurons, resulting in an $RMSE_{real}$ of 14.5123 $\mu g{\cdot}cm^{-2}$. In summary, the BPNN model demonstrated that the LAI estimation model constructed using the RPIOSL-UBM dataset and the LCC estimation model constructed using the PROSAIL dataset performed the best (Table 5).

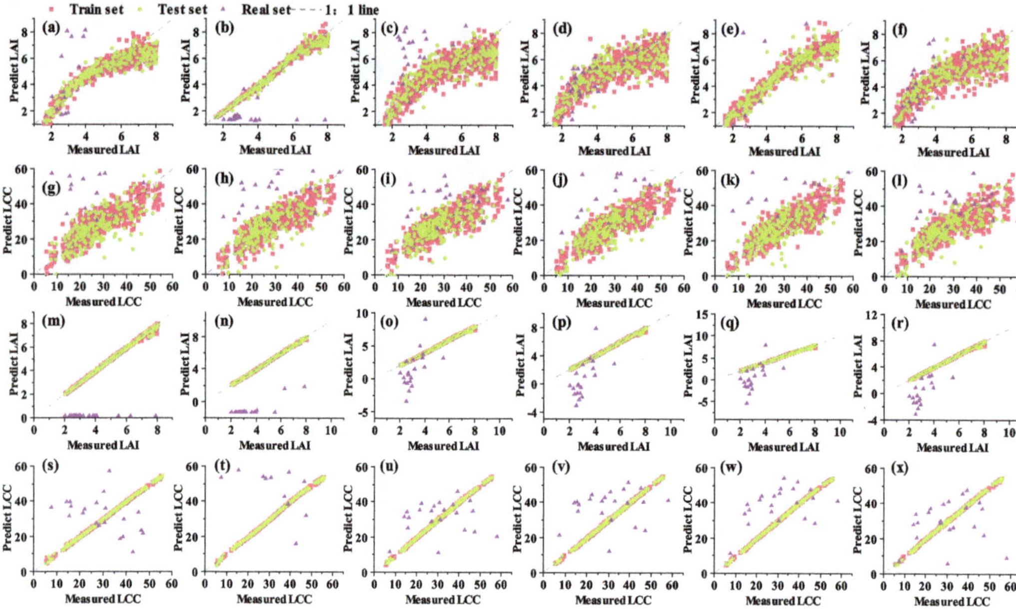

Figure 10. BP neural network-based estimation of LAI and LCC result plots, where (**a–f**) are based on the RPIOSL-UBM model to estimate LAI result plots, with the number of implied layers from 1–6, respectively; (**g–l**) are based on the RPIOSL-UBM model to estimate LCC result plots, with the number of implied layers from 10–60, respectively; (**m–r**) are the result plots of estimated LAI based on the PROSAIL model, with the depth of hidden layers from 1–6, respectively; and (**s–x**) are the result plots of estimated LCC based on the PROSAIL model, with the depth of hidden layers from 1–6, respectively.

Table 5. Table of results of estimating LAI and LCC evaluation indexes based on BPNN.

	Model	Evaluation Indicator	1	2	3	4	5	6
LAI	RPIOSL-UBM	Train set R^2	0.8476	0.9864	0.7484	0.7081	0.9354	0.7478
		Test set R^2	0.8106	0.9785	0.6871	0.6401	0.8655	0.6720
		Train set RMSE	0.74	0.2201	0.9460	1.0279	0.4793	0.9468
		Test set RMSE	0.8461	0.2846	1.0847	1.1719	0.7202	1.1067
		Real set RMSE	5.7549	3.9280	3.4980	1.4288	9.0464	2.5146
	PROSAIL	Train set R^2	0.9991	0.9997	0.9997	0.9997	0.9996	0.9996
		Test set R^2	0.9988	0.9997	0.9996	0.9995	0.9995	0.9994
		Train set RMSE	0.0515	0.028	0.0279	0.0313	0.0325	0.0334
		Test set RMSE	0.0593	0.029	0.0317	0.0389	0.0387	0.0408
		Real set RMSE	3.5525	4.5736	6.4012	5.7027	6.0567	6.2243
LCC	RPIOSL-UBM	Train set R^2	0.7228	0.7033	0.6692	0.7135	0.7071	0.6756
		Test set R^2	0.6012	0.6147	0.6036	0.6369	0.6194	0.6258
		Train set RMSE	5.6530	5.8467	6.1743	5.7407	5.8084	6.1070
		Test set RMSE	7.0133	6.6393	6.7994	6.3914	6.6278	6.4353
		Real set RMSE	37.5623	22.9874	19.0587	26.2064	29.0904	18.0800
	PROSAIL	Train set R^2	0.9994	0.9993	0.9993	0.9994	0.9994	0.9993
		Test set R^2	0.9993	0.9992	0.9993	0.9994	0.9994	0.9993
		Train set RMSE	0.2490	0.2631	0.2558	0.2443	0.2435	0.2503
		Test set RMSE	0.2657	0.2896	0.2677	0.2516	0.2582	0.2690
		Real set RMSE	19.7256	54.3931	14.5123	16.1608	14.9091	15.9118

3.4. Model Results Based on ELM Method

To develop a rice phenotypic parameter estimation model for predicting the LCC and LAI, the ELM model was employed. The dataset was partitioned into training and test sets in a 7:3 ratio and validated against empirical data. Due to the differing mechanisms of the two RTMs, the number of neurons required in the hidden layer varied. For the LAI and LCC estimation models based on the RPIOSL-UBM dataset, the number of hidden layer neurons ranged from 10 to 60, whereas for the models based on the PROSAIL dataset, the number of neurons ranged from one to five and included 10. The results of the model training, as depicted in Figure 11, indicate that the LAI estimation model utilizing the RPIOSL-UBM dataset achieved optimal performance with 10 neurons in the hidden layer, achieving an $RMSE_{real}$ of 0.6357, while the PROSAIL-based model performed best with two neurons, achieving an $RMSE_{real}$ of 0.7433. Similarly, the LCC estimation model using the RPIOSL-UBM dataset was optimal with 10 neurons, achieving an $RMSE_{real}$ of 6.0101 $\mu g \cdot cm^{-2}$, whereas the PROSAIL-based model was optimal with one neuron, achieving an $RMSE_{real}$ of 12.5478 $\mu g \cdot cm^{-2}$. Overall, the ELM model showed that the estimation models for LAI and LCC constructed using the RPIOSL-UBM dataset were the most effective, outperforming those based on the PROSAIL dataset (Table 6).

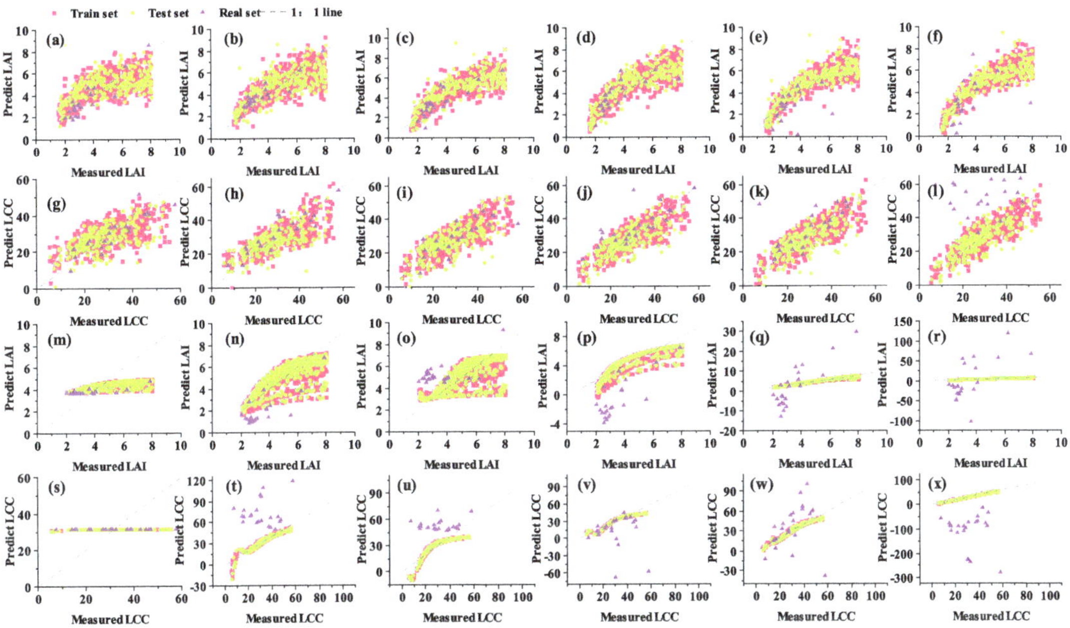

Figure 11. Estimated LAI and LCC result plots based on ELM, where (**a–f**) are estimated LAI result plots based on the RPIOSL-UBM model, with the depth of hidden layers from 10–60 respectively; (**g–l**) are estimated LCC result plots based on the RPIOSL-UBM model, with the depth of hidden layers from 10–60 respectively; (**m–r**) are estimated LCC result plots based on the PROSAIL model estimated LAI result plots, with the depth of hidden layers from 1–5 and 10, respectively; and (**s–x**) are estimated LCC result plots based on the PROSAIL model, with the depth of hidden layers from 1–5 and 10, respectively.

Table 6. Table of results of estimating LAI and LCC evaluation indexes based on ELM.

	Model	Evaluation Indicator	1	2	3	4	5	6
LAI	RPIOSL-UBM	Train set R^2	0.4369	0.6088	0.7128	0.7390	0.7776	0.8071
		Test set R^2	0.3373	0.5151	0.6158	0.6622	0.6879	0.7140
		Train set RMSE	1.4139	1.1785	1.0098	0.9627	0.8886	0.8276
		Test set RMSE	1.5739	1.3470	1.2025	1.1272	1.0799	1.0348
		Real set RMSE	0.6357	0.6672	0.7760	0.9928	1.7747	1.9839
	PROSAIL	Train set R^2	0.6612	0.6813	0.7009	0.8065	0.9847	0.9988
		Test set R^2	0.6021	0.6253	0.6545	0.7897	0.9783	0.9984
		Train set RMSE	1.5761	0.9756	0.9453	0.7604	0.2136	0.0603
		Test set RMSE	1.5501	1.0275	0.9891	1.7705	0.2472	0.0677
		Real set RMSE	1.2377	0.7433	2.0863	4.4998	8.9954	48.2324
LCC	RPIOSL-UBM	Train set R^2	0.4044	0.4675	0.6385	0.6603	0.6751	0.7227
		Test set R^2	0.4082	0.3638	0.5715	0.6389	0.6238	0.6542
		Train set RMSE	8.2733	7.8232	6.4453	6.2484	6.1111	5.6448
		Test set RMSE	7.9128	8.2650	6.8419	6.2044	6.5088	6.2459
		Real set RMSE	6.0101	6.1523	7.2157	9.1982	13.9596	29.1397
	PROSAIL	Train set R^2	0.5128	0.7263	0.8922	0.9351	0.9618	0.9973
		Test set R^2	0.5276	0.7372	0.8903	0.9303	0.9627	0.9973
		Train set RMSE	9.7402	5.1313	3.2179	2.4976	1.9157	0.5109
		Test set RMSE	9.9350	5.1196	3.3117	2.6359	1.9289	0.5210
		Real set RMSE	12.5478	26.0820	35.8104	46.3862	31.1645	156.3313

3.5. Model Results Based on BLS Method

In order to build a rice phenotypic parameter estimation model to estimate the LCC and LAI, this subsection was modeled using a BLS framework, with the dataset partitioned into training and test sets at a 7:3 ratio and, subsequently, validated against the measured dataset. Due to the different mechanisms of the two RTMs, the regularization parameters for sparse regularization in building the estimation model are also different. In the LAI and LCC estimation model developed with the RPIOSL-UBM dataset, the regularization parameters were set from 2^{-40} to 2^{-10}. In the LAI and LCC estimation model developed with the PROSAIL dataset, the regularization parameters were configured to span from 2^{-5} to 2^{-10} to 2^{-30}. The outcomes of the model training are illustrated in Figure 12. The evaluation indexes are demonstrated in Table 7. As can be seen in the graphs, the LAI estimation model developed with the RPIOSL-UBM dataset is the most effective when the regularization parameter is 2^{-10} and the $RMSE_{real}$ is 4.5924; the LAI estimation model developed with the PROSAIL dataset is the most effective when the regularization parameter is 2^{-5} and the $RMSE_{real}$ is 4.9139. The LCC estimation model developed with the RPIOSL-UBM dataset is the most effective when the $RMSE_{real}$ is 20.9618 $\mu g \cdot cm^{-2}$; and the LCC estimation model developed with the PROSAIL dataset is the most effective when the $RMSE_{real}$ is 12.3398 $\mu g \cdot cm^{-2}$, when the regularization parameter is 2^{-5}. In conclusion, the BLS model, the LAI estimation model based on RPIOSL-UBFM dataset and the LCC estimation model based on PROSAIL dataset have the best results.

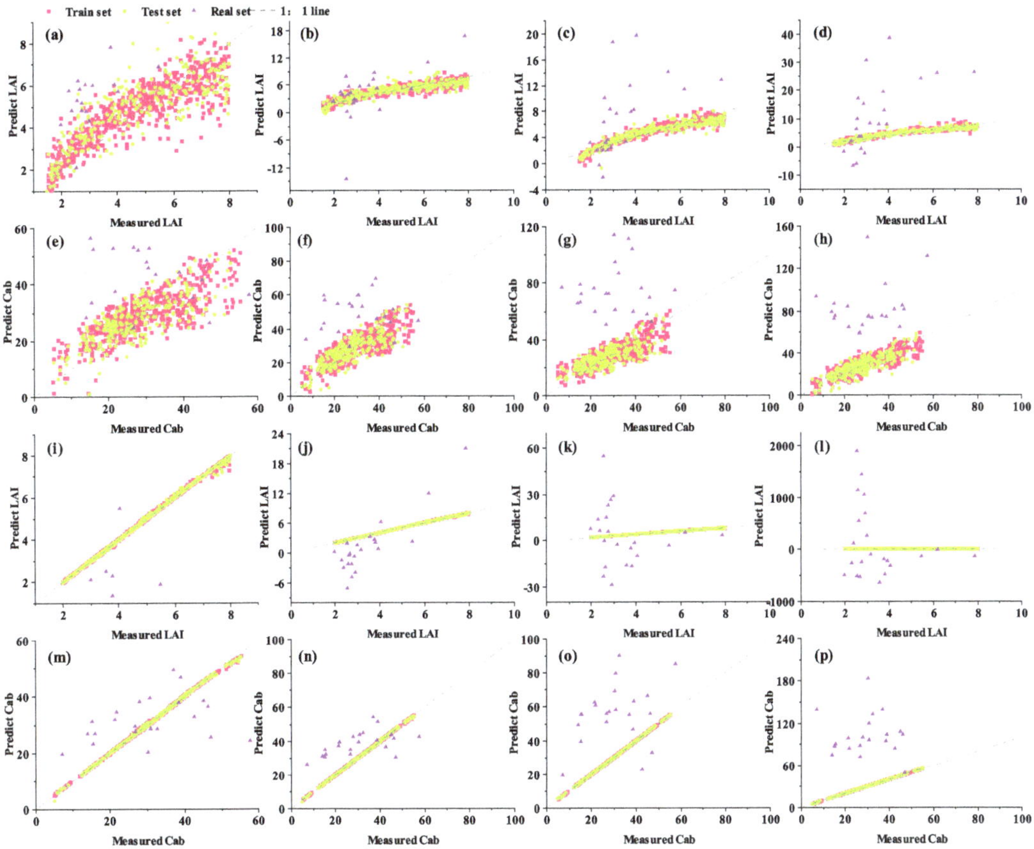

Figure 12. BLS-based estimation of LAI and LCC result plots, where (**a**–**d**) are the LAI result plots based on the RPIOSL-UBM model, with regularization parameters from 2^{-10} to 2^{-40}, respectively; (**e**–**h**) are the LCC result plots based on the RPIOSL-UBM model, with regularization parameters from 2^{-10} to 2^{-40}, respectively; (**i**–**l**) are the LAI result plots based on the PROSAIL model to estimate LAI resultant plots, with regularization parameters from 2^{-5} to 2^{-10} to 2^{-30}; and (**m**–**p**) are PROSAIL model based to estimate LCC resultant plots, with regularization parameters from 2^{-10} to 2^{-40}, respectively.

Table 7. Table of results of estimating LAI and LCC evaluation indexes based on BLS.

	Model	Evaluation Indicator	1	2	3	4
LAI	RPIOSL-UBM	Train set R^2	0.7448	0.8294	0.8697	0.8922
		Test set R^2	0.6449	0.7127	0.8223	0.8777
		Train set RMSE	0.9539	0.7789	0.6830	0.6186
		Test set RMSE	1.1550	1.0377	0.8176	0.6796
		Real set RMSE	4.5924	4.8772	6.2856	13.6650
	PROSAIL	Train set R^2	0.9994	0.9999	0.9997	1.0000
		Test set R^2	0.9990	0.9998	0.9994	1.0000
		Train set RMSE	0.0438	0.0201	0.0293	0.0083
		Test set RMSE	0.0533	0.0266	0.0413	0.0104
		Real set RMSE	4.9139	5.098	19.1130	69.1963

Table 7. *Cont.*

	Model	Evaluation Indicator	1	2	3	4
LCC	RPIOSL-UBM	Train set R^2	0.6193	0.6523	0.5987	0.7067
		Test set R^2	0.6026	0.6676	0.5885	0.7019
		Train set RMSE	6.6385	6.3224	6.7917	5.8070
		Test set RMSE	6.4649	5.9309	6.5804	5.6870
		Real set RMSE	20.9618	24.4485	49.3468	56.2261
	PROSAIL	Train set R^2	0.9993	0.9998	1.0000	1.0000
		Test set R^2	0.9991	0.9998	1.0000	1.0000
		Train set RMSE	0.2631	0.1280	0.0488	0.0092
		Test set RMSE	0.2944	0.1506	0.0476	0.0107
		Real set RMSE	12.3398	13.2870	31.0316	95.7500

4. Discussion

4.1. Discussion of the Accuracy of the Spectral Simulation

The RPIOSL model is a leaf RTM developed with the PROSPECT model, combined with the layered optics assumption and improvements to the rice leaf structure. It was shown that the RPIOSL model was better than the PROSPECT model in simulating the reflectance of rice leaf. Canopy reflectance is mainly composed of leaf reflectance and background reflectance, so the accuracy of the canopy RTM depends not only on the accuracy of leaf reflectance and transmittance but also on whether the simulation mechanism of the canopy RTM is reasonable [50,51]. In this study, the RPIOSL-UBM model, constructed by applying the RPIOSL model coupled with the UBM model, and the PROSAIL model were applied to simulate the hyperspectral reflectance of the rice canopy, respectively, and compared with the measured data. The simulation accuracy of the RPIOSL-UBM model was found to be better than that of the PROSPECT model. In the 500–700 nm band range, the spectra simulated by the RPIOSL-UBM model were closer to the measured data. This is because the RPIOSL model takes into account the actual physiological characteristics of the leaf and the distribution of chlorophyll within the leaf by layering, which makes its simulation better in the visible light range. In the 750–1000 nm band, the spectra simulated by the RPIOSL-UBM model are also closer to the measured data. This is primarily due to the UBM model's more precise consideration of the impact of background reflectance on canopy reflectance. In the SAIL model, only the soil can be selected as wet or dry, and the specific reflectance of the soil cannot be input. On the contrary, rice, unlike dryland crops, spends most of its growing period above a shallow water layer, so it is crucial to input accurate background reflectance in the RTM. Moreover, the SAIL model is based on the assumption of uniform distribution in the canopy, whereas rice, a crop with a ridge structure, is unsealed at the tillering stage and pre-tillering and tasseling stage, and is not uniformly distributed in the canopy, so the simulation results of the SAIL model are not as good as those of the UBM model at the tillering stage and pre-tillering and tasseling stage. The advantage of the coupled canopy radiative transfer model is that it takes into account both the multilayer characteristics of the internal structure of rice leaves and the canopy structure characteristics of rice, a crop with monopoly row structure, thus improving the simulation accuracy. In conclusion, the RPIOSL-UBM model shows higher accuracy in simulating the canopy reflectance of rice by taking the leaf structure, canopy structure, and background reflectance into fine consideration.

4.2. Discussion of Feature Wavelength Extraction

In this study, sensitivity analyses of two canopy RTMs were conducted, revealing that the LCC and LAI exhibited different distributions of sensitivity regions across the two models. The RPIOSL-UBM model included more physicochemical parameters compared to the PROSAIL model. Since the RPIOSL-UBM model divides the LCC into two layers and introduces the parameter of the stratified proportion of LCC, the contribution of th eLCC was divided into the contribution of LCC and the stratified proportion of LCC in the LCC sensitivity analysis. Overall, the results of the LCC sensitivity analysis in the two models did not differ much. Since the UBM model and the SAIL model are not based on the same evolutionary model, there are differences in the sensitive bands of the LAI in the sensitivity analysis. In this study, hyperspectral reflectance was interpolated to 5 nm intervals in order to improve the running speed of the algorithm, so the results of the characteristic wavelength screening basically do not have the problem of covariance between neighboring wavelengths. The characteristic wavelengths of chlorophyll are predominantly concentrated in the 400–700 nm range, a distribution determined by the light absorption properties of chlorophyll molecules. In this wavelength range, chlorophyll has strong absorption in the blue-violet (430–470 nm) and red (640–660 nm) regions, while it has weak absorption in the green region, which is the reason for the green color of the plant leaves. In the results of the characteristic band screening for LCC, bands within the range of 430–470 nm and 640–660 nm bands appeared, which is consistent with the results of Ban et al. [52] indicating that the characteristic band screening results retained most of the information related to the LCC, and the estimation model of the LCC can be developed with these characteristic band screening results.

The LAI is a critical parameter for quantifying vegetation canopy density and vegetation cover. In the red light band (620–700 nm), chlorophyll absorbs light more strongly, the reflectance of leaves is lower, and the overall reflectance of red light decreases with increasing leaf density, so the reflectance of red light is generally negatively correlated with the LAI [53]. In the near-infrared band (700–1300 nm), the reflectance of leaves is very high due to the strong scattering of near-infrared light by the cellular structure of leaves, and the canopy reflectance increases with an increasing LAI. The red-edge band (680–750 nm) encapsulates the combined effects of chlorophyll absorption and cellular structure scattering. The position and slope of the red edge are highly sensitive to variations in the LAI, making it a crucial band for monitoring the LAI. The reflectance of the green light band (500–570 nm), although less affected by chlorophyll absorption, can still provide some information related to the LAI, which in turn improves the estimation accuracy. Therefore, mechanically speaking, the sensitive band range of the LAI should basically cover the 500–1300 nm band. It is evident that the characteristic wavelength selection results of the RPIOSL-UBM model retain LAI-related information more comprehensively than those of the PROSAIL model.

4.3. Discussion of Model Accuracy Results

In this study, the BPNN, ELM, and BLS methods were used to construct LAI and LCC inversion models, respectively. The specific parameters in the models are shown in Table 8, and the computation times of the training and test sets are shown in Figure 13a and Figure 13b, respectively. Various numbers of hidden layers were utilized to construct the rice phenotypic parameter estimation model based on the BPNN. Analysis of the results indicates that the LCC estimation model, developed using the RPIOSL-UBM dataset, progressively enhanced its validation accuracy on the real dataset as the depth of hidden layers increased. However, the accuracy of the training and validation sets is lower than that of the model with fewer hidden layers. This phenomenon may be attributed to the fact that additional hidden layers enhance the model's ability to capture complex patterns, while simultaneously increasing the risk of overfitting. The LAI estimation model developed with the PROSAIL dataset increases the validation accuracy of the model on the real dataset as the depth of hidden layers decreases. As can be seen from the subplot of Figure 10m, the model validates better on the real dataset, mainly because the output results are all between 0 and 1, resulting in a lower overall RMSE. However, the results of the model are not distributed around the 1:1 line, indicating that the model is not optimal despite the low RMSE. The LAI estimation model developed with the RPIOSL-UBM dataset showed oscillations in model accuracy, and the R^2 of the training and validation sets did not show a monotonic change with the depth of hidden layers. The model performs better with a medium number of hidden layers. This is because too few hidden layers cannot capture complex patterns, while too many hidden layers tend to lead to overfitting. Therefore, a moderate number of hidden layers strikes a balance between complexity and generalization ability. The LCC estimation model developed with the PROSAIL dataset showed little change in the R^2 and RMSE for the validation and training sets as the depth of hidden layers was changed. Although the results of the validation and training sets look good, the RMSE is larger when validated on the real dataset, and the RMSE of the optimal model for the real dataset is still larger than 14. For LCC estimation, such an error is large and is not suitable to be applied in practical scenarios. In summary, different numbers of hidden layers have different effects on model accuracy. A moderate number of hidden layers can strike a balance between complexity and generalization ability, thus showing better results on the training set, validation set, and real dataset. However, the performance of the model on real datasets needs to be considered comprehensively to ensure the practical application of the model.

Table 8. Model parameter list.

	Static Parameters	Variation Parameters
BPNN	Number of training: 1000; Target error: 0.0001; Learning rate: 0.05.	Number of neurons in the hidden layer: LAI: 1–6; LCC: 10–60.
ELM	Activation function: sig; Regularization factor: 0.	Number of neurons in the hidden layer: RPIOSL-UBM:10–60; PROSAIL: 1–5, 10.
BLS	Shrinkage parameter for enhancement nodes: 0.8; Number of iterations: 200.	Regularization parameter: RPIOSL-UBM: 2^{-10}–2^{-40}; PROSAIL-LAI: 2^{-5}, 2^{-10}–2^{-30}; PROSAIL-LCC: 2^{-10}–2^{-40}.

In developing rice phenotypic parameter estimation models using the ELM, various numbers of hidden layers were employed for analysis. The results indicate that for models estimating the LCC and LAI based on the RPIOSL-UBM dataset, the precision of both the training and validation sets increases with the depth of hidden layers. However, the validation accuracy on the real dataset deteriorates as the depth of hidden layers increases. The best validation performance on the real dataset is observed with the fewest hidden layers, resulting in an RMSE of 0.6357 for LAI estimation and 6.0101 $\mu g \cdot cm^{-2}$ for LCC estimation. At this point, the R^2 values for both the training and validation sets are low, both below 0.5. As the depth of hidden layers increases, the R^2 values for the training and validation sets gradually rise, reflecting the sensitivity of the ELM method to the depth of hidden layers and neuron selection. However, the validation accuracy on the real dataset continues to decrease. Similarly, for LCC and LAI estimation models developed with the PROSAIL dataset, the accuracies of the training and validation sets improve with an increasing number of hidden layers. Nevertheless, the accuracy on the real dataset decreases with more hidden layers. Although the RMSE for both training and validation sets is less than 1 when the depth of hidden layers is 10, the RMSE for the real dataset is very high, indicating that the model performs well on the training and validation sets but poorly in real-world scenarios. The reason for this is that as the depth of hidden layers increases, the complexity of the model also increases, leading to good performance on the training and validation sets but poor performance on the real dataset. This is a typical overfitting phenomenon, where the model overfits the noise and details in the training data and lacks generalization. The model performs well on the training and validation sets but does not generalize effectively on the real dataset, leading to a decrease in validation accuracy. The ELM has the advantage of fast training but is more sensitive to the number of hidden layers and the choice of neurons. Too many hidden layers may lead to excessive model complexity and increase the risk of overfitting. In summary, although the ELM model performs better on the training and validation sets, the validation accuracy on the real dataset decreases, mainly due to overfitting and dataset differences. By introducing techniques such as regularization, cross-validation, and data enhancement, the effectiveness of the model in real scenarios can be improved.

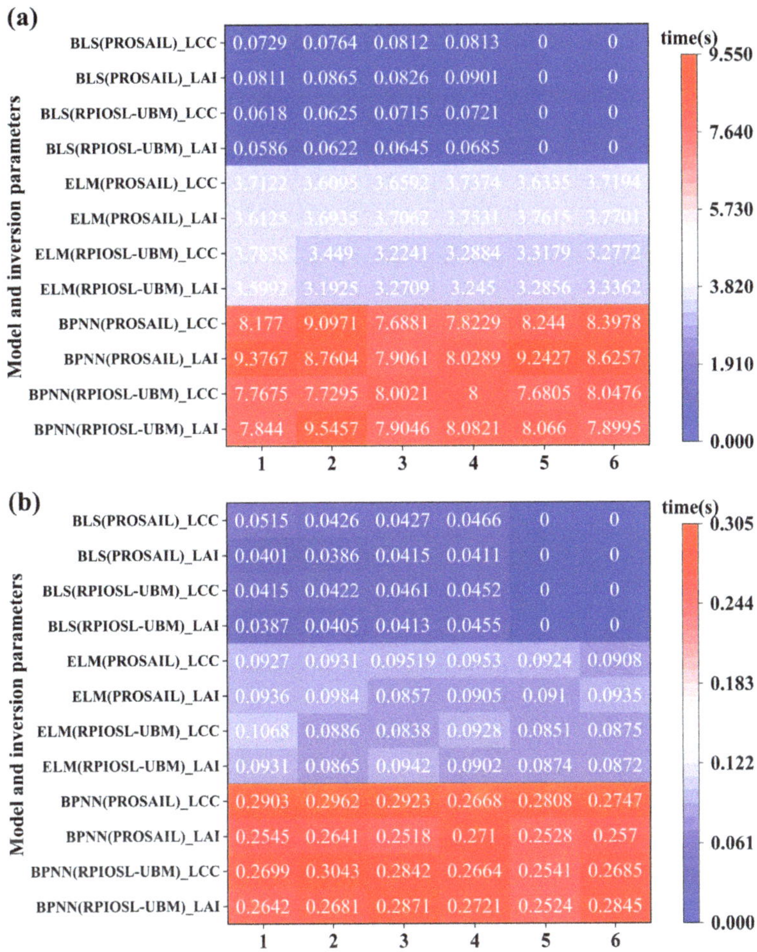

Figure 13. Model runtime graph. Subfigure (**a**) shows the training set runtime heatmap and subfigure (**b**) shows the validation set runtime heatmap, where 1–6 denotes sets 1–6 of parameters.

Different regularization parameters were used for modeling when constructing the rice phenotypic parameter estimation model based on the BLS (broad learning system). The results of the analysis showed that the accuracy of the model in the training and validation sets gradually increased as the regularization parameter was reduced. However, in the model developed with the PROSAIL dataset, the RMSE of the real dataset is very high, despite the R^2 of both training and validation sets being equal to 1, indicating that the model undergoes a serious overfitting phenomenon and has a very poor generalization ability. Furthermore, the RMSE of the LAI and LCC in all models constructed using the BLS method were higher than those constructed using the BP neural network and ELM methods, showing that the BLS method is much inferior to the other two methods in terms of generalizability. The overfitting problem is mainly due to the increase in model complexity caused by the regularization parameter being too small, which makes the model perform well in the training data but poorly on the real dataset. Discrepancies between datasets may also lead to a model performing well on the training and validation sets, yet failing to generalize effectively to the real dataset.

In terms of inversion accuracy, Zhang et al. [54] performed LAI inversion based on RGB and multispectral data, and the results showed that the RMSE ranged from 0.810 to 0.881, whereas the LAI inversion in this study resulted in an RMSE of 0.6357. To analyze the reason for this, this study simulated the effect of LAI changes on the spectra in the range of 700–1000 nm more efficiently by means of the radiative transfer model. In contrast, RGB and multispectral data have less information in the near-infrared band, which leads to a lower accuracy of their inversion. Xu et al. [55] inverted the chlorophyll content of rice leaves based on the PROSAIL radiative transfer model look-up table, and the RMSE of the model was 9.2 $\mu g{\cdot}cm^{-2}$, while the LCC inversion in this study resulted in an RMSE of 6.0101 $\mu g{\cdot}cm^{-2}$, which showed a higher accuracy. This enhancement may be attributed to the coupling of the RPIOSL model and the UBM model in this study, which is able to simulate the rice canopy reflectance more accurately compared to the PROSAIL model, thus improving the data accuracy of the look-up table and the inversion accuracy. In summary, further improvement of the simulation accuracy of the radiative transfer model will help to improve the accuracy of the inversion model, which is a direction worthy of in-depth research. The improvement of the model lies not only in the technical innovation, but also in the finer processing of the spectral data, with a view to achieving superior performance in future applications.

In summary, the overfitting phenomenon occurred in both the rice phenotypic parameter estimation models developed with the RPIOSL-UBM dataset and the PROSAIL dataset. The reasons for the overfitting phenomenon can be summarized in two points: First, the models did not select appropriate parameters, such as the quantity of hidden layers and the tuning of regularization parameters; second, there are differences between the model datasets. By observing the construction results of the two RTMs, it can be found that although an overfitting phenomenon exists in both models, the degree of overfitting in the training results based on the RPIOSL-UBM model is better than that of the PROSAIL model, which should be attributed to the fact that the simulation accuracy of the rice canopy hyperspectral spectrum of the RPIOSL-UBM model is better than that of the PROSAIL model. When constructing the model based on the ELM method, setting the number of implied layers to 30 can obtain a more ideal estimation model, and at the same time, the results in the real data validation will not be too bad, and the RMSE is within the acceptable range, which can be applied in the actual production. Therefore, to develop an accurate rice phenotype estimation model based on the RTM, it is imperative to further refine the RTM to ensure that the simulated hyperspectral data closely align with the measured hyperspectral data; on the other hand, it is necessary to find the appropriate parameters of the model to improve the generalization ability of the model and reduce the risk of overfitting.

4.4. Discussion of Limitations

In this study, an inverse model of LAI and LCC in rice was constructed by coupling leaf and canopy radiative transfer models and based on a machine learning approach. Although the model showed some accuracy in validation, there are still some limitations that need to be further explored. First, in the coupling part of the leaf and canopy radiative transfer models, certain leaf radiative transfer model parameters rely on the results of the optimization algorithm rather than the measured data [27]. This limitation suggests that future research should be devoted to exploring how these parameters can be obtained from measured data to enhance the reliability of the model. In addition, the simulation results of the current radiative transfer model in the 700–1000 nm band still have errors, which may lead to a decrease in the accuracy of LAI inversion. For this reason, future studies should further optimize the canopy radiative transfer model, especially considering the effect of shallow water background on canopy radiative transfer and reflectance when rice is a non-dryland crop. In terms of the inversion model, this study only relied on machine learning, neural network, and wide learning methods to construct the model and did not use optimization algorithms for further optimization. The introduction of optimization algorithms in future studies is expected to improve the model accuracy, thus providing more accurate and reliable data support for field production. In addition, the present model has not been tested in other rice varieties and growing areas, and its generalizability still needs to be further verified and discussed. These limitations provide a clear direction for subsequent research with a view to enhancing the application value and promotion potential of the model.

5. Conclusions

In this study, the RPIOSL model and the UBM model were coupled for the first time to construct a canopy RTM. The accuracy of canopy spectral reflectance simulated by the RPIOSL-UBM model was compared with that of the PROSAIL model. Characteristic wavelengths were extracted using the Sobol sensitivity analysis method and the CARS method. A simulated dataset was selected based on measured data, and rice phenotype estimation models were constructed using BP neural networks and ELM and BLS methods.The results demonstrated that the rice LAI and LCC estimation models, constructed using the RPIOSL-UBM dataset and the ELM method, were optimal. The validation RMSE for the measured dataset was 0.6357 for LAI and 6.0101 $\mu g \cdot cm^{-2}$ for LCC, indicating that the model is suitable for estimating rice phenotypic parameters from UAV hyperspectral data. Compared to models using the PROSAIL dataset, the RMSE for the measured dataset improved by 0.1076 for LAI and 6.3297 $\mu g \cdot cm^{-2}$ for LCC. Future research should focus on selecting the appropriate number of hidden layers to prevent overfitting and improve the accuracy of the RTM simulation. Enhancing the simulation accuracy of the RTM will make it more closely aligned with actual data, thereby improving the precision of rice phenotypic parameter estimation models based on the canopy RTM.

Author Contributions: Z.J.: Methodology, Writing—original draft. H.L.: Visualization. H.C.: Data acquisition. S.L.: Supervision. F.Y.: Conceptualization, Writing—review and editing. T.X.: Funding acquisition, Validation. All authors have read and agreed to the published version of the manuscript.

Funding: This research was supported by the Natural Science Foundation of Liaoning Provincial (Grant No. 2023-MSLH-283), the National Science Foundation of China (Grant No. 32201652), and the Liaoning Province 'Xingliao Talent Program' Project (Grant No. XLYC2203005).

Institutional Review Board Statement: Not applicable.

Data Availability Statement: The raw data supporting the conclusions of this article will be made available by the authors on request.

Acknowledgments: We would like to thank the editors and reviewers for their professional advice on this manuscript.

Conflicts of Interest: The authors declare no conflicts of interest.

References

1. Zhang, B.; Gu, L.; Dai, M.; Bao, X.; Sun, Q.; Zhang, M.; Qu, X.; Li, Z.; Zhen, W.; Gu, X. Estimation of grain filling rate of winter wheat using leaf chlorophyll and LAI extracted from UAV images. *Field Crop. Res.* **2024**, *306*, 109198. [CrossRef]
2. Zhai, W.; Li, C.; Cheng, Q.; Ding, F.; Chen, Z. Exploring Multisource Feature Fusion and Stacking Ensemble Learning for Accurate Estimation of Maize Chlorophyll Content Using Unmanned Aerial Vehicle Remote Sensing. *Remote Sens.* **2023**, *15*, 3454. [CrossRef]
3. Li, W.; Li, D.; Liu, S.; Baret, F.; Ma, Z.; He, C.; Warner, T.; Guo, C.; Cheng, T.; Zhu, Y.; et al. RSARE: A physically-based vegetation index for estimating wheat green LAI to mitigate the impact of leaf chlorophyll content and residue-soil background. *ISPRS-J. Photogramm. Remote Sens.* **2023**, *200*, 138–152. [CrossRef]
4. Zhou, J.; Li, F.; Wang, X.; Yin, H.; Zhang, W.; Du, J.; Pu, H. Hyperspectral and Fluorescence Imaging Approaches for Nondestructive Detection of Rice Chlorophyll. *Plants* **2024**, *13*, 1270. [CrossRef] [PubMed]
5. Ma, Y.; Qiu, C.; Zhang, J.; Pan, D.; Zheng, C.; Sun, H.; Feng, H.; Song, X. Potato Leaf Chlorophyll Content Estimation through Radiative Transfer Modeling and Active Learning. *Agronomy* **2023**, *13*, 3071. [CrossRef]

6. Zhang, S.; Tian, J.; Lu, X.; Tian, Q.; He, S.; Lin, Y.; Li, S.; Zheng, W.; Wen, T.; Mu, X.; et al. Monitoring of chlorophyll content in local saltwort species Suaeda salsa under water and salt stress based on the PROSAIL-D model in coastal wetland. *Remote Sens. Environ.* **2024**, *306*, 114117. [CrossRef]
7. Liu, H.; Lei, X.; Liang, H.; Wang, X. Multi-Model Rice Canopy Chlorophyll Content Inversion Based on UAV Hyperspectral Images. *Sustainability* **2023**, *15*, 7038. [CrossRef]
8. Yuan, W.; Meng, Y.; Li, Y.; Ji, Z.; Kong, Q.; Gao, R.; Su, Z. Research on rice leaf area index estimation based on fusion of texture and spectral information. *Comput. Electron. Agric.* **2023**, *211*, 108016. [CrossRef]
9. Castro-Valdecantos, P.; Apolo-Apolo, O.; Perez-Ruiz, M.; Egea, G. Leaf area index estimations by deep learning models using RGB images and data fusion in maize. *Precis. Agric.* **2022**, *23*, 1949–1966. [CrossRef]
10. Wang, Z.; Chen, J.; Raza, M.; Zhang, J.; Tan, X.; Saeed, A.; Ma, J.; Yang, F.; Yang, W. Predicting maize leaf area index by partial least square combined with wavelet transform. *Agron. J.* **2022**, *114*, 2860–2873. [CrossRef]
11. Li, S.; Jin, Z.; Bai, J.; Xiang, S.; Xu, C.; Yu, F. Research on fertilization decision method for rice tillering stage based on the coupling of UAV hyperspectral remote sensing and WOFOST. *Front. Plant Sci.* **2024**, *15*, 1405239. [CrossRef] [PubMed]
12. Dai, S.; Luo, H.; Hu, Y.; Zheng, Q.; Li, H.; Li, M.; Yu, X.; Chen, B. Retrieving leaf area index of rubber plantation in Hainan Island using empirical and neural network models with Landsat images. *J. Appl. Remote Sens.* **2023**, *17*, 014503. [CrossRef]
13. Sun, J.; Ren, Z.; Cui, J.; Luo, T.; Chen, T.; Yang, W.; Song, P. A high-throughput method for accurate extraction of intact rice panicle traits. *Plant Phenomics* **2024**, *6*, 0213. [CrossRef] [PubMed]
14. Yue, J.; Li, T.; Feng, H.; Fu, Y.; Liu, Y.; Tian, J.; Yang, H.; Yang, G. Enhancing field soil moisture content monitoring using laboratory-based soil spectral measurements and radiative transfer models. *Agric. Commun.* **2024**, *2*, 100060. [CrossRef]
15. Yu, F.; Bai, J.; Jin, Z.; Zhang, H.; Yang, J.; Xu, T. Estimating the rice nitrogen nutrition index based on hyperspectral transform technology. *Front. Plant Sci.* **2023**, *14*, 1118098. [CrossRef]
16. Wang, X.; Xu, G.; Feng, Y.; Peng, J.; Gao, Y.; Li, J.; Han, Z.; Luo, Q.; Ren, H.; You, X.; et al. Estimation Model of Rice Aboveground Dry Biomass Based on the Machine Learning and Hyperspectral Characteristic Parameters of the Canopy. *Agronomy* **2023**, *13*, 1940. [CrossRef]
17. Wang, J.; Wu, B.; Kohnen, V.; Lin, D.; Yang, C.; Wang, X.; Qiang, A.; Liu, W.; Kang, J.; Li, H.; et al. Classification of Rice Yield Using UAV-Based Hyperspectral Imagery and Lodging Feature. *Plant Phenomics* **2021**, *2021*, 9765952. [CrossRef]
18. Song, Y.; Cao, S.; Chu, X.; Zhou, Y.; Xu, Y.; Sun, T.; Zhou, G.; Liu, X. Non-destructive detection of moisture and fatty acid content in rice using hyperspectral imaging and chemometrics. *J. Food Compos. Anal.* **2023**, *121*, 105397. [CrossRef]
19. Xu, T.; Wang, F.; Shi, Z.; Miao, Y. Multi-scale monitoring of rice aboveground biomass by combining spectral and textural information from UAV hyperspectral images. *Int. J. Appl. Earth Obs. Geoinf.* **2024**, *127*, 103655. [CrossRef]
20. Wu, G.; Fang, Y.; Jiang, Q.; Cui, M.; Li, N.; Ou, Y.; Diao, Z.; Zhang, B. Early identification of strawberry leaves disease utilizing hyperspectral imaging combing with spectral features, multiple vegetation indices and textural features. *Comput. Electron. Agric.* **2023**, *204*, 107553. [CrossRef]
21. Qiao, L.; Gao, D.; Zhao, R.; Tang, W.; An, L.; Li, M.; Sun, H. Improving estimation of LAI dynamic by fusion of morphological and vegetation indices based on UAV imagery. *Comput. Electron. Agric.* **2022**, *192*, 106603. [CrossRef]
22. Zou, M.; Liu, Y.; Fu, M.; Li, C.; Zhou, Z.; Meng, H.; Xing, E.; Ren, Y. Combining spectral and texture feature of UAV image with plant height to improve LAI estimation of winter wheat at jointing stage. *Front. Plant Sci.* **2024**, *14*, 1272049. [CrossRef] [PubMed]
23. Tang, Z.; Chen, Z.; Gao, Y.; Xue, R.; Geng, Z.; Bu, Q.; Wang, Y.; Chen, X.; Jiang, Y.; Chen, F.; et al. A Strategy for the Acquisition and Analysis of Image-Based Phenome in Rice during the Whole Growth Period. *Plant Phenomics* **2023**, *5*, 0058. [CrossRef] [PubMed]
24. Chen, Q.; Zheng, B.; Chen, T.; Chapman, S. Integrating a crop growth model and radiative transfer model to improve estimation of crop traits based on deep learning. *J. Exp. Bot.* **2022**, *73*, 6558–6574. [CrossRef]
25. Li, X.; Yu, H.; Yu, Y.; Wang, H.; Zhang, L.; Zhang, X.; Sui, Y. Inversion Model of Clorophyll Content in Rice Based on a Bonic Optimization Algorithm. *Spectrosc. Spectr. Anal.* **2023**, *43*, 93–99. [CrossRef]
26. Jiang, J.; Comar, A.; Weiss, M.; Baret, F. FASPECT: A model of leaf optical properties accounting for the differences between upper and lower faces. *Remote Sens. Environ.* **2021**, *253*, 112205. [CrossRef]
27. Xiang, S.; Jin, Z.; Li, J.; Yu, F.; Xu, T. RPIOSL: Construction of the radiation transfer model for rice leaves. *Plant Methods* **2024**, *20*, 1. [CrossRef]
28. Xu, X.; Fan, W.; Li, J.; Zhao, P.; Chen, G. A unified model of bidirectional reflectance distribution function for the vegetation canopy. *Sci. China-Earth Sci.* **2017**, *60*, 463–477. [CrossRef]
29. Meng, F.; Li, J.; Zhang, Y.; Qi, S.; Tang, Y. Transforming unmanned pineapple picking with spatio-temporal convolutional neural networks. *Comput. Electron. Agric.* **2023**, *214*, 108298. [CrossRef]
30. Du, R.; Lu, J.; Xiang, Y.; Zhang, F.; Chen, J.; Tang, Z.; Shi, H.; Wang, X.; Li, W. Estimation of winter canola growth parameter from UAV multi-angular spectral-texture information using stacking-based ensemble learning model. *Comput. Electron. Agric.* **2024**, *222*, 109074. [CrossRef]
31. Shao, M.; Nie, C.; Zhang, A.; Shi, L.; Zha, Y.; Xu, H.; Yang, H.; Yu, X.; Bai, Y.; Liu, S.; et al. Quantifying effect of maize tassels on LAI estimation based on multispectral imagery and machine learning methods. *Comput. Electron. Agric.* **2023**, *211*, 108029. [CrossRef]

32. Ji, S.; Gu, C.; Xi, X.; Zhang, Z.; Hong, Q.; Huo, Z.; Zhao, H.; Zhang, R.; Li, B.; Tan, C. Quantitative Monitoring of Leaf Area Index in Rice Based on Hyperspectral Feature Bands and Ridge Regression Algorithm. *Remote Sens.* **2022**, *14*, 2777. [CrossRef]
33. Luo, L.; Chang, Q.; Gao, Y.; Jiang, D.; Li, F. Combining Different Transformations of Ground Hyperspectral Data with Unmanned Aerial Vehicle (UAV) Images for Anthocyanin Estimation in Tree Peony Leaves. *Remote Sens.* **2022**, *14*, 2271. [CrossRef]
34. Zhu, H.; Liu, Z.; Chen, C.; Liang, Y. An Efficient Algorithm for the Incremental Broad Learning System by Inverse Cholesky Factorization of a Partitioned Matrix. *IEEE Access* **2021**, *9*, 19294–19303. [CrossRef]
35. Qiu, C.; Ding, F.; He, X.; Wang, M. Apply Physical System Model and Computer Algorithm to Identify Osmanthus Fragrans Seed Vigor Based on Hyperspectral Imaging and Convolutional Neural Network. *Inf. Technol. Control* **2023**, *52*, 887–897. [CrossRef]
36. Wenjing, G.; Xue, C.; Xiaohan, L.; Yusheng, H.; Zhenhui, R. Apple firmness detection method based on hyperspectral technology. *Food Control* **2024**, *166*, 110690. [CrossRef]
37. Li, X.; Wei, Z.; Peng, F.; Liu, J.; Han, G. Non-destructive prediction and visualization of anthocyanin content in mulberry fruits using hyperspectral imaging. *Front. Plant Sci.* **2023**, *14*, 1137198. [CrossRef]
38. Xiao, Q.; Tang, W.; Zhang, C.; Zhou, L.; Feng, L.; Shen, J.; Yan, T.; Gao, P.; He, Y.; Wu, N. Spectral Preprocessing Combined with Deep Transfer Learning to Evaluate Chlorophyll Content in Cotton Leaves. *Plant Phenomics* **2022**, *2022*, 9813841. [CrossRef]
39. Amanah, H.; Wakholi, C.; Perez, M.; Faqeerzada, M.; Tunny, S.; Masithoh, R.; Choung, M.; Kim, K.; Lee, W.; Cho, B. Near-Infrared Hyperspectral Imaging (NIR-HSI) for Nondestructive Prediction of Anthocyanins Content in Black Rice Seeds. *Appl. Sci.* **2021**, *11*, 4841. [CrossRef]
40. Peanusaha, S.; Pourreza, A.; Kamiya, Y.; Fidelibus, M.; Chakraborty, M. Nitrogen retrieval in grapevine (*Vitis vinifera* L.) leaves by hyperspectral sensing. *Remote Sens. Environ.* **2024**, *302*, 113966. [CrossRef]
41. Huang, Q.; Wang, X.; Gao, Q.; Carraro, A.; Sozzi, M.; Marinello, F. Indicators to Digitization Footprint and How to Get Digitization Footprint (Part 2). *Comput. Electron. Agric.* **2024**, *224*, 109206. [CrossRef]
42. Su, X.; He, J.; Li, W.; Pan, Y.; Li, D.; Yao, X.; Cheng, T.; Zhu, Y.; Cao, W.; Tian, Y. Monitoring Rice Leaf Nitrogen Content Based on the Canopy Structure Effect Corrected With a Novel Model PROSPECT-P. *IEEE Trans. Geosci. Remote Sens.* **2024**, *62*, 4414317. [CrossRef]
43. Li, X.; Sun, Z.; Lu, S.; Omasa, K. PROSPECULAR: A model for simulating multi-angular spectral properties of leaves by coupling PROSPECT with a specular function. *Remote Sens. Environ.* **2023**, *297*, 113754. [CrossRef]
44. Xue, H.; Xu, X.; Yang, Y.; Hu, D.; Niu, G. Rapid and Non-Destructive Prediction of Moisture Content in Maize Seeds Using Hyperspectral Imaging. *Sensors* **2024**, *24*, 1855. [CrossRef]
45. Yuan, X.; Zhang, X.; Zhang, N.; Ma, R.; He, D.; Bao, H.; Sun, W. Hyperspectral Estimation of SPAD Value of Cotton Leaves under Verticillium Wilt Stress Based on GWO-ELM. *Agronomy* **2023**, *13*, 1779. [CrossRef]
46. Liu, T.; Xu, T.; Yu, F.; Yuan, Q.; Guo, Z.; Xu, B. A method combining ELM and PLSR (ELM-P) for estimating chlorophyll content in rice with feature bands extracted by an improved ant colony optimization algorithm. *Comput. Electron. Agric.* **2021**, *186*, 106177. [CrossRef]
47. Chu, F.; Wang, G.; Wang, J.; Chen, C.; Wang, X. Learning broad learning system with controllable sparsity through L regularization. *Appl. Soft. Comput.* **2023**, *136*, 110068. [CrossRef]
48. Liu, L.; Liu, T.; Chen, C.; Wang, Y. Modal-Regression-Based Broad Learning System for Robust Regression and Classification. *IEEE Trans. Neural Netw. Learn. Syst.* **2023**, *35*, 12344–12357. [CrossRef]
49. Wang, X.; Ling, B.; Zhao, H.; Liu, S. The Tensor Discriminant Ridge Regression Model With Extreme Learning Machine for Hyperspectral Image Classification. *IEEE J. Sel. Top. Appl. Earth Observ. Remote Sens.* **2023**, *16*, 8102–8114. [CrossRef]
50. Viskari, T.; Shiklomanov, A.; Dietze, M.C.; Serbin, S.P. The influence of canopy radiation parameter uncertainty on model projections of terrestrial carbon and energy cycling. *PLoS ONE* **2019**, *14*, e0216512. [CrossRef]
51. Hovi, A.; Janoutová, R.; Malenovský, Z.; Schraik, D.; Gastellu-Etchegorry, J.P.; Lauret, N.; Novotný, J.; Rautiainen, M. Physically based modelling of spectral transmittance through forest canopies. *Methods Ecol. Evol.* **2024**, *15*, 1859–1872. [CrossRef]
52. Ban, S.; Liu, W.; Tian, M.; Wang, Q.; Yuan, T.; Chang, Q.; Li, L. Rice Leaf Chlorophyll Content Estimation Using UAV-Based Spectral Images in Different Regions. *Agronomy* **2022**, *12*, 2832. [CrossRef]
53. He, J.; Zhang, N.; Su, X.; Lu, J.; Yao, X.; Cheng, T.; Zhu, Y.; Cao, W.; Tian, Y. Estimating Leaf Area Index with a New Vegetation Index Considering the Influence of Rice Panicles. *Remote Sens.* **2019**, *11*, 1809. [CrossRef]
54. Zhang, Y.; Jiang, Y.; Xu, B.; Yang, G.; Feng, H.; Yang, X.; Yang, H.; Liu, C.; Cheng, Z.; Feng, Z. Study on the Estimation of Leaf Area Index in Rice Based on UAV RGB and Multispectral Data. *Remote Sens.* **2024**, *16*, 3049. [CrossRef]
55. Yang, X.; Lu, X.; Shi, J.; Li, J.; Ju, W. Inversion of Rice Leaf Chlorophyll Content Based on Sentinel-2 Satellite Data. *Spectrosc. Spectr. Anal.* **2022**, *42*, 866–872. [CrossRef]

agriculture

MDPI

Article

Multi-Genotype Rice Yield Prediction Based on Time-Series Remote Sensing Images and Dynamic Process Clustering

Qian Li [1], Shaoshuai Zhao [1], Lei Du [1] and Shanjun Luo [1,2,*]

[1] Aerospace Information Research Institute, Henan Academy of Sciences, Zhengzhou 450046, China; liqian@hnas.ac.cn (Q.L.); zss@hnas.ac.cn (S.Z.); dulei@hnas.ac.cn (L.D.)
[2] School of Remote Sensing and Information Engineering, Wuhan University, Wuhan 430079, China
* Correspondence: luoshanjun@hnas.ac.cn

Abstract: Predicting rice yield in a timely, precise, and efficient manner is crucial for directing agricultural output and creating food policy. The goal of this work was to create a stable, high-precision estimate model for the yield prediction of multi-genotype rice combined with dynamic growth processes. By obtaining RGB and multispectral data of the rice canopy during the whole development stage, several bands of reflectance, vegetation index, canopy height, and canopy volume were retrieved. These remote sensing properties were used to define several curves of the rice-growing process. The k-shape technique was utilized to cluster the various characteristics based on rice growth features, and data from different groups were subsequently employed to create a yield estimation model. The results demonstrated that, in comparison to utilizing solely spectral and geometric factors, the accuracy of the multi-genotype rice estimate model based on dynamic process clustering was much higher. With a root mean square error of 315.39 kg/ha and a coefficient of determination of 0.82, the rice yield calculation based on canopy volume temporal characteristics was the most accurate. The proposed approach can support precision agriculture and improve the extraction of characteristics related to the rice growth process.

Keywords: yield estimation; vegetation indices; canopy height; canopy volume; UAV; dynamic process clustering

1. Introduction

Rice serves as a staple diet for almost half of the world's population, particularly in Asia [1]. It is a vital component of everyday nutrition and is high in proteins, carbohydrates, vitamins, and minerals [2]. Rice is a staple crop in many nations, and the state of its development and output has a direct impact on the food security of each nation [3]. In addition to aiding in the development of national food security-related policy decisions, macro-control of grain market prices, and international grain trade, a quick and accurate understanding of pre-harvest yield data is crucial for the precise provision of agricultural insurance and wise management of farmland [4,5]. Predicting rice yield is so crucial for ensuring food security, assisting in agricultural decision-making, advancing science and technology, adjusting to climate change, preserving social stability, and facilitating international commerce.

Crop yield estimation is complicated, lagging, and not feasible on a large scale due to the time-consuming, labor-intensive, and expert knowledge-required nature of traditional methods, which primarily involve field sampling surveys, meteorological forecasts, and agronomical forecasts [6]. Furthermore, conventional on-the-ground manual yield assessment techniques are ineffective and vulnerable to plant damage, making them unsuitable for yield estimation [7]. As a quick monitoring, analysis, and diagnostic tool that can reliably gather crop image data across large regions, remote sensing is extensively utilized in many facets of smart agriculture [8]. Since the 1970s, optical satellite data with certain properties, like spatial, temporal, and spectral resolution, have been widely employed for large-scale crop production prediction due to advancements in remote sensing technology [9,10]. However, the timeliness of data collection cannot be guaranteed due to the coarse and weather-sensitive geographical and temporal resolutions of satellite data, which have a greater impact on regional agricultural output prediction. In recent years, crop growth monitoring has become more efficient owing to unmanned aerial vehicle (UAV) remote sensing technology, which can flexibly carry various sensors and efficiently capture high spatial and temporal resolution image data [11]. UAV-based remote sensing offers new prospects for remote sensing technologies by monitoring a greater range than ground-based measurement methods, better spatial resolution, more frequent observation opportunities, and lower costs than satellite and airplane observations [12]. Thus, there is much promise for rice yield estimation in the field using UAV remote sensing technologies.

Differentiated field data configurations are used in the majority of current crop remote sensing studies for yield estimation. Most field studies are planned using irrigation, planting techniques, and fertilizer gradient control [13–15]. However, it is challenging to match the experimental design in actual crop field production. This makes it challenging to use current estimating models in real-world field settings. Field managers adequately fertilize the soil before planting. Varieties and planting dates may vary among rice fields grown by different farmers. Producers will manage their acreage in a more sophisticated manner, particularly given China's current cropland fragmentation scenario [16]. Because of this, inconsistent irrigation or fertilizer use is quite uncommon. Therefore, there are few existing studies on remote sensing for yield estimation of data under the natural growing state, which makes it difficult to meet the needs of actual farmland management.

The vegetation index (VI), which is computed using UAV image reflectance, has been shown to be an effective crop yield forecast indicator [17]. The rapid development of UAVs has also enhanced the acquisition frequency and spatial and temporal resolution of crop image data. For instance, Zhou et al. employed a UAV fitted with a digital camera and a multispectral camera to capture images of rice at various stages. They then used multiple linear regression (MLR) to analyze the relationship between different VIs and rice yield. According to the findings, the visible atmospherically resistance index (VARI), which was computed using MLR and digital imagery, performed best during the jointing and booting stages, while the normalized difference vegetation index (NDVI), which was computed using MLR and multispectral imagery, performed best during the booting and heading stages [18]. Furthermore, data, including canopy temperature, height, and texture, have been suggested for crop yield estimation [13,15,19]. However, for rice, canopy changes are very complicated as the reproductive cycle shifts, and it is difficult to provide generalizable indications for yield prediction utilizing the aforementioned indicators. Vegetation indices perform poorly in predicting yield at later stages of crops because it has been argued that yield is the result of the nonlinear accumulation of crop photosynthetic products, and traditional linear regression models are unable to adequately capture this complex nonlinear relationship. As a result, when predicting agricultural yield, researchers choose nonlinear methods like machine learning [19,20]. Machine learning can better handle nonlinear relationships between large amounts of data. However, it is weak in handling complex nonlinear relationships and time-series data and is ineffective in predicting yield for multiple varieties with large variations in morphological structure and growth stage [21]. The performance of machine learning models is affected by a variety of factors, including training data, input variables, crop type, and growth stage. One of the most popular techniques for estimating yield is linear regression, which frequently works well because of its high interpretability [22].

In recent years, phenology has been shown to provide critical information for crop yield prediction [23]. Studies have indicated that dividing the time window by phenological stage allows for a more accurate extraction of environmental variables to capture the complex interactions between crop growth and external factors [24]. Most current research on crop yield estimation focuses on the use of single-period variables or the integration of multi-period variables [4]. When using single-period variables, the correlation between variables and yield from sowing to maturity is often analyzed, and finally, the variables with high correlation are filtered out for direct yield prediction. When multi-period variables are employed, a matrix of variables from multiple periods is often obtained as inputs for machine learning or multiple regression models for yield estimation. However, information on crop variables in different periods has distinct growth dimensions and cannot be directly compared and integrated. Therefore, determining the phenological period of a crop is essential to guarantee the accuracy of growth monitoring and yield prediction. The threshold, maximum slope, and curve fitting methods of optical remote sensing have been utilized to monitor crop phenology [25]. These approaches can only detect the stage of obvious change in greenness based on inflection points and cannot monitor other key stages closely related to agricultural practices. Moreover, accurate real-time monitoring of phenology can be realized based on remote sensing data and classification algorithms. However, this requires a large amount of known phenological data. The essence of classifying different phenological periods is to distinguish variable features at various stages. This problem can be solved if a suitable division method of variables is found to distinguish their differences. The k-shape clustering algorithm is a typical classification technique based on the changing features of a time series, which has the advantage of dealing with the signals of diverse domains. The basic idea is to calculate the similarity between time series based on the distance of the shape to realize clustering [26]. Remote sensing feature variables are characterized by a time series. Therefore, there is potential for the classification of remote sensing features based on time series.

Two separate experiments that simulated rice cultivation under natural growing conditions were created for this investigation. A UAV remote sensing platform was equipped with both an RGB and a multispectral camera to obtain high-frequency observations of rice throughout its growth stage. The k-shape approach was utilized to accomplish high-precision prediction of multi-genotype (multi-species) rice yield based on temporal growth feature clustering by analyzing the contribution of spectral and structural information to the yield estimation of multi-genotype rice. The specific goals of this study were to (1) compare the effects of geometric and spectral information on multi-genotype rice yield estimation, (2) choose variables that are appropriate for characterizing the features of the rice growth process, and (3) forecast multi-genotype rice yield by clustering growth process features.

2. Materials and Methods

2.1. Experimental Design

The data used in this investigation came from three field-independent investigations that used multiple rice genotypes and replicated rice cultivation under natural growth conditions, as shown in Figure 1. Different hybrid varieties of rice were cultivated in each of the 289 plots in Experiment 1 (2022, Exp. 1). Each plot had a one-square-meter area. In Experiment 2 (2019, Exp. 2), 48 plots representing 48 distinct rice varieties were planted. Each field plot had a total area of roughly 40 square meters. Except for the various rice genotypes, all field management procedures were the same. The uniform rate of nitrogen fertilizer application was 180 kg/ha. Before transplanting, 50% of the nitrogen fertilizer was applied as a basal fertilizer, 25% was applied during the tillering stage, and 25% was applied during the booting stage. Phosphorus and potash fertilizers were applied as one-time basal fertilizers at 90 kg/ha and 180 kg/ha, respectively. In Experiment 3 (2022, Exp. 3), three nitrogen gradient levels were set up, N1/4, N1, and N2, representing nitrogen applications of 36.3, 144, and 288 kg/ha. Meanwhile, three replications were set up, and the three varieties were randomized. In total, there were 27 plots with an area of about 15 m^2 each. The management practices remained the same as in Experiments 1 and 2, except for the differences in varieties and N fertilization levels. This study was conducted on a plot scale. Each plot was planted with an individual rice variety.

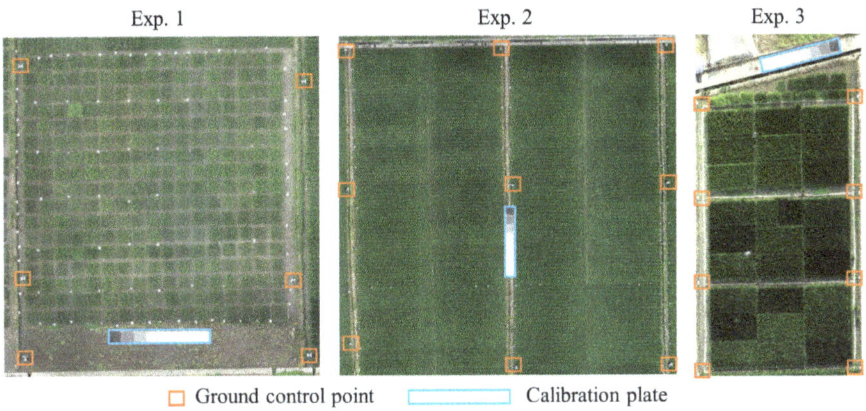

Figure 1. Experimental arrangement and plot layout.

2.2. Data Acquisition and Processing

2.2.1. UAV RGB Image

RGB images of the rice canopy were acquired using a Phantom 4 Pro quadcopter drone manufactured by DJI Innovation (SZ DJI Technology Co., Ltd., Shenzhen, China). The altitude of the UAV was set to 30 m, and the overlap was 90% in heading and 70% in side direction. The average flight speed of the UAV was set to 5 m/s. The data acquisition time required per unit area (1 m^2) was calculated to be approximately 0.6 s based on the experimental area. The gimbal of the UAV ensured that the camera was always vertically downward during image acquisition. The camera has a field of view of 84°, an image size of 5472 × 3648 pixels, and a ground resolution of about 1 cm/pixel. The aperture size and ISO sensitivity were set before aerial photography according to the actual lighting conditions in the field, and the camera parameters remained unchanged throughout the aerial photography image acquisition process.

After acquiring the RGB images of the experimental area, Agisoft Photoscan Professional software (version 1.4.5, Agisoft LLC, St. Petersburg, Russia) was used for image stitching and 3D reconstruction to generate a dense 3D point cloud, digital elevation model (DEM), digital surface model (DSM), and orthomosaic products of the experimental area based on the coordinates of the ground control points. The Photoscan software is based on the Structure from Motion (SfM) and Multi-View Stereo (MVS) algorithms for image processing. RGB data were collected during 10 periods (denoted as S1–S10), including the tillering, jointing, booting, heading, and ripening stages of rice, with an interval of 5–10 days between each collection.

2.2.2. UAV Multispectral Image

An S1000 UAV (S1000, SZ DJI Technology, Co., Ltd., Shenzhen, China) equipped with an MCA series multispectral camera (Tetracam, Inc., Chatsworth, CA, USA) was used to collect the multispectral data. It was clear, cloudless, and windless when the UAV mission was selected. The time frame for gathering the data was consistent from 10:00 to 14:00 local time. A 12-band MCA (center bands: 490, 520, 550, 570, 670, 680, 700, 720, 800, 850, 900, and 950 nm) was the multispectral camera utilized in this investigation. The RGB and multispectral image acquisition times were identical.

The UAV multispectral image processing involves three steps: geometrical processing, radiative handling, and spectral information acquisition. The geometrical processing of UAV multispectral images acquired based on the MCA camera includes halation calibration, waveband registration, and distortion modification, which is accomplished using the MCA image-specific programming tool PixelWrech2 (Tetracam, Inc., Chatsworth, CA, USA). Radiative handling consists mainly of radiometric calibration. In this work, eight calibrators with available known reflectances (3%, 6%, 12%, 24%, 36%, 48%, 56%, and 80%) were used for radiometric calibration, as shown in Figure 1. The radiometric calibration approach was based on the PEL method [23]. Spectral information acquisition comprises region of interest (ROI) outlining and reflectance retrieval.

2.2.3. Rice Yield

After the rice of all genotypes had matured, the rice yield was measured in each plot by manual sampling. After manual harvesting, threshing, drying, water content determination, and weighing, the measured rice yield was calculated based on the number of samples taken, weight reading of the samples, transplanting density, and water content.

2.3. *Vegetation Indices Construction*

Vegetation indices have been proposed to reflect dynamic alternation in the full growth cycle of vegetation through the combination of different bands of reflectance. They are related to leaf pigmentation, photosynthesis, and plant nutrient status and are useful for monitoring rice growth. In this study, six vegetation indices that proved to be effective in monitoring vegetation growth and yield prediction were selected, as shown in Table 1.

Table 1. The vegetation indices selected in this study.

Vegetation Indices	Formula	Reference
NDVI	(R850 nm − R670 nm)/(R850 nm + R670 nm)	[27]
GNDVI	(R850 nm − R550 nm)/(R850 nm + R550 nm)	[28]
NDRE	(R850 nm − R720 nm)/(R850 nm + R720 nm)	[29]
$CI_{reg\ edge}$	R850 nm/R720 nm − 1	[30]
EVI2	2.5 × (R850 nm − R670 nm)/(R850 nm + 2.4 × R670 nm + 1)	[31]
CI_{green}	R850 nm/R550 nm − 1	[32]

2.4. *Rice Canopy Height and Canopy Volume Extraction*

To obtain an accurate canopy height (CH) and reduce the effect of ground undulation, the DEM of the base ground was acquired before rice was transplanted to the field. After the seedlings are transplanted, the DSM product generated from each aerial photograph is subtracted from the base ground DEM, which is the rice canopy height model (CHM). On the CHM image, the rice canopy area was selected by outlining the ROIs, and the average value of CH of all pixels in the range of each ROI was computed as the canopy height of the plot. The acquisition process of rice CH is shown in Figure 2.

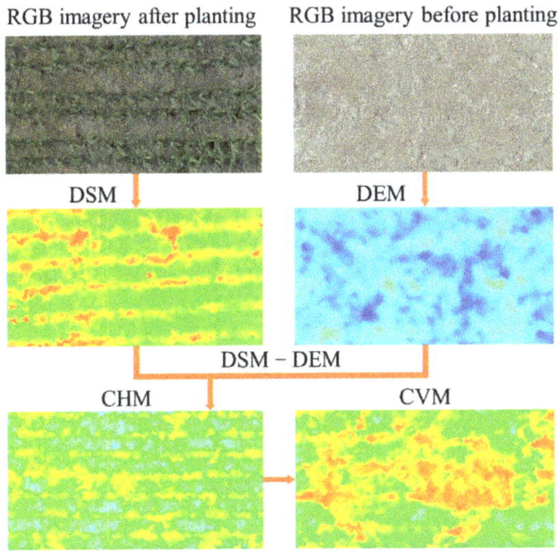

Figure 2. Canopy height and canopy volume extraction process.

After obtaining the canopy CHM, the canopy volume model (CVM) can be obtained by combining the ground sampling distance (*GSD*) information of each pixel. Similar to *CH*, the *CV* of each plot can be calculated using the ROI tool. The formula for *CV* is shown in Equation (1).

$$CV = \sum CH_i \times GSD^2 \tag{1}$$

where CH_i is the canopy height of the *i*th pixel.

2.5. K-Shape Clustering Method

An accurate, scalable, and domain-independent time-series clustering approach used in this study is the k-shape algorithm [33]. The program can calculate the distances for shapes and has a distance measure that is independent of movement and scaling. The iterative enhancement mechanism at the core of the algorithm creates homogeneous and better-separated clusters. To update the cluster assignments of the time series in each iteration, a method that the algorithm uses to compute the cluster centers is provided, based on the features of the standard inter-correlation distance measure [26]. The specific steps are as follows: (1) Computation of the mutual correlation function. The mutual correlation function reflects the degree to which the two sequences match each other at different relative positions. (2) Normalization of the correlation function. (3) Calculation of the shape-based distance (SBD). The larger the correlation function, the smaller the SBD. (4) Calculating the mass center of the class based on SBD. (5) Implementation of k-shape clustering. Initially, sequences are randomly assigned to clusters, k sequences are randomly selected, and the mass center of each cluster is computed. Subsequently, the SBD of each sequence with the mass center of the existing clusters is computed from scratch, and when the SBD is the smallest, it is classified into the cluster, and the mass center of each cluster is updated dynamically. Finally, iterations are performed until the change in the mass center of each cluster is less than a threshold or a specified number of iterations is reached.

2.6. Model Evaluation and Technology Roadmap

In this study, a ten-fold cross-validation method was used for accuracy statistics, and the model calibration and validation processes are shown in Figure 3. Ten-fold cross-validation is a widely used method for model evaluation. It divides the dataset into ten equal parts, and in each iteration, nine of them are taken as the training set and the remaining one as the test set. This is performed in a cycle until each copy of the data is used as a test set. Eventually, the test results of the ten iterations are averaged to obtain an assessment of the model performance. This approach makes full use of the data, reduces the variance in model assessment, and improves the stability and reliability of the assessment results. In Exp. 1, a ten-fold cross-validation method was used. Exp. 2 and Exp. 3 measure the migration ability of the model as independent validation data. The coefficient of determination (R^2) and root mean square error (RMSE) were selected for the assessment of rice yield prediction models. The technology roadmap for rice yield prediction in this study is shown in Figure 4.

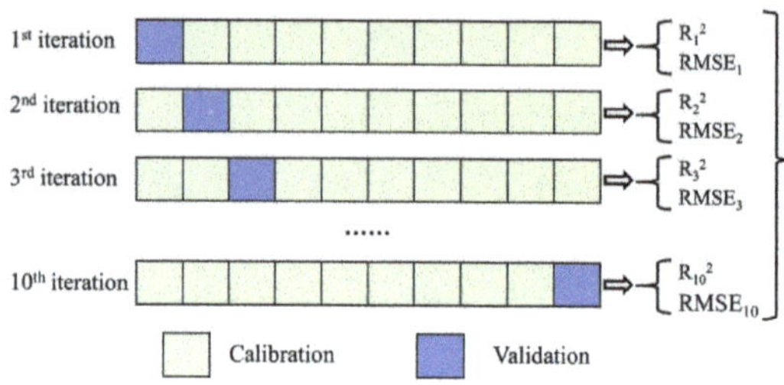

$$R^2 = \frac{1}{10}\sum_{i=1}^{10} R_i^2$$

$$RMSE = \frac{1}{10}\sum_{i=1}^{10} RMSE_i^2$$

Figure 3. Ten-fold cross-validation schematic diagram.

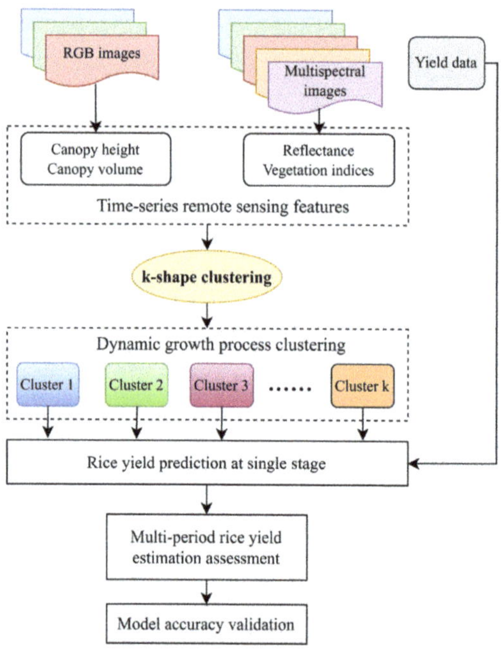

Figure 4. Technology roadmap for rice yield estimation.

3. Results

3.1. Canopy Height Extraction Results

Due to the time-consuming and labor-intensive measurement of rice canopy height using manual methods, the timely acquisition of real data for a large number of samples could not be accomplished. Taking Exp. 1 as an example, the actual canopy heights of different parts of the samples were measured in ten periods, and 765 sample data were finally obtained. UAV remote sensing technology was used to obtain the rice canopy height of the corresponding actual measured plots, and the comparison results are shown in Figure 5. It can be seen that the rice canopy height obtained by UAV remote sensing technology has a very high precision, with an overall RMSE of 0.04 m. All sample points are distributed near the 1:1 line. Therefore, the rice CH obtained by remote sensing methods can replace the measured data. The UAV-acquired CH was used for all calculations in the subsequent modeling process.

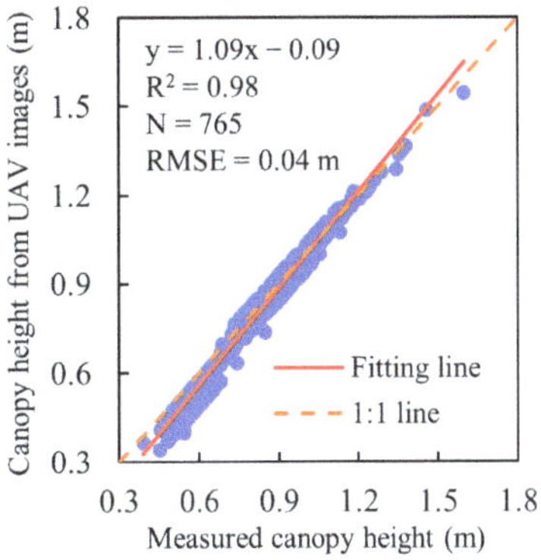

Figure 5. Comparison of rice canopy heights acquired from UAV RGB images with measured values.

3.2. Rice Yield Prediction Based on VIs, CH, and CV

Before predicting rice yield, it is necessary to analyze the changes in each predictor variable over time. The 720 nm band reflectance, NDRE, CI_{green}, and CH of some plots were taken as an example to be analyzed, and the results are shown in Figure 6. It can be seen that the variations in red-edge band reflectance with time show a general trend of gradual increase. However, there is obvious volatility. NDRE showed an overall trend of first increasing, then remaining relatively stable, and finally decreasing over time. Compared to reflectance, volatility is weakened. CI_{green} shows a consistent trend with NDRE overall, but there is spurious volatility. Compared to red-edge reflectance, NDRE, and CI_{green}, CH exhibits the weakest volatility, showing an overall trend of increasing and then stabilizing. It is worth noting that there is an apparent commonality in the selected indicators, i.e., there are several samples with a consistent trend in volatility but with a large difference in trend from the others. In the case of the NDRE, for example, it is clear that some samples show a curve of dramatic growth, followed by stabilization, and finally a sharp decline. Another class of samples exists that shows a stable and constant curve, followed by a gradual increase, and finally, a decrease in volatility. Moreover, in the middle stage of the growth stage, the indicators show more complex patterns of change, especially the red-edge band reflectance and CI_{green}. The overall pattern of change in these variables can be divided into more similar combinations of samples.

The correlation of the six vegetation indices, CH and CV, constructed in this study, with the final yield at different stages was analyzed, and the results are shown in Figure 7. In the correlation heatmap, darker colors indicate higher Pearson correlation coefficients. * indicates a significant correlation at a 0.05 confidence level. In terms of individual periods, almost all remotely sensed variables showed an insignificant correlation with yield, except for EVI2 in period S3. In cases where multiple period variables jointly predicted rice yield, multiple linear regression methods were used to fuse variables from different stages. It can be seen that all the variables were significantly correlated with rice yield except NDVI, GNDVI, and CI_{green}. Among these, NDRE, CH, and CV showed the strongest correlations.

This indicates that multi-period remote sensing data have the potential to improve the accuracy of rice yield prediction. However, the correlation coefficients are still below 0.6, and further accuracy improvement is needed.

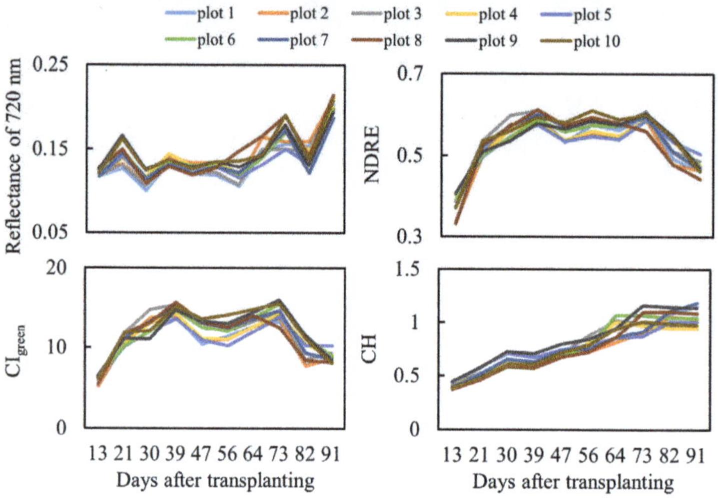

Figure 6. Time-series variation curves of canopy reflectance, VI, and CH in the selected plots.

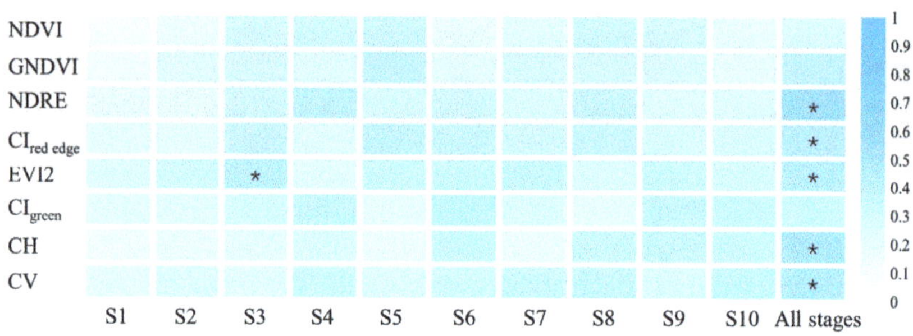

Figure 7. Correlation of remote sensing variables with rice yield at different periods (* indicates significant correlation at 0.05 confidence level).

The rice yield prediction models using NDRE, CH, and CV variables and multiple linear regression are shown in Figure 8. It can be observed that accurate rice yield prediction results cannot be obtained by directly utilizing remote sensing variables over multiple periods. The R^2 of the models are all lower than 0.4, and the RMSE are all more than 1500 kg/ha. As can be seen from the normality test of the measured data, the yield data of the 289 plots conform to the standard normal distribution. The prediction results based on NDRE, CH, and CV show that there is an overestimation of rice yield in most of the plots, and the yield prediction values of the vast majority of the plots are greater than 9000 kg/ha. From the perspective of the distribution of yield, the results of yield prediction based on NDRE and CH show that there is a large number of clustering phenomena in the sample points, which cannot conform to the standard normal distribution. In the CV-based model, the phenomenon is modified. This shows the potential of CV to estimate rice yield with high accuracy.

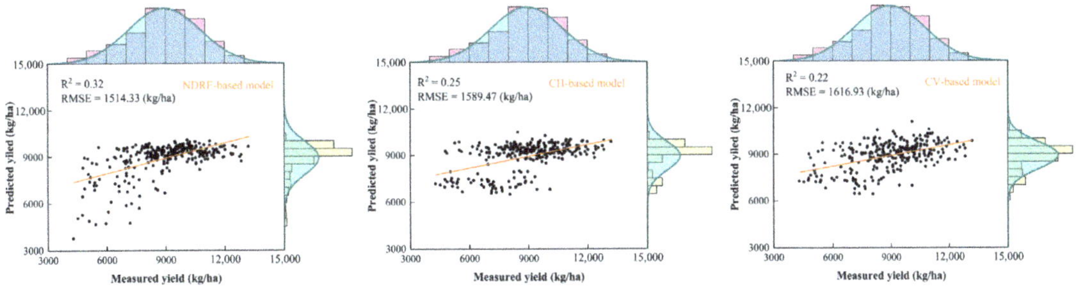

Figure 8. Comparison of rice yield estimation results based on multi-period NDRE, CH, and CV.

3.3. Rice Yield Prediction Based on Dynamic Process Clustering

3.3.1. Clustering Based on Time-Series Reflectance Curves

To reduce the mutual impact among several sample groups, samples with similar curve trends were clustered. The k-shape technique was used to cluster the reflectance curves of various bands based on the SBD-based mass center calculation method. Figure 9 displays the results of using the corresponding variables from multiple periods to forecast the yield in each sample group. The prediction of rice yield is not significantly and consistently improved by clustering reflectance curves in any of the bands other than the red-edge bands (700 and 720 nm). The optimal rice yield prediction accuracy using this indicator is about 0.5 for R^2 and about 1200 kg/ha for RMSE. The accuracy of estimating rice yield fluctuates irregularly as the number of clustering categories increases. In terms of local effects, the prediction accuracy of rice yield may show some improvement after realizing sample clustering. For instance, the accuracy R^2 is increased by around 0.2, and the RMSE is decreased by roughly 600 kg/ha after using the 490 nm band reflectance curve to actualize the sample division of 5 and 8 categories. Following the sample division of two and four categories using the 800 nm band reflectance curve, the RMSE is decreased by about 800 kg/ha, and the accuracy R^2 is increased by around 0.2. The accuracy R^2 is increased by around 0.3, and the RMSE is decreased by more than 600 kg/ha after the 4- and 7-class sample division is realized using the 550 nm band reflectance curve. It goes without saying that improper clustering will reduce accuracy.

It was discovered that the accuracy of predicting rice yield considerably increased and stabilized after the samples were clustered using red-edge band reflectance curves. Clustering into six classes of samples improves the model accuracy the most when utilizing the 700 nm band. When compared to clustering into just two classes of samples, the R^2 is increased by around 0.3, and the RMSE is decreased by roughly 700 kg/ha. The model's accuracy essentially remains the same as the number of clustering classes is increased. The model accuracy increased the most when using the 720 nm band and clustering into eight classes of samples. When only two classes of samples are clustered, the RMSE decreases by around 800 kg/ha, and the R^2 improves by approximately 0.4. The accuracy of the model stops increasing as the clustering categories continue to grow. According to the aforementioned findings, rice growth may be described using red-edge band reflectance profiles.

3.3.2. Clustering Based on Time-Series Vegetation Index Curves

Similar to the temporal reflectance curve clustering, different categories were clustered using the k-shape algorithm for different vegetation indices. In each category of samples, the rice yield was predicted using the corresponding variables in multiple periods, and the results are shown in Figure 10. It can be found that with the increase of clustering categories, the accuracy of rice yield estimation for different vegetation indices shows an obvious and stable improvement. Except for the obvious accuracy improvement pattern, compared with the results of clustering using spectral curve features, the accuracy of rice yield prediction using vegetation index feature clustering is substantially improved, with the highest accuracy of R^2 close to 0.8 and RMSE close to 400 kg/ha. With the increase in clustering categories, the accuracy of rice yield prediction firstly increases significantly and then basically remains stable. It is worth mentioning that when the highest rice yield prediction accuracy is obtained, the number of clustering categories characterized by different time-series vegetation index curves varies, and the number of categories maybe six, seven, or eight.

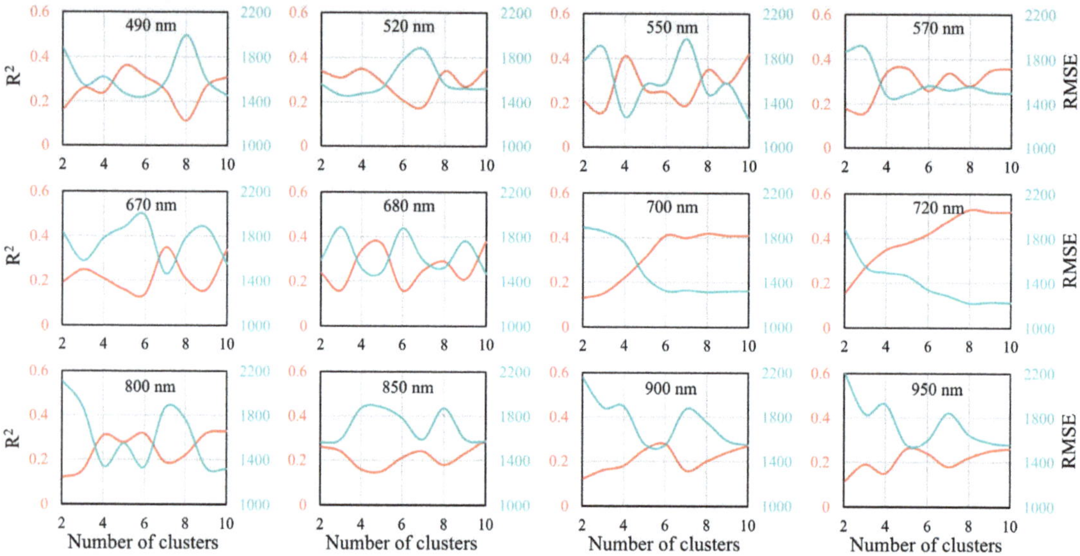

Figure 9. Trends in multi-period rice yield estimation results based on time-series feature clustering of reflectance curves in different bands.

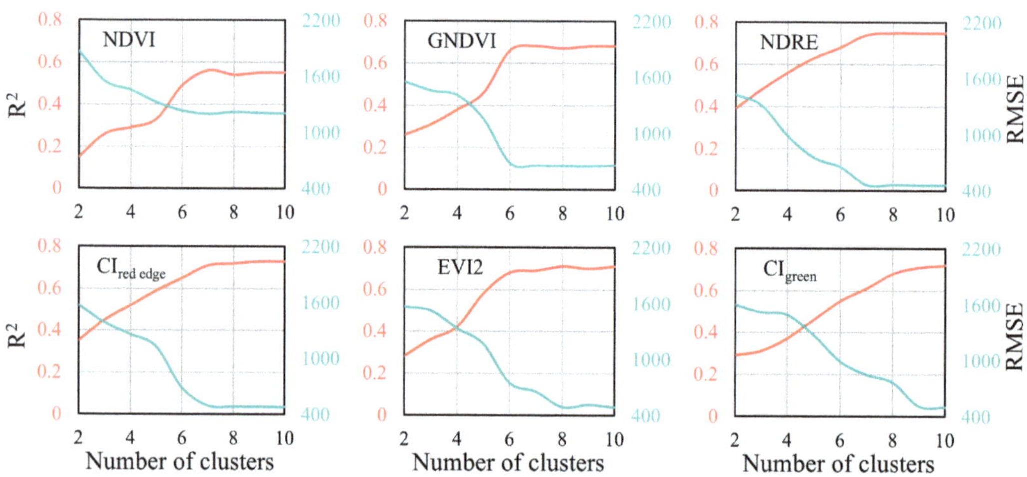

Figure 10. Trends in multi-period rice yield estimation results based on time-series vegetation indices curves clustering.

GNDVI only needs 289 samples to be clustered into six distinct groups, which is the smallest number of categories needed to achieve the best rice yield forecast accuracy. However, CI_{green} needs to be clustered into nine groups to attain the best estimation accuracy. When the NDVI is grouped into seven groups, the best accuracy is achieved. Nevertheless, there is room for improvement in the precision of rice yield estimation when compared to other vegetation indices. When estimating the yield using the NDVI curve, the highest accuracy R^2 was less than 0.6, and the RMSE was greater than 1200 kg/ha. Based on the time-series curves of other vegetative indices, the maximum yield estimation accuracy R^2 was approximately 0.7, with an RMSE of roughly 500 kg/ha. With an R^2 of nearly 0.75, and an RMSE of roughly 400 kg/ha, the red-edge index curve-based estimation of rice yield exhibits the highest accuracy overall. Previous results have shown that the time-series features of vegetation indices, particularly red-edge indices, which have the greatest impact on rice yield estimation, can accurately describe the growth characteristics of rice over the entire period.

3.3.3. Clustering Based on Time-Series CH and CV Curves

Similar to the temporal reflectance curve and vegetation index curve clustering, different categories were clustered using the k-shape algorithm for CH and CV. In each category of samples, the corresponding variables of multiple periods were utilized to predict the yield, and the results are shown in Figure 11. It can be found that with the increase of clustering categories, the change rule of rice yield prediction accuracy based on CH and CV time-series curve characteristics shows a similar trend. The yield estimation accuracy reaches its highest when the number of clustering categories increases from two to six. When continuing to increase the clustering categories, the yield estimation accuracy remains stable. The R^2 of the rice estimation model based on the clustering of CV temporal features is more than 0.8, and the RMSE is about 300 kg/ha. After utilizing the CH temporal curve to realize the division of the samples into two and six categories, the accuracy of R^2 is increased by more than 0.4, and the RMSE is reduced by more than 1000 kg/ha. After utilizing the CV temporal curve to realize the division of the samples into two and six categories, the accuracy of R^2 is increased by about 0.5, and the RMSE is reduced by more than 1200 kg/ha. The above results show that the CH and CV features of the time series can well characterize the growth of rice over the whole period. The accuracy of the rice yield estimation based on CV time-series curves was higher than that based on CH features. Rice yield estimation based on CH and CV time-series curves was more accurate than that based on reflectance and vegetation index characteristics.

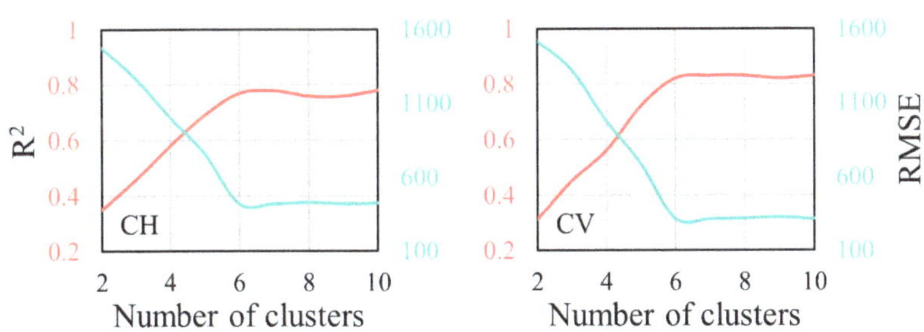

Figure 11. Trends in multi-period rice yield estimation results based on time-series CH and CV curve clustering.

Figure 12 displays the findings of the estimation of rice yield in Exp. 1 based on the numbers seven, six, and six for the NDRE, CH, and CV clustering groups, respectively. With an R^2 of 0.82 and an RMSE of 315.39 kg/ha, it is evident that the rice yield estimation based on CV temporal features has the highest accuracy. The accuracy of rice yield estimation based on NDRE and CH temporal features is somewhat worse. The model that is based on the clustering of NDRE time-series curve features has a lower RMSE of 1054.95 kg/ha and an improved R^2 of 0.42 when compared to the accuracy of rice yield estimation using multi-period NDRE. The model that is based on the clustering of CH time-series curve features has a lower RMSE of 1165.79 kg/ha and an improved R^2 of 0.52 when compared to the accuracy of rice yield estimation using multi-period CH. With a lowered RMSE of 1301.54 kg/ha and an improved R^2 of 0.6, the model based on CV time-series curve feature clustering outperforms the accuracy of rice yield estimation using multi-period CV. From the distribution of predicted rice yield values, the results of yield prediction based on NDRE, CH, and CV time-series features all show a standard normal distribution, which is consistent with the distribution of measured values. This also indicates that the method shows excellent performance in both high- and low-yield value estimations without obvious overestimation and underestimation. When comparing the spectral and structural features, the accuracy of rice yield estimation based on CH and CV temporal features was 35.67 kg/ha and 143.96 kg/ha lower than the RMSE of the model accuracy based on NDRE temporal features, respectively. This demonstrates the prominent role of structural parameter growth features in rice yield estimation.

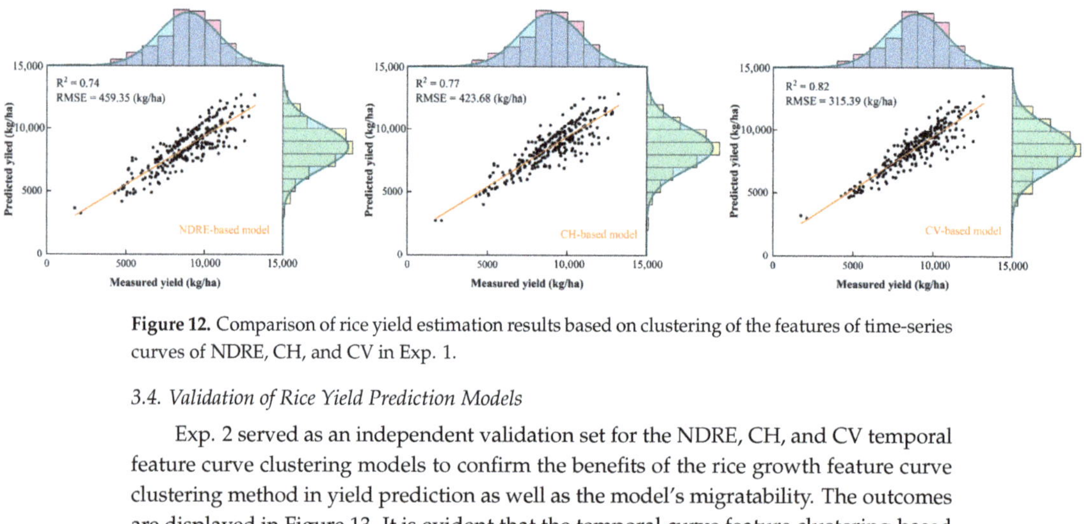

Figure 12. Comparison of rice yield estimation results based on clustering of the features of time-series curves of NDRE, CH, and CV in Exp. 1.

3.4. Validation of Rice Yield Prediction Models

Exp. 2 served as an independent validation set for the NDRE, CH, and CV temporal feature curve clustering models to confirm the benefits of the rice growth feature curve clustering method in yield prediction as well as the model's migratability. The outcomes are displayed in Figure 13. It is evident that the temporal curve feature clustering-based method performs well when calculating the multi-genotype rice yield. Similar to the findings of Exp. 1, the rice yield estimation model based on CV temporal characteristics achieves the best validation accuracy with R^2 = 0.85, RMSE = 282.41 kg/ha. R^2 = 0.82, RMSE = 309.62 kg/ha, and R^2 = 0.78, RMSE = 463.69 kg/ha are the results of the rice yield estimation model based on CH and NDRE temporal characteristics, respectively. The distribution of Exp. 2's measured yield data shows that the rice yield values follow a normal distribution. The distribution of the predicted rice values also matches a standard normal distribution. The conclusions show that the technique of using clustering of rice growth characteristic curves may successfully increase the precision of yield estimation in multi-genotype rice.

Like Exp. 2, the data obtained from Exp. 3 were used for independent validation, and the results are shown in Figure 13. Unlike Exp. 2, Exp. 3 contained fewer rice genotypes. However, Exp. 3 included more pronounced genotypic variability because one variety was Japonica rice. It can be seen that the method based on time-series remote sensing feature clustering showed satisfactory accuracy. The order of rice yield prediction accuracy for different features remains consistent with that in Experiments 1 and 2. The results further demonstrate the feasibility of the proposed method for estimating rice yield in complex scenarios.

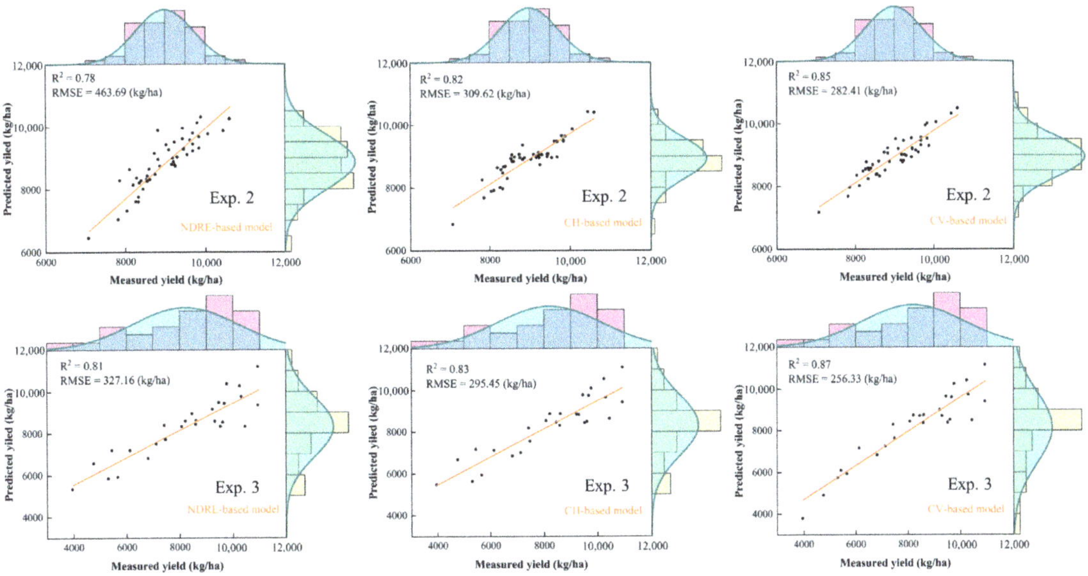

Figure 13. Comparison of rice yield estimation results based on multi-period NDRE, CH, and CV curve feature clustering in Exp. 2 and Exp. 3.

4. Discussion

The formation of rice yield is a long-term accumulation process that is affected by multiple factors [34]. In remote sensing yield estimation, yield estimation models can be obtained based on a single growth stage, but the spectral information of multiple growth stages within a rice-growing season can more comprehensively reflect the yield formation process [7,35]. In this study, based on two years of independent field experiments with multiple genotypes of rice, the growth process of different genotypes of rice was characterized using growth characterization parameters, including vegetation index, canopy height, and canopy volume, based on the acquisition of RGB and multispectral images throughout the entire growth stage. The k-shape algorithm was applied to realize the clustering of rice genotypes with different similar growth characteristics. Ultimately, high-precision yield prediction of multi-genotype rice was achieved using multi-period remote sensing features. Compared with traditional yield prediction using spectral, vegetation index, or geometric features directly, the model has higher accuracy and stability.

Spectral information, especially vegetation indices, has long been recognized as a useful indicator of crop growth parameters and yield estimation [36,37]. For example, the leaf area index, chlorophyll content, and biomass of rice, wheat, and maize can be extracted with high accuracy using vegetation indices [38–40]. As different vegetation indices have been used for more refined studies, red-edge band-based vegetation indices are considered to have higher accuracy and more stable results in crop growth monitoring [41,42]. Red-edge indices have also shown better results than traditional vegetation indices for crop yield estimation [43,44]. Furthermore, some structural parameters such as canopy cover, canopy height, and canopy volume have been proposed to enhance crop growth parameters and yield estimation [15]. Numerous studies have shown that in densely growing vegetation, structural parameters can compensate for the lack of spectral information and help improve the estimation of crop growth trait parameters [17,45,46].

In this study, it was found that the model accuracy was low when estimating rice yield using single-period vegetation indices and structural parameters. After combining the multi-period remote sensing indicators, the correlation with yield was significantly improved (Figure 7). Since remote sensing indicators in multiple periods carry different information on rice growth, and rice yield is the comprehensive result of biomass accumulation and distribution in various periods [5]. The expression for yield differences is facilitated by utilizing monitoring data at individual stages [18]. This demonstrates the importance of multi-period growth characteristics in the prediction of final rice yield. However, multi-species rice exhibits different growth characteristics when simulating rice cultivation under actual field conditions. As a result, the accuracy of yield estimation using a combination of multi-period vegetation indices remains poor (Figure 8). Direct comparisons of yield differences could not be made due to the variation in the growth cycles of different rice genotypes, resulting in the data observed not being within the same growth dimension. In this context, the accuracy of rice yield estimation based on multi-period remote sensing features was significantly improved after clustering the rice growth characteristics using a k-shape. The division of varieties with distinct growth characteristics enables the direct comparison of multiple variety yields within the same dimension. From Figure 9, we observe that the accuracy of rice yield estimation based on the red-edge band reflectance time-series curve features is significantly better than that using other band features. The results in Figure 10 indicate that the yield estimation models clustered with time-series characteristic curves of the red-edge indices (NDRE and $CI_{red\ edge}$) have higher accuracy and stability compared to other vegetation indices. These findings further demonstrate the prominent role of the red-edged bands in rice yield estimation. The accuracy of rice yield estimation was further improved after utilizing CH and CV time-series curve feature clustering (Figure 11). Compared with the NDRE feature clustering model, the model based on structural feature clustering only needs to be clustered into six groups to obtain a higher and more stable model accuracy. It indicates that the temporal characteristics of structural parameters can better reflect the growth characteristics of different genotypes of rice. This conclusion is consistent with the findings of previous studies that used structural parameters to improve the accuracy of crop yield estimation [47].

In this study, the data obtained from Exp. 1 was utilized for ten-fold cross-validation, which resulted in a highly accurate estimation model. On this basis, Exp. 2 was used for independent validation. The results show that the estimation accuracy in Exp. 2 is higher than the model accuracy in Exp. 1 based on the corresponding NDRE, CH, and CV temporal feature models. It also shows that the accuracy of the model proposed in this study is affected by the number of samples. Exp. 2 contained 48 different rice varieties, which was significantly lower than the 289 samples in Exp. 1. This also indirectly indicates that the complexity of the growth characteristics of the different genotypes of rice in Exp. 2 is lower than that of rice in Exp. 1. From the clustering of different remote sensing indicators, it can be observed that there are differences in the number of growth feature clusters of different complexities when obtaining the highest rice yield estimation accuracy. For example, the yield estimation accuracy based on spectral reflectance curve feature clustering is unstable. The number of categories based on vegetation index curve feature clustering is large. This is most likely due to the fact that spectral information is susceptible to light variations and canopy structure, which results in overly complex curve features [48,49]. The extracted rice structural features are less affected by factors such as light; therefore, a more stable model accuracy can be obtained. This can also be verified in Exp. 3.

In the next step of this study, more variables that can effectively characterize the rice growth process will be explored. Meanwhile, the factors affecting the growth characteristics of rice will be emphasized. Examples include the growth stage, field management practices, planting density, and variety type. Based on this, additional genotype clustering methods that can be interpreted will be developed. Additionally, we will study exactly which periods have an impact on final yield as a way to simplify the data acquisition cycle.

The object of this study is plot-scale multi-genotype rice. Experiments and validation have not been conducted in other scenarios, such as nitrogen gradient, stress environments, different planting densities, and cropping styles. In existing yield estimation studies, linear regression models are mainly used for a single variety as well as for nitrogen fertilizer control experimental scenarios [17]. Machine learning and deep learning models are mostly used for multi-genotype crop yield estimations [22,50]. Studies similar to the present study on estimating yield after automatic classification of multiple rice genotypes have not been reported.

5. Conclusions

In this study, a high-precision prediction method for multi-genotype rice based on time-series remote sensing images and dynamic growth process clustering was proposed. The structural and spectral information of the rice canopy, including CH, CV, and some vegetation indices, were extracted for the whole period using RGB and multispectral images, respectively. The time-series reflectance, VIs, CH, and CV curves were used as representatives of the rice growth process to cluster multi-genotype rice. The results showed that the red-edge bands were superior to the other bands in clustering the reflectance time-series curves for yield estimation. When estimating rice yield using VIs time-series curve feature clustering, the accuracy of rice yield estimation was substantially improved compared to the reflectance model, especially when using red-edge indices. When using CH and CV time-series feature clustering for rice yield estimation, the model accuracy was further improved, and the predicted yield distribution conformed to the standard normal distribution, as did the measured data, demonstrating that it can be well adapted to the prediction of both high- and low-value rice yield. The rice yield estimation based on CV temporal features had the highest accuracy with an R^2 of 0.82 and RMSE of 315.39 kg/ha. The proposed method can effectively solve the problem of low-yield estimation accuracy of multi-genotype rice and assist in fine management under natural rice-growing conditions.

Author Contributions: Conceptualization, methodology, writing—original draft preparation, Q.L.; software, validation, data curation, S.Z. and L.D. writing—review and editing, S.L. All authors have read and agreed to the published version of the manuscript.

Funding: This research was funded by the Joint Fund of Henan Province Science and Technology R&D Program, grant number 235200810069; the Science and Technology Tackling Project of Henan Province, grant number 242102210011; the Basic Research Operating Expenses Program of Henan Academy of Sciences, grant number 240625002; and the Scientific Research Initiation Program for High-level Talents of Henan Academy of Sciences, grants numbers 241825015 and 241824205.

Institutional Review Board Statement: Not applicable.

Data Availability Statement: Related data are available upon reasonable request.

Conflicts of Interest: The authors declare no conflicts of interest.

References

1. Sagart, L. How Many Independent Rice Vocabularies in Asia? *Rice* **2011**, *4*, 121–133. [CrossRef]
2. Satoh, R.; Tsuge, I.; Tokuda, R.; Teshima, R. Analysis of the distribution of rice allergens in brown rice grains and of the allergenicity of products containing rice bran. *Food Chem.* **2019**, *276*, 761–767. [CrossRef]
3. Liao, C.J.; Fang, S.L.; Zhang, H.D.; Liu, L.S.; Xie, J.X.; Li, X.; Cao, F.B.; Chen, J.N.; Huang, M. Grain Yield and Yield Attributes of Currently Popular Hybrid Rice Varieties Compared to Representative Super Hybrid Rice Varieties in Subtropical Environments. *Agronomy* **2024**, *14*, 11. [CrossRef]
4. Xue, H.Y.; Xu, X.G.; Zhu, Q.Z.; Meng, Y.; Long, H.L.; Li, H.L.; Song, X.Y.; Yang, G.J.; Yang, M.; Li, Y.F.; et al. Rice yield and quality estimation coupling hierarchical linear model with remote sensing. *Comput. Electron. Agric.* **2024**, *218*, 12. [CrossRef]
5. dela Torre, D.M.G.; Gao, J.; Macinnis-Ng, C. Remote sensing-based estimation of rice yields using various models: A critical review. *Geo-Spat. Inf. Sci.* **2021**, *24*, 580–603. [CrossRef]
6. Wang, F.L.; Wang, F.M.; Zhang, Y.; Hu, J.H.; Huang, J.F.; Xie, J.K. Rice Yield Estimation Using Parcel-Level Relative Spectra Variables From UAV-Based Hyperspectral Imagery. *Front. Plant Sci.* **2019**, *10*, 12. [CrossRef]
7. Yang, Q.; Shi, L.S.; Han, J.Y.; Zha, Y.Y.; Zhu, P.H. Deep convolutional neural networks for rice grain yield estimation at the ripening stage using UAV-based remotely sensed images. *Field Crop. Res.* **2019**, *235*, 142–153. [CrossRef]
8. Wang, F.M.; Yao, X.P.; Xie, L.L.; Zheng, J.Y.; Xu, T.Y. Rice Yield Estimation Based on Vegetation Index and Florescence Spectral Information from UAV Hyperspectral Remote Sensing. *Remote Sens.* **2021**, *13*, 19. [CrossRef]
9. Franch, B.; San Bautista, A.; Fita, D.; Rubio, C.; Tarrazó-Serrano, D.; Sánchez, A.; Skakun, S.; Vermote, E.; Becker-Reshef, I.; Uris, A. Within-Field Rice Yield Estimation Based on Sentinel-2 Satellite Data. *Remote Sens.* **2021**, *13*, 22. [CrossRef]
10. Soriano-González, J.; Angelats, E.; Martínez-Eixarch, M.; Alcaraz, C. Monitoring rice crop and yield estimation with Sentinel-2 data. *Field Crop. Res.* **2022**, *281*, 11. [CrossRef]
11. Yang, Q.; Shi, L.S.; Han, J.Y.; Chen, Z.W.; Yu, J. A VI-based phenology adaptation approach for rice crop monitoring using UAV multispectral images. *Field Crop. Res.* **2022**, *277*, 13. [CrossRef]
12. Xu, S.Z.; Xu, X.A.; Zhu, Q.Z.; Meng, Y.; Yang, G.J.; Feng, H.K.; Yang, M.; Zhu, Q.L.; Xue, H.Y.; Wang, B.B. Monitoring leaf nitrogen content in rice based on information fusion of multi-sensor imagery from UAV. *Precis. Agric.* **2023**, *24*, 2327–2349. [CrossRef]
13. Li, B.; Xu, X.M.; Zhang, L.; Han, J.W.; Bian, C.S.; Li, G.C.; Liu, J.G.; Jin, L.P. Above-ground biomass estimation and yield prediction in potato by using UAV-based RGB and hyperspectral imaging. *ISPRS-J. Photogramm. Remote Sens.* **2020**, *162*, 161–172. [CrossRef]
14. Maimaitijiang, M.; Sagan, V.; Sidike, P.; Hartling, S.; Esposito, F.; Fritschi, F.B. Soybean yield prediction from UAV using multimodal data fusion and deep learning. *Remote Sens. Environ.* **2020**, *237*, 20. [CrossRef]
15. Ashapure, A.; Jung, J.H.; Chang, A.J.; Oh, S.; Yeom, J.; Maeda, M.; Maeda, A.; Dube, N.; Landivar, J.; Hague, S.; et al. Developing a machine learning based cotton yield estimation framework using multi-temporal UAS data. *ISPRS-J. Photogramm. Remote Sens.* **2020**, *169*, 180–194. [CrossRef]
16. Xu, L.; Ming, D.P.; Du, T.Y.; Chen, Y.Y.; Dong, D.H.; Zhou, C.H. Delineation of cultivated land parcels based on deep convolutional networks and geographical thematic scene division of remotely sensed images. *Comput. Electron. Agric.* **2022**, *192*, 16. [CrossRef]
17. Feng, A.J.; Zhou, J.F.; Vories, E.D.; Sudduth, K.A.; Zhang, M.N. Yield estimation in cotton using UAV-based multi-sensor imagery. *Biosyst. Eng.* **2020**, *193*, 101–114. [CrossRef]
18. Zhou, X.; Zheng, H.B.; Xu, X.Q.; He, J.Y.; Ge, X.K.; Yao, X.; Cheng, T.; Zhu, Y.; Cao, W.X.; Tian, Y.C. Predicting grain yield in rice using multi-temporal vegetation indices from UAV-based multispectral and digital imagery. *ISPRS-J. Photogramm. Remote Sens.* **2017**, *130*, 246–255. [CrossRef]
19. Marcone, A.; Impollonia, G.; Croci, M.; Blandinières, H.; Pellegrini, N.; Amaducci, S. Garlic yield monitoring using vegetation indices and texture features derived from UAV multispectral imagery. *Smart Agric. Technol.* **2024**, *8*, 13. [CrossRef]
20. Yuan, J.H.; Zhang, Y.L.; Zheng, Z.J.; Yao, W.; Wang, W.S.; Guo, L.F. Grain Crop Yield Prediction Using Machine Learning Based on UAV Remote Sensing: A Systematic Literature Review. *Drones* **2024**, *8*, 27. [CrossRef]
21. Fan, J.H.; Zhou, J.; Wang, B.W.; de Leon, N.; Kaeppler, S.M.; Lima, D.C.; Zhang, Z. Estimation of Maize Yield and Flowering Time Using Multi-Temporal UAV-Based Hyperspectral Data. *Remote Sens.* **2022**, *14*, 16. [CrossRef]
22. Shi, G.W.; Du, X.; Du, M.W.; Li, Q.Z.; Tian, X.L.; Ren, Y.T.; Zhang, Y.; Wang, H.Y. Cotton Yield Estimation Using the Remotely Sensed Cotton Boll Index from UAV Images. *Drones* **2022**, *6*, 23. [CrossRef]
23. Zhang, C.S.; Diao, C.Y. A Phenology-guided Bayesian-CNN (PB-CNN) framework for soybean yield estimation and uncertainty analysis. *ISPRS-J. Photogramm. Remote Sens.* **2023**, *205*, 50–73. [CrossRef]
24. Pei, J.; Tan, S.F.; Zou, Y.P.; Liao, C.H.; He, Y.N.; Wang, J.; Huang, H.B.; Wang, T.X.; Tian, H.F.; Fang, H.J.; et al. The role of phenology in crop yield prediction: Comparison of ground-based phenology and remotely sensed phenology. *Agric. For. Meteorol.* **2025**, *361*, 14. [CrossRef]
25. Zhou, M.; Zheng, H.B.; He, C.; Liu, P.; Awan, G.M.; Wang, X.; Cheng, T.; Zhu, Y.; Cao, W.X.; Yao, X. Wheat phenology detection with the methodology of classification based on the time-series UAV images. *Field Crop. Res.* **2023**, *292*, 12. [CrossRef]

26. Martinez-Tejada, I.; Riedel, C.S.; Juhler, M.; Andresen, M.; Wilhjelm, J.E. k-Shape clustering for extracting macro-patterns in intracranial pressure signals. *Fluids Barriers CNS* **2022**, *19*, 13. [CrossRef] [PubMed]
27. Rouse, J.W. Monitoring the vernal advancement and retrogradation (greenwave effect) of natural vegetation. In *Technical Report, Progress Report RSC 1978-2 for NASA, Greenbelt, USA*; NASA: Washington, DC, USA, 1974.
28. Gitelson, A.A.; Merzlyak, M.N. Signature analysis of leaf reflectance spectra: Algorithm development for remote sensing of chlorophyll. *J. Plant Physiol.* **1996**, *148*, 494–500. [CrossRef]
29. Fitzgerald, G.J.; Rodriguez, D.; Christensen, L.K.; Belford, R.; Sadras, V.O.; Clarke, T.R. Spectral and thermal sensing for nitrogen and water status in rainfed and irrigated wheat environments. *Precis. Agric.* **2006**, *7*, 233–248. [CrossRef]
30. Gitelson, A.A.; Gritz, Y.; Merzlyak, M.N. Relationships between leaf chlorophyll content and spectral reflectance and algorithms for non-destructive chlorophyll assessment in higher plant leaves. *J. Plant Physiol.* **2003**, *160*, 271–282. [CrossRef] [PubMed]
31. Jiang, Z.Y.; Huete, A.R.; Didan, K.; Miura, T. Development of a two-band enhanced vegetation index without a blue band. *Remote Sens. Environ.* **2008**, *112*, 3833–3845. [CrossRef]
32. Gitelson, A.A.; Keydan, G.P.; Merzlyak, M.N. Three-band model for noninvasive estimation of chlorophyll, carotenoids, and anthocyanin contents in higher plant leaves. *Geophys. Res. Lett.* **2006**, *33*, 5. [CrossRef]
33. Wang, X.; Song, R.B.; Xiao, J.M.; Li, T.; Li, X.Q. Accelerating k-Shape Time Series Clustering Algorithm Using GPU. *IEEE Trans. Parallel Distrib. Syst.* **2023**, *34*, 2718–2734. [CrossRef]
34. Wang, F.M.; Wang, F.L.; Hu, J.H.; Xie, L.L.; Yao, X.P. Rice Yield Estimation Based on an NPP Model With a Changing Harvest Index. *IEEE J. Sel. Top. Appl. Earth Observ. Remote Sens.* **2020**, *13*, 2953–2959. [CrossRef]
35. Yang, R.; Zhou, J.; Lu, X.Y.; Shen, J.X.; Chen, H.Z.; Chen, M.Y.; He, Y.; Liu, F. A robust rice yield estimation framework developed by grading modeling and normalized weight decision-making strategy using UAV imaging technology. *Comput. Electron. Agric.* **2023**, *215*, 13. [CrossRef]
36. Wang, Z.L.; Tan, X.M.; Ma, Y.M.; Liu, T.; He, L.M.; Yang, F.; Shu, C.H.; Li, L.L.; Fu, H.; Li, B.; et al. Combining canopy spectral reflectance and RGB images to estimate leaf chlorophyll content and grain yield in rice. *Comput. Electron. Agric.* **2024**, *221*, 15. [CrossRef]
37. Guo, Y.H.; Wang, H.X.; Wu, Z.F.; Wang, S.X.; Sun, H.Y.; Senthilnath, J.; Wang, J.Z.; Bryant, C.R.; Fu, Y.S. Modified Red Blue Vegetation Index for Chlorophyll Estimation and Yield Prediction of Maize from Visible Images Captured by UAV. *Sensors* **2020**, *20*, 16. [CrossRef] [PubMed]
38. Li, S.Y.; Yuan, F.; Ata-Ui-Karim, S.T.; Zheng, H.B.; Cheng, T.; Liu, X.J.; Tian, Y.C.; Zhu, Y.; Cao, W.X.; Cao, Q. Combining Color Indices and Textures of UAV-Based Digital Imagery for Rice LAI Estimation. *Remote Sens.* **2019**, *11*, 21. [CrossRef]
39. Wang, A.C.; Song, Z.S.; Xie, Y.W.; Hu, J.; Zhang, L.Y.; Zhu, Q.Z. Detection of Rice Leaf SPAD and Blast Disease Using Integrated Aerial and Ground Multiscale Canopy Reflectance Spectroscopy. *Agriculture* **2024**, *14*, 19. [CrossRef]
40. Li, F.; Piasecki, C.; Millwood, R.J.; Wolfe, B.; Mazarei, M.; Stewart, C.N. High-Throughput Switchgrass Phenotyping and Biomass Modeling by UAV. *Front. Plant Sci.* **2020**, *11*, 15. [CrossRef] [PubMed]
41. Qiao, L.; Zhao, R.M.; Tang, W.J.; An, L.L.; Sun, H.; Li, M.Z.; Wang, N.; Liu, Y.; Liu, G.H. Estimating maize LAI by exploring deep features of vegetation index map from UAV multispectral images. *Field Crop. Res.* **2022**, *289*, 14. [CrossRef]
42. Cheng, J.P.; Yang, H.; Qi, J.B.; Sun, Z.D.; Han, S.Y.; Feng, H.K.; Jiang, J.Y.; Xu, W.M.; Li, Z.H.; Yang, G.J.; et al. Estimating canopy-scale chlorophyll content in apple orchards using a 3D radiative transfer model and UAV multispectral imagery. *Comput. Electron. Agric.* **2022**, *202*, 15. [CrossRef]
43. Ali, N.; Mohammed, A.; Bais, A.; Berraies, S.; Ruan, Y.F.; Cuthbert, R.D.; Sangha, J.S. Field-Scale Precision: Predicting Grain Yield of Diverse Wheat Breeding Lines Using High-Throughput UAV Multispectral Imaging. *IEEE J. Sel. Top. Appl. Earth Observ. Remote Sens.* **2024**, *17*, 11419–11433. [CrossRef]
44. Camenzind, M.P.; Yu, K. Multi temporal multispectral UAV remote sensing allows for yield assessment across European wheat varieties already before flowering. *Front. Plant Sci.* **2024**, *14*, 19. [CrossRef]
45. Yu, D.Y.; Zha, Y.Y.; Shi, L.S.; Jin, X.L.; Hu, S.; Yang, Q.; Huang, K.; Zeng, W.Z. Improvement of sugarcane yield estimation by assimilating UAV-derived plant height observations. *Eur. J. Agron.* **2020**, *121*, 16. [CrossRef]
46. Liu, T.; Wu, F.; Mou, N.N.; Zhu, S.L.; Yang, T.L.; Zhang, W.J.; Wang, H.; Wu, W.; Zhao, Y.Y.; Sun, C.M.; et al. The estimation of wheat yield combined with UAV canopy spectral and volumetric data. *Food Energy Secur.* **2024**, *13*, 17. [CrossRef]
47. Zhou, W.Q.; Song, C.; Liu, C.L.; Fu, Q.; An, T.H.; Wang, Y.J.; Sun, X.B.; Wen, N.; Tang, H.; Wang, Q. A Prediction Model of Maize Field Yield Based on the Fusion of Multitemporal and Multimodal UAV Data: A Case Study in Northeast China. *Remote Sens.* **2023**, *15*, 22. [CrossRef]
48. Luo, S.J.; Jiang, X.Q.; Yang, K.L.; Li, Y.J.; Fang, S.H. Multispectral remote sensing for accurate acquisition of rice phenotypes: Impacts of radiometric calibration and unmanned aerial vehicle flying altitudes. *Front. Plant Sci.* **2022**, *13*, 19. [CrossRef] [PubMed]

49. Muramatsu, K.; Yoneda, E.; Soyama, N.; Thanyapraneedkul, J.; López-Ballesteros, A. Use of light response curve parameters to estimate gross primary production capacity from chlorophyll indices of global observation satellite and flux data. *Sci. Remote Sensing* **2024**, *10*, 16. [CrossRef]
50. Li, D.H.; Sun, X.X.; Jia, Y.H.; Yao, Z.W.; Lin, P.Y.; Chen, Y.Y.; Zhou, H.B.; Zhou, Z.Q.; Wu, K.X.; Shi, L.L.; et al. A longan yield estimation approach based on UAV images and deep learning. *Front. Plant Sci.* **2023**, *14*, 17. [CrossRef]

agriculture

MDPI

Article

Combining UAV Multispectral Imaging and PROSAIL Model to Estimate LAI of Potato at Plot Scale

Shuang Li [1], Yongxin Lin [1], Ping Zhu [1], Liping Jin [1,2], Chunsong Bian [1,*] and Jiangang Liu [1,*]

[1] State Key Laboratory of Vegetable Biobreeding, Institute of Vegetables and Flowers, Chinese Academy of Agricultural Sciences, Beijing 100081, China; shuanglimailbox@163.com (S.L.); linyongxin1554@163.com (Y.L.); zhuping9717@163.com (P.Z.); jinliping@caas.cn (L.J.)

[2] Inner Mongolia Academy of Science and Technology, Hohhot 010021, China

* Correspondence: bianchunsong@caas.cn (C.B.); liujiangang@caas.cn (J.L.)

Abstract: Accurate and rapid estimation of the leaf area index (LAI) is essential for assessing crop growth and nutritional status, guiding farm management, and providing valuable phenotyping data for plant breeding. Compared to the tedious and time-consuming manual measurements of the LAI, remote sensing has emerged as a valuable tool for rapid and accurate estimation of the LAI; however, the empirical inversion modeling methods face challenges of low efficiency for actual LAI measurements and poor model interpretability. The integration of radiative transfer models (RTMs) can overcome these problems to some extent. The aim of this study was to explore the potential of combining the PROSAIL model with high-resolution unmanned aerial vehicle (UAV) multispectral imaging to estimate the LAI across different growth stages at the plot scale. In this study, four inversion strategies for estimating the LAI were tested. Firstly, two types of lookup tables (LUTs) were built to estimate potato LAI of different varieties across different growth stages. Specifically, LUT1 was based on band reflectance, and LUT2 was based on vegetation index. Secondly, the hybrid models combining LUTs generated by PROSAIL and two machine learning algorithms (random forest (RF), Partial Least Squares Regression (PLSR)) are built to estimate potato LAI. The determination of coefficient (R^2) of models for estimating LAI by LUTs ranged from 0.24 to 0.64. The hybrid method that integrates UAV multispectral, PROSAIL, and machine learning significantly improved the accuracy of LAI estimation. Compared to the results based on LUT2, the hybrid model achieved higher accuracy with the R^2 of the inversion model improved by 30% to 263%. The LAI retrieval model using the PROSAIL model and PLSR achieved an R^2 as high as 0.87, while the R^2 using the RF algorithm ranged from 0.33 to 0.81. The proposed hybrid model, integrated with UAV multispectral data, PROSAIL, and PLSR can achieve approximate accuracy compared with the empirical inversion models, which can alleviate the labor-intensive process of handheld LAI measurements for building inversion models. Thus, the hybrid approach provides a feasible and efficient strategy for estimating the LAI of potato varieties across different growth stages at the plot scale.

Keywords: potato; leaf area index; UAV multispectral imaging; PROSAIL; phenotyping

1. Introduction

As the third largest food crop in the world, the potato industry plays a crucial role in global food security [1]. As a shallow-rooted tuber crop, the harvested organ of potato is the underground tuber. There is a significant covariance between canopy and tuber, making canopy growth assessment critical for assessing potato nutritional status and predicting yield. The leaf area index (LAI) is a crucial parameter that can be directly employed to depict the canopy structure [2]. It is closely related to the physiological functions of crops and the nutrient and water cycles within ecosystems. It has been shown that potato yield is positively correlated to the leaf area index to a certain extent [3]. Meanwhile, the LAI is of great significance in characterizing the canopy structure of vegetation and the growth status of vegetation [4]. Since the 1960s, the LAI has been used to quantify the interception of light by vegetation, and the interactions between features and light form the basis for vegetation monitoring through remote sensing [5]. Consequently, the leaf area index plays a crucial role in the remote-sensing monitoring of vegetation. Accurate monitoring of the LAI is beneficial for enhancing production efficiency, understanding the growth dynamic differences in different regions, and predicting the yield of potatoes, etc. This important application can promote the sustainable development of the potato industry and bring greater economic and social benefits to agricultural production.

Traditional methods for determining the LAI have included direct measurement, the use of optical instruments such as the LAI-2000 [6], and point quadrat techniques [7]. These methods, which are suitable for point-like areas, become impractical and inefficient when scaled up due to their lack of representativeness and the extensive time and labor they require. In contrast, remote-sensing technology enables LAI estimation over broader temporal and spatial scales, facilitating the accurate and dynamic monitoring of vegetation status. This technology serves as an essential tool for high-throughput phenotypic analysis in precision agriculture and breeding contexts [8].

Presently, LAI inversion models that employ remote-sensing technology are developed through two main methodologies: empirical statistical modeling and physical inversion modeling using RTMs [9]. Empirical models rely on establishing regression relationships between spectral reflectance or vegetation indices and measured data. Machine learning (ML) algorithms are the most commonly used methods for empirical modeling. ML not only trains models to automatically recognize and analyze spectral data—thereby improving the accuracy and generalization of LAI estimation—but also integrates data from different sensors and spectral bands for multidimensional analysis, providing a more comprehensive understanding of crop canopy characteristics and further enhancing LAI estimation accuracy. However, this approach can be significantly influenced by factors such as growth stage, ecological zone, and sensor type, which limits its applicability across different crops or varieties [10]. RTM-based models use physical laws to elucidate the causal relationships between plant components and radiation photon interactions, considering factors like crop canopy structure, growth status, and environmental conditions. The inversion of physiological indices based on RTMs is typically achieved through lookup tables and numerical optimization but both methods require substantial computational effort [11], limiting their use in hyperspectral scenarios. However, the hybrid inversion method, which combines RTMs with ML algorithms, capitalizes on the strengths of both approaches [12].

As a commonly used RTM, the PROSAIL model comprehensively accounts for the optical properties of soil and the geometric characteristics of vegetation [8,9]. It includes both forward simulation and inverse retrieval processes. By changing the input parameter values, the model simulates a large amount of hyperspectral data in the range of 400–2500 nm, completing the spectral forward simulation. Subsequently, it combines lookup tables or machine learning algorithms to estimate vegetation physiological and biochemical indices. The PROSAIL model is currently used in the inversion of various indices, such as the LAI, leaf chlorophyll content, canopy chlorophyll content, and canopy water content [13–16]. Research has shown that during the inversion of the LAI, optical remote-sensing signals can interfere with the optical features associated with chlorophyll content, leading to uncertainty in the inversion results of these two agronomic parameters [17]. Researchers have defined the red-edge position based on the abrupt changes in the reflectance curve between 680 and 750 nm. Reflectance at this position primarily arises from multiple reflections between the leaf layers and chlorophyll absorption [18]. Sun et al. have incorporated red-edge reflectance into the construction of vegetation indices, effectively improving the accuracy of crop LAI estimation [15].

The combination of RTMs with hyperspectral or multispectral imaging provides an effective approach for monitoring plant physiological and biochemical characteristics. Previous RTM-based inversions of physiological indicators have primarily utilized hyperspectral and satellite multispectral data. The REGFLEC model, combined with SPOT satellite data, has been used to estimate the LAI and chlorophyll content (Cab) for a wide range of crops, such as maize, wheat, and soybean [19]. The PROSAIL model, in conjunction with canopy hyperspectral information, has also been used to estimate chlorophyll content in potato leaves [20]. Highly accurate inversions of the LAI and chlorophyll content can be obtained using the PROSAIL model when incorporating multi-source satellite data [21]. In recent years, unmanned aerial vehicles (UAVs) have been playing an increasingly significant role in crop phenotyping. Compared to satellite remote sensing, UAV remote sensing offers greater flexibility and higher spatial and temporal resolution, making it a crucial tool for monitoring crop growth in the field [8,9]. Duan et al. evaluated the applicability of the LAI inversion using UAV hyperspectral data combined with PROSAIL modeling, including for potatoes [22]. While hyperspectral equipment provides rich spectral data, multispectral sensors generate less spectral information, reducing computational demands and data redundancy; however, a downside is that they may lack some relevant spectral bands. In contrast, integrating UAV-based multispectral imaging with RTMs offers significant advantages in addressing these limitations. Nevertheless, there is still limited research on the precise estimation of potato LAI using UAV multispectral remote sensing and canopy radiative transfer modeling, particularly in breeding and field trial plots.

Therefore, the objective of this study was to explore the potential of combining the PROSAIL model with UAV multispectral imaging to estimate potato LAI across key growing stages under different cultivars and nitrogen rates. Specifically, this study aimed to achieve the following: 1. Determine the sensitive model parameters of PROSAIL and the optimal lookup table size for potato LAI inversion. 2. Explore the potential of combining PROSAIL and UAV multispectral imaging for potato LAI inversion at plot scale. 3. Evaluate the performance of the hybrid method for estimating the LAI, compared to traditional empirical models based on the ground-truth measurements at different growth stages.

2. Materials and Methods

2.1. Experiment Design

The experiment was conducted in Chabei, Zhangjiakou, Hebei Province, China, in 2023 (Figure 1). This region is located in the temperate arid and semi-arid zone of East Asia's continental monsoon climate, with an altitude of 1390 m. The soil type is calcium chestnut. Two potato varieties, Zhongshu 5 and Zhongshu 49 (D681), were used in the experiment, along with five nitrogen fertilizer treatments (0, 50, 100, 250, and 400 $kg{\cdot}ha^{-1}$), each with four replications. The crops were sown on 5 May and harvested on 8 September. Eight ground control points (GCPs) were placed around the experimental field, and the three-dimensional coordinates of the GCPs were determined using high-precision RTK GPS.

2.2. Data Acquisition

2.2.1. Remote-Sensing Data Acquisition and Pre-Processing

A DJI Inspire 2 (DJI Technology Co., Shenzhen, China) UAV equipped with a RedEdge-P multispectral camera (MicaSense, Seattle, WA, USA) was used as the remote-sensing platform (Figure 2). The spectral band information (Table 1) of the multispectral sensor is provided in Table 1.

In order to minimize the interference of background factors on the test results, the UAV was operated between 10:00 and 14:00. The flight altitude of the mounted multispectral sensor was 30 m, with both heading overlap and side-to-side overlap set at 75%. Calibration plates were photographed both before takeoff and after landing, and the images were radiometrically calibrated using a light sensor mounted on top of the UAV [8]. Multispectral image pre-processing (including radiometric and geometric correction) and image stitching (including alignment, optimizing alignment, generating dense point clouds, generating meshes, generating textures, generating digital elevation models, and digital orthophotos) were performed using Agisoft Metashape Professional 2.0.2 software. ArcMap 10.8 software was used to realize image segmentation, and PyCharm Community Edition 2023.2.3 software was used to complete image background removal and spectral reflectance extraction in each band.

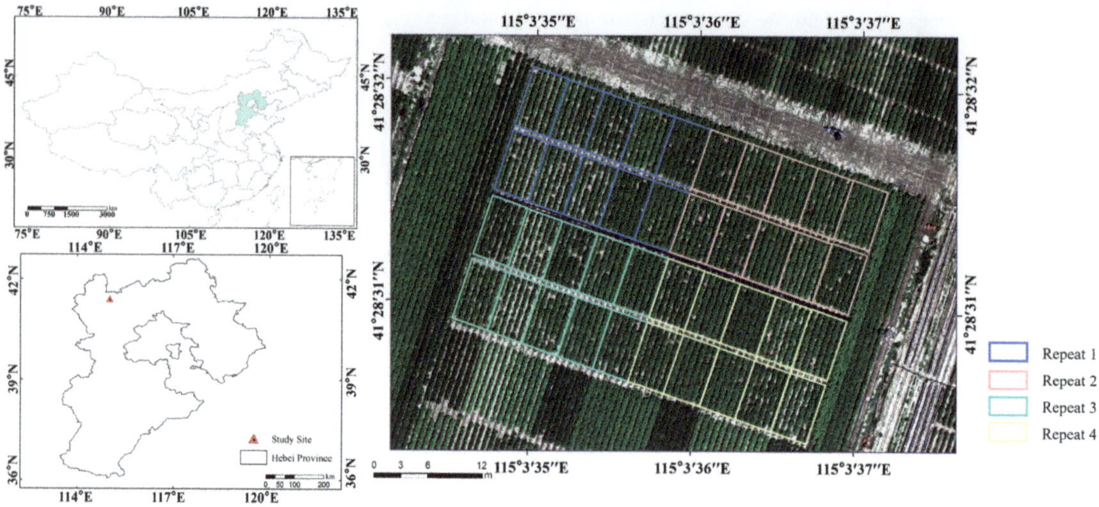

Figure 1. Location of the study area and field plot distribution.

Figure 2. Unmanned aerial vehicle multispectral image acquisition system.

Table 1. Spectral characterization of the MicaSense RedEdge-P camera for multispectral image acquisition.

Bands	Center Bands	Bandwidth	Resolution	Field of View
Blue	475 nm	32 nm	1456 × 1088 (1.58 MP per multispectral band)	49.6° × 38.3° VFOV
Green	560 nm	27 nm	1456 × 1088 (1.58 MP per multispectral band)	49.6° × 38.3° VFOV
Red	668 nm	16 nm	1456 × 1088 (1.58 MP per multispectral band)	49.6° × 38.3° VFOV
Red-edge	717 nm	12 nm	1456 × 1088 (1.58 MP per multispectral band)	49.6° × 38.3° VFOV
Near-infrared	842 nm	57 nm	1456 × 1088 (1.58 MP per multispectral band)	49.6° × 38.3° VFO
Panchromatic	634.5 nm	463 nm	2464 × 2056 (5.1 MP panchromatic band)	44.5° × 37.7° VFOV

The spectral response function (SRF) for each band was calculated based on the transmittance of the respective band filter of the RedEdge-P multispectral sensor. Simulated spectral reflectance was then resampled to the center wavelength of the RedEdge-P sensor according to the SRF (Figure 3), in order to construct the equivalent spectral reflectance of the simulated band information. The equivalent spectral reflectance based on the RedEdge-P spectral response function is calculated as follows [23]:

$$R_{rs}(band_i) = \frac{\int_{\lambda_1}^{\lambda_2} R_{rs}(\lambda)SRF(\lambda)d(\lambda)}{\int_{\lambda_1}^{\lambda_2} SRF(\lambda)d(\lambda)} \quad (1)$$

where $R_{rs}(band_i)$ is the equivalent spectral reflectance in $band_i$ of the sensor; λ_1 and λ_2 are the band range of the band; $R_{rs}(\lambda)$ is the simulated optical reflectance; and $SRF(\lambda)$ is the spectral responsivity at λ wavelength.

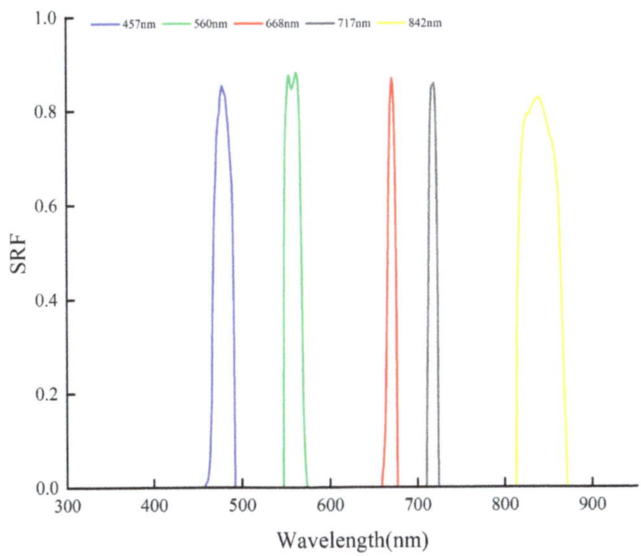

Figure 3. Spectral response function of the RedEdge-P multispectral sensor used.

2.2.2. Agronomic Data Acquisition

A total of four plant canopy biomass collections were completed across 40 plots during the potato tuber initiation and tuber bulking stages. Simultaneously, data on the leaf area index, equivalent water thickness, chlorophyll content, and carotenoid content were also collected (Table 2).

Table 2. Overview of agronomic data acquisition.

Growth STAGE	Time	Number of Subdivisions (Number)	Parameter
Tuber initiation stage	4 July 2023	80	Biomass, LAI, chlorophyll content, carotenoid content, equivalent water thickness
Tuber initiation stage	15 July 2023	80	Biomass, LAI, equivalent water thickness
Tuber bulking stage	3 August 2023	80	Biomass, LAI, chlorophyll content, carotenoid content, equivalent water thickness
Tuber bulking stage	14 August 2023	80	Biomass, LAI, chlorophyll content, carotenoid content, equivalent water thickness

Six plants were collected from each plot. The leaves, stems, roots, underground stems (excluding the tuber), and tubers were separated. The leaves were then killed at 105 °C for 30 min, followed by drying at 85 °C until the biomass reached a constant weight. Afterward, the dry matter weight was measured. Dry matter content (g·cm^{-2}) was calculated as the above-ground biomass per unit area. Before weighing the fresh weight of the samples, leaf images were captured using a camera. Leaf image extraction was then performed by separating the plant from the background through threshold segmentation (Figure 4). The leaf area index was derived from the pixel occupancy of the leaf area. Equivalent water thickness and dry matter content were calculated from the measured leaf area, dry weight, and fresh weight. During the same period, three plants were selected from each plot, and four leaves from each plant were brought back to the laboratory. Each leaf sample, with an area of 2.5 cm^2, was weighed to 0.1 g. The samples were then immersed in 96% ethanol until the material turned white. Absorbance measurements were taken with a UV spectrophotometer at 470, 649, and 665 nm wavelengths. These measurements were used to calculate the chlorophyll and carotenoid content (in mg/g) by combining the absorbance data with the mass of the samples. The calculation formula is as follows:

$$C_a = 13.95D_{665} - 6.88D_{649} \quad (2)$$

$$C_b = 24.96D_{649} - 7.32D_{665} \quad (3)$$

$$C_{x,c} = \frac{1000D_{470} - 2.05C_a - 114.8C_b}{245} \quad (4)$$

$$C_{ab} = \frac{(C_a + C_b) \times \mathrm{V} \times \mathrm{N}}{1000 \times \mathrm{S}} \quad (5)$$

$$C_{ar} = \frac{C_{x,c} \times \mathrm{V} \times \mathrm{N}}{1000 \times \mathrm{S}} \quad (6)$$

where C_a and C_b are the concentrations of chlorophyll a and chlorophyll b (mg·L^{-1});

Figure 4. Leaf area photo background removal effect.

$C_{x,c}$ is the concentration of carotenoids (mg·L^{-1});
C_{ab} is the chlorophyll content (μg·cm^{-2});
Car is the carotenoid content (μg·cm^{-2});
D_{665}, D_{649}, and D_{470} represent the extinction of chloroplast pigment extracts at wavelengths of 665 nm, 649 nm, and 470 nm;
V is the total volume of the extract (mL); N is the dilution factor; S is the leaf area (cm^2).

2.3. PROSAIL Model

The PROSAIL model, which integrates the leaf radiative transfer model PROSPECT and the canopy radiative transfer model SAIL, is the most commonly used RTM for simulating crop canopy reflectance as a function of the LAI, leaf angle distribution function, chlorophyll content, dry matter content, carotenoid content, leaf equivalent water thickness, canopy reflectance background, sensor viewing angle, sun zenith, and azimuth angles [9]. The PROSPECT-5 and 4SAIL models (http://teledetection.ipgp.jussieu.fr/prosail/, accessed on 30 September 2024) were used in this study. The PROSPECT model assumes the leaf blade structure as a multilayer flat plate with a rough surface. It also assumes that light rays are both isotropic and parallel, and simulates Lambertian scattering of light rays between the flat plates by inputting the physical and chemical parameters of the leaves. This results in the calculation of the leaf reflectance and transmittance over the 400 to 2500 nm spectral range. The leaf spectral information simulated by the PROSPECT model is then used as input for the SAIL model. The SAIL model assumes that the vegetation canopy is a homogeneous, infinitely extensible mixed medium with isotropic leaves. It simulates the radiative transfer process within the canopy using radiative transfer equations as the theoretical basis to obtain the canopy-scale reflectance. There are two commonly used inversion methods for radiative transfer modeling, the LUT-based method and the hybrid inversion method that combines machine learning [20]. Due to the "same effect with different parameters" problem in RTM inversion, combining sensitivity analysis results, a priori knowledge, and measured data can effectively reduce the occurrence of this phenomenon—where different parameters lead to the same spectral response [14].

2.3.1. Sensitivity Analysis

Sensitivity analysis is an important method for qualitatively and quantitatively assessing how changes in model parameters affect the model's output. By combining measured data with a priori knowledge, the ranges and fixed values for model parameters used in sensitivity analysis are determined. Based on the results of this analysis, the input parameter ranges and fixed values for constructing the final lookup table are established.

A local sensitivity analysis of the 14 model parameters was conducted, treating each parameter individually as a variable while fixing the others. This analysis qualitatively evaluated how the input parameter ranges influenced the reflectance in the desired spectral band. The sensitive model parameters were identified from the local sensitivity analysis, and a global sensitivity analysis was then performed on these parameters using the Sobol method to quantitatively assess how changes in the model parameters impact the model's output. The ranges of the sensitivity analysis parameters and the settings for fixed values are presented in Appendix A Table A1.

2.3.2. Lookup Tables (LUTs)

In PROSAIL model inversion, the number of parameters determined by a priori knowledge or fixed values is typically much larger than the number of field-obtained parameters within the setup range. This discrepancy makes it difficult for radiative transfer models to directly invert the desired vegetation growth parameters based solely on spectral information; however, LUTs provide a solution to this issue [24]. With the LUT-based inversion method, the optimal combination of parameters corresponding to the simulated spectrum that most closely matches the measured spectrum can be identified through a simple search process. In this study, the LAI was retrieved at two stages—the tuber initiation stage and the tuber bulking stage—for both the late-maturing variety D681 and the early-maturing variety Zhongshu 5. The simulated spectral reflectance of the PROSAIL model was combined with the spectral response function of the RedEdge-P sensor to calculate the equivalent spectral reflectance, which is referred to as the simulated spectral reflectance. Two types of lookup tables were constructed: LUT1, which was based on five bands of simulated spectral reflectance; and LUT2, which contained six simulated vegetation indices derived from five bands of simulated spectral reflectance (see Table 3).

Table 3. Vegetation index used in this study.

Name	Formulas	References
Optimized soil-adjusted vegetation index (OSAVI)	$(1+0.16)\frac{NIR-R}{NIR+R+0.16}$	[25]
Red-Edge Normalized Difference Vegetation Index (NDVIre)	$\frac{\rho_{RE}-\rho_{Red}}{\rho_{RE}+\rho_{Red}} \times \rho_{NIR}$	[15]
Red-Edge Modified Simple Ratio (MSRre)	$\frac{\rho_{RE}/\rho_{Red}-1}{\sqrt{\rho_{RE}/\rho_{Red}+1}} \times \rho_{NIR}$	[15]
Soil-adjusted vegetation index (SAVI)	$(1+0.5)\frac{(NIR-R)}{(NIR+R+0.5)}$	[26]
Enhanced Vegetation Index (EVI)	$2.5\frac{NIR-R}{(NIR+6R-7.5B)+1}$	[27]
Modified Triangular Vegetation Index 2 (MTVI2)	$1.5\frac{(1.2(NIR-G)-2.5(R-G))}{\sqrt{(2NIR+1)^2-(6NIR-5\sqrt{R})-0.5}}$	[28]

In the LUT-based inversion, the LAI was estimated when the root mean square error (*RMSE*) and mean absolute error (*MAE*) between the UAV-measured values and the simulated spectra in the lookup table were minimized, based on the cost function. The parameter combination with the smallest mean *RMSE* and *MAE* was then chosen as the inversion result.

The cost function used to establish the relationship between the measured spectra (or vegetation indices) and the modeled spectra (or vegetation indices) is defined as follows:

$$RMSE = \sqrt{\frac{1}{n}\sum(R_{simulated} - R_{measured})^2} \quad (7)$$

$$MAE = \frac{1}{n}\sum_{i=1}^{n}|R_{simulated} - R_{measured}| \quad (8)$$

where n is the number of bands or vegetation indices; $R_{simulated}$ is the simulated reflectance value or vegetation index constructed by simulated reflectance; $R_{measured}$ is the measured band reflectance value or vegetation index constructed by measured reflectance.

To minimize the impact of lookup table size on the final inversion results, the full-life data for the two varieties were used as examples for pre-inversion lookups based on the distribution ranges of the model parameters provided in Appendix A Table A2. Lookup tables containing 1000, 5000, 10,000, 20,000, and 50,000 simulated spectral reflectance were constructed using the Latin hypercube sampling method. The optimal lookup table size was determined by comparing the inversion results of LUT1, and the construction of each lookup table (LUT) was completed using this optimal size.

2.3.3. Machine Learning Algorithms

RF and PLSR are widely used to estimate potato LAI, demonstrating strong performance in previous research. This study emphasizes the potential of empirical statistical modeling and radiation modeling methods in estimating potato leaf area index at the community scale, thus, RF and PLSR were chosen.

Random Forest Algorithm

The random forest (RF) algorithm introduces the concept of bagging, which involves constructing a series of unrelated decision trees by randomly selecting samples and features [29]. In addition, during the construction of each decision tree, each node randomly selects a subset of features and chooses the optimal features for splitting. The model demonstrates good predictive ability, high tolerance to noise and outliers, and can avoid overfitting to some extent. Each decision tree makes predictions based on the selected samples and features. By averaging the regression predictions of all decision trees, the overall regression prediction for the forest is obtained. Training the RF model requires setting several parameters, including the number of trees, the number of random features, and the stopping criterion. The RF model is built using the scikit-learn library in Python, and the entire process is carried out in PyCharm Community Edition 2023.2.3. The number of decision trees is set to 100, and the number of features is determined by the square root of the total number of features. The training process stops when the minimum number of samples in the tree nodes is one, and the minimum impurity is zero.

Partial Least Squares Regression Algorithm

Partial Least Squares Regression (PLSR) is a statistical method for modeling linear regression between multivariate data. PLSR is able to handle multiple response variables simultaneously and can effectively solve the multicollinearity problem by finding the direction that explains the maximum covariance between the independent and dependent variables to reduce the dimensionality of the data and construct predictive models [30]. PLSR model construction and validation were accomplished by loading the pls package using the R version 4.2.2 language.

The equivalent spectral reflectance was used to construct the vegetation index; the simulated vegetation index and the corresponding parameter input range were used as the modeling set; and the measured data were used as the validation set. The machine learning algorithm was combined to realize the potato LAI inversion based on the simulated data.

Hybrid Modeling Strategy

Using LUT2 simulation data as the modeling set, and RMSE and MAE as the cost functions, we screened out the lookup table information with the smallest mean values of RMSE and MAE compared to the UAV multispectral vegetation index. We combined the spectral index with RF and PLSR algorithms to construct hybrid inversion models. The field-measured LAI in 2023 was used as the validation set. The inversion model constructed using PROSAIL simulated spectral data and the machine learning algorithm with the field-measured LAI were compared to verify the feasibility of the hybrid modeling method for estimating potato LAI.

2.4. Model Evaluation and Statistical Analysis

The inversion of the LAI during the tuber initiation stage and tuber bulking stage, for two varieties, as well as the comprehensive LAI inversion for the entire growth period of the two varieties, was achieved using simulated spectral data and input model parameter ranges. The inversion accuracy was validated using actual measured multispectral data from UAV and ground-truth data. The model performance was evaluated using two statistical indicators: the coefficient of determination (R^2) and *RMSE*. The formulas for the evaluation criteria are as follows:

$$R^2 = 1 - \frac{\sum_{i=1}^{m}(\hat{y}_i - \overline{y})^2}{\sum_{i=1}^{m}(y_i - \overline{y})^2} \tag{9}$$

$$RMSE = \sqrt{\frac{1}{m}\sum_{i=1}^{m}(y_i - \hat{y}_i)^2} \tag{10}$$

where yi represents the observed LAI values; $\overline{y}$ represents the mean of the observed LAI values; $\hat{y}_i$ represents the predicted LAI values; and m represents the number of prediction points.

3. Results

3.1. Sensitivity Analysis of the PROSAIL Model Parameters

3.1.1. Local Sensitivity Analysis

In order to localize the parameters of the PROSAIL model, the numerical range and fixed value are determined based on the measured data and prior knowledge during sensitivity analysis. As shown in Figure 5, when the LAI is less than 3 and when the LAI is between 3 and 6, it exhibits a varying impact on the spectral reflectance response in the

400 nm to 2500 nm bands. Specifically, an increase in the LAI is associated with an increase in reflectance in the visible, red-edge, and near-infrared regions, with the effect being more pronounced when the LAI is less than three. Chlorophyll content (Cab) significantly affects the reflectance in the visible and red-edge bands, with reflectance in the visible region decreasing as chlorophyll content increases. Carotenoid content (Car) only influences reflectance in the visible band. The dry matter content (cm) affects reflectance in the 780 nm to 2500 nm range, in addition to the visible spectrum. Water content (Cw) notably affects reflectance between 860 nm and 2500 nm. The presence of brown matter (Cbrown) alters reflectance in both the visible and near-infrared (NIR) spectra. Leaf area (ALA), nitrogen content (N), and hotspot factor (hspot) significantly affect reflectance between 760 nm and 2400 nm. Reflectance decreases with increasing ALA but increases with higher N and hspot values. Sky reflectance (Skyl), soil reflectance (psoil), and leaf thickness (tts) mainly influence the NIR spectrum up to 1000 nm, with minimal impact on reflectance fluctuations. The value of leaf thickness (tto) affects reflectance across the full spectral range but has little effect on the visible spectrum. Since the tto is not the main focus of this study, a value of 0 is used as the standard in model construction. Finally, the parameter psi has no significant effect on reflectance across the full band range.

The analysis shows that the LAI, ALA, hspot, N, Cab, Car, Cm, Cbrown, and Cw have a significant effect on reflectance in the visible and red-edge bands. Although Cbrown also influences reflectance at wavelengths shorter than 1000 nm, the actual measurement data for Cbrown are unavailable. Based on previous studies, Cbrown is set to a constant value of 0 when constructing the lookup table. The parameters psoil, skyl, ts, to, and psi have negligible effects on reflectance; therefore, they are set to constant values of 0 during the global sensitivity analysis.

3.1.2. Global Sensitivity Analysis

The results of the local sensitivity analysis showed that the spectral response in the visible region varied with the LAI value. The global sensitivity analysis is discussed in terms of 0 < LAI < 3 and 3 < LAI < 6, respectively. The global sensitivity analysis shows that when the LAI < 3, the reflectance at the bands shown in Table 1 is mostly affected by the LAI, and that 842 nm is mainly affected by Cm (69.16%). The percentage of LAI effect on canopy reflectance at 475 nm, 560 nm, 668 nm, and 717 nm was 99.79%, 94.93%, 99.58%, and 74.62%, respectively. When the LAI > 3, the inverse at the bands shown in Table 1 is mainly affected by the LAI, ALA, and Cab, and at 842 nm, it is still mainly affected by Cm (73.14%). The canopy reflectance at 475 nm was mainly affected by ALA (83.64%), followed by the LAI (9.83%). The 560 nm canopy reflectance was mainly affected by the Cab (76.66%). The spectral reflectance at 668 nm is affected by ALA, LAI, Cab, and hspot in the order of 37.23%, 31.18%, 15.67%, and 14.07%, respectively, and the spectral reflectance at 717 nm is mainly affected by the Cab, which affects the results by 60.73% (Figure 6). The results showed that the canopy structural parameters and chlorophyll content had a great influence on the visible light and near-infrared reflectance during the vigorous shoot growth stage, and it was very important to understand and reduce the influence of chlorophyll content on reflectance in the LAI retrieval.

3.2. Effect of Lookup Table Size on Inversion Results

With the increase in the number of simulated spectra included in the lookup table, the accuracy of the LAI inversion model based on PROSAIL improves (Figure 7); however, when the number of simulated spectra exceeds 10,000, the time required to construct the LUTs increases significantly, while the accuracy of the LAI inversion model starts to decrease. Figure 7 shows that the construction times for LUTs containing 1000, 5000, 10,000, 20,000, and 50,000 spectral data took 88.577 s, 440.864 s, 889.426 s, 1761.24 s, and 4568.293 s, respectively. Using LUT1 with 1000 simulated data, the modeling R^2 is 0.28 and RMSE is 1.81. When the simulated spectral data in LUT1 increased to 10,000, R^2 increased by 89.82% and the RMSE reduced by 57.51%. In addition, when the simulated spectra in the LUT exceeded 10,000 and continued to increase, the accuracy of the LAI inversion model decreased. This may be due to the larger lookup table amplifying the effects of the phenomenon where "different parameters have the same spectral reflectance" on the model results. Based on the above results, LAI retrieval was conducted using the LUT containing 10,000 simulated spectra.

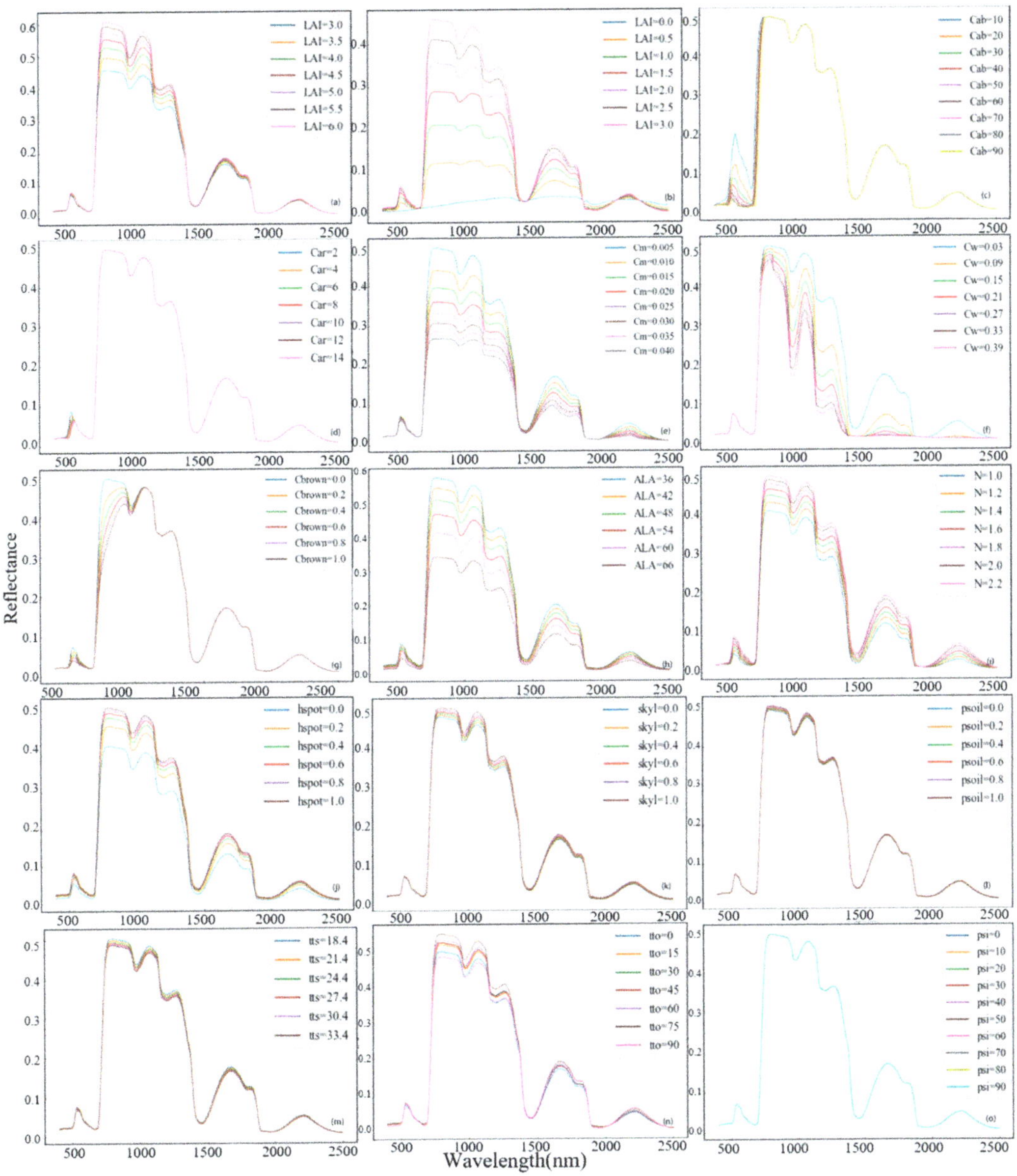

Figure 5. Local sensitivity analysis of PROSAIL model parameters. Figures (**a**,**b**) show the variation in spectral reflectance at 400–2500 nm for 3 < LAI < 6 and 0 < LAI < 3; (**c**–**o**) show the effects of Cab, Car, Cm, Cw, Cbrown, hspot, ALA, N, skyl, psoil, tts, tto, and psi on the spectral reflectance at 400 nm–2500 nm, respectively.

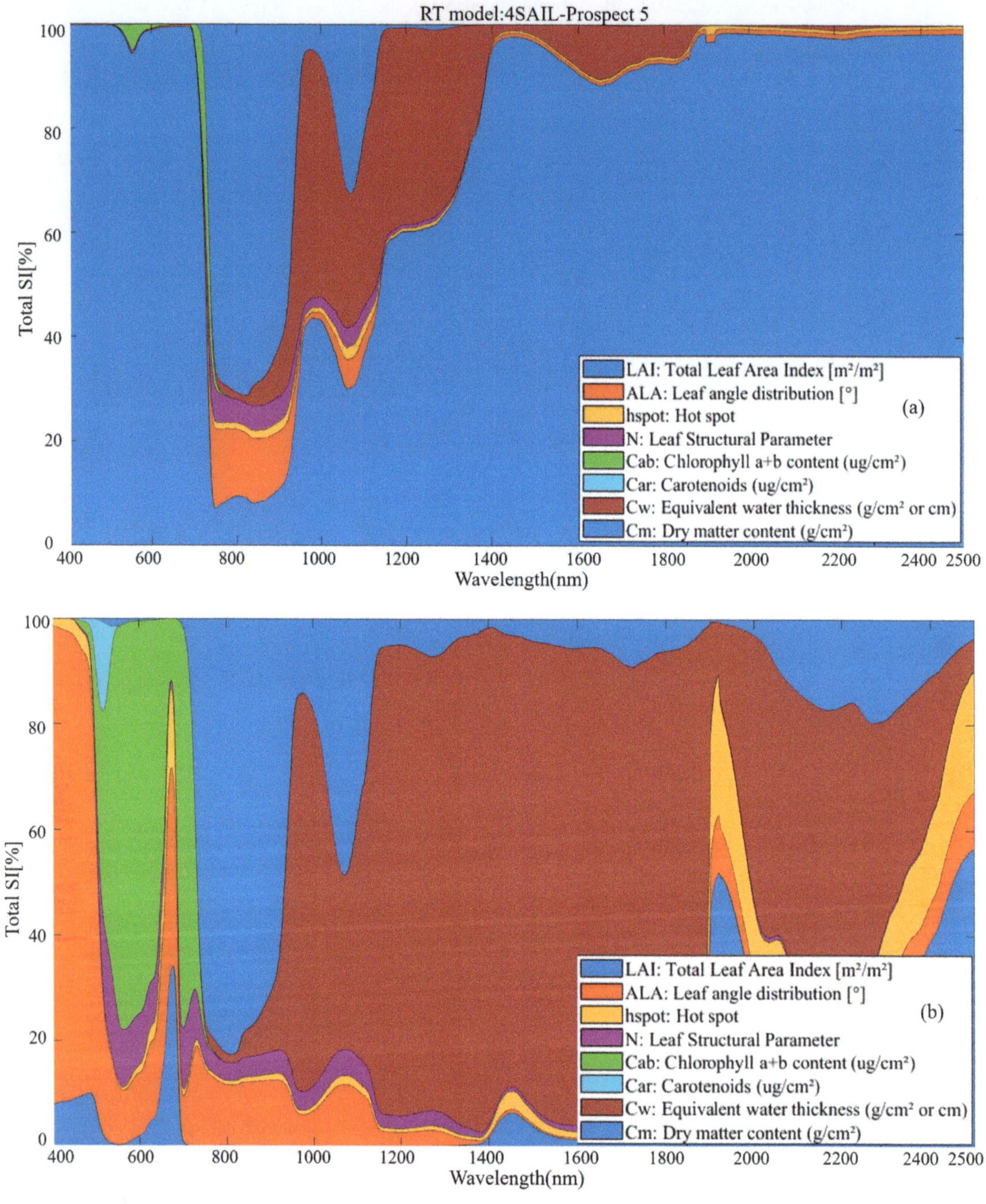

Figure 6. Global sensitivity analysis of the main PROSAIL model parameters: (**a**) the result of global sensitivity analysis for 0 < LAI < 3; (**b**) the result of global sensitivity analysis for 3 < LAI < 6.

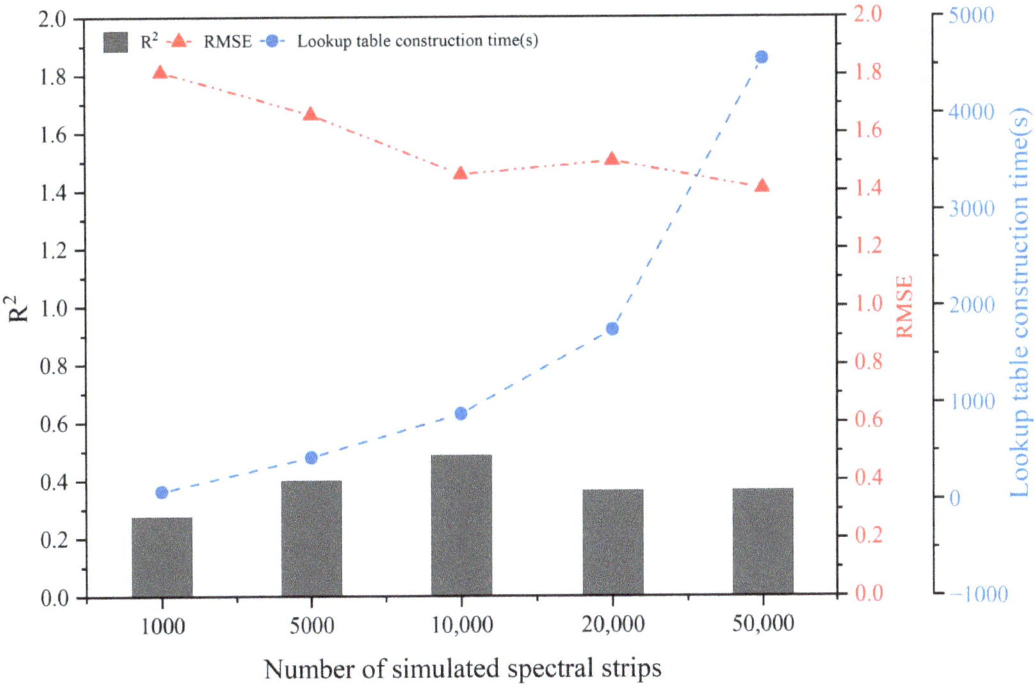

Figure 7. Results of LAI inversion using LUT1.

3.3. Potato LAI Inversion Based on Different Methods

The results of potato LAI inversion based on the PROSAIL model are shown in Table 4 and Figure 8; the hybrid inversion method using the PROSAIL model combined with the machine learning algorithm significantly improves the accuracy of model inversion. The accuracy of LAI inversion using LUT1 was stable for each growth stage and each variety, while LUT2 had a poor inversion effect for the tuber bulking stage. However, except for the tuber bulking stage, the inversion results based on LUT2 were better than LUT1 at each stage. The modeling accuracy of the hybrid inversion method based on LUT2 is significantly higher than that of the previous two methods. Except for the tuber bulking stage, the validation R^2 of the hybrid model of PROSAIL and RF is between 0.53 and 0.81 but the validation R^2 of this modeling method for the tuber bulking stage is only 0.33. The inversion accuracy of the hybrid model of PROSAIL combined with PLSR at each stage of the growth periods of potato is generally good, and the R^2 of the LAI verification at each stage and for both varieties based on this method is 0.67–0.88, and RMSE is 0.28–1.18. Compared with the inversion results using LUT2, the model R^2 of the tuber initiation stage, the tuber bulking stage, D681, Zhongshu5, and the whole growth stage increased by 30%, 263%, 49%, 47%, and 47%, respectively. The hybrid modeling method of PROSAIL + PLSR solves the problem of the low modeling accuracy and overfitting of PROSAIL + RF in the tuber expansion stage, significantly improves the accuracy of the LAI inversion model, and improves the stability of the LAI inversion model in different periods and varieties.

Table 4. Inversion of LAI results based on LUT1, LUT2, and hybrid methods.

Modeling Period/Species	LUT1		LUT2		PROSAIL + RF				PROSAIL + PLSR			
					Modeling Set		Validation Set		Modeling Set		Validation Set	
	R^2	RMSE	R^2	RMSE	R^2	RMSE	R^2	RMSE	R^2	RMSE	R^2	RMSE
M1	0.42	0.25	0.64	0.56	0.96	0.12	0.81	0.51	0.76	0.30	0.83	0.46
M2	0.43	1.24	0.24	1.80	0.90	0.49	0.33	1.66	0.56	0.85	0.87	1.18
D681	0.56	0.80	0.45	1.23	0.93	0.33	0.53	1.07	0.73	0.64	0.67	0.89
Z5	0.56	0.37	0.60	0.56	0.92	0.20	0.74	0.47	0.74	0.35	0.88	0.28
ALL	0.52	0.77	0.51	1.06	0.93	0.28	0.60	0.94	0.70	0.56	0.75	0.80

Note: M1, M2, Z5, and ALL represent all data during tuber initiation stage, tuber bulking stage, for zhongshu5, and for the full-life span of the two varieties, respectively.

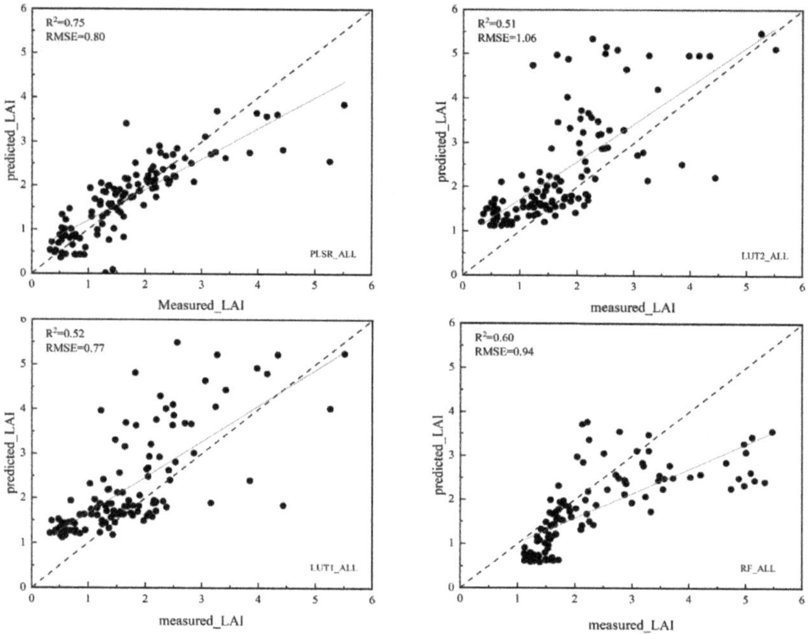

Figure 8. LAI inversion results of potato varieties across all growth stages using four strategies. The above results are for the model validation set, and the hybrid model results are for model validation using measured data.

3.4. Comparison of LAI Inversion Results Based on PROSAIL and Empirical Modeling

The LAI inversion results for each stage or variety based on field-measured data showed that the validation R^2 of the RF model for the LAI estimation across five stages or varieties ranged from 0.41 to 0.80 (Table 5). The model using the PLSR algorithm for the LAI inversion was more stable than those of RF, and the LAI inversion result was the best for the different stages or varieties, with the R^2 of the model verification ranging from 0.57 to 0.94.

Table 5. Empirical modeling results based on measured data.

Modeling Period/Species	RF				PLSR			
	Modeling Set		Validation Set		Modeling Set		Validation Set	
	R^2	RMSE	R^2	RMSE	R^2	RMSE	R^2	RMSE
M1	0.84	0.24	0.75	0.29	0.79	0.28	0.69	0.31
M2	0.76	0.51	0.65	0.55	0.79	0.63	0.57	0.79
D681	0.70	0.53	0.41	0.65	0.85	0.35	0.73	0.58
Z5	0.90	0.14	0.80	0.19	0.92	0.15	0.94	0.12
ALL	0.79	0.36	0.63	0.48	0.72	0.45	0.70	0.71

Note: M1, M2, Z5, and ALL represent all data during tuber initiation stage, tuber bulking stage, for zhongshu5, and for the full-life span of the two varieties, respectively.

These results indicate that the proposed hybrid inversion method, which combines potato simulation data with the empirical model based on measured data, achieves excellent accuracy. Moreover, the simulated data modeling approach requires only a small number of measured samples to define the range of the LAI indicators and verify the model. This can effectively reduce the challenges in constructing the inversion model, especially in cases where there is a low measured sample size or difficulties with measurements in large-scale scenarios.

4. Discussion

4.1. Performance of Inversion Models for Potato LAI Estimation

The combination of multispectral data and the PROSAIL model can accurately estimate the LAI at different growth stages and for different potato varieties, avoiding the problems of limited feasibility and model instability caused by small or insufficient sample sizes in a single growth stage. Spectral indices usually exhibit insensitivity at earlier growth stages, and saturation at later growth stages [25,26]. When using optical imaging to invert the leaf area index, it is prone to saturation in areas with high LAI, resulting in low inversion accuracy [31]. In the inversion results using lookup tables and PROSAIL combined with RF, the lower accuracy of the tuber bulking stage may be due to spectral saturation at large LAI values—which reduces the sensitivity of reflectance in the visible, red-edge, and near-infrared bands to LAI changes—and the increased interference of indicators such as chlorophyll content and average leaf inclination on spectral reflectance. Future studies should aim to mitigate the influence of these factors on LAI retrieval results by optimizing parameters or introducing novel vegetation indices.

The observed LAI is necessary for the empirical inversion strategy, which must be collected with manually handled measurements. As we know, LAI measurements can be conducted using devices such as a Plant Canopy Analyzer (LAI-2000, LI-COR, Lincoln, NE, USA), AccuPAR LP-80 ceptometer (METER Group, Pullman, WA, USA), and LI-3100C leaf area meter (LI-COR, Lincoln, NE, USA), which is also time-consuming and labor-intensive at the plot scale [9,10]. The hybrid strategy proposed in this manuscript combines the PROSAIL model, high-resolution unmanned aerial vehicle multispectral imaging, and machine learning algorithms to estimate potato LAI at the plot scale, which can be estimated without observed LAI data collection. The accuracy of LAI estimation models by the hybrid method and empirical modeling was compared, which displayed that the hybrid method can provide a similar estimation accuracy compared to empirical modeling. The hybrid approach offers substantial practical benefits due to reduced labor demands, which can improve the LAI estimation efficiency at the plot scale.

The hybrid inversion method used in this study can be implemented based on simulated data, greatly reducing the dependence on field data and proposing a feasible method for large-scale estimation of potato LAI, which is worthy of further validation in a broader agricultural scenario. When using PROSAIL and RF to estimate potato LAI, there exists a sharp drop in the accuracy of the training and validation of models, with the R^2 dropping from 0.93 to 0.60. Both the modeling set and validation set were chosen by random sampling, so this drop may be caused by overfitting of the RF model. This can be attributed to insufficient training datasets or overly complex training models [15,19,22]. Overfitting is a common problem in machine learning—while it performs well on the training set and poorly on the test data [10]. Building a random forest model using methods such as bagging and booting may be a potential strategy to improve the model's generalization ability [18]. Moreover, increasing the amount of datasets may be helpful for improving the LAI inversion accuracy using the random forest algorithm in future research. Moreover, the contribution of the model structures (e.g., different deep learning algorithms) to the LAI estimation can be explored with specific themes in the future.

4.2. Impact of Sensitive Parameter Determination on Model Results

Sensitivity analysis revealed that canopy reflectance is predominantly influenced by ALA and Cab when the LAI exceeds three, corroborating results from previous studies [14].

External factors such as weather conditions [32], remote-sensing data acquisition angle [23], and brown pigment content [33] at the time of image acquisition have a great impact on LAI estimation. This suggests that differentiating between cloudy and clear weather conditions [34,35] can enhance inversion accuracy for high LAI values. However, this study's scope was limited to the effects of model parameter changes under singular angles and ideal weather conditions, without considering variables like climate or light changes and increased flight angles that deviate from ideal conditions in practical applications.

A preliminary classification of the LAI by fertility stage was conducted without a detailed examination of the varying impacts of LAI sizes on spectral reflectance. Besides the LAI, ALA emerges as a critical canopy structure parameter in the PROSAIL model [29], with sensitivity analyses indicating significant effects of Cab on spectral reflectance at specific wavelengths and ALA's influence exceeding 50% at certain wavelengths when LAI > 3. Therefore, acquiring precise canopy structure measurements and detailed spectral data is crucial for minimizing the impact of Cab and other parameters to refine LAI inversion accuracy. The RedEdge-P sensor contains only one band at the red-edge position, which presents a challenge in constructing a valid vegetation index. Future research should explore the extent of influence from variations in Cab data range and other canopy structure parameters on LAI inversion, aiming to optimize vegetation indices or model parameters to reduce their impact on LAI inversion outcomes and enhance overall accuracy.

4.3. Necessity of PROSAIL Model Parameter Calibration

During the whole growth cycle, the shoot of potatoes varies significantly. When retrieving the LAI for different growth stages or varieties, determining the model parameter ranges based on the measured data and prior knowledge can significantly improve the accuracy of LAI inversion [6]. Compared to the LAI retrieval method that uses only the reflectance of LAI-sensitive spectral bands, retrieving the LAI using the reflectance of five bands results in higher model accuracy. Therefore, multispectral sensors that capture more band information can be used to refine the data from each band, potentially further improving the accuracy of the inversion model.

4.4. Effect of Lookup Table Size on Model Results

The empirical modeling method of using the spectral vegetation index to invert crop physiological and biochemical parameters is severely limited due to the lack of physical principles and the small amount of radiation information [11]. The use of a radiative transfer model to invert vegetation parameters takes into account the optical characteristics of leaves and the radiative transfer characteristics of the canopy, which is a mechanistic method for vegetation parameter inversion [16]. LUT is a method of determining inversion parameters from a table driven by the distribution and co-distribution patterns of defined input variable sets and reflectance table sizes. The cost function was used to minimize the distance between the simulated reflectance and measured reflectance and then to determine the entire set of primary input variables corresponding to the radiative transfer model based on LUTs [35]. At present, the lookup table size in the PROSAIL model is generally between 2500 and 100,000 [36]. Therefore, in order to compare the accuracy and computational efficiency of inverting the leaf area index with different lookup table sizes, this paper set five strategies ranging from 1000 to 50,000. The results show that when the lookup table size is 10,000, using the lookup table to invert the leaf area index has the best accuracy and the shortest calculation time. The density of numerical input for model parameters and the number of simulated spectra in the lookup tables significantly influence the inversion results [37]. Based on the sensitivity analysis, we constructed five lookup tables of different sizes to determine the optimal number of simulated spectra to include in the final lookup table; however, due to the large number of model parameters and the high density of model parameters, 10,000 simulated spectra had to be selected from over 10 million spectra using Latin hypercube sampling. Given the time constraints, only two types of LUTs were adopted in this study. Future research could focus on investigating the impact of lookup table size and the type of lookup tables on model accuracy. Efforts should also be made to mitigate the issue of poor model stability, which can arise from insufficient information in the lookup table and from a small number of lookup tables.

5. Conclusions

In this study, the ability of PROSAIL models combined with UAV multispectral imaging to estimate potato LAI at the plot scale was explored. The LAI has a significant influence on spectral reflectance. When the LAI is less than three, the contribution of potato LAI to the spectral reflectance in the visible light and red-edge bands ranges from 74.62% to 99.79%. The use of a lookup table containing 10,000 simulated spectra results in desirable model accuracy in a relatively short time. Based on the simulated spectral data, the LAI retrieval results using LUT1 for different growth stages and potato varieties demonstrated strong stability. The accuracy of the potato LAI retrieval model based on LUT2 was significantly higher than that of the LUT1, except during the tuber bulking stage.

The fusion of UAV multispectral imagery, the radiation transfer model, and machine learning algorithms significantly improves accuracy. Among the four inversion strategies tested, the hybrid model integrating UAV multispectral, PROSAIL, and PLSR yielded the most accurate and stable performance. Compared to the results obtained with LUT2, the hybrid model achieved higher accuracy, with the R^2 of the inversion model improving by 30% to 263%. Notably, the validation R^2 of the hybrid model combining PROSAIL and PLSR during the tuber bulking stage reached 0.87, which effectively overcame the low inversion accuracy observed with LUTs during the tuber bulking stage.

When compared with the empirical modeling method based on measured data, the hybrid method using simulated spectra also yielded good results for potato LAI retrieval. This suggests that PROSAIL has great potential for estimating potato LAI. Furthermore, the hybrid method can effectively reduce the challenges associated with constructing inversion models when sample sizes are insufficient or when measurement difficulties arise with larger numbers of plots. This approach presents a potential strategy for estimating potato LAI at the plot scale.

Author Contributions: Conceptualization, J.L. and S.L.; methodology, S.L.; formal analysis, S.L. and Y.L.; writing—original draft preparation, S.L. and J.L.; writing—review and editing, S.L., J.L., P.Z. and L.J.; supervision, J.L. and C.B.; funding acquisition, J.L. All authors have read and agreed to the published version of the manuscript.

Funding: This research was funded by National Key R&D Program of China (2023YFD2302100), the National Natural Science Foundation of China (32372232), an earmarked fund for CARS (CARS-09-P12), the Industrial Technology Innovation Program of IMAST (2024RCYJ04004), and Key Scientific and Technological Projects of Heilongjiang Province in China (2021ZXJ05A05-03).

Institutional Review Board Statement: Not applicable.

Data Availability Statement: Data will be made available upon request.

Conflicts of Interest: The authors declare no conflicts of interest.

Appendix A

Table A1. Parameterization of the PROSAIL model for sensitivity analysis.

Model	Abbr.	Variable	Unit	Data/Range (Local Sensitivity Analysis)	Data/Scope (Global Sensitivity Analysis)
PROSPECT-5	N	Leaf structure parameter	Unitless	1–2 (0.2), 1.5	1–2
	Cab	Chlorophyll a + b content	$\mu g \cdot cm^{-2}$	10–90 (10), 40	31–89
	Car	Carotenoids	$\mu g \cdot cm^{-2}$	2–14 (2), 5	6.3–14.1
	Cbrown	Brown pigments	$\mu g \cdot cm^{-2}$	0–1 (0.1), 0	-
	Cm	Dry matter content	$g \cdot cm^{-2}$	0.005–0.040 (0.005), 0.005	0.005–0.040
	Cw	Equivalent water thickness	$g \cdot cm^{-2}$	0.030–0.400 (0.01), 0.03	0.030–0.400
4SAIL	LAI	Leaf area index	$m^2 \cdot m^{-2}$	0–3 (0.5); 3–6 (0.5), 3.5	0–3; 3–6
	ALA	Average leaf inclination angle	°	36–65 (5), 50	36–65
	skyl	Diffuse/Direct light	Unitless	0–1 (0.2), 0.2	-
	psoil	Soil brightness coefficient	Unitless	0–1 (0.2), 0.2	-
	hspot	Hot spot	Unitless	0–1 (0.2), 0.33	0–1
	tts	Solar Zenith Angle	°	18.4–33.4 (3), 25	-
	tto	View Zenith Angle	°	0–90 (10), 0	-
	psi	Relative Azimuth Angle	°	0–90 (10), 0	-

Note: The data to the right of the sensitivity analysis column "," are the data used when setting fixed values; the data inside "()" are the step size when this parameter is a variable, e.g., LAI: 0–3 (0.5); 3–6 (0.5), 3.5. It is shown that when LAI is used as the variable to fix the other parameters, LAI is set in the ranges of 0–3 and 3–6, respectively, and local sensitivity analyses are performed in steps of 0.5.

Table A2. Constructing lookup table model parameter settings.

Model	Abbr.	Variable	Unit	M1	M2	Z5	D681	ALL
PROSPECT-5	N	Leaf structure parameter	Unitless	1–1.5 (0.1)	1–2 (0.1)	1–2 (0.1)	1–1.5 (0.1)	1–2 (0.1)
	Cab	Chlorophyll a + b content	$\mu g \cdot cm^{-2}$	55–88.1 (5)	31–76 (5)	31–83 (5)	33.7–88.1 (5)	31–88.1 (5)
	Car	Carotenoids	$\mu g \cdot cm^{-2}$	6–14.1 (0.5)	6.4–12.2 (0.5)	6–14.1 (0.5)	6–14.1 (0.5)	6.3–14.1 (0.5)
	Cbrown	Brown pigments	$\mu g \cdot cm^{-2}$	0	0	0	0	0
	Cm	Dry matter content	$g \cdot cm^{-2}$	0.004–0.037 (0.002)	0.008–0.05 (0.002)	0.004–0.032 (0.002)	0.004–0.05 (0.002)	0.004–0.05 (0.005)
	Cw	Equivalent water thickness	$g \cdot cm^{-2}$	0.03	0.03	0.03	0.03	0.03
4SAIL	LAI	Leaf area index	$m^2 \cdot m^{-2}$	0.3–2.4 (0.1)	0.6–5.5 (0.2)	0.3–3.5 (0.2)	0.3–5.5 (0.2)	0.3–5.5 (0.2)
	ALA	Average leaf inclination angle	°	57–60 (1)	60–65 (1)	57–65 (1)	57–65 (10)	57–65 (1)
	skyl	Diffuse/Direct light	Unitless	20	20	20	20	20

Table A2. *Cont.*

Model	Abbr.	Variable	Unit	M1	M2	Z5	D681	ALL
	psoil	Soil brightness coefficient	Unitless	0.2	0.2	0.2	0.2	0.2
	hspot	Hot spot	Unitless	0–1 (0.1)	0–1 (0.1)	0–1 (0.1)	0–1 (0.1)	0–1 (0.1)
	tts	Solar Zenith Angle	°	30	30	30	30	30
	tto	View Zenith Angle	°	0	0	0	0	0
	psi	Relative Azimuth Angle	°	0	0	0	0	0

Note: M1, M2, Z5, and ALL denote tuber initiation stage, tuber bulking stage, Zhongshu5, and full-life stage of the two varieties, respectively. The data in "()" are the parameter steps set when constructing the lookup table.

References

1. Devaux, A.; Goffart, J.-P.; Kromann, P.; Andrade-Piedra, J.; Polar, V.; Hareau, G. The potato of the future: Opportunities and challenges in sustainable agri-food systems. *Potato Res.* **2021**, *64*, 681–720. [CrossRef] [PubMed]
2. Watson, D. Comparative Physiological Studies on the Growth of Field Crops: II. The Effect of Varying Nutrient Supply on Net Assimilation Rate and Leaf Area. *Ann. Bot.* **1947**, *11*, 375–407. [CrossRef]
3. Begum, F.; Kundu, B.; Hossain, M. Physiological analysis of growth and yield of potato in relation to planting date. *J. Bangladesh Acad. Sci.* **2015**, *39*, 45–51. [CrossRef]
4. Xiao, Z.; Liang, S.; Wang, J.; Xiang, Y.; Zhao, X.; Song, J. Long-Time-Series Global Land Surface Satellite Leaf Area Index Product Derived from MODIS and AVHRR Surface Reflectance. *IEEE Trans. Geosci. Remote Sens.* **2016**, *54*, 5301–5318. [CrossRef]
5. Allen, W.; Richardson, A. Interaction of Light with a Plant Canopy. *J. Opt. Soc. Am.* **1968**, *58*, 1023–1028. [CrossRef]
6. Nathalie, B. Ground-based measurements of leaf area index: A review of methods, instruments and current controversies. *J. Exp. Bot.* **2003**, *54*, 2403–2417.
7. Wilson, J.W. Estimation of foliage dense-ness and foliage angle by inclined point quadrats. *Aust. J. Bot.* **1963**, *11*, 95–105. [CrossRef]
8. Impollonia, G.; Croci, M.; Blandinières, H.; Marcone, A.; Amaducci, S. Comparison of PROSAIL Model Inversion Methods for Estimating Leaf Chlorophyll Content and LAI Using UAV Imagery for Hemp Phenotyping. *Remote Sens.* **2022**, *14*, 5801. [CrossRef]
9. Roosjen, P.; Brede, B.; Suomalainen, J.; Bartholomeus, H.; Kooistra, L.; Clevers, J. Improved estimation of leaf area index and leaf chlorophyll content of a potato crop using multi-angle spectral data—Potential of unmanned aerial vehicle imagery. *Int. J. Appl. Earth Obs. Geoinf.* **2018**, *66*, 14–26. [CrossRef]
10. Yu, T.; Zhou, J.; Fan, J.; Wang, Y.; Zhang, Z. Potato Leaf Area Index Estimation Using Multi-Sensor Unmanned Aerial Vehicle (UAV) Imagery and Machine Learning. *Remote Sens.* **2023**, *15*, 4108. [CrossRef]
11. Berger, K.; Atzberger, C.; Danner, M.; D'Urso, G.; Mauser, W.; Vuolo, F.; Hank, T. Evaluation of the PROSAIL Model Capabilities for Future Hyperspectral Model Environments: A Review Study. *Remote Sens.* **2018**, *10*, 85. [CrossRef]
12. Gustau, C.; Dino, S.; Jakob, R.; Markus, R. A perspective on Gaussian processes for Earth observation. *Natl. Sci. Rev.* **2019**, *6*, 616–618.
13. Su, W.; Wu, J.; Wang, X.; Xie, Z.; Zhang, Y.; Tao, W.; Jin, T. Retrieving Corn Canopy Leaf Area Index Based on Sentinel-2 Image and PROSAIL Model Parameter Calibration. *Spectrosc. Spectr. Anal.* **2021**, *41*, 1891–1897.
14. Sun, J.; Wang, L.; Shi, S.; Li, Z.; Yang, J.; Gong, W.; Wang, S.; Tagesson, T. Leaf pigment retrieval using the PROSAIL model: Influence of uncertainty in prior canopy-structure information. *Crop J.* **2022**, *10*, 1251–1263. [CrossRef]
15. Sun, Y.; Wang, B.; Zhang, Z. Improving Leaf Area Index Estimation with Chlorophyll Insensitive Multispectral Red-Edge Vegetation Indices. *IEEE J. Sel. Top. Appl. Earth Obs. Remote Sens.* **2023**, *16*, 3568–3582. [CrossRef]
16. Zhang, C.; Liu, X.; Wang, R.; Wei, N.; Liu, J.; Yu, K.; Wang, F. A Study on Canopy Water Content Inversion of *Phyllostachys edulis* Forest Based on PROSAIL Model. *J. Northwest For. Univ.* **2023**, *38*, 224–232+249.
17. Wang, R.; Chen, J.M.; He, L.; Liu, J.; Shang, J.; Liu, J.; Dong, T. A novel semi-empirical model for crop leaf area index retrieval using SAR co- and cross-polarizations. *Remote Sens. Environ.* **2023**, *296*, 113727. [CrossRef]
18. David, H.; Urte, S.; Andreas, W. Machine Learning Techniques for Predicting Crop Photosynthetic Capacity from Leaf Reflectance Spectra. *Mol. Plant* **2017**, *10*, 878–890.
19. Houborg, R.; Anderson, C. Utility of an image-based canopy reflectance modeling tool for remote estimation of LAI and leaf chlorophyll content at regional scales. *J. Appl. Remote Sens.* **2009**, *3*, 033529.
20. Elizabeth, B.; Brigitte, L.; Bernie, Z.; James, W. Non-destructive estimation of potato leaf chlorophyll from canopy hyperspectral reflectance using the inverted PROSAIL model. *Int. J. Appl. Earth Obs. Geoinf.* **2007**, *9*, 360–374.
21. Su, W.; Sun, Z.; Chen, W.-H.; Zhang, X.; Yao, C.; Wu, J.; Huang, J.; Zhu, D. Joint Retrieval of Growing Season Corn Canopy LAI and Leaf Chlorophyll Content by Fusing Sentinel-2 and MODIS Images. *Remote Sens.* **2019**, *11*, 2409. [CrossRef]

22. Duan, S.; Li, Z.; Wu, H.; Tang, B.; Ma, L.; Zhao, E.; Li, C. Inversion of the PROSAIL model to estimate leaf area index of maize, potato, and sunflower fields from unmanned aerial vehicle hyperspectral data. *Int. J. Appl. Earth Obs. Geoinf.* **2014**, *26*, 12–20. [CrossRef]
23. Luo, W.; Li, R.; Shen, F.; Liu, J. HY-1C/D CZI Image Atmospheric Correction and Quantifying Suspended Particulate Matter. *Remote Sens.* **2023**, *15*, 386. [CrossRef]
24. Zhang, M.; Su, W.; Zhu, D. Retrieval of LAI and LCC in Summer Corn Canopy Based on the PROSAIL Model Using an Improved Inversion Strategy. *Geogr. Geo-Inf. Sci.* **2019**, *35*, 28–33.
25. Jin, X.; Diao, W.; Xiao, C.; Wang, F.; Chen, B.; Wang, K.; Li, S. Estimation of Wheat Agronomic Parameters using New Spectral Indices. *PLoS ONE* **2013**, *8*, e72736. [CrossRef]
26. Zhen, Z.; Chen, S.; Yin, T.; Chavanon, E.; Lauret, N.; Guilleux, J.; Henke, M.; Qin, W.; Cao, L.; Li, J.; et al. Using the Negative Soil Adjustment Factor of Soil Adjusted Vegetation Index (SAVI) to Resist Saturation Effects and Estimate Leaf Area Index (LAI) in Dense Vegetation Areas. *Sensors* **2021**, *21*, 2015. [CrossRef]
27. Qiao, K.; Zhu, W.; Xie, Z.; Li, P. Estimating the Seasonal Dynamics of the Leaf Area Index Using Piecewise LAI-VI Relationships Based on Phenophases. *Remote Sens.* **2019**, *11*, 689. [CrossRef]
28. Xie, Q.; Huang, W.; Liang, D.; Chen, P.; Wu, C.; Yang, G.; Zhang, D. Leaf Area Index Estimation Using Vegetation Indices Derived from Airborne Hyperspectral Images in Winter Wheat. *IEEE J. Sel. Top. Appl. Earth Obs. Remote Sens.* **2014**, *7*, 3586–3594. [CrossRef]
29. Jiao, Q.; Sun, Q.; Zhang, B.; Huang, W.; Ye, H.; Zhang, Z.; Zhang, X.; Qian, B. A Random Forest Algorithm for Retrieving Canopy Chlorophyll Content of Wheat and Soybean Trained with PROSAIL Simulations Using Adjusted Average Leaf Angle. *Remote Sens.* **2022**, *14*, 98. [CrossRef]
30. Wold, S.; Sjöström, M.; Eriksson, L. PLS-regression: A basic tool of chemometrics. *Chemom. Intell. Lab. Syst.* **2001**, *58*, 109–130. [CrossRef]
31. Mutanga, O.; Masenyama, A.; Sibanda, M. Spectral saturation in the remote sensing of high-density vegetation traits: A systematic review of progress, challenges, and prospects. *ISPRS J. Photogramm. Remote Sens.* **2023**, *198*, 297–309. [CrossRef]
32. Li, W.; Weiss, M.; Waldner, F.; Defourny, P.; Demarez, V.; Morin, D.; Hagolle, O.; Baret, F. A Generic Algorithm to Estimate LAI FAPAR and FCOVER Variables from SPOT4 HRVIR and Landsat Sensors: Evaluation of the Consistency and Comparison with Ground Measurements. *Remote Sens.* **2015**, *7*, 15494–15516. [CrossRef]
33. Danner, M.; Berger, K.; Wocher, M.; Mauser, W.; Hank, T. Fitted PROSAIL Parameterization of Leaf Inclinations, Water Content and Brown Pigment Content for Winter Wheat and Maize Canopies. *Remote Sens.* **2019**, *11*, 1150. [CrossRef]
34. Xu, Z.; He, A.; Zhang, Y.; Hao, Z.; Li, Y.; Xiang, S.; Li, B.; Chen, L.; Yu, H.; Shen, W.; et al. Retrieving chlorophyll content and equivalent water thickness of Moso bamboo (*Phyllostachys pubescens*) forests under *Pantana phyllostachysae* Chao-induced stress from Sentinel-2A/B images in a multiple LUTs-based PROSAIL framework. *For. Ecosyst.* **2023**, *10*, 100108. [CrossRef]
35. Weiss, M.; Frédéric, B.; Myneni, B.; Agnès, P.; Knyazikhin, Y. Investigation of a model inversion technique to estimate canopy biophysical variables from spectral and directional reflectance data. *Agronomie* **2000**, *20*, 3–22. [CrossRef]
36. He, W.; Yang, H.; Pan, J.; Xu, P. Exploring optimal design of look-up table for prosail model inversion with multi-angle modis data. *Proc. SPIE Int. Soc. Opt. Eng.* **2012**, *8524*, 852420.
37. Wang, Z.; Skidmore, A.K.; Wang, T.; Darvishzadeh, R.; Hearne, J. Applicability of the PROSPECT model for estimating protein and cellulose plus lignin in fresh leaves. *Remote Sens. Environ.* **2015**, *168*, 205–218. [CrossRef]

agriculture

MDPI

Article

Segmentation and Proportion Extraction of Crop, Crop Residues, and Soil Using Digital Images and Deep Learning

Guangfu Gao [1], Shanxin Zhang [2], Jianing Shen [1], Kailong Hu [3], Jia Tian [4], Yihan Yao [1], Qingjiu Tian [5], Yuanyuan Fu [1], Haikuan Feng [6], Yang Liu [6,7] and Jibo Yue [1,*]

1 College of Information and Management Science, Henan Agricultural University, Zhengzhou 450002, China; gaoguangfu@stu.henau.edu.cn (G.G.); shenjianing@stu.henau.edu.cn (J.S.); yaoyihan@stu.henau.edu.cn (Y.Y.); yuanyuanfu@henau.edu.cn (Y.F.)

2 School of Information Science and Technology, Beijing Forestry University, Beijing 100083, China; zhangshanxin@bjfu.edu.cn

3 Key Laboratory of Emergency Satellite Engineering and Application, Ministry of Emergency Management, Beijing 100124, China; hklong_gis@163.com

4 School of Instrumentation and Optoelectronic Engineering, Beihang University, Beijing 100191, China; tianjia@buaa.edu.cn

5 International Institute for Earth System Science, Nanjing University, Nanjing 210023, China; tianqj@nju.edu.cn

6 Key Laboratory of Quantitative Remote Sensing in Agriculture, Ministry of Agriculture, Beijing Research Center for Information Technology in Agriculture, Beijing 100097, China; fenghaikuan@nercita.org.cn (H.F.); liuyanghe810@cau.edu.cn (Y.L.)

7 Key Lab of Smart Agriculture System, Ministry of Education, China Agricultural University, Beijing 100083, China

* Correspondence: yuejibo@henau.edu.cn

Abstract: Conservation tillage involves covering the soil surface with crop residues after harvest, typically through reduced or no-tillage practices. This approach increases the soil organic matter, improves the soil structure, prevents erosion, reduces water loss, promotes microbial activity, and enhances root development. Therefore, accurate information on crop residue coverage is critical for monitoring the implementation of conservation tillage practices. This study collected "crop–crop residues–soil" images from wheat-soybean rotation fields using mobile phones to create calibration, validation, and independent validation datasets. We developed a deep learning model named crop–crop residue–soil segmentation network (CCRSNet) to enhance the performance of cropland "crop–crop residues–soil" image segmentation and proportion extraction. The model enhances the segmentation accuracy and proportion extraction by extracting and integrating shallow and deep image features and attention modules to capture multi-scale contextual information. Our findings indicated that (1) lightweight models outperformed deeper networks for "crop–crop residues–soil" image segmentation. When CCRSNet employed a deep network backbone (ResNet50), its feature extraction capability was inferior to that of lighter models (VGG16). (2) CCRSNet models that integrated shallow and deep features with attention modules achieved a high segmentation and proportion extraction performance. Using VGG16 as the backbone, CCRSNet achieved an mIoU of 92.73% and a PA of 96.23% in the independent validation dataset, surpassing traditional SVM and RF models. The RMSE for the proportion extraction accuracy ranged from 1.05% to 3.56%. These results demonstrate the potential of CCRSNet for the accurate, rapid, and low-cost detection of crop residue coverage. However, the generalizability and robustness of deep learning models depend on the diversity of calibration datasets. Further experiments across different regions and crops are required to validate this method's accuracy and applicability for "crop–crop residues–soil" image segmentation and proportion extraction.

Keywords: image segmentation; proportion extraction; deep learning; crop residue coverage

1. Introduction

Crop residues are one of the important solid waste resources in farmlands, playing a crucial role in sustaining the ecological environment of agricultural fields [1]. Crop residues can increase the soil organic matter, improve the soil structure, prevent soil erosion, reduce soil and water loss, promote microbial activity, and enhance the development of crop roots [2–6]. The crop residue coverage is vital for implementing conservation tillage practices. China places great importance on the comprehensive utilization of crop residues and vigorously promotes policies for crop residue incorporation into the soil [7]. Reasonable crop residue coverage can increase the soil organic matter by 7.59–14.60% and the crop yield by 4.11–11.8% [8]. Therefore, understanding the information on crop residue coverage is essential for maintaining farmland ecology and increasing crop yields [1].

Image classification and line-point transect methods are two primary manual techniques for assessing field crop residue coverage [6]. However, these manual methods are time-consuming and labor-intensive, and their low accuracy presents a significant limitation. In recent years, image segmentation algorithms have been increasingly applied in agriculture [9–11]. Image segmentation, a core task in computer vision, initially focused on basic image processing techniques. Early segmentation methods primarily relied on simple thresholding, where images were divided into regions based on grayscale values [12]. While thresholding is computationally simple, its effectiveness is limited by the image quality and lighting conditions [13]. Later, segmentation techniques began incorporating statistical models and graph theory. For instance, Gaussian mixture models (GMMs) and Markov random fields (MRFs) were developed for more complex segmentation tasks [14,15]. GMMs differentiate regions using probabilistic pixel modeling, while MRFs address local consistency by considering spatial relationships between pixels [16,17]. These approaches, however, are computationally intensive and require a precise initialization. As computing power advanced, segmentation methods evolved to include shape- and edge-detection techniques. Edge-based methods, such as the Canny edge detector and Sobel operator, became popular for detecting image edges [5,18]. These methods perform image segmentation by detecting edges within the image. Additionally, active contour models (e.g., Snakes) and level set methods were developed, improving the detection of complex shapes and boundaries [19,20]. These models enhance segmentation accuracy, especially in images with well-defined boundaries [21]. These methods effectively address challenges related to varying scales and complex structures that earlier approaches struggled with. However, manually defined image features often fail to capture the full complexity of environments, limiting traditional algorithms to specific image types and hindering their performance in more intricate scenes. Although these methods are simple and interpretable, they remain competitive in certain applications.

Machine learning methods have also been introduced into image segmentation, with support vector machine (SVM) and random forest (RF) algorithms emerging as important tools [22,23]. SVM perform classification and segmentation by constructing a hyperplane in high-dimensional feature spaces, while RF enhances robustness and accuracy by integrating multiple decision trees for random feature selection and sample classification [7,24]. Nevertheless, when processing images of soil and crop residues with similar color features, traditional machine learning algorithms often suffer from poor generalization, resulting in frequent over-segmentation and under-segmentation.

Deep learning-based image segmentation has increasingly been applied to real-world scenarios [25]. The fully convolutional networks (FCNs) replace traditional network structures with convolutional layers, enabling spatial mapping rather than merely predicting class probabilities for each pixel [26]. More advanced convolutional neural networks, such as ResNet and MobileNet, achieve better performance by stacking convolutional layers and utilizing depthwise separable convolution to improve model efficiency and speed while maintaining high accuracy [27]. Ronneberger et al. [28] developed U-Net, which utilizes skip connections between the encoder and decoder to capture contextual information, particularly for medical image segmentation. Chen et al. [29] introduced DeepLab, which incorporates atrous convolution to improve multi-scale perception capabilities. However, deep learning models often overlook the semantic context across different scales, leading to inadequate segmentation accuracy, particularly in distinguishing similar features [30]. This issue becomes more pronounced in agricultural applications, where crop residues and soil often have similar characteristics, resulting in a lower segmentation accuracy compared to natural or man-made environments.

In recent years, the introduction of attention mechanisms and self-attention models, such as the Transformer, has significantly advanced image segmentation technology [31]. Methods like the Vision Transformer (ViT), which integrate self-attention mechanisms, have further improved segmentation accuracy and generalization [32]. While increasing the number of convolutional layers enhances the model's feature extraction capabilities, deepening the network structure raises the computational costs and demands higher hardware performance for model deployment. Existing research often emphasizes deep feature extraction, overlooking shallow feature information. This over-reliance on deep features can degrade model performance in areas rich in details or with ambiguous boundaries. For instance, the color similarity between crop residues and soil, combined with varying camera angles, results in complex distributions of "soil–crop residue" targets in farmland images. Therefore, when designing deep learning-based image segmentation models for separating and extracting the proportions of "crop–crop residue–soil" in farmland, it is crucial to balance deep and shallow features and fully leverage semantic context at multiple scales to achieve accurate information extraction.

In recent years, many machine learning algorithms have been applied to the work of crop residue coverage extraction [33–35]. For example, Zhou et al. proposed a method to extract crop residue coverage from UAV (Unmanned Aerial Vehicle) images by using an improved deep learning model; Yue et al. proposed to use the radiative transfer model and a deep learning algorithm to draw crop residue coverage maps with the help of remote sensing images, etc. [3,36]. These research results show that for different image types (such as UAV images and remote sensing images), using appropriate models and algorithms can effectively carry out the extraction and mapping work of crop residue coverage.

The primary aim of this study was to propose a method for segmenting and extracting the proportions of crops, crop residues, and soil from digital images using deep learning. A deep learning model, crop–crop residue–soil segmentation network (CCRSNet), was developed to improve the performance of image segmentation and proportion extraction in cropland areas. CCRSNet integrates both shallow and deep image features and incorporates a pyramid pooling module to capture contextual information at multiple scales. The study compared the performance of current machine learning-based segmentation methods, including RF and SVM, with the proposed CCRSNet model. The results demonstrate that CCRSNet, by leveraging shallow feature information and the pyramid pooling module, achieves superior segmentation and proportion extraction of crops, crop residues, and soil.

2. Materials and Methods

2.1. Study Area and Experimental Design

2.1.1. Study Area

The study area is located in Yuanyang County, Xinxiang City, Henan Province (Figure 1a, 113°36′~114°15′ E, 134°55′~35°11′ N), China. Yuanyang County is situated in a mid-latitude zone, characterized by a warm temperate continental monsoon climate, with an average annual precipitation of 490 mm. The local agriculture primarily involves wheat-corn and wheat-soybean rotations, with wheat typically sown in mid-October and both soybeans and corn generally planted in late June.

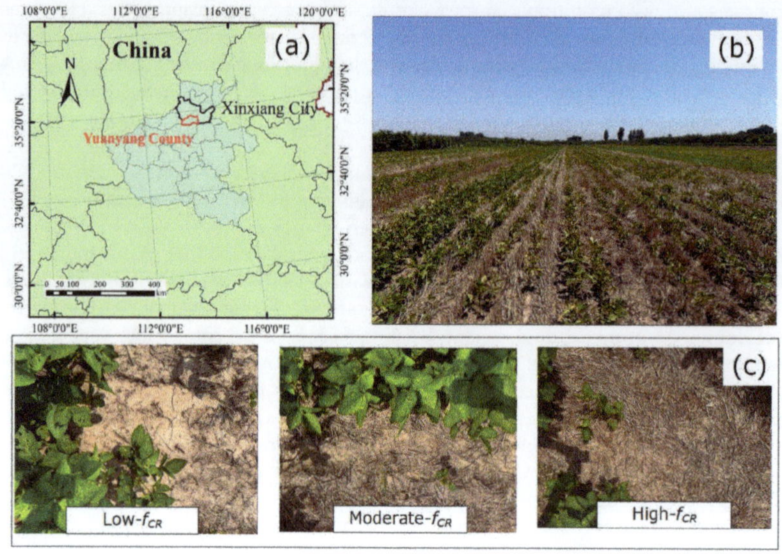

Figure 1. Study area and experimental sites. (**a**) Location of the study area. (**b**) Soybean experimental field. (**c**) Field "crop–crop residue–soil" digital images, f_{CR} (crop residue coverage).

2.1.2. Field Experimental Design

We collected the field "crop–crop residue–soil" images for the two stages of soybean growth stages during the summer of 2023, from seeding (23 July) to flowering (25 August) stages. This is because there are rarely "crop–crop residue–soil" scenarios under medium to high soybean cover. This study employed an Apple iPhone 14 Pro (48-megapixel mode) to capture field images of "crop–crop residue–soil." The images were collected under sunny conditions in a conservation tillage soybean field (Figure 1b), with the goal of obtaining high-definition digital images of the soil, crop residue, and crops. At the time of collection, the crop height ranged between 20 and 30 cm, and the phone was held manually at a height of 100–110 cm (from ground surface), oriented vertically downward (Figure 1c), This ensures the picture quality is as good as possible and reduces the errors caused by image distortion. A total of 200 images depicting "crop–crop residue–soil" scenes was taken. However, due to unavoidable distortions and human interference, shadows from personnel and other artifacts, such as shoes, appeared at the edges of the images. As a result, it was necessary to manually crop these edge-affected areas for deep learning model calibration, quantitative validation, and visual assessment. The cropping process was carried out in two ways:

1. For constructing the training dataset and performing quantitative validation, images with a pixel size of 256 × 256 × 3 were extracted from the central region of the original images and labeled according to land cover categories.
2. For field image segmentation applications and visual evaluations, only the edge-affected areas were manually removed.

2.2. Data Pre-Processing

2.2.1. Data Annotation

The Labelme annotation platform was employed to manually label the cropped images [37]. Upon completion of the annotation, the exported json files were converted to generate single-channel grayscale label masks, which provided labels for subsequent deep learning model calibration. The images were categorized into three classes: soil, crop, crop residue (Table 1). Figure 2 illustrates the original images and their corresponding labels during the dataset annotation process.

Table 1. Annotation standards for agricultural crops, crop residue, and soil images.

Label	Category	Description
L0	Crop	The green plants in farmland are mainly soybeans and a small amount of weeds.
L1	Crop residue	The residue after wheat harvesting, mainly consisting of stems; small residues may labeled as soil.
L2	Soil	Dry, moist, shaded, and illuminated soil; small pieces of soil region may be labeled as crop residue under high crop residue coverage.

Figure 2. Original image and annotated image.

2.2.2. Data Augmentation

After data annotation, we divided the dataset into a training and validation dataset (TVD; n = 160) and an independent validation dataset (IVD; n = 40). The TVD dataset was used to calibrate and validate the machine learning and deep learning models, while the IVD dataset, containing 40 digital images, was employed for independent evaluation to further assess the model's performance in real-world scenarios. This step was essential for evaluating the model's generalization ability by testing its effectiveness on unseen data.

The TVD dataset consisted of 160 digital farmland images, which were augmented in various ways to increase diversity and complexity, thereby improving the dataset's representativeness. Specifically, three augmentation techniques were applied:

- Rotation: A random angle between -90° and 90° was used to rotate the images, altering the positions of the categories to be segmented.
- Horizontal mirroring: This technique was applied to create left-right symmetrical versions of the original images.
- Vertical mirroring: This technique generated top–bottom symmetrical versions of the original images.

After augmentation, we obtained 960 digital farmland images along with their corresponding annotation results. Of these, 75% (n = 720) were designated as the calibration set for model training, while the remaining 25% (n = 240) were allocated as the validation set for initial performance assessment and tuning.

2.3. Technical Workflow

This study focused on a dataset of images featuring crops, crop residue, and soil from various agricultural fields, applying different machine learning and deep learning models for image segmentation. The primary goal was to extract the proportions of each category and compare the models' performance. The technical workflow, illustrated in Figure 3, consisted of the following four steps:

1. Image acquisition: Images of crops, crop residue, and soil were collected at different times from agricultural fields within a specified region. The TVD dataset was used for calibration and validation, while the IVD dataset served as an independent validation set to assess the models' generalization performance and robustness.
2. Data preprocessing: The dataset was manually annotated, categorizing the images into three classes: "soil–crop–crop residue". Data augmentation techniques, such as rotation and mirroring, were applied to enhance the dataset.
3. Model construction: The proposed CCRSNet model architecture utilized VGG16 and ResNet50 as backbone networks.
4. Accuracy verification: Based on the TVD and IVD datasets, the segmentation accuracies of CCRSNet, RF, and SVM for "soil–crop–crop residue" in farmland were compared. Ablation experiments were also conducted to assess the contributions of different components within CCRSNet.

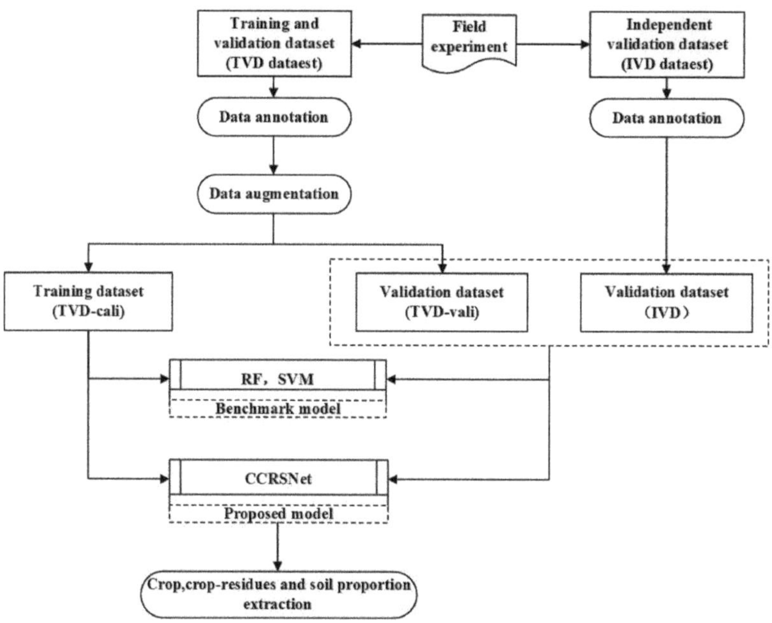

Figure 3. Methodology framework.

2.4. CCRSNet Segmentation Model

Semantic segmentation is a core task in the field of computer vision, aiming to assign a distinct class label to each pixel in an image, thereby generating a segmentation image of the same size as the original. The rapid development of CNN-based semantic segmentation models has led to the emergence of many innovative network architectures, such as PSPNet, the DeepLab series, and the U-Net series [38,39].

2.4.1. Backbone Network

The backbone network is a crucial component of deep learning networks responsible for feature extraction from input images. The extracted features are subsequently fed into other parts of the network, and the backbone network can be replaced with various architectures. Commonly utilized backbone networks include VGG16 and ResNet50, which are primarily classification networks known for their superior performance [40].

VGG16 was first proposed by the Visual Geometry Group at the University of Oxford [41]. The VGG model is composed of multiple 2×2 pooling layers and 3×3 convolution kernels. It has a simple and clear structure and is an excellent network for image recognition and classification. Although the VGG model has a large number of parameters and high computational cost, its contribution to deep learning and computer vision research is still significant, especially in understanding the effectiveness of the neural network hierarchical structure.

ResNet50 network introduced the concept of the residual network [42]. Due to the powerful feature extraction ability of the proposed residual structure, it is widely used in various deep learning networks. The deep residual network effectively overcomes the problems of reduced learning efficiency and ineffective improvement of accuracy caused by the increase in network depth. ResNet is mainly composed of convolution residual blocks (conv block) and skip residual blocks (identity block). Among them, the convolution residual block is used to change the network dimension, and the skip residual block is used to deepen the network. Therefore, the ResNet network has good performance in image recognition and classification.

2.4.2. CCRSNet Model Architecture

This study introduces a novel network architecture named CCRSNet, which employs ResNet50 or VGG16 as the backbone and incorporates channel and spatial attention mechanisms and a pyramid pooling module during upsampling. Current research often focuses on the deep features of convolutional networks, while CCRSNet enhances performance by integrating both shallow and deep image features from the backbone network, allowing for a more comprehensive capture of various feature information within images. This design enables CCRSNet to efficiently extract and utilize rich information from images, thereby improving segmentation accuracy and the performance and generalization ability of proportion extraction for crops, crop residue, and soil in farmland. The specific network architecture is depicted in Figure 4.

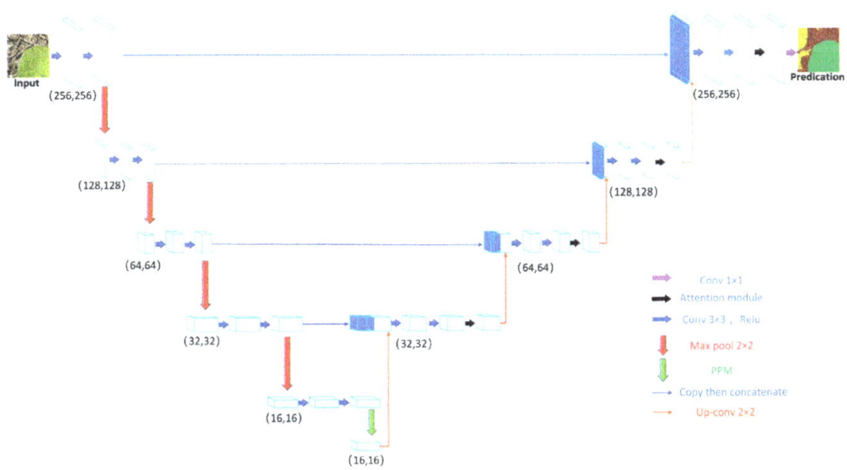

Figure 4. CCRSNet architecture.

The following is an explanation of part of the structure of CCRSNet:

1. Input: The input image size is 256 × 256 × 3.
2. Backbone: VGG16 and ResNet50 were selected as the backbone networks for CCRSNet.
3. Pyramid pooling module (PPM): PPM is composed of multiple pooling layers, each using windows of different sizes (including 1 × 1, 2 × 2, 3 × 3, and 6 × 6 pooling windows in this study) to extract contextual information of images at different scales. Subsequently, the pooled information is adjusted to the same size and concatenated through upsampling [43].
4. Attention module: The attention mechanism module in this study includes channel attention and spatial attention mechanisms, with lightweight characteristics and minimal impact on model complexity [44].

2.5. Baseline Models

This study selected two machine learning models, RF and SVM, as baseline models to achieve segmentation-like effects by classifying image pixels and analyzing the resulting confusion matrices. The proposed CCRSNet segmentation model's performance in segmenting and proportionally extracting crops, crop residue, and soil in farmland was explored.

RF is an ensemble learning method. RF constructs multiple decision trees and aggregates their results to improve prediction accuracy and stability [45]. The fundamental concept combines several decision trees to mitigate overfitting issues and enhance prediction accuracy. In RF, each decision tree is trained using a random subset of the data and a random subset of features, thus increasing model diversity and generalization capacity.

SVM is widely used in machine learning and pattern recognition. It optimizes classification accuracy by maximizing the margin between the hyperplane and the nearest data points (support vectors), which helps enhance the model's generalization ability and reduce classification errors. When data are not linearly separable, SVM employs kernel functions (such as gaussian kernel) to map data to a higher-dimensional space, achieving linear separability in the new space [46].

2.6. Deep Learning Model Parameter Settings

This study used a workstation equipped with an Intel i7-13650HX processor, 24 GB of RAM, and an RTX 4070 GPU (8 GB VRAM) for model calibration. During the deep learning model calibration, the first five epochs employed transfer learning with pretrained parameters from the backbone networks (VGG16 and ResNet50), with 100 training epochs set. The number of decision trees for the RF model calibration was 100, and the random seed parameter was 42. A linear kernel function was selected in SVM calibration, with the random seed parameter also set to 42. Each model underwent three calibration and validation iterations, retaining the optimal result.

During model calibration, a batch size of 2 was set when freezing parameters, and a batch size 16 was employed when unfreezing parameters. The optimizer was configured as 'adam', with a maximum learning rate of 1×10^{-6} and a minimum of 1×10^{-4}, controlling the learning rate's range. Cross-entropy loss was introduced into the loss function to address the issue of extremely imbalanced sample sizes across categories.

2.7. Segmentation and Classification Accuracy Evaluation Metrics

The confusion matrix is a widely used tool for evaluating model performance. Table 2 presents the confusion matrix for a binary classification problem. In the confusion matrix, TP, TN, FP, and FN represent true positives, true negatives, false positives, and false negatives, respectively. The confusion matrix can be applied to both binary and multi-class classification problems.

Table 2. Confusion matrix.

Type		Prediction	
	Label	Positive	Negative
Actual	Positive	true positives (TPs)	false negatives (FNs)
	Negative	false positives (FPs)	true negatives (TNs)

Additionally, standard evaluation metrics for semantic segmentation derived from the confusion matrix include intersection over union (IoU), mean IoU (mIoU), recall, and pixel accuracy (PA).

1. The ratio of the intersection of predicted results and true annotations to their union, reflecting the model's prediction performance for each category.

$$IoU = \frac{TP}{TP + FP + FN} \tag{1}$$

2. The average of IoUs across all categories, indicating the model's average segmentation performance across all categories, serving as a crucial metric for assessing segmentation performance.

$$mIoU = \frac{1}{N}\sum_{i=1}^{N} IoU_i \tag{2}$$

3. The proportion of correctly predicted pixels to the total number of pixels reflects the model's overall prediction accuracy, although it does not consider the performance of each category.

$$PA = \frac{TP + TN}{TP + FP + FN + TN} \tag{3}$$

4. The proportion of correctly predicted positive samples among all actual positives reflects the model's ability to detect true positives.

$$Recall = \frac{TP}{TP + FN} \tag{4}$$

Generally, higher values of mIoU, IoU, recall, and PA indicate better model performance.

2.8. Proportion Extraction Evaluation Metrics

To evaluate the accuracy of proportion extraction for the three categories of "soil–crop–crop residue", we employed RMSE and the coefficient of determination (R^2).

$$RMSE = \sqrt{\frac{1}{m}\sum_{i=1}^{m}(y_i - \hat{y}_i)^2} \tag{5}$$

$$R^2 = 1 - \frac{\sum_{i=1}^{m}(\hat{y}_i - y_i)^2}{\sum_{i=1}^{m}(\overline{y}_i - y_i)^2} \tag{6}$$

where y_i represents the actual measured value, $\overline{y}_i$ is the sample mean, $\hat{y}_i$ denotes the estimated value, and m indicates the sample size. For the same sample data, a higher R^2 and a lower RMSE generally indicate better model accuracy.

3. Results

3.1. Model Calibration and Validation Based on the TVD Dataset

Table 3 presents the RF and SVM models' validation accuracy based on the TVD dataset. The RF model achieved the highest accuracy (mIoU: 71.29%), while the SVM model had the lowest accuracy (mIoU: 21.64%). We also trained and validated the proposed CCRSNet model. The loss curves of the CCRSNet segmentation network during calibration are shown in Figure 5. It can be seen from Figure 5 that the CCRSNet model with VGG16 as the backbone network shows a relatively good training effect. During the training process, the loss of this model decreased more rapidly and had a smaller value. Table 3 also presents the accuracy evaluation results based on the TVD dataset. Our findings demonstrate that the CCRSNet model, using VGG16 as the backbone network, achieved the best performance (mIoU: 87.84%, PA: 93.70%). Compared to the RF model, the mIoU of CCRSNet improved by 16.55%. Moreover, compared with the ResNet50 model, the VGG16 network structure is relatively simple, has a relatively small number of parameters, and requires less storage space and computing resources. Therefore, it can perform better in scenarios with smaller datasets.

Table 3. Performance evaluation based on the TVD dataset.

Model and Backbone		RF	SVM	CCRSNet	
				VGG16	ResNet50
Recall	L0 (crop)	99.11%	82.24%	99.21%	99.37%
	L1 (crop residue)	62.55%	45.56%	90.41%	92.93%
	L2 (soil)	82.87%	4.8%	92.67%	91.41%
PA		80.70%	33.54%	93.70% *	93.54%
mIoU		71.29%	21.64%	87.84% *	87.72%

* indicates the highest mIoU and PA.

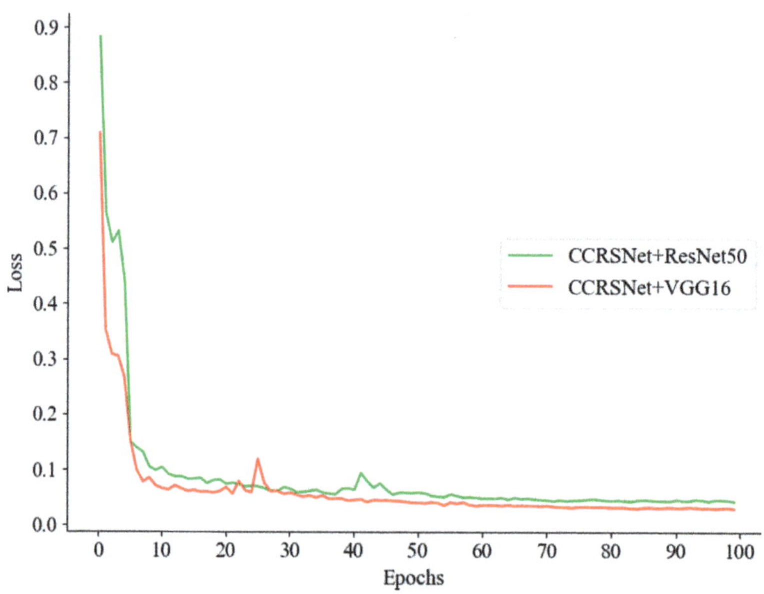

Figure 5. mIoU and loss curves of CCRSNet semantic segmentation network with different backbone networks during calibration.

3.2. Model Evaluation Based on the IVD Dataset

We compared the segmentation accuracy of different models based on the IVD dataset (Table 4). The experimental results (Table 4) indicated that the deep learning models had a higher accuracy than the traditional machine learning models. The results indicate that the CCRSNet model, with VGG16 as the backbone network, performed the best on the IVD datasets. Specifically, the CCRSNet model combined with VGG16 achieved the highest performance on the IVD dataset (mIoU: 92.73%, PA: 96.23%). The CCRSNet model can effectively extract feature information from segmentation targets even when the number of validation samples is relatively small.

Table 4. Performance evaluation based on the IVD dataset.

Model and Backbone		RF	SVM	CCRSNet	
				VGG	ResNet50
Recall	L0 (crop)	98.22%	87.87%	98.56%	98.51%
	L1 (crop residues)	64.35%	45.56%	94.27%	95.43%
	L2 (soil)	78.83%	4.85%	96.16%	94.46%
	PA	82.47%	58.00%	96.23% *	96.19%
	mIoU	66.86%	32.98%	92.73% *	92.65%

* indicates the highest mIoU and PA.

3.3. *CCRSNet Ablation Study Based on the TVD and IVD Datasets*

To further validate the effectiveness of (1) the attention module and (2) the deep and shallow feature structure module in the proposed CCRSNet, this study conducted ablation experiments using the TVD and IVD datasets. The three comparative ablation experiments and their respective architectures were as follows:

(i) Exp. 1: CCRSNet (Figure 4);
(ii) Exp. 2: CCRSNet without the deep and shallow feature structure (Appendix A, Figure A1a);
(iii) Exp. 3: CCRSNet without the attention module (Appendix A, Figure A1b).

Table 5 presents the segmentation accuracy for each category and the mIoU based on the TVD and IVD datasets. The results show that for the TVD dataset, the segmentation accuracy and mIoU for farmland images in Experiments 2 and 3 were lower than in Experiment 1. Experiment 3, which lacked the attention module, demonstrated a 0.15% improvement in mIoU on the independent validation set compared to Experiment 2 (which did not utilize shallow features). This indicates that integrating shallow feature information enhanced the model's generalization capability and robustness.

Table 5. Ablation experiments based on the TVD and IVD datasets.

	Type	Exp. 1		Exp. 2		Exp. 3	
	Label	TVD-vali	IVD	TVD-vali	IVD	TVD-vali	IVD
Recall	L0 (crop)	99.21%	98.56%	98.87%	97.73%	98.95%	98.66%
	L1 (crop residues)	90.41%	94.27%	90.45%	94.34%	92.18%	93.64%
	L2 (soil)	92.67%	96.16%	92.10%	95.62%	91.79%	95.74%
	PA	93.70% *	96.23% **	93.30%	95.83%	93.50%	95.91%
	mIoU	87.84% *	92.73% **	87.20%	91.98%	87.57%	92.13%

* indicates the highest mIoU and PA based on the TVD validation dataset; ** indicates the highest mIoU and PA based on the IVD dataset.

3.4. *Segmentation Results and Proportional Extraction Accuracy Based on CCRSNet*

Based on the model's performance on the TVD and IVD datasets, we ultimately selected the CCRSNet model with VGG16 as the backbone network (TVD dataset: mIoU of 87.84%, PA of 93.70%; IVD dataset: mIoU of 92.73%, PA of 96.23%) to perform "crop–crop residues–soil" image segmentation and proportional extraction for farmland images. Figure 6 shows two randomly selected farmland images, along with their annotation and prediction results, while Figure 7 displays the original farmland images and their corresponding predictions to illustrate the model's performance under real-world conditions. Figure 8 shows the visual explanations provided by highlighting the image regions that the model considers crucial for a specific prediction through Grad-CAM. It can be seen from the figure that the model pays the highest attention to crop residue. Our results demonstrate that the CCRSNet model, using VGG16 as the backbone, is highly effective in achieving "crop–crop residues–soil" image segmentation for farmland images.

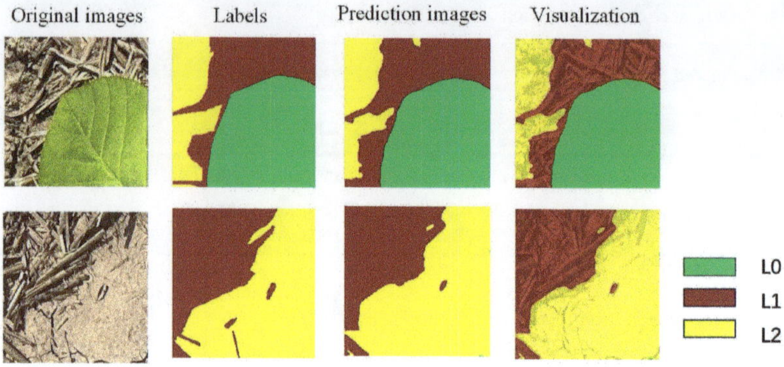

Figure 6. Visualization of segmentation results for processed images using the CCRSNet model with VGG16 as the backbone network.

Figure 7. Visualization of segmentation results for original images using the CCRSNet model with VGG16 as the backbone network.

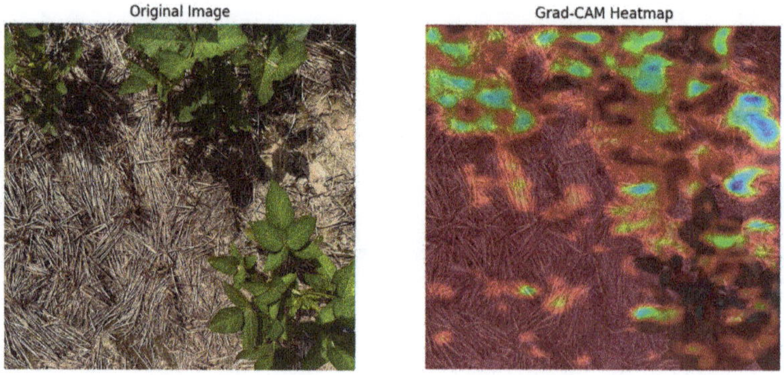

Figure 8. Class activation mapping using the CCRSNet model with VGG16 as the backbone network.

We performed a statistical analysis and accuracy evaluation of the model's proportional extraction results based on the TVD dataset. Figure 9a–c show scatter plots comparing the model's predicted proportions with the actual proportions in the TVD dataset. Figure 9a–c corresponds to the proportional extraction of the three categories, respectively. Our results show that the R^2 for all three categories exceeded 0.99. Using the RMSE as the metric, the crop proportion extraction performed best (RMSE = 0.55%), followed by crop residues (RMSE = 0.80%), while soil extraction showed the lowest performance (RMSE = 0.89%). We also conducted a statistical analysis and accuracy evaluation on the model's proportional extraction results using the IVD dataset. Figure 9d–f shows scatter plots comparing the predicted and actual proportions in the IVD dataset. Figure 9d–f represents the proportional extraction of the three categories, respectively. Similar to the TVD dataset, our results demonstrate that the R^2 for all three categories was above 0.99. In terms of the RMSE, the crop proportion extraction again performed best (RMSE = 1.05%), followed by crop residues (RMSE = 3.13%), and soil (RMSE = 3.56%) showed the weakest performance. The CCRSNet model provided high-accuracy proportional extraction results for the three categories.

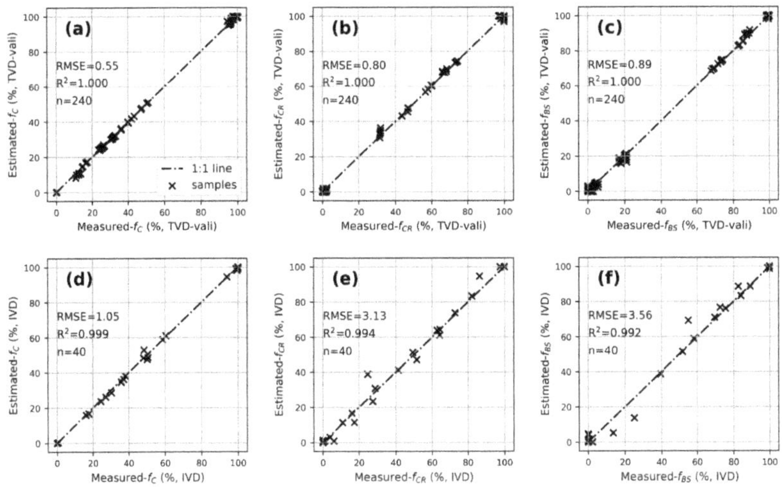

Figure 9. Proportion extraction of crop, crop residues, and soil using digital images and deep learning based on the TVD and IVD datasets. (**a**) crop (TVD-vali). (**b**) crop residues (TVD-vali). (**c**) soil (TVD-vali). (**d**) crop (IVD). (**e**) crop residues (IVD). (**f**) soil (IVD).

4. Discussion

4.1. Advantages of Deep Learning in Image Segmentation and Proportion Extraction

Traditional machine learning algorithms for image segmentation typically rely on expert experience for feature selection and extraction, which is time-consuming and labor-intensive. Moreover, when facing large-scale datasets, these algorithms have high computational demands and limited generalization capabilities, making it challenging to model nonlinear data. In contrast, deep learning models trained on large-scale data can learn more refined features, resulting in higher segmentation accuracy and stable performance across different complex backgrounds. Compared to traditional machine learning algorithms (such as RF and SVM), deep learning models (like CCRSNet) can automatically learn and extract multi-level features from images without the need for manual feature design [47].

Compared to benchmark models such as RF and SVM, the deep learning model CCRSNet designed in this study stands out for its ability to extract and integrate features from both shallow and deep layers of images. Furthermore, it incorporates an attention module to capture contextual information at different scales within the image. This enhances its generalization capabilities and robustness, allowing the model to adapt to various agricultural environments. As shown in Table 4, the CCRSNet model, utilizing VGG16 as its backbone network, delivers high-performance segmentation and proportion extraction of crop, crop residues, and soil in farmlands. The model achieved an mIoU of 87.84% on the TVD dataset and 93.70% on the IVD dataset, making it the most accurate model among those tested. In summary, the CCRSNet model exhibits significant advantages over traditional machine learning algorithms regarding accuracy, generalization capability, and overall performance, particularly for complex tasks such as digital image segmentation and the proportion extraction of crop, crop residues, and soil in agricultural settings.

Numerous studies have demonstrated that segmentation algorithms based on deep learning can provide high-precision segmentation results in various natural scene images, such as those of buildings and people [48,49]. The CCRSNet model mentioned in this paper achieved an mIoU of 87.84% and a PA of 93.70% on the TVD dataset. Consequently, our research further indicates that the deep learning-based CCRSNet can distinguish between similar features, such as crop residues and soil, in digital images of farmlands. Additionally, our findings show that the RMSE for the proportion extraction accuracy of crop, crop residues, and soil using CCRSNet ranged from 1.05% to 3.56%. This suggests that the designed deep learning model can offer remarkably high precision in providing information on crop residue coverage, potentially aiding agricultural experts in implementing conservation tillage practices.

4.2. Disadvantages of Deep Learning for Crop, Crop Residues, and Soil Proportion Extraction

Deep learning models' reliance on a large volume of manually annotated data during calibration notably impacts their performance in segmentation tasks. The model must be trained using extensive, high-quality annotated data to achieve satisfactory segmentation results. This typically involves considerable workforce and time investment in the dataset preparation phase to collect and annotate sufficient agricultural image data. This process is cumbersome and highly time-consuming, especially when dealing with targets with similar features, as the workload for annotation can substantially increase. Additionally, obtaining high-quality annotated data in practical applications poses various challenges. For instance, seasonal changes may cause inconsistencies in target features across different seasons, affecting the model's calibration effectiveness. Weather conditions can also impact data collection; for example, rainy or foggy weather might reduce image quality, affecting the data's accuracy and reliability [50]. The high cost of data collection equipment is another significant factor, particularly in agricultural production, where high-precision remote sensing devices or drones may require substantial financial investments, posing a formidable barrier for small farms or research institutions with limited resources.

The calibration of deep learning models depends on extensive labeled data and substantial computational resources. The calibration of deep neural networks typically requires high-performance computing hardware, such as GPUs. Moreover, the model's inference stage also demands certain computational capabilities, which could be a limiting factor for some low-cost devices or field application scenarios. In real-time applications, insufficient computational resources could lead to delays in model inference, potentially affecting the efficiency of final decision-making processes [51].

The "black box" nature of deep learning models makes their internal decision-making processes opaque, leading to poor interpretability [52]. In application fields like agriculture, users often desire to understand the basis of the model's decisions to make more accurate management decisions. The decision-making processes of deep learning models are usually difficult to intuitively comprehend, and this lack of interpretability could limit their practical application. If the model's decision-making process cannot be explained, users might question the model's reliability.

Deep learning models' universality and generalization ability heavily depend on the comprehensiveness of the calibration data. Validation under broader conditions is necessary to ensure excellent performance across different regions, environments, and crops. Furthermore, updating and optimizing the model is a continuous process. As new data and knowledge accumulate, the model needs ongoing adjustments and improvements to maintain its performance and accuracy. This process requires not only technical support, but also sustained research efforts. Continuous optimization and updates ensure the model remains effective in constantly changing environments.

5. Conclusions

In this study, we designed the CCRSNet network model to enhance the segmentation and proportional extraction performance of crop, crop residues, and soil based on high-resolution digital images. CCRSNet improves the performance by extracting and fusing both shallow and deep image features and integrating an attention module to capture multi-scale contextual information. The main conclusions of this study are as follows:

(i) Compared to traditional machine learning models (e.g., RF and SVM), deep learning models are more suitable for the segmentation and proportional extraction of farmland "crop–crop residues–soil." When using VGG16 as the backbone network for the CCRSNet segmentation model, CCRSNet achieved a segmentation accuracy of 96.23%, which is notably higher than traditional models like SVM (58.00%) and RF (82.47%).

(ii) The CCRSNet model, which is capable of fusing shallow and deep image features and incorporates an attention module, provides high-performance results for farmland "crop–crop residues–soil" image segmentation and proportional extraction. On the IVD independent validation dataset, the CCRSNet model with a lightweight backbone network achieved an mIoU of 92.73%, a PA of 96.23%, and proportional extraction RMSE values between 1.05% and 3.56%.

The generalization and robustness of machine learning models are dependent on the comprehensiveness of the calibration dataset. However, the method proposed in this study was only tested on the constructed TVD and IVD datasets. Future research should conduct experiments in additional regions and on a wider variety of crops to validate the accuracy and generalizability of the proposed method for "crop–crop residues–soil" image segmentation and proportional extraction.

Author Contributions: Methodology, G.G. and J.Y.; validation, G.G.; investigation, G.G., J.S., Y.Y., Y.F. and J.Y.; writing—original draft, G.G.; writing—review and editing, G.G., S.Z., J.S., K.H., J.T., Y.Y., Q.T., Y.F., H.F., Y.L. and J.Y.; funding acquisition, J.Y. All authors have read and agreed to the published version of the manuscript.

Funding: This research was supported by a grant from Key Laboratory of Emergency Satellite Engineering and Application, Ministry of Emergency Management, and the National Natural Science Foundation of China (42101362, 42101321).

Institutional Review Board Statement: Not applicable.

Data Availability Statement: The dataset is available on request from the authors.

Conflicts of Interest: The authors declare no conflicts of interest.

Appendix A

To further verify the effectiveness of (1) the attention module and (2) the deep and shallow feature structure module in the proposed CCRSNet, we conducted ablation experiments based on the TVD and IVD datasets. The ablation experiments (Exp. 2 and Exp. 3) and corresponding architectures are shown in Figure A1.

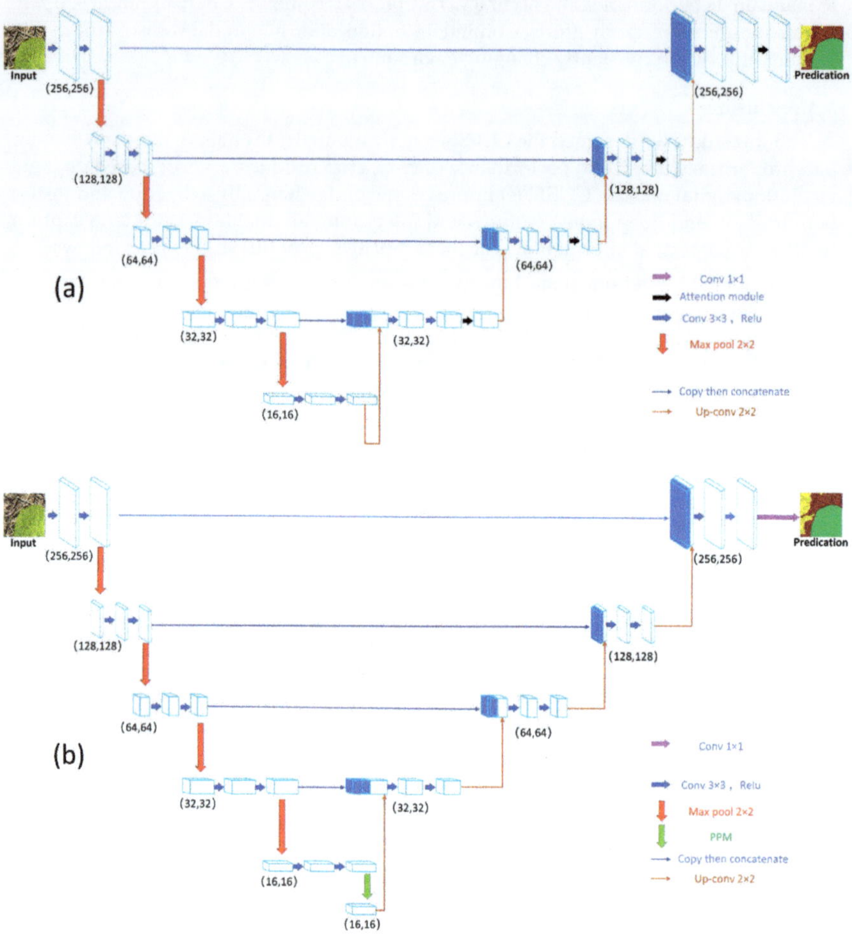

Figure A1. Ablation experiment architectures. (**a**) CCRSNet without the deep and shallow feature structure, (**b**) CCRSNet without the attention module.

References

1. Liu, J.; Qiu, T.; Peñuelas, J.; Sardans, J.; Tan, W.; Wei, X.; Cui, Y.; Cui, Q.; Wu, C.; Liu, L.; et al. Crop Residue Return Sustains Global Soil Ecological Stoichiometry Balance. *Glob. Chang. Biol.* **2023**, *29*, 2203–2226. [CrossRef] [PubMed]
2. Delandmeter, M.; Colinet, G.; Pierreux, J.; Bindelle, J.; Dumont, B. Combining Field Measurements and Process-based Modelling to Analyse Soil Tillage and Crop Residues Management Impacts on Crop Production and Carbon Balance in Temperate Areas. *Soil Use Manag.* **2024**, *40*, 13098. [CrossRef]
3. Yue, J.; Tian, Q.; Liu, Y.; Fu, Y.; Tian, J.; Zhou, C.; Feng, H.; Yang, G. Mapping Cropland Rice Residue Cover Using a Radiative Transfer Model and Deep Learning. *Comput. Electron. Agric.* **2023**, *215*, 108421. [CrossRef]
4. Su, Y.; Gabrielle, B.; Makowski, D. The Impact of Climate Change on the Productivity of Conservation Agriculture. *Nat. Clim. Chang.* **2021**, *11*, 628–633. [CrossRef]
5. Gao, P.; Song, Y.; Minhui, S.; Qian, P.; Su, Y. Extract Nanoporous Gold Ligaments from SEM Images by Combining Fully Convolutional Network and Sobel Operator Edge Detection Algorithm. *SSRN Electron. J.* **2021**, *365*, 536–538. [CrossRef]
6. Yue, J.; Tian, Q.; Tang, S.; Xu, K.; Zhou, C. A Dynamic Soil Endmember Spectrum Selection Approach for Soil and Crop Residue Linear Spectral Unmixing Analysis. *Int. J. Appl. Earth Obs. Geoinf.* **2019**, *78*, 306–317. [CrossRef]
7. Belgiu, M.; Drăguţ, L. Random Forest in Remote Sensing: A Review of Applications and Future Directions. *ISPRS J. Photogramm. Remote Sens.* **2016**, *114*, 24–31. [CrossRef]
8. Islam, M.U.; Guo, Z.; Jiang, F.; Peng, X. Does Straw Return Increase Crop Yield in the Wheat-Maize Cropping System in China? A Meta-Analysis. *F. Crop. Res.* **2022**, *279*, 108447. [CrossRef]

9. Yue, J.; Tian, Q.; Dong, X.; Xu, N. Using Broadband Crop Residue Angle Index to Estimate the Fractional Cover of Vegetation, Crop Residue, and Bare Soil in Cropland Systems. *Remote Sens. Environ.* **2020**, *237*, 111538. [CrossRef]
10. Dolata, P.; Wróblewski, P.; Mrzygłód, M.; Reiner, J. Instance Segmentation of Root Crops and Simulation-Based Learning to Estimate Their Physical Dimensions for on-Line Machine Vision Yield Monitoring. *Comput. Electron. Agric.* **2021**, *190*, 106451. [CrossRef]
11. Mishra, S.; Mishra, D.; Santra, G.H. Applications of Machine Learning Techniques in Agricultural Crop Production: A Review Paper. *Indian J. Sci. Technol.* **2016**, *9*, 1–14. [CrossRef]
12. Song, H.; Wang, J.; Bei, J.; Wang, M. Modified Snake Optimizer Based Multi-Level Thresholding for Color Image Segmentation of Agricultural Diseases. *Expert Syst. Appl.* **2024**, *255*, 124624. [CrossRef]
13. Shang, C.; Zhang, D.; Yang, Y. A Gradient-Based Method for Multilevel Thresholding. *Expert Syst. Appl.* **2021**, *175*, 114845. [CrossRef]
14. Gupta, L.; Sortrakul, T. A Gaussian-Mixture-Based Image Segmentation Algorithm. *Pattern Recognit.* **1998**, *31*, 315–325. [CrossRef]
15. Panjwani, D.K.; Healey, G. Markov Random Field Models for Unsupervised Segmentation of Textured Color Images. *IEEE Trans. Pattern Anal. Mach. Intell.* **1995**, *17*, 939–954. [CrossRef]
16. Chen, Y.; Cheng, N.; Cai, M.; Cao, C.; Yang, J.; Zhang, Z. A Spatially Constrained Asymmetric Gaussian Mixture Model for Image Segmentation. *Inf. Sci.* **2021**, *575*, 41–65. [CrossRef]
17. Trombini, M.; Solarna, D.; Moser, G.; Dellepiane, S. A Goal-Driven Unsupervised Image Segmentation Method Combining Graph-Based Processing and Markov Random Fields. *Pattern Recognit.* **2023**, *134*, 109082. [CrossRef]
18. Yang, Y.; Zhao, X.; Huang, M.; Wang, X.; Zhu, Q. Multispectral Image Based Germination Detection of Potato by Using Supervised Multiple Threshold Segmentation Model and Canny Edge Detector. *Comput. Electron. Agric.* **2021**, *182*, 106041. [CrossRef]
19. Hashim, F.A.; Hussien, A.G. Snake Optimizer: A Novel Meta-Heuristic Optimization Algorithm. *Knowledge-Based Syst.* **2022**, *242*, 108320. [CrossRef]
20. Ding, Z.; Li, C.; Huang, R.; Gatenby, C.J.; Metaxas, D.N.; Gore, J.C. A Level Set Method for Image Segmentation in the Presence of Intensity Inhomogeneities with Application to MRI. *IEEE Trans. Image Process.* **2011**, *20*, 2007–2016. [CrossRef]
21. Wang, Z.; Wan, L.; Xiong, N.; Zhu, J.; Ciampa, F. Variational Level Set and Fuzzy Clustering for Enhanced Thermal Image Segmentation and Damage Assessment. *NDT E Int.* **2021**, *118*, 102396. [CrossRef]
22. Yue, J.; Tian, Q. Estimating Fractional Cover of Crop, Crop Residue, and Soil in Cropland Using Broadband Remote Sensing Data and Machine Learning. *Int. J. Appl. Earth Obs. Geoinf.* **2020**, *89*, 102089. [CrossRef]
23. Guerrero, J.M.; Pajares, G.; Montalvo, M.; Romeo, J.; Guijarro, M. Support Vector Machines for Crop/Weeds Identification in Maize Fields. *Expert Syst. Appl.* **2012**, *39*, 11149–11155. [CrossRef]
24. Xu, J.; Zhou, S.; Xu, A.; Ye, J.; Zhao, A. Automatic Scoring of Postures in Grouped Pigs Using Depth Image and CNN-SVM. *Comput. Electron. Agric.* **2022**, *194*, 106746. [CrossRef]
25. Wang, H.; Ma, Z.; Ren, Y.; Du, S.; Lu, H.; Shang, Y.; Hu, S.; Zhang, G.; Meng, Z.; Wen, C.; et al. Interactive Image Segmentation Based Field Boundary Perception Method and Software for Autonomous Agricultural Machinery Path Planning. *Comput. Electron. Agric.* **2024**, *217*, 108568. [CrossRef]
26. Li, Y.; Zhao, H.; Qi, X.; Wang, L.; Li, Z.; Sun, J.; Jia, J. Fully Convolutional Networks for Panoptic Segmentation. In Proceedings of the 2021 IEEE/CVF Conference on Computer Vision and Pattern Recognition (CVPR), Nashville, TN, USA, 20–25 June 2024; 2021; pp. 214–223.
27. Shaheed, K.; Mao, A.; Qureshi, I.; Kumar, M.; Hussain, S.; Ullah, I.; Zhang, X. DS-CNN: A Pre-Trained Xception Model Based on Depth-Wise Separable Convolutional Neural Network for Finger Vein Recognition. *Expert Syst. Appl.* **2022**, *191*, 116288. [CrossRef]
28. Ronneberger, O.; Fischer, P.B.T. U-Net: Convolutional Networks for Biomedical Image Segmentation. In Proceedings of the Medical Image Computing and Computer-Assisted Intervention–MICCAI, Munich, Germany, 5–9 October 2015; pp. 234–241.
29. Chen, L.; Papandreou, G.; Kokkinos, I.; Murphy, K.; Yuille, A.L. DeepLab: Semantic Image Segmentation with Deep Convolutional Nets, Atrous Convolution, and Fully Connected CRFs. *IEEE Trans. Pattern Anal. Mach. Intell.* **2018**, *40*, 834–848. [CrossRef]
30. Beeche, C.; Singh, J.P.; Leader, J.K.; Gezer, N.S.; Oruwari, A.P.; Dansingani, K.K.; Chhablani, J.; Pu, J. Super U-Net: A Modularized Generalizable Architecture. *Pattern Recognit.* **2022**, *128*, 108669. [CrossRef]
31. Qi, J.; Liu, X.; Liu, K.; Xu, F.; Guo, H.; Tian, X.; Li, M.; Bao, Z.; Li, Y. An Improved YOLOv5 Model Based on Visual Attention Mechanism: Application to Recognition of Tomato Virus Disease. *Comput. Electron. Agric.* **2022**, *194*, 106780. [CrossRef]
32. Chen, H.; He, Y.; Zhang, L.; Yao, S.; Yang, W.; Fang, Y.; Liu, Y.; Gao, B. A Landslide Extraction Method of Channel Attention Mechanism U-Net Network Based on Sentinel-2A Remote Sensing Images. *Int. J. Digit. Earth* **2023**, *16*, 552–577. [CrossRef]
33. Yue, J.; Tian, Q.; Dong, X.; Xu, K.; Zhou, C. Using Hyperspectral Crop Residue Angle Index to Estimate Maize and Winter-Wheat Residue Cover: A Laboratory Study. *Remote Sens.* **2019**, *11*, 807. [CrossRef]
34. Ding, Y.; Zhang, H.; Wang, Z.; Xie, Q.; Wang, Y.; Liu, L.; Hall, C.C. A Comparison of Estimating Crop Residue Cover from Sentinel-2 Data Using Empirical Regressions and Machine Learning Methods. *Remote Sens.* **2020**, *12*, 1470. [CrossRef]
35. Yue, J.; Fu, Y.; Guo, W.; Feng, H.; Qiao, H. Estimating Fractional Coverage of Crop, Crop Residue, and Bare Soil Using Shortwave Infrared Angle Index and Sentinel-2 MSI. *Int. J. Remote Sens.* **2022**, *43*, 1253–1273. [CrossRef]
36. Zhou, D.; Li, M.; Li, Y.; Qi, J.; Liu, K.; Cong, X.; Tian, X. Detection of Ground Straw Coverage under Conservation Tillage Based on Deep Learning. *Comput. Electron. Agric.* **2020**, *172*, 105369. [CrossRef]

37. Torralba, A.; Russell, B.C.; Yuen, J. LabelMe: Online Image Annotation and Applications. *Proc. IEEE* **2010**, *98*, 1467–1484. [CrossRef]
38. Zhang, S.; Zhang, C. Modified U-Net for Plant Diseased Leaf Image Segmentation. *Comput. Electron. Agric.* **2023**, *204*, 107511. [CrossRef]
39. Chen, J.; Mei, J.; Li, X.; Lu, Y.; Yu, Q.; Wei, Q.; Luo, X.; Xie, Y.; Adeli, E.; Wang, Y.; et al. TransUNet: Rethinking the U-Net Architecture Design for Medical Image Segmentation through the Lens of Transformers. *Med. Image Anal.* **2024**, *97*, 103280. [CrossRef]
40. Qiang, J.; Liu, W.; Li, X.; Guan, P.; Du, Y.; Liu, B.; Xiao, G. Detection of Citrus Pests in Double Backbone Network Based on Single Shot Multibox Detector. *Comput. Electron. Agric.* **2023**, *212*, 108158. [CrossRef]
41. Simonyan, K.; Zisserman, A. Very Deep Convolutional Networks for Large-Scale Image Recognition. *3rd Int. Conf. Learn. Represent. ICLR 2015—Conf. Track Proc.* **2014**, 1–14. [CrossRef]
42. Hattiya, T.; Dittakan, K.; Musikasuwan, S. Diabetic Retinopathy Detection Using Convolutional Neural Network: A Comparative Study on Different Architectures. *Eng. Access* **2021**, *7*, 50–60. [CrossRef]
43. Lian, X.; Pang, Y.; Han, J.; Pan, J. Cascaded Hierarchical Atrous Spatial Pyramid Pooling Module for Semantic Segmentation. *Pattern Recognit.* **2021**, *110*, 107622. [CrossRef]
44. Du, L.; Lu, Z.; Li, D. Broodstock Breeding Behaviour Recognition Based on Resnet50-LSTM with CBAM Attention Mechanism. *Comput. Electron. Agric.* **2022**, *202*, 107404. [CrossRef]
45. Bai, J.; Li, Y.; Li, J.; Yang, X.; Jiang, Y.; Xia, S.-T. Multinomial Random Forest. *Pattern Recognit.* **2022**, *122*, 108331. [CrossRef]
46. Dong, S. Multi Class SVM Algorithm with Active Learning for Network Traffic Classification. *Expert Syst. Appl.* **2021**, *176*, 114885. [CrossRef]
47. Wang, P.; Fan, E.; Wang, P. Comparative Analysis of Image Classification Algorithms Based on Traditional Machine Learning and Deep Learning. *Pattern Recognit. Lett.* **2021**, *141*, 61–67. [CrossRef]
48. Wang, C.; Antos, S.E.; Triveno, L.M. Automatic Detection of Unreinforced Masonry Buildings from Street View Images Using Deep Learning-Based Image Segmentation. *Autom. Constr.* **2021**, *132*, 103968. [CrossRef]
49. Zhao, H.; Zheng, J.; Wang, Y.; Yuan, X.; Li, Y. Portrait Style Transfer Using Deep Convolutional Neural Networks and Facial Segmentation. *Comput. Electr. Eng.* **2020**, *85*, 106655. [CrossRef]
50. Barbedo, J.G.A. Impact of Dataset Size and Variety on the Effectiveness of Deep Learning and Transfer Learning for Plant Disease Classification. *Comput. Electron. Agric.* **2018**, *153*, 46–53. [CrossRef]
51. Ghasemi, F.; Mehridehnavi, A.; Pérez-Garrido, A.; Pérez-Sánchez, H. Neural Network and Deep-Learning Algorithms Used in QSAR Studies: Merits and Drawbacks. *Drug Discov. Today* **2018**, *23*, 1784–1790. [CrossRef]
52. Liang, Y.; Li, S.; Yan, C.; Li, M.; Jiang, C. Explaining the Black-Box Model: A Survey of Local Interpretation Methods for Deep Neural Networks. *Neurocomputing* **2021**, *419*, 168–182. [CrossRef]

agriculture

MDPI

Article

Influence of Vegetation Phenology on the Temporal Effect of Crop Fractional Vegetation Cover Derived from Moderate-Resolution Imaging Spectroradiometer Nadir Bidirectional Reflectance Distribution Function–Adjusted Reflectance

Yinghao Lin [1,2], Tingshun Fan [1], Dong Wang [3], Kun Cai [1], Yang Liu [1], Yuye Wang [1,*], Tao Yu [3,*] and Nianxu Xu [4]

1 Henan Key Laboratory of Big Data Analysis and Processing, School of Computer and Information Engineering, Henan University, Kaifeng 475001, China; linyh@henu.edu.cn (Y.L.); fantingshun@163.com (T.F.); ckhenu@vip.henu.edu.cn (K.C.); sea@vip.henu.edu.cn (Y.L.)

2 Shenzhen Research Institute of Henan University, Shenzhen 518000, China

3 Aerospace Information Research Institute, Chinese Academy of Sciences, Beijing 100094, China; wangdong201232@aircas.ac.cn

4 Department of Public Security Management, Jiangsu Police Institute, Nanjing 210031, China; xunianxu@jspi.cn

* Correspondence: wangyuye@henu.edu.cn (Y.W.); yutao@irsa.ac.cn (T.Y.)

Abstract: Moderate-Resolution Imaging Spectroradiometer (MODIS) Nadir Bidirectional Reflectance Distribution Function (BRDF)-Adjusted Reflectance (NBAR) products are being increasingly used for the quantitative remote sensing of vegetation. However, the assumption underlying the MODIS NBAR product's inversion model—that surface anisotropy remains unchanged over the 16-day retrieval period—may be unreliable, especially since the canopy structure of vegetation undergoes stark changes at the start of season (SOS) and the end of season (EOS). Therefore, to investigate the MODIS NBAR product's temporal effect on the quantitative remote sensing of crops at different stages of the growing seasons, this study selected typical phenological parameters, namely SOS, EOS, and the intervening stable growth of season (SGOS). The PROBA-V bioGEOphysical product Version 3 (GEOV3) Fractional Vegetation Cover (FVC) served as verification data, and the Pearson correlation coefficient (PCC) was used to compare and analyze the retrieval accuracy of FVC derived from the MODIS NBAR product and MODIS Surface Reflectance product. The Anisotropic Flat Index (AFX) was further employed to explore the influence of vegetation type and mixed pixel distribution characteristics on the BRDF shape under different stages of the growing seasons and different FVC; that was then combined with an NDVI spatial distribution map to assess the feasibility of using the reflectance of other characteristic directions besides NBAR for FVC correction. The results revealed the following: (1) Generally, at the SOSs and EOSs, the differences in PCCs before vs. after the NBAR correction mainly ranged from 0 to 0.1. This implies that the accuracy of FVC derived from MODIS NBAR is lower than that derived from MODIS Surface Reflectance. Conversely, during the SGOSs, the differences in PCCs before vs. after the NBAR correction ranged between −0.2 and 0, suggesting the accuracy of FVC derived from MODIS NBAR surpasses that derived from MODIS Surface Reflectance. (2) As vegetation phenology shifts, the ensuing differences in NDVI patterning and AFX can offer auxiliary information for enhanced vegetation classification and interpretation of mixed pixel distribution characteristics, which, when combined with NDVI at characteristic directional reflectance, could enable the accurate retrieval of FVC. Our results provide data support for the BRDF correction timescale effect of various stages of the growing seasons, highlighting the potential importance of considering how they differentially influence the temporal effect of NBAR corrections prior to monitoring vegetation when using the MODIS NBAR product.

Keywords: fractional vegetation cover; MODIS NBAR; temporal effect; vegetation phenology; BRDF; dimidiate pixel model

1. Introduction

With rapid advances in multi-angle observation satellite-based sensors, such as Polarization and Directionality of the Earth's Reflectances, Multi-angle Imaging SpectroRadiometer, and Moderate-Resolution Imaging Spectroradiometer (MODIS), whose detection bands extend beyond the visible and near-infrared (NIR) to the thermal infrared, researchers can now obtain richer spectral and structural information, which greatly improves the capability of multi-angle optical remote sensing in modeling and inversion [1]. The solar radiation reflected by most ground objects is anisotropic, with directionality varying according to solar incidence and the geometric conditions of satellite observations. The Bidirectional Reflectance Distribution Function (BRDF) is a key model for multi-angle optical remote sensing studies that is often used to characterize such changes. Studying the surface BRDF is significant for robust progress in the quantitative remote sensing of vegetation, which can describe the three-dimensional structural characteristics of ground objects and retrieve various surface parameters based on it, such as the Leaf Area Index and Fractional Vegetation Cover (FVC) [2]. Furthermore, bidirectional reflectance characteristics of the ground surface may be used to obtain the reflectance normalized to different angles, which can eliminate the reflectance discrepancies caused by distinct incidence or observation angles, paving the way for subsequent quantitative remote sensing applications [3]. Due to its advantages of a broad spectral range coupled with high temporal and spatial resolution, MODIS is widely used in surface cover detection, vegetation growth monitoring, and vegetation phenology change research [4,5]. The MODIS Nadir BRDF-Adjusted Reflectance (NBAR) product effectively adjusts the impact introduced by the BRDF effect and is commonly used for detecting shifts in vegetation phenology [6–8].

The MODIS NBAR product has a 16-day retrieval period, and its inversion model assumes that surface anisotropy remains unchanged during this period. Yet this assumption may be unreliable for areas that undergo rapid surface changes, such as floods or fires [9]. Moreover, various vegetation types such as crops, forests, shrubs, and grasses exhibit distinctive phenological characteristics, and the canopy structure of each vegetation type will change significantly at the start of season (SOS) and again at the end of season (EOS), which may also undermine that assumption's reliability. Accordingly, Proud et al. proposed a modified version of the MODIS BRDF algorithm for the Spinning Enhanced Visible and InfraRed Imager data aboard the geostationary Meteosat Second Generation (MSG) satellites, which markedly shortened the retrieval period and enabled the usage of MSG BRDF data to examine short-term and rapidly evolving phenomena [9]. To investigate the appropriate retrieval period of the EVI2 time series after the BRDF correction of the Advanced Baseline Imager (ABI) data onboard the Geostationary Operational Environmental Satellite-R series satellites, Shen et al. used NBAR data of the Visible Infrared Imaging Radiometer Suite (VIIRS) for evaluation; they found that the ABI data retrieval period was shortened to 3 days, which is crucial for near-real-time monitoring of crop phenology vis-à-vis the 16-day retrieval period of the polar-orbiting satellite [10]. Hasegawa et al. constructed a BRDF observation system for forests to determine the relationship between vegetation phenology and BRDF, reporting a greater BRDF influence in summer [11]. However, that study did not explore whether the influence of the BRDF correction of quantitative remote sensing retrieval of vegetation at different stages of the growing seasons. Overall, the body of research addressing the relationship between vegetation phenology and BRDF has mostly focused on vegetation types such as forests, woodlands, and pastures [12–14], leaving crops vastly understudied.

As a pivotal indicator of surface vegetation conditions, FVC and its alteration—one of the main manifestations of land cover change—indirectly conveys the degree of human activities' impact on natural ecology [15]. As the backbone of food production, cropland not only ensures the food security of a country but also is a critical ecosystem component, and shifts in FVC could substantially affect agricultural production and the stability of surface ecosystems. Common methods for retrieving fractional vegetation coverage from remote sensing images include the dimidiate pixel model and machine learning algorithms [16–18]. Due to the ±55° across-track scanning angle of MODIS, its images exhibit a more pronounced BRDF effect. Hence, to better apply MODIS NBAR product to dynamically monitor the growth status of crops, it is imperative to better understand in depth the temporal effect of the FVC derived from MODIS NBAR at different stages of the crops' growing seasons.

The overarching goal of this study was to investigate the temporal effect of MODIS NBAR-derived FVC across distinct stages of the crops' growing seasons. Specifically, the NDVI and EVI fitting curves of the MOD13Q1 product were first utilized to acquire the calendar date of crop phenological parameters, namely SOS and EOS as well as their intervening stable growth of season (SGOS). Next, we used the MODIS Surface Reflectance product (MOD09GA) and MODIS NBAR product (MCD43A4) to derive the FVC at the calendar date of those phenological parameters. Finally, using the PROBA-V bioGEOphysical product Version 3 (GEOV3) FVC as the verification data, the FVC's retrieval accuracy was compared and analyzed to explore the temporal effect of the MODIS NBAR correction at each stage of the crops' growing seasons.

2. Materials and Methods

2.1. Study Area

The study area is located in the Wancheng District, Nanyang City, Henan Province (China), encompassing 112°28′9″–112°49′52″ E and 32°37′51″–33°9′45″ N, in the middle of the Nanyang Basin. Lying in the transition between the subtropics and warm temperate zone, this region has a humid climate, with an average annual temperature of 14.9 °C and an average annual precipitation of 805.8 mm, which is conducive to the growth of various plants. The crop maturity system follows an annual double-cropping pattern, with wheat, corn, and peanuts predominately cultivated. The land cover types, sampling points distribution, and true-color images of the three mixed pixels in the study area are shown in Figure 1. The crop phenology extraction sampling points were used to subsequently acquire the NDVI/EVI average fitting curve to extract phenological parameters, with the BRDF sampling points (savanna pixel, grass pixel, crop pixel, and mixed pixels) then used to analyze the BRDF patterns of various land cover types.

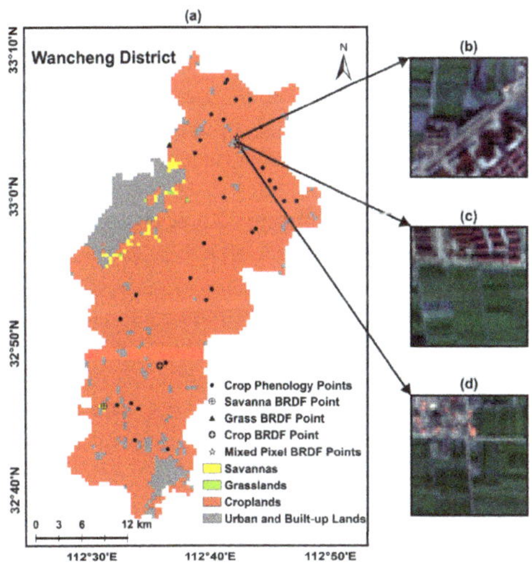

Figure 1. Spatial extent of the Wancheng District study area (in Henan Province, China). (**a**) Map of land cover types showing the location of sampling points across the study area. This map came from MCD12Q1 (v061). (**b**–**d**) True-color images of the three mixed pixels, obtained from Sentinel-2. The distribution characteristics are as follows: crops above with buildings below (**b**); crops below with buildings above (**c**); and buildings in the upper-left corner, crops in the remainder (**d**).

Temperature and precipitation are the primary factors driving phenological shifts, but their influence on vegetation phenology varies across regions [19]. Here, the study area's precipitation and temperature data were collected from the ERA5-Land monthly averaged product for 2017–2021 (Figure 2). Overall, the temperature from 2017 through 2021 showed clear seasonal fluctuations, whose pattern was generally similar during the period; precipitation also displayed seasonal fluctuations, with relatively low precipitation in the summer of 2019, which may have led to the advancement of stages of the crops' growing seasons [20].

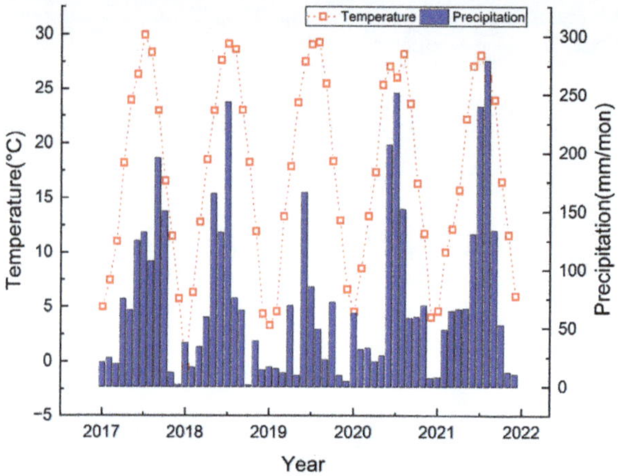

Figure 2. Monthly average temperature and monthly total precipitation in the study area, from 2017 to 2021.

2.2. Data

The remote sensing datasets used in this study are listed in Table 1. MOD13Q1 [21] is a MODIS vegetation indices product. Since that data have been processed already (with respect to water bodies, cloud cover, and heavy aerosols), their quality is guaranteed, spurring widespread use in studies of vegetation cover change [22,23]. We selected the NDVI and EVI time series from which to extract the crop phenological parameters of the study area. MOD09GA [24] is a MODIS Surface Reflectance product corrected for atmospheric conditions (such as gas, aerosol, and Rayleigh scattering), used here to retrieve the FVC without BRDF correction. MCD43A4 [25] is a MODIS NBAR product, whose view zenith angle is normalized to the nadir, while its solar zenith angle is adjusted to the local solar noon of the day to eliminate the impact of varying view zenith angles, it used in this study to retrieve the NBAR-corrected FVC.

The GEOV3 FVC product [26] is an FVC product generated by filtering, gap filling, and smoothing data based on a neural network model [27]. Compared with GEOV1 and GEOV2, the GEOV3 product has superior spatial resolution via algorithmic improvements. Several studies have evaluated its performance, showing that it performs well and has reliable accuracy [27–29]; hence, it was used in this study to evaluate MODIS-derived FVC. For comparative purposes, ArcMap was used to reproject and resample the GEOV3 FVC data to match the coordinate system and spatial resolution of MODIS data.

MCD12Q1 [30] is a MODIS land cover type product, which provides land cover classification information on a global scale. It is now one of the most widely used land cover products, containing a total of 13 scientific datasets, of which the IGBP classification scheme was used here. MCD43A1 [31] is a MODIS BRDF Model Parameters product, which supplies weighting parameters associated with the semi-empirical RTLSR (Ross Thick-LiSparse Reciprocal) BRDF model.

Table 1. Remote sensing datasets used in this study.

Datasets	Temporal Resolution	Spatial Resolution	Purpose
MODIS vegetation indices product (MOD13Q1 v061)	16 days	250 m	To extract crop phenological parameters
MODIS Surface Reflectance product (MOD09GA v061)	daily	500 m	To provide surface reflectance and solar zenith angle
MODIS NBAR product (MCD43A4 v061)	daily	500 m	To provide NBAR reflectance
MODIS Land Cover product (MCD12Q1 v061)	yearly	500 m	To obtain cropland pixels
MODIS BRDF Model Parameters product (MCD43A1 v061)	daily	500 m	To provide RTLSR model kernel parameters
GEOV3 FVC product	10 days	300 m	To serve as validation data

2.3. Methodology

This study sought to explore the temporal effect of MODIS NBAR correction at different stages of the growing seasons, which entailed three major processes: crop phenological parameters extraction, FVC retrieval, and accuracy evaluation. Their data processing flow is presented in Figure 3. Firstly, TIMESAT was used to fit the MOD13Q1-NDVI and MOD13Q1-EVI time series, resulting in the average fitting curve used to extract crop phenological parameters. Next, MOD09GA and MCD43A4 data collected under clear weather conditions were selected according to the previously acquired crop phenological parameters, then NDVI was calculated through band math, and the respective FVC estimated by using the dimidiate pixel model. Finally, the GEOV3 FVC product was used as verification data to compare and analyze the retrieval accuracy of the FVC derived from MOD09GA and MCD43A4.

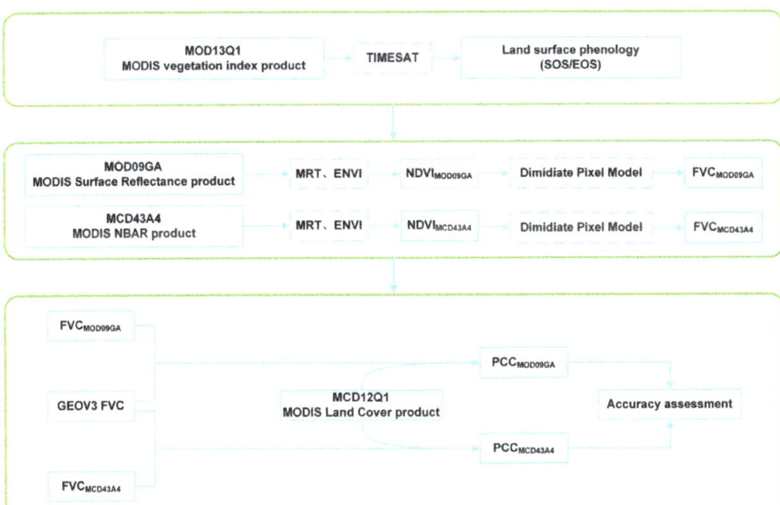

Figure 3. Data processing flow chart. The green rectangles from top to the bottom represent three steps: crop phenological parameters extraction with TIMESAT; Fractional Vegetation Cover (FVC)

derived from MOD09GA and MCD43A4; and accuracy evaluation, respectively. Blue solid rectangles refer to a used product or derived results, while blue dashed rectangles refer to the software or model used in this study. $NDVI_{MOD09GA}$: NDVI derived from MOD09GA, $NDVI_{MCD43A4}$: NDVI derived from MCD43A4, $FVC_{MOD09GA}$: FVC derived from MOD09GA, $FVC_{MCD43A4}$: FVC derived from MCD43A4. $PCC_{MOD09GA}$: Pearson correlation coefficient (PCC) calculated for $FVC_{MOD09GA}$ and GEOV3 FVC, $PCC_{MCD43A4}$: PCC calculated for $FVC_{MCD43A4}$ and GEOV3 FVC.

2.3.1. Crop Phenological Parameters' Extraction

TIMESAT (v3.3) is recognized for being a robust, efficient software tool for phenology studies. With its graphical user interface (GUI), TIMESAT is user-friendly in which key parameters can be easily set [32]. The SOS and EOS refer to the point at which the curve intersects a proportion of the seasonal amplitude as measured from the left minimum and right minimum, respectively. However, because the results of the first and last year's phenological extraction were insufficiently accurate when using TIMESAT, the MOD13Q1 data from 2017 to 2022 were instead selected to extract crop phenological parameters from 2018 to 2021. MODIS-NDVI and MODIS-EVI are widely employed in regional or global phenology studies given their notable advantages, e.g., a high temporal and spatial resolution [12,33]. In the land cover type map, a total of 30 sampling points were selected across the study area's cropland (Figure 1a) with reference to the Sentinel-2 true-color image, after which the average fitting curve of NDVI and EVI were obtained to extract the crop phenological parameters. The average value was taken as the final result to bolster the accuracy of phenological extraction. To reconstruct time series data, S-G (Savitzky–Golay) filtering is commonly used [34,35]. Following the suggestions of Jonsson et al. [36], who originally proposed the dynamic threshold, and by referring to other scholars' experiences [37,38], we decided on setting the dynamic threshold to a value of 0.2, whose calculation formula is defined as follows:

$$VI_{lim} = (VI_{max} – VI_{min})\ S \tag{1}$$

where VI_{lim} is the extraction threshold of SOS (EOS) NDVI/EVI; VI_{max} is the maximum value of NDVI/EVI in the vegetation growth cycle; VI_{min} is the minimum value of NDVI/EVI in the rising or falling stage of that growth cycle; and S is the percentage coefficient, set to 20% here.

Lacking ground-based phenological observations, this study relied on the time series curve filtering method and dynamic threshold—given their good phenological extraction accuracy as demonstrated in previous studies [34,35,37,38]—and compared the phenological extraction results of two different vegetation indices: NDVI and EVI. Finally, their average value of crop phenological parameters was selected as the result. Based on the ground field survey of Ma et al. and known field details of the study area, the SOS of overwintering crops usually spans the end of October to the end of November [39]. Our other phenological results were consistent with those found relevant in the study area in previous years [37,38]. Further, our other phenological results for 2018 and 2019 showed high consistency with the phenological dataset from 2000 to 2019, released by Luo et al. [40].

2.3.2. Fractional Vegetation Cover (FVC) Retrieval

The phenological parameters derived from the two vegetation indices consisted of SOS, EOS, and SGOS. According to these, the MOD09GA and MCD43A4 data with clear weather near them were identified via the Google Earth Engine to retrieve the FVC. Next, MODIS Reprojection Tools and The Environment for Visualizing Images software (v5.3) were used to preprocess the NIR and RED bands data for the NDVI calculation. Then, based on this NDVI, the FVC was estimated by the dimidiate pixel model, which is the most widely used and simple linear mixture decomposition model. It assumes that each pixel's information consists of vegetation as well as no vegetation, which greatly weakens the influence of soil background, atmosphere, and vegetation type, making it an effective method for retrieving FVC [17,41]. The FVC calculation formula is as follows:

$$FVC = (NDVI - NDVI_{soil}) / (NDVI_{veg} - NDVI_{soil}) \quad (2)$$

where $NDVI_{soil}$ denotes the NDVI value of bare soil or no vegetation coverage area, and $NDVI_{veg}$ denotes the NDVI value of a pure vegetation coverage pixel. In this study, we counted the NDVI and used those NDVI values with cumulative probabilities of 5% and 95% to represent $NDVI_{soil}$ and $NDVI_{veg}$, respectively.

2.3.3. Data Analysis

This section describes the methods employed to assess the FVC's accuracy and the BRDF's shape. The linear correlation between the MODIS-derived FVC and GEOV3 FVC was quantified using the Pearson correlation coefficient (PCC) to explore the temporal effect of the MODIS NBAR correction. The Anisotropic Flat Index (AFX) was used to assess the shape change in BRDF and thereby determine the relationship between geometric–optical scattering and volumetric scattering characteristics.

(1) FVC Accuracy Assessment: GEOV3 FVC was used to evaluate MODIS-derived FVC. Although the two datasets are not exactly the same, differing in terms of their (i) spatial resolution and spectral responses, as well as (ii) FVC retrieval algorithms, the GEOV3 FVC can still provide a sound reference for the MODIS-derived FVC. The all-cropland pixels in the study area were obtained using MCD12Q1, and the FVC derived from MOD09GA and MCD43A4 in Section 2.3.2 was statistically analyzed vis-à-vis GEOV3 FVC by the PCC, to explore the temporal effect of MODIS NBAR correction for crops at the different stages of the growing seasons. Specifically, the PCC was used to determine the magnitude of consistency between the MODIS-derived FVC and GEOV3 FVC. The PCC is calculated this way:

$$PCC = \frac{\sum_{i=1}^{n}\left(FVC_{MODIS}^{i} - \overline{FVC_{MODIS}}\right)\left(FVC_{GEOV3}^{i} - \overline{FVC_{GEOV3}}\right)}{\sqrt{\sum_{i=1}^{n}\left(FVC_{MODIS}^{i} - \overline{FVC_{MODIS}}\right)^{2}}\sqrt{\sum_{i=1}^{n}\left(FVC_{GEOV3}^{i} - \overline{FVC_{GEOV3}}\right)^{2}}} \quad (3)$$

where FVC_{MODIS}^{i} is the FVC derived from MOD09GA or MCD43A4; the FVC_{GEOV3}^{i} is the FVC provided by GEOV3 FVC; and n is the number of all cropland pixels in the study area.

(2) BRDF shape assessment: Unlike a spectral vegetation index, such as NDVI, the MODIS BRDF shape indicator AFX contains pertinent information about vegetation structure. AFX conveys the BRDF shape based on its value around unity. An AFX < 1 indicates that geometric–optical scattering is dominant, implying a dome-shaped BRDF curve with a prominent reflectance peak (hotspot) in the retro-solar direction. An AFX > 1 indicates that volumetric scattering is dominant, implying a bowl-shaped BRDF curve where reflectance near the nadir is lower than for larger scattering angles, with the minimum usually displaced towards the forward scattering direction in the principal plane. An AFX ≈ 1 indicates a relatively flat BRDF curve. Importantly, AFX varies by band and phenological date, and is related to land cover type along with land surface structure. The general AFX formula is as follows [42]:

$$AFX = 1 + \frac{f_{vol}(\lambda)}{f_{iso}(\lambda)} \times 0.189184 - \frac{f_{geo}(\lambda)}{f_{iso}(\lambda)} \times 1.377622 \quad (4)$$

where $f_{iso}(\lambda)$, $f_{geo}(\lambda)$, and $f_{vol}(\lambda)$ are constant coefficients that, respectively, represent the weights of isotropic scattering, geometric-optical scattering, and volumetric scattering. The values 0.189184 and 1.377622 are the bi-hemispherical integral of the Ross Thick kernel and the reciprocal LiSparse kernel, respectively.

3. Results

3.1. Extraction of Phenological Parameters via NDVI and EVI

The fitted curves of the preprocessed NDVI and EVI time series generated by TIMESAT, along with phenological parameters, are shown in Figure 4. Evidently, the NDVI and EVI time series curves follow the same general fluctuation pattern, depicting similar seasonal variation in crop phenology; however, the EVI profile is always positioned below the NDVI profile. Meanwhile, as Figure 4 shows, their extracted SOS points lie close to each other, and likewise for EOS. After a comparative consideration, the midpoint of the NDVI and EVI phenological timing was taken and this designated as the crop phenological parameters results for 2018–2021. The annual phenological parameters of the NDVI time series curves in Figure 4 included two SOSs and EOSs, as well as four SGOSs. However, factors such as cloud cover prevented the identification of the phenological parameter SGOS during the rise in NDVI in the second growing season of 2020.

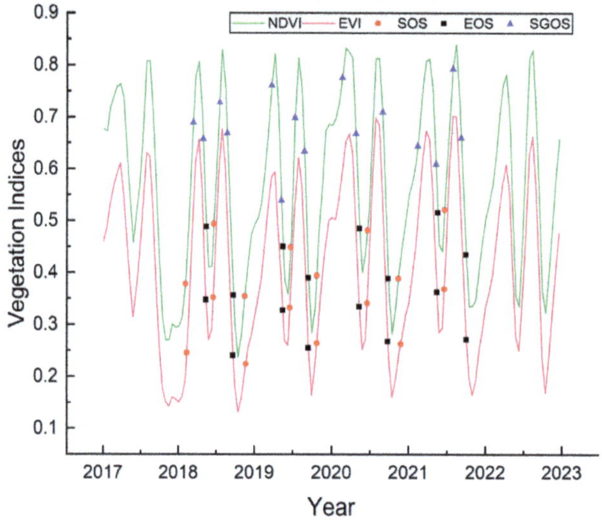

Figure 4. NDVI and EVI time series fitted curves and phenological parameters of crops. SOS: start of season; EOS: end of season; SGOS: stable growth of season.

The extraction results of SOS and EOS in 2018–2021 are presented in Table 2. The study area follows an annual double-cropping pattern, resulting in two growing seasons per year. Evidently, the first SOS in 2018 differed substantially from that in the other three years. Our investigation revealed that, from 28 August to 19 October 2017, Henan Province experienced its most serious sustained rainy weather in the last decade. This situation is evinced in Figure 2, where precipitation rose abnormally during this period, which severely impacted the harvesting of the autumn crop and strongly delayed the sowing of the overwintering crop. Hence, we speculated that could be why the first SOS in 2018 came so late.

Table 2 also indicates that the second EOS in 2019, along with both the SOS and EOS in the first growing season of 2020, happened earlier than in other years. Based on our investigation, this was mainly because the average temperature in the study area was above normal with precipitation less than normal since the sowing of the autumn crop in June 2019. This reasoning is also supported by the trends in Figure 2, which led to an earlier-than-normal harvest of the summer crop followed by the subsequent winter wheat being sown sooner than normal.

Table 2. The SOS (start of season) and EOS (end of season) of crop phenological parameters, from 2018 to 2021.

Year	SOS_1 [1]	EOS_1 [1]	SOS_2 [1]	EOS_2 [1]
2018	5 February 2018	14 May 2018	17 June 2018	22 September 2018
2019	18 November 2018	17 May 2019	20 June2019	15 September 2019
2020	25 October 2019	8 May 2020	19 June2020	24 September 2020
2021	18 November 2020	16 May 2021	18 June2021	30 September 2021

[1] SOS_1 and EOS_1 refer to crop phenological parameters in the first growing season; SOS_2 and EOS_2 refer to crop phenological parameters in the second growing season.

3.2. *Overview of Fractional Vegetation Cover Estimation*

After determining the calendar date of crop phenological parameters from the time series fitted curves shown in Figure 2, and given that cloud cover will reduce the quality and availability of remote sensing images, we selected MODIS data with clear-sky weather near the calendar date of phenological parameters. This calendar date information on typical phenological points in 2021 is provided, as an example, in Table 3 (these corresponding to those points in Figure 4).

Table 3. Typical crop phenological parameters' temporal information (2021, example).

MODIS Data: Calendar Date of Phenology	GEOV3 Data: Calendar Date of FVC
15 November 2020 (SOS)	20 November 2020
10 February 2021 (SGOS)	10 February 2021
9 May 2021 (SGOS)	10 May 2021
22 May 2021 (EOS)	20 May 2021
22 June 2021 (SOS)	20 June 2021
30 July 2021 (SGOS)	31 July 2021
8 September 2021 (SGOS)	10 September 2021
30 September 2021 (EOS)	30 September 2021

From Table 3, three distinct phenological parameters—15 November 2020 (SOS), 10 February 2021 (SGOS), and 30 September 2021 (EOS)—were selected as examples. The FVC was derived from MOD09GA and MCD43A4, and the visualized differences in FVC values generated accordingly (Figure 5). These results revealed that the spatial distribution of FVC derived from MOD09GA and MCD43A4 is generally similar (Figure 5a,b,d,e,g,h, respectively). Some blank (white) data did appear in the middle of the left side in Figure 5b,e,h, and this is due to a river in the area, which led to missing data in the MCD43A4 product. According to Figure 5c,f,i, in general, the difference between MOD09GA and MCD43A4 is greater than zero. The difference in FVC between Figure 5c,i (SOS and EOS, respectively) is notably higher than that in Figure 5f (SGOS).

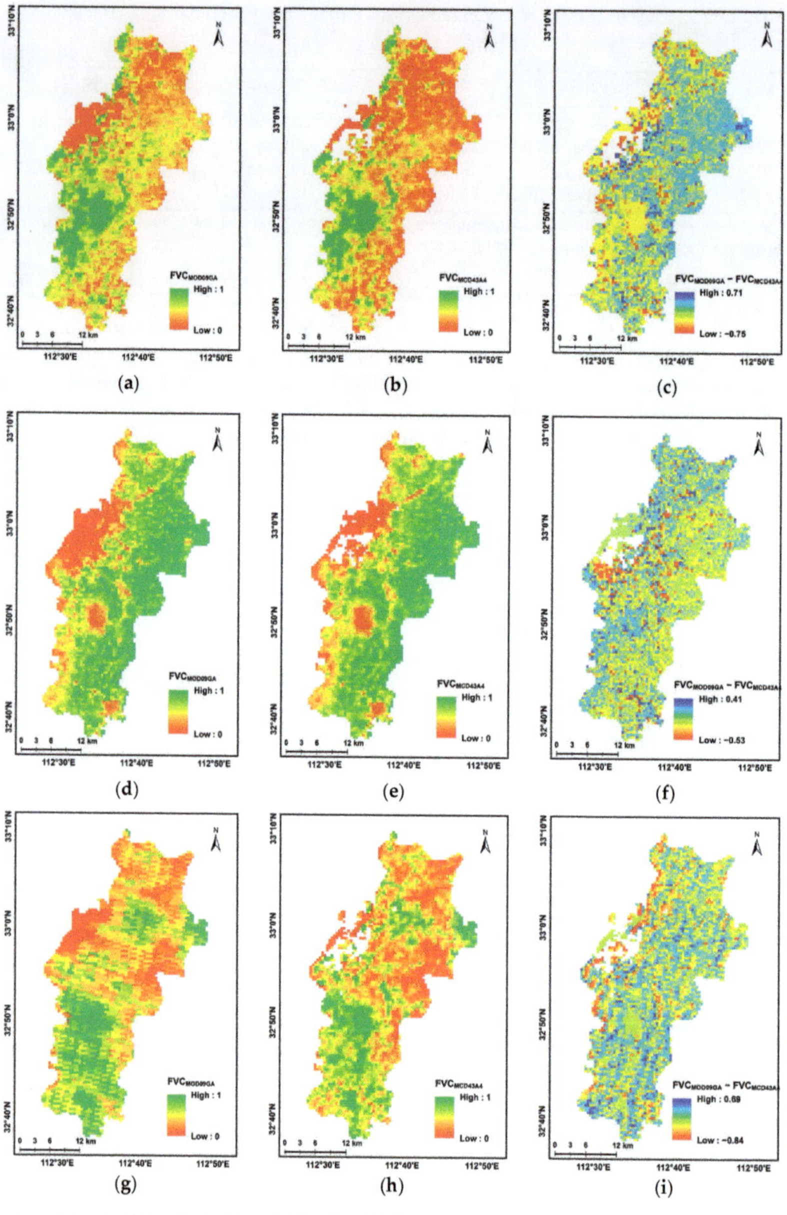

Figure 5. Spatial distribution of Fractional Vegetation Cover (FVC) derived from MOD09GA and MCD43A4, and the difference images of FVC. $FVC_{MOD09GA}$: FVC derived from MOD09GA, $FVC_{MCD43A4}$: FVC derived from MCD43A4. (**a–c**) FVC derived from MOD09GA, MCD43A4, and the difference between $FVC_{MOD09GA}$ and $FVC_{MCD43A4}$ on 15 November 2020, respectively; (**d–f**) FVC derived from MOD09GA, MCD43A4, and the difference between $FVC_{MOD09GA}$ and $FVC_{MCD43A4}$ on 10 February 2021, respectively; (**g–i**) FVC derived from MOD09GA, MCD43A4, and the difference between $FVC_{MOD09GA}$ and $FVC_{MCD43A4}$ on 30 September 2021, respectively.

3.3. Effects of the NBAR Correction at Different Stages of the Growing Seasons on Fractional Vegetation Cover Retrieval Results

The Pearson correlation coefficients of MOD09GA and MCD43A4 with the GEOV3 FVC, respectively, and their differences are shown in Figure 6. The Pearson correlation coefficients, $PCC_{MOD09GA}$ and $PCC_{MCD43A4}$, between $FVC_{MOD09GA}$, $FVC_{MCD43A4}$, and GEOV3 FVC at selected phenological parameters from 2018 through 2021 are plotted in Figure 6a. These phenological parameters correspond to those identified by the NDVI average fitting curve shown in Figure 4. From Figure 6a, it can be seen how the temporal effect of the retrieved FVC varies before and after NBAR correction at different stages of the growing seasons. The reason for the breakpoint in 2020 was mentioned in Section 3.1.

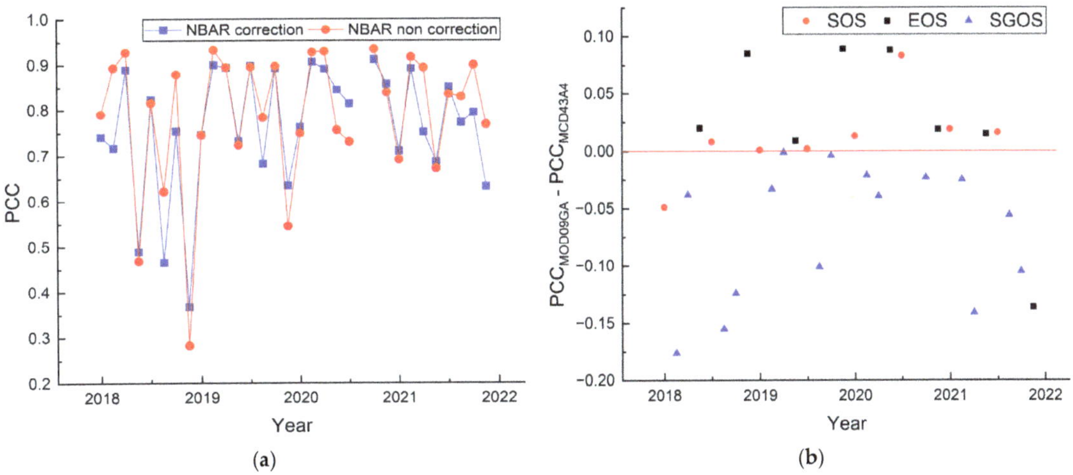

Figure 6. Pearson correlation coefficients (PCCs) of Fractional Vegetation Cover (FVC) derived before and after the NBAR correction with GEOV3 FVC at different stages of the growing seasons. $FVC_{MOD09GA}$: FVC derived from MOD09GA. $FVC_{MCD43A4}$: FVC derived from MCD43A4. $PCC_{MOD09GA}$: PCC calculated for $FVC_{MOD09GA}$ and GEOV3 FVC, $PCC_{MCD43A4}$: PCC calculated for $FVC_{MCD43A4}$ and GEOV3 FVC. (**a**) $PCC_{MOD09GA}$ and $PCC_{MCD43A4}$ in 2018–2021; (**b**) Scatterplot of numerical differences between $PCC_{MOD09GA}$ and $PCC_{MCD43A4}$. SOS: start of season; EOS: end of season; SGOS: stable growth of season.

The relationship between the differences in $PCC_{MOD09GA}$ and $PCC_{MCD43A4}$ is depicted in Figure 6b. When the difference is >0, this would indicate that the retrieval accuracy of the FVC derived before the NBAR correction exceeds that after the NBAR correction; and vice versa when the difference is <0. Overall, Figure 6b shows that, during SGOS of the crop, the differences between $PCC_{MOD09GA}$ and $PCC_{MCD43A4}$ ranged between −0.2 and 0, indicating a generally stronger correlation between $FVC_{MCD43A4}$ and GEOV3 FVC. This result suggested the FVC derived from MCD43A4 (NBAR) was more consistent with GEOV3 FVC. However, for most SOSs and EOSs, the differences between $PCC_{MOD09GA}$ and $PCC_{MCD43A4}$ mainly ranged between 0 and 0.1. This implied a weaker correlation between $FVC_{MCD43A4}$ and GEOV3 FVC, demonstrating that despite NBAR correction, the MCD43A4 product was less consistent with GEOV3 FVC than $FVC_{MOD09GA}$ was with GEOV3 FVC.

4. Discussion

4.1. Effects of Different Stages of the Growing Seasons on the Temporal Effect of Fractional Vegetation Cover Retrieved from MODIS NBAR

Normalizing the multi-angular reflectances or spectral indices to a common solar and view angle using BRDF models has been demonstrated to effectively mediate the BRDF impacts, thus enabling a more accurate intercomparison of satellite observations, both spatially and temporally [9,43]. Therefore, the MCD43A4 product is now widely used to study vegetation phenology. Common BRDF models, such as the Roujean model, the Walthall model, and the RTLSR model, are designed particularly for polar-orbiting satellite observations conducted under a wide range of angular conditions (MODIS, VIIRS, etc.) [44]. But high-quality BRDF modeling requires a sufficient number of clear-sky observations within a short time span, such that no significant changes in vegetation properties have occurred. The polar-orbiting satellite retrieval time period usually spans multiple days, typical 8–16 days, but it could be unreliable for regions known to undergo rapid land surface variations, such as fires and floods [9]. For some of the rapid developmental stages in vegetation phenology, vegetation characteristics will change, albeit not as drastically as when fires or floods occur, yet the model assumption of surface anisotropy remains unchanged over the retrieval period may still be unreliable.

As Figure 6b shows, most of the correlations between the FVC derived from the MCD43A4 product and the GEOV3 FVC are weaker when the crop is at SOS or EOS, which will impair the monitoring of crop phenology by MODIS NBAR. This negative impact is primarily due to the fact that MODIS is a polar-orbiting satellite sensor with a 16-day retrieval period for the NBAR product, for which the model assumption that the surface anisotropy remains unchanged during the period imposes an intrinsic uncertainty, especially during key stages of the growing seasons such as SOS and EOS when vegetation characteristics undergo rapid alterations.

4.2. Analysis of the Influence of Vegetation Types on the BRDF for Different Stages of the Growing Seasons

To explore the influence of different vegetation types on BRDF patterns in the different stages of the growing seasons, this study obtained the MCD43A1 product of the three vegetation type pixels with different stages of the growing seasons shown in Figure 1a to create NDVI polarization maps. These new results are shown in Figure 7. The data are formatted in a polar coordinate system, with the polar angle representing the relative azimuth angle (ranging from 0° to 360° with an interval of 1°) and the distance from the center of the circle representing the viewing zenith angle (ranging from 0° to 70° with an interval of 0.5°). The backscattering direction corresponds to an azimuth angle of 0°, while the forward scattering direction corresponds to an azimuth angle of 180°. Satellite observations with a high sun/view zenith angle (>70°) will reduce accuracy in the atmospheric correction process and further negatively influence BRDF modeling [45], so the view zenith angle is limited here to between 0° and 70°. To comprehensively consider the different BRDF patterns of the NIR and RED bands, we used the RTLSR model to simulate both bands and thereby generate an NDVI spatial distribution map. The SOS and EOS of crop phenological parameters in 2021 are employed as examples for analysis.

From the perspective of NDVI patterns, we find that various vegetation types exhibit distinct patterns in their NDVI at different stages of the growing seasons. Figure 7a–d show that winter and summer crops feature differential NDVI patterns at SOS and EOS. The shape of the high-value area in the NDVI pattern of winter crop undergoes a more pronounced change, whereas for summer crop, it changes less markedly. In Figure 7e–h, with shifts in vegetation phenology, the shape of the high-value area in the NDVI pattern of savanna pixel changes less, indicating it is less affected by seasonal changes. In contrast Figure 7i–l reveal that for a grassland pixel, the shape of the high-value area in the NDVI pattern changes more noticeably with shifts in vegetation phenology. Figure 7i,l also show that NDVI patterns differ starkly from those found for crop pixel and savanna pixel.

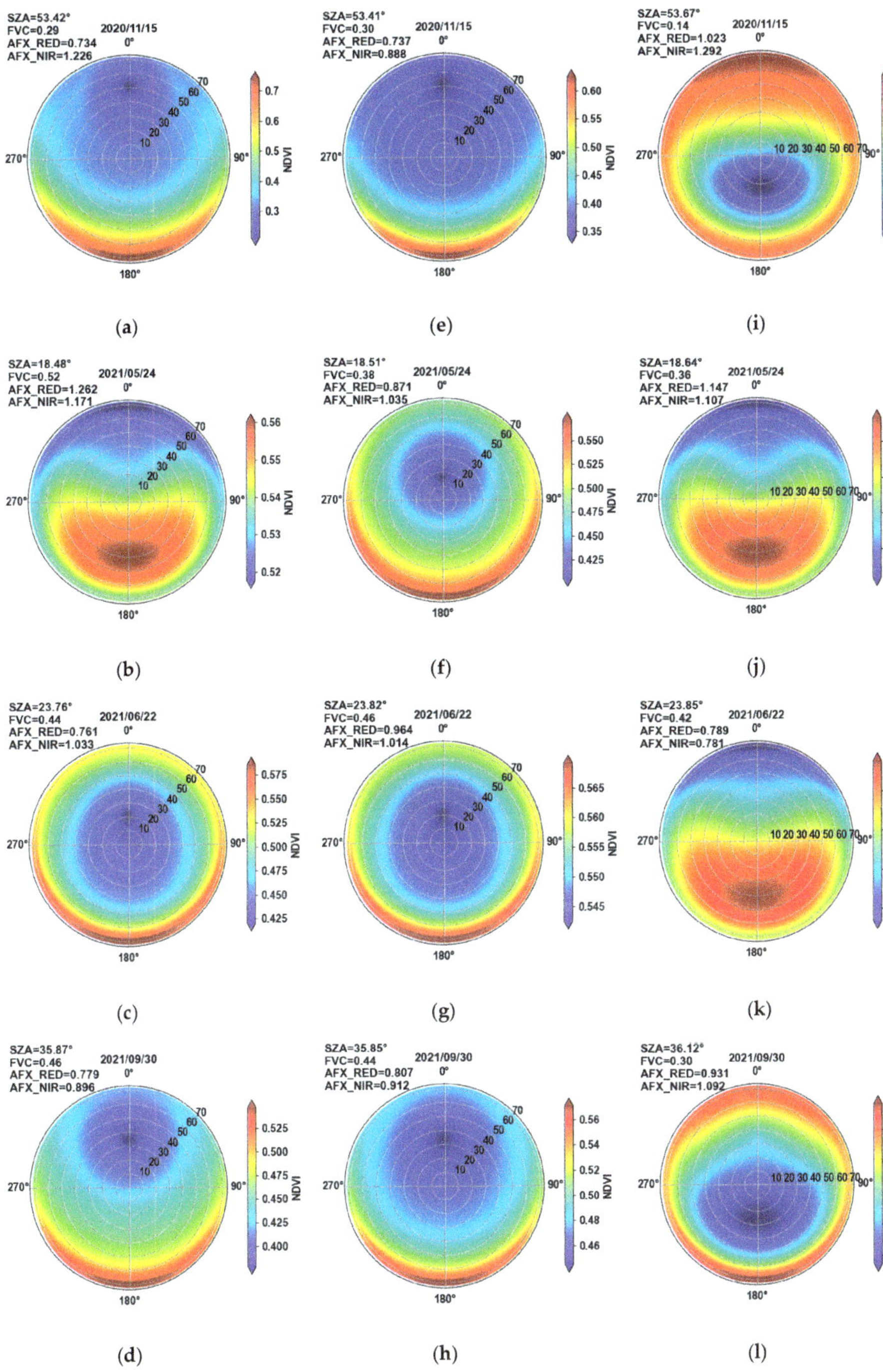

Figure 7. NDVI spatial distribution maps of crop pixel, savanna pixel, and grassland pixel in different stages of the growing seasons. (**a**–**d**) Crop. (**e**–**h**) Savanna. (**i**–**l**) Grassland. SZA: Solar Zenith Angle, FVC: Fractional Vegetation Cover, AFX_RED: Anisotropic Flat Index (AFX) in the red band, AFX_NIR: AFX in the near-infrared band.

From the perspective of AFX, as vegetation phenology shifts, there is a growth and decline in vegetation, which would affect the relative size relationship between volumetric and geometric–optical scattering. Meanwhile, the NIR and RED bands have distinct characteristics for each vegetation type in the different stages of the growing seasons. For example, on 15 November 2020, for crop pixel the AFX_RED = 0.734 and AFX_NIR = 1.226 (Figure 7a), indicating a dome-shaped BRDF for the RED band, but a bowl-shaped for the NIR band; for savanna pixel the AFX_RED = 0.737 and AFX_NIR = 0.888 (Figure 7e), indicating a dome-shaped BRDF for both bands; for grassland pixel the AFX_RED = 1.023 and AFX_NIR = 1.292, likewise indicating a bowl-shaped BRDF for both bands.

NDVI is arguably the most commonly used remote sensing index to quantify FVC [46]. Here, the FVC values in the figures come from the GEOV3 FVC product. Figure 7 shows that the values of NDVI vary with characteristic directional reflectance (i.e., reflectance under the corresponding characteristic direction), while the values of FVC are not the same in different stages of the growing seasons. The differences between the NDVI patterns and AFX reflect the complex influence of different vegetation types and seasonal changes on the BRDF patterns, which can provide valuable auxiliary information for the accurate identification and classification of vegetation types. By combining the NDVI under the characteristic directional reflectance, it becomes possible to accurately estimate the FVC of different vegetation types.

4.3. Analysis of the Influence of Mixed Pixel Distribution Characteristics on the BRDF for Different Stages of the Growing Seasons

To explore the influence of the distribution characteristics of the mixed pixels on the BRDF patterns in the different stages of the growing seasons, this study obtained the MCD43A1 product of the three mixed pixels with different stages of the growing seasons in Figure 1a, to create NDVI polarization maps. The distribution characteristics of the three mixed pixels are shown in Figure 1b–d. The results are shown in Figure 8. The format for drawing the NDVI polarization map is the same as that in Section 4.2.

From the perspective of NDVI patterns, the distribution characteristics of different mixed pixels can evidently affect the patterns of NDVI, with the mixing of buildings and crops leading to greater pattern complexity. Figure 8a–d show that the direction of the high-value area in these NDVI patterns undergoes a reversal, from the backscattering direction to the forward scattering direction as the vegetation phenology shifts. Figure 8e–h show that the shape of the high-value area in these NDVI patterns is altered more markedly by the change shifts in vegetation phenology. Figure 8i–l show that with shifts in vegetation phenology, there is a more pronounced modification of the shape and direction of the high-value area in these NDVI patterns. Also, as seen in Figure 8a,b,e,f under the same stage of the growing seasons, the high-value areas of these NDVI patterns for the two sets of mixed pixels are distributed in opposite directions. This outcome may be caused by the opposing distribution of characteristics in mixed pixels.

From the perspective of AFX, as vegetation phenology shifts, crops in mixed pixels undergo growth and decline, altering the relative size relationship between the volumetric and geometric–optical scattering. Meanwhile, we find that NIR and RED bands display different characteristics for the mixed pixels in different stages of the growing seasons. For example, on 15 November 2020, Figure 8a shows an AFX_RED = 0.911 and AFX_NIR = 0.874, indicating a dome-shaped BRDF for either band; Figure 8e shows an AFX_RED = 0.934 and AFX_NIR = 1.067, indicating a dome-shaped BRDF for the RED band, yet a bowl-shaped for NIR band; Figure 8i shows an AFX_RED = 0.960 and AFX_NIR = 0.902, indicating a dome-shaped BRDF for both bands.

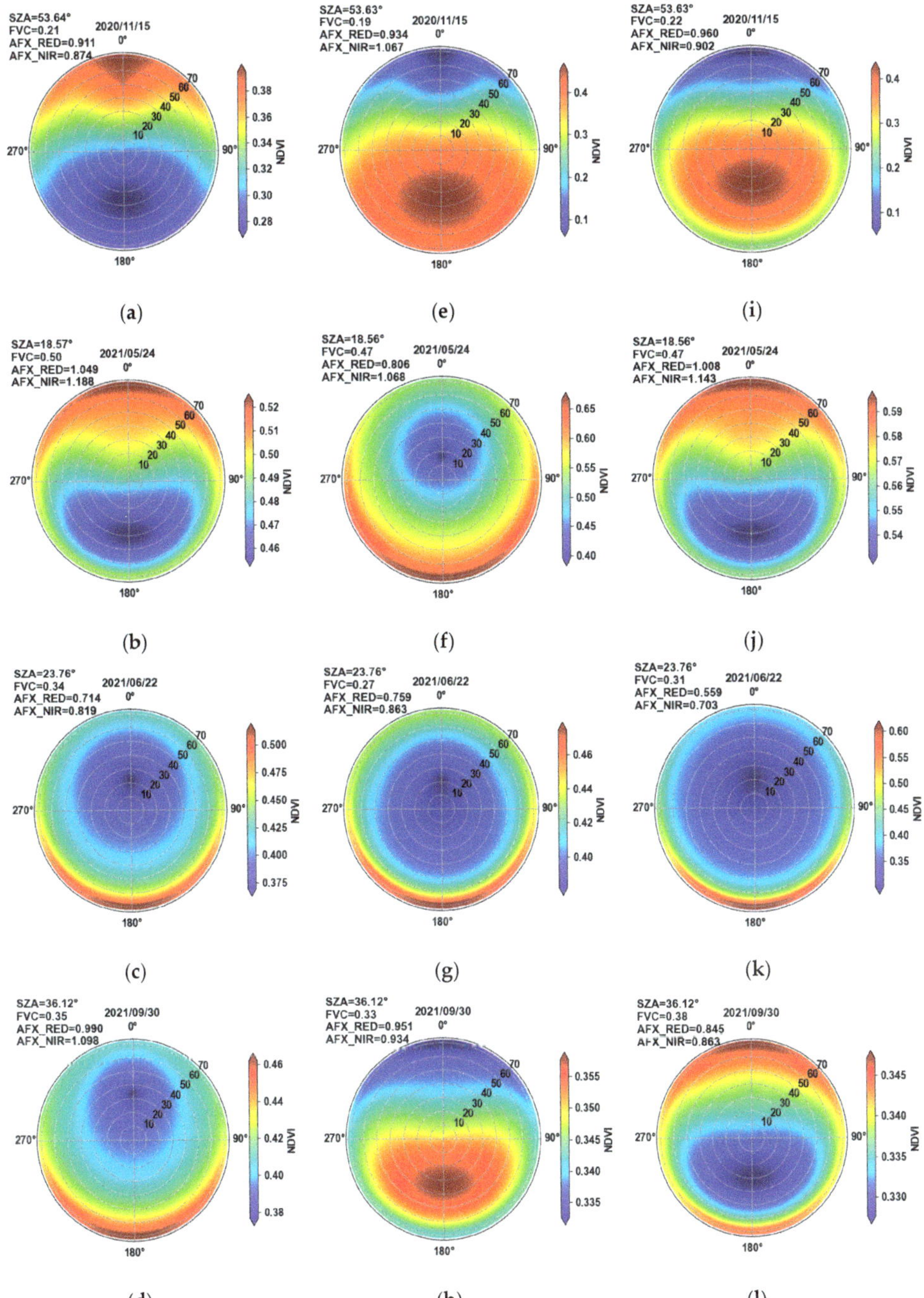

Figure 8. NDVI spatial distribution maps of mixed pixels in different stages of the growing seasons. (**a–d**) Crops above and buildings below. (**e–h**) Crops below and buildings above. (**i–l**) Buildings in the upper-left corner and crops in the remainder. SZA: Solar Zenith Angle, FVC: Fractional Vegetation Cover, AFX_RED: Anisotropic Flat Index (AFX) in the red band, AFX_NIR: AFX in the near-infrared band.

Figure 8 also depicts how the NDVI values vary with characteristic directional reflectance, with the FVC values obviously changing in different stages of the growing seasons. The differences between the NDVI patterns and AFX reflect the complex influence of mixed pixels' distribution characteristics and seasonal changes on the BRDF patterns, which can provide valuable auxiliary information for the accurate interpretation of not only the distribution characteristics but also coverage ratio of the mixed pixels. So, by combining the NDVI under the characteristic directional reflectance could provide an opportunity for the accurate estimation of the FVC for mixed pixels.

4.4. Limitations and Future Prospects

By studying the temporal effect of the MODIS NBAR product when crops are in different stages of the growing seasons, we have gained a better understanding of the relationship between the MODIS NBAR product and crop phenology, which should enable a more accurate monitoring of vegetation. Nonetheless, it is worthwhile to consider this study's limitations. (1) Different crop types exhibit varying spectral characteristics, growth cycles, and structural characteristics, which can lead to discrepancies in vegetation index time series curves. As the study area expands, the diversity of crop types in the same period increases; this could reduce accuracy of phenological identification, thereby enlarging the uncertainty of this study's results. Additionally, significantly expanding the study area makes it harder to acquire MODIS data that meets observation conditions because of factors such as cloud cover. For those reasons, we restricted the study area to the Wancheng District.

(2) The dimidiate pixel model has the advantages of a simple principle and strong operability, but it also harbors certain disadvantages. In particular, the selection of NDVI values for bare soil and pure vegetation pixels is affected by subjective factors. At the same time, it is inappropriate to divide mixed pixels into bare soil and photosynthetic vegetation in areas covered by extensive non-photosynthetic vegetation. However, these shortcomings do not outweigh the model's benefits, which also include straightforward, reliable calculations; universal and easy-to-obtain data parameters; and high retrieval accuracy. Therefore, it is still widely used in FVC retrieval [17,41]. (3) Discrepancies between the phenological periods acquired at the pixel scale from remote sensing data and those recorded at the species level from ground observations, can lead to significant uncertainties in the validation of phenological extraction results based on remote sensing data [47]. Lacking ground-based phenological observations, this study employed robust extraction methods with high phenological periods' accuracy in previous studies. Indirect methods were then applied to validate the phenology extraction results, demonstrating a good correlation [37,38,40]. Consequently, the vegetation phenology derived from the MODIS vegetation indices product can be considered to have a certain degree of reliability.

High-quality BRDF modeling requires not only obtaining enough clear-sky observations within a short time span, but also considering the representativeness of angular sampling [48,49]. Polar-orbiting satellites have a longer retrieval period, but this allows for more representative angular sampling. Geostationary satellites can obtain more clear-sky observations in a short-term period with a large spread of illumination conditions. Still, the inherently invariant viewing geometry of the geostationary platform reduces the anisotropic variations within an observed reflectance time series. Considering the high complementarities of geostationary and polar-orbiting satellite observations, their robust integration will offer new opportunities for vegetation monitoring. In tandem, their integration creates opportunities to enhance the accuracy of remote sensing extraction of vegetation phenology.

5. Conclusions

This study examined the Wancheng District from 2018 to 2021, comparing the correlation between the crop FVC (Fractional Vegetation Cover) derived from MOD09GA and MCD43A4 with the GEOV3 FVC to quantitatively assess the temporal effect of MODIS

NBAR across different stages of the growing seasons. The results demonstrate that using MODIS NBAR to retrieve crop FVC is less effective at SOS or EOS, which poses a challenge for accurate vegetation dynamics monitoring. This study improves our understanding of the relationship between MODIS NBAR and vegetation phenology and provides a basis for more accurate monitoring of crop phenology using MODIS data in the future. Meanwhile, under different stages of the growing seasons, the differences in NDVI patterns and AFX can provide auxiliary information useful for vegetation classification and interpretation of mixed pixel distribution characteristics. Combining this with the NDVI at characteristic directional reflectance should bolster the accurate retrieval of FVC. Further study is warranted regarding the accuracy and applicability of MODIS NBAR in monitoring other vegetation types in different regions and various phenological conditions, as well as investigating the influence of characteristic directional reflectance on the temporal effect of the MODIS FVC correction. Pursuing such work will augment the scope of MODIS data's application in quantitative remote sensing products for vegetation and will be the focus of our future research efforts.

Author Contributions: Conceptualization, Y.L. (Yinghao Lin), T.Y. and T.F.; methodology, Y.L. (Yinghao Lin), Y.W. and T.F.; software, T.F., N.X. and K.C.; validation, K.C., Y.L. (Yang Liu) and Y.W.; formal analysis, Y.L. (Yang Liu), D.W. and K.C.; investigation, T.F. and N.X.; resources, Y.L. (Yinghao Lin) and N.X.; data curation, Y.L. (Yinghao Lin) and T.F.; writing—original draft preparation, T.F.; writing—review and editing, Y.L. (Yinghao Lin) and T.Y.; visualization, Y.W., D.W. and N.X.; supervision, Y.L. (Yinghao Lin) and T.Y.; project administration, T.Y.; funding acquisition, Y.L. (Yinghao Lin) and N.X. All authors have read and agreed to the published version of the manuscript.

Funding: This research was funded by the Science and Technology Development Program of Henan Province (No. 242300421639); the Shenzhen Science and Technology Program (No. JCYJ20220530162001003); the Key R&D and Promotion Projects of Henan Province (No. 232102210071); the National Science and Technology Major Project (No. 80-Y50G19-9001-22/23); the Science and Technology Program of Ministry of Public Security (No. 2022JC32); and the Scientific and Technological Innovation Team of Universities in Henan Province (No. 24IRTSTHN021).

Institutional Review Board Statement: Not applicable.

Data Availability Statement: The MODIS data can be downloaded from: https://ladsweb.modaps.eosdis.nasa.gov (accessed on 22 August 2024), while the GEOV3 FVC data can be downloaded from: https://land.copernicus.eu/global/products/fcover (accessed on 22 August 2024).

Acknowledgments: The author would like to thank all contributors to this study.

Conflicts of Interest: The authors declare no conflicts of interest.

References

1. Yan, G.; Jiang, H.; Yan, K.; Cheng, S.; Song, W.; Tong, Y.; Liu, Y.; Qi, J.; Mu, X.; Zhang, H.; et al. Review of optical multi-angle quantitative remote sensing. *Natl. Remote Sens. Bull.* **2021**, *25*, 83–108. [CrossRef]
2. Jiang, H.; Jia, K.; Wang, Q.; Shang, J.; Liu, J.; Xie, X.; Dong, T. Angular effect correction for improved LAI and FVC retrieval using GF-1 wide field view data. *IEEE Trans. Geosci. Remote Sens.* **2023**, *61*, 1–14. [CrossRef]
3. Han, Y.; Wen, J.; Xiao, Q.; Bao, Y.; Chen, X.; Liu, Q.; He, M. Review of the land surface BRDF inversion methods based on remotely sensed satellite data. *Natl. Remote Sens. Bull.* **2023**, *27*, 2024–2040. [CrossRef]
4. Peng, M.; Li, C.; Wang, P.; Dai, X. Spatio-Temporal Variation and Future Sustainability of Net Primary Productivity from 2001 to 2021 in Hetao Irrigation District, Inner Mongolia. *Agriculture* **2024**, *14*, 613. [CrossRef]
5. Zhao, F.; Yang, G.; Yang, H.; Long, H.; Xu, W.; Zhu, Y.; Meng, Y.; Han, S.; Liu, M. A method for prediction of winter wheat maturity date based on modis time series and accumulated temperature. *Agriculture* **2022**, *12*, 945. [CrossRef]
6. Cui, K.; Yang, J.; Dong, J.; Zhao, G.; Cui, Y. Comparing different spatial resolutions and indices for retrieving land surface phenology for deciduous broadleaf forests. *Remote Sens.* **2023**, *15*, 2266. [CrossRef]
7. Ingty, T.; Erb, A.; Zhang, X.; Schaaf, C.; Bawa, K.S. Climate change is leading to rapid shifts in seasonality in the himalaya. *Int. J. Biometeorol.* **2023**, *67*, 913–925. [CrossRef]
8. Norris, J.R.; Walker, J.J. Solar and sensor geometry, not vegetation response, drive satellite NDVI phenology in widespread ecosystems of the western United States. *Remote Sens. Environ.* **2020**, *249*, 112013. [CrossRef]

9. Proud, S.R.; Zhang, Q.; Schaaf, C.; Fensholt, R.; Rasmussen, M.O.; Shisanya, C.; Mutero, W.; Mbow, C.; Anyamba, A.; Pak, E. The normalization of surface anisotropy effects present in SEVIRI reflectances by using the MODIS BRDF method. *IEEE Trans. Geosci. Remote Sens.* **2014**, *52*, 6026–6039. [CrossRef]
10. Shen, Y.; Zhang, X.; Gao, S.; Zhang, H.K.; Schaaf, C.; Wang, W.; Ye, Y.; Liu, Y.; Tran, K.H. Analyzing GOES-R ABI BRDF-adjusted EVI2 time series by comparing with VIIRS observations over the CONUS. *Remote Sens. Environ.* **2024**, *302*, 113972. [CrossRef]
11. Hasegawa, K.; Izumi, T.; Matsuyama, H.; Kajiwara, K.; Honda, Y. Seasonal change of bidirectional reflectance distribution function in mature Japanese larch forests and their phenology at the foot of Mt. Yatsugatake, central Japan. *Remote Sens. Environ.* **2018**, *209*, 524–539. [CrossRef]
12. Li, Y.; Jiao, Z.; Zhao, K.; Dong, Y.; Zhou, Y.; Zeng, Y.; Xu, H.; Zhang, X.; Hu, T.; Cui, L. Influence of varying solar zenith angles on land surface phenology derived from vegetation indices: A case study in the harvard forest. *Remote Sens.* **2021**, *13*, 4126. [CrossRef]
13. Ma, X.; Huete, A.; Tran, N.N. Interaction of seasonal sun-angle and savanna phenology observed and modelled using MODIS. *Remote Sens.* **2019**, *11*, 1398. [CrossRef]
14. Ma, X.; Huete, A.; Tran, N.N.; Bi, J.; Gao, S.; Zeng, Y. Sun-angle effects on remote-sensing phenology observed and modelled using himawari-8. *Remote Sens.* **2020**, *12*, 1339. [CrossRef]
15. Li, J.; Zhang, J.; Wang, X.; Wang, G. Long term observation of fractional vegetation cover in Qingyang of Gansu Province and its response to climate change. *Atmosphere* **2022**, *13*, 288. [CrossRef]
16. Gao, S.; Castellazzi, P.; Vervoort, R.W.; Doody, T.M. Fine scale mapping of fractional tree canopy cover to support river basin management. *Hydrol. Process.* **2021**, *35*, e14156. [CrossRef]
17. Liu, C.; Zhang, X.; Wang, T.; Chen, G.; Zhu, K.; Wang, Q.; Wang, J. Detection of vegetation coverage changes in the Yellow River Basin from 2003 to 2020. *Ecol. Indic.* **2022**, *138*, 108818. [CrossRef]
18. Song, D.-X.; Wang, Z.; He, T.; Wang, H.; Liang, S. Estimation and validation of 30 m fractional vegetation cover over China through integrated use of Landsat 8 and Gaofen 2 data. *Sci. Remote Sens.* **2022**, *6*, 100058. [CrossRef]
19. Zhang, J.; Chen, S.; Wu, Z.; Fu, Y.H. Review of vegetation phenology trends in China in a changing climate. *Prog. Phys. Geogr.* **2022**, *46*, 829–845. [CrossRef]
20. Liu, Y.; Qin, Y.; Ge, Q.; Dai, J.; Chen, Q. Reponses and sensitivities of maize phenology to climate change from 1981 to 2009 in Henan Province, China. *J. Geogr. Sci.* **2017**, *27*, 1072–1084. [CrossRef]
21. Didan, K. MODIS/Terra Vegetation Indices 16-Day L3 Global 250m SIN Grid V061. 2021. Available online: https://lpdaac.usgs.gov/products/mod13q1v061/ (accessed on 9 August 2024).
22. He, C.; Yan, F.; Wang, Y.; Lu, Q. Spatiotemporal Variation in Vegetation Growth Status and Its Response to Climate in the Three-River Headwaters Region, China. *Remote Sens.* **2022**, *14*, 5041. [CrossRef]
23. Xu, B.; Li, J.; Luo, Z.; Wu, J.; Liu, Y.; Yang, H.; Pei, X. Analyzing the spatiotemporal vegetation dynamics and their responses to climate change along the Ya'an–Linzhi section of the Sichuan–Tibet Railway. *Remote Sens.* **2022**, *14*, 3584. [CrossRef]
24. Vermote, E.; Wolfe, R. MODIS/Terra Surface Reflectance Daily L2G Global 1 km and 500 m SIN Grid V061. 2021. Available online: https://lpdaac.usgs.gov/products/mod09gav061/ (accessed on 9 August 2024).
25. Schaaf, C.; Wang, Z. MODIS/Terra + Aqua BRDF/Albedo Nadir BRDF Adjusted Ref Daily L3 Global—500 m V061. 2021. Available online: https://lpdaac.usgs.gov/products/mcd43a4v061/ (accessed on 9 August 2024).
26. Baret, F.; Weiss, M.; Verger, A.; Smets, B. ATBD for FCOVER from PROBA-V products at 300 m resolution (GEOV3). Available online: https://land.copernicus.eu/en/technical-library/product-user-manual-fraction-of-green-vegetation-cover-333-m-version-1-1/@@download/file (accessed on 9 August 2024).
27. Liu, D.; Jia, K.; Wei, X.; Xia, M.; Zhang, X.; Yao, Y.; Zhang, X.; Wang, B. Spatiotemporal comparison and validation of three global-scale fractional vegetation cover products. *Remote Sens.* **2019**, *11*, 2524. [CrossRef]
28. Chen, J.; Huang, R.; Yang, Y.; Feng, Z.; You, H.; Han, X.; Yi, S.; Qin, Y.; Wang, Z.; Zhou, G. Multi-scale validation and uncertainty analysis of GEOV3 and MuSyQ FVC products: A case study of an alpine grassland ecosystem. *Remote Sens.* **2022**, *14*, 5800. [CrossRef]
29. Fuster, B.; Sánchez-Zapero, J.; Camacho, F.; García-Santos, V.; Verger, A.; Lacaze, R.; Weiss, M.; Baret, F.; Smets, B. Quality assessment of PROBA-V LAI, fAPAR and fCOVER collection 300 m products of copernicus global land service. *Remote Sens.* **2020**, *12*, 1017. [CrossRef]
30. Friedl, M.; Sulla-Menashe, D. MODIS/Terra + Aqua Land Cover Type Yearly L3 Global 500 m SIN Grid V061. 2022. Available online: https://lpdaac.usgs.gov/products/mcd12q1v061/ (accessed on 9 August 2024).
31. Schaaf, C.; Wang, Z. MODIS/Terra + Aqua BRDF/Albedo Model Parameters Daily L3 Global—500 m V061. 2021. Available online: https://lpdaac.usgs.gov/products/mcd43a1v061/ (accessed on 9 August 2024).
32. Stanimirova, R.; Cai, Z.; Melaas, E.K.; Gray, J.M.; Eklundh, L.; Jönsson, P.; Friedl, M.A. An empirical assessment of the MODIS land cover dynamics and TIMESAT land surface phenology algorithms. *Remote Sens.* **2019**, *11*, 2201. [CrossRef]
33. Zhang, H.; Wang, X.; Peng, D. Evaluation of urban vegetation phenology using 250 m MODIS vegetation indices. *Photogramm. Eng. Remote Sens.* **2022**, *88*, 461–467. [CrossRef]
34. Feng, Z.; Chen, J.; Huang, R.; Yang, Y.; You, H.; Han, X. Spatial and temporal variation in alpine vegetation phenology and its response to climatic and topographic factors on the Qinghai–Tibet Plateau. *Sustainability* **2022**, *14*, 12802. [CrossRef]

35. Liu, Y.; Zhou, W.; Gao, S.; Ma, X.; Yan, K. Phenological responses to snow seasonality in the qilian mountains is a function of both elevation and vegetation types. *Remote Sens.* **2022**, *14*, 3629. [CrossRef]
36. Jonsson, P.; Eklundh, L. Seasonality extraction by function fitting to time-series of satellite sensor data. *IEEE Trans. Geosci. Remote Sens.* **2002**, *40*, 1824–1832. [CrossRef]
37. Hou, X.; Sui, X.; Liang, S.; Wang, M.; Dong, M. Comparison of Five Methods for Phenology Extraction of Winter Wheat. *Remote Sens. Inf.* **2017**, *32*, 65–70. [CrossRef]
38. Wu, W.; Yang, P.; Tang, H.; Zhou, Q.; Zhang, L. Monitoring Spatial Patterns of Cropland Phenology in North China Based on NOAA NDVI Data. *Sci. Agric. Sin.* **2009**, *42*, 552–560.
39. Ma, X.; Zhang, X.; Qiao, L.; Zheng, Z.; Pan, L.; Peng, J.; Yang, H.; Xia, H. A dataset of winter crop distribution maps in Henan Province from 2019 to 2021. *China Sci. Data* **2022**, *7*, 290–302. [CrossRef]
40. Luo, Y.; Zhang, Z. ChinaCropArea1km: A High-Resolution Crop Distribution Dataset for Three Staple Crops in China from 2000–2019. Available online: http://www.nesdc.org.cn/sdo/detail?id=627dfc4b7e28172589c2df9b (accessed on 9 August 2024).
41. Zhang, H.; He, Z.; Xu, J.; Mu, W.; Chen, Y.; Wang, G. Analysis of Spatial and Temporal Changes in Vegetation Cover and Driving Forces in the Wuding River Basin, Loess Plateau. *Forests* **2023**, *15*, 82. [CrossRef]
42. Jiao, Z.; Li, X.; Wang, J.; Zhang, H. Assessment of MODIS BRDF shape indicators. *Natl. Remote Sens. Bull.* **2021**, *15*, 432–456. [CrossRef]
43. Schaaf, C.B.; Gao, F.; Strahler, A.H.; Lucht, W.; Li, X.; Tsang, T.; Strugnell, N.C.; Zhang, X.; Jin, Y.; Muller, J.-P. First operational BRDF, albedo nadir reflectance products from MODIS. *Remote Sens. Environ.* **2002**, *83*, 135–148. [CrossRef]
44. Lavergne, T.; Kaminski, T.; Pinty, B.; Taberner, M.; Gobron, N.; Verstraete, M.M.; Vossbeck, M.; Widlowski, J.-L.; Giering, R. Application to MISR land products of an RPV model inversion package using adjoint and Hessian codes. *Remote Sens. Environ.* **2007**, *107*, 362–375. [CrossRef]
45. Lyapustin, A.; Wang, Y.; Korkin, S.; Huang, D. MODIS collection 6 MAIAC algorithm. *Atmos. Meas. Tech.* **2018**, *11*, 5741–5765. [CrossRef]
46. Tian, Q.; Min, X. Advances in study on vegetation indices. *Adv. Earth Sci.* **1998**, *13*, 327–333.
47. Fan, D.; Zhao, X.; Zhu, W.; Zheng, Z. Review of influencing factors of accuracy of plant phenology monitoring based on remote sensing data. *Prog. Geogr.* **2016**, *35*, 304–319. [CrossRef]
48. Gao, F.; Schaaf, C.B.; Strahler, A.H.; Lucht, W. Using a multikernel least-variance approach to retrieve and evaluate albedo from limited bidirectional measurements. *Remote Sens. Environ.* **2001**, *76*, 57–66. [CrossRef]
49. Lucht, W.; Lewis, P. Theoretical noise sensitivity of BRDF and albedo retrieval from the EOS-MODIS and MISR sensors with respect to angular sampling. *Int. J. Remote Sens.* **2000**, *21*, 81–98. [CrossRef]

agriculture

MDPI

Article

Detection of Mechanical Damage in Corn Seeds Using Hyperspectral Imaging and the ResNeSt_E Deep Learning Network

Hua Huang [1,†], Yinfeng Liu [1,†], Shiping Zhu [1,*], Chuan Feng [1], Shaoqi Zhang [2], Lei Shi [2], Tong Sun [2] and Chao Liu [2]

1 College of Engineering and Technology, Southwest University, Chongqing 400716, China; huahuang@swu.edu.cn (H.H.); liuyfln@163.com (Y.L.); fengchuan2021@126.com (C.F.)
2 College of Information and Management Science, Henan Agricultural University, Zhengzhou 450002, China; zsq@henau.edu.cn (S.Z.); shilei@henau.edu.cn (L.S.); suntong@henau.edu.cn (T.S.); cliu@henau.edu.cn (C.L.)
* Correspondence: zspswu@126.com
† These authors contributed equally to this work and should be considered co-first authors.

Abstract: Corn is one of the global staple grains and the largest grain crop in China. During harvesting, grain separation, and corn production, corn is susceptible to mechanical damage including surface cracks, internal cracks, and breakage. However, the internal cracks are difficult to observe. In this study, hyperspectral imaging was used to detect mechanical damage in corn seeds. The corn seeds were divided into four categories that included intact, broken, internally cracked, and surface-crackedtv. This study compared three feature extraction methods, including principal component analysis (PCA), kernel PCA (KPCA), and factor analysis (FA), as well as a joint feature extraction method consisting of a combination of these methods. The dimensionality reduction results of the three methods (FA + KPCA, KPCA + FA, and PCA + FA) were combined to form a new combined dataset and improve the classification. We then compared the effects of six classification models (ResNet, ShuffleNet-V2, MobileNet-V3, ResNeSt, EfficientNet-V2, and MobileNet-V4) and proposed a ResNeSt_E network based on the ResNeSt and efficient multi-scale attention modules. The accuracy of ResNeSt_E reached 99.0%, and this was 0.4% higher than that of EfficientNet-V2 and 0.7% higher than that of ResNeSt. Additionally, the number of parameters and memory requirements were reduced and the frames per second were improved. We compared two dimensionality reduction methods: KPCA + FA and PCA + FA. The classification accuracies of the two methods were the same; however, PCA + FA was much more efficient than KPCA + FA and was more suitable for practical detection. The ResNeSt_E network could detect both internal and surface cracks in corn seeds, making it suitable for mobile terminal applications. The results demonstrated that detecting mechanical damage in corn seeds using hyperspectral images was possible. This study provides a reference for mechanical damage detection methods for corn.

Keywords: corn seed; hyperspectral image; mechanical damage; combined dataset; ResNeSt_E

1. Introduction

Corn, along with rice and wheat, is one of the three major food crops worldwide. Corn is an indispensable raw material for light, chemical, and other industries. In 2012, the corn production in China exceeded its rice production for the first time and it has since become the largest grain crop in China [1]. Compared to rice and wheat, corn has a significantly higher grain yield [2]. Since the 21st century, the expansion of corn acreage areas has accelerated. Based on current trends, corn is expected to replace wheat as the most widely grown crop of the world by 2030 [3]. Mechanical damage is an important factor that affects the quality of corn seeds. From harvest to sowing, during mechanical harvesting, seed separation, drying, processing, and other processes [4–7], corn seeds are susceptible to mechanical damage. Common forms of mechanical damage include surface cracks, internal cracks, breaks, and other damage [8,9]. This damage shortens the shelf life of corn seeds and reduces their germination rate and seed vigor.

With the development of detection technology, an increasing number of non-destructive detection techniques have been applied to agricultural detection [10]. Spectral and imaging technologies are the most widely used methods for identifying crop seeds. Santana et al. [11] used hyperspectral sensors and machine learning to classify Asian soybean rust. Xuan et al. [12] used hyperspectral technology to determine the protein content in rice grains. Zhao et al. [13] collected images of wheat grains and achieved the rapid detection of wheat grain quality by improving the YOLOv5 model. Many studies have been conducted examining detection of corn seeds. Liu et al. [14] used visible/near-infrared spatially resolved spectroscopy to predict individual corn-seed vigor with an accuracy of 91.67%. Javanmardi et al. [15] classified corn seed varieties based on computer vision and deep learning with an accuracy of 98.1%. Based on hyperspectral imaging, Yang et al. [16] proposed a spectral and spatial attention module that enabled the detection of defective corn seeds with an accuracy of 94.56% on a test set. Yang et al. [17] used near-infrared spectroscopy combined with deep learning to determine the quality of corn, with an accuracy of 96.46%.

Mechanical damage to crop seeds is typically divided into surface and internal damage, with surface cracks and breaks being easier to detect. Wang et al. [18] proposed an improved BCK-YOLOv7 model to solve the problem of dense distribution of corn seeds during harvesting and this successfully detected broken and intact corn seeds under high-density conditions with a recognition accuracy of 96.9%. Based on the YOLOv4-small model, Li et al. [19] designed a device to detect broken grains and damaged corn seeds with an accuracy of 93%. Wang et al. [20] collected near-infrared spectra of soybean seeds, used principal component analysis (PCA) and random forest variable selection, and classified surface-cracked and normal seeds with an accuracy of 84%. In contrast to surface cracks, certain cracks arise inside corn seed, extend only to the pericarp, and are not visible on the surface [21]. These types of internal cracks are difficult to detect and can cause further harm. The detection of internal cracks requires the observation of the internal structure. This was achieved by placing a bright light source under the corn seeds and a camera above the corn to collect images. Internal crack detection in corn seeds has been achieved using deep learning [22,23]. Wang et al. [24] used near-infrared spectroscopy to detect internal cracks in rice seeds with an accuracy of 91.3%. Chen et al. [25] used an X-ray imaging system to collect maize seed images and classified damaged and intact seeds with an average accuracy of 99.66% based on the improved YOLOv8 model. X-ray microcomputed tomography (μCT) can be used to obtain high-precision three-dimensional images of samples. Dong et al. [26] observed and studied internal cracks in corn kernels using μCT and analyzed the relationship between cracks and the kernel breakage rate. Jiao et al. [27] used μCT technology to study the variation of endosperm cracks in corn seeds during soaking and proposed the R-YOLOv7-small model to determine the number and length of cracks in corn seeds. The μCT technology can capture the three-dimensional microstructure of corn seeds with good detection results, but its high costs make it unsuitable for application in agricultural production lines.

Hyperspectral imaging exhibits a wide range of applications for the detection of corn seed quality. Hyperspectral imaging combines the advantages of spectroscopy and imaging, obtains the spectral and spatial information of the target, and meets the requirements of rapid nondestructive detection [28]. Zhang et al. [29] collected the hyperspectral images of several types of corn seeds and identified corn varieties by comprehensively considering their spatial, spectral, and textural features. Zhang et al. [30] combined the spatial and spectral information of hyperspectral images and proposed a deep one-class learning network to identify counterfeit corn seeds. Qiao et al. [31] collected hyperspectral images of corn seeds, combined the spectral and textural information, and determined the starch and protein contents of corn seeds without drying. Xue et al. [32] obtained spectral images of corn seeds using hyperspectral imaging technology and achieved rapid and nondestructive detection of the moisture content of corn seeds. Regarding to the detection of corn seed quality using hyperspectral technology, few reports are available regarding the detection of mechanical damage.

Based on previous studies and an analysis of the literature, three problems have been observed regarding the detection of mechanical damage in corn seeds. First, few studies have been conducted examining the detection of internal cracks in corn seeds, and only a few have reported detection methods. Secondly, hyperspectral datasets containing mechanical damage to corn seeds are lacking, thus making it difficult to develop models suitable for detecting mechanical damage. Finally, research investigating the detection of mechanical damage to corn seed slack has identified both internal and surface cracks. In this study, hyperspectral imaging technology was used to detect mechanical damage in corn seeds. The hyperspectral image, containing both spatial and spectral information, was used to improve the detection of internal cracks and detect both internal and surface cracks.

2. Materials and Methods

2.1. Sample Preparation

The corn samples used in this study were obtained from Anhui Province. All samples were stored at room temperature in a dry area away from light. The specific process of corn seed classification is as follows:

(1) Pick up a single seed and observe the appearance. If the appearance is broken, mark it as surface cracked; if the appearance is intact, proceed to the next step;
(2) Place the experimental seeds flatly on the transmitted light source, move and observe the seeds to ensure that all areas of the seeds can be transmitted;
(3) If cracks are observed, mark the current seed as internally cracked; if no cracks are observed, proceed to the next step;
(4) Turn the seed over and repeat steps (2) and (3); if no cracks are observed, the current seed is labeled as intact;
(5) Repeat the above steps until all seeds have been screened.

The 2496 kernels were divided into four categories that included intact (IN; 600 kernels), broken (BR; 552 kernels), internally cracked (IC; 720 kernels), and surface cracked (SC; 624 kernels). All seed images were divided according to the ratio of training:validation:test sets = 4:1:1 and a hyperspectral mechanical damage dataset for corn seeds was constructed. The composition of the dataset is shown in Table 1. Hyperspectral true color images of seeds of various categories are shown in Figure 1.

Table 1. Datasets.

	Training	Validation	Test	Total
IN	400	100	100	600
BR	368	92	92	552
IC	480	120	120	720
SC	416	104	104	624
total	1664	416	416	2496

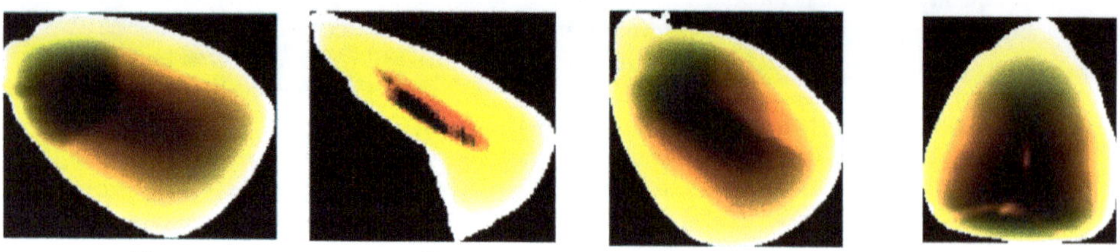

(a) (b) (c) (d)

Figure 1. Hyperspectral true-color images of corn seeds: (**a**) IN, (**b**) BR, (**c**) IC, and (**d**) SC.

2.2. Hyperspectral Image Acquisition

An HIS-VNIR-B1621 visible/near-infrared hyperspectral imaging system was used for data acquisition. The system consisted of a CCD camera (Raptor EM285CL, Raptor Photonics Incorporated, USA), 363–1025 nm spectral imager (Imspector V10E, Specim, Oulu, Finland), an IT 3900 150 W halogen light source, a mobile platform, and a dark box. The samples were then placed on a movable glass platform. A halogen lamp was placed below the glass platform, light was passed vertically through the sample, and the lens was placed above the sample. Hyperspectral imaging software Hyper Spectral Image was used to control the camera and mobile platform to acquire hyperspectral images. The image resolution was 1632 × 1232 pixels.

2.3. Hyperspectral Image Preprocessing

To eliminate the influence of ambient noise, ambient light, and dark current of the device, performing a black-white correction for the hyperspectral data was necessary. Correction was performed according to Formula (1):

$$R = \frac{R_0 - D}{W - D} \times 100\% \tag{1}$$

where R is the corrected hyperspectral image, W is the whiteboard calibration image captured when the dark door is closed, the light source is turned on, and no sample is present; D is the blackboard calibration image taken when the dark door is closed, the light source is turned off, the lens cover is covered, and no sample is present; and R_0 is the original hyperspectral image captured when the dark door is closed, the light source is turned on, and the sample is placed.

As the acquired hyperspectral image contained noisy areas around the sample, it was cropped to preserve only the sample area. As the acquired hyperspectral image exhibited noise at the beginning and end bands, these bands were removed to maintain 1113 bands in the range of 400.3854–1000.5995 nm.

2.4. Standardization

The images were standardized prior to processing. Standardization allows the original data to be proportionally shifted within a certain range, and this can improve the speed of image processing and accuracy of the results. The formula for standardization is as follows:

$$x' = \frac{x - \mu}{\sigma} \tag{2}$$

where x' is the standardized image matrix, x is the original image matrix, μ is the mean of the image matrix, and σ is the standard deviation of the image matrix.

2.5. Hyperspectral Image Feature Extraction

Hyperspectral images are characterized by numerous bands. The information is rich; however, the correlation between adjacent bands is very large, resulting in significant information redundancy. Therefore, feature extraction from hyperspectral images is required [33].

2.5.1. Principal Component Analysis

PCA is a classic method for the dimensionality reduction of data [34]. PCA calculates the covariance matrix of the original data and determines the optimal projection based on the covariance matrix to identify new features, called principal components (PC). The obtained PCs were orthogonal and independent.

2.5.2. Factor Analysis

Factor analysis (FA) is a dimensionality reduction method that extracts potential common factors from multiple variables [35]. The FA examines the relationship between the original variables. The FA assumes that the presence of a few main factors among the variables affects external performance. These factors reflected most of the information in the original data without missing important information, thereby reducing dimensionality.

Compared with PCA, both seek to respond to most of the information in the original data with a few variables. Both methods seek new variables that are not present in the original variables. The difference is that the new variables identified by PCA are linear combinations of the original variables. The FA, on the other hand, decomposes the original variables to obtain common and special factors. The common factors are the factors that are common to all the original variables and the special factors are the factors that are unique to each original variable. The FA is to extract these common factors.

2.5.3. Kernel PCA (KPCA)

PCA is a linear dimensionality-reduction method [36]. KPCA is a nonlinear extension of PCA that achieves the nonlinear dimensionality reduction of data. KPCA first maps the data nonlinearly to a high-dimensional feature space, and then performs PCA on the feature space, maps the PCs back to the original space, and obtains reduced-dimensional data.

2.6. Sobel Edge Detection

To highlight the edge details of the internal and surface cracks in corn seeds, performing edge detection on a reduced-dimensional image is necessary. The Sobel operator is a classic first-order edge detection operator. The Sobel operator exhibits a low computational complexity, high accuracy, and the ability to suppress noise. The Sobel operator performs gradient detection in both horizontal and vertical directions of an image. The formula used is as follows:

$$G_x = \begin{bmatrix} -1 & 0 & +1 \\ -2 & 0 & +2 \\ -1 & 0 & +1 \end{bmatrix} * A \quad (3)$$

$$G_y = \begin{bmatrix} -1 & -2 & -1 \\ 0 & 0 & 0 \\ +1 & +2 & +1 \end{bmatrix} * A \quad (4)$$

$$G = \sqrt{G_x^2 + G_y^2} \quad (5)$$

where G_x and G_y are the horizontal and vertical gradient maps, A is the original image, and G is the final edge-detection image.

2.7. Laplace Edge Detection

The Laplace operator is a second-order differential operator that detects edges based on the gray value of the image. The Laplace operator is suitable for fuzzy detection. The Laplace operator is expressed as:

$$\begin{bmatrix} 0 & -1 & 0 \\ -1 & 4 & -1 \\ 0 & -1 & 0 \end{bmatrix} \quad (6)$$

2.8. Linear Stretching

As the storage format of hyperspectral data is different from that of RGB image data, the pixel values of the hyperspectral image must be stretched to a range of 0–255 to save them in the RGB format. The stretching formulas are as follows:

$$R = \frac{max_o - min_o}{max_i - min_i} \times gray + min_o \quad (7)$$

where R is the stretched image; max_o is the maximum value of the output image, typically 255; min_o is the minimum value of the output image, typically 0; max_i is the maximum value of the input image, that is the gray value corresponding to 95% in this study; min_i is the minimum value of the input image, which is the gray value corresponding to 5% in this study; and $gray$ is the gray value of a pixel.

2.9. Classification Networks

Traditional deep neural networks are equipped with deep network structures for feature extraction. These designs can improve network detection; however, the requirements for storage devices and computational resources are high. Therefore, considering practical applications, the networks chosen in this study are lightweight networks with fewer layers.

2.9.1. ResNet

The ResNet model exhibits a low network complexity and introduces residual modules that reduce the difficulty of training, speed up training, make network models easier to deploy and train, and can be better applied to devices.

ResNet was proposed by Kaiming He's team in 2015 [37]. As the layers of the convolutional neural network become deeper, the network becomes difficult to train and tends to cause problems such as gradient explosion and gradient vanishing, that degrade the network performance. ResNet uses a residual structure to effectively alleviate these problems. ResNet has various versions, such as ResNet-18 and ResNet-152, with the main difference being the number of layers used. The ResNet-18 network was used in this study.

2.9.2. ShuffleNet-V2

ShuffleNet-V2 was proposed by the Megvii Technology (Beijing, China) team in 2018 [38]. They proposed four design guidelines for efficient networks, improved ShuffleNet-V1 based on these guidelines. Channel separation divides an input channel into two branches. The left branch was neither manipulated nor displayed identically. The right branch performs three consecutive convolutions and maintains the same input and output channels. ShuffleNet-V2 enabled efficient and accurate detection. ShuffleNet-V2-1.0x was used in this study.

2.9.3. MobileNet-V3

Google released MobileNet-V3 in 2019 [39], which added SE modules to the core blocks of MobileNet-V2 and updated its activation functions. The SE module was relatively simple. Each channel is pooled and passed through two fully connected layers to obtain the output vector. Additionally, the activation function was redesigned. This paper proposes an activation function called h-swish. Compared to the original Swish activation function, h-swish improves the inference speed of the network and is more friendly to the quantization process. The MobileNetv3-large network was used in this study.

2.9.4. ResNeSt

ResNeSt, that is, an improved version of ResNet, was proposed by Amazon's Mu Li team (Amazon, Seattle, WA, USA) in 2020 [40]. This study proposed a split attention block and combined it with ResNet to create ResNeSt. The ResNeSt block divides the input into k parts, denoted as Cardinal 1~k, and subsequently splits each cardinal into r parts. Following these operations, kr groups were obtained. In this way, the network has many convolutional kernel branches in the same layer that extract features separately so that the network can obtain more features. The minimal network provided in the original paper was ResNeSt50. In this study, we refer to the ResNet18 network structure and constructed the ResNeSt18 network.

2.9.5. EfficientNet-V2

Google proposed EfficientNet-V2 in April 2021 [41]. In EfficientNet-v1, the authors reported that the use of Depthwise Convolutions was slow in the shallow layers of the network. Although Depthwise Convolutions possess fewer parameters and smaller floating-point operations (FLOPs), they cannot fully utilize the existing accelerators. Therefore, a fused MBConv module was proposed. This module used an accelerator to accelerate the network. The EfficientNetv2-s network was used in this study.

2.9.6. MobileNet-V4

Google launched MobileNet-V4 in 2024 [42]. The core of MobileNet-V4 is the proposed Universal Inverted Bottleneck (UIB) structure. The UIB introduces two optional depthwise convolutions into the original inverted bottleneck block, with one located before the expansion layer and the other between the expansion and projection layers. This simple change unifies several important existing modules, including the original inverted bottleneck block, ConvNext, and FFN in the ViT. A MobileNetv4-medium network was used in this study.

2.10. Overview of the Entire Methodology

As presented in Figure 2, hyperspectral images are first preprocessed after acquisition. Then, a binary mask was obtained based on the 1000.5995 nm gray scale image. Based on the mask, it is cropped to one image per seed. These seed images were divided into datasets by species and scale. Feature extraction is performed separately for each seed picture, followed by Sobel edge detection and Laplace edge detection. The image after edge detection is linearly stretched and then resized to 224 × 224 and then saved as a jpg. Each feature extraction method receives its respective corresponding jpg dataset. The corresponding jpg images obtained by different feature extraction methods are input into the six classification models. The classification results of the six models are synthesized and the three jpg datasets with the best results are filtered to form a combined dataset. The combined dataset is put into the six models and the ResNeSt model is selected by considering other metrics. The improved ResNeSt_E model is proposed on the basis of ResNeSt.

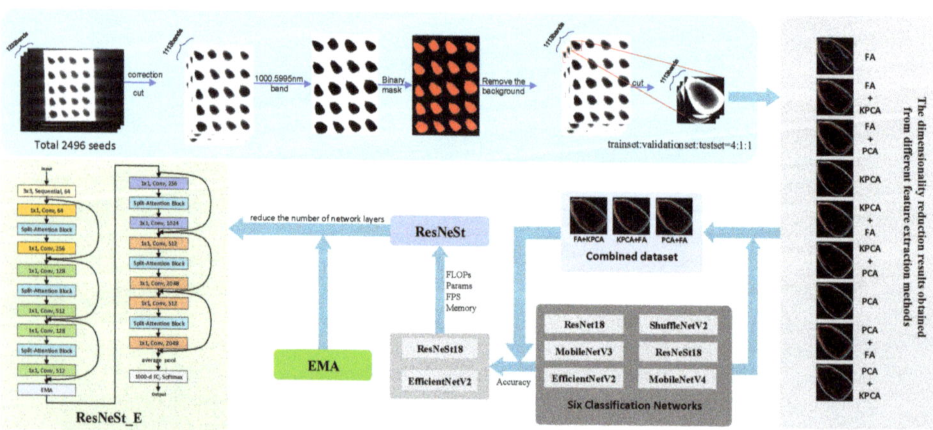

Figure 2. Overall process.

2.11. Model Implementation

The hardware environment of the experimental platform was designed, where the CPU model was Intel® Core^{TM} i5-13600KF (Intel, Mountain View, CA, USA), and GPU model was NVIDIA GeForce RTX 4060 Ti (Nvidia, Santa Clara, CA, USA). The software environment used was a Windows 11 23H2 operating system, CUDA version 12.1, programming language Python 3.6, and deep learning framework Pytorch 1.10. All subsequent experiments were conducted using this platform.

2.12. Performance Evaluation

In this study, accuracy was used to evaluate the training results of the model. The accuracy was calculated as follows:

$$ACC = \frac{TP + TN}{TP + FP + FN + TN} \tag{8}$$

where ACC is the accuracy, TP is the number of true positive samples, TN is the number of true negative samples, FP is the number of false positive samples, and FN is the number of false negative samples.

3. Results

3.1. Creating a Dataset

To facilitate the analysis, a preprocessed hyperspectral image was processed. An image with a wavelength of 1000.5995 nm was selected. The sample exhibited a relatively clear outline in the band image. A grayscale histogram is used to separate the sample from the image, obtain an outline of each seed, and generate a binary mask. A hyperspectral image with the background removed was obtained by multiplying the binary mask by the image of all bands. The image was then cut using a binary mask to obtain the hyperspectral image of each seed. The flowchart is presented in Figure 3.

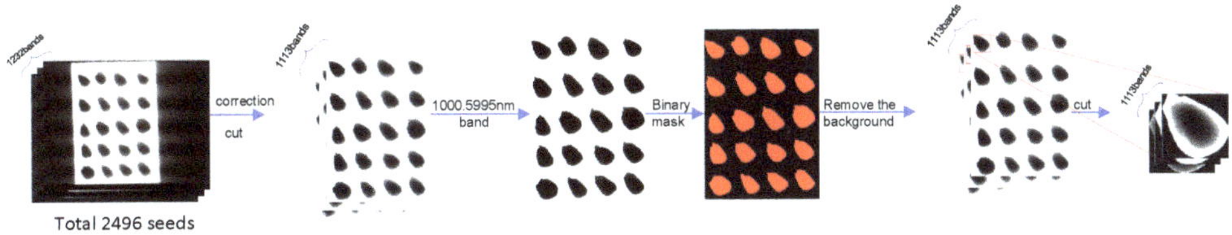

Figure 3. Hyperspectral image processing procedure.

3.2. Hyperspectral Image Dimensionality Reduction

In this study, PCA, FA, and KPCA were used to extract features. The feature extraction process is presented in Figure 4.

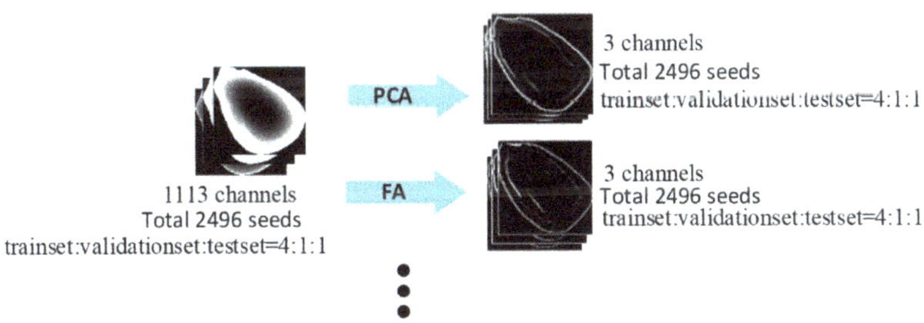

Figure 4. Feature extraction.

3.2.1. Determination of the Number of Components

We randomly selected hyperspectral images of some seeds and downscaled them using PCA, FA, and KPCA, and the explained variance of each component calculated. Table 2 presented the results for one of the seeds. It can be seen that the cumulative explained variance of the first three components exceeds 99% in all three methods. Therefore, we set the final number of components to three.

Table 2. Explained variance of each component.

Components	1	2	3	4	5	6	7
PCA	0.9506	0.0389	0.0055	0.0020	0.0010	0.0008	0.0003
FA	0.9413	0.0478	0.0059	0.0020	0.0013	0.0010	0.0003
KPCA	0.9510	0.0389	0.0055	0.0020	0.0010	0.0008	0.0003

3.2.2. Combined Feature Extraction

Considering that different feature extraction methods extract features with different emphases, combinations of two of the three methods were used to extract the features together. We first use one method to go down to some (>3) dimensions and then use another method to go to 3 dimensions. After a comparative study, we determined that we would first drop to 12 dimensions. This number of dimensions retains the majority of information and avoids the noise associated with more components.

3.2.3. Edge Detection and Linear Stretching

After feature extraction for each corn seed image, we obtain the corresponding three-channel image. First, we perform Sobel edge detection on this three-channel image. The result of Sobel edge detection is still a three-channel image. We perform Laplace edge detection on the grayscale image of each channel of this image, and then perform linear stretching so that the value of each pixel of the grayscale map is between 0 and 255. The three grayscale maps are then synthesized into a three-channel image to obtain the processed result. Finally, the synthesized image was resized to a uniform size of 224 × 224 and saved in JPG format.

3.3. Classification Results

3.3.1. Comparison of Dimensionality Reduction Methods

For the dimension reduction results obtained from different feature extraction methods, ResNet-18, ShuffleNet-V2, MobileNet-V3, ResNeSt-18, EfficientNet-V2, and MobileNet-V4 were used for training. The cross-entropy loss function was used uniformly, with a batch size of 32 and training epoch of 60. The optimizer was selected as Adam and the learning rate was adjusted using the StepLR function, where the number of learning rate decrease intervals was set to five and the learning rate adjustment multiple was set to 0.5. The results of the validation set are presented in Table 3:

Table 3. Accuracy of the validation set.

	ResNet18	ShuffleNetV2	MobileNetV3	ResNeSt18	EfficientNetV2	MobileNetV4
FA	0.933	0.928	0.930	0.938	0.918	0.921
FA + KPCA	0.938	**0.952**	0.947	0.935	0.940	0.938
FA + PCA	0.935	0.945	0.930	0.940	0.925	0.923
KPCA	0.918	0.930	0.925	0.933	0.930	0.918
KPCA + FA	**0.954**	0.947	0.930	**0.957**	**0.954**	**0.945**
KPCA + PCA	0.925	0.933	0.938	0.928	0.928	0.918
PCA	0.925	0.928	0.933	0.947	0.925	0.899
PCA + FA	0.947	0.945	**0.954**	0.950	0.942	0.916
PCA + KPCA	0.923	0.928	0.925	0.933	0.940	0.918

Bold numbers in Table 3 indicate the results with the highest classification accuracy for each network. As presented in this Table, these results correspond to three feature extraction methods, including FA + KPCA, KPCA + FA, and PCA + FA. Where FA + KPCA means FA down to 12 dimensions, then KPCA down to 3 dimensions; KPCA + FA means KPCA down to 12 dimensions, then FA down to 3 dimensions; PCA + FA means PCA down to 12 dimensions, then FA down to 3 dimensions.

3.3.2. Combined Dataset

In machine vision, images are typically processed by adding noise and rotations. This enables one image to be augmented into multiple images, ultimately allowing the limited data to produce a value equal to that of the additional data. In this study, different feature extraction methods were used to extract different features from original hyperspectral images. Combining these different dimensionality reduction results enabled the classification network to obtain more features and improve the accuracy of the classification results. The above three-dimensional reduction results for FA + KPCA, KPCA + FA, and PCA + FA were combined into a new dataset. The composition of the combined dataset is presented in Table 4. Notice from Table 4 that unlike the training and calibration sets, the test set does not combine the downscaling results corresponding to the three methods but are independent of each other.

Table 4. Combined dataset.

Set		IN	BR	IC	SC	Total
Training		1200	1104	1440	1248	4992
Validation		300	276	360	312	1248
	FA + KPCA	100	92	120	104	416
Test	KPCA + FA	100	92	120	104	416
	PCA + FA	100	92	120	104	416

3.3.3. Classification Results for Combined Datasets

Six models were trained using the combined dataset. The highest accuracies in the test set corresponding to FA + KPCA, KPCA + FA, and PCA + FA are listed in Table 5.

Table 5. Classification accuracy for the combined dataset.

	ResNet18	Shufflenetv2	Mobilenetv3	ResNest18	Efficientnetv2	Mobilenetv4
FA + KPCA	0.978	0.971	0.945	0.971	0.986	0.933
KPCA + FA	0.978	0.978	0.945	0.983	0.986	0.947
PCA + FA	0.978	0.978	0.950	0.983	0.986	0.964

As presented in Table 5, the network with the best classification performance was Efficientnetv2, with an accuracy of 98.6%, and this was followed by ResNeSt (98.3%).

3.4. Model Comparison

The accuracy of Efficientnetv2 reached 98.6% and the accuracy of ResNest reached 98.3%. The difference between the two was not significant. Therefore, we compared the two in terms of FLOPs, the total number of parameters to be trained in the network model (Params), frames per second (FPS), and the memory required for inference (memory). The results of these comparisons are presented in Table 6. Efficientnetv2 exhibited lower FLOPs than did ResNest18, whereas ResNest18 outperformed Efficientnetv2 in terms of Params, FPS, and Memory. A higher FPS indicated that more images were processed simultaneously. A smaller Memory implies that fewer resources are available. Therefore, considering practical applications, we recommend using ResNest18 as the classification network.

Table 6. Model comparison.

	Efficientnetv2	ResNeSt18	ResNeSt_E
Accuracy	0.986	0.983	0.990
FLOPs (M)	2925.85	3663.96	3454.79
Params (M)	22.10	17.07	15.82
FPS (img/s)	12.7	17.0	19.2
Memory (M)	139.00	97.19	80.37

3.5. *Model Improvements*

3.5.1. Efficient Multi-Scale Attention Module

Efficient multi-scale attention (EMA) is an efficient attention mechanism introduced in 2023 [43]. In machine-vision tasks, channel or spatial attention mechanisms can produce clearer feature representations. Based on coordinate attention (CA), the authors improved the sequential processing through a grouping structure and proposed an EMA module without dimensionality reduction. The goal of EMA is to reduce the computational cost while preserving the information of each channel. The EMA transforms parts of the channels into batch dimensions and divides the channel dimension into several subfeatures so that the spatial semantic features are evenly distributed in each feature group.

3.5.2. ResNeSt_E

Based on ResNeSt and the EMA, this study proposes an improved ResNeSt_E network, the structure of which is illustrated in Figure 5. We reduced the number of network layers of ResNeSt and added an EMA module to improve accuracy while simultaneously reducing the memory of the model and improving the FPS, and this made the model more suitable for end devices.

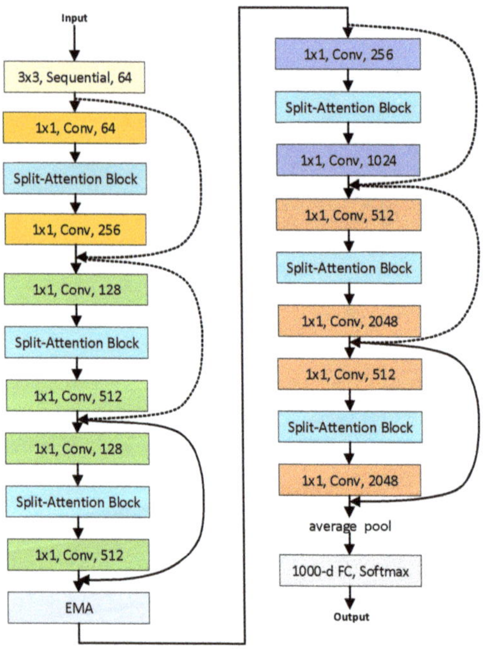

Figure 5. Schematic depicting the functioning of ResNeSt_E.

3.5.3. Training Model

Training ResNeSt_E on the combined dataset. The hyperparameters of the training process are set as follows: the batch size is 32; the epoch is 60; the loss function is the cross-entropy loss function; the optimizer is Adam; the learning rate is adjusted by using the StepLR function; the number of learning rate descent intervals is set to 5; and the learning rate adjustment multiplier is set to 0.5. The training process and results are presented in Figure 6.

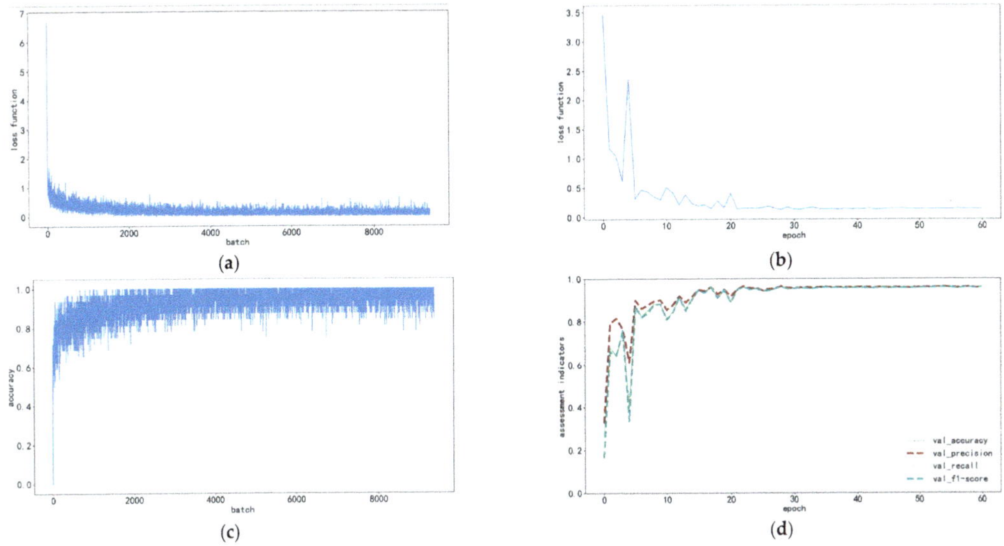

Figure 6. Training process of ResNeSt_E on combined dataset: (**a**) training set loss function, (**b**) validation set loss function, (**c**) training set accuracy, (**d**) assessment indicators for the classification of validation set.

3.5.4. Test Set Results

The confusion matrix obtained by predicting the test set using the trained ResNeSt_E is presented in Figure 7.

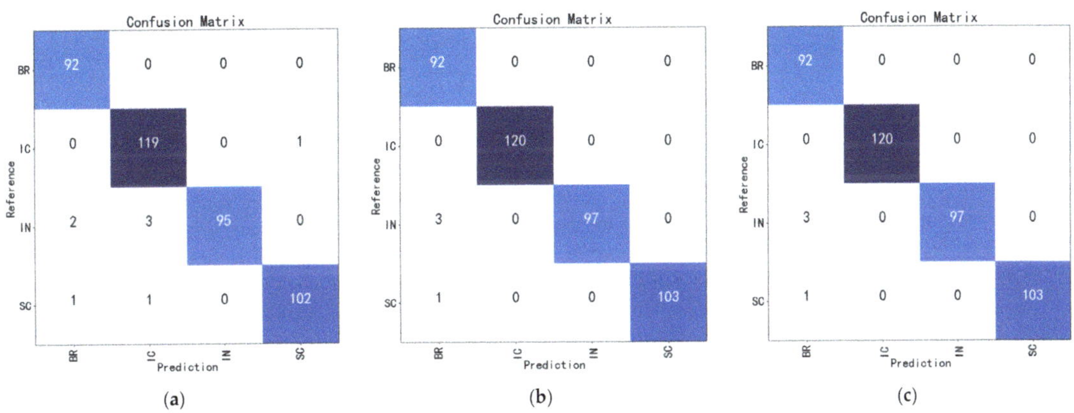

Figure 7. Confusion matrix of ResNeSt_E on the test set: (**a**) FA + KPCA, (**b**) KPCA + FA, (**c**) PCA + FA.

In Figure 7, it can be concluded that the accuracy of FA + KPCA is 0.981, KPCA + FA is 0.990 and PCA + FA is 0.990. The FLOPs, Params, FPS, and Memory of ResNeSt_E were calculated and compared to those of the ResNeSt18 and Efficientnetv2 models. The results are summarized in Table 6.

As listed in Table 6, ResNeSt_E achieved the highest accuracy of 99.0%. Compared to ResNeSt18, the highest accuracy, FLOPs, Params, FPS, and Memory of ResNeSt_E were all improved. Compared with Efficientnetv2, ResNeSt_E exhibited larger FLOPs but higher accuracy and FPS, fewer parameters and less memory, and was more suitable for end devices.

3.6. Selection of Dimensionality Reduction Methods

The accuracies of the classification results of Efficientnetv2, ResNeSt18, and ResNeSt_E for KPCA + FA and PCA + FA are the same for the test set. Therefore, the operational efficiencies of the two models were compared.

For each of the four seed categories, 25 hyperspectral images were captured for a total of 100 images. KPCA + FA and PCA + FA were used to reduce the dimensionality of 100 hyperspectral images, and the completion times were compared. The results demonstrated that PCA + FA took 47.86 s and KPCA + FA took 12354.25 s. Thus, PCA + FA was much more efficient than was KPCA + FA. Therefore, when applying the trained model in practice, we recommend using PCA + FA, as that can significantly improve efficiency while ensuring accuracy.

4. Discussion

In studies that use hyperspectral images to detect crop quality, the average spectrum of each sample area is typically obtained as the spectral curve of the target, and detection is subsequently performed based on this [44,45]. In this study, cracks in corn seeds, particularly internal cracks, occupied a very small area throughout the seeds. If the average spectrum of each seed is extracted for detection, large errors are produced. Therefore, the detection in this study was primarily based on spatial texture features.

We compared the performance of the three feature extraction methods and six joint methods in each classification network and then selected three feature extraction methods that included FA + KPCA, KPCA + FA, and PCA + FA. We combined the dimensionality reduction results of the three methods into a single dataset, and this allowed the classification network to obtain more features and improve the classification results. We compared the performances of six classification networks on the combined dataset and selected two classification networks, Efficientnetv2 and ResNeSt18. We compared the accuracy of the two models, including FLOPs, Params, FPS, and memory. Although the accuracy of Efficientnetv2 was slightly higher than that of ResNeSt18, the parameters, FPS, and memory of ResNeSt18 were better than that of Efficientnetv2, and this made ResNeSt18 more suitable for application in end-devices. Therefore, we chose to improve it using ResNeSt18. We propose an improved ResNeSt_E network based on the ResNeSt and EMA modules. ResNeSt_E achieved higher accuracy with a higher number of parameters, FPS, and Memory than did Efficientnetv2.

We compare studies related to mechanical damage to crop seeds in Table 7. It can be seen that our work is of interest. We used hyperspectral imaging to identify mechanical damage in corn seeds, and we identified both internal and surface damage in corn seeds with 99% accuracy. Our study provides a reference for related work.

Table 7. Comparison of related studies.

Research Object	Location of Damage	Detection Technology	Classification Algorithm	Accuracy	Ref.
corn	surface	image	improved BCK-YOLOv7	96.9%	Wang et al [18]
corn	surface	image	YOLOv4-small	93%	Li et al. [19]
soybean	surface	near-infrared spectra	random forest	84%	Wang et al. [20]
corn	internal	image	Cascsde model	92.7%	Li et al. [22]
corn	internal	image	Optimized S2ANet	95.91%	Zhang et al [23]
rice	internal	near-infrared spectra	PLS-DA, KNN, SVM, RF	91.3%	Wang et al. [24]
corn	internal	X-ray imaging	improved YOLOv8	99.66%	Chen et al. [25]
corn	Internal and surface	Hyperspectral Imaging	ResNeSt_E	99%	this study

5. Conclusions

Hyperspectral imaging was used to identify mechanical damage in corn seeds. Few existing studies have investigated mechanical damage using hyperspectral technology for seed quality detection. Furthermore, the detection of mechanical damage in corn seeds typically involves only one aspect. For example, identification only occurs in the case of internal cracks, or only in the case of surface damage. In this study, we divided corn seeds into four categories that included intact, broken, internally cracked, and surface cracked, and we successfully identified both internal and surface cracks. We compared multiple feature extraction methods, and based on the comparison results, we recommended using three feature extraction methods (FA + KPCA, KPCA + FA, and PCA + FA) in the model training process. PCA + FA was used to apply the trained model to the device. We propose combining the dimensionality reduction results of different feature extraction methods to form a combined dataset that can provide additional features to the network during training. We compared common classical lightweight networks and proposed a ResNeSt_E classification network based on ResNeSt, that achieved 99.0% accuracy while optimizing the parameters, FPS, and memory. This study identified the mechanical damage to corn seeds and provided a new method for identifying internal and surface cracks in corn seeds. This study has some limitations. Although we considered this situation in an actual application, we could not deploy it in a terminal, and this does not represent the actual situation. This study used more spatial texture features and did not fully explore features in the spectral dimension. These shortcomings should be addressed in future studies.

Author Contributions: Writing the original draft, Writing—review and editing, Resources, Data Curation, Funding acquisition, Investigation, H.H.; Writing the original draft, Conceptualization, Methodology, Formal analysis, Software, Validation, Investigation, Y.L.; Validation, Resources, Data curation, writing—review and editing, Supervision, Project administration, and funding acquisition, S.Z. (Shiping Zhu); investigation and methodology, C.F.; Investigation, Formal analysis, S.Z. (Shaoqi Zhang); Resources, Funding acquisition, and project administration, L.S.; Project administration and resources, T.S.; Investigation, Data curation, C.L. All authors have read and agreed to the published version of the manuscript.

Funding: This work was supported by Research on Rapid Detection and Evaluation Methods for Seed Displacement Quality of Planters under the Major Science and Technology Project of Henan Province: R&D and Industrialization of Key Equipment for High-Performance Tillage, Planting, and Harvesting of Major Grain Crops funded by the Henan Provincial Department of Science and Technology (Project No. 231100110200).

Institutional Review Board Statement: Not applicable.

Data Availability Statement: The original contributions presented in the study are included in the article; further inquiries can be addressed to the corresponding author.

Acknowledgments: We would like to thank the editors and reviewers for their professional advice on this manuscript.

Conflicts of Interest: The authors declare no conflicts of interest.

References

1. Deng, H.; Zheng, W.; Shen, Z.; Štreimikienė, D. Does fiscal expenditure promote green agricultural productivity gains: An in-vestigation on corn production. *Appl. Energy* **2023**, *334*, 120666. [CrossRef]
2. Erenstein, O.; Jaleta, M.; Sonder, K.; Mottaleb, K.; Prasanna, B. Global maize production, consumption and trade: Trends and R&D implications. *Food Secur.* **2022**, *14*, 1295–1319. [CrossRef]
3. Erenstein, O.; Chamberlin, J.; Sonder, K. Estimating the global number and distribution of maize and wheat farms. *Glob. Food Secur.* **2021**, *30*, 100558. [CrossRef]
4. Hundal, J.; Takhar, P.S. Experimental study on the effect of glass transition on moisture profiles and stress-crack formation during continuous and time-varying drying of maize kernels. *Biosyst. Eng.* **2010**, *106*, 156–165. [CrossRef]
5. Zheng, Z.; Ren, L.; Fu, H.; Yang, P.; Lv, L.; Xu, J.; Yang, D. Effect of glass transition on the formation of drying cracks in the component parts of maize kernels. *Biosyst. Eng.* **2023**, *236*, 131–146. [CrossRef]

6. Rocha-Villarreal, V.; Hoffmann, J.F.; Vanier, N.L.; Serna-Saldivar, S.O.; García-Lara, S. Hydrothermal treatment of maize: Changes in physical, chemical, and functional properties. *Food Chem.* **2018**, *263*, 225–231. [CrossRef]
7. Sun, T.; Cao, R.; Liu, J.; Wang, K. Mechanism of crack formation in corn during microwave drying process. *Cereal Chem.* **2024**, *101*, 563–576. [CrossRef]
8. Kruszelnicka, W.; Leda, P.; Tomporowski, A.; Ambrose, K. Breakage behavior of corn kernels subjected to repeated loadings. *Powder Technol.* **2024**, *435*, 119372. [CrossRef]
9. Shahbazi, R.; Shahbazi, F. Effects of cushion box and closed let-down ladder usage on mechanical damage during corn kernel handling: Cracking. *J. Stored Prod. Res.* **2022**, *99*, 102006. [CrossRef]
10. Neri, I.; Caponi, S.; Bonacci, F.; Clementi, G.; Cottone, F.; Gammaitoni, L.; Figorilli, S.; Ortenzi, L.; Aisa, S.; Pallottino, F.; et al. Real-Time AI-Assisted Push-Broom Hyperspectral System for Precision Agriculture. *Sensors* **2024**, *24*, 344. [CrossRef]
11. Santana, D.C.; de Queiroz Otone, J.D.; Baio, F.H.R.; Teodoro, L.P.R.; Alves, M.E.M.; da Silva Junior, C.A.; Teodoro, P.E. Machine learning in the classification of asian rust severity in soybean using hyperspectral sensor. *Spectrochim. Acta Part A Mol. Biomol. Spectrosc.* **2024**, *313*, 124113. [CrossRef]
12. Xuan, G.; Jia, H.; Shao, Y.; Shi, C. Protein content prediction of rice grains based on hyperspectral imaging. *Spectrochim. Acta Part A Mol. Biomol. Spectrosc.* **2024**, *320*, 124589. [CrossRef]
13. Zhao, W.; Liu, S.; Li, X.; Han, X.; Yang, H. Fast and accurate wheat grain quality detection based on improved YOLOv5. *Comput. Electron. Agric.* **2022**, *202*, 107426. [CrossRef]
14. Liu, W.; Luo, B.; Kang, K.; Xia, Y.; Zhang, H. Non-destructive detection of single corn seed vigor based on visible/near-infrared spatially resolved spectroscopy combined with chemometrics. *Spectrochim. Acta Part A Mol. Biomol. Spectrosc.* **2024**, *312*, 124089. [CrossRef] [PubMed]
15. Javanmardi, S.; Miraei Ashtiani, S.-H.; Verbeek, F.J.; Martynenko, A. Computer-vision classification of corn seed varieties using deep convolutional neural network. *J. Stored Prod. Res.* **2021**, *92*, 101800. [CrossRef]
16. Yang, D.; Zhou, Y.; Jie, Y.; Li, Q.; Shi, T. Non-destructive detection of defective maize kernels using hyperspectral imaging and convolutional neural network with attention module. *Spectrochim. Acta Part A Mol. Biomol. Spectrosc.* **2024**, *313*, 124166. [CrossRef]
17. Yang, J.; Ma, X.; Guan, H.; Yang, C.; Zhang, Y.; Li, G.; Li, Z.; Lu, Y. A quality detection method of corn based on spectral technology and deep learning model. *Spectrochim. Acta Part A Mol. Biomol. Spectrosc.* **2024**, *305*, 123472. [CrossRef] [PubMed]
18. Wang, Q.; Yang, H.; He, Q.; Yue, D.; Zhang, C.; Geng, D. Real-Time Detection System of Broken Corn Kernels Based on BCK-YOLOv7. *Agronomy* **2023**, *13*, 1750. [CrossRef]
19. Li, X.; Du, Y.; Yao, L.; Wu, J.; Liu, L. Design and Experiment of a Broken Corn Kernel Detection Device Based on the Yolov4-Tiny Algorithm. *Agriculture* **2021**, *11*, 1238. [CrossRef]
20. Wang, L.; Huang, Z.; Wang, R. Discrimination of cracked soybean seeds by near-infrared spectroscopy and random forest variable selection. *Infrared Phys. Technol.* **2021**, *115*, 103731. [CrossRef]
21. Wei, S.; Xiao, B.; Xie, W.; Wang, F.; Chen, P.; Yang, D. Stress simulation and cracking prediction of corn kernels during hot-air drying. *Food Bioprod. Process.* **2020**, *121*, 202–212. [CrossRef]
22. Li, J.; Zhao, B.; Wu, J.; Zhang, S.; Lv, C.; Li, L. Stress-Crack detection in maize kernels based on machine vision. *Comput. Electron. Agric.* **2022**, *194*, 106795. [CrossRef]
23. Zhang, Y.; Lv, C.; Wang, D.; Mao, W.; Li, J. A novel image detection method for internal cracks in corn seeds in an industrial in-spection line. *Comput. Electron. Agric.* **2022**, *197*, 106930. [CrossRef]
24. Wang, L.; Wang, W.; Huang, Z.; Zhen, S.; Wang, R. Discrimination of internal crack for rice seeds using near infrared spectroscopy. *Spectrochim. Acta Part A Mol. Biomol. Spectrosc.* **2024**, *319*, 124578. [CrossRef] [PubMed]
25. Chen, S.; Li, Y.; Zhang, Y.; Yang, Y.; Zhang, X. Soft X-ray image recognition and classification of maize seed cracks based on image enhancement and optimized YOLOv8 model. *Comput. Electron. Agric.* **2024**, *216*, 108475. [CrossRef]
26. Dong, P.-F.; Xie, R.-Z.; Wang, K.-R.; Ming, B.; Hou, P.; Hou, J.-F.; Xue, J.; Li, C.-H.; Li, S.-K. Kernel crack characteristics for X-ray computed microtomography (μCT) and their relationship with the breakage rate of maize varieties. *J. Integr. Agric.* **2020**, *19*, 2680–2689. [CrossRef]
27. Jiao, Y.; Wang, Z.; Shang, Y.; Li, R.; Hua, Z.; Song, H. Detecting endosperm cracks in soaked maize using μCT technology and R-YOLOv7-tiny. *Comput. Electron. Agric.* **2023**, *213*, 108232. [CrossRef]
28. Saha, D.; Manickavasagan, A. Machine learning techniques for analysis of hyperspectral images to determine quality of food products: A review. *Curr. Res. Food Sci.* **2021**, *4*, 28–44. [CrossRef] [PubMed]
29. Zhang, W.; Li, Z.; Sun, H.-H.; Zhang, Q.; Zhuang, P.; Li, C. SSTNet: Spatial, Spectral, and Texture Aware Attention Network Using Hyperspectral Image for Corn Variety Identification. *IEEE Geosci. Remote Sens. Lett.* **2022**, *19*, 5514205. [CrossRef]
30. Zhang, L.; Wei, Y.; Liu, J.; An, D.; Wu, J. Maize seed fraud detection based on hyperspectral imaging and one-class learning. *Eng. Appl. Artif. Intell.* **2024**, *133*, 108130. [CrossRef]
31. Qiao, M.; Cui, T.; Xia, G.; Xu, Y.; Li, Y.; Fan, C.; Han, S.; Dong, J. Integration of spectral and image features of hyperspectral imaging for quantitative determination of protein and starch contents in maize kernels. *Comput. Electron. Agric.* **2024**, *218*, 108718. [CrossRef]
32. Xue, H.; Xu, X.; Yang, Y.; Hu, D.; Niu, G. Rapid and Non-Destructive Prediction of Moisture Content in Maize Seeds Using Hy-perspectral Imaging. *Sensors* **2024**, *24*, 1855. [CrossRef] [PubMed]

33. Lu, B.; Dao, P.D.; Liu, J.; He, Y.; Shang, J. Recent Advances of Hyperspectral Imaging Technology and Applications in Agriculture. *Remote. Sens.* **2020**, *12*, 2659. [CrossRef]
34. Bro, R.; Smilde, A.K. Principal component analysis. *Anal. Methods* **2014**, *6*, 2812–2831. [CrossRef]
35. Gaskin, C.J.; Happell, B. On exploratory factor analysis: A review of recent evidence, an assessment of current practice, and recommendations for future use. *Int. J. Nurs. Stud.* **2014**, *51*, 511–521. [CrossRef]
36. Schölkopf, B.; Mika, S.; Smola, A.; Rätsch, G.; Müller, K.R. Kernel Principal Component Analysis. In Proceedings of the International Conference on Artificial Neural Networks—ICANN '97: 7th International, Lausanne, Switzerland, 8–10 October 1997.
37. He, K.; Zhang, X.; Ren, S.; Sun, J. Deep Residual Learning for Image Recognition. In Proceedings of the IEEE Conference on Computer Vision and Pattern Recognition, Las Vegas, NV, USA, 27–30 June 2016; pp. 770–778.
38. Ma, N.; Zhang, X.; Zheng, H.-T.; Sun, J. ShuffleNet V2: Practical Guidelines for Efficient CNN Architecture Design. In Proceedings of the European Conference on Computer Vision (ECCV), Munich, Germany, 8–14 September 2018; pp. 116–131. [CrossRef]
39. Howard, A.; Sandler, M.; Chu, G.; Chen, L.C.; Chen, B.; Tan, M.; Wang, W.; Zhu, Y.; Pang, R.; Vasudevan, V.; et al. Searching for Mobilenetv3. In Proceedings of the IEEE/CVF International Conference on Computer Vision, Seoul, Republic of Korea, 27 October–2 November 2019; pp. 1314–1324.
40. Zhang, H.; Wu, C.; Zhang, Z.; Zhu, Y.; Lin, H.; Zhang, Z.; Sun, Y.; He, T.; Mueller, J.; Manmatha, R.; et al. Resnest: Split-Attention Networks. In Proceedings of the IEEE/CVF Conference on Computer Vision and Pattern Recognition, New Orleans, LA, USA, 19–24 June 2022; pp. 2736–2746.
41. Tan, M.; Le, Q. Efficientnetv2: Smaller Models and Faster Training. In Proceedings of the International Conference on Machine Learning, Online, 18–24 July 2021; pp. 10096–10106.
42. Qin, D.; Leichner, C.; Delakis, M.; Fornoni, M.; Luo, S.; Yang, F.; Wang, W.; Banbury, C.; Ye, C.; Akin, B.; et al. Mobilenetv4-universal models for the mobile ecosystem. *arXiv* **2024**, arXiv:2404.10518.
43. Ouyang, D.; He, S.; Zhang, G.; Luo, M.; Guo, H.; Zhan, J.; Huang, Z. Efficient Multi-Scale Attention Module with Cross-Spatial Learning. In Proceedings of the ICASSP 2023—2023 IEEE International Conference on Acoustics, Speech and Signal Processing, Rhodes Island, Greece, 4–10 June 2023; pp. 1–5.
44. Yuan, W.; Zhou, H.; Zhou, Y.; Zhang, C.; Jiang, X.; Jiang, H. In-field and non-destructive determination of comprehensive maturity index and maturity stages of *Camellia oleifera* fruits using a portable hyperspectral imager. *Spectrochim. Acta Part A Mol. Biomol. Spectrosc.* **2024**, *315*, 124266. [CrossRef]
45. Wu, N.; Weng, S.; Xiao, Q.; Jiang, H.; Zhao, Y.; He, Y. Rapid and accurate identification of bakanae pathogens carried by rice seeds based on hyperspectral imaging and deep transfer learning. *Spectrochim. Acta Part A Mol. Biomol. Spectrosc.* **2024**, *311*, 123889. [CrossRef]

agriculture

MDPI

Article

Vegetation Phenology Changes and Recovery after an Extreme Rainfall Event: A Case Study in Henan Province, China

Yinghao Lin [1,2], Xiaoyu Guo [1], Yang Liu [1], Liming Zhou [1], Yadi Wang [1,2], Qiang Ge [1,*] and Yuye Wang [1]

1 Henan Key Laboratory of Big Data Analysis and Processing, School of Computer and Information Engineering, Henan University, Kaifeng 475001, China; linyh@henu.edu.cn (Y.L.); guoxy718@163.com (X.G.); sea@vip.henu.edu.cn (Y.L.); lmzhou@henu.edu.cn (L.Z.); yadiwang@henu.edu.cn (Y.W.); wangyuye@henu.edu.cn (Y.W.)

2 Shenzhen Research Institute of Henan University, Shenzhen 518000, China

* Correspondence: gq@henu.edu.cn

Abstract: Extreme rainfall can severely affect all vegetation types, significantly impacting crop yield and quality. This study aimed to assess the response and recovery of vegetation phenology to an extreme rainfall event (with total weekly rainfall exceeding 500 mm in several cities) in Henan Province, China, in 2021. The analysis utilized multi-sourced data, including remote sensing reflectance, meteorological, and crop yield data. First, the Normalized Difference Vegetation Index (NDVI) time series was calculated from reflectance data on the Google Earth Engine (GEE) platform. Next, the 'phenofit' R language package was used to extract the phenology parameters—the start of the growing season (SOS) and the end of the growing season (EOS). Finally, the Statistical Package for the Social Sciences (SPSS, v.26.0.0.0) software was used for Duncan's analysis, and Matrix Laboratory (MATLAB, v.R2022b) software was used to analyze the effects of rainfall on land surface phenology (LSP) and crop yield. The results showed the following. (1) The extreme rainfall event's impact on phenology manifested directly as a delay in EOS in the year of the event. In 2021, the EOS of the second growing season was delayed by 4.97 days for cropland, 15.54 days for forest, 13.06 days for grassland, and 12.49 days for shrubland. (2) Resistance was weak in 2021, but recovery reached in most areas by 2022 and slowed in 2023. (3) In each year, SOS was predominantly negatively correlated with total rainfall in July (64% of cropland area in the first growing season, 53% of grassland area, and 71% of shrubland area). In contrast, the EOS was predominantly positively correlated with rainfall (51% and 54% area of cropland in the first and second growing season, respectively, and 76% of shrubland area); however, crop yields were mainly negatively correlated with rainfall (71% for corn, 60% for beans) and decreased during the year of the event, with negative correlation coefficients between rainfall and yield (−0.02 for corn, −0.25 for beans). This work highlights the sensitivity of crops to extreme rainfall and underscores the need for further research on their long-term recovery.

Keywords: crop yield; Duncan analysis; Google Earth Engine; NDVI; vegetative growth; phenological parameters; climate variability

1. Introduction

Vegetation phenology, the study of seasonal changes in plant communities, is crucial for understanding ecosystem functioning and strongly influences the carbon balance of ecosystems [1]. Phenological changes serve as primary cues for species to adjust to climate anomalies and such changes are sensitive to extreme climate events. However, the response mechanisms involved vary depending on the study area and vegetation types [2,3]. For instance, Shen et al. [4] found that alpine vegetation had the greatest temperature sensitivity (−3.3 °C/day) but the lowest rainfall sensitivity (−0.024 day/mm) for the start of the growing season (SOS), while steppe vegetation had the lowest temperature sensitivity (−1.9 °C/day) yet the greatest rainfall sensitivity (−0.108 day/mm). Piao et al. [5]

demonstrated that extreme cold conditions have led to a delay in SOS and an advance at the end of the growing season (EOS). Gong et al. [6] investigated the impacts of Hurricane Michael—it struck the U.S. Gulf of Mexico on 10 October 2018—on vegetation phenology in local subtropical longleaf pine forest sites, finding that this hurricane hastened post-storm fall senescence, leading to a 33-day advancement in EOS and 95-day reduction in the length of the growing season (LOS) at xeric sites. Liu et al. [7] identified a positive correlation between pre-season mean air temperature, total rainfall, and EOS by investigating vegetation phenology in China's temperate regions from 1982 to 2011. Most recently, Sun et al. [8] investigated how vegetation phenology responded to extreme temperature and rainfall events that differed in intensity on the Tibetan Plateau, from 2000 to 2018. Their work showed that high-intensity rainfall has advanced the SOS in about 54% of the region's area and delayed the EOS in 65% of it, that hot weather has advanced both the SOS and EOS in about 60% of the region, and that severe cold weather has delayed the SOS but advanced the EOS in 60% of the region.

Henan Province, located in the middle and lower reaches of the Yellow River Basin in east-central China, has a well-developed agricultural industry and a cropland area of about 81,500 km^2, ranking it second among the country's provincial cropland areas. Several scholars have studied the vegetation phenology in this province. Zhang et al. [9] quantified the effects of temperature, rainfall, solar radiation, and wind on maize phenology, from 1971 to 2020, by using a comprehensive climate suitability model. This revealed temperature and rainfall as the main climatic factors affecting yield variability, while low sunshine and high winds could adversely impact crop yield to some extent. Liu et al. [10] quantitatively analyzed the spatiotemporal changes in maize phenology and its sensitivity to changes in major climatic factors, from 1981 to 2009, by using a climate tendency rate and sensitivity analysis. Their findings uncovered a rate of change of −0.01 day/a to −0.17 day/a for the seedling-to-maturity phase of maize, with the LOS changing (increasing) at a rate of 0.04 day/a. Yet far fewer studies have addressed the mechanisms by which extreme climatic events alter phenology, whose research is imperative [3,11].

On or around 20 July 2021, Henan Province experienced a rare and large-scale extreme rainfall disaster, known as the "7.20" event. According to the China Meteorological Administration, the heavy rainfall was caused chiefly by an immense volume of water vapor brought by Typhoon In-Fa. The terrain exacerbated the risk situation, leading to huge amounts of rainfall falling on windward slopes. Waterlogged crops incurred oxygen deficiency in their roots, growth inhibition, dieback, and collapse, as well as greater susceptibility to pests and diseases. Altogether, this caused severe damage to crops such as corn and soybeans, culminating in stark declines in their yield and quality, serious economic losses for farmers, and extensive damage to the province's agroecosystems [12].

Remote sensing technology, due to its capacity for large-scale observations at relatively low costs, has become an essential tool in disaster and risk monitoring [13,14]. The Normalized Difference Vegetation Index (NDVI), derived from the Moderate Resolution Imaging Spectroradiometer (MODIS), has been widely used to invert land surface phenology (LSP) [15]. Using the Google Earth Engine (GEE) platform, Pan et al. [16] analyzed Landsat 7/8 and Sentinel 2A/B surface reflectance data NDVI to extract the phenological characteristics of different vegetation types to delineate the planted area of winter crops in their study area. Agriculture is the economic backbone of Henan Province, and flooding there caused by extreme rainfall is a prominent threat to its crop yields. This paper takes the extreme rainfall event in July 2021 as an example and Henan Province as the study area. The NDVI time series was first generated using surface reflectance data from 2018–2023. Next, the SOS and EOS of these six years were extracted and the changes in phenology and recovery after the event were calculated. Finally, corn and bean yield data along with meteorological data were combined to examine correlations between rainfall and phenology or yield. The results can provide valuable insights for improving ecological protection, management, ecosystem services, and disaster prevention and mitigation policy-making in Henan Province.

2. Materials and Methods

2.1. Study Area

Henan Province spans 31°23′ N to 36°22′ N in latitude and 110°21′ E to 116°39′ E in longitude, encompassing 167,000 km^2. Henan has a continental monsoon climate, transitioning from a warm temperate zone in its north to a subtropical zone in its south [17]. The east-central region of Henan is experiencing an increasing frequency of extreme rainfall events. Over the past 50 years, rainfall has gradually declined from south to north, resulting in marked differences between the regions, with an average annual rainfall of 735.94 mm [18]. Rainfall is largely concentrated in June, July, and August, which together account for 60% to 70% of the annual total. Henan is one of the political, economic, and cultural centers of China. By the end of 2023, its permanent population reached 98.15 million, ranking it third in total population at the provincial level [19].

Henan is also a typical Chinese province with multiple growing seasons per calendar year. The single-growing season is prevalent in the western and southern mountainous regions of Henan, with forests and natural grasslands predominating in the west, and single-season rice fields dominant in the south. The double-growing season region is mainly located in the eastern plains of Henan, which is prime agricultural land, with the first growing season used to cultivate winter wheat and the second for corn, peanuts, and soybeans. The triple-growing-season region is less common, being sporadically distributed in Henan's northern part in which vegetables are mainly cultivated [20]. As shown in Figure 1, the vegetation types in the study areas where the total rainfall exceeded 500 mm in the week before and after the '7.20' extreme rainfall event (hereon referred to as the extreme rainfall zone) consist mostly of cropland, followed by shrubland, with a few patches of forest and grassland. Representative sample points were labeled representative sample points for four different vegetation types: cropland, shrubland, forest, and grassland (in both extreme and non-extreme rainfall zones).

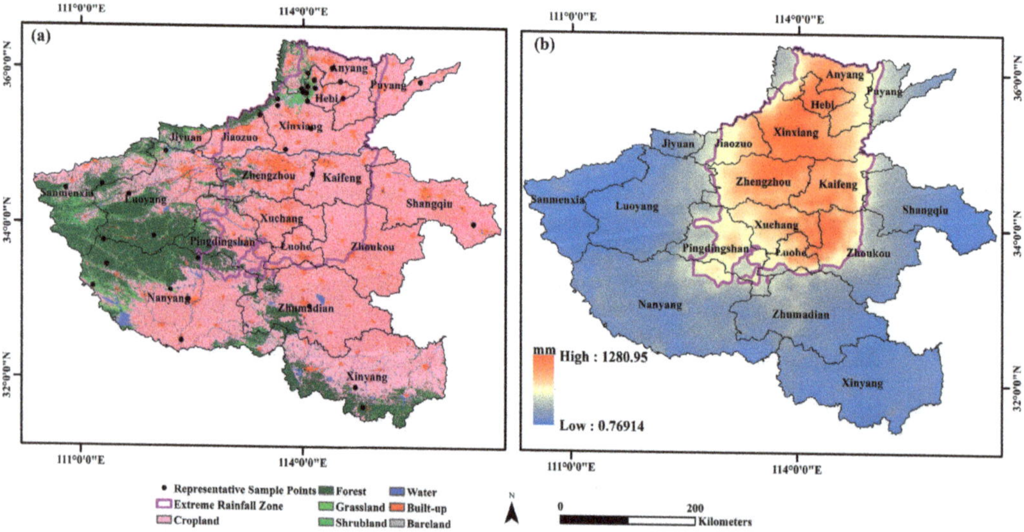

Figure 1. (**a**) Map of the study area, Henan Province (China), and the distribution of its land cover types. (**b**) Cumulative rainfall from 17 July to 23 July 2021. The irregular purple line-demarcated zone is where the cumulative rainfall exceeded 500 mm, with its cities delineated by gray lines.

2.2. Data

This study used the 2020 version of the 30-m global surface coverage data GlobeLand30, published by the National Geomatics Center of China [21]. They were produced by the Ministry of Natural Resources of China and donated to the United Nations on 15 September 2020, the 75th anniversary of the latter's founding. The three-season vegetable growing areas mentioned in this study are subsumed under the cropland category of this dataset.

When using the Maximum Value Composite approach, the 8-d or 16-d resolution MODIS vegetation index products may lose values for important phenological transition dates [22,23]. Further, NDVI is more sensitive than other metrics in detecting differences in LSP parameters [24]. So, based on the GEE platform [25] and using the atmospherically corrected "MODIS/Terra Surface Reflectance Daily L2G Global 1 km and 500 m SIN Grid v061" (MOD09GA) [26] product, NDVI time series with a temporal resolution of 3 days and a spatial resolution of 500 m for the 2018–2023 period were batch computed [27]:

$$\mathrm{NDVI} = \frac{\mathrm{NIR} - \mathrm{RED}}{\mathrm{NIR} + \mathrm{RED}} \tag{1}$$

In the above equation, NIR is the reflectance value for the near-infrared band (841–876 nm), and RED is the reflectance value for the red band (620–670 nm). The value of NDVI can range from -1 to 1, with larger positive values representing greater vegetation greenness, and smaller positive values representing less vegetation greenness; negative values represent non-vegetation types, such as clouds, water, and snow as ground cover [28,29].

The annual production (weight) data and planted area data of corn and bean in the study area were obtained from the statistical yearbook compiled by the Henan Provincial Bureau of Statistics [30]. Yield in this study was defined as weight divided by planted area, in units of 'tons ha^{-1}'.

The Climate Prediction Center Morphing Technique (CMORPH), developed by the National Oceanic and Atmospheric Administration's Climate Prediction Centre of the United States of America (NOAA/CPC, [31]), was used to visualize rainfall and associated data calculations in this study. This dataset has a temporal resolution of 30 min and a spatial resolution of 8 km. The calculation of total rainfall was performed in MATLAB (v.R2022b) software, using the 'cmorph' band of the rainfall NetCDF file, with a data matrix of 2 $\times$ number of rows $\times$ number of columns, where 2 corresponds to the two values of rainfall for one hour. The total rainfall was calculated by adding up the two layers, with the spatial resolution resampled to the same as that of the NDVI data.

2.3. Methods

The GEE platform and a personal desktop computer were used to conduct this study. As illustrated in Figure 2, NDVI time series were first calculated from reflectance data in the GEE platform. Next, the R environment (R v.4.3.3 and R Studio v.2023.06.2+561, [32]) was used for the phenology parameters' extraction, with SPSS (v.26.0.0.0) software used for Duncan's analysis and MATLAB (v.R2022b) software to analyze the effects of total rainfall upon NDVI and LSP [33,34].

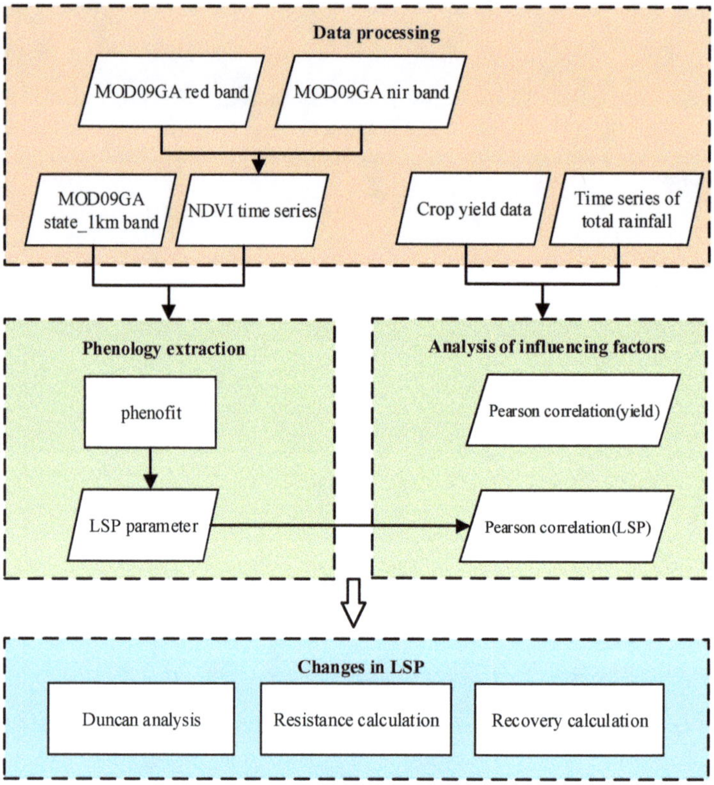

Figure 2. The flowchart of this vegetation phenology study.

2.3.1. Extraction of Phenology Indicators

To extract the phenology indicators, the 'phenofit' package of Kong et al. [20] was used because it can categorize the number of growing seasons per pixel and is suitable for phenology extraction in multi-season crop areas. The 'qc_StateQA' function was used to initialize the weights based on the quality assessment band "state_1km" of MOD09GA data; pixel weights were set to 1 (no cloud, snow, aerosol), 0.2 (cloud, snow, aerosol), and 0.5 (all other cases) based on a pixel's value in this band.

The 'check_input' function was utilized to discard any spikes and missing values for the time-series NDVI. The boundary ylu was defined as the upper and lower quartiles of the data, and those point values outside the boundary were designated the lower ylu boundary, with 0.02 assigned as their point weights. To delineate the number of growing seasons, a coarse fit was performed using the 'wSG' function with the parameter frame set to 48. A fine fit was then performed using the 'Beck' function to capture the rapid changes in vegetation during each growing season. The 'wTSM weight update' function was applied to adjust the weight values during the fitting process. Finally, the 'TRS' thresholding method was employed to extract the phenology parameters.

2.3.2. Resistance and Recovery Rates of Vegetation and Rainfall Recovery Rates

Two evaluation metrics of ecosystem resilience were used to assess the resistance, R_t, and recovery, R_c, of forest, grassland, and shrubland vegetation to the extreme rainfall event. For crops, given that these are annual plants, the recovery rate R_{cp} of rainfall in 2022 and 2023 was considered to measure the stability of the environment of such plots. The equations for each are as follows [35–37]:

$$R_t = \frac{NDVI_1}{NDVI_0} \quad (2)$$

$$R_c = \frac{NDVI_i - NDVI_1}{NDVI_0 - NDVI_1} \quad (3)$$

$$R_{cp} = \frac{p_i - p_1}{p_0 - p_1} \quad (4)$$

where, $NDVI_0$ is the NDVI before the extreme rainfall event (2020); $NDVI_1$ is the NDVI in the year of the extreme rainfall event (2021); and $NDVI_i$ is the NDVI in each year after the event (2022, 2023). The p_0 is the rainfall before the extreme rainfall event (2020); p_1 is the rainfall in the year of the extreme rainfall event (2021); and p_i is the rainfall in each year after the event (2022, 2023). Larger values indicate greater resistance. Recovery can then be categorized into six ratings, as shown in Table 1, based on the R_c and R_{cp} values obtained [38].

Table 1. Recovery rating scores and their quantification and qualification.

Rating	Range of Recovery	Recovery
1	<0	Poor
2	0–0.25	Relatively poor
3	0.25–0.5	Average
4	0.5–0.75	Relatively good
5	0.75–1.0	Good
6	>1	Fully

2.3.3. Data Analysis

Many research methods have been used to study changes in vegetation phenology and correlations between variables [39,40]. The present study relied on three methods:

(1) For each vegetation type, a one-way analysis of variance (ANOVA) was used to determine the temporal effect of extreme rainfall on each phenological parameter. That is, whether the SOS differed among three subperiods: before and during the extreme (2018~2021), one year (2022) after extreme rainfall, and two years (2023) after extreme rainfall; and whether EOS differed among four subperiods: before the extreme rainfall (2018~2020), the year of extreme rainfall (2021), the year after extreme rainfall (2022), and two years after extreme rainfall (2023). Before performing the ANOVA, tests for normality and homogeneity of variances were conducted to ensure the validity of the analysis. Then, after each ANOVA, Duncan's multiple range test—which can provide careful analysis of between-group differences—was used for the pairwise statistical comparisons of the mean values of each phenological parameter between the treatment groups (i.e., subperiods).

(2) The spatial correlation of rainfall data from 2018 to 2023 with SOS or EOS, as well as that from 2018 to 2022 with crop yield, was analyzed using Pearson's correlation coefficient, which was calculated in MATLAB (v.R2022b) software using Equation (4) [39]:

$$r = \frac{\sum_{i=1}^{n} (p_i - \overline{p})(x_i - \overline{x})}{\sqrt{\sum_{i=1}^{n} (p_i - \overline{p})^2 \sum_{i=1}^{n} (x_i - \overline{x})^2}} \quad (5)$$

where p_i is the total rainfall in July of the year i; x_i is the phenological parameter (SOS or EOS) or yield data of year i; and $\overline{p}$ and $\overline{x}$ are the average values of rainfall and phenology or the mean yield of year n, respectively. The value of r ranges from −1 to

1, and the larger the absolute value of *r* is, the larger the effect of rainfall on phenology or yield, and vice versa.

(3) The correlation between rainfall and crop yield for a given year was calculated using the Pearson correlation coefficient in SPSS (v.26.0.0.0) software [41], as per Equation (5):

$$\rho_{m,n} = \frac{cov(m,n)}{\sigma_m \sigma_n} \tag{6}$$

In the above equation, *m* is the total rainfall in July annually, and *n* is the annual corn or bean yield.

3. Results

3.1. Changes in Phenology after Extreme Rainfall

The changes in the NDVI of representative pixels of each vegetation type from 2018 to 2023 are shown in Figure 3, since shrubland pixels are all distributed in the extreme rainfall zone, there is no non-extreme rainfall zone data for shrubland. Irrespective of type, the vegetation index in the extreme rainfall zone decreased after the extreme rainfall event of "7.20" in 2021. Furthermore, for both cropland and grassland, their curves are lower in the extreme rainfall zone than in the non-extreme rainfall zone.

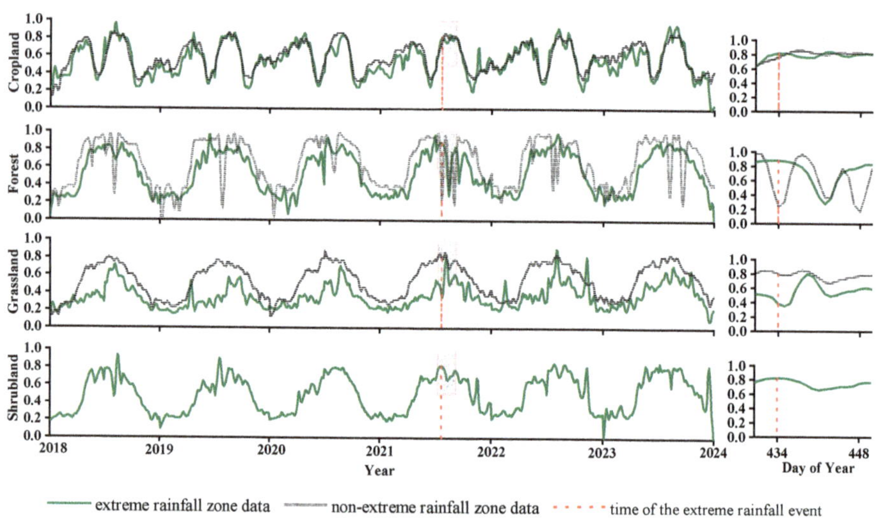

Figure 3. Trends in the NDVI of each vegetation type, from 2018 to 2023. Green curves show representative sample point values in the extreme rainfall zone while gray curves show those in non-extreme rainfall zone; the vertically dashed red lines and red rectangles mark the occurrence of the extreme rainfall event in 2021 in Henan Province (China).

These trends in NDVI highlight the immediate impact of extreme rainfall events on vegetation health. To further quantify this effect and assess the impact on the phenology of each vegetation type, ANOVA analyses were conducted, with the results summarized in Table 2.

The mean values of SOS (SOS1) for the first growing season of cropland were significantly different from those for pre-extreme rainfall, advancing by 2.33 days in 2022, but delayed significantly in 2023. Mean values for EOS (EOS1) were significantly delayed by 3.04 days in 2022 and by another 0.37 days in 2023. Mean values of SOS for the second growing season (SOS2) differed significantly from those for pre-extreme rainfall with a delay of 1.4 days in 2022 and another significant delay in 2023. Although the mean EOS

(EOS2) was significantly delayed by 4.97 days after extreme rainfall in 2021, it arrived significantly earlier in 2022 but then significantly later in 2023.

Table 2. Results of the variance analysis (ANOVA) testing the temporal impact of an extreme rainfall event on LSP parameters. Different letters indicate significant differences within each column subset at the $p < 0.05$ level, with a to d corresponding to increasing mean values.

Vegetation Type	LSP	*p* Value	Years	Mean
Cropland	SOS1 *	0	2018–2021	32.28 (b)
			2022	29.95 (a)
			2023	42.39 (c)
	EOS1 *	0.006	2018–2021	144.40 (a)
			2022	147.44 (b)
			2023	147.81 (c)
	SOS2 *	0	2018–2021	180.82 (a)
			2022	182.22 (c)
			2023	181.62 (b)
	EOS2 *	0	2018–2020	272.73 (a)
			2021	277.70 (c)
			2022	275.47 (b)
			2023	283.00 (d)
Forest	SOS	0	2018–2021	85.58 (a)
			2022	85.91 (b)
			2023	88.09 (c)
	EOS	0	2018–2020	318.02 (a)
			2021	333.56 (d)
			2022	321.80 (b)
			2023	325.63 (c)
Grassland	SOS	0.101	2018–2021	86.60 (a)
			2022	86.36 (a)
			2023	88.34 (b)
	EOS	0.954	2018–2020	315.60 (a)
			2021	328.66 (c)
			2022	324.09 (b)
			2023	323.94 (b)
Shrubland	SOS	0.063	2018–2021	99.46 (b)
			2022	96.86 (a)
			2023	100.14 (c)
	EOS	0.998	2018–2020	313.90 (a)
			2021	326.39 (c)
			2022	316.61 (b)
			2023	326.28 (c)

* SOS1 and EOS1 represent the phenology parameters for the first growing season, whereas SOS2 and EOS2 correspond to the phenology parameters for the second growing season.

For forest vegetation, the mean SOS was significantly delayed by 0.33 days in 2022, the year after the extreme rainfall event, in comparison to the pre-extreme rainfall mean, and then significantly delayed by 2.18 days in 2023. The mean EOS in 2021 was significantly different from the pre-extreme rainfall mean, with a delay of 15.54 days on average; however, in 2022, one year after the event, the EOS had significantly advanced by 11.76 days. Nevertheless, in 2023, the EOS mean value was again significantly delayed vis-à-vis the previous year, but still earlier than 2021, which may be attributed to the greater total rainfall in 2023.

Grassland vegetation exhibited a mean SOS in 2022 that was comparable to pre-extreme rainfall conditions, with an average advance of 0.24 days. However, there was a significant difference between the grassland's mean SOS in 2023 and that before the event, corresponding to a delay of 1.98 days. Compared with mean values for 2018 to 2020, the mean EOS in 2021 was significantly delayed by 13.06 days, and in 2022 it was significantly advanced by 4.57 days, albeit not returning to pre-extreme rainfall levels. No significant differences were found between 2023 and 2022.

For shrubland vegetation, the mean SOS in 2022 differed significantly from that for pre-extreme rainfall, coming 2.6 days earlier on average, and then delayed significantly in 2023. The mean EOS was significantly different between pre-extreme rainfall versus after the event in 2021, being delayed by 12.49 days on average. Although the EOS did come significantly earlier in 2022, it did not recover to pre-rainstorm levels, and it was significantly delayed again in 2023.

3.2. Spatiotemporal Patterns of Resistance and Recovery

The results for the resistance (R_t) and recovery (R_c) of forest, grassland, and shrubland vegetation after the extreme rainfall event are illustrated in Figure 4. The overall resistance of the forest (R_tNDVImean = 0.91) indicated a reduction in its NDVI across the study area. In 2022, the forest recovery was not ideal (R_cNDVImean = −1.99); however, good forest recovery occurred in 2023 (R_cNDVImean = 0.89). For grassland, the overall resistance (R_tNDVImean = 0.90) revealed a decrease in NDVI. The NDVI did not recover in 2022 (R_cNDVImean = −1.65), but it did recover well in 2023 (R_cNDVImean = 0.99). Shrubland resistance also indicated a decrease in NDVI (R_tNDVImean = 0.88), with no recovery of NDVI in 2022 (R_cNDVImean = −1.21) followed by a good recovery in 2023 (R_cNDVImean = 0.77).

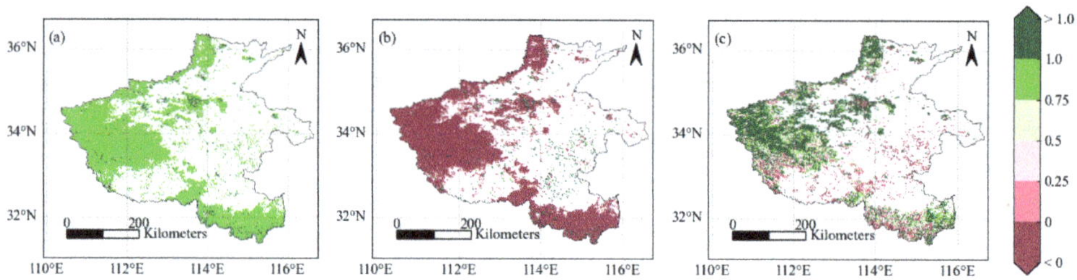

Figure 4. (**a**) Spatial distribution of resistance values of vegetation after the extreme rainfall event in 2021, in Henan Province, China. In (**b**,**c**) are the patterns of vegetation recovery in 2022 and 2023, respectively.

The mean values for the resistance and recovery of forest, grassland, and shrubland vegetation in the extreme rainfall zone are detailed in Table 3, indicating significant differences in recovery among the vegetation types. The potential reasons for these differences in sensitivity are discussed in Section 4.2.

Table 3. Mean resistance and recovery of forest, grassland, and shrubland vegetation in the extreme rainfall zone.

Vegetation Type	Resistance	Recovery in 2022	Recovery in 2023
Forest	0.90	−1.60	1.06
Grassland	0.92	−1.28	1.26
Shrubland	0.88	−1.21	0.77

Results for the recovery (R_{cp}) of rainfall in the distribution area of cropland after the extreme rainfall event are shown in Figure 5, revealing a moderate recovery in 2022 (R_{cp}mean = 0.59) and good recovery in 2023 (R_{cp}mean = 0.77) compared to the period before the extreme event.

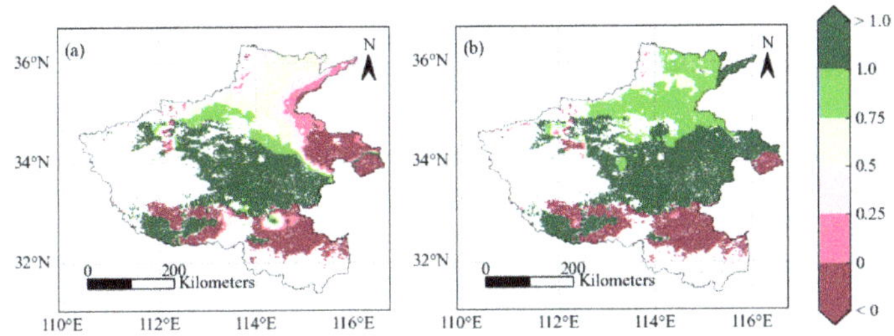

Figure 5. The patterns of rainfall recovery in (**a**) 2022 and (**b**) 2023, respectively.

3.3. Correlation between Rainfall and LSP

The spatial distribution of Pearson's correlation coefficients between cropland phenology and rainfall is shown in Figure 6. The proportion of pixels with a negative correlation between the SOS for cropland vegetation in the first growing season and the total rainfall in July was 64%, i.e., the SOS happened earlier as rainfall increased. However, 51% of the pixels featured a positive correlation between the EOS and the total rainfall in July, i.e., the EOS was delayed by more rainfall. In the second growing season, 53% and 54% of the pixels were, respectively, distinguished by positive correlations of SOS and EOS with total rainfall in July. Taken together, these results were consistent with the trends in phenology changes of cropland vegetation (top of Table 2).

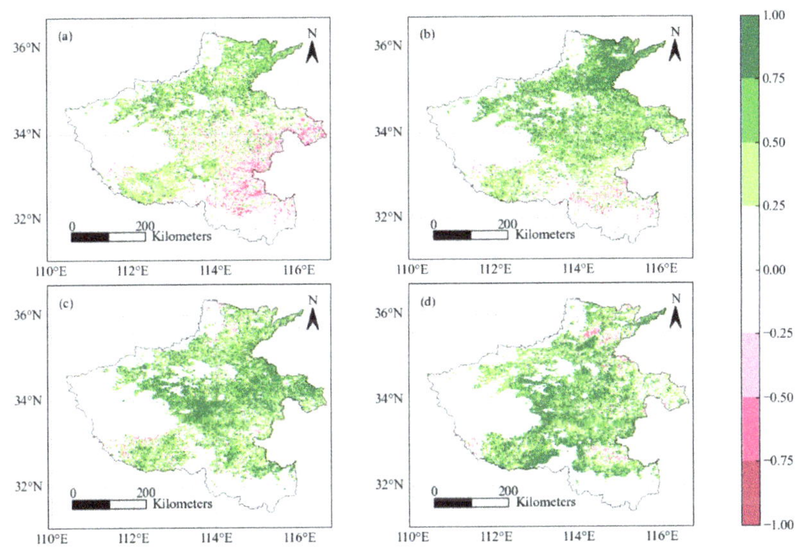

Figure 6. Spatial distribution of Pearson's r coefficient values in cropland: (**a**–**d**) are the correlations of SOS1, EOS1, SOS2, and EOS2 with rainfall, respectively.

The spatial distribution of Pearson's correlation coefficients between forest phenology and rainfall is shown in Figure 7. The analysis indicates that 39% of the pixels showed a negative correlation between the SOS of forest vegetation and total rainfall in July, whereas the proportion of pixels with a positive correlation was noticeably higher, at 59%. The proportion of pixels with a negative correlation between the EOS in July and total rainfall reached 55%, exceeding those with a positive correlation (43%).

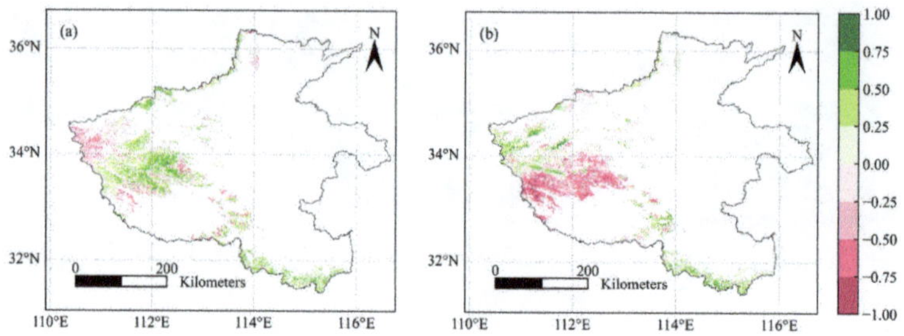

Figure 7. Spatial distribution of Pearson's *r* coefficient values for the forest (**a**) SOS and (**b**) EOS correlations with rainfall, in Henan Province, China.

The spatial distribution of Pearson's correlation coefficients between grassland phenology and rainfall is shown in Figure 8. Overall, 53% of the pixels had a negative correlation between the SOS of grassland vegetation and total rainfall in July, this is higher than those with a positive correlation (43%). The proportion of pixels with a negative correlation between the EOS and total rainfall in July reached 49%, only slightly higher than those with a positive correlation (47%).

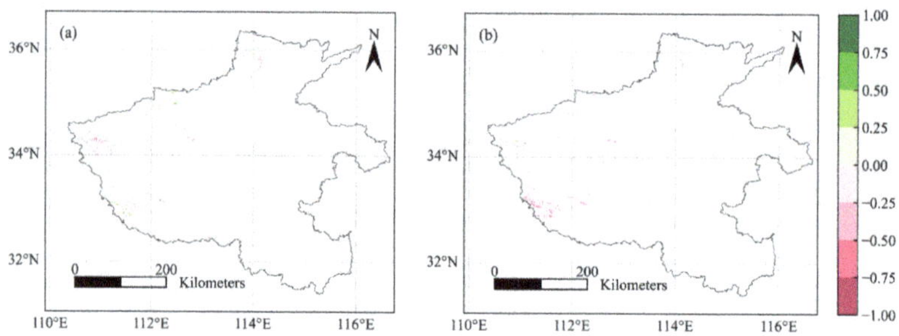

Figure 8. Spatial distribution of Pearson's *r* coefficient values for the grassland (**a**) SOS and (**b**) EOS correlations with rainfall, in Henan Province, China.

The spatial distribution of Pearson's correlation coefficients between shrubland phenology and rainfall is shown in Figure 9. The proportion of pixels with a negative correlation between the SOS of shrubland vegetation and total rainfall in July reached 71%, whereas the proportion of pixels with a positive correlation was much lower, at 26%. Conversely, 22% of the pixels showed a negative correlation between the EOS and total rainfall in July, with 76% of pixels being positively correlated.

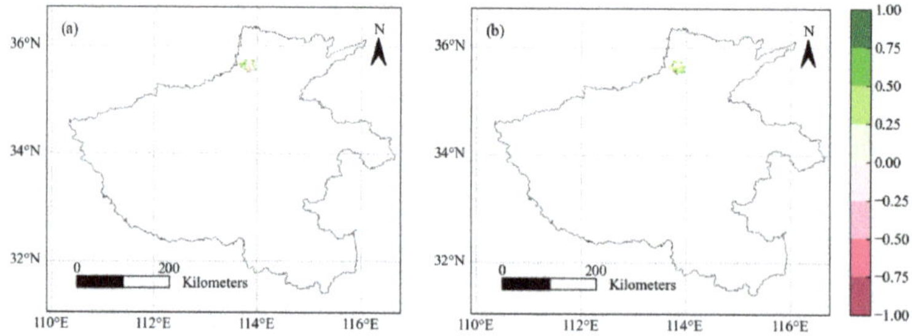

Figure 9. Spatial distribution of Pearson's *r* coefficient values for the shrubland (**a**) SOS and (**b**) EOS correlations with rainfall, in Henan Province, China.

3.4. Relationship between Rainfall and Crop Yield

The spatial distribution of Pearson's correlation coefficients for corn and bean yields vis-à-vis the 2018–2022 July rainfall is shown in Figure 10. Across the cropland region, 71% of the pixels showed a negative correlation between corn yield and rainfall, while the proportion of pixels that had a negative correlation between bean yield and rainfall was even higher, at 60%. These results indicated an increase in rainfall was associated with a decrease in yield.

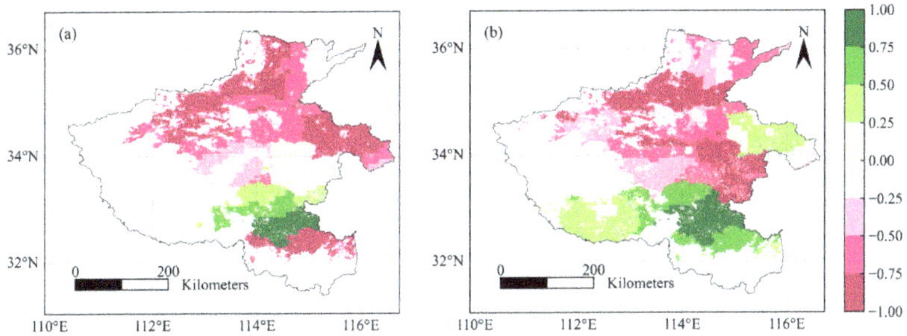

Figure 10. Spatial distribution of Pearson's r coefficients for the (**a**) corn yield and (**b**) bean yield correlations with rainfall, in Henan Province, China.

In the extreme rainfall zone, about 90% of the regions displayed a negative correlation between corn yield and rainfall, as shown in Table 4. Though not as pronounced, 98% of the regions also featured a negative correlation between bean yield and rainfall, and 10% of the pixels had a significant negative correlation.

Table 4. Percentage of correlation coefficients between crop yield and rainfall. Significant positive correlation: $r > 0$, $p < 0.05$. Significant negative correlation: $r < 0$, $p < 0.05$.

Crop	Correlation	Proportion
Corn	Positive correlation	9.9%
	Negative correlation	90.1%
	Significant positive correlation	0%
	Significant negative correlation	3.8%
Bean	Positive correlation	1.3%
	Negative correlation	98.4%
	Significant positive correlation	0%
	Significant negative correlation	10.0%

The correlation coefficients between rainfall and crop yield in a given year are detailed in Table 5 and were negative for both in 2021, indicating that the increase in rainfall led to decreased yields.

Table 5. Pearson correlations between crop yield and rainfall within each year.

Year	Corn Yield	Bean Yield
2018	0.09	0.25
2019	0.11	0.07
2020	−0.08	−0.52
2021	−0.02	−0.25
2022	0.49	0.56

4. Discussion

4.1. Changes in Rainfall by City

The average rainfall in July for each city from 2018 to 2023 is shown in Figure 11. Specifically, in 2021, the average rainfall exceeded 500 mm everywhere except Luoyang City, Sanmenxia City, and Jiyuan City, while rainfall was lowest in Sanmenxia City, which could explain why crop yield there did not decrease in 2021. In 2018 and 2019, the years preceding the heavy rainfall event of this study, the average July rainfall in each city did not exceed 400 mm. In 2020, under the influence of the north-south oscillation of the main rain belt in the Huaihe River Basin, six cities in southeastern Henan (Luohe, Nanyang, Shangqiu, Xinyang, Zhoukou, Zhumadian) received heavy rainfall, with rainfall exceeding 500 mm from 17–19 July [42]. In 2022, the year right after that (2021) of the heavy rainfall event, seven more cities (Kaifeng, Anyang, Hebi, Xinxiang, Puyang, Shangqiu, Zhumadian) received more than 500 mm of rainfall in July [21,43]. For example, the average rainfall in Hebi in July 2023 was nearly 1.8 times that for the same period over many years before [44], reaching 516 mm, while rainfall in the rest of Henan's affected cities returned to normal levels in that year.

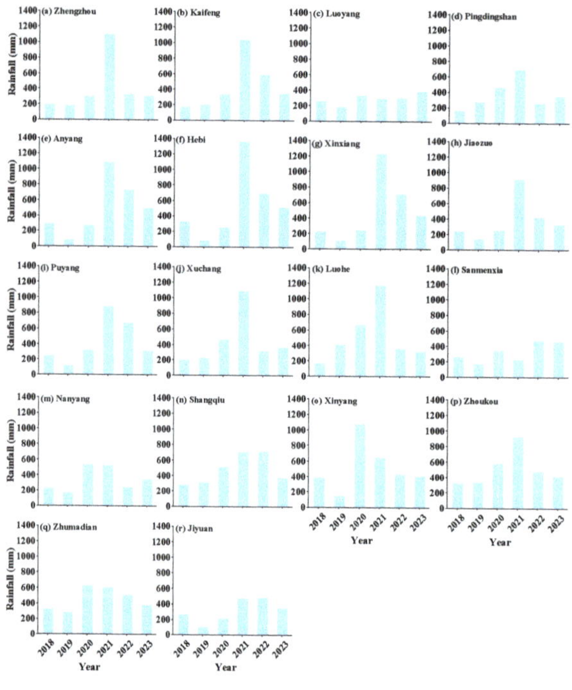

Figure 11. The average rainfall per city in July each year from 2018 to 2023.

4.2. Effects of Extreme Rainfall on Vegetation Phenology

Surprisingly few studies have investigated the response of vegetation phenology to extreme rainfall events. In this case study, MODIS reflectance data were used to calculate vegetation indices from which vegetation phenology parameters were derived. Specifically, this study explored changes in the phenology, resistance, and recovery of vegetation types after an extreme rainfall event and analyzed the factors affecting phenology in combination with climate data. The results indicate that, after the event, the temporal vegetation index curves of various vegetation types in the extreme rainfall area display a decrease, which can be explained by the low NDVI values of pixels caused by vegetation being submerged by flooding. The decrease in forests and shrubs is likely due to changes caused by plant lodging and soil moisture saturation. Further, vegetation's resistance is weaker and the EOS is delayed. The phenological response strategy is affected by rainfall, and the recovery of vegetation differs between different municipalities 1 and 2 years after the event. This study found compelling evidence that the effect of extreme rainfall on the EOS in the same year of the event was mainly a postponement effect.

After the extreme rainfall event in 2021, generally, the SOS occurred earlier and the EOS was delayed. Furthermore, by 2023, vegetation conditions had not yet recovered to their pre-extreme rainfall levels, for which work by Hogan et al. [45] provides a valuable perspective on this phenomenon, pointing out that biodiversity and resilience together influence the recovery time of ecosystems.

Given that the extreme rainfall event occurred in July 2021, the correlation between vegetation phenology and total rainfall in July for each year was further explored. This set of results revealed that rainfall tends to be negatively related to the SOS and positively related to the EOS. This pattern is consistent with the findings of some scholars [8,46,47], yet it contradicts those of other studies [5,40,48,49]. This can be explained by different factors such as drought, fire, hurricanes, extreme cold, soil erosion, and anthropogenic disturbances (e.g., land use and land cover changes). For example, hurricanes can cause sudden loss of foliage and a rapid decline in the leaf area index of the plant community, so that the end of the growing season comes earlier for that vegetation [6,50]. There is also substantial heterogeneity in the interactions between extreme climatic events and different vegetation types [47,51,52]. The influence of climate on phenology is now undeniable. Huang et al. [53] demonstrated that the relative contribution of flooding to SOS2 was 80.1%. Work by Zhang et al. [54] showed that cumulative rainfall reached a certain threshold to stimulate vegetation greening, with a lag in vegetation dormancy of up to 84 days. Using multiple models, Zscheischler et al.'s [55] simulation results enable them to elucidate how ecosystem productivity is increased by extreme rainfall, which enhances the carbon sequestration capacity of terrestrial ecosystems.

4.3. Effects of Extreme Rainfall on Crop Yields

Henan is an important grain-producing province. This study's investigation of the rate of recovery of rainfall in its cropland distribution areas suggests that rainfall is recovering to pre-extreme-event levels on a yearly basis. The research on yield changes in the province shows that, in 2021, the total annual crop yields of all cities were lower than their prior mean, except for bean yields in Nanyang, Shangqiu, Xinyang and Zhumadian, which remained stable. Both corn and bean yields in 2022 rose in comparison to 2021, except for a drop in bean yield in Luoyang City, Pingdingshan, Nanyang, Shangqiu, and Zhumadian City, as shown in Table 6. However, the 2022 yields in most regions remain low compared to their 2018–2020 yields on average. According to the crop planted areas in each city, as detailed in Table 7, the planted areas in Zhengzhou, Pingdingshan, Anyang, Hebi, Xinxiang, Jiaozuo, Shangqiu, and Jiyuan cities did not decrease in 2021 compared to the average of the previous three years, but their grain yields decreased, indicating a generally negative impact of rainfall on crop yields. This phenomenon is consistent with the findings of Liu et al. [56], who pointed out that the physical damage caused by extreme rainfall events during the critical growth period of crops, accompanied by root hypoxia caused by oversaturated soils, can significantly affect the growth and development of crops, culminating in reduced yields. In contrast, the lower rainfall Sanmenxia and Luoyang cities still had lower crop yields, which correlated with the reduction in the planted areas of crops in those two cities.

The correlation analysis between yield and rainfall for 2018–2022 revealed that an increase in rainfall usually leads to a decrease in yield. This is similar to the findings of previous studies; for example, when Pantaleoni et al. [57] examined the impact of an extreme rainfall event on crop yields in Indiana in 2003, soybean yields were significantly lower after the event. The study also showed that although yields recovered in individual areas in some years, overall, the long-term effects of extreme rainfall events on cropland vegetation remained significant. Taken together, this emphasizes the importance of considering extreme weather events in agricultural management and disaster prevention.

Table 6. Annual crop yield of various cities in Henan Province, China.

Cities	Mean Yield * (tons ha^{-1})		Yield in 2021 (tons ha^{-1})		Yield in 2022 (tons ha^{-1})	
	Corn	Beans	Corn	Beans	Corn	Beans
Zhengzhou	4.94	1.90	4.48	1.67	4.81	1.81
Kaifeng	5.37	2.05	4.97	1.94	5.34	2.04
Luoyang	5.29	2.32	4.60	2.10	4.83	1.99
Pingdingshan	5.08	2.78	4.82	2.31	4.82	2.25
Anyang	6.67	2.39	4.70	2.05	6.36	2.54
Hebi	7.23	2.35	2.54	1.16	7.19	2.17
Xinxiang	6.22	3.17	4.55	1.88	5.96	2.78
Jiaozuo	7.33	3.05	5.40	2.11	7.09	2.74
Puyang	6.72	2.85	6.27	2.37	7.01	2.76
Xuchang	6.89	2.83	6.19	2.18	6.67	2.36
Luohe	7.60	2.66	6.99	2.40	7.20	2.46
Sanmenxia	4.76	2.16	4.75	1.78	4.85	1.84
Nanyang	5.03	1.67	4.71	2.18	4.93	1.85
Shangqiu	6.38	2.56	5.25	2.81	6.04	2.61
Xinyang	6.14	1.17	5.68	1.55	5.91	1.95
Zhoukou	6.45	2.42	6.29	2.12	6.38	2.17
Zhumadian	5.79	1.90	5.73	2.13	5.91	2.12
Jiyuan	5.38	2.78	4.75	2.22	5.15	2.26

* Mean yield from 2018 to 2020.

Table 7. Annual crop planted areas of various cities in Henan Province, China.

Cities	Mean Planted Areas * (kha)		Planted Areas in 2021 (kha)		Planted Areas in 2022 (kha)	
	Corn	Beans	Corn	Beans	Corn	Beans
Zhengzhou	134.57	6.26	127.87	4.22	127.64	4.85
Kaifeng	189.32	13.19	187.67	12.00	186.41	14.28
Luoyang	182.16	29.95	196.55	19.90	194.40	23.48
Pingdingshan	198.00	14.09	197.36	13.82	196.73	15.29
Anyang	247.33	4.76	251.56	4.01	253.29	6.30
Hebi	77.90	0.52	78.21	0.37	77.76	1.68
Xinyang	293.59	14.80	309.27	9.62	310.12	12.63
Jiaozuo	121.33	4.41	126.39	1.97	126.96	3.08
Puyang	145.86	23.72	153.27	22.74	155.33	24.70
Xuchang	151.04	42.97	153.59	41.57	155.24	42.03
Luohe	85.68	34.13	92.88	29.58	93.40	30.53
Sanmenxia	58.01	20.95	60.27	19.39	60.20	19.52
Nanyang	454.36	49.97	467.86	33.74	470.35	37.48
Shangqiu	429.03	52.23	445.71	35.74	439.51	42.86
Xinyang	20.99	7.15	15.62	4.40	18.90	3.13
Zhoukou	511.48	104.54	542.82	75.76	544.11	76.67
Zhumadian	435.87	26.19	438.83	25.07	434.85	30.59
Jiyuan	19.91	1.32	20.05	1.34	20.53	1.32

* Mean planted areas from 2018 to 2020.

4.4. Limitations and Outlook

The second-growing season crops in Henan have been boosted by subsidy policies in recent years, so their plantings are increasing annually. According to the 2023 Statistical Yearbook released by the Henan Provincial People's Government, the area of fall crops in the province expanded by 17.84 kha in 2022. This shift not only affected local agricultural yield but also contributed to advancing the SOS to a certain extent. This trend of varietal switching and altered planting density introduces a slew of new challenges and opportunities for both ecological environment and climate response patterns in Henan, which deserves further in-depth study and exploration. The data covered in this study were limited to 3 years after the extreme rainfall event occurred, and the yield data for 2023 are not yet available online and so could not be analyzed in conjunction with other factors, such as sunshine hours and wind speed. Moreover, the effect of soil moisture on NDVI values may be significant at local scales, especially in sparsely vegetated areas, where wetter soils may lead to higher reflectance. It should be noted that this paper is based on statistical analyses performed on a whole-province scale, which did not specifically consider soil moisture effects. Hence, a comprehensive understanding of vegetation restoration dynamics requires continued observation and research over the long term. Future research activity could consider a wider range of environmental variables, including factors such as soil moisture, wind speed, temperature fluctuations, and human intervention, to better understand the long-term effects of extreme rainfall events on vegetation phenology.

5. Conclusions

This unique case study provides insight into differential phenology responses to an extreme rainfall event among vegetation types in Henan Province, China. Vegetation phenology in Henan was extracted from MODIS reflectance data from 2018 to 2023. Significant differences between SOS and EOS after and before the event were analyzed, along with the resistance and recovery of vegetation, the recovery rate of rainfall, the factors affecting NDVI, and the relationships of rainfall to phenological indicators and crop yield. The main conclusions are as follows:

(1) The application of Duncan's analysis was crucial in detecting significant differences between treatment groups after extreme rainfall events, providing robust statistical support for the results. The effect of an extreme rainfall event on phenology directly manifested as a delay in the EOS of the year of the event. In 2021, the EOS of the second growing season was delayed by 4.97 days for cropland, 15.54 days for forest, 13.06 days for grassland, and 12.49 days for shrubland.

(2) Resistance decreased in forest, grassland, and shrubland after the extreme rainfall event. Recovery was good in most areas 1 year after the event, and phenology parameters did not recover 2 years after the event.

(3) The extreme rainfall event negatively impacted crop yields in autumn 2021, and the correlation between yield and rainfall was negative in most areas. The study underscores the need for effective disaster management strategies in agricultural regions prone to extreme weather, particularly in economically vital areas like Henan Province.

There is a clear correlation between phenology and rainfall, which is generally expressed as a negative correlation between SOS and rainfall of the first growing season in cropland, grassland, and shrubland, but as a positive correlation between EOS and rainfall of the first and second growing seasons in cropland and shrubland. The results of this study suggest that attention should be paid to the significant losses caused by extreme rainfall to society and to finding ways to minimize the impact of associated flooding. The government of Henan, given its status as a nationally important economic and grain-producing province, should aim to strengthen disaster prevention and improve urban planning to lessen the potential impact of future extreme weather events on its society and economy.

Author Contributions: Conceptualization, Y.L. (Yinghao Lin), Q.G. and Y.W. (Yuye Wang); methodology, Y.L. (Yinghao Lin), Q.G. and Y.W. (Yuye Wang); software, X.G.; validation, Q.G., Y.L. (Yang Liu) and Y.W. (Yadi Wang); formal analysis, L.Z.; investigation, X.G.; resources, Y.L. (Yinghao Lin); data curation, Y.L. (Yinghao Lin) and X.G.; writing—original draft preparation, X.G.; writing—review and editing, Y.L. (Yinghao Lin) and Q.G.; visualization, Y.W. (Yadi Wang); supervision, Q.G.; project administration, Q.G.; funding acquisition, Y.L. (Yinghao Lin). All authors have read and agreed to the published version of the manuscript.

Funding: This research was funded by the Science and Technology Development Program of Henan Province (No. 242300421639); the Shenzhen Science and Technology Program (No. JCYJ20220530162001003); the Key R&D and Promotion Projects of Henan Province (No. 232102210071); the National Science and Technology Major Project (No. 80-Y50G19-9001-22/23); and a Scientific and Technological Innovation Team of Universities in Henan Province (No. 24IRTSTHN021).

Institutional Review Board Statement: Not applicable.

Data Availability Statement: The dataset used in this paper can be found through the National Basic Geographic Information Center of China: https://www.ngcc.cn/ (accessed on 10 March 2024), the National Oceanic and Atmospheric Administration: https://www.ncei.noaa.gov/ (accessed on 29 March 2024), the Google Earth Engine: https://code.earthengine.google.com/ (accessed on 15 April 2024), and the Henan Provincial Bureau of Statistics: https://tjj.henan.gov.cn/tjfw/tjcbw/tjnj/ (accessed on 15 May 2024).

Acknowledgments: The author would like to thank all contributors to this study.

Conflicts of Interest: The authors declare no conflicts of interest.

References

1. Barichivich, J.; Briffa, K.R.; Osborn, T.J.; Melvin, T.M.; Caesar, J. Thermal growing season and timing of biospheric carbon uptake across the Northern Hemisphere. *Glob. Biogeochem. Cycles* **2012**, *26*, GB4015. [CrossRef]
2. Badeck, F.W.; Bondeau, A.; Böttcher, K.; Doktor, D.; Lucht, W.; Schaber, J.; Sitch, S. Responses of spring phenology to climate change. *New Phytol.* **2004**, *162*, 295–309. [CrossRef]
3. Zhang, J.; Chen, S.; Wu, Z.; Fu, Y. Review of vegetation phenology trends in China in a changing climate. *Prog. Phys. Geogr.* **2022**, *46*, 829–845. [CrossRef]
4. Shen, M.; Piao, S.; Cong, N.; Zhang, G.; Jassens, I.A. Precipitation impacts on vegetation spring phenology on the Tibetan Plateau. *Glob. Chang. Biol.* **2015**, *21*, 3647–3656. [CrossRef] [PubMed]
5. Piao, S.; Zhang, X.; Chen, A.; Liu, Q.; Lian, X.; Wang, X.; Peng, S.; Wu, X. The impacts of climate extremes on the terrestrial carbon cycle: A review. *Sci. China Earth Sci.* **2019**, *62*, 1551–1563. [CrossRef]
6. Gong, Y.; Staudhammer, C.L.; Kenney, G.; Wiesner, S.; Zhang, Y.; Starr, G. Vegetation structure drives forest phenological recovery after hurricane. *Sci. Total Environ.* **2021**, *774*. [CrossRef]
7. Liu, Q.; Fu, Y.H.; Zeng, Z.; Huang, M.; Li, X.; Piao, S. Temperature, precipitation, and insolation effects on autumn vegetation phenology in temperate China. *Glob. Chang. Biol.* **2016**, *22*, 644–655. [CrossRef]
8. Sun, M.; Li, P.; Ren, P.; Tang, J.; Zhang, C.; Zhou, X.; Peng, C. Divergent response of vegetation phenology to extreme temperatures and precipitation of different intensities on the Tibetan Plateau. *Sci. China Earth Sci.* **2023**, *66*, 2200–2210. [CrossRef]
9. Zhang, N.; Qu, Y.; Song, Z.; Chen, Y.; Jiang, J. Responses and sensitivities of maize phenology to climate change from 1971 to 2020 in Henan Province, China. *PLoS ONE* **2022**, *17*, e0262289. [CrossRef]
10. Liu, Y.; Qin, Y.; Ge, Q.; Dai, J.; Chen, Q. Reponses and sensitivities of maize phenology to climate change from 1981 to 2009 in Henan Province, China. *J. Geogr. Sci.* **2017**, *27*, 1072–1084. [CrossRef]
11. He, Z.; Du, J.; Chen, L.; Zhu, X.; Lin, P.; Zhao, M.; Fang, S. Impacts of recent climate extremes on spring phenology in arid-mountain ecosystems in China. *Agric. For. Meteorol.* **2018**, *260–261*, 31–40. [CrossRef]
12. Zhang, Q.; Li, R.; Sun, J.; Lu, F.; Xu, J.; Zhang, F. A Review of Research on the Record-Breaking Precipitation Event in Henan Province, China, July 2021. *Adv. Atmos. Sci.* **2023**, *40*, 1485–1500. [CrossRef]
13. Lan, Q.; Dong, J.; Lai, S.; Wang, N.; Zhang, L.; Liao, M. Flood Inundation Extraction and its Impact on Ground Subsidence Using Sentinel-1 Data: A Case Study of the "7.20" Rainstorm Event in Henan Province, China. *IEEE J. Sel. Top. Appl. Earth Obs. Remote Sens.* **2024**, *17*, 2927–2938. [CrossRef]
14. Rahman, M.S.; Di, L. A Systematic Review on Case Studies of Remote-Sensing-Based Flood Crop Loss Assessment. *Agriculture* **2020**, *10*, 131. [CrossRef]
15. Himani Kanwar, S.S. Phenology and Global Climate Change: A Comprehensive Review. *eJournal Appl. For. Ecol. (eJAFE)* **2023**, *11*, 20–30.
16. Pan, L.; Xia, H.; Zhao, X.; Guo, Y.; Qin, Y. Mapping Winter Crops Using a Phenology Algorithm, Time-Series Sentinel-2 and Landsat-7/8 Images, and Google Earth Engine. *Remote Sens.* **2021**, *13*, 2510. [CrossRef]
17. Shi, B.; Zhu, X.; Hu, Y.; Yang, Y. Drought characteristics of Henan province in 1961-2013 based on Standardized Precipitation Evapotranspiration Index. *J. Geogr. Sci.* **2017**, *27*, 311–325. [CrossRef]
18. Huang, J.; Zhou, L.; Zhang, F.; Hu, Z.; Tian, H. Responses of yield variability of summer maize in Henan province, north China, to large-scale atmospheric circulation anomalies. *Theor. Appl. Climatol.* **2021**, *143*, 1655–1665. [CrossRef]
19. The People's Government of Henan Province. Provincial Situation. Available online: https://www.henan.gov.cn/2024/08-08/3033664.html (accessed on 26 August 2024).
20. Kong, D.; McVicar, T.R.; Xiao, M.; Zhang, Y.; Peña-Arancibia, J.L.; Filippa, G.; Xie, Y.; Gu, X. phenofit: An R package for extracting vegetation phenology from time series remote sensing. *Methods Ecol. Evol.* **2022**, *13*, 1508–1527. [CrossRef]

21. NGCC. National Geomatics Center of China. Available online: https://www.ngcc.cn/ (accessed on 10 March 2024).
22. Testa, S.; Soudani, K.; Boschetti, L.; Borgogno Mondino, E. MODIS-derived EVI, NDVI and WDRVI time series to estimate phenological metrics in French deciduous forests. *Int. J. Appl. Earth Obs. Geoinf.* **2018**, *64*, 132–144. [CrossRef]
23. Zeng, L.; Wardlow, B.D.; Hu, S.; Zhang, X.; Zhou, G.; Peng, G.; Xiang, D.; Wang, R.; Meng, R.; Wu, W. A Novel Strategy to Reconstruct NDVI Time-Series with High Temporal Resolution from MODIS Multi-Temporal Composite Products. *Remote Sens.* **2021**, *13*, 1397. [CrossRef]
24. Liu, W. The Response of NDVI to Drought at Different Temporal Scales in the Yellow River Basin from 2003 to 2020. *Water* **2024**, 16. [CrossRef]
25. Gorelick, N.; Hancher, M.; Dixon, M.; Ilyushchenko, S.; Thau, D.; Moore, R. Google Earth Engine: Planetary-scale geospatial analysis for everyone. *Remote Sens. Environ.* **2017**, *202*, 18–27. [CrossRef]
26. Vermote, E.; Wolfe, R. MODIS/Terra Surface Reflectance Daily L2G Global 1 km and 500 m SIN Grid V061. 2021. Available online: https://lpdaac.usgs.gov/products/mod09gav061/ (accessed on 15 April 2024).
27. Joshi, R.; Singh, A.; Parab, T.; Mandy, J.; Pande, C. Assessing the Impact of Recent Climate Dynamics on Land Since the Last Two Decades (1991–2021) Using LST and NDVI. In *Natural Resource Monitoring, Planning and Management Based on Advanced Programming*; Advances in Geographical and Environmental Sciences; Springer: Singapore, 2024; pp. 269–308.
28. Rocha, A.V.; Shaver, G.R. Advantages of a two band EVI calculated from solar and photosynthetically active radiation fluxes. *Agric. For. Meteorol.* **2009**, *149*, 1560–1563. [CrossRef]
29. Jiang, Z.; Huete, A.; Didan, K.; Miura, T. Development of a two-band enhanced vegetation index without a blue band. *Remote Sens. Environ.* **2008**, *112*, 3833–3845. [CrossRef]
30. Statistical Yearbook of Henan Provincial Bureau of Statistics. Available online: https://tjj.henan.gov.cn/tjfw/tjcbw/tjnj/ (accessed on 15 May 2024).
31. Xie, P.; Robert, J.; Wu, S.; Yoo, S.-H.; Yarosh, Y.; Sun, F.; Lin, R. NOAA CDR Program. NOAA Climate Data Record (CDR) of CPC Morphing Technique (CMORPH) High Resolution Global Precipitation Estimates, Version 1. 2019. 2024. Available online: https://www.ncei.noaa.gov/access/metadata/landing-page/bin/iso?id=gov.noaa.ncdc:C00948 (accessed on 29 March 2024).
32. R Core Team. *R: A Language and Environment for Statistical Computing*; R Foundation for Statistical Computing: Vienna, Austria, 2024; Available online: https://www.R-project.org/ (accessed on 11 May 2024).
33. Kim, S.; Ouyang, M.; Zhang, X. Compute spearman correlation coefficient with Matlab/CUDA. In Proceedings of the 2012 IEEE International Symposium on Signal Processing and Information Technology (ISSPIT), Ho Chi Minh City, Vietnam, 12–15 December 2012; pp. 000055–000060.
34. Rodrigues, L.; Paixao, E. Risk of Zika-related microcephaly: Stable or variable? *Lancet* **2017**, *390*, 824–826. [CrossRef]
35. Portela, A.P.; Goncalves, J.F.; Durance, I.; Vieira, C.; Honrado, J. Riparian forest response to extreme drought is influenced by climatic context and canopy structure. *Sci. Total Environ.* **2023**, *881*, 163128. [CrossRef]
36. Lin, C.-Y.; Lo, H.-M.; Chou, W.-C.; Lin, W.-T. Vegetation recovery assessment at the Jou-Jou Mountain landslide area caused by the 921 Earthquake in Central Taiwan. *Ecol. Model.* **2004**, *176*, 75–81. [CrossRef]
37. Hong, Y.; Zhao, Y.; Wang, Y.; Xin, C.; Zhao, Y. Temporal and spatial variation characteristics of vegetation restoration based on MODIS-NDVI Wenchuan earth quake region in ten years. *Sci. Tecnol. Eng.* **2019**, *19*, 64–71.
38. Li, M.; Li, G.; Xie, Z. Post-flood recovery assessment based on multi-source remote sensing data: A case study of the "7·20" rainstorm in Henan. *Remote Sens. Nat. Resour.* **2024**, *36*, 250–266. [CrossRef]
39. Ying, H.; Zhang, H.; Zhao, J.; Shan, Y.; Zhang, Z.; Guo, X.; Rihan, W.; Deng, G. Effects of spring and summer extreme climate events on the autumn phenology of different vegetation types of Inner Mongolia, China, from 1982 to 2015. *Ecol. Indic.* **2020**, *111*, 105974. [CrossRef]
40. Karimi, S.; Heydari, M.; Mirzaei, J.; Karami, O.; Heung, B.; Mosavi, A. Assessment of Post-Fire Phenological Changes Using MODIS-Derived Vegetative Indices in the Semiarid Oak Forests. *Forests* **2023**, *14*, 590. [CrossRef]
41. Weaver, B.; Wuensch, K.L. SPSS and SAS programs for comparing Pearson correlations and OLS regression coefficients. *Behav. Res. Methods* **2013**, *45*, 880–895. [CrossRef]
42. Elephant Entertainment. How Heavy Is the Rainfall in Henan during This Year's Flood Season? Rainfall in Multiple Areas Breaks Historical Records. Available online: https://baijiahao.baidu.com/s?id=1673085675293448809&wfr=spider&for=pc (accessed on 2 April 2024).
43. Henan Hydrological and Water Resources Monitoring and Reporting Center. Monthly Water Situation Report for July 2022. Available online: http://www.hnssw.com.cn/sqwater1/31705.jhtml (accessed on 3 April 2024).
44. Henan Hydrological and Water Resources Monitoring and Reporting Center. Monthly Water Situation Report for July 2023. Available online: http://www.hnssw.com.cn/l1SwfwL2Sqxx/34398.jhtml (accessed on 5 April 2024).
45. Hogan, J.A.; Feagin, R.A.; Starr, G.; Ross, M.; Lin, T.-C.; O'connell, C.; Huff, T.P.; Stauffer, B.A.; Robinson, K.L.; Lara, M.C.; et al. A Research Framework to Integrate Cross-Ecosystem Responses to Tropical Cyclones. *BioScience* **2020**, *70*, 477–489. [CrossRef]
46. LI, R.; Zhou, G. Responses of woody plants phenology to air temperature in Northeast China in 1980–2005. *Chin. J. Ecol.* **2010**, *29*, 2317–2326. [CrossRef]
47. Piao, S.; Fang, J.; Zhou, L.; Ciais, P.; Zhu, B. Variations in satellite-derived phenology in China's temperate vegetation. *Glob. Chang. Biol.* **2006**, *12*, 672–685. [CrossRef]

48. Jeong, S.-J.; Ho, C.-H.; Gim, H.-J.; Brown, M.E. Phenology shifts at start vs. end of growing season in temperate vegetation over the Northern Hemisphere for the period 1982–2008. *Glob. Chang. Biol.* **2011**, *17*, 2385–2399. [CrossRef]
49. Hwang, T.; Song, C.; Vose, J.M.; Band, L.E. Topography-mediated controls on local vegetation phenology estimated from MODIS vegetation index. *Landsc. Ecol.* **2011**, *26*, 541–556. [CrossRef]
50. Renton, K.; Salinas-Melgoza, A.; Rueda-Hernández, R.; Vázquez-Reyes, L.D. Differential resilience to extreme climate events of tree phenology and cavity resources in tropical dry forest: Cascading effects on a threatened species. *Forest Ecol.* **2018**, *426*, 164–175. [CrossRef]
51. Hu, X.; Huang, B.; Cherubini, F. Impacts of idealized land cover changes on climate extremes in Europe. *Ecol. Indic.* **2019**, *104*, 626–635. [CrossRef]
52. Li, C.; Wang, J.; Hu, R.; Yin, S.; Bao, Y.; Ayal, D.Y. Relationship between vegetation change and extreme climate indices on the Inner Mongolia Plateau, China, from 1982 to 2013. *Ecol. Indic.* **2018**, *89*, 101–109. [CrossRef]
53. Huang, Y.; Chen, X.S.; Zou, Y.A.; Zhang, P.Y.; Li, F.; Hou, Z.Y.; Li, X.; Zeng, J.; Deng, Z.M.; Zhong, J.R.; et al. Exploring the relative contribution of flood regimes and climatic factors to Carex phenology in a Yangtze River-connected floodplain wetland. *Sci. Total Environ.* **2022**, *847*, 157568. [CrossRef] [PubMed]
54. Zhang, X.; Friedl, M.A.; Schaaf, C.B.; Strahler, A.H.; Liu, Z. Monitoring the response of vegetation phenology to precipitation in Africa by coupling MODIS and TRMM instruments. *J. Geophys. Res. Atmos.* **2005**, *110*, 1–14. [CrossRef]
55. Zscheischler, J.; Michalak, A.M.; Schwalm, C.; Mahecha, M.D.; Huntzinger, D.N.; Reichstein, M.; Berthier, G.; Ciais, P.; Cook, R.B.; El-Masri, B.; et al. Impact of large-scale climate extremes on biospheric carbon fluxes: An intercomparison based on MsTMIP data. *Glob. Biogeochem. Cycles* **2014**, *28*, 585–600. [CrossRef]
56. Liu, Y.; Shi, W. The quantitative impacts of drought and flood on crop yields and production in China. In Proceedings of the 2019 8th International Conference on Agro-Geoinformatics (Agro-Geoinformatics), Istanbul, Turkey, 16–19 July 2019; pp. 1–6.
57. Pantaleoni, E.; Engel, B.A.; Johannsen, C.J. Identifying agricultural flood damage using Landsat imagery. *Precis. Agric.* **2007**, *8*, 27–36. [CrossRef]

agriculture

MDPI

Article

Effects of Variety and Growth Stage on UAV Multispectral Estimation of Plant Nitrogen Content of Winter Wheat

Meiyan Shu [1], Zhiyi Wang [1], Wei Guo [1], Hongbo Qiao [1], Yuanyuan Fu [1], Yan Guo [2,3], Laigang Wang [2,3,*], Yuntao Ma [4] and Xiaohe Gu [5]

1 College of Information and Management Science, Henan Agricultural University, Zhengzhou 450002, China; smy511@henau.edu.cn (M.S.); 18838197107@163.com (Z.W.); guowei@henau.edu.cn (W.G.); qiaohb@henau.edu.cn (H.Q.); fyy0201@163.com (Y.F.)
2 Institute of Agricultural Information Technology, Henan Academy of Agricultural Sciences, Zhengzhou 450002, China; guoyan@hnagri.org.cn
3 Key Laboratory of Huang-Huai-Hai Smart Agricultural Technology, Ministry of Agriculture and Rural Affairs, Zhengzhou 450002, China
4 College of Land Science and Technology, China Agricultural University, Beijing 100091, China; yuntao.ma@cau.edu.cn
5 Information Technology Research Center, Beijing Academy of Agriculture and Forestry Sciences, Beijing 100097, China; guxh@nercita.org.cn
* Correspondence: wanglaigang@hnagri.org.cn

Abstract: The accurate estimation of nitrogen content in crop plants is the basis of precise nitrogen fertilizer management. Unmanned aerial vehicle (UAV) imaging technology has been widely used to rapidly estimate the nitrogen in crop plants, but the accuracy will still be affected by the variety, the growth stage, and other factors. We aimed to (1) analyze the correlation between the plant nitrogen content of winter wheat and spectral, texture, and structural information; (2) compare the accuracy of nitrogen estimation at single versus multiple growth stages; (3) assess the consistency of UAV multispectral images in estimating nitrogen content across different wheat varieties; (4) identify the best model for estimating plant nitrogen content (PNC) by comparing five machine learning algorithms. The results indicated that for the estimation of PNC across all varieties and growth stages, the random forest regression (RFR) model performed best among the five models, obtaining R^2, RMSE, MAE, and MAPE values of 0.90, 0.10%, 0.08, and 0.06%, respectively. Additionally, the RFR estimation model achieved commendable accuracy in estimating PNC in three different varieties, with R^2 values of 0.91, 0.93, and 0.72. For the dataset of the single growth stage, Gaussian process regression (GPR) performed best among the five regression models, with R^2 values ranging from 0.66 to 0.81. Due to the varying nitrogen sensitivities, the accuracy of UAV multispectral nitrogen estimation was also different among the three varieties. Among the three varieties, the estimation accuracy of SL02-1 PNC was the worst. This study is helpful for the rapid diagnosis of crop nitrogen nutrition through UAV multispectral imaging technology.

Keywords: winter wheat; variety; unmanned aerial vehicle (UAV); multispectral image; plant nitrogen content (PNC); machine learning

1. Introduction

Winter wheat is one of the significant food crops [1,2]. Nitrogen is a crucial nutrient for crop growth, yield, and quality [3,4]. The improper application of nitrogen fertilizer has detrimental effects on both crops and the farm environment. Nitrogen deficiency will hinder photosynthesis and reduce yield, while excessive nitrogen fertilizer will reduce fertilizer utilization and pollute the environment [5]. Hence, accurate and real-time monitoring of nitrogen content is essential for precise fertilization decision-making and for maintaining stable yields.

Remote sensing has been widely applied for monitoring crop nitrogen status over extensive areas, relying on the correlation between the nitrogen content in plants and canopy spectral responses. Nitrogen affects the composition and content of chlorophyll, which subsequently alters the leaf spectrum. In nitrogen-deficient conditions, plants exhibit reduced height and yellowing leaves. Conversely, in nitrogen-sufficient conditions, crops grow taller and display greener leaves, resulting in spectral responses in the near-infrared and red bands [6]. Numerous studies have utilized non-imaging hyperspectral data to estimate nitrogen status in various crops, including wheat [7], maize [8], and paddy rice [9], yielding promising results. Handheld sensors, such as Greenseeker and CropCircle, based on crop spectral response principles, can rapidly assess crop nitrogen status [10,11]. However, both near-ground non-imaging hyperspectral and handheld sensors only provide point information. Although these methods can effectively indicate nitrogen status in some plants, the spatial distribution of the nitrogen status of all plants cannot be obtained, thus affecting the effect of precise nitrogen fertilizer application.

In recent years, the application of UAV imaging technology in crop monitoring has increased significantly. Drones can be equipped with various sensors, including digital, multispectral, thermal infrared, hyperspectral, and LiDAR systems. These UAV imaging technologies are now extensively employed to monitor various aspects of crop growth, including the seedling emergence rate [12], growth trends [13], nutritional status [14], disease detection [15,16], and yield estimation [17]. Digital imaging has inherent limitations, lacking the red-edge and near-infrared bands that are more sensitive to crop nutrient status. Thermal infrared imaging, while effective for monitoring surface temperatures and estimating crop or soil moisture, does not provide detailed spectral information. In contrast, the data acquired through hyperspectral and LiDAR sensing can deliver high-precision estimations of crop physiological parameters, although these instruments are costly and require complex processing. UAV multispectral imaging combines high spatial resolution with a relatively rich array of spectral bands, rendering it the most cost-effective sensor for diagnosing crop nutrition.

To date, several studies have applied UAV multispectral imaging to assess crop nitrogen status, such as leaf nitrogen content, plant nitrogen content, leaf nitrogen density, plant nitrogen density, and nitrogen nutrient index. Previous research on crop nitrogen estimation via UAV imaging has mainly focused on the spectrum, texture, and vegetation indices derived from the spectrum. The plant nitrogen content (PNC) of crops is an important factor affecting the canopy spectrum. Texture describes the spatial distribution of brightness among adjacent pixels [18,19]. Similarly, differences in PNC affect texture parameters. The estimation of the nitrogen status of crops by integrating the spectrum, vegetation indices, and texture has been widely reported [20,21]. Crop canopy structure is highly correlated with PNC, including canopy coverage and plant height [22,23]. The higher the PNC, the greater the canopy cover and plant height, especially in the early and middle stages of growth. Therefore, we believe that canopy structure information can be used as one of the features to estimate PNC. It is relatively easy to extract plant height and canopy coverage from UAV images [24]. There have been few relevant reports where structure information was employed in PNC estimation. Therefore, we intend to introduce canopy structure information in combination with the spectrum and texture to estimate PNC.

Due to differences among varieties, the nitrogen content of crop plants will show different time-series changes with the progress of the growth stage. The nitrogen content of crop plants in the same growth period is also affected by water and fertilizer treatment. Previous studies on crop plant nitrogen estimation by UAV technology have mainly focused on the same variety or a multi-variety combination [25,26]. There are few reports on the effects of the growth stage and variety on the nitrogen content estimation of winter wheat plants by UAV technology.

According to the previous research on crop trait estimation by UAV imaging, the features that can be extracted from images mainly include spectral reflectance [27], vegetation indices [28], and texture [29]. There is a certain degree of collinearity among these features. Therefore, selecting an appropriate algorithm is the basis for accurately estimating crop PNC. According to previous studies, five representative machine learning algorithms were selected to explore the optimal model for estimating PNC. Partial least squares regression (PLSR) is the most commonly used linear algorithm, which is suitable for multicollinearity between independent variables [30]. Random forest regression (RFR) can integrate multiple decision tree models to reduce the overfitting of any single model [31]. Support vector regression (SVR) can effectively handle high-dimensional data and model nonlinear relationships [32]. Gaussian process regression (GPR) can alleviate the "black box" problem, which often occurs in machine learning regression methods [33]. It has achieved considerable success in vegetation feature detection. Oliveira [34] compared the outcomes of multiple linear regression with the estimation of the tillering number, plant height, and stem diameter of wheat, finding that models based on random forest algorithms exhibited superior accuracy and precision compared to multiple linear regression models. Liu et al. [35] utilized support vector machine, random forest, random tree, and linear regression models to estimate the physiological parameters of rice varieties based on multispectral remote sensing data, concluding that support vector machine demonstrated better adaptability and higher precision in predicting SPAD values than the other models. In Ding et al.'s [32] study, three common machine learning algorithms—RFR, SVR, and PLSR—were employed to construct nitrogen content estimation models for winter wheat, revealing that random forest outperformed the other methods. Accordingly, the selection of an appropriate modeling approach is necessary for enhancing the accuracy of crop parameter estimation. In this study, we selected five common algorithms, including random forest regression, support vector machine regression, partial least squares regression, Gaussian process regression, and neural network regression, to estimate the PNC of winter wheat, aiming to find the optimal method.

The objective of this study was to analyze the effects of the variety and growth stage on the UAV multispectral estimation of the PNC of winter wheat. The experimental dataset we used in this study included three varieties and five nitrogen fertilizer levels. The specific objectives included (1) analyzing the correlations between spectral, texture, and structural information and wheat plant nitrogen; (2) comparing the accuracy of nitrogen content estimation in wheat plants during single and multiple growth stages; (3) assessing the consistency of UAV multispectral image in estimating plant nitrogen content across different wheat varieties; (4) evaluating the performance of five machine learning methods for estimating the PNC of winter wheat to find the optimal estimation model.

2. Materials and Methods

2.1. Study Area and Experimental Design

Field experiments were conducted during the 2022–2023 growing season of winter wheat in Xinji City, Hebei Province, China (33°24′ N, 114°44′ E). The experimental site has a warm temperate semi-humid monsoon continental climate characterized by four distinct seasons. The predominant soil type is tidal soil. The annual average temperature is 12.5 °C, while the annual average rainfall is 488.2 mm, with the majority occurring during summer months, specifically from June to August, which accounts for over 67.9% of the total annual precipitation. The primary crops cultivated in this area are wheat and corn.

The experimental design comprised three wheat varieties and five levels of nitrogen fertilizer application. The selected wheat varieties were Malan No. 1 (ML 1), Hengguan 35 (HG 35), and Shiluan 02-1 (SL 02-1). The nitrogen application levels were 0, 180, 240, 300, and 360 kg N hm^{-2}, designated as N0, N1, N2, N3, and N4, respectively. Each treatment was replicated three times, resulting in a total of 45 experimental units. Nitrogen fertilizer was applied in equal quantities at multiple intervals. In addition, nitrogen, phosphorus, and potassium fertilizers were applied prior to sowing at a rate of 120 kg·ha^{-1}. The seedling density for the field trial was 3.75 million plants per hectare. The geographical location and layout of the experimental units in the study area are illustrated in Figure 1.

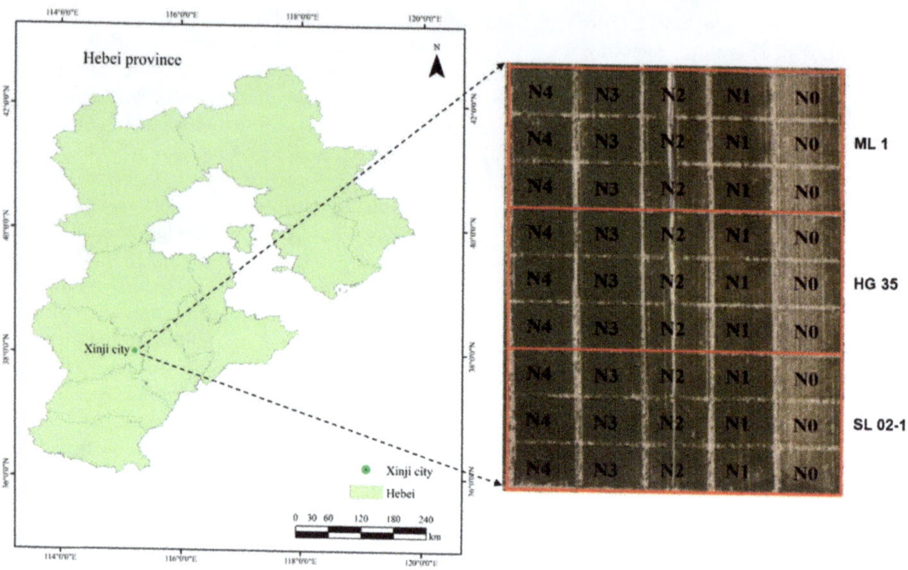

Figure 1. The geographical location of the study area and the distribution of experimental plots.

2.2. Data Acquisition

We collected the field data at the jointing stage, booting stage, anthesis stage, and filling stage. The acquired data included the plant height, plant nitrogen content, and UAV multispectral imaging. A tape measure was employed to assess the heights of five uniformly growing wheat plants that represented the growth level of each plot. Subsequently, destructive sampling was conducted, and the samples were transported to the laboratory for drying, where the nitrogen content of the plants was analyzed. The dried wheat plants were crushed, and nitrogen content was determined using the Kjeldahl method. A total of 180 nitrogen samples were collected from wheat plants throughout the entire growth period.

Multispectral data from the UAV in the study area were acquired synchronously on the day of field sampling, utilizing a DJI Phantom 4 (SZ DJI Technology Co. Ltd., Shenzhen, China) multispectral drone. The drone was equipped with six 1/2.9-inch CMOS sensors with an effective pixel number of 2.08 million, including one visible-light sensor (RGB) for visible-light imaging and five single-band sensors (MS) for multispectral imaging, with multispectral bands of red, green, blue, near-red, and red edge, respectively. The central wavelengths were 450 nm, 560 nm, 650 nm, 730 nm, and 840 nm, respectively. The UAV multispectral data collection was conducted between 10:00 a.m. and 14:00, and the day was cloudless, and the wind was less than level 3. We set the course overlap of the drone flight to 80%, the side overlap to 80%, and the flight height to 30 m (1.6 cm/pix). Eight ground control points were set up using black and white tiles in field trials. Before UAV imaging, the ground control points (GCPs) were evenly arranged in the field using black and white tiles with a size of 30 cm in length and width. Intelligent RTK (CHCNAV-T8, Shanghai, China) was used to obtain the accurate geographical positions of each control point. Before the imaging process, a whiteboard was used for the radiometric calibration of the multispectral sensor. The UAV multispectral imaging system is equipped with a sunshine sensor, which can automatically calibrate the image according to the light condition. The duration of flight was about 10 min, and the sunlight was almost constant during the imaging process.

2.3. Feature Extraction of UAV Multispectral Images

The stitching of UAV multispectral images was conducted using Pix4Dmapper software v4.4.12 (Pix4D, Lausanne, Switzerland). The primary steps involved include the creation of a dense point cloud, the addition of control points, the establishment of mesh and texture, and the generation of both the digital elevation model (DEM) and the digital surface model (DSM). During the image-stitching process, a calibration plate was utilized to facilitate the radiometric calibration of the multispectral images. The features extracted from the UAV multispectral images comprised spectral reflectance, vegetation indices, texture, canopy coverage, and plant height. The principal technical workflow of this study is illustrated in Figure 2.

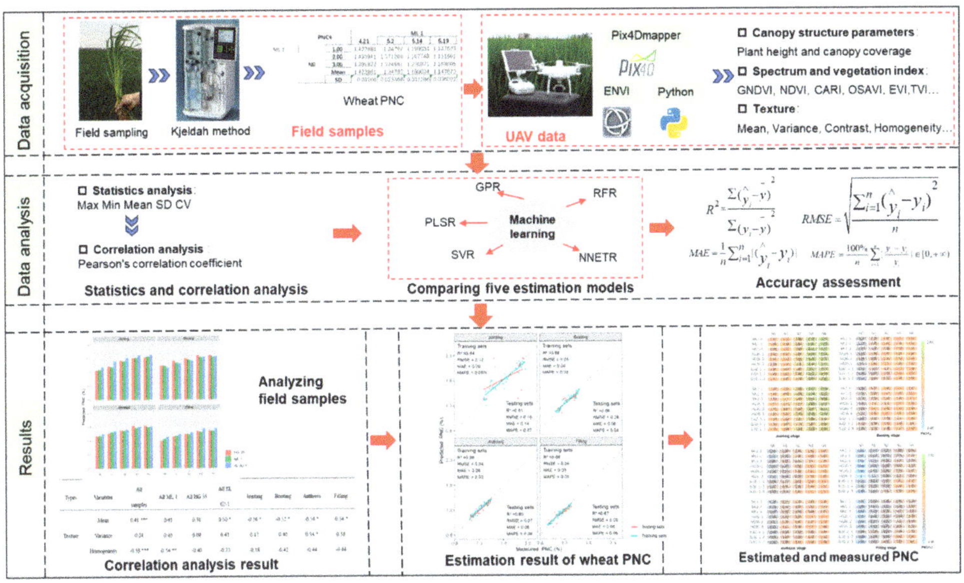

Figure 2. The main technical flowchart of this study. Note: PNC, plant nitrogen content; UAV, unmanned aerial vehicle; GNDVI, green-band normalized vegetation index; NDVI, normalized difference vegetation index; CARI, chlorophyll absorption ratio index; OSAVI, optimized soil-adjusted vegetation index; EVI, enhanced vegetation index; TVI, triangle vegetation index; SD, standard deviation; CV, variable coefficient; PLSR, partial least squares regression; RFR, random forest regression; SVR, support vector machine regression; GPR, Gaussian process regression; NNETR, neural network regression model; R^2, coefficient of determination; RMSE, root mean square error; MAE, mean absolute error; MAPE, mean absolute percentage error. *, **, and *** indicate significant differences at $p < 0.05$, $p < 0.01$, and $p < 0.001$.

2.3.1. Spectral Bands and Vegetation Indices

In the ENVI 5.3 (ExelisVisual Information Solutions, Inc., Boulder, CO, USA) software, the random forest algorithm was employed to classify the UAV multispectral images, resulting in images that exclusively contained pixels corresponding to wheat plants. Subsequently, the reflectance data from five bands of the wheat plants were extracted, and a range of vegetation indices were calculated. Drawing on prior research, 13 vegetation indices were selected for estimating the nitrogen content of the wheat plants. The specific bands and vegetation index details are listed in Table 1.

Table 1. The calculation formulas of vegetation indices.

Vegetation Index	Formulas	References
Green-band normalized vegetation index (GNDVI)	$(R_{nir} - R_{green})/(R_{nir} + R_{green})$	[36]
Normalized difference vegetation index (NDVI)	$(R_{nir} - R_{red})/(R_{nir} + R_{red})$	[37]
Chlorophyll absorption ratio index (CARI)	$(R_{red\ edge} - R_{red}) - 0.2 \times (R_{red\ edge} + R_{red})$	[38]
Optimized soil-adjusted vegetation index (OSAVI)	$(R_{nir} - R_{red})/(R_{nir} + R_{red} + 0.16)$	[38]
Normalized blue–green difference index (NGBDI)	$(R_{green} - R_{blue})/(R_{green} + R_{blue})$	[39]
Enhanced vegetation index (EVI)	$2.5 \times (R_{nir} - R_{red})/(R_{nir} + 6 \times R_{red} - 7.5 \times R_{blue} + 1)$	[40]
Triangle vegetation index (TVI)	$0.5 \times (120 \times (R_{nir} - R_{green}) - 200 \times (R_{red} - R_{green}))$	[41]
Atmospherically resistant vegetation index (VARI)	$(R_{green} - R_{red})/(R_{red} + R_{green} - R_{blue})$	[42]
Excessive green index (EXG)	$2 \times R_{green} - R_{red} - R_{blue}$	[43]
Ratio vegetation index (RVI)	R_{nir}/R_{red}	[42]
Soil-adjusted vegetation index (SAVI)	$1.5 \times (R_{nir} - R_{red})/(R_{nir} + R_{red} + 0.5)$	[44]
Normalized blue–green band difference vegetation index (GBNDVI)	$(R_{nir} - (R_{green} + R_{blue}))/(R_{nir} + R_{green} + R_{blue})$	[43]
Difference vegetation index (DVI)	$R_{nir} - R_{red}$	[45]

2.3.2. Texture Information

In addition to spectral reflectance and vegetation indices, texture information from the images was selected as an independent variable for estimating the nitrogen content of wheat plants. First, the multispectral image was converted into an image. Subsequently, the texture information in each cell was calculated and extracted, which included the mean value (Mea), variance (Var), homogeneity (Hom), contrast (Con), dissimilarity (Dis), information entropy (Ent), second moment (Sec), and correlation (Cor). The size of the sliding window was set to 5 × 5 pixels.

2.3.3. Canopy Structure Parameters

The terrain of the study area is characterized by a flat topography, and the DSM obtained via UAV is effective in reflecting the variations in wheat plant height. The DSM for the experimental area encompasses not only the vegetation but also the underlying soil, with each pixel value representing the elevation of the corresponding point. The pixel percentiles of the DSM images indicate varying positions within the canopy, where lower percentiles correspond to ground level and higher percentiles denote the upper boundary of the plant canopy. Percentile refers to the value associated with the cumulative distribution of the data. In this context, the 99th percentile of DSM pixel values is designated as the upper boundary of the wheat plants, while the 2nd percentile is regarded as ground level. Consequently, the height of wheat plants can be calculated using the DSM values acquired during the study period [46].

Canopy coverage refers to the percentage of the total area represented by the vertical projection of vegetation onto the ground [47]. Wheat plant pixels were extracted from UAV multispectral images by a classification method, and the proportion of wheat plant pixels in each plot to the whole plot was calculated.

2.4. Modeling Method

The spectral reflectance, vegetation indices, texture, plant height, and canopy coverage extracted from UAV images were utilized as independent variables for estimating the nitrogen content of wheat plants throughout the growth period. The ratio of training to test set samples was established at 2:1. Four evaluation metrics—coefficient of determination (R^2), root mean square error (RMSE), mean absolute error (MAE), and mean absolute percentage error (MAPE)—were employed to assess the performance of the various models.

Five widely used algorithms were selected for estimating the nitrogen content in wheat plants: partial least squares (PLS), support vector machine (SVM), random forest (RF), neural network regression (NNet), and Gaussian process regression (GPR).

Partial least squares regression (PLSR) is a statistical technique adept at addressing multiple regression challenges, particularly when the number of independent variables exceeds the number of samples or when multicollinearity is present among the independent variables [48]. PLSR integrates the strengths of principal component analysis (PCA) and least squares regression to effectively distill the essential information from the dataset.

Random forest regression (RFR) is a method based on the random forest algorithm, which is an ensemble learning technique. This approach constructs multiple decision tree models and integrates them to mitigate the overfitting risk associated with any single model while enhancing predictive performance [49]. Each decision tree is trained on a random subset of the original data, known as a bootstrap sample, and is split using a random subset of features.

Support vector machine regression (SVR) is another regression approach grounded in support vector machines [50]. Compared to traditional linear regression and other regression techniques, SVR exhibits superior flexibility and robustness, enabling it to handle high-dimensional data and model nonlinear relationships effectively. By selecting different kernel functions, SVR can adapt to various data distributions and demonstrates a degree of resilience to outliers.

Gaussian process regression (GPR) employs a non-parametric methodology that utilizes Gaussian processes for data modeling and prediction. In GPR, it is assumed that the distribution of the target variable adheres to a multivariate Gaussian distribution. The probability distribution of the target variable can be inferred by modeling the training data and facilitating predictions for new data points [51]. Consequently, GPR partly alleviates the "black box" issue frequently encountered in machine learning regression methods. In recent years, GPR has seen considerable success in vegetation feature retrieval.

The neural network regression model (NNet) adeptly addresses complex nonlinear relationships, resulting in improved data fitting [52]. This methodology also boasts high computational efficiency, enabling the completion of training and prediction processes in a relatively short time frame. However, neural network regression is not devoid of limitations; it is sensitive to noisy data and involves intricate parameter tuning. In this study, a neural network regression model was developed using the multinom function from the NNet package, which automatically fine-tunes parameters based on the training data to optimize model performance.

3. Results

3.1. PNC under Different Growth Stages, Nitrogen Fertilizers, and Varieties

Figure 3 illustrates the nitrogen content of wheat plants across various nitrogen application levels and growth stages. It is evident that an increase in nitrogen application corresponds with a rise in the nitrogen content of the wheat plants, which is unaffected by the growth stage or wheat variety. With the development of the growth stage, the PNC of HG35 and ML1 first increases and then decreases, reaching the maximum at the booting stage. The PNC of SL02-1 shows a continuous decline. With the increase in nitrogen supply, the PNC of all varieties shows an increasing trend, but the amplitudes of the increases are different. During both the early and later stages of growth, specifically at the jointing and filling stages, the nitrogen content of SL02-1 wheat was the highest across the different nitrogen application levels. At the booting stage, the nitrogen content of HG 35 wheat surpassed that of the ML 1 and SL02-1 varieties. Furthermore, at the flowering stage, as nitrogen application rates increased, the growth rate of nitrogen content in HG 35 wheat outpaced those of ML 1 and SL02-1.

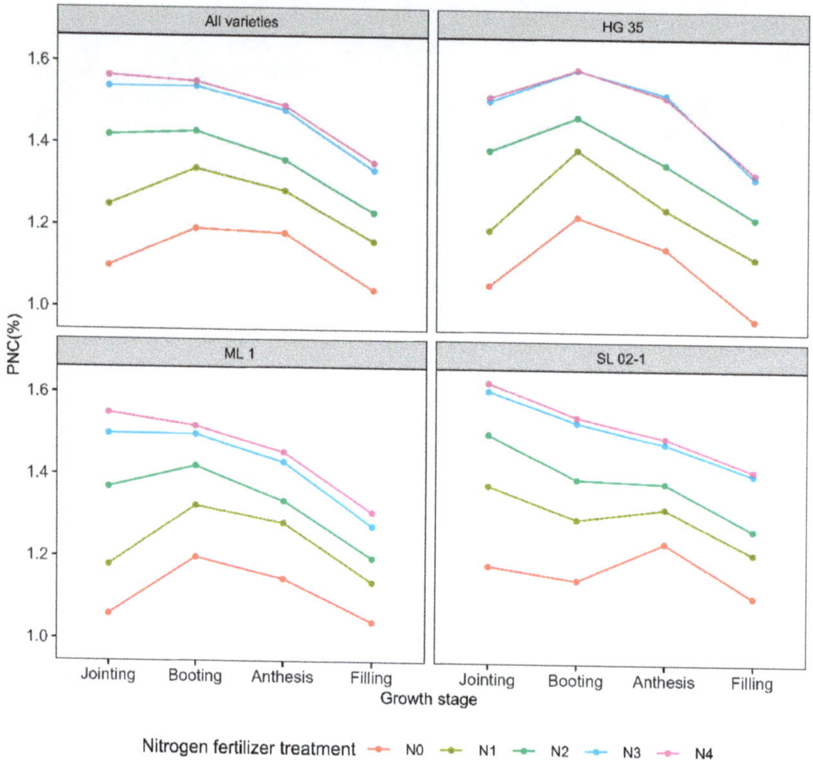

Figure 3. Plant nitrogen content of wheat at different nitrogen levels and growth stages. Note: PNC, plant nitrogen content; three wheat varieties: HG 35, Hengguan 35; ML 1, Malan No. 1; SL 02-1, Shiluan 02-1.

The nitrogen content data from 180 wheat plants were subjected to statistical analysis, revealing a range of values from 0.96% to 2.266%, with an average of 1.46% and a coefficient of variation of 490.57. According to the maximum, minimum, and coefficient of variation values of the samples, significant differences in the PNC of winter wheat were observed. Similarly, statistical analyses were performed on samples from the three wheat varieties throughout the entire growth period, as well as on all samples within individual growth periods, indicating that the nitrogen content varied significantly across each sample set. Table 2 presents a summary of the statistical information concerning the nitrogen content of different wheat plant samples.

Table 2. Partitioning of wheat plant nitrogen datasets (%).

Datasets	Sample Numbers	Max	Min	Mean	SD	CV
Jointing all samples	45	2.27	1.39	1.84	0.30	605.06
Booting all samples	45	1.62	1.12	1.41	0.14	996.32
Anthesis all samples	45	1.55	1.11	1.36	0.13	1076.44
Filling all samples	45	1.45	0.96	1.23	0.13	962.49
All ML 1 samples	60	2.27	1.025	1.44	0.31	458.15
All HG 35 samples	60	2.21	0.96	1.46	0.31	472.02
All SL 02-1 samples	60	2.13	1.08	1.47	0.27	545.77
All samples	180	2.27	0.96	1.46	0.30	490.57

Note: Three wheat varieties: HG 35, Hengguan 35; ML 1, Malan No. 1; SL 02-1, Shiluan 02-1; Max, maximum; Min, minimum; SD, standard deviation; CV, variable coefficient.

3.2. Correlation Analysis between Features and PNC

We analyzed the Pearson correlation coefficients between spectral reflectance, vegetation indices, texture, canopy structure parameters, and the nitrogen content of wheat plants (Table 3). Overall, irrespective of whether the entire growth period or specific growth stages were considered, the correlation between spectral and vegetation indices and the nitrogen content of wheat plants was robust and unaffected by wheat varieties. In comparison to individual growth stages, the overall single-band spectral reflectance (such as red, green, blue, and red edge) exhibited a stronger correlation with the nitrogen content of wheat plants across multiple growth stages. Notably, among the selected vegetation indices, NDVI, GNDVI, RVI, GBNDVI, and EXG demonstrated a greater correlation with nitrogen content in wheat plants. Within the dataset for individual growth stages, most vegetation indices were found to have a strong correlation with nitrogen content in wheat, except for EXG, which showed no correlation with nitrogen content during the booting and filling periods.

Table 3. Correlation between three types of features extracted from UAV images and PNC.

Types	Variables	All Samples	All ML 1	All HG35 35	All SL 02-1	Jointing	Booting	Anthesis	Filling
Texture	Mean	0.41 ***	0.41	0.31	0.50 *	−0.56 *	−0.52 *	−0.56 *	−0.54 *
	Variance	0.24	0.43	0.09	0.43	0.17	0.40	0.54 *	0.36
	Homogeneity	−0.33 ***	−0.54 **	−0.40	−0.23	−0.18	−0.42	−0.44	−0.44
	Contrast	0.28 *	0.47 *	0.15	0.43	0.13	0.46	0.52 *	0.36
	Dissimilarity	0.32 **	0.50 *	0.24	0.36	0.15	0.45	0.50	0.39
	Entropy	0.24	0.45 *	0.44	0.02	0.30	0.46	0.39	0.50
	Second moment	−0.20	−0.43	−0.44	0.05	−0.29	−0.44	−0.36	−0.50
	Correlation	0.18	0.35	−0.24	0.40	−0.37	−0.55 *	0.35	−0.13
Canopy structure parameters	CC	0.54 ***	0.54 **	0.60 ***	0.47 *	0.15	0.18	−0.74 ***	0.09
	Plant height	−0.43 ***	−0.46 *	−0.36 ***	−0.48 *	0.55 *	0.73 ***	0.20	0.13
Reflectance spectra and vegetation indices	R_{450}	−0.75 ***	−0.74 ***	−0.79***	−0.72 ***	−0.57 ***	−0.78 ***	−0.65 **	−0.70 ***
	R_{550}	−0.77 ***	−0.79 ***	−0.82 ***	−0.71 ***	−0.62 ***	−0.73 ***	−0.73 ***	−0.73 ***
	R_{660}	−0.77 ***	−0.77 ***	−0.83 ***	−0.70 ***	−0.59 **	−0.75 ***	−0.72 ***	−0.81 ***
	R_{735}	−0.70 ***	−0.72 ***	−0.72 ***	−0.66 ***	−0.63 *	−0.39	−0.69 ***	−0.44
	R_{790}	−0.52 ***	−0.52 ***	−0.49 ***	−0.56 ***	0.67 **	0.79 ***	0.30	0.20
	GNDVI	0.64 ***	0.69 ***	0.85 ***	0.31	0.64 ***	0.81 ***	0.73 ***	0.79 ***
	NDVI	0.58 ***	0.65 ***	0.81 ***	0.19	0.61 **	0.79 ***	0.71 ***	0.77 ***
	CARI	−0.20	−0.25	−0.02	−0.32	0.54 *	0.76 ***	0.55 *	0.61 **
	OSAVI	0.08	0.11	0.37	−0.25	0.63 ***	0.81 ***	0.70 ***	0.73 ***
	NGBDI	−0.62 ***	−0.66 ***	−0.67 ***	−0.56 **	−0.67 ***	0.42	−0.55*	0.44
	EVI	−0.12	−0.12	0.08	−0.32	0.65 ***	0.80 ***	0.66 ***	0.66 ***
	TVI	−0.27 *	−0.27	−0.12	−0.40	0.64 ***	0.81 ***	0.61 **	0.59 **
	VARI	0.34 ***	0.39	0.70 ***	−0.16	0.51 *	0.60 **	0.56 *	0.57 *
	EXG	−0.64 ***	−0.74 ***	−0.70 ***	−0.57 ***	−0.53 *	0.35	−0.63 ***	0.11
	RVI	0.63 ***	0.71 ***	0.86 ***	0.15	0.63 ***	0.75 ***	0.65 ***	0.70 ***
	SAVI	−0.16	−0.15	0.05	−0.37	0.64 ***	0.81 ***	0.67 ***	0.68 ***
	GBNDVI	0.55 ***	0.63 ***	0.81 ***	0.12	0.63 ***	0.81 ***	0.72 ***	0.78 ***
	DVI	−0.30 ***	−0.30	−0.18	−0.42	0.65 ***	0.81 ***	0.60 **	0.58 **

Note: *, **, and *** indicate significant differences at $p < 0.05$, $p < 0.01$, and $p < 0.001$. R_{450}, R_{550}, R_{660}, R_{735}, and R_{790}, the spectral reflectance of 450, 550, 660, and 735 bands; CC, canopy coverage.

3.3. Estimation of PNC of Multiple Varieties in Single Stage

Table 4 presents the estimation results of five regression models for the nitrogen content of wheat plants at a single growth stage. According to the results from the training set, the NNet regression model yielded the most accurate estimates across all periods. However, its performance on the test set was the least effective among the five models evaluated. Overall, the NNet regression model demonstrated significant overfitting, showing better results on the training set and poorer performance on the test set. The results from the PLSR model exhibited relatively stable performance on both the training and test sets; nevertheless, the overall accuracy remained low. Among the remaining three methods—GPR, SVR, and RFR—performance on the test set ranked as follows: GPR exhibited the highest efficacy, followed by SVR and RFR in descending order. During the jointing and anthesis periods, the estimated R^2 of the GPR regression model reached 0.8 on the test set. Conversely, during the booting and filling periods, the estimated R^2 for the test set of the model was 0.66 and 0.67. Among the five algorithms, GPR performed the best when modeling PNC at a single growth stage. GPR requires that the target variables adhere to the multivariate Gaussian distribution. Different wheat varieties have different nitrogen absorption abilities, resulting in a higher CV of PNC at a single growth stage than across multiple growth stages (Table 2). The PNC at a single stage is more in line with the multivariate Gaussian distribution, resulting in the best effect of GPR for PNC estimation being obtained at a single growth stage. There were some differences in nitrogen estimation for wheat plants at different growth stages. The accuracy of plant nitrogen estimation, from high to low, for different growth stages was jointing, anthesis, filling, and booting. Figure 4 shows the optimal estimation of the PNC of winter wheat with multiple varieties in a single growth stage.

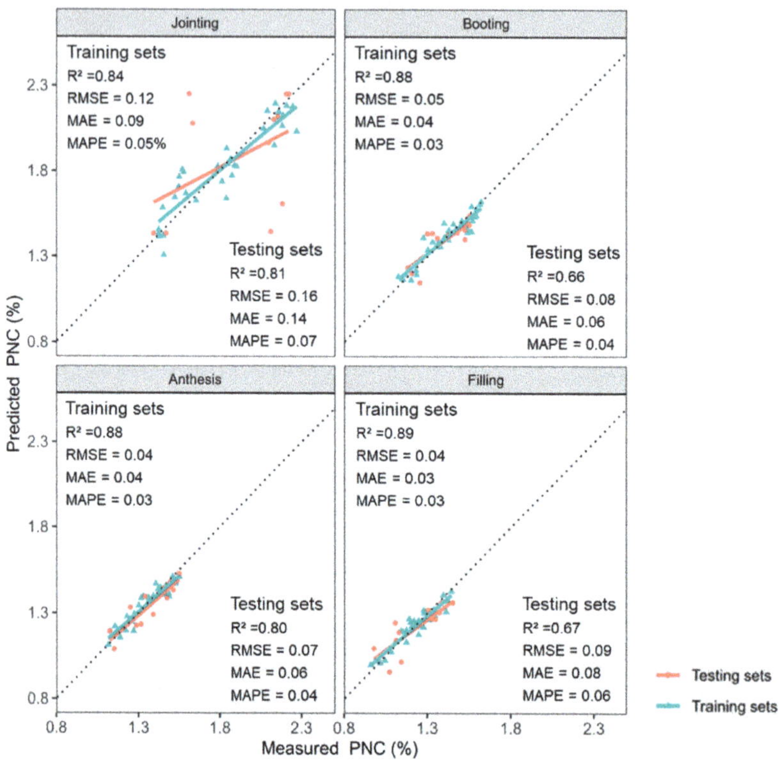

Figure 4. Estimation results of the PNC of multiple varieties in a single growth stage based on GPR. Note: PNC, plant nitrogen content; GPR, Gaussian process regression.

Table 4. Estimation results of nitrogen in wheat plants of multiple varieties in single stage.

Growth Stages	Datasets	Evaluation Indices	SVR	RFR	GPR	PLSR	NNETR
Jointing	Training set	R^2	0.88	0.95	0.84	0.54	0.99
		RMSE (%)	0.10	0.08	0.12	0.20	0.01
		MAE	0.06	0.06	0.09	0.15	0.01
		MAPE (%)	0.03	0.03	0.05	0.08	0.00
	Testing set	R^2	0.76	0.79	0.81	0.45	0.24
		RMSE (%)	0.23	0.18	0.16	0.28	0.34
		MAE	0.19	0.15	0.14	0.24	0.23
		MAPE (%)	0.09	0.08	0.07	0.12	0.12
Booting	Training set	R^2	0.88	0.93	0.88	0.68	1.00
		RMSE (%)	0.05	0.04	0.05	0.08	0.01
		MAE	0.04	0.03	0.04	0.06	0.01
		MAPE (%)	0.03	0.02	0.03	0.04	0.00
	Testing set	R^2	0.63	0.60	0.66	0.48	0.05
		RMSE (%)	0.08	0.08	0.08	0.09	0.25
		MAE	0.07	0.07	0.06	0.07	0.19
		MAPE (%)	0.04	0.05	0.04	0.06	0.12
Anthesis	Training set	R^2	0.92	0.95	0.88	0.54	1.00
		RMSE (%)	0.04	0.03	0.04	0.09	0.01
		MAE	0.03	0.03	0.04	0.09	0.01
		MAPE (%)	0.02	0.02	0.03	0.06	0.00
	Testing set	R^2	0.77	0.64	0.80	0.43	0.32
		RMSE (%)	0.07	0.09	0.07	0.09	0.19
		MAE	0.06	0.07	0.06	0.08	0.15
		MAPE (%)	0.04	0.05	0.04	0.07	0.11
Filling	Training set	R^2	0.89	0.94	0.89	0.61	0.99
		RMSE (%)	0.04	0.03	0.04	0.07	0.01
		MAE	0.03	0.03	0.03	0.06	0.01
		MAPE (%)	0.03	0.02	0.03	0.05	0.00
	Testing set	R^2	0.59	0.56	0.67	0.48	0.55
		RMSE (%)	0.10	0.11	0.09	0.12	0.16
		MAE	0.09	0.10	0.08	0.11	0.14
		MAPE (%)	0.07	0.08	0.06	0.09	0.11

Note: PLSR, partial least squares regression; RFR, random forest regression; SVR, support vector machine regression; GPR, Gaussian process regression; NNETR, neural network regression model; R^2, coefficient of determination; RMSE, root mean square error; MAE, mean absolute error; MAPE, mean absolute percentage error.

3.4. Nitrogen Estimation of Single Wheat Variety in Multiple Growth Periods

Table 5 presents the estimated nitrogen content of three wheat varieties across multiple growth periods. A significant discrepancy exists between the accuracy of the training set and the test set derived from the NNet regression model. Among the various models utilized, PLSR exhibited the lowest accuracy for the training set constructed from the three wheat varieties. In contrast, the performance of the other three methods—GPR, SVR, and RFR—ranked as follows based on the test set results: RFR, GPR, and SVR, in descending order of effectiveness. Specifically, for the nitrogen content of wheat plants in ML 1, the test set metrics for RFR yielded an R^2 of 0.91, RMSE of 0.11%, MAE of 0.07, and a MAPE of 0.04%. For HG-35 wheat plants, the test set results were R^2 = 0.93, RMSE = 0.14%, MAE = 0.11, and MAPE = 0.06%. In the case of SL02-1 wheat plants, the R^2, RMSE, MAE, and MAPE were 0.72, 0.14%, 0.12, and 0.08%, respectively. Overall, different wheat varieties achieved high precision in estimating nitrogen content. However, the estimation accuracy for the SL02-1 variety was notably poor, which may be attributed to its relatively low sensitivity to nitrogen. Figure 5 illustrates these findings.

Table 5. Estimation results of nitrogen in wheat plants of single wheat variety across multiple growth stages.

Varieties	Dataset	Indices	SVR	RFR	GPR	PLSR	NNETR
ML 1	Training set	R^2	0.88	0.97	0.91	0.81	0.99
		RMSE (%)	0.12	0.05	0.09	0.13	0.01
		MAE	0.07	0.04	0.06	0.09	0.01
		MAPE (%)	0.04	0.02	0.04	0.06	0.00
	Testing set	R^2	0.86	0.91	0.89	0.77	0.77
		RMSE (%)	0.14	0.11	0.12	0.16	0.61
		MAE	0.09	0.07	0.09	0.11	0.36
		MAPE (%)	0.06	0.04	0.06	0.08	0.21
HG 35	Training set	R^2	0.98	0.99	0.96	0.92	0.99
		RMSE (%)	0.05	0.04	0.06	0.09	0.01
		MAE	0.03	0.04	0.05	0.07	0.01
		MAPE (%)	0.02	0.02	0.04	0.05	0.00
	Testing set	R^2	0.87	0.93	0.88	0.78	0.58
		RMSE (%)	0.16	0.14	0.14	0.19	0.24
		MAE	0.12	0.11	0.10	0.15	0.18
		MAPE (%)	0.08	0.06	0.08	0.10	0.12
SL 02-1	Training set	R^2	0.81	0.96	0.83	0.49	0.99
		RMSE (%)	0.13	0.06	0.11	0.19	0.03
		MAE	0.09	0.05	0.08	0.15	0.02
		MAPE (%)	0.05	0.03	0.05	0.10	0.01
	Testing set	R^2	0.46	0.72	0.52	0.26	0.36
		RMSE (%)	0.18	0.14	0.18	0.22	0.30
		MAE	0.14	0.12	0.15	0.19	0.205
		MAPE (%)	0.09	0.08	0.10	0.14	0.15

Note: Three wheat varieties: HG 35, Hengguan 35; ML 1, Malan No. 1; SL 02-1, Shiluan 02-1. PLSR, partial least squares regression; RFR, random forest regression; SVR, support vector machine regression; GPR, Gaussian process regression; NNETR, neural network regression model; R^2, coefficient of determination; RMSE, root mean square error; MAE, mean absolute error; MAPE, mean absolute percentage error.

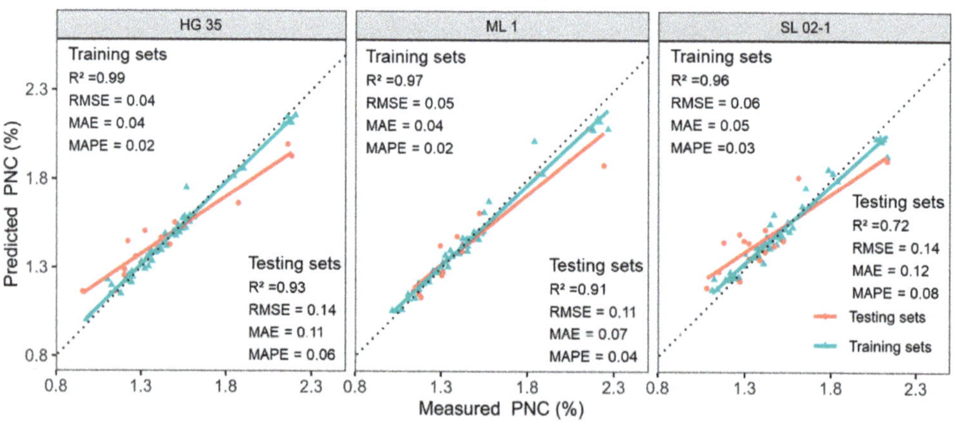

Figure 5. Optimal nitrogen estimation results of wheat plants of a single variety in multiple growth periods. Note: PNC, plant nitrogen content; three wheat varieties: HG 35, Hengguan 35; ML 1, Malan No. 1; SL 02-1, Shiluan 02-1.

3.5. PNC Estimation of Multiple Varieties during the Entire Growth Period

Firstly, the effect of estimating nitrogen content in wheat plants with all samples from four growth periods put together was analyzed (Table 6). Table 6 shows the estimation results of the five regression methods for nitrogen content in wheat plants constructed using all the extracted features. Regardless of whether the training set or the test set was used, the performance of the constructed model was RFR, NNETR, SVR, GPR, and PLSR, in order from high to low, with RFR performing best and PLSR performing worst. All four machine learning methods achieve better estimation results than PLSR. With the test set, R^2 obtained by GPR and RFR is 23.44% and 40.63% higher than that obtained by PLSR, respectively. The optimal estimation results of nitrogen content in wheat plants across multiple growth periods and varieties showed training set R^2, RMSE, MAE, and MAPE values of 0.97, 0.05%, 0.04, and 0.02%, respectively, and test set R^2, RMSE, MAE, and MAPE values of 0.90, 0.10%, 0.08, and 0.06%. For the modeling of multiple growth stages, RFR performed best. RFR has a strong fitting ability when the data size is large. As can be seen from Table 2, the sample size of multiple growth stages is large, and the CV is much lower than that of a single growth stage. Therefore, compared with the other four algorithms, RFR is more suitable for constructing a model to estimate PNC across multiple growth stages. Figure 6 shows the estimated nitrogen content and measured values of wheat plants at each growth stage based on RFR.

Table 6. Estimation results of nitrogen in wheat plants of multiple varieties across multiple growth stages.

Datasets	Indices	SVR	RFR	GPR	PLSR	NNETR
Training set	R^2	0.91	0.97	0.86	0.75	0.93
	RMSE (%)	0.09	0.05	0.11	0.15	0.08
	MAE	0.06	0.04	0.08	0.11	0.06
	MAPE (%)	0.04	0.02	0.05	0.07	0.04
Testing set	R^2	0.85	0.90	0.79	0.64	0.85
	RMSE (%)	0.13	0.10	0.14	0.18	0.12
	MAE	0.09	0.08	0.10	0.14	0.90
	MAPE (%)	0.06	0.06	0.07	0.10	0.06

Note: PLSR, partial least squares regression; RFR, random forest regression; SVR, support vector machine regression; GPR, Gaussian process regression; NNETR, neural network regression model; R^2, coefficient of determination; RMSE, root mean square error; MAE, mean absolute error; MAPE, mean absolute percentage error.

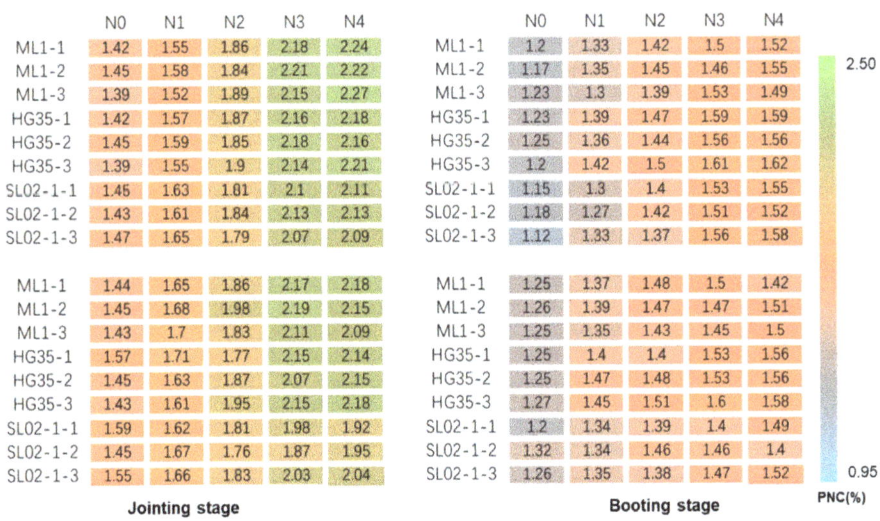

Figure 6. *Cont.*

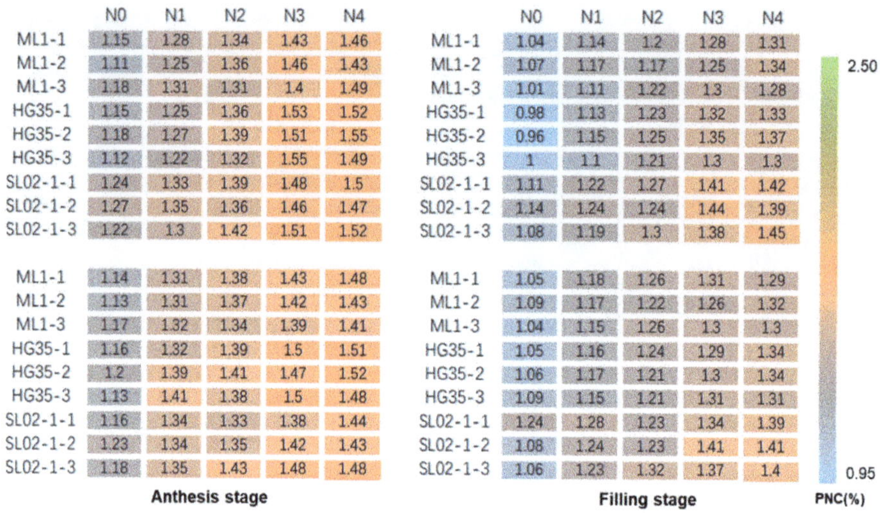

Figure 6. Nitrogen content and measured values of wheat plants at different growth stages estimated based on RFR. Note: PNC, plant nitrogen content; RFR, random forest regression.

4. Discussion

4.1. Correlation of Features Extracted from UAV Images for Estimating Wheat PNC

In previous studies, the main features used to estimate PNC were the spectrum, vegetation indices, and texture. Considering that canopy structure parameters are also closely related to PNC, we introduced two canopy structure parameters, plant height and canopy coverage, to form new feature sets. Our findings showed that spectral information had the best correlation with wheat PNC, while texture and structure information had weak correlations with wheat PNC. Previous studies have shown that the color and brightness information obtained from UAV digital images can be used to estimate crop nitrogen content [33,53]. We found that the absolute value of the correlation coefficient between the three RGB bands and nitrogen content in wheat plants was 0.56 to 0.83. Nitrogen content is a key component of crop chlorophyll, and chlorophyll absorption and reflection are clearly characterized at specific bands, such as 650 nm for red light and 450 nm for blue–violet light [54,55]. Therefore, the spectral information of these bands can directly reflect the nitrogen status of plants.

Vegetation indices performed well in monitoring crop growth and nutritional status. These indices are usually closely related to the above-ground biomass, leaf area index, and chlorophyll content of crops. Determining the relationship between crop nitrogen content and a vegetation index is the basis for the accurate estimation of crop nitrogen status. In this study, 13 vegetation indices were calculated based on multispectral bands to estimate the PNC of winter wheat. Our findings showed that most of the selected vegetation indices were significantly correlated with the nitrogen content of wheat plants. Previous studies have also shown that a vegetation index constructed based on red-edge parameters can accurately estimate crop chlorophyll and nitrogen content [35,56]. Basso et al. [57] found that the red-edge region was closely related to the nitrogen and chlorophyll contents of crops, and the red-edge parameter had a relatively stable mathematical relationship with agronomic components. Our study found that the red-edge band does not perform well compared to the red, green, and blue bands, especially in the booting and filling stages. The correlation between the CARI calculated using the red-edge band and PNC in all samples of multiple varieties or a single variety is worse than that with other indices, such as NDVI, GNDVI, RVI, GBNDVI, and EXG. But, the CARI performed well at the single growth stage. There was a good correlation between plant nitrogen and the CARI in a single growth stage, indicating that fertilizer application had a significant effect on plant nitrogen. The poor correlation between PNC and the CARI in integrated multi-growth stages indicates that PNC is confused in different growth stages. In addition, different varieties had different nitrogen absorption efficiencies, which also reduced the correlation between the CARI and PNC. It is worth noting that, in this study, the vegetation indices calculated from the spectral data of the blue and green regions also had high correlations with the nitrogen content of wheat plants.

At present, most studies estimate crop nitrogen content based on the spectrum and vegetation indices [58,59]. In this study, in addition to the spectrum and vegetation indices, the correlations between texture and canopy structure information (canopy coverage and plant height) and wheat PNC were also analyzed. Our findings showed that most texture information is less correlated with wheat PNC, while some texture parameters, such as mean and entropy, are significantly correlated with the nitrogen content of wheat plants. Canopy coverage and plant height were also significantly correlated with wheat PNC, and the estimated correlation between plant height and PNC in the first two growth stages was especially high because the growth of wheat was more prosperous when the nitrogen status was better, which directly reflected the plant height and plant coverage. In this study, canopy structure and texture information were used to supplement the spectrum and vegetation indices, which effectively realized the high-precision estimation of wheat PNC.

4.2. *Effects of the Variety and Growth Stage on Estimating Wheat PNC*

The samples in this study cover different nitrogen fertilizer treatments and wheat varieties. The dataset of four growth stages of wheat was obtained to estimate wheat PNC at each growth stage. For wheat samples of the single growth stage, from the five regression methods, it can be seen that the jointing and anthesis stages performed better, and the test set R^2 is around 0.8. The test set R^2 for the optimal estimation of nitrogen content in wheat plants in the booting and filling stages was 0.66. This could be due to the jointing stage being on the 4th day after the first nitrogen application and the anthesis stage being on the 5th day after the second nitrogen application. Different nitrogen fertilizer supplies directly reflect the wheat PNC. The results of this study showed that no matter which modeling method was used, the estimation effect of wheat PNC in multiple growth stages was better than that in a single growth stage.

For wheat varieties, the estimation accuracy of the wheat PNC of ML1 and HG35 is similar, and the test set R^2 reached more than 0.9. The accuracy of the test set was 0.72 when estimating the PNC of SL02-1. On the whole, there was a significant positive correlation between the PNC and nitrogen application rate of each wheat variety. The correlation between the PNC and nitrogen application rate of HG 35 was the best, indicating that the nitrogen absorption capacity of this wheat variety was better than that of the other two varieties.

4.3. *Comparison of Modeling Algorithms*

In recent years, machine learning algorithms have shown great practicability in integrating multi-source information to diagnose crop growth and nitrogen status [28,60]. Considering the advantages of the large number of available machine learning algorithms, we tested five algorithms (NNETR, PLSR, GPR, RFR, and SVR) to explore their performance in the estimation of the PNC of winter wheat. Our findings showed that GPR was the best among the five models for estimating wheat PNC at a single growth stage. This indicated that the GPR method had a better application effect on small sample datasets. This was because Gaussian process regression can be used to fit nonlinear data and is a powerful regression method, which has corresponding advantages in dealing with complex data and small sample datasets [33]. We found that the NNETR model was one of the worst-performing algorithms for estimating wheat PNC at a single growth stage. This may be because the sample size of a single growth stage is only 45, which is relatively small, resulting in the poor stability of the model. Neural network regression usually requires a large amount of training data to obtain good performance [52]. If the dataset is insufficient or the training data are not representative, the accuracy of the model will be restrained. The performance of PLSR is weak compared to the RFR, SVR, and GPR models. On the whole, the RFR, SVR, and GPR models outperformed the other two models on the dataset in this study.

For the dataset of multiple growth periods, RFR and SVR performed better than the others. Most of the test set accuracy R^2 values of the SVR and RFR construction models were 0.85 or above. The test set R^2 of the single-growth-stage dataset was also as high as 0.79. In many studies, RFR has yielded high precision in the growth monitoring and N status diagnosis of various crops (including maize, wheat, and sugarcane) [28,34,61].

4.4. Limitations and Future Research

There are some limitations in the study. Firstly, we compared the accuracy of five machine learning algorithms in PNC estimation. But, deep learning has shown a better effect in the estimation of crop traits in recent years. It is necessary to try using deep learning algorithms to estimate the PNC of crops in the subsequent research. Secondly, only three varieties of winter wheat were used in the study. We will increase the number of wheat varieties in future experiments to verify the robustness of the proposed method of estimating PNC. Finally, we only used a dataset from one experimental site. It is necessary to conduct experiments at multiple sites in the future to improve the universality of the proposed method.

The practical application of UAV technology for estimating the nitrogen content of winter wheat plants includes the following steps. Firstly, UAV multispectral images are obtained at each growth stage. Secondly, vegetation indices and texture and canopy structure parameters are calculated. Thirdly, the feature images are input into the optimal model selected in this study for estimating PNC. Fourthly, the spatial distribution of winter wheat PNC is mapped according to the estimation results. In future studies, we will continue to conduct variable irrigation and fertilizer experiments with more varieties to obtain more growth stage data. We will further reveal the effects of the variety and growth stage on the estimation of winter wheat PNC using UAV-based multispectral images.

5. Conclusions

The main contribution of this work is that we employed UAV multispectral images to estimate the nitrogen content of various wheat cultivars at different growth stages using spectral reflectance, vegetation indices, and texture and canopy structure parameters with five regression methods. The following conclusions were drawn: (1) The correlation between spectral and vegetation indices and wheat PNC was robust. The correlations between texture and structural information and the nitrogen content of wheat plants were weak, and only some texture and structural parameters were significantly correlated with wheat PNC. (2) The accuracy of nitrogen content estimation for wheat plants across the multiple growth stages exceeded that in a single growth stage. (3) The wheat variety had an influence on PNC estimation. Compared with HG 35 and ML 1, the estimation accuracy for the SL02-1 variety was notably poor. (4) Among the models, RFR and SVR exhibited the highest overall accuracy on multiple-growth-period datasets, while GPR yielded the best results for a single growth stage.

According to our findings, the following three aspects can be improved in the practical application and future directions of UAV-based PNC estimation. Firstly, it is necessary to add canopy structure information to the feature set, such as the spectrum, vegetation indices, and texture. Secondly, facing the PNC estimation of multiple varieties, it is necessary to construct a model with a single variety. Thirdly, collaborative modeling of data from multiple growth stages helps to improve accuracy. We can obtain UAV multispectral images before topdressing fertilizer, quickly estimate PNC, and then calculate the nitrogen application rate for each management unit. Therefore, it is feasible to use UAV multispectral imaging technology to manage nitrogen fertilizer in real time.

Author Contributions: Conceptualization, M.S., H.Q. and L.W.; methodology, M.S. and W.G.; software, M.S. and H.Q.; validation, M.S. and Z.W.; formal analysis, M.S.; investigation, M.S., Z.W. and Y.F.; resources, Y.G. and L.W.; data curation, M.S. and Z.W.; writing—original draft preparation, M.S.; writing—review and editing, M.S.; visualization, Z.W.; supervision, X.G., Y.M. and L.W.; project administration, M.S.; funding acquisition, M.S. and Y.G. All authors have read and agreed to the published version of the manuscript.

Funding: This research was funded by the open subject of the Key Laboratory of Smart Agricultural Technology of HuangHuaihai, Ministry of Agriculture and Rural Affairs, in 2024 (No. 202409); the Henan Province Science and Technology Research Project (242102110357); the Henan Province Key R&D and Promotion Projects (No. 232102111030); the Science and Technology Innovation Leading Talent Cultivation Program of the Institute of Agricultural Information Technology, Henan Academy of Agricultural Sciences (No. 2022KJCX01); and the National Funded Postdoctoral Researcher Program Class C (No. GZC202307).

Institutional Review Board Statement: Not applicable.

Data Availability Statement: The data presented in this study are available on request from the corresponding author due to the need for follow-up studies.

Conflicts of Interest: The authors declare no conflicts of interest.

References

1. Karabak, S.; Kan, M. *Wheat Landraces*; Springer International Publishing: Cham, Switzerland, 2021; pp. 121–146.
2. Tian, Z.; Zhang, Y.; Zhang, H.; Li, Z.; Li, M.; Wu, J.; Liu, K. Winter wheat and soil total nitrogen integrated monitoring based on canopy hyperspectral feature selection and fusion. *Comput. Electron. Agric.* **2021**, *201*, 107285. [CrossRef]
3. Liu, Z.; Gao, J.; Zhao, S.; Sha, Y.; Huang, Y.; Hao, Z.; Ke, L.; Chen, F.; Yuan, L.; Mi, G. Nitrogen responsiveness of leaf growth, radiation use efficiency and grain yield of maize (*Zea mays* L.) in Northeast China. *Field Crops Res.* **2023**, *291*, 108806. [CrossRef]
4. Kong, L.; Xie, Y.; Hu, L.; Feng, B.; Li, S. Remobilization of vegetative nitrogen to developing grain in wheat (*Triticum aestivum* L.). *Field Crop. Res.* **2016**, *196*, 134–144. [CrossRef]
5. Calderon, R.; Rajendiran, K.; Kim, U.J.; Palma, P.; Arancibia-Miranda, N.; Silva-Moreno, E.; Corradini, F. Sources and fates of perchlorate in soils in Chile: A case study of perchlorate dynamics in soil-crop systems using lettuce (*Lactuca sativa*) fields. *Environ. Pollut.* **2020**, *264*, 7. [CrossRef] [PubMed]
6. Shu, M.; Zhu, J.; Yang, X.; Gu, X.; Li, B.; Ma, Y. A spectral decomposition method for estimating the leaf nitrogen status of maize by UAV-based hyperspectral imaging. *Comput. Electron. Agric.* **2023**, *212*, 108100.
7. Feng, W.; Guo, B.; Wang, Z.; He, L.; Song, X.; Wang, Y.; Guo, T. Measuring leaf nitrogen concentration in winter wheat using double-peak spectral reflection remote sensing data. *Field Crops Res.* **2014**, *159*, 43–52. [CrossRef]
8. Wen, P.; Shi, Z.; Li, A.; Ning, F.; Zhang, Y.; Wang, R.; Li, J. Estimation of the vertically integrated leaf nitrogen content in maize using canopy hyperspectral red edge parameters. *Precis. Agric.* **2021**, *22*, 984–1005. [CrossRef]
9. Lee, Y.; Yang, C.; Chang, K.; Shen, Y. A simple spectral index using reflectance of 735 nm to assess nitrogen status of rice canopy. *Agron. J.* **2008**, *100*, 205–212. [CrossRef]
10. Cao, Q.; Miao, Y.; Wang, H.; Huang, S.; Cheng, S.; Khosla, R.; Jiang, R. Non-destructive estimation of rice plant nitrogen status with Crop Circle multispectral active canopy sensor. *Field Crops Res.* **2013**, *154*, 133–144. [CrossRef]
11. Zhang, N.; Qi, B.; Zhao, J.; Zhang, X.; Wang, S.; Zhao, T.; Gai, J. Prediction for Soybean Grain Yield Using Active Sensor GreenSeeker. *Acta Agron. Sin.* **2014**, *40*, 657–666. [CrossRef]
12. Yuan, J.; Li, X.; Zhou, M.; Zheng, H.; Liu, Z.; Liu, Y.; Yao, X. Rapidly count crop seedling emergence based on waveform Method (WM) using drone imagery at the early stage. *Comput. Electron. Agric.* **2024**, *220*, 108867. [CrossRef]
13. Yue, J.; Tian, J.; Philpot, W.; Tian, Q.; Feng, H.; Fu, Y. VNAI-NDVI-Space and Polar Coordinate Method for Assessing Crop Leaf Chlorophyll Content and Fractional Cover. *Comput. Electron. Agric.* **2023**, *207*, 107758. [CrossRef]
14. Yue, J.; Feng, H.; Tian, Q.; Zhou, C. A Robust Spectral Angle Index for Remotely Assessing Soybean Canopy Chlorophyll Content in Different Growing Stages. *Plant Methods* **2020**, *16*, 104. [CrossRef] [PubMed]
15. Vélez, S.; Ariza-Sentís, M.; Valente, J. Mapping the spatial variability of Botrytis bunch rot risk in vineyards using UAV multispectral imagery. *Eur. J. Agron.* **2022**, *142*, 126691. [CrossRef]
16. Fajardo, J.U.; Maridueña-Zavala, M.; Cevallos-Cevallos, J.; Donoso, D.O. Early Detection of Plant Viral Disease Using Hyperspectral Imaging and Deep Learning. *Plants-Basel* **2022**, *11*, 2581.
17. Walsh, O.; Marshall, J.; Nambi, E.; Jackson, C.; Ansah, E.; Lamichhane, R. Wheat Yield and Protein Estimation with Handheld and Unmanned Aerial Vehicle-Mounted Sensors. *Agronomy* **2023**, *13*, 207. [CrossRef]
18. Zhang, J.; Cheng, T.; Shi, L.; Wang, W.; Niu, Z.; Guo, W.; Ma, X. Combining spectral and texture features of UAV hyperspectral images for leaf nitrogen content monitoring in winter wheat. *Int. J. Remote Sens.* **2022**, *43*, 2335–2356. [CrossRef]
19. Fan, Y.; Feng, H.; Yue, J.; Jin, X.; Liu, Y.; Chen, R. Using an optimized texture index to monitor the nitrogen content of potato plants over multiple growth stages. *Comput. Electron. Agric.* **2023**, *212*, 108147. [CrossRef]

20. Fu, Y.; Yang, G.; Pu, R.; Li, Z.; Li, H.; Xu, X.; Song, X.; Yang, X.; Zhao, C. An overview of crop nitrogen status assessment using hyperspectral remote sensing: Current status and perspectives. *Eur. J. Agron.* **2021**, *124*, 126241. [CrossRef]
21. Zhang, S.; Duan, J.; Qi, X.; Gao, Y.; He, L.; Liu, L. Combining spectrum, thermal, and texture features using machine learning algorithms for wheat nitrogen nutrient index estimation and model transferability analysis. *Comput. Electron. Agric.* **2024**, *222*, 109022. [CrossRef]
22. Bronson, K.; French, A.; Conley, M.; Barnes, E. Use of an ultrasonic sensor for plant height estimation in irrigated cotton. *Agronomy* **2021**, *113*, 2175–2183. [CrossRef]
23. Li, H.; Li, D.; Xu, K.; Cao, W.; Jiang, X.; Ni, J. Monitoring of Nitrogen Indices in Wheat Leaves Based on the Integration of Spectral and Canopy Structure Information. *Agronomy* **2022**, *12*, 833. [CrossRef]
24. Xie, J.; Zhou, Z.; Zhang, H.; Zhang, L.; Li, M. Combining Canopy Coverage and Plant Height from UAV-Based RGB Images to Estimate Spraying Volume on Potato. *Sustainability* **2022**, *14*, 6473. [CrossRef]
25. Flynn, K.; Baath, G.; Lee, T.; Gowda, P.; Northup, B. Hyperspectral reflectance and machine learning to monitor legume biomass and nitrogen accumulation. *Comput. Electron. Agric.* **2023**, *211*, 107991. [CrossRef]
26. Guo, Y.; He, J.; Huang, J.; Jing, Y.; Xu, S.; Wang, L.; Li, S.; Zheng, G. Effects of the Spatial Resolution of UAV Images on the Prediction and Transferability of Nitrogen Content Model for Winter Wheat. *Drones* **2022**, *6*, 299. [CrossRef]
27. Blekanov, I.; Molin, A.; Zhang, D.; Mitrofanov, E.; Mitrofanova, O.; Li, Y. Monitoring of grain crops nitrogen status from uav multispectral images coupled with deep learning approaches. *Comput. Electron. Agric.* **2023**, *212*, 108047. [CrossRef]
28. Jiang, J.; Atkinson, P.; Zhang, J.; Lu, R.; Zhou, Y.; Cao, Q.; Tian, Y.; Zhu, Y.; Cao, W.; Liu, X. Combining fixed-wing UAV multispectral imagery and machine learning to diagnose winter wheat nitrogen status at the farm scale. *Eur. J. Agron.* **2022**, *138*, 126537. [CrossRef]
29. Yang, F.; Liu, Y.; Yan, J.; Guo, L.; Tan, J.; Meng, X.; Xiao, Y.; Feng, H. Winter Wheat Yield Estimation with Color Index Fusion Texture Feature. *Agriculture* **2024**, *14*, 581. [CrossRef]
30. Cao, Q.; Yang, G.; Duan, D.; Chen, L.; Wang, F.; Xu, B.; Zhao, C.; Niu, F. Combining multispectral and hyperspectral data to estimate nitrogen status of tea plants (*Camellia sinensis* (L.) O. Kuntze) under field conditions. *Comput. Electr. Agricult.* **2022**, *198*, 107084. [CrossRef]
31. Li, Z.; Zhou, X.; Cheng, Q.; Fei, S.; Chen, Z. A Machine-Learning Model Based on the Fusion of Spectral and Textural Features from UAV Multi-Sensors to Analyse the Total Nitrogen Content in Winter Wheat. *Remote Sens.* **2023**, *15*, 2152. [CrossRef]
32. Ding, F.; Li, C.; Zhai, W.; Fei, S.; Cheng, Q.; Chen, Z. Estimation of Nitrogen Content in Winter Wheat Based on Multi-Source Data Fusion and Machine Learning. *Agriculture* **2022**, *12*, 1752. [CrossRef]
33. Fu, Y.; Yang, G.; Li, Z.; Song, X.; Li, Z.; Xu, X.; Wang, P.; Zhao, C. 2020. Winter Wheat Nitrogen Status Estimation Using UAV-Based RGB Imagery and Gaussian Processes Regression. *Remote Sens.* **2020**, *12*, 3778. [CrossRef]
34. Oliveira, R.; Barbosa, M.; Pinto, A.; Oliveira, J.; Zerbato, C.; Furlani, C. Predicting Sugarcane Biometric Parameters by UAV Multispectral Images and Machine Learning. *Agronomy* **2022**, *12*, 1992. [CrossRef]
35. Liu, S.; Zhang, B.; Yang, W.; Chen, T.; Zhang, H.; Lin, Y.; Tan, J.; Li, X.; Gao, Y.; Yao, S.; et al. Quantification of Physiological Parameters of Rice Varieties Based on Multi-Spectral Remote Sensing and Machine Learning Models. *Remote Sens.* **2023**, *15*, 453. [CrossRef]
36. Gitelson, A.; Kaufman, Y.; Merziyak, M. Use of a green channel in remote sensing of global vegetation from EOS-MODIS. *Remote Sen. Environ.* **1996**, *58*, 289–298. [CrossRef]
37. Rouse, J. *Monitoring the Vernal Advancement of Retrogradation (Green Wave Effect) of Natural Vegetation*; NASA/GSFC Type III. Final Report; NASA/GSFC: Greenbelt, MD, USA, 1974; p. 371.
38. Rondeaux, G.; Baret, F.; Steven, M. Optimization of soil-adjusted vegetation indices. *Remote Sens. Environ.* **1996**, *55*, 95–107. [CrossRef]
39. Gitelson, A.; Vina, A.; Caganda, V.; Rundquist, D.; Arkebauer, T. Remote estimation of canopy content in crops. *Geophys. Res. Lett.* **2005**, *32*, 1–4. [CrossRef]
40. Huete, A.; Justice, C.; Leeuwen, W. MODIS vegetation index (MOD13). *Algorithm Theor. Basis Doc.* **1999**, *3*, 295–309.
41. Deering, D.; Rouse, J.; Hass, R.; Schell, J. Measuring "Forage Production" of grazing units from Landsat MSS data. In Proceedings of the 10th International Symposium on Remote Sensing of Environment, Ann Arbor, MI, USA, 6 October 1975; pp. 169–1178.
42. Erunova, M.; Pisman, T.; Shevyrnogov, A. The technology for detecting weeds in agricultural crops based on vegetation index VARI (PlanetScope). Journal of Siberian Federal University. *Eng. Technol.* **2021**, *14*, 347–353.
43. Lamm, R.; Slaughter, D.; Giles, D. Precision weed control system for cotton. *Trans. Am. Soc. Agric. Biol. Eng.* **2002**, *45*, 231–238.
44. Huete, A.; Hua, G.; Qi, J.; Chehbouni, A.; Leeuwen, W. Normalization of multidirectional red and NIR reflectances with the SAVI. *Remote Sen. Environ.* **1992**, *41*, 143–154. [CrossRef]
45. Jordan, C.F. Derivation of leaf-area index from quality of light on the forest floor. *Ecology* **1969**, *50*, 663–666. [CrossRef]
46. Hu, P.; Chapman, S.; Wang, X.; Potgieter, A.; Duan, T.; Jordan, D.; Guo, Y.; Zheng, B. Estimation of plant height using a high throughput phenotyping platform based on unmanned aerial vehicle and self-calibration: Example for sorghum breeding. *Eur. J. Agron.* **2018**, *95*, 24–32. [CrossRef]
47. Sun, B.; Wang, C.; Yang, C.; Xu, B.; Zhou, G.; Li, X. Retrieval of rapeseed leaf area index using the PROSAIL model with canopy coverage derived from UAV images as a correction parameter. *Int. J. Appl. Earth Obs. Geoinf.* **2021**, *102*, 102373. [CrossRef]

48. Berger, K.; Verrelst, J.; F'eret, J.-B.; Wang, Z.; Wocher, M.; Strathmann, M.; Danner, M.; Mauser, W.; Hank, T. Crop nitrogen monitoring: Recent progress and principal developments in the context of imaging spectroscopy missions. *Remote Sens. Environ.* **2020**, *242*, 111758. [CrossRef]
49. Breiman, L. Random forests, Machine Learning. *J. Clin. Microbiol.* **2001**, *45*, 199–228.
50. Vapnik, V. *Statistical Learning Theory*; Chapters 10–11; Wiley: New York, NY, USA, 1998; pp. 401–492.
51. Camps-Valls, G.; Verrelst, J.; Munoz-Mari, J.; Laparra, V.; Mateo-Jimenez, F.; Gomez-Dans, J. A survey on Gaussian processes for earth-observation data analysis: A comprehensive investigation. *IEEE Geosci. Remote Sens. Mag.* **2016**, *4*, 58–78. [CrossRef]
52. Soric, J.; Stanic, M.; Lesicar, T. On Neural Network Application in Solid Mechanics. *Trans. Famena* **2023**, *47*, 45–66. [CrossRef]
53. Maimaitijiang, M.; Ghulam, P.; Sidike, S.; Hartling, M.; Maimaitiyiming, K.; Peterson, E.; Shavers, E.; Fishman, J.; Peterson, J.; Kadam, S.; et al. Unmanned Aerial System (uas)-based Phenotyping of Soybean Using Multi-sensor Data Fusion and Extreme Learning Machine. *ISPRS J. Photogramm. Remote Sens.* **2017**, *134*, 43–58. [CrossRef]
54. Zhang, L.; Song, X.; Niu, Y.; Zhang, H.; Wang, A.; Zhu, Y.; Zhu, X.; Chen, L.; Zhu, Q. Estimating Winter Wheat Plant Nitrogen Content by Combining Spectral and Texture Features Based on a Low-Cost UAV RGB System throughout the Growing Season. *Agriculture* **2024**, *14*, 456. [CrossRef]
55. Yang, X.; Yang, R.; Ye, Y.; Yuan, Z.; Wang, D.; Hua, K. Winter wheat SPAD estimation from UAV hyperspectral data using cluster-regression methods. *Int. J. Appl. Earth Obs. Geoinf.* **2021**, *105*, 102618. [CrossRef]
56. Su, X.; Nian, Y.; Yue, H.; Zhu, Y.; Li, J.; Wang, W.; Sheng, Y.; Ma, Q.; Liu, J.; Wang, W.; et al. Improving Wheat Leaf Nitrogen Concentration (LNC) Estimation across Multiple Growth Stages Using Feature Combination Indices (FCIs) from UAV Multispectral Imagery. *Agronomy* **2024**, *14*, 1052. [CrossRef]
57. Basso, B.; Cammarano, D.; De, V.P. Remotely sensed vegetation indices: Theory and applications for crop management. *Riv. Ital. Agrometeorol.* **2004**, *1*, 36–53.
58. Liao, Z.; Dai, Y.; Wang, H.; Quirine, M.; Lu, J.; Zhang, F.; Liu, Z.; Fan, J. A double-layer model for improving the estimation of wheat canopy nitrogen content from unmanned aerial vehicle multispectral imagery. *J. Integr. Agric.* **2023**, *22*, 2248–2270. [CrossRef]
59. Fan, Y.; Feng, H.; Yue, J.; Liu, Y.; Jin, X.; Xu, X.; Song, X.; Ma, Y.; Yang, G. Comparison of Different Dimensional Spectral Indices for Estimating Nitrogen Content of Potato Plants over Multiple Growth Periods. *Remote Sens.* **2023**, *15*, 602. [CrossRef]
60. Grinberg, N.; Orhobor, O.; King, R. An evaluation of machine-learning for predicting phenotype: Studies in yeast, rice, and wheat. *Mach. Learn.* **2020**, *109*, 251–277. [CrossRef]
61. Fan, C.; Zhang, D.; Yang, L.; Cui, T.; He, X.; Qiao, M. Improving Nitrogen Status Diagnosis and Recommendation of Maize Using UAV Remote Sensing Data. *Biosyst. Eng.* **2023**, *236*, 212–223. [CrossRef]

agriculture

MDPI

Article

Refinement of Cropland Data Layer with Effective Confidence Layer Interval and Image Filtering

Reza Maleki [1], Falin Wu [1,*], Amel Oubara [1], Loghman Fathollahi [2] and Gongliu Yang [3]

[1] SNARS Laboratory, School of Instrumentation and Optoelectronic Engineering, Beihang University, Beijing 100191, China; maleki@buaa.edu.cn (R.M.); oubara@buaa.edu.cn (A.O.)
[2] Meteorological Department of West Azerbaijan Province, Iran Meteorological Organization (IRIMO), Orumiyeh 670056, Iran; l.fathollahi@buaa.edu.cn
[3] School of Mechanical Engineering, Zhejiang University, Hangzhou 310030, China; yanggl007@zju.edu.cn
* Correspondence: falin.wu@buaa.edu.cn; Tel.: +86-10-82313929

Abstract: Various systems have been developed to process agricultural land data for better management of crop production. One such system is Cropland Data Layer (CDL), produced by the National Agricultural Statistics Service of the United States Department of Agriculture (USDA). The CDL has been widely used for training deep learning (DL) segmentation models. However, it contains various errors, such as salt-and-pepper noise, and must be refined before being used in DL training. In this study, we used two approaches to refine the CDL for DL segmentation of major crops from a time series of Sentinel-2 monthly composite images. Firstly, different confidence intervals of the confidence layer were used to refine the CDL. Secondly, several image filters were employed to improve data quality. The refined CDLs were then used as the ground-truth in DL segmentation training and evaluation. The results demonstrate that the CDL with +45% and +55% confidence intervals produced the best results, improving the accuracy of DL segmentation by approximately 1% compared to non-refined data. Additionally, filtering the CDL using the majority and expand–shrink filters yielded the best performance, enhancing the evaluation metrics by about 1.5%. The findings suggest that pre-filtering the CDL and selecting an effective confidence interval can significantly improve DL segmentation performance, contributing to more accurate and reliable agricultural monitoring.

Keywords: Cropland Data Layer (CDL); crop mapping; confidence layer; segmentation; deep learning; Sentinel-2

1. Introduction

The agricultural sector has historically met food production demands; however, concerns about its ability to sustain this role for an expanding global population persist in food security discussions [1]. While significant strides have been made in reducing hunger globally, substantial challenges remain [2,3]. Achieving effective situational awareness in food production necessitates a comprehensive understanding of the earth as an integrated system, a capability that is uniquely provided by satellite technology [4]. Satellites offer the ability to map farmland areas and crop types, estimate planted areas and yields and provide early warnings for droughts and floods. Consequently, numerous monitoring systems have been developed in recent years to utilize these satellite data. Among these, Cropland Data Layer (CDL), published annually by the United States Department of Agriculture (USDA), stands out by offering 30 m resolution crop type maps derived from extensive labeled training samples [5–7]. A comprehensive overview of various global agricultural monitoring systems is available in the work of Fritz, et al. [8].

The CDL is widely regarded as the primary source for ground-truth data in machine learning model training owing to its advanced system architecture and adherence to geospatial web services standards within a publicly accessible web environment [9]. Numerous studies affirm the CDL's credibility as a reliable ground-truth for crop mapping [10–13].

Currently, the CDL represents the most comprehensive national crop type map available for free use and download, offering exceptional overall accuracy for major crops, particularly corn and soybeans, with accuracy rates exceeding 95% [5]. However, several studies have highlighted defects within the CDL, primarily due to its reliance on remote sensing datasets, which raises concerns regarding the quality of CDL products [9,14–18]. To address these concerns, the USDA National Agricultural Statistics Service (NASS) has provided an accuracy rating since 2008 and introduced the confidence layer in 2017 to enhance data reliability [5].

The use of various CDL confidence layer percentages has been explored in some studies to utilize the CDL as ground-truth data [13,19]. For instance, Hao et al. [13] employed a 95% confidence interval, rejecting all CDLs below this threshold. However, there is no clear justification for selecting the 95% threshold, and similar studies lack a rationale for their chosen confidence intervals. Additionally, a review of the CDL reveals significant errors, some resembling salt-and-pepper noise, even within the 100% confidence interval. These inaccuracies negatively impact deep learning (DL) data outcomes, necessitating the removal of erroneous CDLs through refining techniques. While some studies [9,14] have attempted to address this issue, fully accurate results have yet to be achieved, indicating a need for further research and the development of alternative approaches.

To refine the CDL and improve DL training outcomes, this research had two primary objectives. The first objective was to establish effective confidence intervals for refining the CDL to enhance DL segmentation accuracy. Various confidence interval values were applied to the CDL of major crops in the study area, and the resulting data were used as the ground-truth in a DL model. The effectiveness of these intervals was analyzed using multi-criteria decision analysis (MCDA) to determine the best approach for future applications. Additionally, the generalizability of these confidence intervals was tested in a different study area, confirming the robustness of our method across different geographical regions. The second objective was to evaluate the effectiveness of different image filtering techniques in mitigating errors within the CDL. By applying these filters, we assessed their contribution to improving the quality of the CDL and subsequently enhancing DL model accuracy for mapping croplands using Sentinel-2 imagery. This research also involved comparing our methods with the refined CDL (R-CDL) from Lin et al. [9], further demonstrating the efficiency and practicality of our approach.

2. Materials and Methods

2.1. Study Area

In this study, we focused on a specific region within the Mississippi Delta, highlighted in Figure 1, selected for its agricultural diversity and distinct seasonal phenological stages [20]. In 2021, soybeans were predominantly cultivated in this area, covering 31.7% of the landscape, along with significant portions of corn, cotton and rice, illustrating its agricultural variety. This diverse region, covering approximately 575,908 square kilometers and featuring various land cover types and surface features, provides an ideal environment for evaluating CDL refinements and the effectiveness of image filtering techniques in improving DL segmentation accuracy for precise agricultural monitoring.

To evaluate the generalizability of our method and conclusions, we conducted additional testing in a different geographical region named T14TNK, identified by its UTM Zone 14 within the Military Grid Reference System (MGRS). This area, covering approximately 100 km by 100 km, is located between Nebraska and Kansas, defined by the coordinates 97°42′ W–99°0′ W and 39°40′ N–40°38.5′ N, and includes parts of the Republican River. The major crops in this region are corn and soybeans, making it an ideal candidate for validating our methodology across different agricultural landscapes. By applying the same confidence interval and image filtering techniques, we aimed to assess the consistency and reliability of our approach. The results from this additional region further support the applicability of our method to diverse agricultural settings.

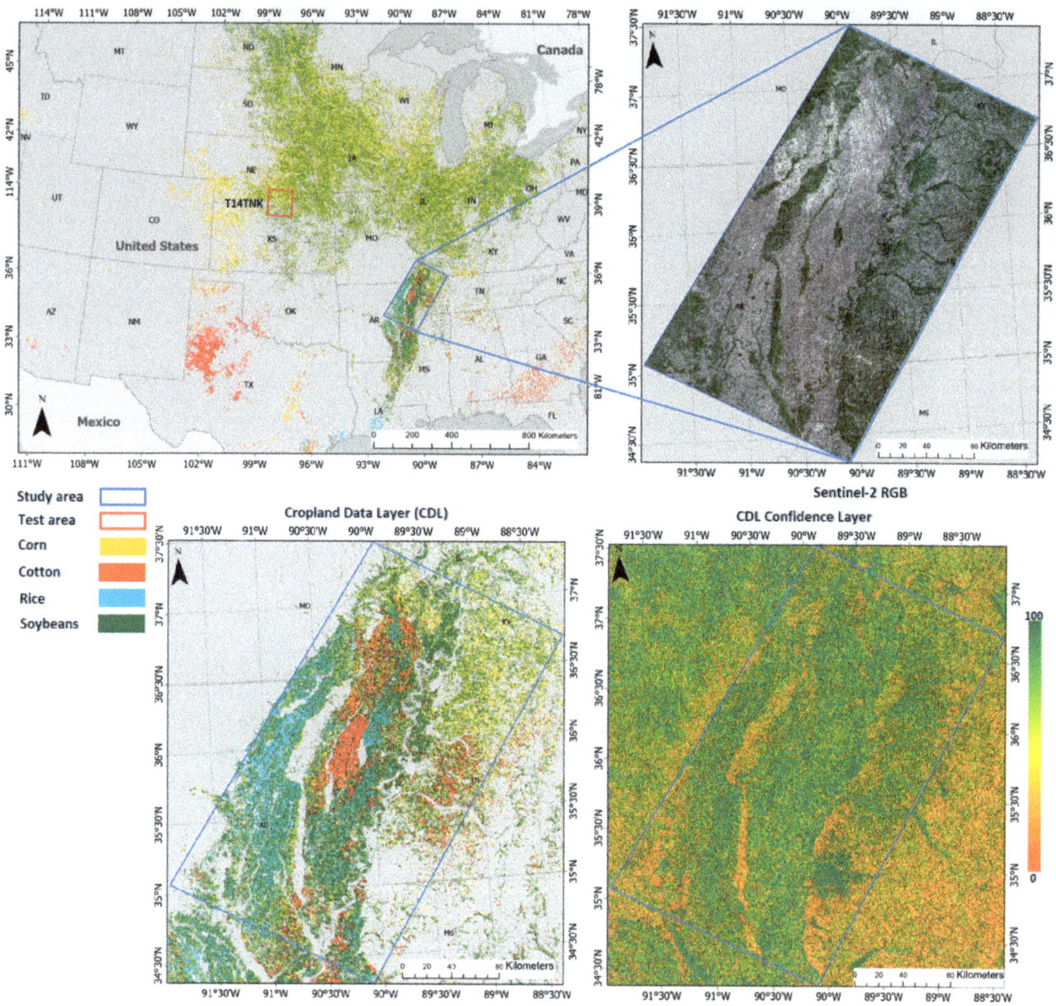

Figure 1. Geographic overview and data layers used in the study. The top-left map shows the study area within the Mississippi Delta (blue rectangle) and T14TNK test area (red rectangle). The top-right image displays Sentinel-2 composite imagery from May 2021. The bottom-left map illustrates the distribution of crops in the CDL. The bottom-right map depicts the CDL confidence layer, indicating the confidence values associated with the CDL.

2.2. Materials

2.2.1. Sentinel-2 Imagery

To utilize satellite images, we selected multispectral images from the European Sentinel-2 sensors. These images are widely used in large-scale vegetation extraction, both in research and various application systems, due to their comprehensive optical spectrum for crop identification and acceptable spatial resolution compared to the CDL [21,22]. The red (B4), green (B3), blue (B2) and near-infrared (B8) bands have a spatial resolution of 10 m. Additionally, the three red-edge bands (B5, B6 and B7), two short-wave infrared bands (B11, B12) and one narrow NIR band (B8a) offer spatial resolutions that can exceed 20 m, adding extra band attributes for classification [21–24]. Bands 1, 9 and 10 correspond to coastal aerosols, water vapor and cirrus clouds, respectively [22]. These bands have a

60 m resolution, which makes accurate recording of the reflectance of minor surface objects challenging. Therefore, after excluding bands 1, 9 and 10, we selected a total of 10 bands for our investigation.

Utilizing Google Earth Engine (GEE) [21,23], we processed monthly minimum composite datasets from May to September, comprising 872 tiles in Mississippi Delta and 29 tiles in T14TNK. This period aligns with the peak growing season in the study area, as indicated by the Normalized Difference Vegetation Index (NDVI) [25] in Figure 2. To provide a comprehensive view of vegetation dynamics, NDVI curves for the entire year of 2021 were generated, contrasting growing and non-growing periods. The NDVI for each major crop was calculated using Sentinel-2 satellite imagery, with cloud masking applied to remove cloudy pixels. The data were composited into 15-day intervals over 2021, and NDVI was computed. Stratified random sampling selected 10,000 sample points for each major crop based on the CDL with 100% confidence interval, extracting NDVI values to provide a detailed temporal profile for each crop.

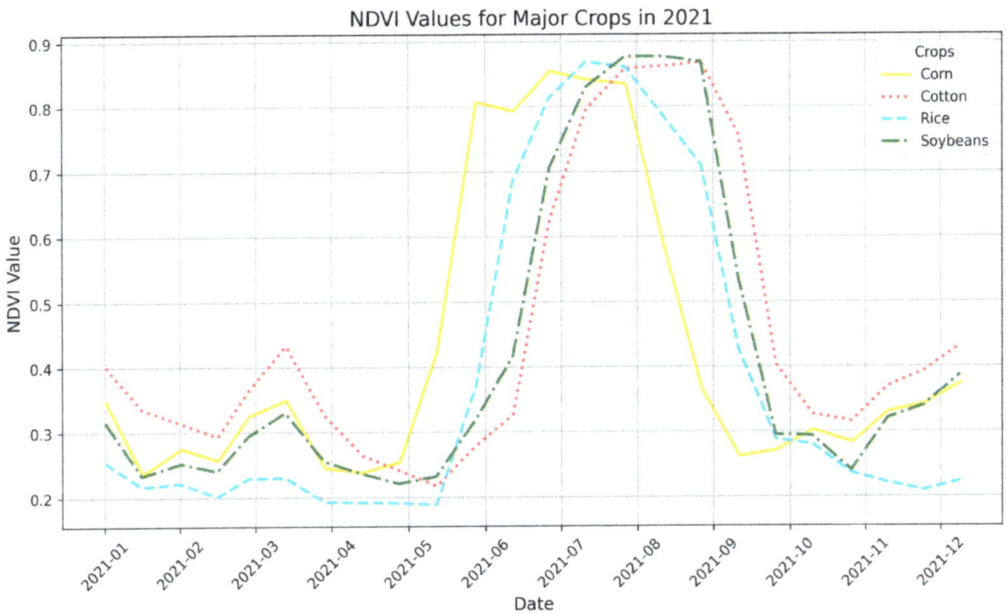

Figure 2. NDVI profiles for the major crops in the study area throughout the year 2021.

2.2.2. Cropland Data Layer (CDL)

Training and validation ground-truth data were derived from the CDL. The USDA—NASS produces the CDL, which offers an annual crop type for the United States at a 30 m resolution with more than 100 crop classes [6]. Since 2006, the state-level CDL classification has been conducted using the supervised RuleQuest See5.0 [26] decision tree classification approach [27,28]. Each US state's metadata include producer accuracy (PA), user accuracy (UA) and Kappa score, and the CDL is evaluated using a subset of ground-truth data. According to Boryan et al. [27], the primary crops in the CDL have excellent classification accuracy ranging from 85% to 95% [5]. The chart in Figure 3 displays the distribution of various land cover types in Mississippi Delta, highlighting major crops such as soybeans, corn, cotton and rice. Additionally, we included the "other" class to account for non-crop areas and different crop types from major crops.

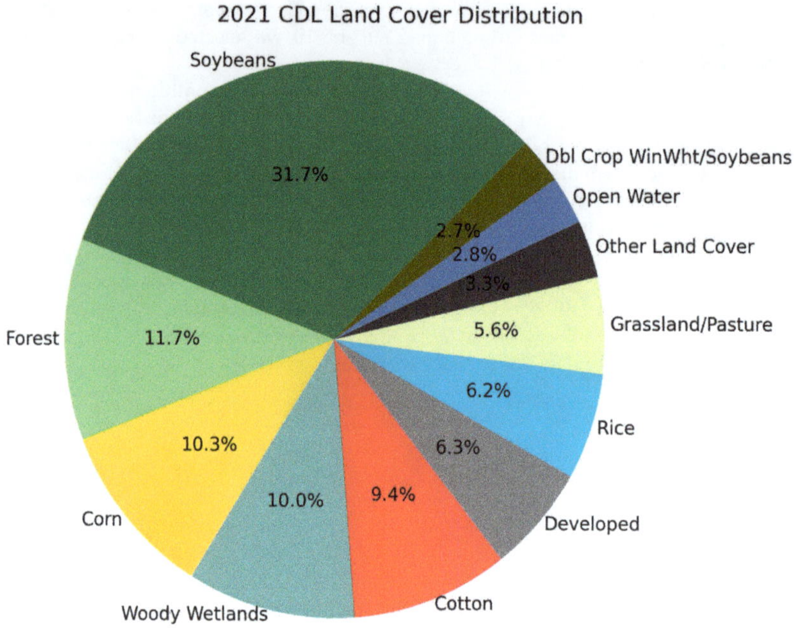

Figure 3. The 2021 CDL land cover distribution in the study area.

To compare the effectiveness of our method, we utilized refined CDL data based on the methodology outlined in Lin et al.'s study [9]. This study aimed to identify and resolve inaccuracies in CDL crop classifications by employing a decision tree method to detect and refine questionable pixels using spatial and temporal crop information. The refined CDL (R-CDL) data were validated against high-resolution satellite images and USDA's official acreage estimates, ensuring their robustness. By incorporating this refined dataset, we were able to benchmark our proposed methods against a well-validated standard, providing a comprehensive evaluation of our approach in relation to existing techniques.

2.2.3. CDL Confidence Layer

The confidence layer is an additional layer provided alongside the CDL, which was evaluated in this study. This layer geographically indicates the expected confidence associated with each output pixel based on the classification rules applied. It offers a visual representation of the distribution and magnitude of classification confidence or error, which is highly beneficial for users. The confidence layer represents classification accuracies as a confidence interval, where a rating of 100 signifies very high confidence, and a rating of 0 signifies very low confidence. Essentially, the confidence value measures how well a pixel fits into the decision tree ruleset, rather than the absolute accuracy of a specific pixel [5].

By utilizing the confidence layer, users can better assess the reliability of the CDL for different applications. In this study, we employed various confidence interval thresholds to refine the CDL, which was then used as the ground-truth for training DL models. The impact of these confidence intervals on the quality of training data and DL performance was systematically evaluated to identify the most effective threshold for accurate crop segmentation from Sentinel-2 imagery.

2.3. Research Approaches

This section delineates the research methodology, with a flowchart in Figure 4 summarizing the essential steps, inputs and outputs. The inputs include monthly minimum composites of Sentinel-2 time series during the growing season, while the outputs encompass various DL segmentation evaluation metrics and maps of major crops under different conditions of confidence layer data and CDL refinements. To enhance the quality of the CDL for use as the ground-truth in the DL, two approaches are proposed: utilizing different confidence intervals of the CDL confidence layer and applying various image filters to mitigate noise and errors. Initially, CDL crop data are refined using specified confidence intervals and overlaid with Sentinel-2 imagery to create a comprehensive database. The DL model is then trained on these datasets, with accuracy metrics compared through MCDA. In the second approach, different image filters are applied to the major crops of the CDL. These refined datasets are subsequently used to train the DL model, and the results are compared to identify the most effective refinement technique.

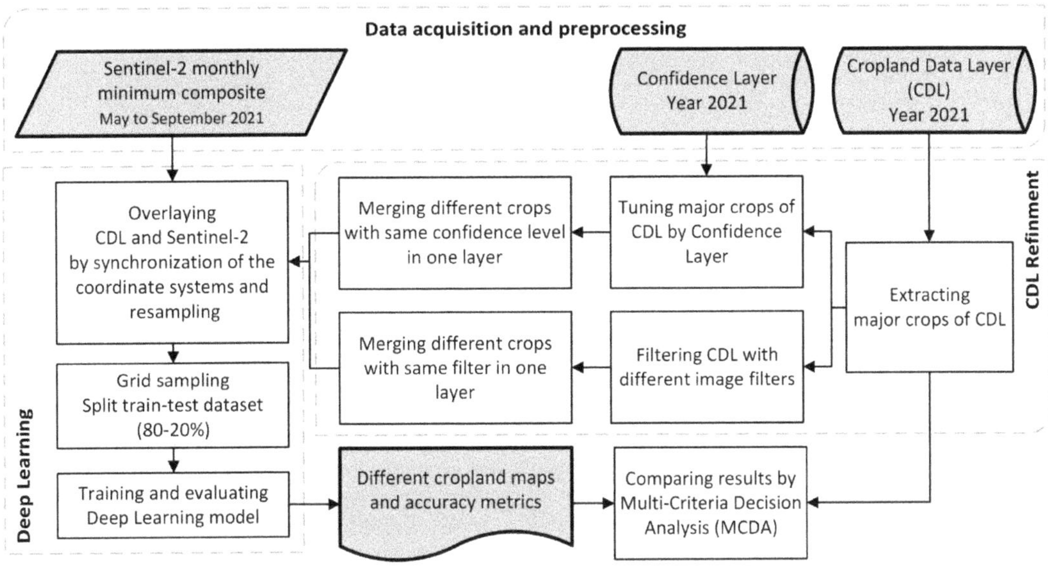

Figure 4. Flowchart summarizing the research approach for major crop mapping from Sentinel-2 imagery using various CDL confidence levels and image filters.

2.3.1. CDL Refinement Using the Confidence Layer

Given the focus on major crops, the initial step involves extracting crop data with varying confidence levels by querying the CDL under different confidence level values. For example, a +75% confidence layer includes crop data with confidence intervals of 75% and higher (e.g., 95%) while excluding data with confidence values below 75%. This method retains higher quality data and discards lower quality data. However, removing low-quality data can sometimes weaken the dataset for DL applications, whereas using all available data may negatively impact the DL by incorporating erroneous data. Numerous studies have explored varying confidence intervals within the confidence layer [13,19], while others have opted to utilize the entire dataset [20]. A critical aim of this research is to determine the most effective confidence interval for refining the CDL as ground-truth data in DL cropland segmentation. To address this, an experiment was designed using crop layer data with confidence intervals from 0% to 100%.

2.3.2. CDL Refinement Using Image Filters

Despite the CDL having defined confidence levels, substantial amounts of erroneous data persist, even at the 100% confidence level [9]. Visual inspection of data in respect of different crops reveals defects such as salt-and-pepper noise and errors [14,17]. These issues are apparent across various confidence intervals. Additionally, the CDL erroneously classifies field borders and roads as croplands, contributing to significant noise and inaccuracies. To address the pervasive issues of noise and errors within the CDL, the next step involves refining the CDL using an image filter to establish a more accurate ground-truth for DL applications. The aim of this process is to eliminate noise, incorrect border areas between fields and other unknown defects. Initially, each major crop from the CDL was separated, and various image filters were applied individually, including the following:

- Aggregation [29]: This filter smooths the data by combining small, isolated patches of classified pixels into larger, contiguous regions, thereby reducing salt-and-pepper noise.
- Boundary cleaning [30]: This filter simplifies the raster by smoothing zone boundaries using expansion (dilation) and shrinking (erosion) techniques. This process involves evaluating each input cell based on its orthogonal and diagonal neighbors to achieve the desired smoothing effect.
- Expand [31]: The expand filter increases the size of designated zones within a raster by a certain number of cells. These designated zones are treated as the foreground, while the rest are considered the background, allowing the foreground to grow into the surrounding background areas.
- Shrink [32]: The shrink filter designates specific zone values as the foreground, enabling their expansion into surrounding background zones. This process effectively reduces noise and minor misclassifications, resulting in a more accurate and conservative delineation of crop extents.
- Majority [33]: This filter reclassifies each pixel based on the majority class of its neighbors, helping to correct misclassified pixels by considering local context.
- Expand–shrink: This technique involves initially shrinking the classified regions in an image to remove noise and small misclassified areas and then expanding the remaining areas back to their original size. This process helps in retaining the core areas of the classified regions while minimizing the impact of noise and erroneous small regions.

After filtering, the refined major crop datasets were merged into a single comprehensive layer, similar to the original CDL. This process generated six distinct filtered datasets, each treated with different image filters. These improved data serve as a more reliable input for DL models, thereby enhancing the precision of cropland segmentation. These filtering techniques were selected for their ability to mitigate specific types of errors and noise present in the CDL.

2.4. Data Pre-Processing

A robust pre-processing workflow was applied to each monthly Sentinel-2 dataset using the GEE platform to optimize data for crop segmentation analysis. The initial step involved a cloud-and-shadow masking technique utilizing the satellite's Scene Classification Layer (SCL) [34] and cloud probability data. This step effectively excluded atmospheric obstructions, enhancing image clarity. Following this, the workflow generated minimum composites for each month, selecting the pixel with the lowest reflectance value from all clear observations to minimize cloud interference. Despite a potential increase in shadow presence, this method prioritizes reducing cloud cover due to its significant impact on spectral data accuracy. Simultaneously, the major crops in the CDL were selected to focus on corn, cotton, rice and soybeans. This involved selectively masking the CDL to retain only these crops and clipping it to match the spatial extent of the Sentinel-2 composite. The 256×256 pixel grid sampling generated 977 samples in the study area and 211 in the test area, filtering out less informative samples to optimize data richness. The refined samples were randomly divided into training and validation groups in an 80–20% split and organized into batches of 64 for efficient DL model training.

2.5. Model Architecture and Training

For the crop segmentation task using Sentinel-2 imagery, the Pytorch-based DeepLabV3Plus [35] model with a ResNet34 encoder was employed. This model was selected due to its proven efficacy in semantic segmentation across various applications and ResNet34's robust feature extraction capabilities [36]. The DeepLabV3Plus architecture, with its standard decoder and batch normalization, was adapted to suit the unique requirements of this dataset. The inputs consisted of 5 monthly minimum composites of Sentinel-2 imagery from May to September, each comprising 10 bands, resulting in a 50-layer input. This configuration captures the phenological changes in major crops. The model output was designed to classify five distinct classes corresponding to major crops (corn, cotton, rice, soybeans and other), optimizing it for detailed segmentation in the study area. The Adam optimizer [37] was used with a learning rate of 0.01. During training, cross-entropy loss was employed, with early stopping implemented after 50 epochs of no improvement to prevent overfitting.

2.6. Accuracy Metrics and Comparative Analysis

Overall accuracy (OA), user's accuracy (UA), producer's accuracy (PA) and F1-score (F1) [38,39] accuracy metrics were employed to evaluate the approaches.

$$\mathrm{OA} = \frac{TP + TN}{\text{Total Instances}} \tag{1}$$

$$\mathrm{UA} = \frac{TP}{TP + FP} \tag{2}$$

$$\mathrm{PA} = \frac{TP}{TP + FN} \tag{3}$$

$$\mathrm{F1} = 2 \times \frac{\mathrm{UA} \times \mathrm{PA}}{\mathrm{UA} + \mathrm{PA}} \tag{4}$$

where TP represents the number of true positives; FP represents the number of false positives; FN represents the number of false negatives; and TN represents the number of true negatives.

Also, a confusion matrix (error matrix) [38,40] is used to evaluate the performance of our DL models in classifying different crop types. A confusion matrix is a table that outlines the performance of the model by comparing the actual classes to the predicted classes. Each cell in the matrix represents the proportion of instances (expressed as a percentage) that were correctly or incorrectly classified by the model. Values range from 0 to 100, indicating the percentage of instances that fall into each category. For instance, a value of 95 in the matrix indicates that 95% of the instances of a particular class were correctly predicted, whereas a value of 0.005 might indicate a small proportion of misclassifications. These values provide a detailed insight into the model's accuracy, UA, PA and overall performance in distinguishing between different crop types.

In addition, MCDA in this context involved evaluating multiple criteria (accuracy metrics) across various confidence interval alternatives in the DL metric results. Let A represent the set of confidence interval alternatives and C represent the set of criteria such as UA, PA and F1 [38,39]. Each criterion $c \in C$ was normalized to bring different accuracy metrics onto a comparable scale. The normalization process for a criterion c for alternative a was calculated as

$$n_{ac} = \frac{x_{ac}}{\sqrt{\sum_{a \in A} x_{ac}^2}} \tag{5}$$

where x_{ac} is the original value of criterion c for alternative a, and n_{ac} is the normalized value. Weights w_c were assigned to each criterion c, reflecting its importance in the decision-making process:

$$w_c = \frac{1}{|C|} \tag{6}$$

The weighted normalized value for each criterion of each alternative was calculated as:

$$v_{ac} = n_{ac} \cdot w_c \tag{7}$$

Identification of the ideal best ($A+$) and ideal worst ($A-$) was as follows:

$$A_c^+ = \max_{a \in A} v_{ac} \text{ and } A_c^- = \min_{a \in A} v_{ac} \tag{8}$$

Calculation of the distance to ideal best ($D+$) and ideal worst ($D-$) was as follows:

$$D_a^+ = \sqrt{\sum_{c \in C} \left(v_{ac} - A_c^+\right)^2} \text{ and } D_a^- = \sqrt{\sum_{c \in C} \left(v_{ac} - A_c^-\right)^2} \tag{9}$$

The relative closeness of each alternative to the ideal solution was calculated as

$$RC_a = \frac{D_a^-}{D_a^+ + D_a^-} \tag{10}$$

Alternatives were then ranked based on their relative closeness to the ideal solution, with a higher RC_a indicating a closer proximity to the ideal, and thus, a higher preference. MCDA systematically analyzes DL model performance across different confidence intervals and image filters, integrating metrics like OA, UA, PA and F1.

For the generalizability analysis, significance analysis experiments were conducted to quantify the similarity and statistical significance of the results between the Mississippi Delta and T14TNK areas. The Pearson correlation coefficient [40,41] and paired t-tests [39] were employed to compare the performance of different refining methods between these two regions. The Pearson correlation coefficient measures the strength and direction of the linear relationship between two variables. The paired t-test is used to determine whether the means of two paired samples differ significantly. The p-value associated with the T-statistic indicates whether the difference between the pairs is statistically significant. To ensure the comparison focuses on trends rather than absolute values, data normalization is performed.

$$\text{T-statistic} = \frac{\overline{d}}{\frac{s_d}{\sqrt{n}}} \tag{11}$$

In the T-statistic, $\overline{d}$ is the mean of the differences between paired observations; s_d is the standard deviation of the differences; and n is the number of pairs.

$$\text{Pearson correlation coefficient} = \frac{\Sigma(x_i - \overline{x})(y_i - \overline{y})}{\sqrt{\Sigma(x_i - \overline{x})^2 \Sigma(y_i - \overline{y})^2}} \tag{12}$$

where x_i and y_i are the individual sample points, and $\overline{x}$ and $\overline{y}$ are the means of the sample sets x and y, respectively. A Pearson correlation coefficient close to 1 indicates a strong positive correlation, while a value close to -1 indicates a strong negative correlation.

3. Results

To implement the proposed approaches, the research was divided into three phases. The first phase involved evaluating the approaches using the CDL with varying confidence levels. In the second phase, different image filters were applied to the CDL, and the DL segmentation results were subsequently evaluated. In the third phase, the methodologies were tested on an additional test area, T14TNK, to compare and validate the effectiveness of the approaches in a different geographical and crop context.

3.1. Impact of CDL Confidence Intervals on Segmentation

The confidence interval percentages applied to the major crop of the CDL result in a progressive reduction in the number of crop pixels within the image. As the confidence interval increases toward 100%, the number of pixels representing crops correspondingly decreases. Figure 5 quantifies this reduction, displaying the area (in hectares) occupied by different crops at each confidence interval. Notably, in some scenarios, the pixel count can be reduced by up to two times. It is crucial to understand the impact of this reduction on machine learning applications, as it directly affects the accuracy and reliability of DL segmentation outcomes. Figure 6 illustrates the distribution of major crop pixels at various confidence intervals, showing how increased confidence thresholds progressively refine the CDL.

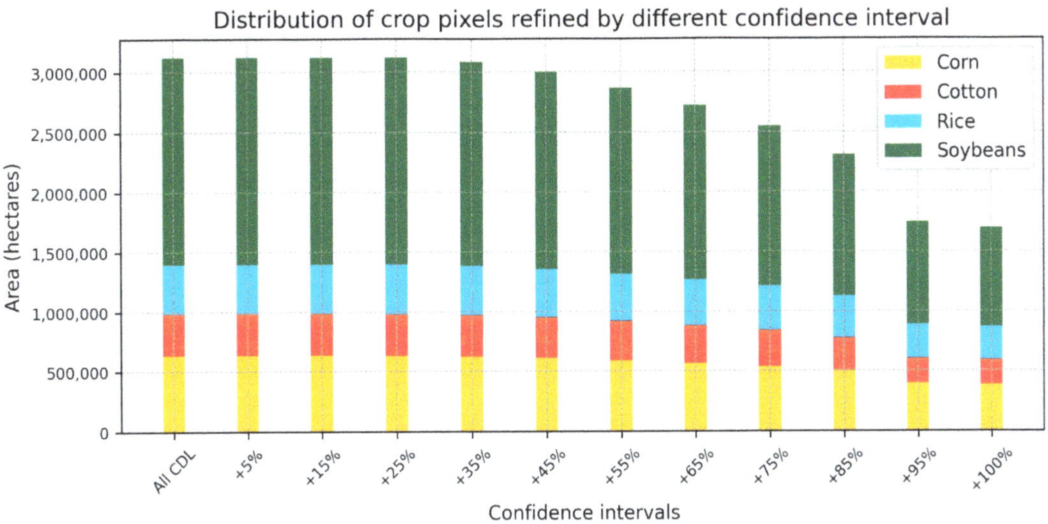

Figure 5. Distribution of crop pixels refined by different confidence levels of major crops within the study area for the year 2021.

Table 1 displays the outcomes (OA, UA, PA and F1) of the DL implementation using different CDL datasets at varying confidence interval percentages. Additionally, the MCDA relative closeness values are provided to indicate the effectiveness of each confidence interval. The best overall performance can be observed at confidence intervals of +45%, +55% and +65%, with OAs of 90.5%–90.6%, indicating that these intervals effectively balance the inclusion of high-quality data while excluding erroneous data. Conversely, the lowest performances are seen at +85%–100% confidence intervals, with OAs less than 88.6%, indicating that excluding too much data adversely impacts the model's performance.

For crop-specific performance, corn and soybeans exhibited the highest F1 at the 55% confidence interval, while cotton and rice achieved the highest F1 at the 45% confidence interval. The MCDA values corroborate these results, showing the highest relative closeness at the 45% and 55% intervals. This reinforces the conclusion that mid-range confidence intervals provide the effective balance by retaining high-quality data and excluding noise. These findings suggest that the 45% and 55% confidence intervals for the CDL strike the best balance, significantly enhancing the DL model's accuracy and reliability for agricultural mapping applications.

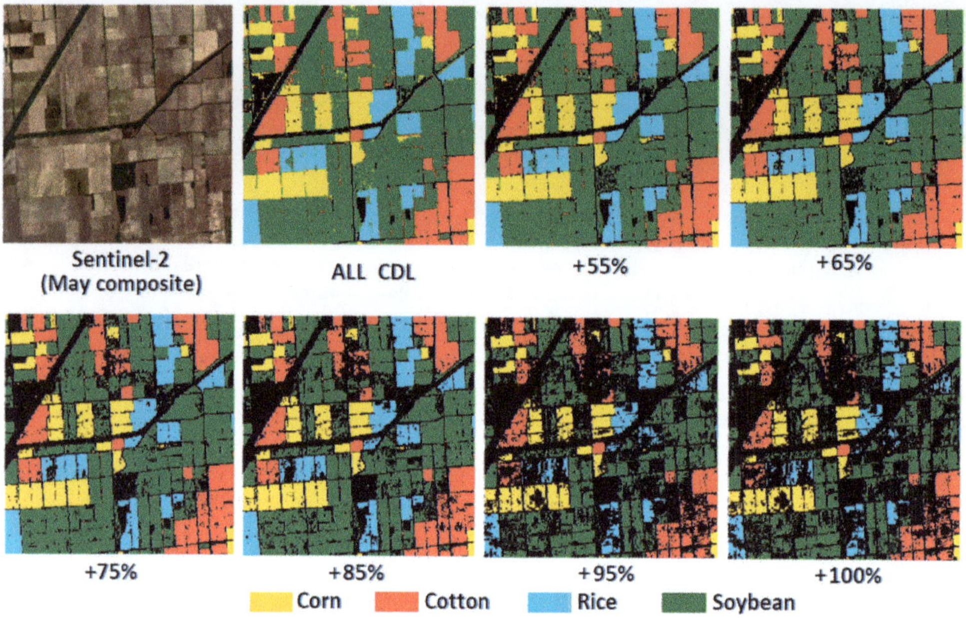

Figure 6. Impact of varying confidence intervals on the refinement of the CDL. The percentages indicate the confidence thresholds used to refine the CDL.

Table 1. Performance metrics of the DL model using CDL datasets at different confidence interval percentages. The metrics include overall accuracy (OA), user's accuracy (UA), producer's accuracy (PA) and F1-score (F1) and MCDA relative closeness. "All CDL" refers to using the entire CDL without any confidence interval filtering, serving as a baseline for comparison.

Confidence	Overall				Corn			Cotton			Rice			Soybeans			Other			
Interval	OA	UA	PA	F1	UA	PA	F1	UA	PA	F1	UA	PA	F1	UA	PA	F1	UA	PA	F1	MCDA
1-21 All CDL	89.4	89.5	89.7	89.6	88.7	88.1	88.4	88.8	91.9	90.3	93.3	91.4	92.3	85.6	86.0	85.8	91.3	91.1	91.2	85.8
+5%	89.5	89.2	89.9	89.5	89.6	86.8	88.2	87.0	93.2	90.0	91.6	92.8	92.2	87.1	84.6	85.8	90.7	92.0	91.4	84.8
+15%	89.7	90.3	89.7	90.0	89.7	87.7	88.7	90.1	91.9	91.0	93.0	92.3	92.6	89.1	83.0	85.9	89.5	93.6	91.5	86.4
+25%	89.9	90.2	90.0	90.1	89.7	88.0	88.8	89.7	92.2	91.0	93.0	92.7	92.8	88.9	83.5	86.1	89.9	93.4	91.6	87.5
+35%	90.0	90.5	89.8	90.2	90.8	87.7	89.2	90.2	91.8	91.0	94.0	91.5	92.7	86.5	85.9	86.2	91.1	92.3	91.7	88.0
+45%	90.5	90.7	90.7	90.7	90.1	89.7	89.9	90.8	91.6	91.2	93.0	93.8	93.4	88.3	85.6	86.9	91.4	92.8	92.1	92.3
+55%	90.6	90.0	91.4	90.7	90.7	89.3	90.0	89.0	93.2	91.0	91.0	95.7	93.3	86.8	87.7	87.2	92.6	91.2	91.9	90.8
+65%	90.6	89.8	91.2	90.4	88.6	91.0	89.8	88.6	92.6	90.6	90.6	95.2	92.8	89.4	84.6	87.0	91.5	92.3	91.9	90.1
+75%	90.3	89.0	90.6	89.8	86.5	92.4	89.4	87.1	91.8	89.3	92.2	91.5	91.9	87.2	85.9	86.5	92.1	91.4	91.7	86.2
+85%	88.6	86.2	87.7	86.9	84.5	88.2	86.3	84.1	85.1	84.5	87.4	92.7	89.9	84.4	81.8	83.1	90.9	90.7	90.8	68.1
+95%	84.7	77.0	79.6	78.1	73.6	81.6	77.4	71.5	75.1	73.2	77.1	87.3	81.9	73.5	64.5	68.7	89.1	89.4	89.2	8.9
+100%	84.9	76.3	79.5	77.8	72.7	81.8	77.0	70.4	75.1	72.6	77.3	82.6	79.8	71.3	69.2	70.2	89.9	88.9	89.4	8.4

The results of the DL segmentation, trained using data with various confidence intervals and the entire CDL dataset, are illustrated in Figure 7. In the segmentation results utilizing the entire dataset without the confidence layer, noise is effectively mitigated, and the original fields are clearly delineated. However, the method encounters challenges in accurately identifying roads and gaps between agricultural fields. In several instances, the segmentation erroneously classified non-cropland areas as cropland, which represents a significant limitation. Conversely, the results for the +85% and higher confidence intervals, while successfully removing noise, also erroneously exclude numerous agricultural fields.

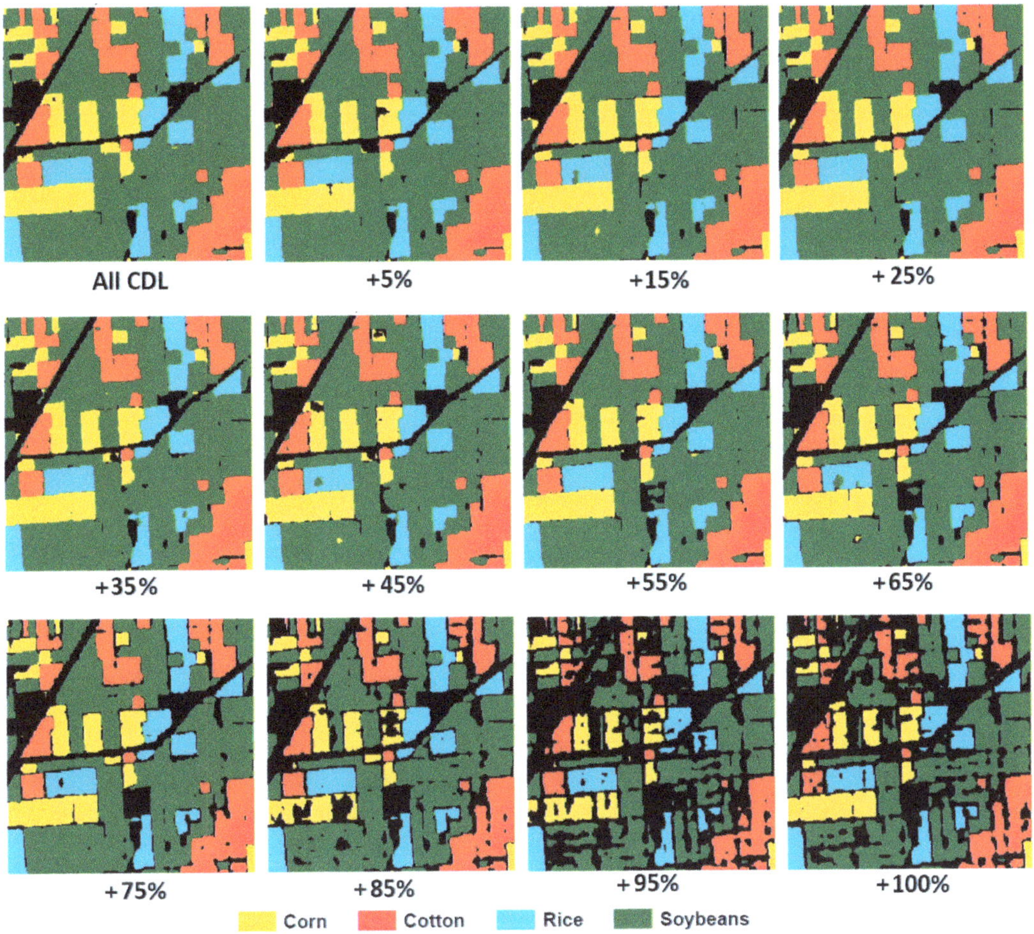

Figure 7. DL segmentation results of croplands from Sentinel-2 imagery. The DL models were trained using different CDL confidence layer intervals.

Conversely, the segmentation results using the +35% to +75% confidence intervals are highly satisfactory. These datasets accurately depict the fields in their entirety, correctly identify gaps between the fields and eliminate non-agricultural areas. There are slight variations between the +45% and +55% confidence intervals; in some cases, the +45% interval outperforms, while in others, the +55% interval yields better results. This suggests that a confidence level within this range could provide the most effective segmentation performance, balancing accuracy and reliability.

The confusion matrices for different confidence intervals of the CDL in Figure 8 reveal various impacts on the performance of DL models in segmenting major crops. The All CDL matrix shows balanced performance across crops but contains some misclassifications, particularly in distinguishing corn and soybeans. As the confidence interval increases to +45% and +55%, there is a slight improvement in the identification of cotton and rice, evidenced by higher UA values in these categories. The +55% confidence level shows a noticeable enhancement in OA, especially for corn and soybeans, reducing false positives and false negatives significantly. The +65% interval continues this trend, with improved accuracy for cotton and rice. However, at the +95% and 100% confidence levels, there is a marked decline in performance across all crops, with increased misclassification rates, particularly for soybeans, indicating that overly stringent confidence levels may exclude valuable data, thereby impairing model accuracy.

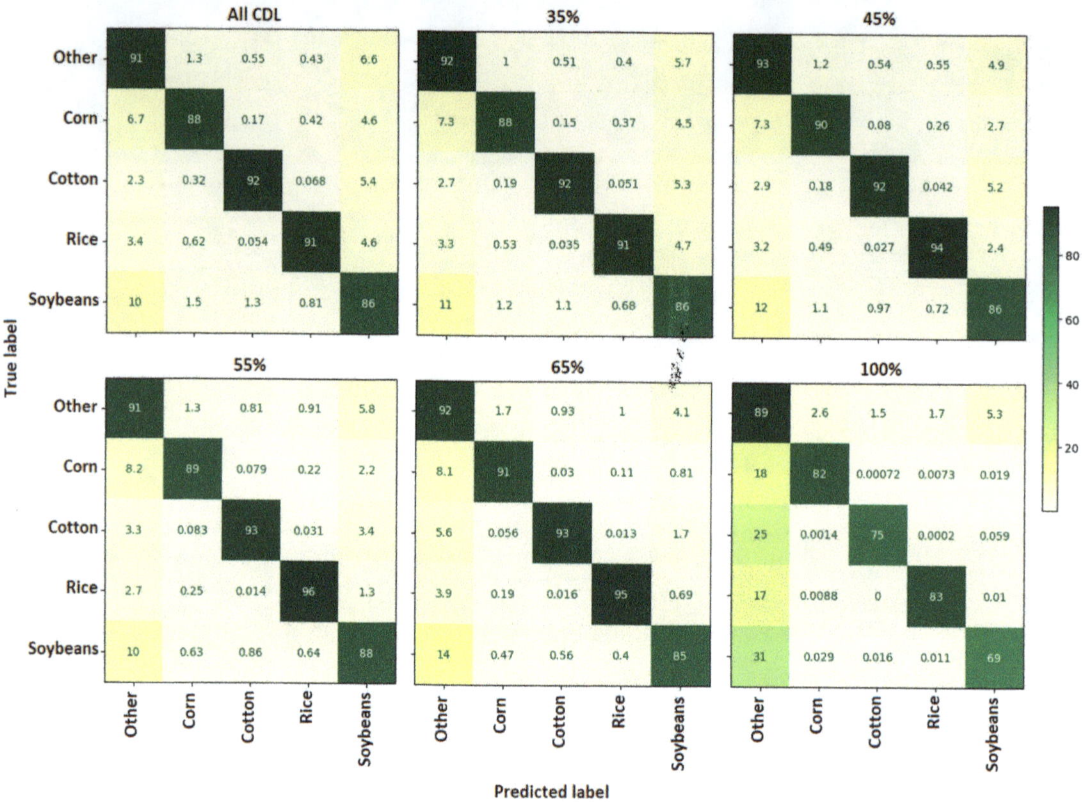

Figure 8. Confusion matrices illustrating the performance of DL models trained with different CDL confidence intervals in segmenting major crops. Diagonal numbers represent the percentage of correctly classified instances for each crop, while non-diagonal numbers indicate the percentage of misclassified instances between different crops.

3.2. Evaluating Filtered CDL

To address the discrepancies in CDL quality, various image filters were applied to enhance the accuracy of the DL models. The aim of these filters is to reduce noise and correct errors within the CDL dataset, ensuring a more reliable ground-truth for DL training. Table 2 presents the outcomes for each filter in terms of OA, UA, PA and F1 for the major crops. The "No Filter" and "R-CDL [9]" results in Table 2 are included for comparison. It should be noted that "No Filter" corresponds to "All CDL" in Table 1.

Applying different image filters to the CDL significantly improved DL model performance over the No Filter baseline. The majority filter and expand–shrink filter each enhanced the OA and F1 by approximately 2%, with similar improvements in user and producer accuracy across all crops. Both filters demonstrated superior effectiveness in refining the CDL for DL applications. The boundary clean filter provided notable enhancements, particularly in OA and F1, showing an approximate 1% improvement over the No Filter results. Although the shrink filter also delivered improvements, it was slightly less effective than the majority and expand–shrink filters, with a modest increase in the OA and F1. The results for R-CDL from Lin et al.'s study [9] show that it achieves competitive performance, indicating its effectiveness in improving CDL quality. Conversely, the expand filter resulted in the lowest performance, highlighting the importance of choosing appropriate filters to avoid amplifying noise. The application of these filters, especially the majority and expand–shrink filters, proved crucial in enhancing the quality of the CDL, thereby improving the DL model's accuracy in segmenting agricultural fields.

Table 2. Performance metrics of DL models using filtered CDL with various image filters. "R-CDL" refers to the CDL refined using the method described in Lin et al.'s study [9]. "No Filter" is equivalent to "All CDL" in Table 1.

	Overall				Corn			Cotton			Rice			Soybeans			Other			
Filters	**OA**	**UA**	**PA**	**F1**	**UA**	**PA**	**F1**	**UA**	**PA**	**F1**	**UA**	**PA**	**F1**	**UA**	**PA**	**F1**	**UA**	**PA**	**F1**	**MCDA**
1-21 Aggregate	90.1	89.5	89.0	89.2	87.3	88.8	88.1	88.7	88.9	88.8	91.8	91.1	91.4	89.2	83.5	86.3	90.6	92.8	91.7	52.9
Boundary Clean	90.3	91.6	90.0	90.7	92.9	85.2	88.9	92.6	91.9	92.2	94.5	91.9	93.2	86.3	88.8	87.5	91.4	92.1	91.8	66.0
Expand	86.7	87.9	85.4	86.5	88.4	78.5	83.1	89.4	85.0	87.2	90.4	87.1	88.7	85.6	81.8	83.7	85.4	94.7	89.8	14.7
Expand–Shrink	91.7	91.5	91.7	91.6	91.7	90.3	91.0	90.1	93.6	91.8	93.2	93.9	93.5	90.7	87.3	89.0	92.0	93.5	92.8	84.0
Majority	91.4	91.8	91.8	91.8	90.2	92.0	91.1	92.5	93.2	92.8	94.0	94.2	94.1	90.9	86.0	88.4	91.4	93.8	92.6	83.8
Shrink	91.4	89.4	89.4	89.3	89.5	85.3	87.4	86.8	89.0	87.9	90.0	93.0	91.4	87.4	85.9	86.6	93.2	93.8	93.5	51.3
R-CDL [9]	90.7	90.8	91.3	91.0	90.0	90.3	90.2	90.0	94.5	92.2	93.5	92.5	93.0	88.8	86.1	87.4	91.4	92.8	92.1	75.9
No Filter	89.4	89.5	89.7	89.6	88.7	88.1	88.4	88.8	91.9	90.3	93.3	91.4	92.3	85.6	86.0	85.8	91.3	91.1	91.2	58.1

The visual comparison of the segmentation results using different image filters on the CDL, as shown in Figure 9, reveals several insights. The No Filter column depicts the raw CDL, displaying significant noise and misclassification, especially along the boundaries of crop fields and roads. The aggregate filter, while effective at smoothing out some noise, still maintains a distinct separation between crop fields and adjacent features, suggesting good performance in boundary areas. Conversely, the shrink filter, although it reduces noise, tends to exaggerate the separation between crop fields and roads, sometimes over-segmenting these areas. The expand filter performs the poorest, as it amplifies noise and leads to over-segmentation, failing to accurately delineate crop fields from non-crop areas. The boundary clean filter, intended to enhance edge detection, shows weaknesses in accurately defining the boundaries of fields, often merging them with surrounding areas, which reduces its effectiveness in precise segmentation.

Overall, the majority and expand–shrink filters stand out. The majority filter shows the highest accuracy in maintaining the integrity of crop fields and effectively reducing noise, making it the best performer overall. The expand–shrink filter also performs well, particularly in maintaining clear boundaries between crop fields and roads, indicating a robust capability in handling complex boundary definitions. These filters significantly improve the segmentation results compared to the No Filter approach, with noticeable enhancements in the clarity and accuracy of the segmented crop fields. This visual analysis aligns with the numerical results, confirming that appropriate filtering techniques can substantially enhance the quality of the CDL for DL applications.

In Figure 10, the confusion matrices for different image filters applied to the CDL reveal distinct variations in the performance of DL models across major crops. The majority filter shows robust performance, particularly in identifying rice and soybeans, with higher UA and PA values compared to the other filters. This filter effectively reduces false positives and false negatives, making it highly reliable for segmenting various crop types. The expand–shrink filter also performs well, particularly in accurately identifying corn and cotton, though its performance slightly lags behind the majority filter.

Conversely, the expand filter exhibits the weakest performance, as evidenced by its higher rates of misclassification, particularly for corn and rice. The boundary clean filter shows moderate effectiveness, with relatively good accuracy for soybeans but less consistency for corn. The aggregate filter performs reasonably well but struggles with distinguishing between crops and non-crop areas, particularly in boundary regions. The majority and expand–shrink filters stand out as the most effective in improving DL segmentation accuracy for the major crops, highlighting their value in enhancing the quality of the CDL for agricultural applications.

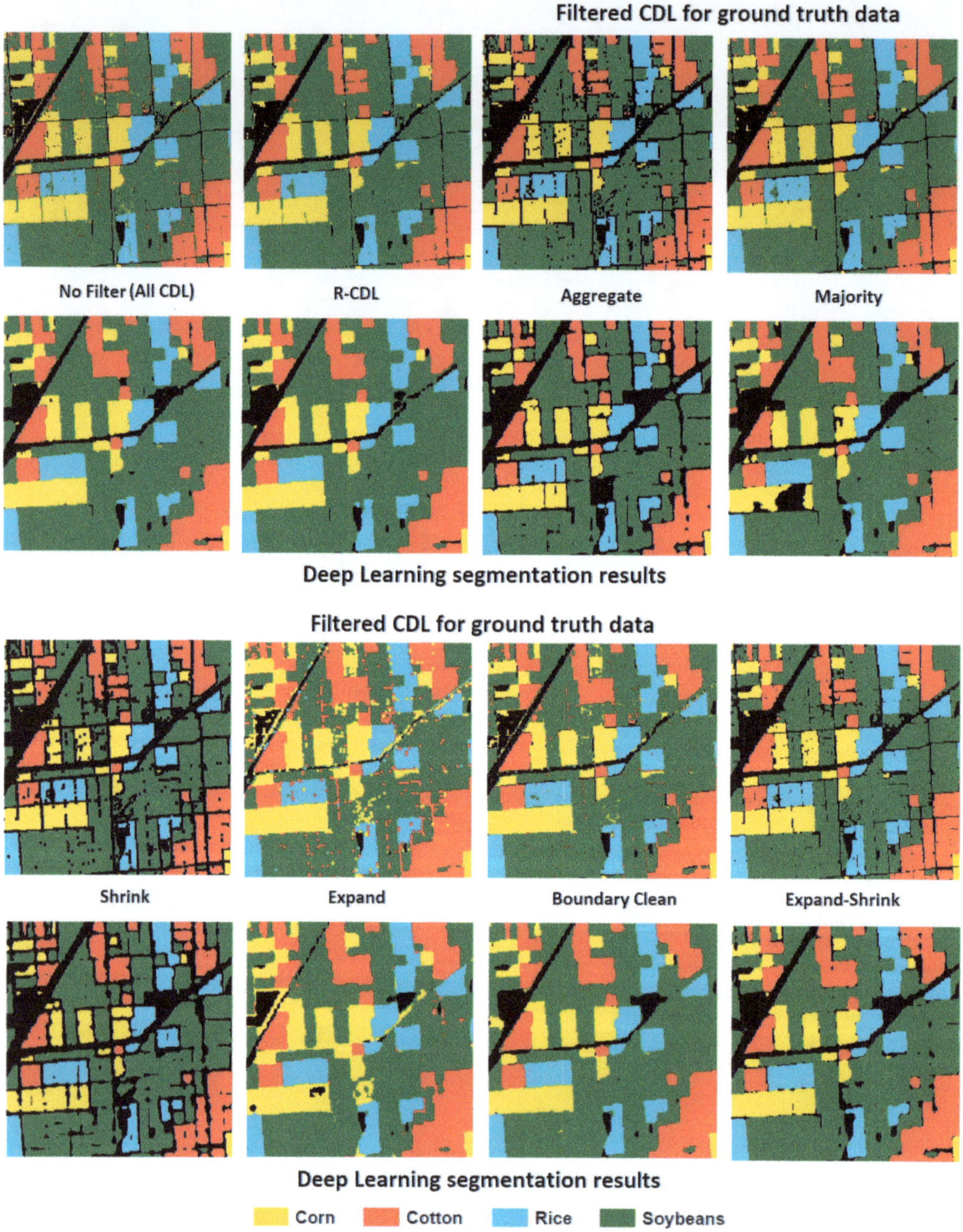

Figure 9. Filtered CDL and corresponding DL segmentation results for major crops using various image filters. The "No Filter" and "R-CDL" results are included for comparison.

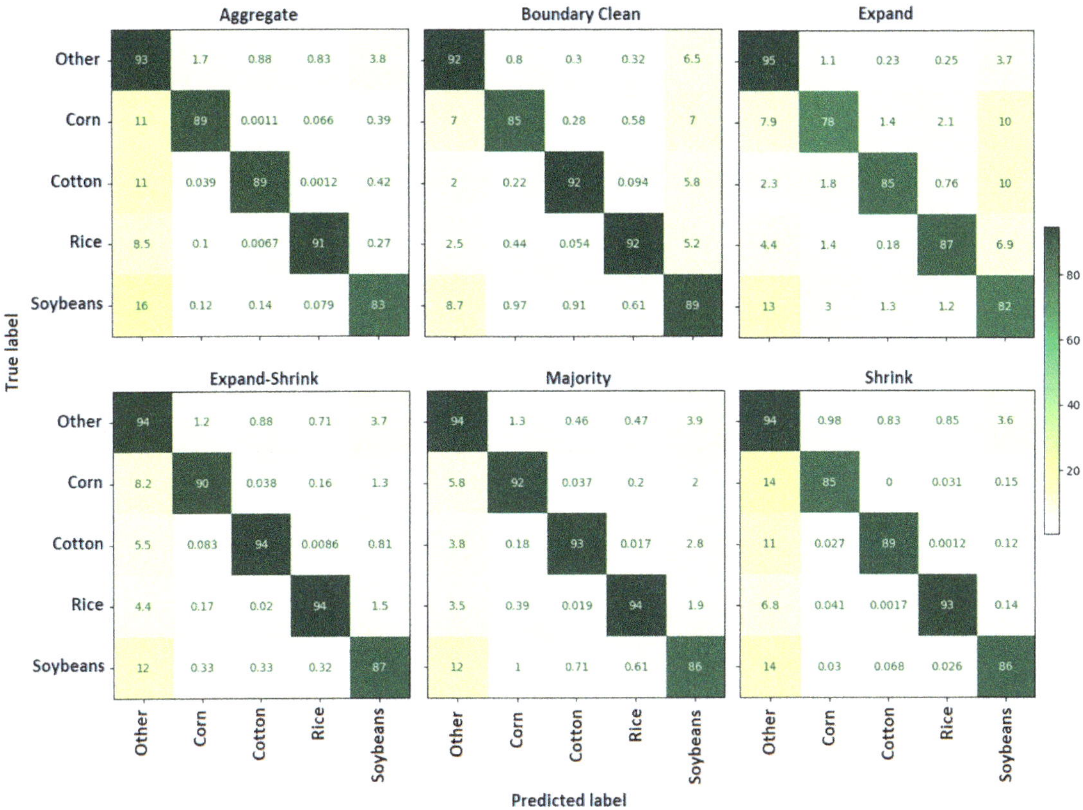

Figure 10. Confusion matrices illustrating the performance of DL models using different image filters on the CDL for major crop segmentation. The values within the matrix represent the percentage of correctly and incorrectly classified instances, ranging from 0 to 100.

3.3. CDL Refinement in T14TNK Area

To ensure the robustness and generalizability of our proposed methodologies in a different geographical and agricultural context, we conducted an additional experiment in the T14TNK test area. The performance metrics of the DL models, trained with the CDL at different confidence intervals, are summarized in Table 3. Notably, the results indicate that the 45% and 55% confidence intervals yield the highest accuracy, suggesting that these intervals effectively balance data quality and noise reduction. This result aligns with our findings in the Mississippi Delta study area, confirming the effectiveness of these confidence intervals across different regions. Conversely, higher confidence intervals, such as 95% and 100%, exhibit the worst results, likely due to excessive exclusion of valid data, thus supporting the importance of selecting appropriate confidence levels to enhance model performance.

The performance metrics of DL models using different image filters on the CDL for the T14TNK area are summarized in Table 4. The results demonstrate that the majority and expand–shrink filters significantly enhance model accuracy, with the OA reaching 93.5% and 93.1%, respectively. The majority filter showed the highest effectiveness, achieving the best results across most metrics. The expand–shrink filter also performed well, indicating that it is a reliable method for improving CDL data quality. In contrast, the expand filter yielded the lowest performance metrics, highlighting the importance of selecting appropriate filtering techniques. The results of the R-CDL from Lin et al.'s study [9] also show competitive accuracy, supporting the robustness of our proposed approaches. These findings align with our previous results in the Mississippi Delta, confirming the generalizability and effectiveness of our methodology across different regions.

Table 3. Performance metrics of DL models trained with the CDL at different confidence intervals for the T14TNK area.

Confidence	Overall				Corn			Soybeans			Other			
Interval	OA	UA	PA	F1	UA	PA	F1	UA	PA	F1	UA	PA	F1	MCDA
All CDL	92.7	91.9	92.2	92.1	92.4	90.3	91.4	88.7	91.8	90.2	94.5	94.6	94.6	92.0
+5%	92.7	92.0	92.1	92.0	91.6	90.9	91.2	90.1	90.6	90.3	94.5	94.7	94.6	92.2
+15%	92.7	92.0	92.2	92.1	93.2	89.7	91.4	88.8	91.8	90.3	94.1	95.1	94.6	91.2
+25%	92.7	92.1	92.1	92.1	92.8	90.0	91.4	89.4	91.3	90.3	94.1	95.0	94.5	92.3
+35%	92.8	92.0	92.3	92.2	91.9	91.1	91.5	89.3	91.5	90.4	94.8	94.4	94.6	93.6
+45%	93.1	92.3	92.6	92.5	92.2	91.5	91.8	89.9	91.7	90.8	94.9	94.6	94.8	96.1
+55%	92.9	92.1	92.5	92.3	91.8	92.1	92.0	89.9	91.2	90.6	94.7	94.0	94.3	94.2
+65%	92.6	91.8	91.9	91.9	91.9	91.9	91.9	89.8	90.3	90.0	93.8	93.6	93.7	91.0
+75%	91.8	90.4	91.6	91.0	91.0	91.4	91.2	86.4	91.2	88.7	93.9	92.2	93.1	82.1
+85%	90.4	88.8	89.1	89.0	88.2	89.9	89.1	85.7	85.7	85.7	92.5	91.8	92.2	63.6
+95%	87.3	82.9	83.4	83.1	80.7	81.7	81.2	77.0	77.8	77.4	91.1	90.6	90.8	6.0
+100%	87.5	82.7	84.1	83.4	78.8	84.8	81.7	77.4	77.5	77.5	91.9	90.0	90.9	9.4

Table 4. Performance metrics of DL models using various image filters on the CDL for the T14TNK area. The R-CDL [9] results are included for comparison, demonstrating the effectiveness of different filtering techniques in enhancing CDL quality.

	Overall				Corn			Soybeans			Other			
Filters	OA	UA	PA	F1	UA	PA	F1	UA	PA	F1	UA	PA	F1	MCDA
Aggregate	92.2	90.7	91.5	91.1	90.5	91.6	91.1	87.2	90.0	88.6	94.2	93.0	93.6	70.3
Boundary Clean	92.5	92.4	91.5	91.9	92.2	96.2	94.1	94.0	88.5	91.2	91.1	89.7	90.4	74.8
Expand	85.6	86.0	85.0	84.6	80.8	98.6	88.8	97.5	73.1	83.5	79.6	83.4	81.5	45.6
Expand–Shrink	93.1	91.8	93.3	92.5	95.7	92.7	94.2	91.3	93.8	92.5	88.2	93.6	90.8	77.7
Majority	93.5	92.7	93.2	93.0	95.4	94.2	94.8	91.8	93.2	92.5	91.1	92.2	91.6	80.7
Shrink	85.6	79.8	91.2	83.7	98.7	79.5	88.1	72.9	97.2	83.3	67.8	96.9	79.8	41.8
R-CDL [9]	92.7	92.2	92.1	92.1	92.1	90.9	91.5	90.5	90.9	90.7	93.9	94.4	94.1	75.5
No Filter	92.7	91.9	92.2	92.1	92.4	90.3	91.4	88.7	91.8	90.2	94.5	94.6	94.6	74.5

4. Discussion

4.1. CDL Refinement Using Confidence Layer

The superior performance observed with the +45% and +55% confidence intervals, as indicated by the highest F1 and MCDA relative closeness, suggests that this level effectively balances the inclusion of high-quality data while minimizing noise. This interval likely provides a robust training set that enhances the model's ability to generalize accurately across different validation samples. In contrast, the decline in performance at the +85%–100% confidence intervals can be attributed to the excessive exclusion of data, which results in a training set that is too limited to capture the full variability in the croplands, thereby impairing the model's performance.

The MCDA relative closeness plays a crucial role in explaining these results by providing a comprehensive evaluation that integrates multiple criteria, such as OA, UA, PA and F1. This holistic approach allows for a more nuanced assessment of the model's performance across different confidence intervals. The high MCDA scores for the +45% and +55% intervals underscore their overall effectiveness, balancing various performance metrics more successfully than other intervals. The insights gained from MCDA highlight the importance of selecting an effective confidence interval that not only maximizes individual accuracy metrics but also achieves a harmonious balance across multiple evaluation criteria, leading to a more reliable and robust model for cropland mapping. This emphasizes the necessity for a strategic approach in choosing confidence intervals to enhance the quality and effectiveness of DL segmentation models in agricultural applications.

4.2. CDL Refinement Using Image Filters

The results of the DL segmentation using various image filters on the CDL underscore the importance of data pre-processing in improving model accuracy. The majority and expand–shrink filters emerged as the top performers due to their ability to effectively reduce noise and preserve the integrity of crop boundaries. The success of the majority filter can be attributed to its ability to smooth out irregularities and enhance the homogeneity of crop areas, thereby improving the model's ability to accurately classify different crop types. This filter's effectiveness in maintaining clear distinctions between crops and non-crop areas, particularly along field boundaries, is crucial for accurate segmentation. Similarly, the expand–shrink filter's ability to manage the complexities of field boundaries and reduce noise without over-segmenting highlights its robustness in handling diverse agricultural landscapes.

However, the poorer performance of the expand filter highlights the risks of amplifying noise during the pre-processing stage. This filter's tendency to over-segment and misclassify non-crop areas as crops underscores the need for careful selection of filtering techniques. The boundary clean filter's moderate performance points to its partial success in edge detection, which, while beneficial, may not be sufficient alone for accurate segmentation. The results indicate that a nuanced approach to data filtering, which balances noise reduction and boundary preservation, is essential for optimizing DL model performance in crop segmentation tasks.

4.3. Comparative Analysis of CDL Refinement Methods

Among the various methods tested, DL segmentation trained with data processed by the majority filter yielded the best results. The findings indicate that approaches utilizing filtered data outperform those using different confidence intervals, with the second-best results achieved using the expand–shrink filter. Conversely, the approaches using data with +95% and 100% confidence intervals produced the worst results, despite their frequent use in other studies. This suggests that high confidence intervals may exclude too much data, leading to poor model performance. Similarly, the DL model trained with expanded data showed significant weaknesses in correct segmentation, with results comparable to the worst-case confidence interval scenarios.

The substantial difference in accuracy between the filter-based approaches and the confidence-interval-based approaches, often around 1%, highlights the importance of pre-processing the CDL with appropriate filters before training DL models. This finding suggests that the application of noise reduction filters on the CDL should be a preliminary step to improve DL performance. Furthermore, combining confidence intervals and filter approaches could potentially enhance CDL quality even further. However, this combined approach requires careful evaluation, as the simultaneous use of filters and confidence intervals might have unforeseen negative effects on DL results.

In comparing the results of our best-performing approach with the R-CDL from Lin et al.'s study [9], our findings demonstrate notable improvements. The R-CDL, which involves sophisticated steps to refine the CDL, was outperformed by the expand–shrink and majority filter approaches, which scored around 1% higher in various accuracy metrics. While our methods using the +45% and +55% confidence intervals resulted in slightly lower accuracies, they still demonstrated significant efficacy. This comparison, as illustrated in the accompanying chart in Figure 11, underscores that our simpler filter-based approaches can achieve superior or comparable accuracy metrics without the complexity of the R-CDL method, thus validating the robustness and effectiveness of our methodologies.

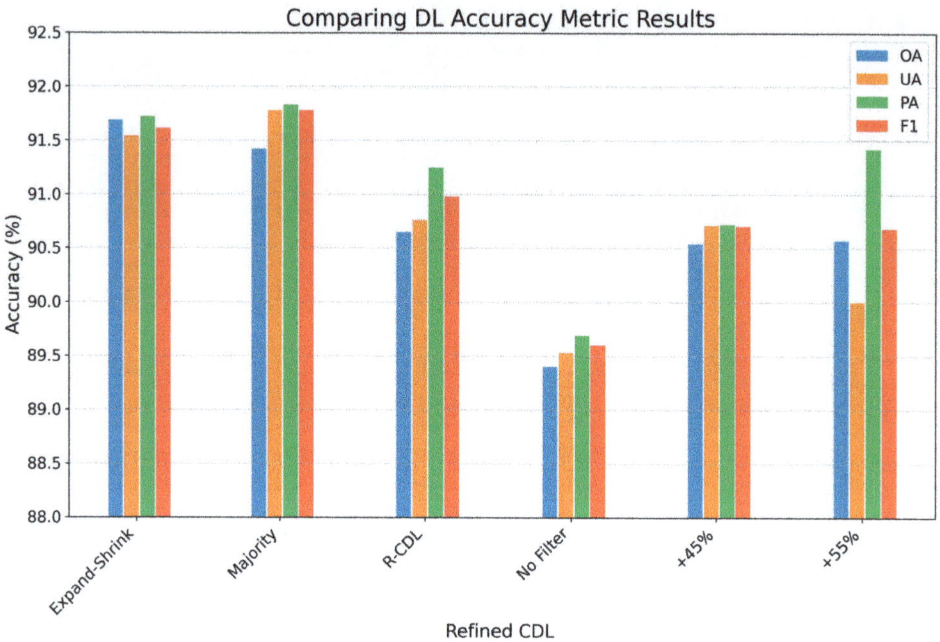

Figure 11. Comparison of DL accuracy metric results using different CDL refinement methods, including the R-CDL from Lin et al.'s study [9].

4.4. *Generalizability Assessment*

To assess the generalizability of our method across different study areas, we conducted a detailed comparative analysis using the F1-score. We used the F1-score as the primary accuracy metric for comparison because it balances precision and recall, providing a comprehensive measure of model performance, especially in the context of imbalanced classes. The study areas included the Mississippi Delta and the T14TNK region. We first normalized the F1-scores to ensure that the trends were the main focus rather than the absolute values. The Pearson correlation coefficient and paired *t*-tests were employed to quantify the similarity and statistical significance of the results between these areas. This approach allowed us to understand whether the trends observed in one region could be replicated in another, thus validating the robustness of our method.

The comparison yielded promising results. For all the approaches, the Pearson correlation coefficient was 0.82, indicating a strong positive correlation between the two study areas. The paired *t*-test resulted in a T-statistic of 3.14×10^{-14} and a *p*-value of 1, suggesting no significant difference between the means of results in the two regions. When focusing on the confidence-interval-based methods, the correlation coefficient was an impressive 0.99, with a T-statistic of 3.68×10^{-15} and a *p*-value of 1, reinforcing the high similarity and consistency of the results. For the filter-based methods, the correlation coefficient was 0.76, and the paired *t*-test yielded a T-statistic of 1.04×10^{-14} and a *p*-value of 1, indicating a robust but slightly less strong correlation compared to the confidence interval methods. This is likely due to the poor performance of the shrink filter in the T14TNK area, which could be attributed to the major crops in that region being corn and soybeans. The shrink filter may have had a detrimental effect on accurately segmenting these crops.

A *p*-value of almost 1 indicates no statistically significant difference between the results, suggesting that the methods' performance in the Mississippi Delta and T14TNK regions is statistically indistinguishable. This reinforces the robustness and generalizability of the methods, showing consistent performance across different regions. Although the trend is similar, the results for T14TNK are generally 1–2% better, except for the shrink and expand filters. This improvement might be due to the DL model having fewer classes to differentiate, allowing it to perform better in T14TNK. Additionally, the major crops in T14TNK, corn and soybeans, may be easier to classify accurately in this region due to their distinct spectral signatures. The chart in Figure 12 visually represents these trends, confirming that our approach is highly generalizable across different geographical regions. To thoroughly analyze the generalizability of our approach, it is essential to test the methods in multiple study areas, which should be undertaken in future research.

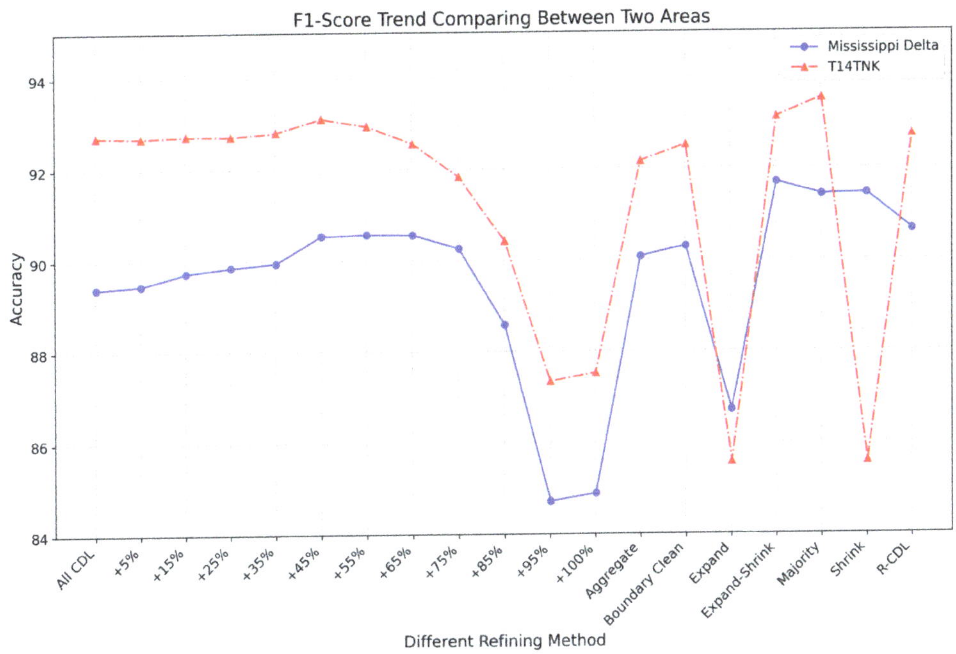

Figure 12. F1-score trends comparing the performance of different refining methods between the Mississippi Delta and T14TNK areas. The chart illustrates the accuracy metrics for various confidence intervals and filtering techniques, highlighting the generalizability and robustness of the methods across different geographical regions.

4.5. Implementation Prospects and Limitations

By integrating the refined CDL with Sentinel-2 imagery, this approach provides a robust framework for creating more accurate and reliable cropland maps. These advancements could play a critical role in agricultural monitoring, enabling better resource management and decision-making processes. The potential to combine these methods with advanced pre-processing techniques further amplifies their utility, potentially leading to more precise segmentation models that can benefit a wide range of agricultural applications.

However, the study has several limitations that must be addressed in future research to fully validate and optimize these methods. A significant constraint is the reliance on the CDL as the sole ground truth, which limits the ability to independently verify the results. Access to additional ground-truth data from different sources would enable a more comprehensive validation of the refined CDL and the effectiveness of the applied filters. Additionally, testing the methods in multiple study areas is essential to ensure that our findings are robust and applicable across different geographical regions. Furthermore, while the current filtering methods have shown efficacy, the development and integration of more advanced filtering techniques could further enhance data quality and segmentation accuracy. Future research should focus on exploring and validating these advanced methods, as well as establishing collaborations to obtain diverse ground-truth datasets, to overcome these limitations and improve the robustness of DL-based cropland segmentation models.

5. Conclusions

Numerous studies have leveraged the CDL and satellite imagery for the automation of cropland classification and segmentation using machine learning models. Despite its utility, the CDL is marred by errors such as salt-and-pepper noise, which adversely affect the performance of DL models in cropland segmentation. Consequently, refining the CDL to mitigate these inaccuracies is crucial. In this research, we investigated two primary approaches for refining the CDL: applying varying confidence intervals to the CDL and employing different image filters. For the time series data, five monthly minimum composites of Sentinel-2 imagery from the Mississippi Delta were used as satellite data for training and testing. To further validate our methods, we tested the approach in a new study area (T14TNK).

The analysis indicates that the CDL with confidence intervals ranging from +45% to +55% yielded the best results in terms of OA, enhancing the accuracy by approximately 1% compared to using the unfiltered CDL. The best results were observed with the CDL processed using the majority and expand–shrink filters, which improved the evaluation metrics by about 1.5%. The application of MCDA further corroborated these findings by providing a comprehensive evaluation across multiple criteria, underscoring the overall efficacy of the majority filter.

The results from T14TNK confirmed the generalizability of our method, showing similar trends in accuracy improvements. The performance metrics in T14TNK were generally around 1%–2% higher compared to the Mississippi Delta, likely due to fewer crop classes in T14TNK, which may have allowed the DL model to perform better. The Pearson correlation coefficient and paired t-tests were employed to quantify the similarity and statistical significance of the results between these areas. The Pearson correlation coefficient for confidence interval methods was 0.99, indicating a very strong correlation, while the paired t-tests yielded a T-statistic close to 0 and a p-value of 1 after normalization, suggesting no significant difference between the performance in the two regions. This reinforces the robustness and generalizability of our methods across different geographical regions.

Based on the findings of this research, it is recommended to filter the CDL with image filters such as majority or expand–shrink before employing it for DL segmentation training to identify crops. Additionally, selecting data with confidence intervals of +45% prior to applying these filters can further enhance the quality and reliability of the training data. Future research should explore the synergistic effects of combining filtering and confidence interval techniques and investigate the potential of integrating advanced CDL pre-processing methods to augment the performance of DL models in agricultural applications. This holistic approach could lead to more precise and dependable segmentation models, thereby benefiting various agricultural mapping and monitoring tasks.

Author Contributions: R.M.: conceptualization, methodology, formal analysis, validation, investigation, data curation, writing—original draft; F.W.: Conceptualization, methodology, validation, resources, writing—review and editing, supervision, projection administration, funding acquisition; A.O.: validation, investigation, writing—review and editing; L.F.: software, validation, writing—review and editing; G.Y.: writing—review and editing, supervision, project administration. All authors have read and agreed to the published version of the manuscript.

Funding: This research received no external funding.

Institutional Review Board Statement: Not applicable.

Data Availability Statement: The Sentinel-2 imagery can be accessed freely using the ESA Copernicus Open Access Hub, and the CDL is available from the USDA NASS website. The R-CDL dataset can be downloaded from Zenodo repository (https://zenodo.org/doi/10.5281/zenodo.5565596, accessed on 17 July 2024). While the Sentinel-2 and CDL are publicly accessible, the derived data supporting the findings of this study are available only upon request due to data sharing restrictions imposed by the license. All of these datasets were accessed and processed using GEE.

Conflicts of Interest: The authors declare no conflicts of interest.

References

1. Čerkasova, N.; White, M.; Arnold, J.; Bieger, K.; Allen, P.; Gao, J.; Meki, M.; Kiniry, J.; Gassman, P. Field scale SWAT+ modeling of corn and soybean yields for the contiguous United States: National Agroecosystem Model Development. *Agric. Syst.* **2023**, *210*, 103695. [CrossRef]
2. FAO. *The State of Food Insecurity in the World—Meeting the 2015 International Hunger Targets: Taking Stock of Uneven Progress*; FAO: Rome, Italy, 2015; pp. 1–54.
3. FAO; IFAD; UNICEF; WFP; WHO. *The State of Food Security and Nutrition in the World: Transforming Food Systems for Affordable Healthy Diets*; FAO: Rome, Italy; IFAD: Rome, Italy; UNICEF: Rome, Italy; WFP: Rome, Italy; WHO: Rome, Italy, 2020.
4. Zhu, Y.; Wu, S.; Qin, M.; Fu, Z.; Gao, Y.; Wang, Y.; Du, Z. A deep learning crop model for adaptive yield estimation in large areas. *Int. J. Appl. Earth Obs. Geoinf.* **2022**, *110*, 102828. [CrossRef]
5. USDA; N.A.S.S. Statewide Agricultural Accuracy Report. Available online: https://www.nass.usda.gov/Research_and_Science/Cropland/metadata/meta.php (accessed on 17 July 2024).
6. Ebrahimy, H.; Zhang, Z. Per-pixel accuracy as a weighting criterion for combining ensemble of extreme learning machine classifiers for satellite image classification. *Int. J. Appl. Earth Obs. Geoinf.* **2023**, *122*, 103390. [CrossRef]
7. Zhang, C.; Di, L.; Lin, L.; Li, H.; Guo, L.; Yang, Z.; Yu, E.G.; Di, Y.; Yang, A. Towards automation of in-season crop type mapping using spatiotemporal crop information and remote sensing data. *Agric. Syst.* **2022**, *201*, 103462. [CrossRef]
8. Fritz, S.; See, L.; Bayas, J.C.L.; Waldner, F.; Jacques, D.; Becker-Reshef, I.; Whitcraft, A.; Baruth, B.; Bonifacio, R.; Crutchfield, J.; et al. A comparison of global agricultural monitoring systems and current gaps. *Agric. Syst.* **2019**, *168*, 258–272. [CrossRef]
9. Lin, L.; Di, L.; Zhang, C.; Guo, L.; Di, Y.; Li, H.; Yang, A. Validation and refinement of cropland data layer using a spatial-temporal decision tree algorithm. *Sci. Data* **2022**, *9*, 63. [CrossRef] [PubMed]
10. Cai, Y.; Guan, K.; Peng, J.; Wang, S.; Seifert, C.; Wardlow, B.; Li, Z. A high-performance and in-season classification system of field-level crop types using time-series Landsat data and a machine learning approach. *Remote Sens. Environ.* **2018**, *210*, 35–47. [CrossRef]
11. Wang, S.; Azzari, G.; Lobell, D.B. Crop type mapping without field-level labels: Random forest transfer and unsupervised clustering techniques. *Remote Sens. Environ.* **2019**, *222*, 303–317. [CrossRef]
12. Zhong, L.; Hu, L.; Zhou, H. Deep learning based multi-temporal crop classification. *Remote Sens. Environ.* **2019**, *221*, 430–443. [CrossRef]
13. Hao, P.; Di, L.; Zhang, C.; Guo, L. Transfer Learning for Crop classification with Cropland Data Layer data (CDL) as training samples. *Sci. Total Environ.* **2020**, *733*, 138869. [CrossRef]
14. Lark, T.J.; Schelly, I.H.; Gibbs, H.K. Accuracy, Bias, and Improvements in Mapping Crops and Cropland across the United States Using the USDA Cropland Data Layer. *Remote Sens.* **2021**, *13*, 968. [CrossRef]
15. Reitsma, K.D.; Clay, D.E.; Clay, S.A.; Dunn, B.H.; Reese, C. Does the US cropland data layer provide an accurate benchmark for land-use change estimates? *Agron. J.* **2016**, *108*, 266–272. [CrossRef]
16. Li, R.; Wei, C.; Afroz, M.D.; Lyu, J.; Chen, G. A GIS-based framework for local agricultural decision-making and regional crop yield simulation. *Agric. Syst.* **2021**, *193*, 103213. [CrossRef]
17. Zhang, C.; Di, L.; Hao, P.; Yang, Z.; Lin, L.; Zhao, H.; Guo, L. Rapid in-season mapping of corn and soybeans using machine-learned trusted pixels from Cropland Data Layer. *Int. J. Appl. Earth Obs. Geoinf.* **2021**, *102*, 102374. [CrossRef]
18. Zhang, C.; Yang, Z.; Di, L.; Lin, L.; Hao, P. Refinement of cropland data layer using machine learning. *Int. Arch. Photogramm. Remote Sens. Spatial Inf. Sci.* **2020**, *42*, 161–164. [CrossRef]
19. Wang, Y.; Feng, L.; Zhang, Z.; Tian, F. An unsupervised domain adaptation deep learning method for spatial and temporal transferable crop type mapping using Sentinel-2 imagery. *ISPRS J. Photogramm. Remote Sens.* **2023**, *199*, 102–117. [CrossRef]
20. Ge, S.; Zhang, J.; Pan, Y.; Yang, Z.; Zhu, S. Transferable deep learning model based on the phenological matching principle for mapping crop extent. *Int. J. Appl. Earth Obs. Geoinf.* **2021**, *102*, 102451. [CrossRef]
21. Yang, G.; Yu, W.; Yao, X.; Zheng, H.; Cao, Q.; Zhu, Y.; Cao, W.; Cheng, T. AGTOC: A novel approach to winter wheat mapping by automatic generation of training samples and one-class classification on Google Earth Engine. *Int. J. Appl. Earth Obs. Geoinf.* **2021**, *102*, 102446. [CrossRef]
22. ESA. MSI User Guide. Available online: https://sentinel.esa.int/web/sentinel/user-guides/sentinel-2-msi (accessed on 17 July 2024).
23. Saad El Imanni, H.; El Harti, A.; Panimboza, J. Investigating Sentinel-1 and Sentinel-2 Data Efficiency in Studying the Temporal Behavior of Wheat Phenological Stages Using Google Earth Engine. *Agriculture* **2022**, *12*, 1605. [CrossRef]

24. Tomíček, J.; Mišurec, J.; Lukeš, P.; Potůčková, M. Retrieval of Harmonized LAI Product of Agricultural Crops from Landsat OLI and Sentinel-2 MSI Time Series. *Agriculture* **2022**, *12*, 2080. [CrossRef]
25. Wang, C.; Zhang, H.; Wu, X.; Yang, W.; Shen, Y.; Lu, B.; Wang, J. AUTS: A Novel Approach to Mapping Winter Wheat by Automatically Updating Training Samples Based on NDVI Time Series. *Agriculture* **2022**, *12*, 817. [CrossRef]
26. Bartschat, A.; Reischl, M.; Mikut, R. Data mining tools. *WIREs Data Min. Knowl. Discov.* **2019**, *9*, e1309. [CrossRef]
27. Boryan, C.; Yang, Z.; Mueller, R.; Craig, M. Monitoring US agriculture: The US Department of Agriculture, National Agricultural Statistics Service, Cropland Data Layer Program. *Geocarto Int.* **2011**, *26*, 341–358. [CrossRef]
28. Rahman, M.S.; Di, L.; Yu, E.; Zhang, C.; Mohiuddin, H. In-Season Major Crop-Type Identification for US Cropland from Landsat Images Using Crop-Rotation Pattern and Progressive Data Classification. *Agriculture* **2019**, *9*, 17. [CrossRef]
29. Dong, W.; Woźniak, M.; Wu, J.; Li, W.; Bai, Z. Denoising aggregation of graph neural networks by using principal component analysis. *IEEE Trans. Ind. Inform.* **2022**, *19*, 2385–2394. [CrossRef]
30. Ilesanmi, A.E.; Ilesanmi, T.O. Methods for image denoising using convolutional neural network: A review. *Complex Intell. Syst.* **2021**, *7*, 2179–2198. [CrossRef]
31. Wade, T.; Wickham, J.; Nash, M.; Neale, A.; Riitters, K.; Jones, K. A Comparison of Vector and Raster GIS Methods for Calculating Landscape Metrics Used in Environmental Assessments. *Photogramm. Eng. Remote Sens.* **2003**, *69*, 1399–1405. [CrossRef]
32. Olivas, E.S.; Guerrero, J.D.M.; Sober, M.M.; Benedito, J.R.M.; Lopez, A.J.S. *Handbook of Research on Machine Learning Applications and Trends: Algorithms, Methods and Techniques—2 Volumes*; IGI Publishing: Hershey, PA, USA, 2009.
33. Soares, D.; Galvão, L.; Formaggio, A. Crop area estimate from original and simulated spatial resolution data and landscape metrics. *Sci. Agric.* **2008**, *65*, 459–467. [CrossRef]
34. European Space Agency. Copernicus Sentinel-2 Collection 1 MSI Level-2A (L2A). Available online: https://sentinels.copernicus.eu/web/sentinel/sentinel-data-access/sentinel-products/sentinel-2-data-products/collection-1-level-2a (accessed on 17 July 2024).
35. Liu, M.; Fu, B.; Xie, S.; He, H.; Lan, F.; Li, Y.; Lou, P.; Fan, D. Comparison of multi-source satellite images for classifying marsh vegetation using DeepLabV3 Plus deep learning algorithm. *Ecol. Indic.* **2021**, *125*, 107562. [CrossRef]
36. Yojana, K.; Thillai Rani, L. OCT layer segmentation using U-NET semantic segmentation and RESNET34 encoder-decoder. *Meas. Sens.* **2023**, *29*, 100817. [CrossRef]
37. Zhang, D.; Pan, Y.; Zhang, J.; Hu, T.; Zhao, J.; Li, N.; Chen, Q. A generalized approach based on convolutional neural networks for large area cropland mapping at very high resolution. *Remote Sens. Environ.* **2020**, *247*, 111912. [CrossRef]
38. Congalton, R.G.; Green, K. *Assessing the Accuracy of Remotely Sensed Data: Principles and Practices*; CRC Press: Boca Raton, FL, USA, 2019.
39. Larsen, A.E.; Hendrickson, B.T.; Dedeic, N.; MacDonald, A.J. Taken as a given: Evaluating the accuracy of remotely sensed crop data in the USA. *Agric. Syst.* **2015**, *141*, 121–125. [CrossRef]
40. Abdali, E.; Valadan Zoej, M.J.; Taheri Dehkordi, A.; Ghaderpour, E. A Parallel-Cascaded Ensemble of Machine Learning Models for Crop Type Classification in Google Earth Engine Using Multi-Temporal Sentinel-1/2 and Landsat-8/9 Remote Sensing Data. *Remote Sens.* **2024**, *16*, 127. [CrossRef]
41. Bahrami, H.; Homayouni, S.; Safari, A.; Mirzaei, S.; Mahdianpari, M.; Reisi-Gahrouei, O. Deep Learning-Based Estimation of Crop Biophysical Parameters Using Multi-Source and Multi-Temporal Remote Sensing Observations. *Agronomy* **2021**, *11*, 1363. [CrossRef]

agriculture

MDPI

Article

Spectral-Frequency Conversion Derived from Hyperspectral Data Combined with Deep Learning for Estimating Chlorophyll Content in Rice

Lei Du [1] and Shanjun Luo [1,2,*]

[1] Aerospace Information Research Institute, Henan Academy of Sciences, Zhengzhou 450046, China; dulei@hnas.ac.cn

[2] School of Remote Sensing and Information Engineering, Wuhan University, Wuhan 430079, China

* Correspondence: luoshanjun@whu.edu.cn or luoshanjun@hnas.ac.cn; Tel.: +86-158-02259980

Abstract: As a vital pigment for photosynthesis in rice, chlorophyll content is closely correlated with growth status and photosynthetic capacity. The estimation of chlorophyll content allows for the monitoring of rice growth and facilitates precise management in the field, such as the application of fertilizers and irrigation. The advancement of hyperspectral remote sensing technology has made it possible to estimate chlorophyll content non-destructively, quickly, and effectively, offering technical support for managing and monitoring rice growth across wide areas. Although hyperspectral data have a fine spectral resolution, they also cause a large amount of information redundancy and noise. This study focuses on the issues of unstable input variables and the estimation model's poor applicability to various periods when predicting rice chlorophyll content. By introducing the theory of harmonic analysis and the time-frequency conversion method, a deep neural network (DNN) model framework based on wavelet packet transform-first order differential-harmonic analysis (WPT-FD-HA) was proposed, which avoids the uncertainty in the calculation of spectral parameters. The accuracy of estimating rice chlorophyll content based on WPT-FD and WPT-FD-HA variables was compared at seedling, tillering, jointing, heading, grain filling, milk, and complete periods to evaluate the validity and generalizability of the suggested framework. The results demonstrated that all of the WPT-FD-HA models' single-period validation accuracy had coefficients of determination (R^2) values greater than 0.9 and RMSE values less than 1. The multi-period validation model had a root mean square error (RMSE) of 1.664 and an R^2 of 0.971. Even with independent data splitting validation, the multi-period model accuracy can still achieve R^2 = 0.95 and RMSE = 1.4. The WPT-FD-HA-based deep learning framework exhibited strong stability. The outcome of this study deserves to be used to monitor rice growth on a broad scale using hyperspectral data.

Keywords: chlorophyll content; frequency-domain signal; deep neural network; hyperspectral data; period adaptation; rice

1. Introduction

Currently, nearly half of the world's population consumes rice as a staple food, and with the worldwide population growth, the demand for rice is expected to continue to grow in the future [1]. As the original rice-producing region, China ranks second in the world in terms of planted area and first in terms of production, so it is evident that China's regional rice production plays a crucial role in the world's food security [2]. The traditional approach to increasing rice yield has relied mainly on breeding and genetic improvement. China has achieved fruitful research results in this area, and rice varieties grown in different regions have gradually achieved a stable level [3]. The quality of development and final yield of rice are closely related to its cropping practices, growing conditions, and growing environment, such as planting density, chlorophyll content, and weed stress [4]. Chlorophyll is the most important indicator pigment in photosynthesis and the power source for plants to convert light energy into chemical energy. From the perspective of precision agriculture, since chlorophyll content is directly related to plant stress and senescence, the real-time monitoring of chlorophyll content is of great significance in grasping the growth status of crops in real time. For example, the chlorophyll content was rapidly and non-destructively estimated to evaluate the wheat drought stress [5].

Conventional sampling survey methods require a large number of samples from rice crops and are destructive. In addition, the poor operating environment of paddy fields can also lead to inefficient data collection, and there is even the possibility of contamination of the samples for testing. These factors greatly increase the degree of sampling difficulty in manual surveys and reduce the credibility of sample data information [6]. At the same time, traditional crop management is highly subjective, relying mainly on the manager's empirical judgment as the basis for decision-making. Such subjective judgments are often less accurate and prone to the excessive application of pesticides or fertilizers, which negatively impacts crop growth and the soil environment. Therefore, there is an urgent need for a comprehensive application of modern information technology, which can effectively enhance the economic benefits of crops, and implement locally adapted field management strategies for crops grown on a wide scale.

The non-destructive monitoring of chlorophyll content in rice has been made possible with the development of spectroscopic techniques [7]. However, spectral monitoring of rice chlorophyll content is not only affected by changes in canopy structure but also by the growth period and soil background factors [8]. Hyperspectral remote sensing technology has shown great advantages in plant remote sensing research and application due to its characteristics of having large spectral information, high resolution, and strong continuity, which can directly quantify the weak spectral differences in crops [9]. Many studies have shown that the use of hyperspectral data to obtain plant biochemical parameters quickly and accurately has become an important means of plant growth monitoring, providing an effective pathway for the rapid, efficient, and non-destructive detection of crop chlorophyll content [10].

The main methods used in modeling the estimation of growth parameters are multiple stepwise regression (MSR), principal component regression, BP neural networks, and random forest regression (RFR) [11–14]. Machine learning and deep learning algorithms have shown strong potential in crop growth monitoring and feature fusion. For instance, the original reflectance, spectral index, and wavelet features were combined by RFR to estimate the chlorophyll content of winter wheat under nitrogen deficiency and powdery mildew stress, and the color features, spectral indices, and chlorophyll fluorescence intensity were fused using multiple linear regression (MLR) and partial least squares regression (PLSR) models to predict sorghum leaf chlorophyll content [15,16]. Existing studies have shown that the spectral indices calculated based on two or more bands correlate well with crop chlorophyll content [17,18]. However, these spectral indices were calculated by utilizing only a few bands of information, which could not comprehensively and effectively extract the hidden weak information and did not reflect the advantages of high spectral resolution of hyperspectral remote sensing data. In terms of hyperspectral data preprocessing techniques, first-order differential, logarithmic, inverse, and wavelet packet transform (WPT) can improve the accuracy of crop growth parameter estimation under specific scenarios (nitrogen fertilizer control and water stress control), such as chlorophyll content prediction at the leaf scale in viroid-inoculated oil palm seedlings, potato leaf area index monitoring under water stress conditions, and carya illinoensis chlorophyll content valuation [19–22]. However, it is difficult to maintain generalization in estimating chlorophyll content at different stages.

Wavelet analysis is one of the promising techniques in hyperspectral weak information extraction, which is often used to solve the problems of spectral noise and unstable inversion parameters by decomposing a complex signal into a functional combination of simple sub-signal components [21]. In order to make full use of the advantage of the informativeness of hyperspectral data, combined with spectral signal preprocessing techniques and the deep neural network (DNN), the harmonic analysis theory was introduced in this paper to perform time-frequency spatial transformation of the traditionally processed spectral data [23]. The data compression effect was achieved by suppressing or eliminating the background noise of the ground feature through harmonic decomposition. The main research objectives are (1) to analyze the correlation between the parameters extracted by different hyperspectral preprocessing techniques and the chlorophyll content of rice; (2) to compare the accuracy of the parameters obtained by different hyperspectral preprocessing techniques using DNN for estimating the rice chlorophyll content; and (3) to analyze the generalized performance of the framework combining spectral preprocessing techniques and DNN for chlorophyll content estimation in different rice periods.

2. Materials and Methods

2.1. Experimental Design and Chlorophyll Content Measurement

Two experiments were conducted from February to May and July to September at the rice experimental bases in the Lingshui Lizu autonomous county, Hainan Province, and Ezhou City, Hubei Province, respectively. In the 42-plot experiment, a total of 42 rice varieties were laid out in the study area, each with an area of 100 m^2. The rice in all plots was transplanted on 8 January and harvested on 20 May. On 4 February (seedling stage), 25 February (tillering stage), 9 March and 19 March (jointing stage), 31 March (heading stage), 17 April (grain filling stage), and 28 April (milk stage), four uniformly distributed points within each plot were selected for chlorophyll content measurements (expressed as SPAD values). The top three leaves were selected on each rice plant, and each point was measured 10 times, and the average of the measurements was taken as the SPAD value of the plot. This experiment was used for the initial validation of the models for estimating chlorophyll content in rice. The 48-plot experiment contained a total of 48 plots planted with different rice varieties, each with an area of about 36 m^2. Rice chlorophyll content was collected on 2 July (seedling stage), 11 July (tillering stage), 21 July (jointing stage), 6 August (heading stage), 21 August (grain filling stage), and 2 September (milk stage), respectively. The collection methods were the same as in the 42-plot experiment. This experiment was used to perform a transportability or robustness validation of the models for estimating chlorophyll content in rice. Except for the different varieties, the other management practices of the two experiments were kept the same. The plots of the different experiments were distributed as shown in Figure 1. In both of the above experiments, the varieties designed were common indica rice. The genotypes of rice in the experiments are not specified because rice genotypes were not a key concern of this study and there is a large number of rice varieties.

2.2. Measurement of Rice Canopy Hyperspectral Data

In this experiment, an ASD FieldSpec 4 spectrometer (Analytical Spectral Devices Inc., Boulder, CO, USA) was used to collect hyperspectral data from the rice canopy. The measurement range of the spectrometer was 350–2500 nm, with a spectral resolution of 3 nm for 350–1000 nm and 8 nm for 1000–2500 nm. The field of view of the spectrometer was 25 degrees. Spectral measurements were performed at six stages: seedling, tillering, jointing, heading, grain filling, and milk stages. At the seedling stage, the rice leaf area index (LAI) was around 1 and the proportion of soil background exposed was high. At the tillering stage, LAI began to exceed 2, and the proportion of soil background occupying the canopy decreased significantly. After the jointing stage, the rice canopy gradually closed (LAI exceeded 5), and the proportion of the canopy occupied by soil background was negligible. During the measurements, the sensor probe was vertically downward, with a vertical height of about 0.5 m from the rice canopy (coverage of approximately 0.04 m^2), and all measurements were corrected with a whiteboard before measurement (the effects of soil background is largely negligible). Four target points were randomly selected in each plot and 10 spectra were collected from each target sampling point, and finally, the average value of the spectra was taken as the spectral measurement value of the target point.

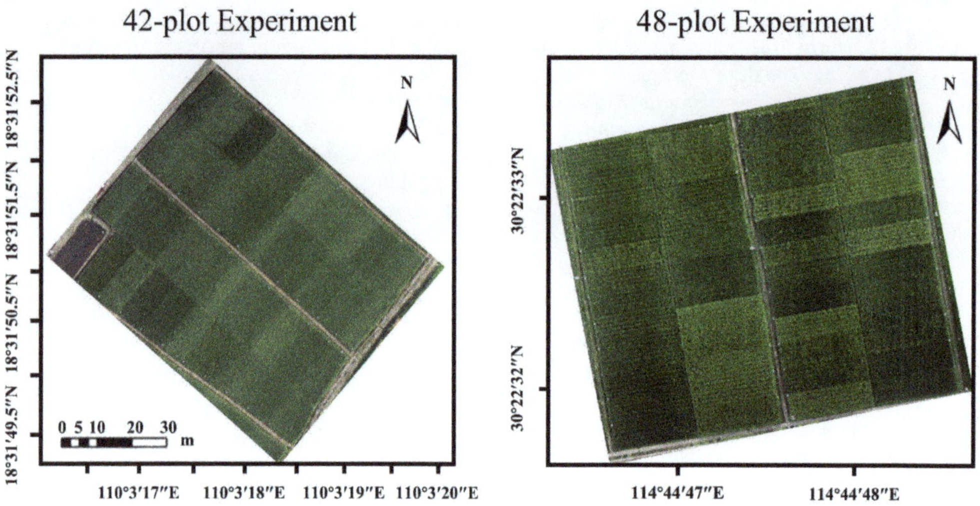

Figure 1. Design for 42- and 48-plot experiments.

2.3. Spectral Preprocessing Techniques

2.3.1. First-Order Differential Processing

The effect of noise on the target can be eliminated by transforming the spectra. A large number of existing studies have shown that differential spectra in characteristic bands have a higher correlation with crop biochemical parameters [24,25]. For vegetation, the spectral measurement is easily affected by the observation angle and illumination, which makes the signal-to-noise ratio of spectral data relatively low. After differential processing, the influence of changing illumination conditions can be reduced, and the effects of background and atmospheric scattering can also be partially or completely eliminated. The biochemical absorption properties of the crop are emphasized by enhancing the spectral differences. The first-order differentiation of the reflectance spectra is calculated as follows:

$$R'(\lambda_i) = [R(\lambda_{i+1}) - R(\lambda_{i-1})]/(\lambda_{i+1} - \lambda_{i-1}), \quad (1)$$

where λ_{i-1}, λ_i, and λ_{i+1} are neighboring wavelengths and $R'(\lambda_i)$ is the first-order differential spectral value corresponding to wavelength λ_i.

2.3.2. Wavelet Packet Transform

Wavelet packet decomposition is often used in signal denoising. The process of decomposing a spectral signal produces information in both low and high frequency parts. Spectral noise is frequently in the high-frequency part. In order to remove the noise in the high-frequency information, the wavelet packet transform (WPT) was adopted in this paper to decompose and reconstruct the high-frequency information more finely. WPT was introduced based on wavelet transform. Compared with wavelet transform, WPT is superior in decomposing and reconstructing high-frequency information, and the information processing result has no redundancy nor omission, so it is more conducive to spectral denoising and original information retention. Daubechies wavelet is a wavelet function constructed by Ingrid Daubechies, a world-renowned scholar of wavelet analysis, and we generally abbreviate it as dbN, where N is the order of the wavelet. The wavelet mother function used in this study was Db10 [26]. Spectral reconstruction was performed based on the optimal wavelet packet basis and the quantized optimal wavelet packet decomposition coefficients to obtain the spectra after WPT noise reduction processing. After WPT processing, the spectra were first-order differentiated to obtain WPT-FD data.

2.3.3. Harmonic Decomposition

Even with the aforementioned data preparation, there are still several noise and redundancy issues in the spectral information. Harmonic analysis (HA) was presented in this work to solve these issues by performing a time-frequency conversion of the spectral data processing as a sequence signal [27]. After harmonic decomposition, the spectra energy characteristic parameters can be found. Any time series function $f(t)$ with respect to time t can be written as a superposition of multiple sine (cosine) waves. This is known as harmonic theory, and it can be defined as fitting the period function $f(t)$ of a digital or time series signal by the superposition of sine (cosine) waves. The spectral profile with N bands can be seen as a function of period N when processing spectral data with HA. The spectral profile of every sample can be understood as the superposition of a sequence of sine (cosine) waves, comprising the harmonic residual term ($A_0/2$), amplitude (A_h, B_h, C_h), and phase (φ), which are the distinctive elements of the energy spectra, according to the HA decomposition. If a set of spectra consisting of N bands is denoted as $V(k) = (v_1, v_2, \ldots, v_N)$, the expansion equation obtained from the h time harmonic decomposition is as follows:

$$\begin{aligned} V(k) &= \frac{A_0}{2} + \sum_{h=1}^{\infty} [A_h cos(2\pi hk/N) + B_h sin(2\pi hk/N)] \\ &= \frac{A_0}{2} + \sum_{h=1}^{\infty} C_h sin(2\pi hk/N + \varphi_h), \end{aligned} \tag{2}$$

The characteristic components of the h-time harmonic decomposition are calculated as follows:

$$A_0/2 = \frac{1}{N}\sum_{k=1}^{N} v_k, \tag{3}$$

$$A_h = \frac{2}{N}\sum_{k=1}^{N} v_k cos(2\pi hk/N), \tag{4}$$

$$B_h = \frac{2}{N}\sum_{k=1}^{N} v_k sin(2\pi hk/N), \tag{5}$$

$$C_h = \sqrt{\left({A_h}^2 + {B_h}^2\right)}, \tag{6}$$

$$\varphi_h = tan^{-1}(A_h/B_h\Big) \tag{7}$$

where $A_0/2$ is the harmonic residual term; $C_h sin(2\pi hk/N + \varphi_h)$ is the harmonic component with h time; and A_h, B_h, C_h, and φ_h are the cosine amplitude, sine amplitude, amplitude of the harmonic component, and the phase of the harmonic component, respectively. Among them, $A_0/2$, C_h, and φ_h reflect the average value of the energy of the spectra in each band, the variation of the energy in different bands, and the position of the band in which the energy appears in amplitude, respectively.

2.4. Deep Learning Model and Validation Methods

The statistical regression modeling-based methods for estimating crop chlorophyll content include both linear and nonlinear models. As agroecosystems are complicated and many of the processes involved are nonlinear, the mechanism of crop growth formation usually behaves nonlinearly [28]. Therefore, nonlinear models are commonly used to monitor crop growth, such as support vector regression, random forest, and partial least squares [29]. However, such traditional machine learning methods are limited in their ability to capture complex nonlinear relationships among data, and deep learning is capable of extracting multi-scale and multi-level features and abstracting combinations of these features into high-level features. Existing studies have shown that deep learning models outperform traditional machine learning and show great potential for growth monitoring using remotely sensed data [30].

Neural networks are based on the extension of perceptual machines, and deep neural network (DNN) can be understood as a neural network with many hidden layers. The neural network layers within DNN are categorized into input, hidden, and output layers by stacking multiple hidden layers to achieve the extraction of higher order feature information, which helps to improve the performance in regression prediction. The DNN model has now become an effective method for solving a variety of classification and regression problems [8]. The network structure designed in this paper contains one input layer, three hidden layers, and one output layer; the layers are directly fully connected to each other, and the neurons between the same layers are not connected (the network structure is shown in Figure 2). The variables obtained based on WPT-FD and WPT-FD-HA screening were converted to one-dimensional vectors corresponding to the measured chlorophyll content of rice, respectively, and used as input layers. The final output was the predicted chlorophyll content. ReLU was selected as the activation function in the DNN model, the root mean square error (RMSE) was used as the optimization function, and the mean square error (MSE) was selected as the loss function for 150 iterations. In this study, Python 3.7 was adopted to build this network structure based on the Keras 2.3.0 framework.

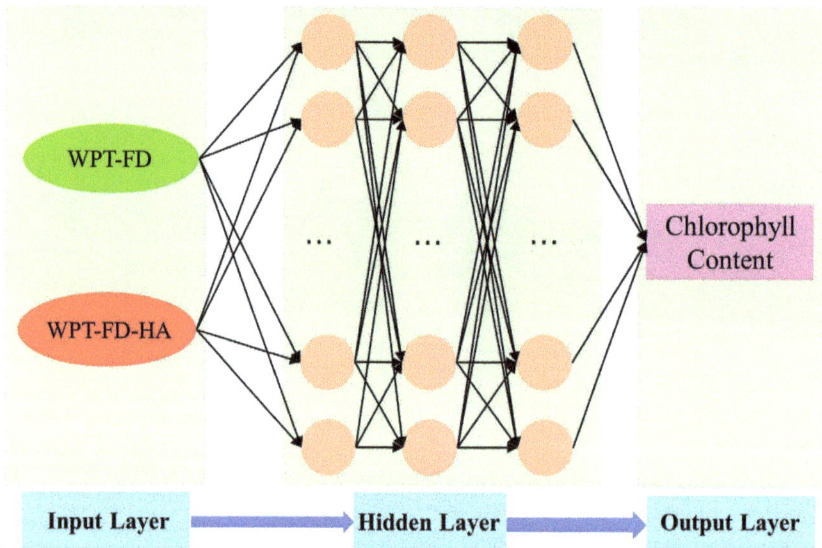

Figure 2. Schematic diagram of the deep learning network framework.

In deep learning models, a common training-test dataset segmentation method is the non-independent data split. For example, within the same experimental region, the data is partitioned into a training set and a test set according to 2:1 or 3:1 [30,31]. If the test set is spatially randomly sampled, spatial autocorrelation can lead to model overfitting. If the test set is spatially blocked, spatial autocorrelation leads to a narrower data distribution in the test set than in the training set. In addition, it does not test the transferability of the model. In this study, based on the traditional validation method, the accuracy and transferability of the model were further tested by combining the independent data split method. The schematic diagram of the two validation methods is shown in Figure 3. It can be seen that a non-independent data split is most likely to have homogeneity of variance. Tests of such homogeneous data do not provide a true indication of the model's transportability [7]. In contrast, an independent data split generally has heterogeneity of variance. The combination of these two methods can improve the effectiveness of the validation results. In this study, the 42-plot experimental data were used for the construction and initial validation of the rice chlorophyll content model (non-independent data split).

The dataset was randomly divided into 2:1 as the model calibration and validation sets, respectively. The 48-plot experimental data were used for model validation across time and location (independent data split). All model accuracy was assessed using the coefficient of determination (R^2) and RMSE.

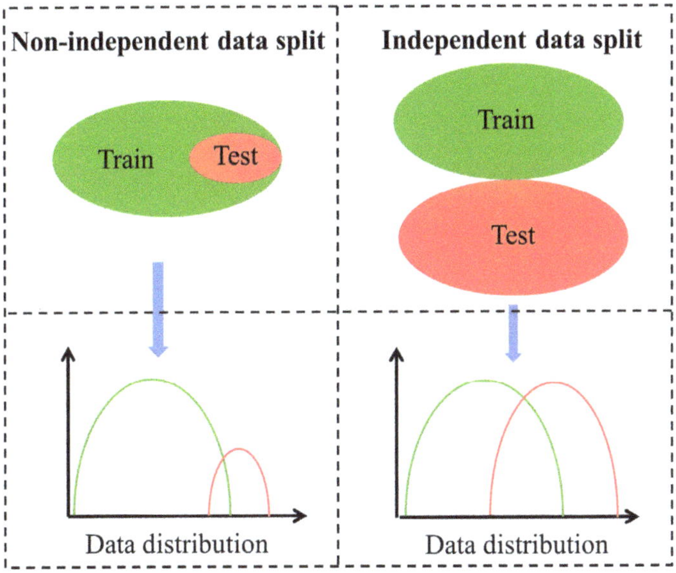

Figure 3. Dataset partitioning and model validation methods.

3. Results

3.1. Analysis of Changes in Rice Canopy Spectra with Chlorophyll Content and Growth Stage

Figure 4a shows the spectral reflectance corresponding to different chlorophyll contents in rice. It can be seen that in the visible bands (about 350–750 nm), the spectral reflectance decreased with increasing chlorophyll content, showing an overall negative correlation between reflectance and SPAD values. In the near-infrared bands (about 750–1750 nm), spectral reflectance was positively correlated with SPAD values. Figure 4b shows the characteristics of rice canopy reflectance changes with growth stages. It is observed that in the visible bands, the spectral reflectance has been increasing from the tillering stage to the grain filling stage, and the increase in magnitude continues to decrease. During the grain tillering stage, rice grew rapidly, the chlorophyll content increased dramatically, and the leaves absorbed lights strongly at red and blue bands, resulting in lower spectral reflectance in these bands. The visible bands showed the largest change in spectral reflectance from the grain filling stage to the milk stage. Figure 4c demonstrates the correlation between the original canopy spectra and the chlorophyll content of rice at different growth stages. It might be noticed that the correlations between the raw spectra and the chlorophyll content of rice at different growth stages varied considerably, with most of the correlations at the jointing stage. The correlation between the first-order derivative spectra and chlorophyll content reached a maximum value near 700 nm during the six growth periods observed.

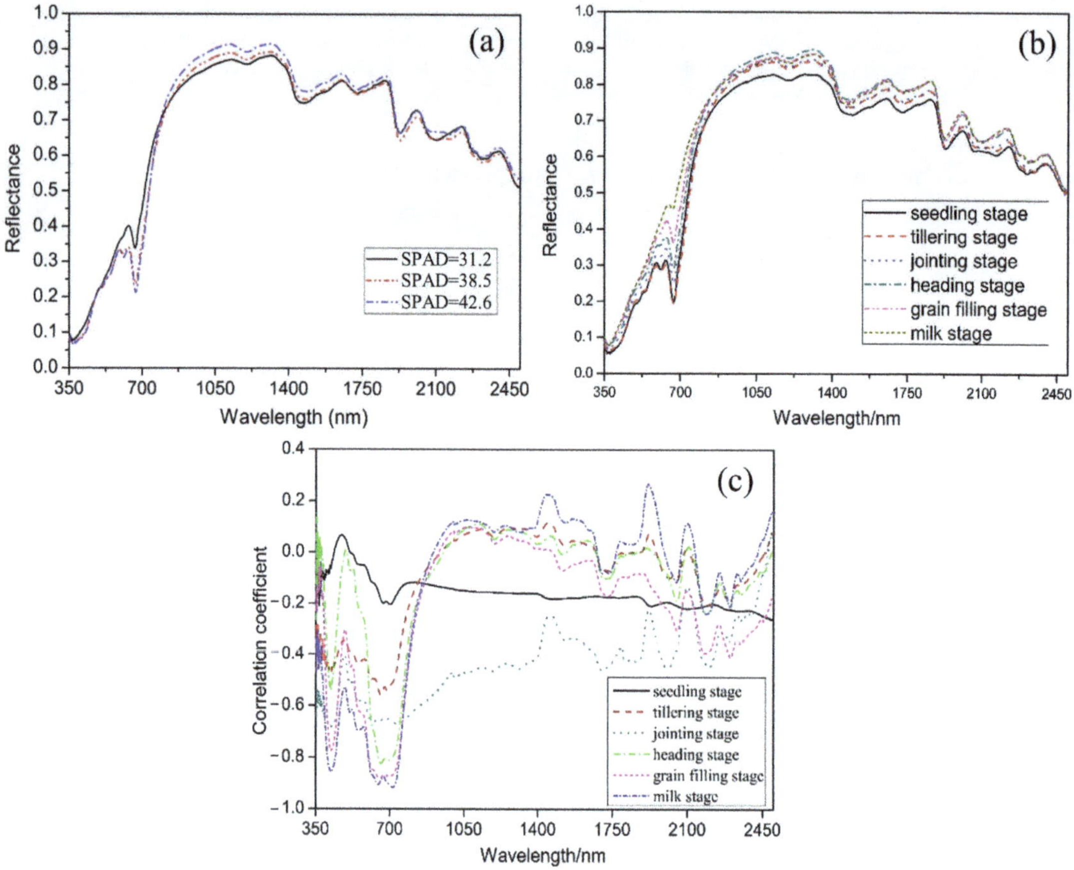

Figure 4. Changes in rice canopy spectra with SPAD and growth stage: (**a**) rice canopy reflectance under different chlorophyll contents; (**b**) changes in rice canopy spectra with growth stage; (**c**) correlation between rice canopy spectra and chlorophyll content.

3.2. Selection of Characteristic Bands

The original spectral data, its first-order differential spectra (FD), and the first-order differential spectral data after wavelet packet reconstruction (WPT-FD) were correlated with the chlorophyll contents of rice for the whole period, and the results are shown in Figure 5. It is evident that the overall negative correlation between the raw spectral reflectance and the rice chlorophyll contents was found. The FD and WPT-FD data can significantly improve the correlation with the rice chlorophyll contents and showed a positive and negative alternating trend. In the process of selecting the characteristic bands, in order to reduce the total number of bands for the estimation of rice chlorophyll content and to achieve the effect of data compression, the principles of selecting the characteristic bands were finally determined as follows: (i) the correlation coefficient was more than 0.8, (ii) the correlation coefficient was selected according to the absolute value from the largest to the smallest, and (iii) the number of bands was moderate. Two hundred and seventy characteristic bands were selected from the FD and WPT-FD data of the whole and each growth period of rice, respectively.

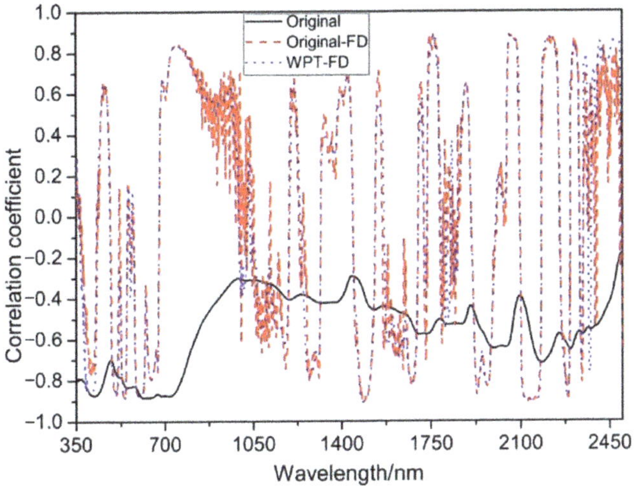

Figure 5. Correlation analysis of different types of data with chlorophyll content in rice.

3.3. Harmonic Decomposition

The WPT-FD data extracted from the rice canopy spectra were decomposed harmonically to obtain the harmonic energy spectra characteristic components $A_0/2$, A_h, B_h, C_h, and φ_h, and their correlation coefficients with leaf chlorophyll content were calculated. The total number of bands in the harmonic decomposition was 270, and, considering the period of the sine (cosine) function, the number of harmonic decompositions was determined to be 270. Figure 6 shows the correlation coefficients between the different harmonic energy spectral characteristic components and the chlorophyll content. It was observed that the correlation between the harmonic components at the beginning and the end of the decomposition number and the chlorophyll content was significantly higher. Finally, the components with correlation coefficients greater than 0.8 were selected from the seedling, tillering, jointing, heading, grain filling, and milk stages of rice, respectively.

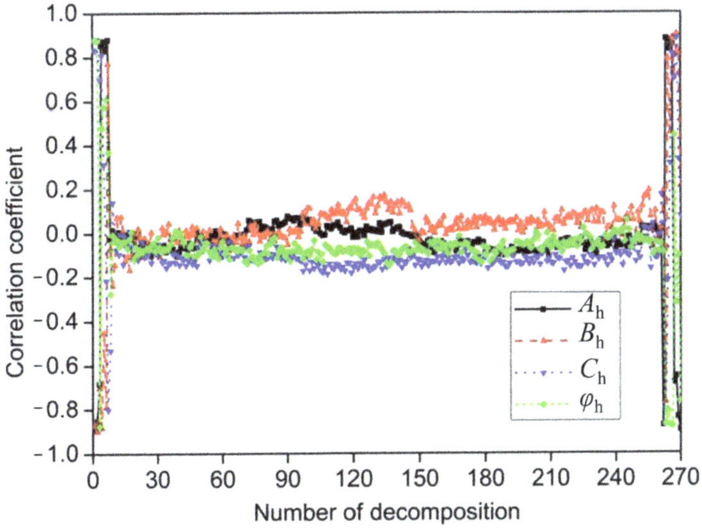

Figure 6. Correlation of HA characterization parameters with chlorophyll content in rice.

3.4. Estimation and Validation of the Chlorophyll Content of Rice at Different Stages Based on Diverse Variables

In this paper, in order to reduce the number of model input variables and improve the estimation performance of the model when estimating the chlorophyll content of rice at different growth stages using DNN, the selected components at six growth stages of rice were treated as the input factors of the deep learning model, respectively. The input variables were randomly divided into calibration and validation sets according to 2:1 to construct the rice chlorophyll prediction model based on WPT-FD and WPT-FD-HA, and the model accuracy is shown in Table 1. It can be found that the validation set accuracies based on WPT-FD variables were significantly lower than those based on the WPT-FD-HA framework when predicting rice chlorophyll content in a single period. As described in more detail, the R^2 of the WPT-FD models was generally lower than 0.8 and the RMSE was greater than 3, while the R^2 of the models based on the WPT-FD-HA framework were all more than 0.9, and the RMSE were all less than 1. When estimating the chlorophyll content of rice in multiple periods, the WPT-FD-HA framework showed comparable accuracies to the single-period models and demonstrated generalization across different periods and the whole period. It was significantly higher than the accuracy of the estimation model based on WPT-FD variables (R^2 = 0.971 vs. 0.707, RMSE = 1.664 vs. 3.334).

Table 1. The results of the DNN models for predicting rice chlorophyll content based on different variables and growth stages.

Growth Stages	Variables	Calibration		Validation	
		R^2	RMSE	R^2	RMSE
Seedling stage (Cal:Val = 28:14)	WPT-FD	0.895	2.467	0.766	2.865
	WPT-FD-HA	0.921	1.596	0.911	0.905
Tillering stage (Cal:Val = 28:14)	WPT-FD	0.946	1.305	0.832	2.304
	WPT-FD-HA	0.992	0.946	0.985	0.975
Jointing stage (Cal:Val = 56:28)	WPT-FD	0.984	1.065	0.863	2.674
	WPT-FD-HA	0.997	0.938	0.994	0.953
Heading stage (Cal:Val = 28:14)	WPT-FD	0.954	1.379	0.845	2.283
	WPT-FD-HA	0.997	0.934	0.991	0.958
Grain filling stage (Cal:Val = 28:14)	WPT-FD	0.941	1.298	0.723	2.984
	WPT-FD-HA	0.990	0.936	0.983	0.962
Milk stage (Cal:Val = 28:14)	WPT-FD	0.946	0.338	0.733	2.863
	WPT-FD-HA	0.990	0.934	0.986	0.958
Whole growth stage (Cal:Val = 200:94)	WPT-FD	0.924	1.406	0.707	3.334
	WPT-FD-HA	0.982	0.947	0.971	1.664

Figures 7 and 8 illustrate the comparison of measured and predicted chlorophyll content values in the single period validation set. From the single-period model, it could be noticed that the chlorophyll estimation error was the largest at the seedling stage (points corresponding to different chlorophyll content values were far away from the 1:1 line). The WPT-FD model showed that the predicted line of rice chlorophyll content at different periods differed from the 1:1 line, whereas the predicted line almost overlapped with the 1:1 line in the WPT-FD-HA model. Excellent estimation was observed at both high and low values when using the WPT-FD-HA framework. As can be seen from the scatter plot of the multi-period model (Figure 9), at low values of chlorophyll content, the WPT-FD-based model showed saturation (a large number of points clustered in the same range). In comparison, no significant aggregation was shown in the WPT-FD-HA model. Combined with the characteristics of rice cultivation during the different periods, it indicated that this framework possessed a certain degree of resistance to soil effects. From the comparison of a single period and full period, the accuracy of the WPT-FD model fluctuated greatly in different periods, and the accuracy in the full period was relatively low. However, the accuracy based on the WPT-FD-HA model showed consistently high accuracy in both the single period and the full period, indicating that the framework has the stability of estimating rice chlorophyll content in different periods.

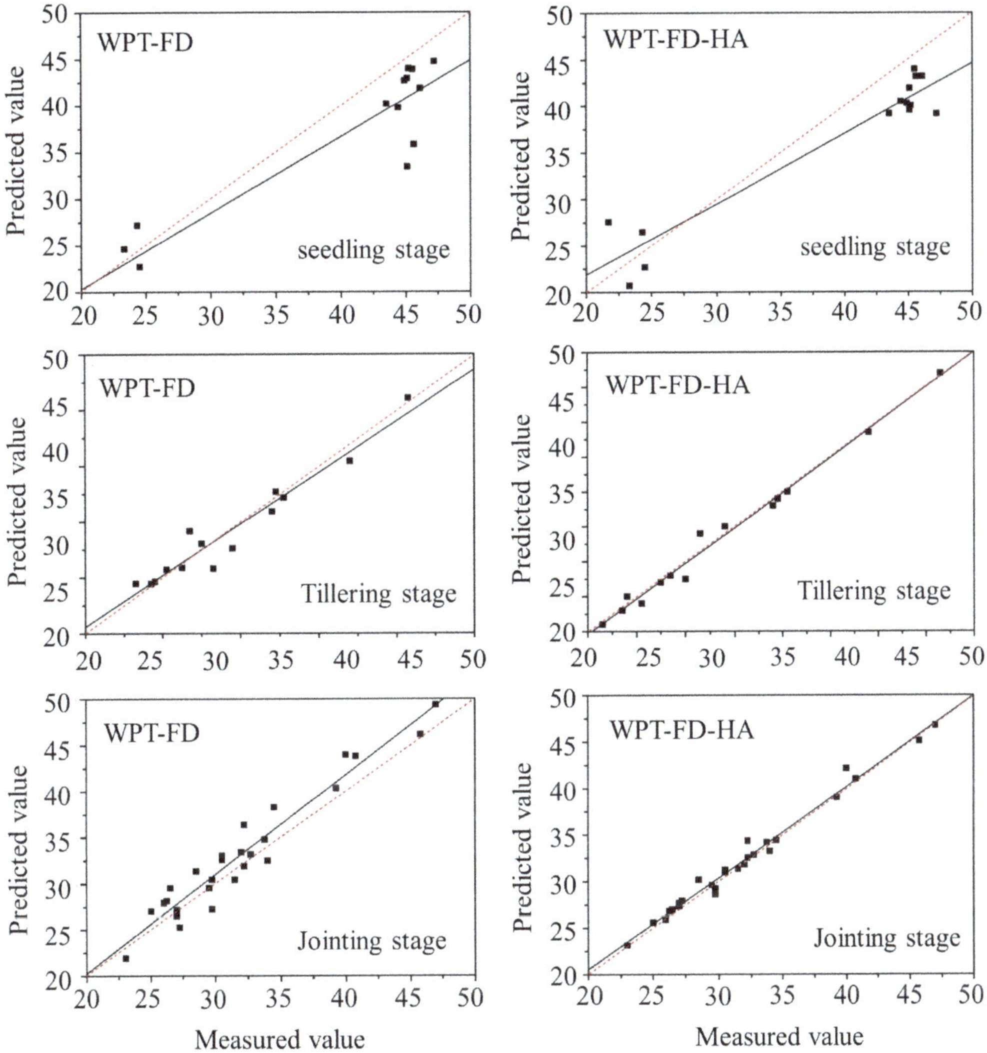

Figure 7. Comparison between measured and predicted chlorophyll content based on the DNN model at the seeding, tillering, and jointing stages in the 42-plot experiment (the black line is the fitting line and the red dotted line is the 1:1 line).

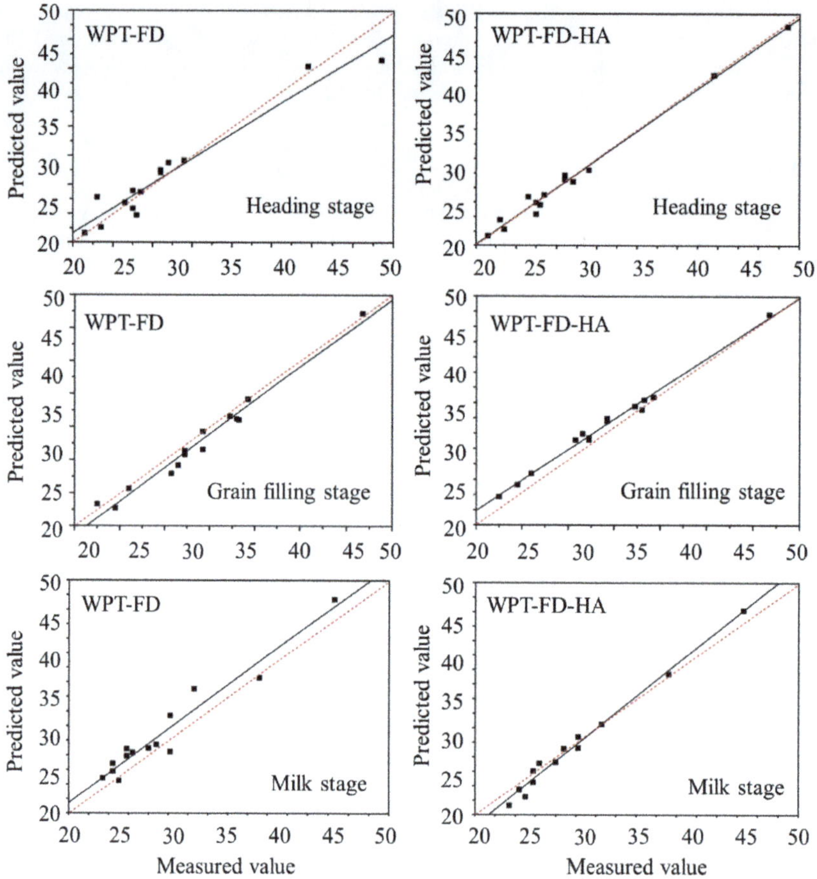

Figure 8. Comparison between measured and predicted chlorophyll content based on the DNN model at the heading, grain filling, and milk stages in the 42-plot experiment (the black line is the fitting line and the red dotted line is the 1:1 line).

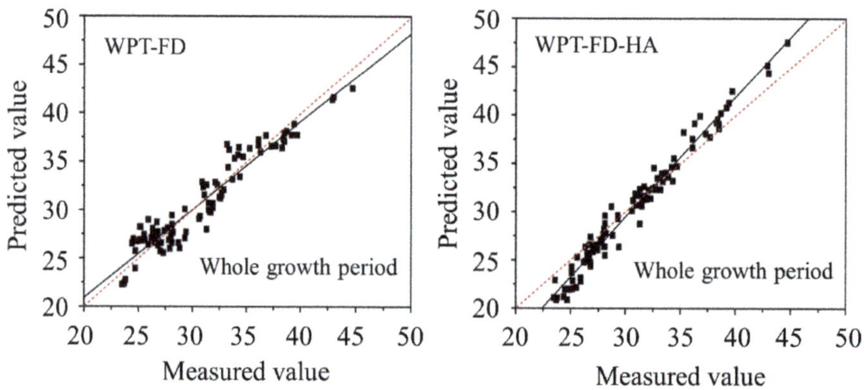

Figure 9. Comparison between measured and predicted chlorophyll content based on the DNN model throughout the whole period in the 42-plot experiment (the black line is the fitting line and the red dotted line is the 1:1 line).

To further prove the stability of the modeling framework proposed in this study for estimating the chlorophyll content of rice in different periods, the method was validated based on the 48-plot experiment, and the results are shown in Figure 10. It was easily seen that the WPT-FD model was less stable in cross-regional experiments, and the fluctuation of model accuracy in a single period was obvious. From the WPT-FD-HA validation model, it can be observed that both the single period and the full period showed high accuracy. The accuracy of the generalized rice chlorophyll model for the full period had an R^2 of 0.95 and an RMSE of 1.4 (N = 288).

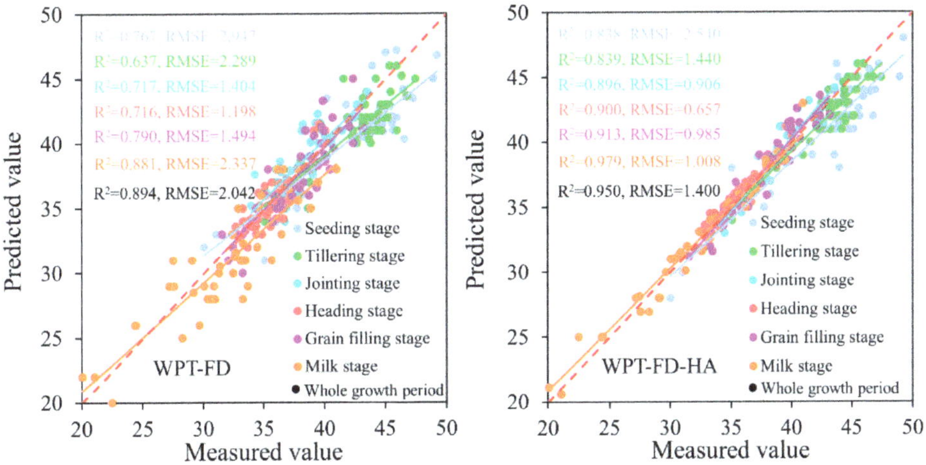

Figure 10. Comparison between measured and predicted chlorophyll content based on the DNN model throughout the whole period in the 48-plot experiment (the red dotted line is the 1:1 line).

4. Discussion

In this paper, the chlorophyll content of rice was estimated for single and multiple periods by spectral data preprocessing techniques, including FD, WPT, and HA decomposition, combined with a deep learning model. The significance of frequency-domain predictors was highlighted. The whole methodology system was applied to hyperspectral data in terms of data processing, parameter selection, and fusion. Furthermore, the technique was generalized to meet the prediction of rice chlorophyll content for different periods as well as across regions.

Most of the current studies on monitoring crop growth parameters are based on the ground, unmanned aerial vehicles (UAVs), or satellite visible and multispectral data [32,33]. Many optical data cannot cover the entire period of crop growth due to cloud cover and revisit cycles. Moreover, the low spatial resolution of satellite imagery is often not applicable to plot-level applications, limiting its use in crop growth monitoring [34]. A ground-based fixed platform can realize crop growth monitoring at the individual and small-plot scale in the field. Compared with satellite platforms, this platform can provide data with higher spatial, temporal, and spectral resolution, but its monitoring scale is small and inefficient, which is only suitable for small-scale applications, constraining its application in large-area crop growth monitoring [35]. Drones can obtain different kinds of images by flying at low altitudes, making them ideal for agricultural applications, while overcoming the shortcomings of satellites and ground platforms, and providing practical tools for precision agriculture. Different sensors carried by UAVs have been used in various scenarios. For example, hyperspectral cameras were utilized for the estimation of leaf area index [36] and chlorophyll content [37]. However, there is still a lack of relevant research. Thermal infrared and LiDAR sensors have been employed in measuring vegetation canopy temperature, water content [38], biomass [39], and yield [40]. However, these sensors are quite heavy for UAVs. They are also relatively expensive, and the data acquired is difficult to process and analyze. Relatively inexpensive RGB cameras are also frequently used in agriculture. However, the lack of highly sensitive red-edge and near-infrared bands that can be used for vegetation monitoring makes it impossible to acquire stable spectral data. Therefore, it is insufficient for in-depth quantitative studies and applications [41]. Multi-spectral sensors only provide information in a small number of bands, which makes it difficult to obtain satisfactory results in complex field scenarios [42]. Concerning crop growth monitoring techniques, there has been a gradual transition from traditional statistical methods to machine learning methods. For example, partial least squares regression (PLS), principal component regression (PCR), stepwise multiple linear regression, and random forest regression were used to construct models for estimating leaf physiological parameters of different crops [43]. In addition, the rapid development of deep learning techniques has also provided effective tools for the prediction of crop growth parameters [31,44]. Therefore, based on the above background, in situ measurement of hyperspectral data was utilized in this study, which was expected to apply the modeling framework to UAV and satellite hyperspectral data.

Vegetation canopy spectra are closely related to vegetation growth, since plant canopy reflectance carries valuable information about canopy interactions with solar radiation, such as vegetation absorption and scattering [45]. In the visible range, vegetation strongly absorbs sunlight and exhibits low reflectance due to the presence of pigments, and in the near-infrared wavelengths, vegetation exhibits relatively high reflectance influenced by thick plant tissues and canopy structures [46]. Currently, optical vegetation indices based on combinations of reflectance in different wavelength bands are widely used for crop growth parameter extraction in the field and regionally [47,48]. For example, the ratio vegetation index has been shown to be the most sensitive in leaf area index estimation, while the red-edge vegetation index has better results in chlorophyll content estimation [47]. However, a single vegetation index makes it difficult to obtain high accuracy in many complex scenarios. For instance, most vegetation indices fail in rice growth monitoring in scenarios with high soil background influence and dense vegetation growth [42,47]. In addition to vegetation indices, height [49,50], texture [51,52], and temperature [40] information have good auxiliary effects in crop growth parameter extraction, but the extraction of this information will inevitably increase the complexity and cost of the UAVs. Furthermore, machine learning or deep learning was used in most of the studies to fuse different types of parameters, which is rarely validated across regions and over time, making it difficult to apply them directly.

In this study, hyperspectral remote sensing technology was applied to the estimation of chlorophyll content in rice, and the theory of harmonic decomposition was invoked to carry out the research by transforming from the spectral domain to the frequency domain. The research method broadens the current research field of remote sensing to diagnose the chlorophyll content of rice and provides a new idea for the estimation of crop chlorophyll content. The innovation of the whole study is that the frequency-domain parameters obtained from harmonic decomposition were substituted for the spectral factors as the final input factors of the model, thus effectively reducing the human errors brought about by the calculation process of the conventional vegetation parameters. The frequency-domain signal is capable of displaying the essential characteristics and different information of the signal more clearly.

The wavelet packet theory was used to decompose the original spectral signals, and the spectra were reconstructed according to the optimal wavelet packet basis and the quantized optimal wavelet packet decomposition coefficients. From Figure 4, it can be seen that the correlation between the wavelet packet reconstructed spectra and the chlorophyll content of rice is better than that of the original spectra near the infrared and near-infrared bands, because wavelet packet decomposition yields a series of high-frequency and low-frequency signals, and some Gaussian noises tend to be contained in the high-frequency components [53]. In wavelet packet reconstruction, the noise contained in the original spectra was effectively reduced by choosing the appropriate wavelet packet basis to calculate the decomposition coefficients and then recombined into a new set of spectral signals.

Chlorophyll content estimation errors come from spectral noise and model input parameters. Vegetation indices were mostly adopted as model input parameters in conventional chlorophyll content estimation models. Different scholars calculated the vegetation index using various wavelengths and could not precisely select a specific wavelength, thus bringing some errors to the estimation model [54,55]. The purpose of introducing the harmonic decomposition is to eliminate the calculation error of the vegetation index due to the non-uniqueness of wavebands. Harmonic decomposition dealt with the whole spectra without involving a specific band reflectance, and finally, a series of harmonic decomposition parameters were obtained. From these parameters, the variables with a higher correlation with chlorophyll content were filtered out to realize the transformation of the input parameters from the spectral domain to the frequency domain.

By comparing the model accuracy of the single-period and full-period estimations of rice chlorophyll based on WPT-FD and WPT-FD-HA variables, it was finally found that the latter exhibited high stability in single-period and full-period estimations and high validation accuracy in experiments at different times and locations. This modeling framework of spectral preprocessing technique combined with DNN is expected to be applied in large-scale hyperspectral crop growth monitoring. Of course, it should be noted that the shortcomings of this study still exist. The ASD spectrometer for measuring rice canopy hyperspectra requires complex optical configurations, which are expensive and difficult to realize for high-throughput data access. However, the method proposed in this study for estimating rice chlorophyll content using hyperspectral data has practical applications. Utilizing airborne or spaceborne hyperspectral sensors for data access will become a future trend and can provide a simple and high-throughput data source for the application of this method [56,57].

5. Conclusions

This paper focuses on the non-destructive monitoring of chlorophyll content in rice at seedling, tillering, jointing, heading, grain filling, and milk stages. By analyzing the correlation between variables obtained by relying on spectral preprocessing techniques and chlorophyll content at each period, two estimation models, WPT-FD and WPT-FD-HA, were constructed based on the DNN algorithm. Through the comparative analysis of the accuracy of the models for a single growth period as well as for the whole period, it can be found that the spectral noise was effectively reduced by WPT reconstruction, and the correlation between rice canopy spectra and chlorophyll content was improved. Moreover, the harmonic decomposition further removes the noise in the first-order differential spectra and has the effect of data compression. After the harmonic decomposition, the correlation between the obtained components and the chlorophyll content of rice was significantly improved. Meanwhile, the harmonic decomposition converted the spectral domain to the frequency domain, which avoided the uncertainty in the calculation of spectral parameters and played a role in reducing parameter calculation errors. It should be emphasized that the rice chlorophyll content estimation model based on DNN and WPT-FD-HA has good adaptability in important individual and entire periods. This suggests that the WPT-FD-HA framework is a chlorophyll content prediction method applicable to the full rice period and has some generalizability. The unified estimation model of rice chlorophyll content proposed in this study is expected to be useful for rice growth monitoring at a large scale using hyperspectral data.

Author Contributions: Formal analysis, L.D.; Funding acquisition, S.L.; Methodology, L.D.; Project administration, S.L.; Resources, L.D.; Validation, S.L.; Writing—original draft, L.D.; Writing—review and editing, S.L. All authors have read and agreed to the published version of the manuscript.

Funding: The research presented in this paper was funded by the Science and Technology Tackling Project of Henan Province (242102210011), Basic Research Operating Expenses Program of Henan Academy of Sciences (240625002), and Scientific Research Initiation Program for High-level Talents of Henan Academy of Sciences (241825015).

Institutional Review Board Statement: Not applicable.

Data Availability Statement: The data reported in this study are contained within the article.

Acknowledgments: The authors sincerely thank Qian Li for their assistance in the modeling and field experiments of this study.

Conflicts of Interest: The authors declare no conflict of interest.

References

1. Zhou, Z.Y.; Jin, J.M.; Liu, J.; Si, Y.J. Covering rice demand in Southern China under decreasing cropping intensities and considering multiple climate and population scenarios. *Sustain. Prod. Consum.* **2023**, *40*, 13–29. [CrossRef]
2. Du, C.C.; Hu, L.L.; Yuan, S.; Xu, L.; Wang, W.B.; Cui, K.H.; Peng, S.B.; Huang, J.L. Ratoon rice-duck co-culture maintains rice grain yield and decreases greenhouse gas emissions in central China. *Eur. J. Agron.* **2023**, *149*, 126911. [CrossRef]
3. Seck, F.; Covarrubias-Pazaran, G.; Gueye, T.; Bartholome, J. Realized Genetic Gain in Rice: Achievements from Breeding Programs. *Rice* **2023**, *16*, 22. [CrossRef]
4. Liu, B.S.; Huang, L.H.; Jiang, X.T.; Liu, Y.; Huang, G.Z.; Yang, C.; Liang, Y.P.; Cai, J.H.; Zhu, G.; Kong, Q.Q. Quantitative evaluation and mechanism analysis of soil chemical factors affecting rice yield in saline-sodic paddy fields. *Sci. Total Environ.* **2024**, *929*, 172584. [CrossRef]
5. Yang, Y.C.; Nan, R.; Mi, T.X.; Song, Y.X.; Shi, F.H.; Liu, X.R.; Wang, Y.Q.; Sun, F.L.; Xi, Y.J.; Zhang, C. Rapid and Nondestructive Evaluation of Wheat Chlorophyll under Drought Stress Using Hyperspectral Imaging. *Int. J. Mol. Sci.* **2023**, *24*, 5825. [CrossRef] [PubMed]
6. Xue, H.Y.; Xu, X.G.; Zhu, Q.Z.; Meng, Y.; Long, H.L.; Li, H.L.; Song, X.Y.; Yang, G.J.; Yang, M.; Li, Y.F.; et al. Rice yield and quality estimation coupling hierarchical linear model with remote sensing. *Comput. Electron. Agric.* **2024**, *218*, 108731. [CrossRef]
7. Wang, Z.L.; Tan, X.M.; Ma, Y.M.; Liu, T.; He, L.M.; Yang, F.; Shu, C.H.; Li, L.L.; Fu, H.; Li, B.; et al. Combining canopy spectral reflectance and RGB images to estimate leaf chlorophyll content and grain yield in rice. *Comput. Electron. Agric.* **2024**, *221*, 108975. [CrossRef]
8. Du, R.Q.; Chen, J.Y.; Xiang, Y.Z.; Zhang, Z.T.; Yang, N.; Yang, X.Z.; Tang, Z.J.; Wang, H.; Wang, X.; Shi, H.Z.; et al. Incremental learning for crop growth parameters estimation and nitrogen diagnosis from hyperspectral data. *Comput. Electron. Agric.* **2023**, *215*, 108356. [CrossRef]
9. Wang, X.K.; Xu, G.L.; Feng, Y.H.; Peng, J.F.; Gao, Y.Q.; Li, J.; Han, Z.L.; Luo, Q.X.; Ren, H.J.; You, X.X.; et al. Estimation Model of Rice Aboveground Dry Biomass Based on the Machine Learning and Hyperspectral Characteristic Parameters of the Canopy. *Agronomy* **2023**, *13*, 1940. [CrossRef]
10. Wei, S.S.; Yin, T.A.; Yuan, B.; Ow, G.L.F.; Yusof, M.L.M.; Gastellu-Etchegorry, J.P.; Whittle, A.J. Estimation of chlorophyll content for urban trees from UAV hyperspectral images. *Int. J. Appl. Earth Obs. Geoinf.* **2024**, *126*, 103617. [CrossRef]
11. Liao, Z.-Q.; Dai, Y.-L.; Wang, H.; Ketterings, Q.M.; Lu, J.-S.; Zhang, F.-C.; Li, Z.-J.; Fan, J.-L. A double-layer model for improving the estimation of wheat canopy nitrogen content from unmanned aerial vehicle multispectral imagery. *J. Integr. Agric.* **2023**, *22*, 2248–2270. [CrossRef]
12. Nian, Y.; Su, X.X.; Yue, H.; Zhu, Y.J.; Li, J.; Wang, W.Q.; Sheng, Y.L.; Ma, Q.; Liu, J.K.; Li, X.W. Estimation of the rice aboveground biomass based on the first derivative spectrum and Boruta algorithm. *Front. Plant Sci.* **2024**, *15*, 13. [CrossRef]
13. Wang, N.; Yang, G.; Han, X.Y.; Jia, G.P.; Li, Q.H.; Liu, F.; Liu, X.; Chen, H.Y.; Guo, X.Y.; Zhang, T.Q. Study of the spectral characters-chlorophyll inversion model of Sabina vulgaris in the Mu Us Sandy Land. *Front. Earth Sci.* **2023**, *10*, 15. [CrossRef]
14. Gu, Q.; Huang, F.D.; Lou, W.D.; Zhu, Y.H.; Hu, H.; Zhao, Y.Y.; Zhou, H.K.; Zhang, X.B. Unmanned aerial vehicle-based assessment of rice leaf chlorophyll content dynamics across genotypes. *Comput. Electron. Agric.* **2024**, *221*, 108939. [CrossRef]
15. Feng, Z.H.; Guan, H.W.; Yang, T.C.; He, L.; Duan, J.Z.; Song, L.; Wang, C.Y.; Feng, W. Estimating the canopy chlorophyll content of winter wheat under nitrogen deficiency and powdery mildew stress using machine learning. *Comput. Electron. Agric.* **2023**, *211*, 107989. [CrossRef]
16. Zhang, H.C.; Ge, Y.F.; Xie, X.Y.; Atefi, A.; Wijewardane, N.K.; Thapa, S. High throughput analysis of leaf chlorophyll content in sorghum using RGB, hyperspectral, and fluorescence imaging and sensor fusion. *Plant Methods* **2022**, *18*, 17. [CrossRef] [PubMed]
17. Liu, L.S.; Xie, Y.C.; Zhu, B.X.; Song, K.S. Rice leaf chlorophyll content estimation with different crop coverages based on Sentinel-2. *Ecol. Inform.* **2024**, *81*, 102622. [CrossRef]
18. Gu, C.P.; Li, J.; Liu, Q.H.; Zhang, H.; Liu, L.Y.; Mumtaz, F.; Dong, Y.D.; Zhao, J.; Wang, X.H.; Liu, C. Retrieving decametric-resolution leaf chlorophyll content from GF-6 WFV by assessing the applicability of red-edge vegetation indices. *Comput. Electron. Agric.* **2023**, *215*, 108455. [CrossRef]

19. Golhani, K.; Balasundram, S.K.; Vadamalai, G.; Pradhan, B. Estimating chlorophyll content at leaf scale in viroid-inoculated oil palm seedlings (*Elaeis guineensis* Jacq.) using reflectance spectra (400 nm–1050 nm). *Int. J. Remote Sens.* **2019**, *40*, 7647–7662. [CrossRef]
20. Luo, S.J.; He, Y.B.; Li, Q.; Jiao, W.H.; Zhu, Y.Q.; Yu, J.K.; Zhao, C.; Xu, R.Y.; Zhang, S.L.; Xu, F.; et al. Assessment of unified models for estimating potato leaf area index under water stress conditions across ground-based hyperspectral data. *J. Appl. Remote Sens.* **2020**, *14*, 12. [CrossRef]
21. Jiang, X.Q.; Luo, S.J.; Fang, S.H.; Cai, B.W.; Xiong, Q.; Wang, Y.Y.; Huang, X.; Liu, X.J. Remotely sensed estimation of total iron content in soil with harmonic analysis and BP neural network. *Plant Methods* **2021**, *17*, 12. [CrossRef] [PubMed]
22. Xu, J.J.; Fu, G.S.; Yan, L.P.; Yu, L.; Kuang, F.; Huang, Q.F.; Tang, X.H. Estimation of the Relative Chlorophyll Content of *Carya illinoensis* Leaves Using Fractional Order Derivative of Leaf and Canopy Scale Hyperspectral Data. *J. Soil Sci. Plant Nutr.* **2024**, *24*, 1407–1423. [CrossRef]
23. Li, X.L.; Lu, K.J.; Zhao, Y.J.; Chen, D.L.; Yi, P.; Hua, W. Incorporating Harmonic-Analysis-Based Loss Minimization Into MPTC for Efficiency Improvement of FCFMPM Motor. *IEEE Trans. Ind. Electron.* **2023**, *70*, 6540–6550. [CrossRef]
24. Svendsen, D.H.; Piles, M.; Muñoz-Mari, J.; Luengo, D.; Martino, L.; Camps-Valls, G. Integrating Domain Knowledge in Data-Driven Earth Observation With Process Convolutions. *IEEE Trans. Geosci. Remote Sens.* **2022**, *60*, 15. [CrossRef]
25. Tang, Z.J.; Guo, J.J.; Xiang, Y.Z.; Lu, X.H.; Wang, Q.; Wang, H.D.; Cheng, M.H.; Wang, H.; Wang, X.; An, J.Q.; et al. Estimation of Leaf Area Index and Above-Ground Biomass of Winter Wheat Based on Optimal Spectral Index. *Agronomy* **2022**, *12*, 1729. [CrossRef]
26. Reum, D.; Zhang, Q. Wavelet based multi-spectral image analysis of maize leaf chlorophyll content. *Comput. Electron. Agric.* **2007**, *56*, 60–71. [CrossRef]
27. Jiang, X.Q.; Luo, S.J.; Ye, Q.; Li, X.C.; Jiao, W.H. Hyperspectral Estimates of Soil Moisture Content Incorporating Harmonic Indicators and Machine Learning. *Agriculture* **2022**, *12*, 1188. [CrossRef]
28. Du, X.Y.; Zheng, L.Y.; Zhu, J.P.; He, Y. Enhanced Leaf Area Index Estimation in Rice by Integrating UAV-Based Multi-Source Data. *Remote Sens.* **2024**, *16*, 1138. [CrossRef]
29. Li, P.L.; Huang, X.J.; Yin, S.; Bao, Y.H.; Bao, G.; Tong, S.Q.; Dashzeveg, G.; Nanzad, T.; Dorjsuren, A.; Enkhnasan, D.; et al. Optimizing spectral index to estimate the relative chlorophyll content of the forest under the damage of *Erannis jacobsoni* Djak in Mongolia. *Ecol. Indic.* **2023**, *154*, 110714. [CrossRef]
30. Han, J.Y.; Shi, L.S.; Yang, Q.; Chen, Z.W.; Yu, J.; Zha, Y.Y. Rice yield estimation using a CNN-based image-driven data assimilation framework. *Field Crops Res.* **2022**, *288*, 108693. [CrossRef]
31. Zhao, R.M.; An, L.L.; Tang, W.J.; Gao, D.H.; Qiao, L.; Li, M.Z.; Sun, H.; Qiao, J.B. Deep learning assisted continuous wavelet transform-based spectrogram for the detection of chlorophyll content in potato leaves. *Comput. Electron. Agric.* **2022**, *195*, 106802. [CrossRef]
32. Huang, J.X.; Gómez-Dans, J.L.; Huang, H.; Ma, H.Y.; Wu, Q.L.; Lewis, P.E.; Liang, S.L.; Chen, Z.X.; Xue, J.H.; Wu, Y.T.; et al. Assimilation of remote sensing into crop growth models: Current status and perspectives. *Agric. For. Meteorol.* **2019**, *276*, 16. [CrossRef]
33. Chen, D.J.; Neumann, K.; Friedel, S.; Kilian, B.; Chen, M.; Altmann, T.; Klukas, C. Dissecting the Phenotypic Components of Crop Plant Growth and Drought Responses Based on High-Throughput Image Analysis. *Plant Cell* **2014**, *26*, 4636–4655. [CrossRef]
34. Deng, L.; Mao, Z.H.; Li, X.J.; Hu, Z.W.; Duan, F.Z.; Yan, Y.N. UAV-based multispectral remote sensing for precision agriculture: A comparison between different cameras. *ISPRS-J. Photogramm. Remote Sens.* **2018**, *146*, 124–136. [CrossRef]
35. Jin, X.L.; Zarco-Tejada, P.J.; Schmidhalter, U.; Reynolds, M.P.; Hawkesford, M.J.; Varshney, R.K.; Yang, T.; Nie, C.W.; Li, Z.H.; Ming, B.; et al. High-Throughput Estimation of Crop Traits: A Review of Ground and Aerial Phenotyping Platforms. *IEEE Geosci. Remote Sens. Mag.* **2021**, *9*, 200–231. [CrossRef]
36. Xie, Q.Y.; Huang, W.J.; Liang, D.; Chen, P.F.; Wu, C.Y.; Yang, G.J.; Zhang, J.C.; Huang, L.S.; Zhang, D.Y. Leaf Area Index Estimation Using Vegetation Indices Derived From Airborne Hyperspectral Images in Winter Wheat. *IEEE J. Sel. Top. Appl. Earth Observ. Remote Sens.* **2014**, *7*, 3586–3594. [CrossRef]
37. Feng, H.K.; Tao, H.L.; Zhao, Y.; Yang, F.Q.; Fan, Y.G.; Yang, G.J. Estimation of Chlorophyll Content in Winter Wheat Based on UAV Hyperspectral. *Spectrosc. Spectr. Anal.* **2022**, *42*, 3575–3580. [CrossRef]
38. Noguera, M.; Millán, B.; Pérez-Paredes, J.J.; Ponce, J.M.; Aquino, A.; Andújar, J.M. A New Low-Cost Device Based on Thermal Infrared Sensors for Olive Tree Canopy Temperature Measurement and Water Status Monitoring. *Remote Sens.* **2020**, *12*, 723. [CrossRef]
39. Andújar, D.; Rueda-Ayala, V.; Moreno, H.; Rosell-Polo, J.R.; Escolà, A.; Valero, C.; Gerhards, R.; Fernández-Quintanilla, C.; Dorado, J.; Griepentrog, H.W. Discriminating Crop, Weeds and Soil Surface with a Terrestrial LIDAR Sensor. *Sensors* **2013**, *13*, 14662–14675. [CrossRef] [PubMed]
40. Maimaitijiang, M.; Sagan, V.; Sidike, P.; Hartling, S.; Esposito, F.; Fritschi, F.B. Soybean yield prediction from UAV using multimodal data fusion and deep learning. *Remote Sens. Environ.* **2020**, *237*, 111599. [CrossRef]
41. Baresel, J.P.; Rischbeck, P.; Hu, Y.C.; Kipp, S.; Hu, Y.C.; Barmeier, G.; Mistele, B.; Schmidhalter, U. Use of a digital camera as alternative method for non-destructive detection of the leaf chlorophyll content and the nitrogen nutrition status in wheat. *Comput. Electron. Agric.* **2017**, *140*, 25–33. [CrossRef]

42. Yao, X.; Wang, N.; Liu, Y.; Cheng, T.; Tian, Y.C.; Chen, Q.; Zhu, Y. Estimation of Wheat LAI at Middle to High Levels Using Unmanned Aerial Vehicle Narrowband Multispectral Imagery. *Remote Sens.* **2017**, *9*, 1304. [CrossRef]
43. Chen, M.C.; Yu, H.Y.; Li, X.K.; Wang, H.J.; Liu, S.; Kong, L.J.; Zhang, L.; Dang, J.M.; Sui, Y.Y. Response Analysis of Hyperspectral Characteristics of Maize Seedling Leaves Under Different Light and Temperature Environment. *Spectrosc. Spectr. Anal.* **2021**, *41*, 3545–3551. [CrossRef]
44. Ye, Z.R.; Tan, X.F.; Dai, M.D.; Chen, X.T.; Zhong, Y.X.; Zhang, Y.; Ruan, Y.J.; Kong, D.D. A hyperspectral deep learning attention model for predicting lettuce chlorophyll content. *Plant Methods* **2024**, *20*, 11. [CrossRef]
45. Verhoef, W. Light-Scattering by Leaf Layers with Application to Canopy Reflectance Modeling–The Sail Model. *Remote Sens. Environ.* **1984**, *16*, 125–141. [CrossRef]
46. Wang, Q.; Sun, D.Y.; Li, Y.M.; Le, C.F.; Huang, C.C. Mechanisms of Remote-Sensing Reflectance Variability and Its Relation to Bio-Optical Processes in a Highly Turbid Eutrophic Lake: Lake Taihu (China). *IEEE Trans. Geosci. Remote Sens.* **2010**, *48*, 575–584. [CrossRef]
47. Wang, W.H.; Zheng, H.B.; Wu, Y.P.; Yao, X.; Zhu, Y.; Cao, W.X.; Cheng, T. An assessment of background removal approaches for improved estimation of rice leaf nitrogen concentration with unmanned aerial vehicle multispectral imagery at various observation times. *Field Crops Res.* **2022**, *283*, 108543. [CrossRef]
48. Li, S.Y.; Yuan, F.; Ata-Ui-Karim, S.T.; Zheng, H.B.; Cheng, T.; Liu, X.J.; Tian, Y.C.; Zhu, Y.; Cao, W.X.; Cao, Q. Combining Color Indices and Textures of UAV-Based Digital Imagery for Rice LAI Estimation. *Remote Sens.* **2019**, *11*, 1763. [CrossRef]
49. Li, B.; Xu, X.M.; Zhang, L.; Han, J.W.; Bian, C.S.; Li, G.C.; Liu, J.G.; Jin, L.P. Above-ground biomass estimation and yield prediction in potato by using UAV-based RGB and hyperspectral imaging. *ISPRS-J. Photogramm. Remote Sens.* **2020**, *162*, 161–172. [CrossRef]
50. Gong, Y.; Yang, K.L.; Lin, Z.H.; Fang, S.H.; Wu, X.T.; Zhu, R.S.; Peng, Y. Remote estimation of leaf area index (LAI) with unmanned aerial vehicle (UAV) imaging for different rice cultivars throughout the entire growing season. *Plant Methods* **2021**, *17*, 16. [CrossRef] [PubMed]
51. Duan, B.; Liu, Y.T.; Gong, Y.; Peng, Y.; Wu, X.T.; Zhu, R.S.; Fang, S.H. Remote estimation of rice LAI based on Fourier spectrum texture from UAV image. *Plant Methods* **2019**, *15*, 12. [CrossRef]
52. Zhou, C.; Gong, Y.; Fang, S.H.; Yang, K.L.; Peng, Y.; Wu, X.T.; Zhu, R.S. Combining spectral and wavelet texture features for unmanned aerial vehicles remote estimation of rice leaf area index. *Front. Plant Sci.* **2022**, *13*, 17. [CrossRef]
53. Song, R.M.; Chen, W.G.; Wang, Y.Y.; Du, L.; Wang, P.Y. Transformer Aging Diagnosis Method Based on Raman Spectroscopy Wavelet Packet-SPCA Feature Extraction. *IEEE Trans. Instrum. Meas.* **2023**, *72*, 8. [CrossRef]
54. Qian, B.X.; Ye, H.C.; Huang, W.J.; Xie, Q.Y.; Pan, Y.H.; Xing, N.C.; Ren, Y.; Guo, A.T.; Jiao, Q.J.; Lan, Y.B. A sentinel-2-based triangular vegetation index for chlorophyll content estimation. *Agric. For. Meteorol.* **2022**, *322*, 109000. [CrossRef]
55. Qiao, L.; Tang, W.J.; Gao, D.H.; Zhao, R.M.; An, L.L.; Li, M.Z.; Sun, H.; Song, D. UAV-based chlorophyll content estimation by evaluating vegetation index responses under different crop coverages. *Comput. Electron. Agric.* **2022**, *196*, 106775. [CrossRef]
56. Qian, S.E. Hyperspectral Satellites, Evolution, and Development History. *IEEE J. Sel. Top. Appl. Earth Observ. Remote Sens.* **2021**, *14*, 7032–7056. [CrossRef]
57. Mo, Y.; Kang, X.D.; Duan, P.H.; Li, S.T. A Robust UAV Hyperspectral Image Stitching Method Based on Deep Feature Matching. *IEEE Trans. Geosci. Remote Sens.* **2022**, *60*, 14. [CrossRef]

agriculture

MDPI

Article

Rapid Detection of Fertilizer Information Based on Near-Infrared Spectroscopy and Machine Learning and the Design of a Detection Device

Yongzheng Ma, Zhuoyuan Wu, Yingying Cheng, Shihong Chen and Jianian Li *

Faculty of Modern Agricultural Engineering, Kunming University of Science and Technology, Kunming 650500, China; 20222114027@stu.kust.edu.cn (Y.M.); 20212214047@stu.kust.edu.cn (Z.W.); chengyingying1@stu.kust.edu.cn (Y.C.); chenshihong@stu.kust.edu.cn (S.C.)

* Correspondence: jianianli@kust.edu.cn

Abstract: The online detection of fertilizer information is pivotal for precise and intelligent variable-rate fertilizer application. However, traditional methods face challenges such as the complex quantification of multiple components and sensor-induced cross-contamination. This study investigates integrating near-infrared principles with machine learning algorithms to identify fertilizer types and concentrations. We utilized near-infrared transmission spectroscopy and applied Partial Least Squares Discriminant Analysis (PLS-DA), Support Vector Machine (SVM), and Back-Propagation Neural Network (BPNN) algorithms to analyze full spectrum data. The BPNN model, using S-G smoothing, demonstrated a superior classification performance for the nutrient ions of four fertilizer solutions: HPO_4^{2-}, NH_4^+, $H_2PO_4^-$ and K^+. Optimization using the competitive adaptive reweighted sampling (CARS) method yielded BPNN model RMSE values of 0.3201, 0.7160, 0.2036, and 0.0177 for HPO_4^{2-}, NH_4^+, $H_2PO_4^-$, and K^+, respectively. Building on this foundation, we designed a four-channel fertilizer detection device based on the Lambert–Beer law, enabling the real-time detection of fertilizer types and concentrations. The test results confirmed the device's robust stability, achieving 93% accuracy in identifying fertilizer types and concentrations, with RMSE values ranging from 1.0034 to 2.4947, all within ±8.0% error margin. This study addresses the practical requirements for online fertilizer detection in agricultural engineering, laying the groundwork for efficient water–fertilizer integration technology aligned with sustainable development goals.

Keywords: near-infrared spectroscopy; Lambert–Beer law; machine learning; fertilizer sensors

1. Introduction

In recent years, China has made strides in water–fertilizer integration technologies, embracing precision fertilizer application and intelligent irrigation [1]. Despite these advancements, there is still ground to cover before the international forefront is reached. The development of an intelligent water–fertilizer integration system is crucial for achieving precision irrigation [2,3]. This system relies on establishing predictive models for water and fertilizer, integrating advanced technologies for the real-time adjustment of variable irrigation, and ensuring the accurate quantitative management of agricultural products. The accurate online detection of each nutrient component in fertilizer solutions is essential for the precise regulation of water and fertilizers in irrigation [4]. However, online fertilizer detection often encounters challenges from environmental factors, leading to issues such as incomplete nutrient data, reduced accuracy, and slower processing speeds. Therefore, achieving dependable online fertilization detection remains a significant challenge for advancing intelligent control technologies in agricultural management.

Fertilizer component information primarily includes the main nutrients and their concentrations within water–fertilizer mixtures. The main online detection methods for fertilizer components at present, both domestically and internationally, include the EC/pH, ion-selective electrode (ISE), and dielectric property detection methods.

The EC/pH method utilizes sensors' electrical conductivity and pH to measure overall ionic composition in fertilizer solutions. However, it lacks precision in differentiating individual ion concentrations [5,6]. The ISE method employs specific electrode membranes to precisely measure target ion concentrations and activities [7], but it may encounter cross-sensitivity issues among ions, potentially affecting measurement accuracy [8]. The dielectric property detection method uses capacitive sensors to measure the solution's relative permittivity, suggesting composition and concentration changes based on variations in dielectric constant. Challenges remain regarding the reliability and stability of frequency prediction techniques.

In addition, near-infrared (NIR) spectroscopy has gained prominence in academia and industry for its ability to selectively absorb light based on functional group characteristics in substances. In recent years, the integration of machine learning methods has revolutionized data analysis, particularly in classification and regression tasks, due to their advanced feature extraction capabilities. Zhi dan Lin et al. undertook a comprehensive spectral scanning and chemical profiling of a substantial volume of soil and fertilizer specimens utilizing visible and near-infrared (VIS/NIR) techniques. Leveraging a genetic algorithm (GA)-based model, precise forecasts were achieved for parameters such as organic matter content (OMC), total nitrogen in soil, as well as nitrogen, phosphorus, and potassium levels in fertilizer [9]. Similarly, Mohammadreza Khanmohammadi et al. employed a chemometric approach amalgamating mid-frequency FTIR spectroscopy with the successive projection algorithm (SPA) for wavelength selection, coupled with a feed-forward back-propagation artificial neural network (BP-ANN) model, to quantify protein content in yogurt samples. The BP-ANN and SPA-BP-ANN methods yielded relative errors (REP) of 7.25 and 3.70, respectively, in predicting the calibration set [10]. Furthermore, Song Le et al. harnessed near-infrared diffuse reflectance spectroscopy to ascertain the composition of compound fertilizers, specifically the content of urea, diurea, and other constituents. Following appropriate preprocessing, partial least squares (PLS) regression achieved initial test coefficients, R^2, of 0.9861 and 0.9713, underscoring its efficacy [11].

The research objective of this paper is to propose a fast and non-destructive method for detecting fertilizer component information based on NIR spectroscopy, and to improve the accuracy and robustness of the model via spectral pre-processing and feature extraction. Three different algorithms, i.e., BPNN, PLS, and SVM models, are compared to construct an optimal model for fertilizer component identification and concentration prediction. Based on this theory, a corresponding detection device is developed and integrated with hardware and software systems to achieve fertilizer type identification and rapid online concentration detection.

2. Materials and Methods

2.1. Sample Selection and Preparation

As the main effective nutrients of the N, P, and K fertilizers that are actually applied to agricultural production crops are NH_4^+, K^+, and total phosphorus (PO_4^{3-}, HPO_4^{2-}, $H_2PO_4^-$) [12], in this paper, potassium sulfate (K_2SO_4, 99%), diammonium hydrogen phosphate ($(NH_4)_2HPO_4$, 99%), potassium dihydrogen phosphate (KH_2PO_4, 99%), and ammonium sulfate ($(NH_4)_2SO_4$, 99%) were purchased from Sinopharm Chemical Reagent Co., Ltd., Shanghai, China. Each fertilizer solution was configured with ten concentration gradients (10–100 mg/L at 10 mg/L intervals) using deionized water, with four samples replicated at each concentration. Finally, all samples were stored at room temperature until measurements were taken. The sample configuration was carried out in the college laboratory.

2.2. Acquisition of Near-Infrared Spectra

The spectral data collection for this study was conducted in the laboratory of Faculty of Environmental Science and Engineering at Kunming University of Science and Technology, using a Cary 5000 NIR spectrophotometer capable of detecting wavelengths from 700 to 2500 nm. The fertilizer solutions under investigation were prepared by adding drops into two-thirds of a quartz cuvette, which was then placed in the instrument's detection tank. The NIR spectrophotometer scanned absorbance spectral curves of the four standard solutions across the entire wavelength range. Each fertilizer solution was scanned five times, and the resulting spectra were averaged to obtain spectral data comprising 1800 wavelengths, each associated with its own absorbance value. Subsequently, 160 sets of wavelength-absorbance spectral data were generated for the four fertilizer solutions. These datasets were then randomly divided into a calibration set and a prediction set in a 3:1 ratio using a random selection method. These sets were employed for the subsequent qualitative and quantitative modeling analyses of the fertilizer solutions (Figure 1a).

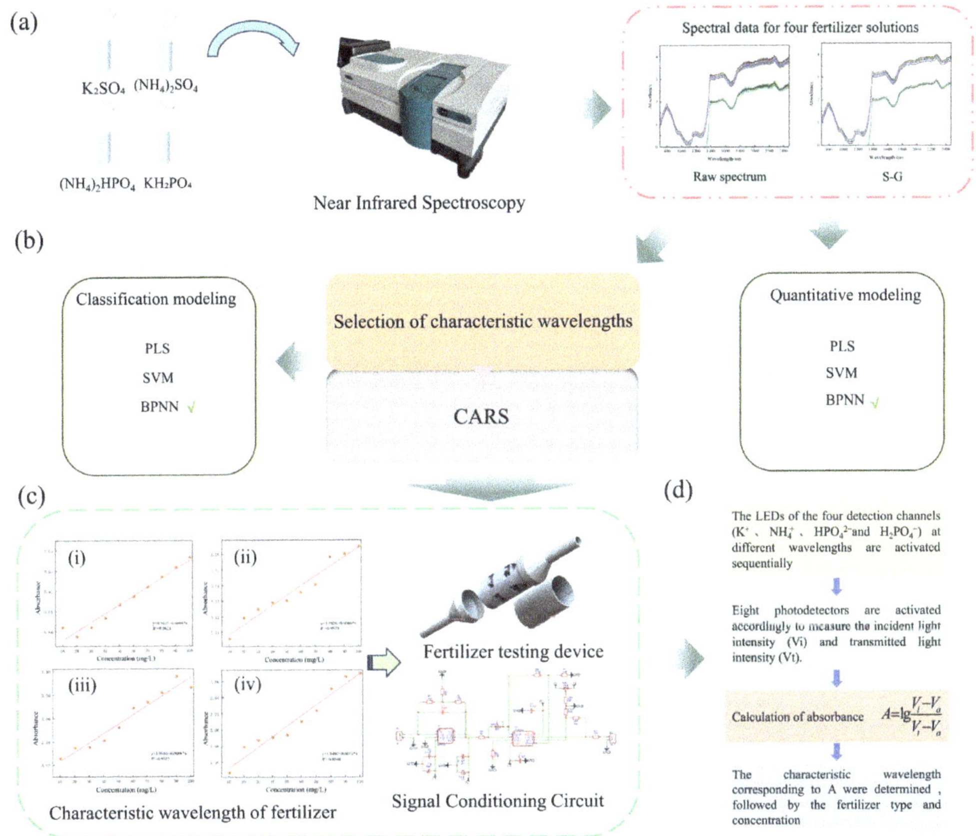

Figure 1. Development strategy of NIR fertilizer detection sensors: (**a**) acquisition and pre-processing of NIR absorption spectra of four fertilizer liquids; (**b**) determination of characteristic wavelengths and construction of qualitative and quantitative models; (**c**) design of sensor structures and amplifier circuits; and (**d**) detection strategy of qualitative analysis followed by quantitative assessment.

2.3. Spectral Pre-Processing and Feature Selection

To mitigate interference from background noise and other unwanted factors in the measured spectra of fertilizer samples [13], the spectral data must undergo preprocessing before modeling. Savitzky–Golay (S-G) smoothing was employed for this purpose, which involves fitting low-order polynomials to adjacent points using least squares. This technique effectively reduces noise, enhances the signal-to-noise ratio, and preserves the essential characteristics of the spectral data [14].

Moreover, this study collects extensive NIR spectral data, which may contain redundancy, covariance, and overlapping information that can impact model accuracy and robustness [15]. Thus, it becomes essential to extract characteristic wavelengths from the raw spectra. Here, Competitive Adaptive Reweighted Sampling (CARS) was utilized to achieve this. CARS operates on a principle akin to natural selection, where variables with higher regression coefficients are given greater weight during iterative feature selection. This approach ensures that emphasis is placed on variables with stronger predictive power in the model [16].

2.4. Classification and Regression Prediction Methods for Spectral Data

In this paper, three different machine learning algorithms, Partial Least Squares Discriminant Analysis (PLS-DA), Support Vector Machine (SVM), and Back-Propagation Neural Network (BPNN), were adopted to treat the prediction model for the construction of nutrient ion species and determination of their concentrations in the measured fertilizer solution. After comprehensively comparing and analyzing the prediction results of the three methods, an optimal classification and regression prediction model was finally selected based on the model evaluation index.

Partial Least Squares Discriminant Analysis (PLS-DA) can effectively extract useful signals from noise by decomposing the spectral information and the corresponding concentration matrices [11], which improves the signal-to-noise ratio and reduces the multicollinearity problem in the data, and significantly improves the reliability and accuracy of the analyzed data.

Support Vector Machine (SVM) focuses on segmenting two independent regions by finding an optimal separating hyperplane to distinguish between different classes of data points, which is based on maximizing the distance between the data points closest to the hyperplane (i.e., the support vectors) [17]. Not only is this approach applicable to classification tasks, but the same principle has been extended to regression problems, called support vector regression (SVR) [18].

The Back-Propagation Neural Network (BPNN) corrects the network using a back-propagation algorithm that gradually adjusts the network weights and biases to minimize the error between the network output and the desired output. In spectral analysis, BPNN is widely used to identify and quantitatively analyze the spectral data of various substances due to its powerful non-linear mapping ability and self-learning capability. The identification of spectral features of different substances by the calibration network can achieve the fast and accurate identification of unknown samples.

2.5. Modeling Assessment

The performance of the classification model is evaluated by sensitivity, specificity, and accuracy for each category [19]. These are calculated using the following equations:

$$Sensitivity\ (\%) = \frac{TP}{TP + FN} \times 100 \quad (1)$$

$$Specificity\ (\%) = \frac{TN}{TN + FP} \times 100 \quad (2)$$

$$Accuracy\ (\%) = \frac{\sum_{i=1}^{n} TP_i}{N} \times 100 \quad (3)$$

TP (true positives) refers to the number of samples correctly classified as 'category 1'; *FN* (false negatives) refers to the number of samples that belonged to 'category 1' but were incorrectly classified as 'category 0'; *TN* (true negatives) refers to the number of samples correctly classified as 'category 0'; and *FP* (false positives) refers to the number of samples correctly classified as 'category 0'. *FN* (false negatives) represents the number of samples that belonged to 'Category 1' but were incorrectly classified as 'Category 0'; *TN* (true negatives) represents the number of samples that were correctly classified as 'Category 0'; FP (false positives) represents the number of samples that belonged to 'Category 0' but were incorrectly classified as 'Category 1'. False positives (*FP*) are the number of samples that belonged to category 0 but were misclassified as category 1. The total number of samples is denoted by *N*, where n is the total number of different categories.

When assessing the performance of regression models, the coefficient of determination (R^2), the root mean square error (RMSE), and the residual prediction deviation (RPD) are commonly used as key indicators of model performance. The value of R^2 ranges from 0 to 1, and the closer the value of R^2 is to 1, the more closely the model predicts the content of nutrient ionic constituents to the actual observations, and the better the fit [20]. Smaller values of RMSEC and RMSEP indicate a smaller deviation between the model predictions and the actual measurements, indicating a higher predictive accuracy of the model [21]. RPD is mainly used to assess the predictive accuracy and overall validity of the model regarding the data. It measures the stability and reliability of the model's predictive ability, with larger RPD values indicating a better predictive performance of the model [22].

2.6. *Development of Fertilizer Detection Sensor*

2.6.1. Fertilizer Detection Sensor Design and Principle

To enhance the detection of fertilizer components, a sensor-based device utilizing near-infrared detection principles was developed. The device's structure is depicted in (Figure 2a); it was designed in a cylindrical format to seamlessly integrate with the fertilizer pipeline. It includes a detector housing, a sensor unit, and a connector for pipeline integration. The sensor features four detection channels, each equipped with components such as LED light-emitting diodes (manufactured by Zhongwei Optoelectronic Technology (Hangzhou) Co., Ltd., ZVISION, Hangzhou, China), quartz glass plates, LED fixed stubs, optoelectronic receiving port bases, and a fertilizer inlet/outlet, as illustrated in (Figure 2b,c). This design ensures robust protection and light control, facilitating precise connection to the delivery line and ensuring the accurate detection of fertilizer solution components.

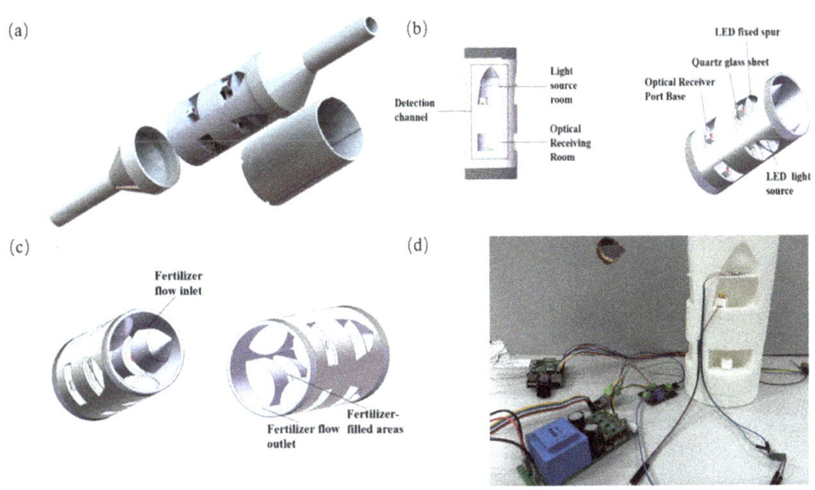

Figure 2. Fertilizer detection sensor; (**a**) overall structure of the sensor; (**b**) exterior structure of the sensor; (**c**) internal structure of the sensor; (**d**) physical drawing of the fertilizer sensor.

The detection device designed in this paper is mainly based on the absorbance of the fertilizer solution to be tested. From the Lambert–Beer law, the relationship between absorbance and incident light and transmitted light is as follows:

$$A = \lg\frac{I_0}{I_t} \quad (4)$$

where A is the absorbance of the measured solution; I_0 is the intensity of incident monochromatic light; I_t is the intensity of transmitted light.

The intensity of incident light and transmitted light in each detection channel are expressed as the output voltage (V_i and V_t) of the two photodetectors. In order to eliminate, as far as possible, the influence of the light in the actual detection environment on the detection results of the device, the photodetector detects and records the ambient light corresponding to the voltage V_a once in advance each time before switching on the LED light source for detection. The formula for calculating the absorbance is as follows:

$$A = \lg\frac{V_i - V_a}{V_t - V_a} \quad (5)$$

where A is the absorbance; V_i is the detection voltage value of the photodetector for detecting the incident light intensity of the channel; V_t is the detection voltage value of the photodetector for detecting the transmitted light intensity of the channel.

2.6.2. Signal Conditioning Circuitry

To address the challenge of noise interference in photodetector output, a signal conditioning circuit (Figure S1, Supplementary Materials) is employed to convert the weak current signal into a specified voltage signal. The initial step involves an (I–V) conversion circuit utilizing a high-precision operational amplifier, AD825 (U1), and a T-shaped feedback network. This circuit efficiently transforms the current output into a voltage signal. Following this, the gain amplifier circuit, centered around the operational amplifier LF353N (U2) and associated resistive–capacitive components, amplifies the voltage signal's amplitude post-conversion. The careful selection of components and adjustment of potentiometer RP1 enable a flexible gain adjustment of up to 100 times, ensuring precise regulation of the output voltage signal's amplitude.

2.6.3. Fertilizer Sensor Stability Analysis

Stability prediction serves as a crucial tool in evaluating the stability of the detection device, as the accuracy of the absorbance measurement hinges directly on the stability of voltage values during the measurement process. To ensure the reliability of the detection device's output, a comprehensive prediction of voltage stability is imperative, focusing primarily on three key components: LED light source stability, transmitted light detection stability, and ambient light. To achieve this, NH_4^+ solutions at five concentrations—20, 40, 60, 80, and 100 mg/L—were employed as the test fertilizer solutions. Each test was conducted continuously for 3 h, with the corresponding photodetectors' output voltage recorded every 15 min.

2.6.4. Detection Strategies for Sensors

This paper proposes a detection method for fertilizer components utilizing detection devices, following a 'first qualitative, then quantitative' approach. The method involves sequentially activating four LED light sources of specific wavelengths within the instrument, each illuminating the corresponding detection channel for a precise spectroscopic analysis of the fertilizer solution under examination. As the characteristic wavelengths of light traverse through the fertilizer solution, the photodetectors sequentially receive the transmission signals of each wavelength and convert them into voltage values. These voltage values are further transformed into absorbance values, enabling the identification of the fertilizer type based on the range of absorbance values. Subsequently, the specific absorbance value is utilized in the appropriate concentration detection model to calculate the specific concentration. The implementation of this detection strategy is depicted in Figure 3.

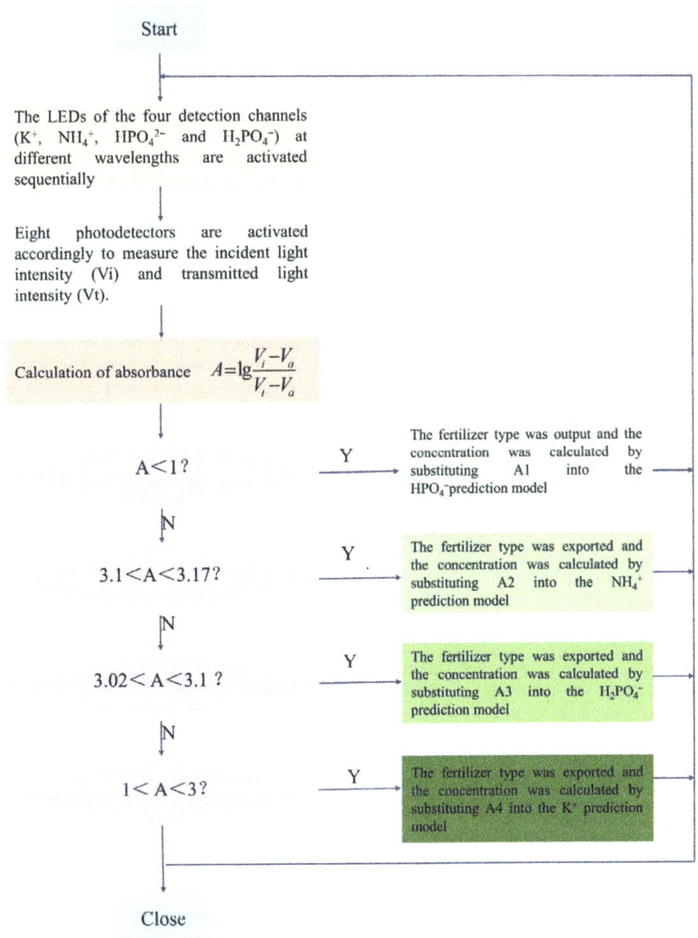

Figure 3. Fertilizer concentration detection strategy.

3. Results and Discussion

3.1. Spectral Pre-Processing and Spectral Characteristics of Four Fertilizer Solutions

Figure 4 depicts the absorbance spectra of all four fertilizer solutions across the entire spectral range. The horizontal coordinate corresponds to the NIR wavelength of the fertilizer solution and the vertical coordinate corresponds to the amount of absorbance produced by the NIR light source illuminating the fertilizer solution. Notably, the spectral curves of distinct nutrient ions exhibit discernible discrepancies in peak and trough patterns at specific wavelengths, alongside variations in peak shape, position, and absorption intensity. To discern the spectral nuances of the four fertilizer solutions and extract pivotal information from the spectral data, the Savitzky–Golay (S-G) smoothing method was employed. This preprocessing step forms the groundwork for the subsequent qualitative and quantitative modeling analyses of the four fertilizers under examination. The resulting spectra post S–G preprocessing are illustrated in (Figure 5).

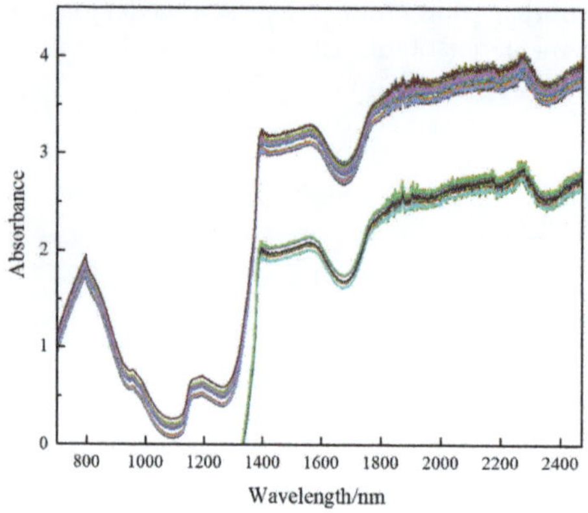

Figure 4. Raw spectra of nutrient ions of four fertilizer solutions to be tested.

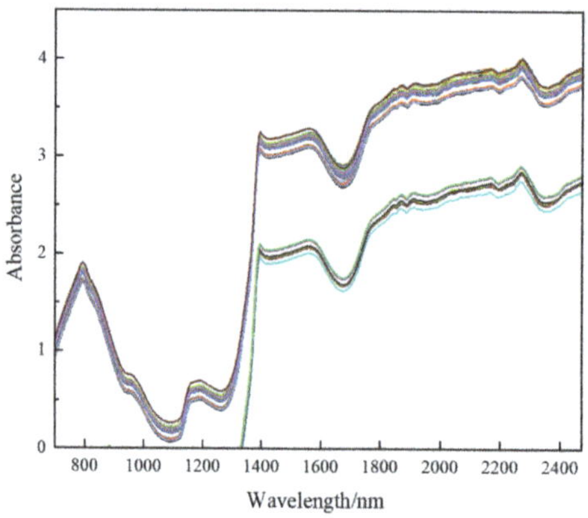

Figure 5. S-G pretreatment spectra of nutrient ions of four fertilizer solutions to be tested.

3.2. Selection of Effective Characteristic Wavelengths for Near-Infrared Spectral Response Data of Fertilizer Solutions

Figure S3 (Supplementary Materials) depicts the competitive adaptive reweighted sampling (CARS) algorithm utilized for screening samples of HPO_4^{2-} fertilizer solution nutrient ions to identify characteristic wavelengths. In Figure S3a, the rapid reduction in the number of selected wavelengths is evident during the initial sampling phase. With the increase in sample size, this reduction gradually decelerates. Concurrently, (RMSECV) exhibits a pattern of initially decreasing and then continuously increasing. The initial decrease signifies the effective removal of irrelevant noise information, while the subsequent increase suggests the potential loss of valid information during the process, as illustrated in Figure S3b. Subsequently, Figure S3c showcases the progression of regression coefficients for each wavelength during feature selection. The blue '*' denotes the optimal sampling point where the lowest RMSECV is achieved, indicating the effectiveness of the selected wavelengths for screening.

The 50 characteristic wavelengths identified by CARS successfully captured the information related to HPO_4^{2-}. These wavelengths are depicted in the average spectral map shown in Figure 6, primarily concentrated in the vicinity of 980 nm. Detailed feature extractions (Figures S4–S6) for the other three fertilizer solutions are available in the Supplementary Materials. Specifically, the feature wavelengths were concentrated around 1450, 1550, and 1600 nm, with selected feature points identified as 70, 60, and 29, respectively.

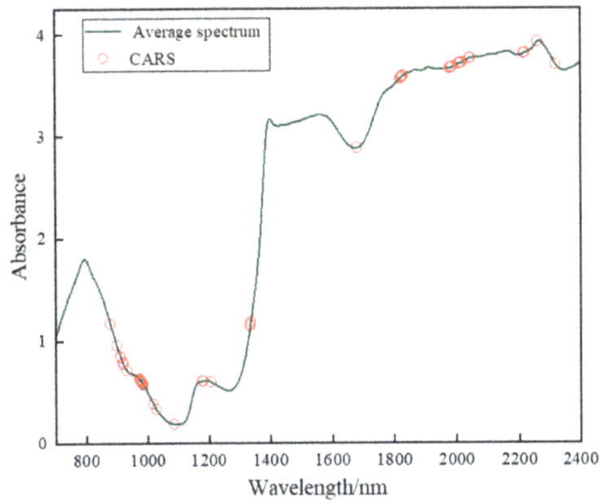

Figure 6. Effective wavelength distribution of HPO_4^- after CARS selection.

By comparing related studies, Lin Zhidan et al. [9] used CARS to select 161, 229, and 161 spectral characteristic wavelengths as the spectral characteristic wavelengths for N, P, and K nutrient contents, respectively. PLS and ELM models were developed. Under the optimal prediction model, R^2 was 0.989, 0.963, and 0.981, respectively. The characteristic wavelength bands selected by Sun Di, Li Mengting et al. [23], based on the near mid-infrared spectroscopy and applying the SIPLS method to the total phosphorus content of faucal water in dairy plants, were also 10,400~9600 cm^{-1} (961~1041 nm), which is similar to the selection of characteristic wavelength points in this paper.

3.3. Fertilizer Component Classification Prediction Model

Three methods, (PLS-DA), (SVM), and (BPNN), as well as a combination of S-G smoothings, were used for the classification-prediction modelling analysis of the nutrient ions of the four fertilizer solutions to be tested. Figure 7 shows the confusion matrices generated by the optimal BPNN, while the other two confusion matrices are presented in Figures S4 and S5 (Supplementary Materials), from which it can be seen that the sensitivities of the K+ samples obtained by the BPNN model are all 100%. Compared to the original spectra, the accuracy of the corrected set of models processed by S-G preprocessing improved from 99.17% to 100%, while that of the predicted set improved significantly, from 87.18% to 98.35%.

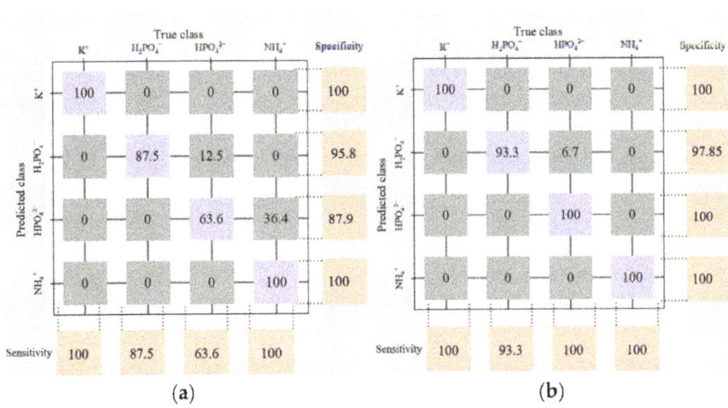

Figure 7. Comparison of the original spectra with the confusion matrix of the four-classification prediction set obtained by S-G preprocessing combined with BPNN: (**a**) raw spectrum; (**b**) S-G preprocessing.

Table 1 shows the classification results of all the models, and it can be seen that the three models obtained after S-G pre-processing achieved a better performance in most cases compared to the models under the original spectra, while the BPNN model after S-G pre-processing achieved very high sensitivity to K^+, HPO_4^{2-}, $H_2PO_4^-$, and NH_4^+ on both the calibration and prediction datasets, with an accuracy of 98.35%, which are all better than the other models. Zhiwei Jiang et al. developed near-infrared spectroscopy (NIRS) combined with five different types of machine learning methods to better identify botanical and geographical sources of AR. The results showed that SNV + BPNN performed best in plant origin classification, identifying both with more than 90% accuracy [24]. Fei Liu et al. investigated visible and near-infrared (Vis/NIR) spectroscopy combined with a back-propagation neural network (BPNN) to achieve the fast discrimination of instant milk tea. The BPNN prediction results showed a 98.7% recognition rate in the validation set [25].

Table 1. Comparison of four classification results obtained by S−G preprocessing combined with PLS-DA, SVM, and BPNN modeling, respectively.

Modeling		Correction Set				Prediction Set			
		K^+	$H_2PO_4^-$	HPO_4^{2-}	NH_4^+	K^+	$H_2PO_4^-$	HPO_4^{2-}	NH_4^+
Raw-PLS	SENS (%)	100	96.90	86.20	100	100	75	81.8	60
	SPEC (%)	100	96.7	85.8	100	100	67.65	83.87	100
	ACC (%)	95.87				84.62			
S-G-PLS	SENS (%)	100	100	100	100	100	83.3	100	100
	SPEC (%)	100	100	100	100	100	93.1	100	100
	ACC (%)	100				94.87			
Raw-SVM	SENS (%)	100	93.90	96	94.10	100	85.70	64.70	63.60
	SPEC (%)	100	96.90	85.70	100	36.40	75	91.70	87.50
	ACC (%)	95.87				71.95			
S-G-SVM	SENS (%)	100	100	100	100	50	100	100	100
	SPEC (%)	100	100	100	100	100	83.3	96.7	100
	ACC (%)	100				87.18			
Raw-BPNN	SENS (%)	100	100	96.9	100	100	87.5	63.6	100
	SPEC (%)	100	98.85	100	100	100	95.8	87.9	100
	ACC (%)	99.17				87.18			
S-G-BPNN	SENS (%)	100	100	100	100	100	93.3	100	100
	SPEC (%)	100	100	100	100	100	97.85	100	100
	ACC (%)	100				98.35			

3.4. Fertilizer Component Concentration Prediction Model

In this study, we used PLSR, SVR, and BPNN for the predictive modelling of nutrient ion concentration in the fertilizer solution and screened the best model. Table 2 shows the evaluation results of the three regression algorithms for predicting the nutrient ion concentrations in the four fertilizer samples based on the wavelengths selected by CARS. For K^+, the CARS BPNN model gave the best prediction, with an R^2 as high as 0.9879, an RMSEP of 0.3201 mg/L, and an RPD of 8.7947. $H_2PO_4^-$ was also better predicted by the CARS-BPNN model, with an R^2 of 0.9592, RMSEP of 0.7160 mg/L, and RPD of 4.2287. For NH_4^+, the BPNN model obtained better correction (R^2: 0.9971 vs. 0.9830) and prediction (R^2: 0.9955 vs. 0.9245) results using CARS than using the full spectrum, suggesting that the use of eigenwave lengths is particularly effective for the BPNN algorithm. The CARS BPNN model was the best predictor of HPO_4^{2-} concentration, with an R^2 of 0.9936, RMSEP of 0.0177 mg/L and RPD of 12.6860.

Table 2. PLSR, SVR, and BPNN statistics for predicting nutrient ion concentrations in four fertilizer samples using full and eigen spectral modeling.

Fertilizer Type	Wavelength Selection Methods	Modeling	Correction Set		Prediction Set		RPD
			R_c^2	RMSEC	R_p^2	RMSEP	
K^+ K_2SO_4	Full	PLSR	0.9031	0.2830	0.9029	0.8180	3.4995
		SVR	0.9355	0.5867	0.7705	1.5367	6.8459
		BPNN	0.9829	0.2035	0.7981	0.9307	2.3104
	CARS	PLSR	0.9927	0.1878	0.9235	0.6140	4.9311
		SVR	0.9585	0.5828	0.9550	0.8202	6.8459
		BPNN	0.9958	0.1848	0.9879	0.3201	8.7947
$H_2PO_4^-$ KH_2PO_4	Full	PLSR	0.9248	0.2705	0.9038	0.8223	3.4817
		SVR	0.9914	0.2667	0.7885	0.9352	2.3370
		BPNN	0.8022	1.9768	0.7102	2.1008	1.4722
	CARS	PLSR	0.9883	0.2372	0.9208	0.7351	3.5614
		SVR	0.9380	0.7452	0.5356	1.6371	1.1029
		BPNN	0.9249	0.7409	0.9592	0.7160	4.2287
NH_4^+ $(NH_4)_2SO_4$	Full	PLSR	0.9895	0.0632	0.9182	0.7102	3.5063
		SVR	0.9809	0.0895	0.9346	0.6814	3.7464
		BPNN	0.9830	0.3780	0.9245	0.7482	3.6503
	CARS	PLSR	0.9987	0.4389	0.9520	0.4903	6.1752
		SVR	0.9962	0.0819	0.7894	0.9803	3.1387
		BPNN	0.9971	0.1522	0.9955	0.2036	14.9451
HPO_4^{2-} $(NH_4)_2HPO_4$	Full	PLSR	0.9885	0.0431	0.9508	0.0589	5.3663
		SVR	0.9982	0.0815	0.7186	3.0436	1.0886
		BPNN	0.9475	0.6710	0.9529	0.5840	4.8282
	CARS	PLSR	0.9998	0.0278	0.9908	0.0374	8.8580
		SVR	0.9970	0.0849	0.9884	0.3280	5.0983
		BPNN	0.9962	0.1824	0.9936	0.0177	12.6860

(Figure 8) shows the correlation between the true and predicted values in the BPNN prediction model for the four fertilizer solutions that were tested. It can be clearly seen that the scattered points are concentrated around the y = x line in both the training and test sets, especially for $(NH_4)_2HPO_4$, indicating a high degree of agreement between the predicted and actual values.

A comprehensive comparison of the performance of the three models in terms of concentration prediction shows that, after optimization using the CARS method, the performance of each model generally achieves a significant improvement, demonstrating the effectiveness of the CARS method in optimizing the performance of regression models. Shen Jengang [26] achieved R^2 values of 0.989, 0.963, and 0.981 in the regression model of fertilizer powder after CARS feature extraction in NIR spectra and construction of PLS, ELM, and SVM, while the RMSEP values were 0.910, 1.724, and 1.393, respectively. Wang Xiaoke [27] completed the regression modelling of the elemental content of nitrogen, phosphorus, and potassium in the NIR spectra of fertilizer samples based on PLS, and the R^2 was greater than 0.83. Wang Lingling [28] proposed a quantitative analytical method for the determination of total nitrogen content in monoammonium phosphate (MAP) fertilizers using Visible–Near-Infrared (Vis-NIR) spectroscopy and LS-SVM. The results showed that LS-SVM calibration using discrete wavelet transform was the best predictor of total nitrogen content in MAP fertilizers with R^2, RMSEP, and RPD values of 0.91, 0.101, and 3.34, respectively.

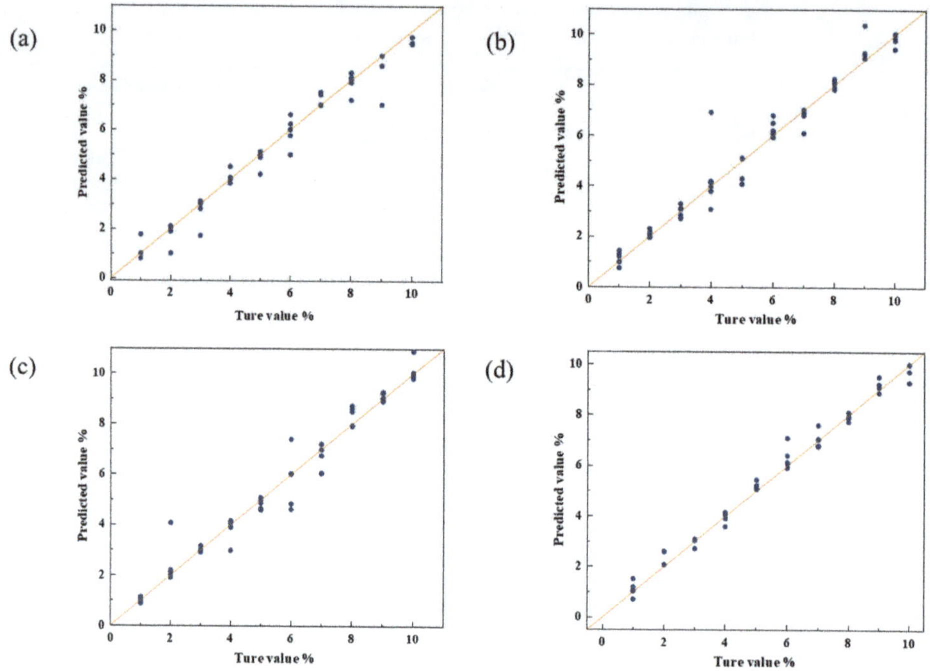

Figure 8. Correlation between true and predicted values in the BPNN prediction model for four fertilizer solutions to be tested. (**a**) KH_2PO_4 quantity contained (**b**) K_2SO_4 quantity contained (**c**) $(NH_4)_2SO$ quantity contained (**d**) $(NH_4)_2HPO_4$ quantity contained.

3.5. Analysis of Characteristic Wavelength Selection and Prediction Modeling of Detection Devices

The analysis reveals that the characteristic wavelengths of the four fertilizer solutions are primarily concentrated around 980, 1450, 1550, and 1600 nm. This concentration suggests that crucial information is prominently expressed at these wavelengths. Consequently, a linear regression analysis was conducted to explore the relationship between concentration and absorbance for each of the four nutrient ions across ten concentration gradients at their respective characteristic wavelengths. The findings indicate a strong correlation between the nutrient ions and their characteristic wavelengths, as depicted in (Figure 9), with R^2 values exceeding 0.95. This high degree of fit demonstrates the efficacy of the linear model in predicting absorbance changes based on wavelength, aligning with the fundamental assumptions of linear regression and fulfilling requirements for both speed and accuracy. Thus, these results offer valuable insights for selecting appropriate light sources and designing the structural framework of fertilizer solution component detection devices.

As can be seen in Figure 9, the absorbance ranges of the four nutrient ions at their respective characteristic wavelengths are also significantly different. the maximum value of absorbance A of HPO_4^{2-} was less than 1; the minimum value of absorbance A of NH_4^+ was greater than 3.1; the absorbance values of $H_2PO_4^-$ were in the range of 3.02–3.09; the absorbance values of K^+ ranged from 1.95 to 2.07. Therefore, when identifying the type of fertilizer to be tested, the fertilizer to be tested can be irradiated by four characteristic wavelengths of 980, 1450, 1550, and 1600 nm in turn, and the absorbance extremes of the nutrient ions at these wavelengths can be used to determine whether or not the fertilizer to be tested contains HPO_4^{2-}, NH_4^+, $H_2PO_4^-$, and K^+. The identification of the type of fertilizer is completed.

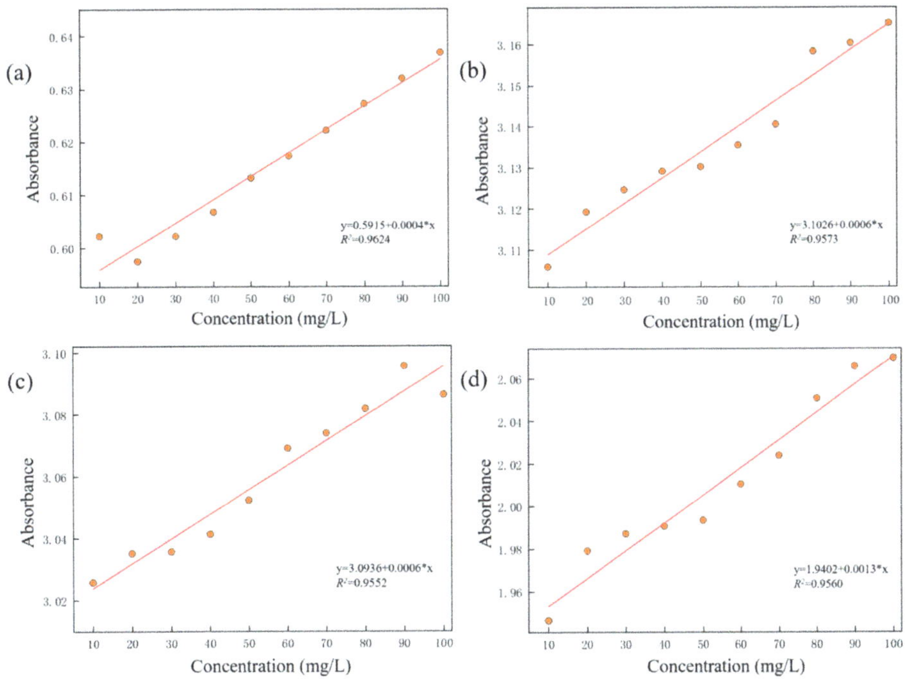

Figure 9. Fitting curves of concentration and absorbance at characteristic wavelengths of four fertilizers to be tested: (**a**) HPO_4^- (980 nm); (**b**) NH_4^+ (1450 nm); (**c**) $H_2PO_4^-$ (1550 nm); (**d**) K^+ (1600 nm).

Based on the relationship between absorbance and concentration of the four ions at their respective characteristic wavelengths, fitting the corresponding linear regression model. As shown in Figure 9, the absorbance of four nutrient ions, HPO_4^{2-}, NH_4^+, $H_2PO_4^-$, and K^+, at the characteristic wavelengths of 980, 1450, 1550, and 1600 nm, respectively, showed a linear positive correlation with the concentration. Through linear regression, the prediction model of the concentration of the fertilizer solution and the absorbance at the characteristic wavelengths was established, as shown in Table 3.

Table 3. Predictive models for ion concentrations of the four fertilizer solutions to be tested.

Nutrient Ion	Characteristic Wavelength Concentration Prediction Model	R^2
HPO_4^{2-}	y = 0.5915 + 0.0004x	0.9624
NH_4^+	y = 3.1026 + 0.00006x	0.9573
$H_2PO_4^-$	y = 3.0936 + 0.0006x	0.9552
K^+	y = 1.9402 + 0.0013x	0.9560

3.6. Stability Analysis of the Fertilizer Sensor

In this paper the stability of the fertilizer sensor has also been analyzed in terms of LED irradiance voltage, transmission voltage, and ambient light voltage. The results are shown in Figure 10, the three voltage values of the fertilizer solution at each concentration do not fluctuate much, so it can be assumed that the effect on the stability of the device is small or negligible.

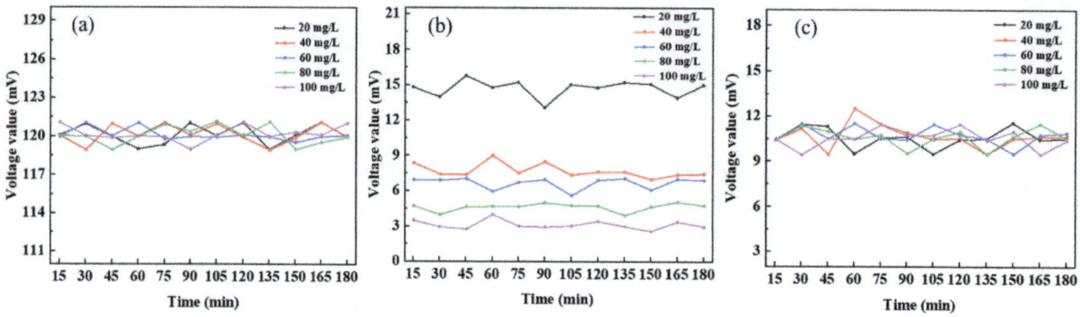

Figure 10. Stability test of fertilizer detection device: (**a**) LED irradiation voltage value; (**b**) transmission voltage value; (**c**) ambient light voltage value.

3.7. Accuracy of Fertilizer Component Type Identification

Ten different concentrations of HPO_4^{2-}, NH_4^+, $H_2PO_4^-$, and K^+ fertilizer solutions were subjected to testing across four detection channels, with each concentration undergoing five repetitions. During each experiment, the voltages corresponding to the incident and transmitted light received by the photodetectors in the four detection channels were recorded. Subsequently, absorbances A_1, A_2, A_3, and A_4 of the four detection channels were calculated using Equation (5), facilitating the judgment of the fertilizer types under examination based on the extremes of absorbance for each nutrient ion at these wavelengths. Ultimately, the accuracy of the fertilizer species identification was determined by tallying the number of correct identifications.

The confusion matrices of the test results are depicted in Figure 11. Notably, $(NH_4)_2HPO_4$ was correctly identified 48 times, resulting in a species identification accuracy of 96%; $(NH_4)_2SO_4$ was correctly identified 45 times, with a species identification accuracy of 90%; KH_2PO_4 was correctly identified 44 times, achieving a species identification accuracy of 88%; K_2SO_4 was correctly identified 49 times, yielding a species identification accuracy of 98%. From the experimental results, it can be seen that the average accuracy of the fertilizer detection device for four types of fertilizer solution for species identification is 93%, showing a better ability to identify the types of fertilizer solution. Wu Hao et al. [29] designed a sensor based on the dielectric properties of a water-soluble fertilizer, in which the detection accuracy of K_2SO_4 solution using e-frequency was 97.43%, slightly lower than that of K^+ (98%) in this paper, while the detection accuracy of the KH_2PO_4 solution was 94.8% higher than that of $H_2PO_4^-$ in this paper.

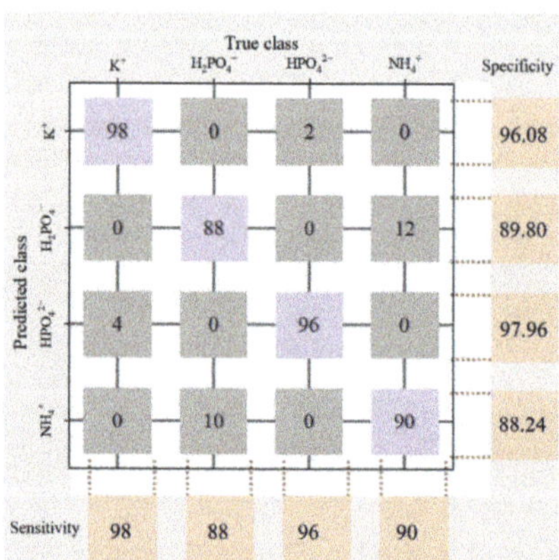

Figure 11. Confusion matrix for identifying nutrient ion types in four fertilizer solutions.

3.8. Fertilizer Component Concentration Detection Accuracy

After identifying the types of fertilizer solutions, the absorbance data obtained from each type were input into the fertilizer concentration prediction model described previously. The measurement results are presented in Table 4, detailing the detected concentrations calculated using the fertilizer solution detection model. The accuracy of the fertilizer concentration detection model was verified by computing the relative error between the actual and measured concentrations, as illustrated in Figure 12.

Table 4. Absorbance and predicted concentration results for four 10–100 mg/L nutrient examples.

Nutrient Ion	Actual Concentration mg/L	Absorbance	Predicted Concentration mg/L	R^2	RMSE
K^+	10	1.954	10.26	0.9953	1.9683
	20	1.966	20.19		
	30	1.977	28.31		
	40	1.991	38.98		
	50	2.003	48.53		
	60	2.020	61.49		
	70	2.033	71.61		
	80	2.049	83.56		
	90	2.057	90.20		
	100	2.065	9.12		
$H_2PO_4^-$	10	3.099	9.68	0.9959	2.4947
	20	3.106	21.18		
	30	3.113	32.07		
	40	3.118	40.05		
	50	3.126	53.21		
	60	3.130	64.12		
	70	3.137	71.54		
	80	3.144	83.96		
	90	3.149	92.72		
	100	3.152	98.07		
NH_4^+	10	3.103	9.52	0.9970	1.6518
	20	3.104	20.62		
	30	3.105	29.87		
	40	3.105	43.06		
	50	3.106	51.09		
	60	3.106	61.33		
	70	3.107	69.82		
	80	3.108	78.09		
	90	3.108	92.78		
	100	3.109	98.29		
HPO_4^{2-}	10	0.596	10.25	0.9991	1.0034
	20	0.600	21.19		
	30	0.603	29.88		
	40	0.608	42.01		
	50	0.612	50.68		
	60	0.615	58.94		
	70	0.620	71.05		
	80	0.624	80.33		
	90	0.628	91.07		
	100	0.631	99.23		

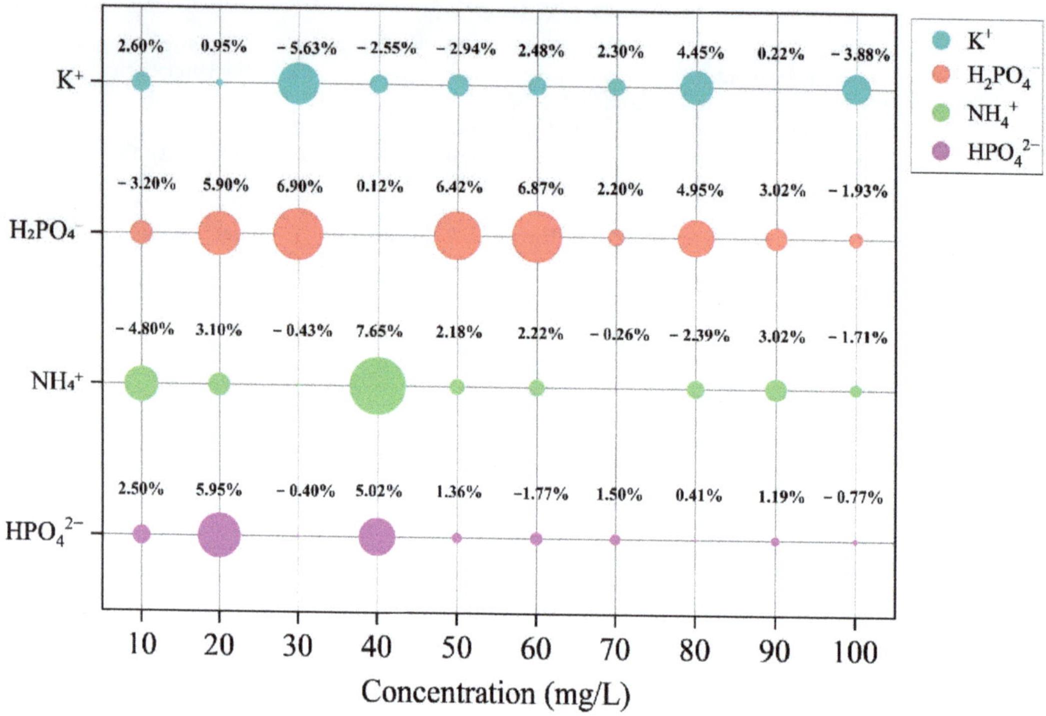

Figure 12. The concentration detection error of the sensor for four kinds of configured fertilizer solution.

Figure 12 illustrates the concentration detection errors of the sensor across the four configurations of fertilizer solutions. Notably, for the K^+ solution, the maximum relative error does not exceed 6%, indicating a highly desirable detection accuracy. Regarding the detection results of the $H_2PO_4^-$ solution, it is observed that within the low-concentration range below 50 mg/L, the detected concentration closely aligns with the actual concentration, with the lowest relative error recorded at 0.12%. In the higher-concentration range, although the detected concentration tends to slightly surpass the actual concentration, the overall relative error remains within the acceptable range (<±7%), reflecting consistent performance. For the NH_4^+ solution, the detected values closely mirror the actual values across most concentrations, except for the 40 mg/L concentration, where the relative error peaks at 7.65%. Lastly, the results for HPO_4^{2-} exhibit excellent agreement, with the detected values almost perfectly matching the actual values.

Li J et al. [30] designed a cylindrical capacitance sensor based on the dielectric properties of fertilizer solutions, with KCL, $Ca(H_2PO_4)_2$-H_2O, and H_2NCONH_2 as the test object, and the maximum relative error of its sensor concentration detection was 7.26%. Li Yunqing et al. [31] designed a NO_3^- selective electrode-based detection device, in which the maximum error caused by $H_2PO_4^-$ in the detection of NO_3^- concentration can reach up to 16%; compared with the sensor designed in this paper, it achieved better results.

4. Conclusions

This paper proposes a rapid detection method using near-infrared spectrophotometry to determine the concentrations of four fertilizer solutions: $(NH_4)_2SO_4$, K_2SO_4, $(NH_4)_2HPO_4$, and KH_2PO_4.

(1) Firstly, qualitative and quantitative prediction models for fertilizer liquid components were developed using NIR spectroscopy and machine learning algorithms to assess

their feasibility. The Back-Propagation Neural Network (BPNN) demonstrated superior qualitative accuracy (98.35%) in identifying all four fertilizer liquids compared to the Partial Least Squares Discriminant Analysis (PLS-DA) model (94.87%) and Support Vector Machine (SVM) model (87.18%). Additionally, the CARS-BPNN model effectively predicted concentrations, achieving RMSE values ranging from 0.01777 to 0.7160.

(2) Subsequently, characteristic wavelengths (980 nm, 1450 nm, 1550 nm, and 1600 nm) were identified through CARS. A four-channel online fertilizer composition testing device was designed using the characteristic wavelength determined by Lambert–Beer's law (980 nm). The detection strategy prioritized qualitative assessment followed by quantitative analysis, achieving 93% accuracy in identifying the four types of fertilizers. Concentration detection RMSE values ranged from 1.0034 to 2.4947, with errors of less than ±8.0%. The sensor's detection accuracy slightly trailed behind that of the full-spectrum BPNN prediction results. These findings collectively enhance the feasibility of practical engineering applications.

To broaden the applicability and versatility of the sensors, future research could extend its scope to include a wider range of fertilizer solution types and concentrations. This study lays a promising technological foundation for the development of sensors capable of efficiently, rapidly, and cost-effectively detecting fertilizer solution information. Future developments might focus on integrating full-spectrum fertilizer solution detection sensors with advanced machine learning models to enhance their accuracy and efficiency, despite potential increased costs. Moreover, this technology holds promise for applications in water–fertilizer integration systems, providing critical support for precise variable-rate fertilizer application.

Supplementary Materials: The following supporting information can be downloaded at: https://www.mdpi.com/article/10.3390/agriculture14071184/s1, Figure S1: Signal conditioning circuit diagram; Figure S2: Device testing platform; Figure S3: CARS process for selecting the effective wavelength of HPO42−; Figure S4: Effective wavelength distribution of NH+ 4after CARS selection; Figure S5: Effective wavelength distribution of H2PO4− after CARS selection; Figure S6: Effective wavelength distribution of K+ after CARS selection; Figure S7: Comparison of the original spectra with the confusion matrix of the four-classified prediction set obtained by S-G preprocessing combined with PLS-DA; Figure S8: Comparison of the original spectra with the confusion matrix of the four-classification prediction set obtained by S-G preprocessing combined with SVM.

Author Contributions: Conceptualization, Y.M. and J.L.; methodology, Z.W. and S.C.; software, Y.M. and S.C.; validation, Y.C. and J.L.; formal analysis, Y.M. and J.L.; investigation, Z.W. and Y.C.; resources, J.L.; data curation, Z.W. and J.L.; writing—original draft preparation, J.L. and Z.W.; writing—review and editing, Y.M. and J.L.; visualization, Y.M.; supervision, J.L.; project administration, Y.M.; funding acquisition, J.L. All authors have read and agreed to the published version of the manuscript.

Funding: This research was funded by the National Natural Science Foundation of China, grant number 52069008, the Yunnan Major Science and Technology Special Plan, grant number 202302AE090024, the Yunnan Fundamental Research Projects, grant number 202101AT070113, the Yunnan Revitalization Talent Support Program.

Institutional Review Board Statement: Not applicable.

Data Availability Statement: The original contributions presented in the study are included in the article/Supplementary Materials, further inquiries can be directed to the corresponding author.

Conflicts of Interest: The authors declare no conflicts of interest.

References

1. Gao, Z.; Du, S.; Zhong, Y.; Wu, Y.; Zhang, G. Water Fertiliser Integration Development Status and Prospects. *China Agric. Inform.* **2015**, *27*, 14–19.
2. Sun, F.; Ma, W.; Li, H.; Wang, S. Research on Water-Fertilizer Integrated Technology Based On Neural Network Prediction and Fuzzy Control. *IOP Conf. Ser. Earth Environ. Sci.* **2018**, *170*, 32168. [CrossRef]

3. Cai, C.; Zheng, P.; Zhang, J. Integrated Monitor System of Water and Fertilizer of Greenhouse Intelligent Irrigation. *Jiangsu Agric. Sci.* **2017**, *45*, 164–166.
4. Lu, H.; Wang, T.; Qiao, D.; Sun, J.; Wu, G.; Tian, C.; Yan, F.; Zhen, B. Internet of Things in Irrigated Agriculture: From Irrigation Automation to Smart Irrigation. *J. Irrig. Drain.* **2023**, *42*, 87–99.
5. Song, J.; Xu, L.; He, D.; Tuskagoshi, S.; Kozai, T.; Shinohara, Y. Estimating EC and Ionic EC Contribution Percentage of Nutrient Solution Based on Ionic Activity. *Int. J. Agric. Biol. Eng.* **2019**, *12*, 42–48. [CrossRef]
6. Moon, T.; Ahn, T.I.; Son, J.E. Long Short-Term Memory for a Model-Free Estimation of Macronutrient Ion Concentrations of Root-Zone in Closed-Loop Soilless Cultures. *Plant Methods* **2019**, *15*, 59. [CrossRef] [PubMed]
7. Chen, F.; Wei, D.; Tang, Y. Virtual Ion Selective Electrode for Online Measurement of Nutrient Solution Components. *IEEE Sens. J.* **2011**, *11*, 462–468. [CrossRef]
8. Cecconi, F.; Reifsnyder, S.; Ito, Y.; Jimenez, M.; Sobhani, R.; Rosso, D. ISE-Ammonium Sensors in WRRFs: Field Assessment of Their Influencing Factors. *Environ. Sci. Water Res. Technol.* **2019**, *5*, 737–746. [CrossRef]
9. Lin, Z.; Wang, R.; Wang, Y.; Wang, L.; Lu, C.; Liu, Y.; Zhang, Z.; Zhu, L. Accurate and Rapid Detection of Soil and Fertilizer Properties Based on Visible/near-Infrared Spectroscopy. *Appl. Opt.* **2018**, *57*, D69–D73. [CrossRef]
10. Khanmohammadi, M.; Garmarudi, A.B.; Ghasemi, K.; Garrigues, S.; de la Guardia, M. Artificial Neural Network for Quantitative Determination of Total Protein in Yogurt by Infrared Spectrometry. *Microchem. J.* **2009**, *91*, 47–52. [CrossRef]
11. Song, L.; Zhang, H.; Ni, X.; Wu, L.; Lin, B.; Yu, L.; Wang, Q.; Wu, Y. Quantitative Analysis of Contents in Compound Fertilizer and Application Research Using Near Infrared Reflectance Spectroscopy. *Spectrosc. Spectr. Anal.* **2014**, *34*, 73–77.
12. Yahaya, S.M.; Mahmud, A.A.; Abdullahi, M.; Haruna, A. Recent Advances in the Chemistry of Nitrogen, Phosphorus and Potassium as Fertilizers in Soil: A Review. *Pedosphere* **2023**, *33*, 385–406. [CrossRef]
13. Bian, X.; Wang, K.; Tan, E.; Diwu, P.; Zhang, F.; Guo, Y. A Selective Ensemble Preprocessing Strategy for Near-Infrared Spectral Quantitative Analysis of Complex Samples. *Chemom. Intell. Lab. Syst.* **2020**, *197*, 103916. [CrossRef]
14. Zhang, G.; Hao, H.; Wang, Y.; Jiang, Y.; Shi, J.; Yu, J.; Cui, X.; Li, J.; Zhou, S.; Yu, B. Optimized Adaptive Savitzky-Golay Filtering Algorithm Based on Deep Learning Network for Absorption Spectroscopy. *Spectrochim. Acta Part A Mol. Biomol. Spectrosc.* **2021**, *263*, 120187. [CrossRef]
15. Jiang, H.; Zhang, H.; Chen, Q.; Mei, C.; Liu, G. Identification of Solid State Fermentation Degree with FT-NIR Spectroscopy: Comparison of Wavelength Variable Selection Methods of CARS and SCARS. *Spectrochim. Acta Part A Mol. Biomol. Spectrosc.* **2015**, *149*, 1–7. [CrossRef]
16. Li, H.; Liang, Y.; Xu, Q.; Cao, D. Key Wavelengths Screening Using Competitive Adaptive Reweighted Sampling Method for Multivariate Calibration. *Anal. Chim. Acta* **2009**, *648*, 77–84. [CrossRef]
17. Liang, L.; Zhang, T.; Wang, K.; Tang, H.; Yang, X.; Zhu, X.; Duan, Y.; Li, H. Classification of Steel Materials by Laser-Induced Breakdown Spectroscopy Coupled with Support Vector Machines. *Appl. Opt.* **2014**, *53*, 544–552. [CrossRef]
18. Yu, C.J.; He, Y.Y.; Quan, T.F. Frequency Spectrum Prediction Method Based on EMD and SVR. *Intell. Syst. Des. Appl.* **2008**, *3*, 39–44.
19. Li, Q.; Zeng, J.; Lin, L.; Zhang, J.; Zhu, J.; Yao, L.; Wang, S.; Yao, Z.; Wu, Z. Low Risk of Category Misdiagnosis of Rice Syrup Adulteration in Three Botanical Origin Honey by ATR-FTIR and General Model. *Food Chem.* **2020**, *332*, 127356. [CrossRef]
20. Li, L.; Ren, T.; Wang, S.; Ming, J.; Liu, Q.; Lu, J. Prediction Models of Winter Oilseed Rape Yield Based on Hyperspectral Data at Pod-Filling Stage. *Trans. Chin. Soc. Agric. Mach.* **2017**, *48*, 221–229.
21. Zhang, Z.; Tai, X.; Yang, N.; Zhang, J.; Huang, X.; Chen, Q. UAV Multispectral Remote Sensing Soil Salinity Inversion Based on Different Fractional Vegetation Coverages. *Trans. Chin. Soc. Agric. Mach.* **2022**, *53*, 220–230.
22. Orrillo, I.; Cruz-Tirado, J.P.; Cardenas, A.; Oruna, M.; Carnero, A.; Barbin, D.F.; Siche, R. Hyperspectral Imaging as a Powerful Tool for Identification of Papaya Seeds in Black Pepper. *Food Control* **2019**, *101*, 45–52. [CrossRef]
23. Sun, D.; Li, M.; Mou, M.; Zhao, R.; Zhang, K. Rapid Determination of Nitrogen and Phosphorus in Dairy Farm Slurry Via Near-Mid Infrared Fusion Spectroscopy Technology. *Spectrosc. Spectr. Anal.* **2021**, *41*, 3092–3098.
24. Jiang, Z.; Jin, K.; Zhong, L.; Zheng, Y.; Shao, Q.; Zhang, A. Near-Infrared Spectroscopy Combined with Machine Learning for Rapid Identification of Atractylodis Rhizoma Decoction Pieces. *Ind. Crops Prod.* **2023**, *197*, 116579. [CrossRef]
25. Liu, F.; Ye, X.; He, Y.; Wang, L. Application of Visible/near Infrared Spectroscopy and Chemometric Calibrations for Variety Discrimination of Instant Milk Teas. *J. Food Eng.* **2009**, *93*, 127–133. [CrossRef]
26. Shen, J.; Qiao, W.; Chen, H.; Zhou, J.; Liu, F. Application of Visible/Near Infrared Spectrometers to Quickly Detect the Nitrogen, Phosphorus, and Potassium Content of Chemical Fertilizers. *Appl. Sci.* **2021**, *11*, 5103. [CrossRef]
27. Wang, X.; Zhao, C.; Dong, D. High-Throughput Online Measurement of Nutrient Contents in Moving Fertilizers-Based on near Infrared Spectrum and Chemometrics. *Jiangsu Agric. Sci.* **2018**, *46*, 238–240.
28. Wang, L.S.; Wang, R.J.; Lu, C.P.; Wang, J.; Huang, W.; Jian, Q.; Wang, Y.B.; Lin, L.Z.; Song, L.T. Quantitative Analysis of Total Nitrogen Content in Monoammonium Phosphate Fertilizer Using Visible-Near Infrared Spectroscopy and Least Squares Support Vector Machine. *J. Appl. Spectrosc.* **2019**, *86*, 465–469. [CrossRef]
29. Wu, H.; Li, J.; Zhang, J.; Ma, Z.; Waleed, E. Development of Rapid Identification Device for Variety of Macronutrient Water Soluble Fertilizers Based on Dielectric Characteristic Frequency. *Trans. Chin. Soc. Agric. Eng. (Trans. CSAE)* **2017**, *33*, 51–58.

30. Li, J.; Gao, Y.; Zeng, J.; Li, X.; Wu, Z.; Wang, G. Online Rapid Detection Method of Fertilizer Solution Information Based on Characteristic Frequency Response Features. *Sensors* **2023**, *23*, 1116. [CrossRef]
31. Li, J.; Li, Y.; Yang, Q.; Lei, L.; Wu, Z. Development of Real-Time Detecting Device for Nitrogen Concentration of Liquid Fertilizer. *Trans. Chin. Soc. Agric. Eng.* **2015**, *31*, 139–145.

agriculture

Article

High-Precision Peach Fruit Segmentation under Adverse Conditions Using Swin Transformer

Dasom Seo [1], Seul Ki Lee [2], Jin Gook Kim [3] and Il-Seok Oh [1,4,*]

1 Department of Computer Science & Artificial Intelligence, Jeonbuk National University, Jeonju-si 54896, Republic of Korea; dasomseo@jbnu.ac.kr
2 Fruit Research Division, National Institute of Horticultural & Herbal Science, Wanju-gun 55365, Republic of Korea; lsk0729@korea.kr
3 Institute of Agriculture and Life Sciences, Gyeongsang National University, Jinju 52157, Republic of Korea; jgkim119@gnu.ac.kr
4 Center for Advanced Image and Information Technology (CAIIT), Jeonbuk National University, Jeonju-si 54896, Republic of Korea
* Correspondence: isoh@jbnu.ac.kr

Abstract: In the realm of agricultural automation, the efficient management of tasks like yield estimation, harvesting, and monitoring is crucial. While fruits are typically detected using bounding boxes, pixel-level segmentation is essential for extracting detailed information such as color, maturity, and shape. Furthermore, while previous studies have typically focused on controlled environments and scenes, achieving robust performance in real orchard conditions is also imperative. To prioritize these aspects, we propose the following two considerations: first, a novel peach image dataset designed for rough orchard environments, focusing on pixel-level segmentation for detailed insights; and second, utilizing a transformer-based instance segmentation model, specifically the Swin Transformer as a backbone of Mask R-CNN. We achieve superior results compared to CNN-based models, reaching 60.2 AP on the proposed peach image dataset. The proposed transformer-based approach specially excels in detecting small or obscured peaches, making it highly suitable for practical field applications. The proposed model achieved 40.4 AP for small objects, nearly doubling that of CNN-based models. This advancement significantly enhances automated agricultural systems, especially in yield estimation, harvesting, and crop monitoring.

Keywords: agricultural automation; computer vision; fruit segmentation; transformer

1. Introduction

The usual tasks in an orchard, such as yield counting, predicting the appropriate harvest time, and picking fruits, are time-consuming and require significant labor. Various automated farming systems and robots have been studied through fusion with other fields to enhance the efficiency of such tasks [1–4]. For automated farming systems in an orchard, especially agricultural robots, computer vision algorithms are required to obtain information on fruit [4,5]. Typically, fruit objects are detected as bounding boxes in orchard images for growth monitoring and yield estimation and to localize positions for harvesting. However, to obtain and use more detailed information, fruits should be segmented at the pixel level. Pixel-level results extend monitoring tasks to estimate size or ripeness. Within the segmentation domain, two main techniques are employed: semantic segmentation, which involves the separation of the foreground and background, and instance segmentation, which identifies and differentiates individual object instances. In this study, we assume that instance segmentation is more suitable for orchard images because many fruits are captured, and robot tasks require separate information for each fruit.

Conventional algorithms have typically been studied using crop images with minimal occlusion or focusing on specific zoomed-in crops [6–9]. However, real field scenes in agricultural environments are often complex, with significant occlusions and variations in crop sizes. Algorithms should be tested on more dense and cluttered images to reflect the real world, and this challenge was acknowledged by [3]. This issue is also crucial for enabling diverse tasks in the application of vision systems or robots. Some tasks, such as monitoring or spraying, also require a wider field of view than that required for traditional crop images. In the agricultural field, there is a tendency to prefer local datasets that mostly comprise zoomed-in images focused on specific targets to open datasets [5]. The MinneApple dataset [10] is unique in that it provides images in which an entire tree is visible, along with individual apple instances annotated at the pixel level.

Several comprehensive peach image datasets have been proposed, although datasets with such images and pixel-level labeling are rare. The authors of [11] presented a dataset for peach image analysis, focusing on instance segmentation and ripeness classification. However, most images in [11] were captured at close range, featuring large object areas and relatively simple backgrounds. Further, the annotation masks provided by [11] covered only visible regions, excluding obscured areas. The authors of [12] presented a dataset with naturally cluttered scenes comprising small objects, but the annotations were bounding boxes only because the dataset was for detection tasks. The authors of [13] provided a large dataset comprising complex peach orchard images to detect immature fruits, so ground truths were annotated with bounding boxes only. In this study, we present a dataset containing various image types, ranging from fruit-focused to whole-tree visible images. For each image, the corresponding fruit instance masks are also annotated. The dataset is specially collected in the peach (*Prunus persica* (L.) Batsch) orchard because peach tree images are highly cluttered with long leaves, lots of bunches, and occlusions.

CNN-based segmentation models have shown significant achievements, but the difficulty in effectively segmenting small or occluded objects exists because of several issues. Typical CNN models can handle small areas well in their initial layers, but the receptive field increases when the layers go deeper, causing a problem in detecting small objects and resulting in inaccurate segmentation due to missing fine details. CNN models usually use pooling layers, such as max pooling, to reduce feature map size, resulting in the loss of information related to small objects. Therefore, CNN-based segmentation models have limitations in accurate segmentation for small or occluded objects. Referencing [4,14,15], most traditional fruit detection methods typically utilize well-known CNN-based models such as YOLO [16], Faster R-CNN [17], mask R-CNN [18], YOLACT [19], SSD [20], and SegNet [21]. These methods commonly face limitations, including difficulty in detecting small fruits, partially hidden or overlapping fruits, and performance degradation under complex natural conditions.

Transformer-based models have been researched and have demonstrated promising performance in solving the aforementioned problems. Transformer-based models use a self-attention mechanism that enables broader context consideration than CNN. Transformers process an entire input sequence at once through self-attention. This feature also enables an enhanced understanding of the global context. Notably, the global context of specific objects is essential in small object segmentation [22]. Despite these advantages, the application of transformer-based models in the agricultural field is currently slow. However, active study is required to develop efficient automated systems (or robots) for agricultural applications. Ref. [15] also points out that transformer models have not been widely explored in fruit analysis within the existing literature, despite the strong representation capabilities of visual transformers. In this study, we specifically apply the Swin Transformer to build a hierarchical model based on shifted windows that contain patches with diverse sizes [23]. Patches in the initial layer windows are small, which is helpful for detecting small objects. While there is example of applying the Swin Transformer for grape detection, note that this application is primarily focused on bounding boxes only [24].

In this paper, we present a peach image dataset and an application of a transformer-based instance segmentation model to accurately detect peach fruits in a cluttered orchard scene. This paper includes the following contributions:

- A novel peach image dataset for instance segmentation, specifically designed to include obscured regions for detailed information and more accurate performance in cluttered orchard environments similar to real orchards.
- An application of a transformer-based instance segmentation model, specially the Swin Transformer, to detect small and obscured peaches more accurately.
- The proposed model achieves an average precision (AP) of 60.2, outperforming CNN-based models, and shows an AP of 40.4 for small objects, nearly doubling that of CNN-based models.

2. Materials and Methods

2.1. Instance Segmentation Based on Transformer

Conventional object detection and instance segmentation models lack detailed segmentation accuracy with small objects or complex background images. To handle diverse situations, the authors of [25] introduced a feature pyramid network (FPN), which serves as the backbone for conventional instance segmentation models, such as mask R-CNN [18] and YOLACT [19]. However, there is a loss of high-resolution feature details, and the potential omission of small or obscured objects still occurs in the down-sampling process of the top–down pathway in the FPN. Because the transformer-based approach can address this issue with large context consideration through self-attention, as mentioned in Section 1, we apply the Swin Transformer [23], a well-known transformer-based instance segmentation method.

Figure 1 depicts the Swin Transformer architecture, shifted window, Swin Transformer block, and vision transformer (ViT) block. First, an input image is partitioned into nonoverlapping patches using a patch split module; 4×4 patches are basically used, and the feature dimension for each patch is $4 \times 4 \times 3$. After the patch partition, the architecture is separated into four stages. Stage 1 comprises a linear embedding layer and Swin Transformer blocks. The linear embedding layer is applied to project features to arbitrary dimension C. The output tokens from the linear embedding layer pass through the SwinTransformer blocks, and the block keeps the number of tokens as $\frac{H}{4} \times \frac{W}{4}$. Stage 2 comprises a patch merging layer and Swin Transformer blocks for feature transformation. The patch merging layer concatenates 2×2 neighborhood patches, and the dimension is increased to $4C$. To reduce the dimension by half, a linear layer is applied. The output tokens pass through the Swin Transformer blocks, and then the output resolution is $\frac{H}{8} \times \frac{W}{8}$. Stages 3 and 4 repeat the process of Stage 2, and the output resolutions become $\frac{H}{16} \times \frac{W}{16}$ and $\frac{H}{32} \times \frac{W}{32}$, respectively. The feature dimensions increase to $2C$, $4C$, and $8C$ for Stages 2, 3, and 4, respectively. In summary, as tokens pass each stage, the number of patches increases and the dimension of each token doubles.

The Swin Transformer blocks in each stage are transformer modules based on ViT [22] (Figure 1a). Although ViT uses a multi-head self-attention (MSA) module, Swin-T applies shifted window-based MSA modules (W-MSA and SW-MSA in Figure 1c). Similar to ViT, LayerNorm (LN) layers come before W-MSA, multilayer perceptron (MLP) blocks are added after W-MSA blocks, and GELU activation is applied between two MLP blocks. The basic transformer architecture computes self-attention globally between a token and all other tokens. However, global computation has quadratic complexity with respect to the number of tokens, posing challenges for tasks requiring large tokens, such as dense prediction and high-resolution images. To address this issue, self-attention between local windows has been proposed [23], where windows are divided evenly into even-sized patches to ensure nonoverlapping windows within an image (Figure 1b). The W-MSA module has a limitation in modeling power due to a lack of connectivity between windows. To address this issue, a method called "Shifted Window Partitioning" has been proposed [23].

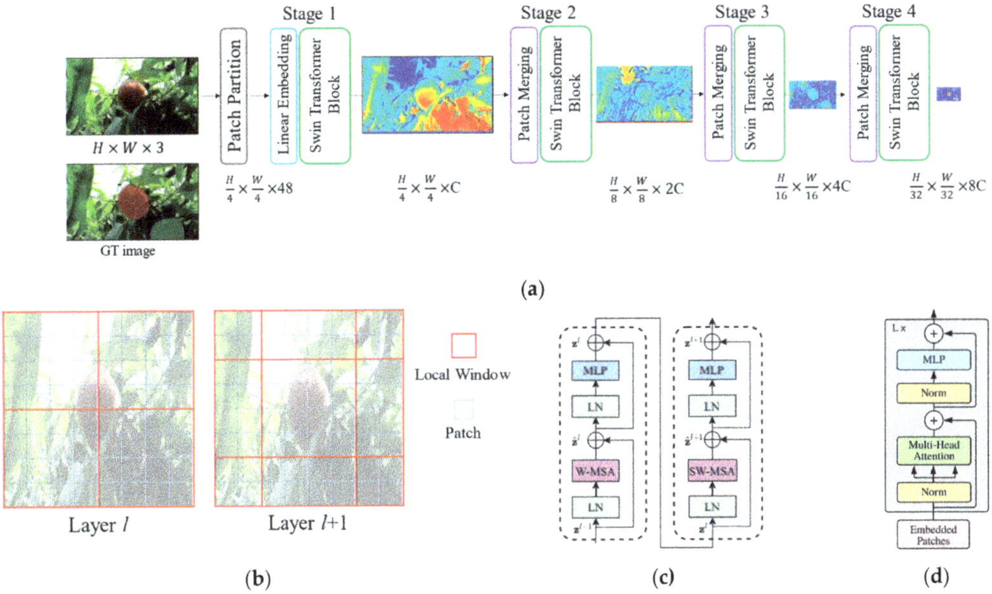

Figure 1. Component illustrations of Swin Transformer. The maps following Swin Transformer blocks are attention maps of each stage. (**a**) Swin Transformer architecture; (**b**) shifted window approach; (**c**) Swin Transformer block; (**d**) ViT block. (**c**,**d**) were extracted from [23] and [22], respectively.

2.2. Dataset Comprising Cluttered Scenes for Peach Segmentation

In this study, we introduce a peach image dataset comprising highly cluttered images. This dataset will serve as a valuable resource for training and evaluating segmentation models. In this subsection, we provide a comprehensive description of the dataset, including its composition, data collection process, and key characteristics.

The dataset comprises 125 RGB images depicting peach trees bearing fruits, each accompanied by corresponding ground-truth annotations in the form of masks for instance segmentation. For experimentation, we partitioned the dataset into three subsets, allocating an 8:1:1 ratio, resulting in 99, 13, and 13 images for training, validation, and testing, respectively. The dataset also includes 1077 peach fruit objects, with an average of eight peaches per image.

The images were captured around the harvest time of 90 days after full bloom, June 2021, in a peach (*Prunus persica* (L.) Batsch) orchard. All images were taken in the morning on the same day under clear weather condition. Canon IXY DIGITAL 220 IS and Samsung MV800 digital cameras were used to acquire images, and the image resolutions encompassed 1600 × 1200, 1920 × 1080, 1440 × 1080, and 4032 × 1024 or their respective inverses. We used various equipment and resolutions to enhance the generalization of the model and robustness in real-world scenarios. The images were captured freely at the standard distances because it was difficult to set a static camera position or location in an orchard environment.

The images were acquired in two types of view: tree- and fruit-bunch-focused. Four trees and nine bunches of peaches were captured; each tree was captured in approximately 20 styles within 1–5 m and each bunch was captured in 5 styles within 0.3 m. Examples of the captured images are shown in the first row of Figure 2. Figure 2a,b show tree-focused images, and Figure 2c shows a fruit-bunch-focused image. Owing to the widely sprawled feature of peach trees, the images could not be captured at a fixed distance, and tree-focused images contained an entire tree or only part of a tree. Fruit-bunch-focused images comprised a few peach fruits, about one or two, in the middle of the image. The numbers of peach fruit objects for each type are listed in Table 1. There are 80 tree-focused and 45 fruit-bunch-focused images, with an average of 12.0 and 2.7 peach objects per image, respectively.

(a) (b) (c)

Figure 2. Examples of image data and corresponding ground-truth masks: (**a**,**b**) tree-focused images; (**c**) fruit-bunch-focused image. The top row presents original images, and the bottom row shows labeled masks.

Table 1. Number of objects and images in the dataset.

	Tree	Fruit Bunch	Total
Objects	957	120	1077
Images	80	45	125
Average number of objects	12.0	2.7	8.6

Instance masks were manually annotated using LabelMe 5.0.1 [26] and labeled as "peach" class, except for dropped fruits. The masks were basically labeled by polygons, and a circle was used if more than 50% of the target was occluded by leaves or other peaches. All masks were annotated, including occluded areas, to apply the dataset to various tasks, such as fruit location and size estimation. Examples of ground-truth masks are shown in the second row of Figure 2.

To clarify clutter and diversity similar to the real field, unlike other datasets, we analyze two characteristics: occlusion and object size. Because the images were captured in an orchard, fruits are often obscured by leaves, branches, and neighborhood fruits. We flagged obscured fruits if the peach edge could not be precisely labeled, and 64.1% of peaches were flagged in total. Figure 3 depicts an image with significant occlusion, where 93.8% of the peaches are occluded.

We analyze the characteristics of object size separately for tree- and fruit-bunch-focused images. Figure 4 shows histograms of the object area ratios of the images. Object size characteristics were analyzed using ratios because each image had a different resolution. Tree-focused images include 957 peach objects; 887 of them, i.e., approximately 92.7% of the total, occupy area ratios smaller than 1% in an image. The minimum and maximum area ratios are 0.0015% and 5.46%, respectively. Images including objects with minimum and maximum area ratios are shown in the first row of Figure 5. Target objects are boxed in a yellow line. Fruit-bunch-focused images include 120 peach objects; 50 peaches are smaller than 1% of the image size. The minimum ratio of fruit-bunch-focused images is also small (0.022%); however, the maximum ratio is 12.22%, and 58.33% of peaches occupy an area larger than 1.0%. Examples of images for each ratio are shown in the second row of Figure 5.

(a) (b)

Figure 3. (**a**) Image with significant occlusion; (**b**) the corresponding ground truth. Most peaches are obscured by leaves.

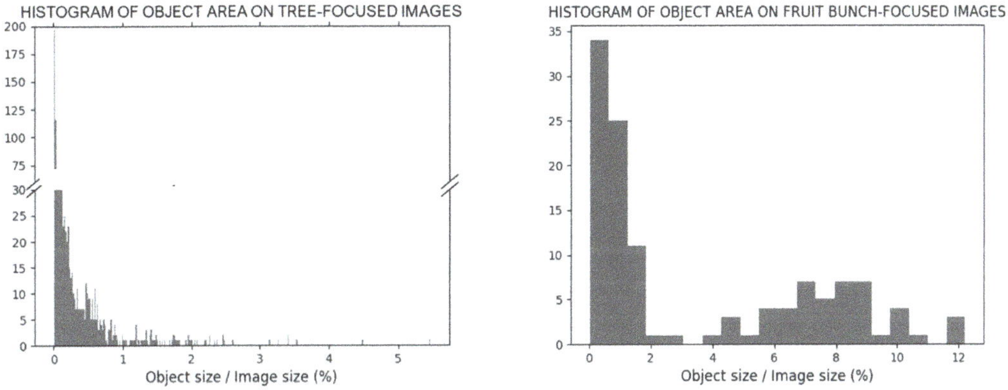

(a) (b)

Figure 4. (**a**) Histograms of object area for tree-focused images; (**b**) and fruit-bunch-focused images.

Statistics about occlusion and object size show how the dataset represents a real field environment not highly controlled. An analysis of object size also shows the diversity of the scenes. We used this dataset to train segmentation models to reflect the real field well; the results are described in Section 3.

Currently, there is a significant shortage of segmentation datasets for agricultural purposes that reflect real field environments. We aim to contribute to the academic community by releasing our dataset to the public. It is available at https://github.com/ssomda21/Dataset-for-Instance-Segmentation-of-Fruits-in-Peach-Tree-Image (accessed on 23 February 2023).

Figure 5. Examples of images containing objects with minimum and maximum areas. Each target object is represented by a yellow box.

2.3. The Metric for Instance Segmentation

To evaluate and compare performance, the standard evaluation metric, average precision (AP), is used. The AP score is derived from the intersection over union (IoU). A prediction is classified as a "true positive (TP)" if IoU between the ground truth and predicted masks exceeds a certain threshold. Typically, an IoU threshold of 0.5 is employed, implying that a prediction is considered TP if the masks overlap by more than half. AP is a metric related to precision–recall, which computes the average value of precision at every recall position, the same as the area under the precision–recall curve. Precision and recall are single-valued metrics based on the prediction results returned by models. The detailed equations are described in Equation (1). Notably, FP and FN mean false positive and false negative, respectively. Mean AP (mAP), which computes the mean value for all categories, is the commonly used metric for object detection/segmentation; however, we use AP because our target category is only "peach."

$$Precision = \frac{\mathrm{TP}}{\mathrm{TP}+\mathrm{FP}} \quad Recall = \frac{\mathrm{TP}}{\mathrm{TP}+\mathrm{FN}} \tag{1}$$

3. Results

In this section, we present the experimental results on peach fruit segmentation within orchard scenes. We trained the Swin-T pretrained model from the Swin Transformer. We trained CNN-based models, specifically Mask R-CNN with a ResNet-50 backbone [18], YOLACT [19], and SOLOv2 [27], for comparative analysis. The experiments were run on an NVIDIA RTX 2080 Ti GPU and an Intel(R) Xeon(R) Gold 6126 CPU. We used the MMDetection 2.25.1 library, supported by OpenMM, to implement the segmentation models [28]. Each model was fine-tuned with a pretrained model from MMDetection and trained on our dataset. We trained all models for 100 epochs, with specific training parameters detailed in Table 2.

Table 2. Parameters of each segmentation model.

Backbone Type	Model	Parameters		
		Optimizer	Learning Rate	Batch Size
CNN	Mask R-CNN (ResNet-50) [18]	SGD	0.02	2
	YOLACT [19]	SGD	0.001	8
	SOLOv2 [27]	SGD	0.001	4
Transformer	Mask R-CNN (Swin-T)	AdamW	0.0001	2

3.1. Evaluation of Peach Fruit Instance Segmentation

The detailed evaluation results for each model are presented in Table 3. Notably, the term "AP" in the table refers to the overall AP score, which is an average across IoU thresholds ranging from 0.5 to 0.95 in increments of 0.05. Mask R-CNN with ResNet-50 backbone [hereinafter, Mask R-CNN(ResNet-50)] recorded an overall AP of 55.1. At IoU thresholds of 0.5 and 0.75, it achieved APs of 83.9 and 56.0, respectively, indicating that while the model exhibits high precision for general overlaps, its performance slightly diminishes at stricter IoU thresholds. YOLACT recorded an overall AP of 52.6. At IoU thresholds of 0.5 and 0.75, it recorded APs of 81.9 and 58.5, respectively. This model's performance tended to decrease as the IoU threshold increased. SOLOv2 recorded an overall AP of 53.2 and recorded 79.6 AP and 55.8 AP at IoU thresholds of 0.5 and 0.75.

Table 3. Evaluation results on the testing set (best performance is shown in bold).

Model	AP	AP@0.5	AP@0.75	Inference Time (ms)
Mask R-CNN(ResNet-50)	55.1	83.9	56	**19.88**
YOLACT	52.6	81.9	58.5	25.92
SOLOv2	53.2	79.6	55.8	27.38
Mask R-CNN(Swin-T)	**60.2**	**87.1**	**65.2**	20.92

Mask R-CNN with the Swin-T backbone (hereinafter, Mask R-CNN(Swin-T)), which incorporates a transformer architecture, notably outperformed the other models. It achieved an overall AP of 60.2. Impressively, when evaluated at an IoU threshold of 0.75, it recorded an AP of 65.2, indicating its ability to maintain high precision, especially in situations that require a close overlap between predictions and ground truth. Although Mask R-CNN(Swin-T) showed the best segmentation performance on the provided dataset, it is essential to note the inference time. Mask R-CNN(ResNet-50) was the swiftest, processing an image in just 19.88 ms. Meanwhile, YOLACT, SOLOv2, and Mask R-CNN(Swin-T) took 25.92, 27.39, and 20.92 ms per image.

Figures 6 and 7, respectively, show the confusion matrix and result images for each model, including only the detection results with a confidence score greater than 0.5. In Figure 6, the order of the boxes is TP, FN, true negative (TN), and FP. Because we consider an instance segmentation problem in this study, we concentrate on TP, FN, and FP. TN should be zero because the models cannot predict background objects. Notably, FN indicates that the model misses existing objects, and FP indicates that the model predicts the wrong region. This analysis was performed on the testing set; the total number of ground-truth objects was 110. Each ratio is calculated based on the number of ground truths, and the numbers in parentheses indicate the real number of predictions. Mask R-CNN(Swin-T) recorded the best performance with 92% TP, while Mask R-CNN (ResNet-50) and YOLACT recorded 87% and 76% TP, respectively. Notably, Mask R-CNN(Swin-T) missed only eight peaches in the entire test dataset. FP predictions often occurred in diseased leaves or dense peach groups. For the first and fifth examples in Figure 7, Mask R-CNN(ResNet-50) predicted duplicate objects in dense peach groups. It also predicted leaves as peaches. YOLACT predicted the least FP among the three models; however, some masks were localized well, but the area was significantly different compared with the ground truth. SOLOv2 misses peach objects similar to YOLACT; however, a FP occurred at least for the examples in Figure 7. In Figure 7, specific examples of FNs and FPs are highlighted by cyan and yellow boxes, respectively.

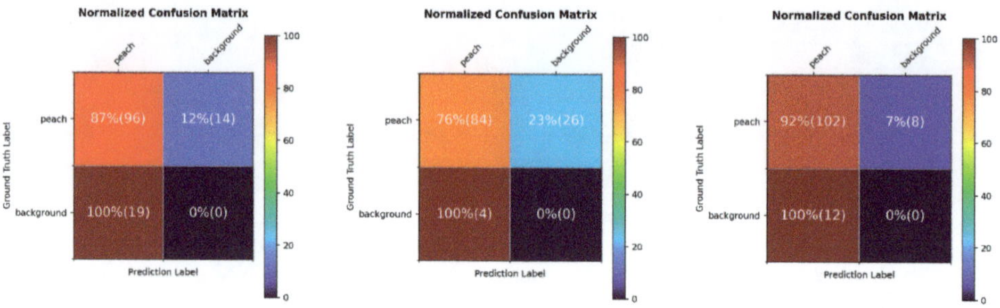

Mask R-CNN(ResNet-50) YOLACT Mask R-CNN(Swin-T)

Figure 6. Confusion matrix for each model. Starting from the top left and moving clockwise, the order is TP, FN, TN, and FP. Each value in the box indicates the ratio with respect to the ground truth, and the values in parentheses indicate the real number of predictions. Mask R-CNN(Swin-T) has the fewest peach misses.

Figure 7. Examples of test images from each model. From left to right, ground-truth images and output images from Mask R-CNN(ResNet-50), YOLACT, SOLOv2, and Mask R-CNN(Swin-T) are shown. FP and FN predictions are highlighted as yellow and cyan boxes, respectively. Mask R-CNN(Swin-T) yields the fewest FPs and FNs.

3.2. Evaluation of Challenging Cases

To find peaches well in cluttered images, the model should be robust to small or occluded objects. We specifically analyze the results by focusing on small and occluded objects. Notably, the "small object" is determined by the condition used by the MS-COCO dataset [29], i.e., smaller than 32 × 32 pixels. Table 4 shows the AP and average recall (AR) scores of the small objects. Mask R-CNN(Swin-T) achieved outstanding performance, scoring 40.4 AP and 40.0 AR, which were more than 1.6 times higher than those of Mask R-CNN(ResNet-50), YOLACT, and SOLOv2. To analyze the robustness of the models for occluded objects, we specifically evaluated only images in the testing set where most objects, exceeding 50%, were obscured. Mask R-CNN(Swin-T) achieved the best performance, 59.2 AP and 63.2 AR, indicating its suitability for cluttered images.

Table 4. Small object segmentation performance.

	Mask R-CNN (ResNet-50)	YOLACT	SOLOv2	Mask R-CNN (Swin-T)
AP	25.2	12.6	20.2	**40.4**
AR	25	25	20	**40**

Additional inferences were performed on unlabeled images; qualitative comparisons are shown in Figure 8. We selected examples that were challenging to count manually, underscoring the difficulty for human observers. YOLACT and SOLOv2 showed lower performance in detecting peaches obscured by leaves in all examples. SOLOv2 also detected significant duplications of peaches. Mask R-CNN(ResNet-50) effectively detected small and obscured peaches; however, some peaches were missed, and the edges of the detected regions were not smooth. These CNN-based models also tended to predict multiple groups of peaches as a single object. Meanwhile, Mask R-CNN(Swin-T) predicted well with lots of objects and well-localized highly obscured objects.

Figure 8. Images from unlabeled inputs. Highlighted regions from the third image are magnified under the images. The region in the white box shows the difference in region separation between Mask R-CNN(ResNet-50) and Mask R-CNN(Swin-T). Mask R-CNN(ResNet-50) detects a group of peaches as a single peach with a high confidence score of 0.72, while Mask R-CNN(Swin-T) detects each peach individually. The white box also shows that YOLACT misses about four peaches and does not separate the peach group on the left side of the image as individual objects. SOLOv2 also misses obscured peaches in the white box and shows significant duplicated detections. The yellow box shows that Mask R-CNN(Swin-T) detects tiny peaches better than other models.

4. Discussion

4.1. Necessity and Limitations of the Dataset

In this study, we present a specialized dataset for peach instance segmentation that is robust to challenging cases, such as occluded and small objects. The ground-truth masks are annotated at the pixel level, including obscured regions, referred to as "amodal masks" [30]. This annotation method helps to develop advanced models for instance segmentation, size estimation, yield estimation, and crop monitoring in the agricultural field.

The primary advantage of the presented dataset is the focus on detailed and complex segmentation scenarios that reflect real field environments because almost all existing datasets for segmentation provide simpler images with large and distinct fruits [3,5,11,31]. This level of detail is unprecedented and offers an invaluable resource for training more sophisticated fruit segmentation algorithms. By providing a dataset that reflects real field environments, we anticipate significant improvements in the real-world applicability of various agricultural technologies. The necessity for such a comprehensive dataset stems from the current limitations in the application of computer vision in agriculture due to the lack of datasets that truly reflect the complexity and variability of field conditions. Our dataset addresses this gap, thereby meeting a critical need for the development of robust peach segmentation models. The implications for agricultural infrastructure are profound, as better segmentation can lead to optimized resource allocation and improved crop management. Unlike other fields, such as medical imaging, which has a wealth of public datasets and challenges [32], the agricultural field faces a shortage of such resources [5]. This deficiency in data availability directly impacts the pace of research progress. To contribute to the agricultural field's growth and overcome these challenges, we have made our dataset openly accessible to facilitate research and foster advancements within the field.

However, the presented dataset has limitations in terms of environmental conditions: images were captured on the same day under the same light and weather conditions. These limitations may reduce the variance but also limit the dataset's ability to generalize across different conditions. In addition, the focus on a single cultivar of peach, although beneficial for in-depth analysis, may not capture the diversity of real-world agricultural scenarios. Future iterations of data acquisition should aim to include a broader variety of cultivars, diverse environmental conditions, and different stages of growth to enhance the generalizability of corresponding segmentation models.

4.2. Robustness for Challenging Cases with Potential for Broad Extension

The transformer-based segmentation model used in this study is robust to challenging cases of agricultural images under adverse conditions [3] and shows a potential for broad extension in automated farming systems. Recently, the agricultural field has consistently shown an interest in restoring obscured areas in detection and segmentation tasks, as this could significantly impact the enhancement of size estimation and growth monitoring performance [33,34]. The proposed model, Mask R-CNN(Swin-T), shows better performance for obscured peaches (see Table 5 and Figures 7 and 8). Mask R-CNN(Swin-T) also outperformed the comparative CNN-based models in terms of occluded area reconstruction. Based on this capability, the transformer-based model can be extended to fruit quality assessments that evaluate quality features, such as size, shape, and color.

Table 5. Segmentation performance on images with more than 50% occlusion.

	Mask R-CNN (ResNet-50)	YOLACT	SOLOv2	Mask R-CNN (Swin-T)
AP	53.9	50.8	51.7	**59.2**
AR	60	56.4	58.9	**63.2**

As shown in Table 4 and Figure 8, Mask R-CNN(Swin-T) achieved outstanding performance in segmenting small peaches and a significant number of peaches, indicating that it effectively localized and identified peach regions even when images were captured from a distance. The region in the yellow box in the third image from Figure 8 shows that Mask R-CNN(Swin-T) detected tiny peaches significantly more than the comparative CNN-based models. This advantage eliminates the need to consider shooting distance when developing agricultural robots. This robustness to small objects also helps shape separations, such as detecting each peach in a fruit bunch. Mask R-CNN(ResNet-50) occasionally detected a group of peaches as a single peach (Figures 7 and 8), whereas Mask R-CNN(Swin-T) detected each peach well. Particularly, the region highlighted with a white box in Figure 8 shows this problem distinctively. Mask R-CNN(ResNet-50) identified a cluster of peaches as a single peach with a high confidence score of 0.72, whereas Mask R-CNN(Swin-T) individually identified each peach in a cluster. YOLACT showed predictions that trespassed neighboring peaches. This separation capability can lead to improved performance in various farming tasks in which the identification of each fruit is crucial, such as fruit counting, robot harvesting, and yield estimation.

4.3. Speed of Two-Stage Detector and Agricultural Robot

In this study, we applied Swin-T to Mask R-CNN, a type of two-stage detector. The two-stage detector is divided into a region proposal network and a detection stage. In Mask R-CNN, the second stage includes pixel-level mask generation to represent precise shapes. Two-stage architectures have advantages such as high accuracy, precise object detection, and flexibility. Flexibility facilitates easy integration with various backbone networks and enables effective application in object segmentation. For these reasons, Mask R-CNN is utilized to verify the Swin Transformer.

However, two-stage detectors are generally slower than one-stage detectors because additional computations are required for the region proposal. Two-stage detectors also require more computational resources, resulting in limitations in applications requiring large datasets or real-time processing ($\geq$30 fps). For these reasons, Mask R-CNN(Swin-T) cannot be appropriate for fast tasks but can be applied to agricultural engineering because agricultural robots usually operate and move slowly [2]. During the harvesting process, it takes a robot between a minimum of 2–3 s to a maximum of 64 s to pick a single fruit, and it moves at a speed of 0.19 m/s, indicating that a transformer model, which requires an average processing time of 20.92 ms per frame, can be adequately applied at this speed. However, improvements in the speed of transformer-based models should be studied because the necessity for real-time processing is increasingly prominent for automated spraying systems [2]. Recently, transformer-based models that show low latency, such as EfficientFormer [35], have been studied.

The transformer-based segmentation approach can be widely applied to some major field operations, such as plant monitoring, phenotyping, spraying, harvesting, yield estimation, and multipurpose robotic systems [1–4]. Particularly, the transformer-based approach can be applied to tasks that require detailed representation, such as phenotyping, because they demonstrate overwhelming performance in challenging cases, as described in Section 3.2. This approach can also be expanded to weeding and disease and insect detection by changing the target from fruit to other objects.

5. Conclusions

In this study, we proposed a transformer-based segmentation model Mask R-CNN (Swin-T) for fruit segmentation in a cluttered orchard. We also presented a novel dataset of peach tree images captured from a peach orchard. This dataset comprises cluttered images including significant obscured objects that reflect real scenes in the agricultural field.

Mask R-CNN(Swin-T), a two-stage detector, shows superior performance over comparative CNN-based models. In particular, Mask R-CNN(Swin-T) recorded an AP of 60.2 and had the fewest missed peaches (FN). The advantage of Mask R-CNN(Swin-T) is revealed in the detection of small and obscured objects, AP 40.4 and 59.2. The proposed model, based on the two-stage detector, is not capable of real-time processing (processing speed of 4.78 fps); however, it can be sufficiently applied because the average speed of agricultural robots is 11.9 s per fruit.

The findings of this study indicate the potential applicability and advantages of transformer-based vision models in agricultural settings, using data that reflect real field environments. Further, transformer-based vision models can be expanded to various intelligent agricultural areas, such as spraying, harvesting, and yield estimation.

Author Contributions: Conceptualization, I.-S.O.; methodology, I.-S.O. and D.S.; software, D.S.; validation, D.S. and I.-S.O.; formal analysis, D.S.; investigation, D.S.; resources, S.K.L. and J.G.K.; data curation, J.G.K.; writing—original draft preparation, D.S.; writing—review and editing, I.-S.O.; visualization, D.S.; supervision, I.-S.O.; project administration, S.K.L.; funding acquisition, S.K.L. and I.-S.O. All authors have read and agreed to the published version of the manuscript.

Funding: This research was funded by the Cooperative Research Program for Agriculture Science and Technology Development (Project No. RS-2021-RD009224), Rural Development Administration, the Republic of Korea.

Institutional Review Board Statement: Not applicable.

Data Availability Statement: The original data presented in the study are openly available in the GitHub repository at https://github.com/ssomda21/Dataset-for-Instance-Segmentation-of-Fruits-in-Peach-Tree-Image (accessed on 23 February 2023).

Conflicts of Interest: The authors declare no conflicts of interest.

References

1. Droukas, L.; Doulgeri, Z.; Tsakiridis, N.L.; Triantafyllou, D.; Kleitsiotis, I.; Mariolis, I.; Giakoumis, D.; Tzovaras, D.; Kateris, D.; Bochtis, D. A Survey of Robotic Harvesting Systems and Enabling Technologies. *J. Intell. Robot. Syst.* **2023**, *107*, 1–29. [CrossRef] [PubMed]
2. Fountas, S.; Mylonas, N.; Malounas, I.; Rodias, E.; Santos, C.H.; Pekkeriet, E. Agricultural Robotics for Field Operations. *Sensors* **2020**, *20*, 2672. [CrossRef]
3. Bac, C.W.; van Henten, E.J.; Hemming, J.; Edan, Y. Harvesting Robots for High-value Crops: State-of-the-art Review and Challenges Ahead. *J. Field Robot.* **2014**, *31*, 888–911. [CrossRef]
4. Yang, Y.Y.; Han, Y.X.; Li, S.; Yang, Y.D.; Zhang, M.; Li, H. Vision based fruit recognition and positioning technology for harvesting robots. *Comput. Electron. Agric.* **2023**, *213*, 108258. [CrossRef]
5. Lu, Y.Z.; Young, S. A survey of public datasets for computer vision tasks in precision agriculture. *Comput. Electron. Agric.* **2020**, *178*, 105760. [CrossRef]
6. Yu, Y.; Zhang, K.L.; Yang, L.; Zhang, D.X. Fruit detection for strawberry harvesting robot in non-structural environment based on Mask-RCNN. *Comput. Electron. Agric.* **2019**, *163*, 104846. [CrossRef]
7. Ge, Y.Y.; Xiong, Y.; From, P.J. Instance Segmentation and Localization of Strawberries in Farm Conditions for Automatic Fruit Harvesting. *IFAC-PapersOnLine* **2019**, *52*, 294–299. [CrossRef]
8. Wang, J.H.; Zhang, Z.Y.; Luo, L.F.; Wei, H.L.; Wang, W.; Chen, M.Y.; Luo, S.M. DualSeg: Fusing transformer and CNN structure for image segmentation in complex vineyard environment. *Comput. Electron. Agric.* **2023**, *206*, 107682. [CrossRef]
9. Wang, D.D.; He, D.J. Fusion of Mask RCNN and attention mechanism for instance segmentation of apples under complex background. *Comput. Electron. Agric.* **2022**, *196*, 106864. [CrossRef]
10. Häni, N.; Roy, P.; Isler, V. MinneApple: A Benchmark Dataset for Apple Detection and Segmentation. *IEEE Robot. Autom. Lett.* **2020**, *5*, 852–858. [CrossRef]
11. Zhao, Z.; Hicks, Y.; Sun, X.F.; Luo, C.X. Peach ripeness classification based on a new one-stage instance segmentation model. *Comput. Electron. Agric.* **2023**, *214*, 108369. [CrossRef]
12. Assunçao, E.T.; Gaspar, P.D.; Mesquita, R.J.M.; Simoes, M.P.; Ramos, A.; Proença, H.; Inacio, P.R.M. Peaches Detection Using a Deep Learning Technique-A Contribution to Yield Estimation, Resources Management, and Circular Economy. *Climate* **2022**, *10*, 11. [CrossRef]
13. Liu, P.Z.; Yin, H. YOLOv7-Peach: An Algorithm for Immature Small Yellow Peaches Detection in Complex Natural Environments. *Sensors* **2023**, *23*, 5096. [CrossRef] [PubMed]
14. Xiao, F.; Wang, H.B.; Xu, Y.Q.; Zhang, R.Q. Fruit Detection and Recognition Based on Deep Learning for Automatic Harvesting: An Overview and Review. *Agronomy* **2023**, *13*, 1625. [CrossRef]
15. Espinoza, S.; Aguilera, C.; Rojas, L.; Campos, P.G. Analysis of Fruit Images with Deep Learning: A Systematic Literature Review and Future Directions. *IEEE Access* **2024**, *12*, 3837–3859. [CrossRef]
16. Redmon, J.; Divvala, S.; Girshick, R.; Farhadi, A. You Only Look Once: Unified, Real-Time Object Detection. In Proceedings of the 2016 IEEE Conference on Computer Vision and Pattern Recognition (CVPR), Las Vegas, NV, USA, 27–30 June 2016; pp. 779–788. [CrossRef]
17. Ren, S.Q.; He, K.M.; Girshick, R.; Sun, J. Faster R-CNN: Towards Real-Time Object Detection with Region Proposal Networks. In Proceedings of the 28th International Conference on Neural Information Processing Systems (NIPS), Montreal, Canada, 7–12 December 2015; pp. 91–99.

18. He, K.M.; Gkioxari, G.; Dollár, P.; Girshick, R. Mask R-CNN. In Proceedings of the 2017 IEEE International Conference on Computer Vision (ICCV), Venice, Italy, 22–29 October 2017; pp. 2980–2988. [CrossRef]
19. Bolya, D.; Zhou, C.; Xiao, F.Y.; Lee, Y.J. YOLACT Real-time Instance Segmentation. In Proceedings of the 2019 IEEE/CVF International Conference on Computer Vision (ICCV), Seoul, Republic of Korea, 27 October–2 November 2019; pp. 9156–9165. [CrossRef]
20. Liu, W.; Anguelov, D.; Erhan, D.; Szegedy, C.; Reed, S.; Fu, C.Y.; Berg, A.C. SSD: Single Shot MultiBox Detector. In Proceedings of the Computer Vision–ECCV 2016: 14th European Conference, Amsterdam, The Netherlands, 11–14 October 2016; Pt I, pp. 21–37.
21. Badrinarayanan, V.; Kendall, A.; Cipolla, R. SegNet: A Deep Convolutional Encoder-Decoder Architecture for Image Segmentation. *IEEE Trans. Pattern Anal. Mach. Intell.* **2017**, *39*, 2481–2495. [CrossRef] [PubMed]
22. Dosovitskiy, A.; Beye, L.; Kolesnikov, A.; Weissenborn, D.; Zhai, X.; Unterthiner, T.; Dehghani, M.; Minderer, M.; Heigold, G.; Gelly, S.; et al. An Image is Worth 16 × 16 Words: Transformers for Image Recognition at Scale. In Proceedings of the International Conference on Learning Representations, Vienna, Austria, 4 May 2021.
23. Liu, Z.; Lin, Y.T.; Cao, Y.; Hu, H.; Wei, Y.X.; Zhang, Z.; Lin, S.; Guo, B.N. Swin Transformer: Hierarchical Vision Transformer using Shifted Windows. In Proceedings of the 2021 IEEE/CVF International Conference on Computer Vision (ICCV), Montreal, QC, Canada, 10–17 October 2021; pp. 9992–10002. [CrossRef]
24. Wang, J.H.; Zhang, Z.Y.; Luo, L.F.; Zhu, W.B.; Chen, J.W.; Wang, W. SwinGD: A Robust Grape Bunch Detection Model Based on Swin Transformer in Complex Vineyard Environment. *Horticulturae* **2021**, *7*, 492. [CrossRef]
25. Lin, T.Y.; Dollár, P.; Girshick, R.; He, K.M.; Hariharan, B.; Belongie, S. Feature Pyramid Networks for Object Detection. In Proceedings of the IEEE Conference on Computer Vision and Pattern Recognition, Honolulu, HI, USA, 21–26 July 2017; pp. 936–944. [CrossRef]
26. Wada, K. Labelme: Image Polygonal Annotation with Python. Available online: https://www.mdpi.com/authors/references (accessed on 1 June 2022).
27. Wang, X.; Zhang, R.; Kong, T.; Li, L.; Shen, C. SOLOv2: Dynamic and Fast Instance Segmentation. *Adv. Neural Inf. Process. Syst.* **2020**, *33*, 17721–17732.
28. Chen, K.; Wang, J.; Pang, J.; Cao, Y.; Xiong, Y.; Li, X.; Sun, S.; Feng, W.; Liu, Z.; Xu, J.; et al. MMDetection: Open MMLab Detection Toolbox and Benchmark. *arXiv* **2019**, arXiv:1906.07155.
29. Lin, T.Y.; Maire, M.; Belongie, S.; Hays, J.; Perona, P.; Ramanan, D.; Dollár, P.; Zitnick, C.L. Microsoft COCO: Common Objects in Context. In *Computer Vision–ECCV 2014*; Lecture Notes in Computer Science; Springer: Cham, Switzerland, 2014; Volume 8693, pp. 740–755. [CrossRef]
30. Follmann, P.; König, R.; Härtinger, P.; Klostermann, M.; Böttger, T. Learning to See the Invisible: End-to-End Trainable Amodal Instance Segmentation. In Proceedings of the 2019 IEEE Winter Conference on Applications of Computer Vision (WACV), Waikoloa, HI, USA, 7–11 January 2019; pp. 1328–1336. [CrossRef]
31. Yao, N.; Ni, F.C.; Wu, M.H.; Wang, H.Y.; Li, G.L.; Sung, W.K. Deep Learning-Based Segmentation of Peach Diseases Using Convolutional Neural Network. *Front. Plant Sci.* **2022**, *13*, 876357. [CrossRef]
32. Tang, X. The role of artificial intelligence in medical imaging research. *BJR Open* **2020**, *2*, 20190031. [CrossRef] [PubMed]
33. Blok, P.M.; van Henten, E.J.; van Evert, F.K.; Kootstra, G. Image-based size estimation of broccoli heads under varying degrees of occlusion. *Biosyst. Eng.* **2021**, *208*, 213–233. [CrossRef]
34. Gené-Mola, J.; Ferrer-Ferrer, M.; Gregorio, E.; Blok, P.M.; Hemming, J.; Morros, J.R.; Rosell-Polo, J.R.; Vilaplana, V.; Ruiz-Hidalgo, J. Looking behind occlusions: A study on amodal segmentation for robust on-tree apple fruit size estimation. *Comput. Electron. Agric.* **2023**, *209*, 107854. [CrossRef]
35. Li, Y.; Yuan, G.; Wen, Y.; Hu, E.; Evangelidis, G.; Tulyakov, S.; Wang, Y.; Ren, J. EfficientFormer: Vision Transformers at MobileNet Speed. *arXiv* **2022**, arXiv:2206.01191.

agriculture

MDPI

Article

Phenotyping the Anthocyanin Content of Various Organs in Purple Corn Using a Digital Camera

Zhengxin Wang [1,†], Ye Liu [2,†], Ke Wang [1], Yusong Wang [1], Xue Wang [1], Jiaming Liu [1], Cheng Xu [3] and Youhong Song [1,4,*]

[1] School of Agronomy, Anhui Agricultural University, Hefei 230036, China; zxwang@ahau.edu.cn (Z.W.); 22721735@stu.ahau.edu.cn (K.W.); wangyusong03@stu.ahau.edu.cn (Y.W.); xuewang@stu.ahau.edu.cn (X.W.); ljming@stu.ahau.edu.cn (J.L.)

[2] Department of Geographical and Earth Sciences, University of Glasgow, Gilmorehill, Glasgow G12 8QQ, UK; liuye5361@163.com

[3] School of Economics and Management, Jingdezhen University, Jingdezhen 333400, China; jgzxc_2005@163.com

[4] Centre for Crop Science, Queensland Alliance for Agriculture and Food Innovation, The University of Queensland, Brisbane, QLD 4072, Australia

* Correspondence: uqysong@163.com

† These authors contributed equally to this work.

Abstract: Anthocyanins are precious industrial raw materials. Purple corn is rich in anthocyanins, with large variation in their content between organs. It is imperative to find a rapid and non-destructive method to determine the anthocyanin content in purple corn. To this end, a field experiment with ten purple corn hybrids was conducted, collecting plant images using a digital camera and determining the anthocyanin content of different organ types. The average values of red (R), green (G) and blue (B) in the images were extracted. The color indices derived from RGB arithmetic operations were applied in establishing a model for estimation of the anthocyanin content. The results showed that the specific color index varied with the organ type in purple corn, i.e., AC_{CR} for the grains, BRT for the cobs, AC_{CB} for the husks, R for the stems, AC_{CB} for the sheaths and BRT for the laminae, respectively. Linear models of the relationship between the color indices and anthocyanin content for different organs were established with R^2 falling in the range of 0.64–0.94. The predictive accuracy of the linear models, assessed according to the NRMSE, was validated using a sample size of 2:1. The average NRMSE value was 11.68% in the grains, 13.66% in the cobs, 8.90% in the husks, 27.20% in the stems, 7.90% in the sheaths and 15.83% in the laminae, respectively, all less than 30%, indicating that the accuracy and stability of the model was trustworthy and reliable. In conclusion, this study provided a new method for rapid, non-destructive prediction of anthocyanin-rich organs in purple corn.

Keywords: purple corn; anthocyanin; digital photography; image analysis

1. Introduction

Anthocyanins are natural pigments with a wide range of colors and represent a major subclass of polyphenols/flavonoids [1]. Such pigments are widely found in natural plants, playing a critical role in alleviating the effect of biotic and abiotic stresses [2–6]. They are also used widely in the food, pharmaceutical and cosmetics industries due to their natural, non-toxic and antioxidant properties [7–10]. As reported, the global market of flavonoids is valued at USD 1.06 billion by 2025, and anthocyanins account for the majority of this share [11]. In the foreseeable future, the demand for anthocyanins in industry will continue to grow [12,13].

The most common way to obtain anthocyanins is to extract them from different plant sources, such as fruits and flowers, but the economic benefit of this is low since such materials are costly [14–16]. Extracting anthocyanins from agricultural by-products such as fruit crops is considered to be a cost-effective method [17,18]. Among them, purple corn (*Zea mays* L.) has attracted significant attention due to the abundance of anthocyanins in its non-grain tissues, such as the cob, in addition to the grain [19,20]. Nevertheless, the procedure of measuring anthocyanin content is cumbersome, as it involves isolating and grinding plant tissues, then the chemical extraction of anthocyanins and analysis of absorbance values or chromatography [14]. It is fairly tedious and costly if many samples are considered in practice [21]. Hence, it is essential to find a simple, convenient method for rapidly estimating the anthocyanin content in different organs in purple corn.

Digital images acquired using sensors such as RGB, multispectral, hyperspectral, thermal infrared and LiDAR have been widely used in monitoring plant height, leaf area indices and plant nutrients [22,23]; the detection of pests and disease [24,25] and the prediction of crop yield [26]. Recently, studies have shown that the color parameters of digital images acquired using RGB cameras can be used to predict the pigment content in plant tissues, such as their content of chlorophyll and anthocyanins [27–29]. In addition, a chlorophyll quantification system based on images from digital cameras such as smartphone and digital single-lens cameras was developed to accurately quantify the chlorophyll content of Chlamydomonas, quinoa and amaranth leaves in situ [30,31]. It has been reported that the color indices of RGB channel values are significantly correlated with the pigment content, indicating that modeling based on such relations is feasible [32–34].

To our knowledge, the anthocyanin content in plant tissues has been estimated using digital images only in black rice [35], sugar maple [36] and some flowers from Spain, including *Borago officinalis* L., *Malva sylvestris* L., *Orchis italica* Poir. and *Silene littorea* Brot [28]. Thus far, there has been no report on purple corn plants. Within this context, we carried out a field study with 10 purple corn hybrids to phenotype the anthocyanin content of various types of organs. Thus, the aim of this study was to (i) examine the relationship between the anthocyanin content in different organs and the color indices of visible light images; (ii) determine the optimal color index for modeling different organs of purple corn and (iii) evaluate the stability of the established predictive model.

2. Materials and Methods

2.1. Plant Materials and Sampling

Ten hybrids of purple corn were sown on 12 June 2022 at the experimental station of Anhui Agricultural University, Hefei (31°86′ N, 117°25′ E, altitude = 27.05 m), Anhui Province, China. We carried out a comparison with the findings in Wang et al. (2022) on meteorological data from different locations in Huaibei Plain, Anhui Province, for 61 years [37]. Among them, the range of $\overline{T}_{max}$ is 29.97–32.94 °C, while the range of $\overline{T}_{min}$ is 20.99–25.08 °C, and the range of $\overline{T}_{mean}$ is 25.04–28.59 °C. Our data are consistent with the historical law of this region with similar climate attributes (see Figure S1 and Table S1). Therefore, it can be considered a typical year.

The soil at the experimental field was a yellow brown type with medium fertility. The planting density was 52,500 plants·ha^{-1}, with 60 cm spacing between rows. A random complete block design was adopted with 3 replicates for each variety. Fertilizer was applied with a mixture of urea, calcium superphosphate and potassium sulfate, adding up to 60.0 kg·ha^{-1} of P_2O_5, 75.0 kg·ha^{-1} of K_2O, 187.5 kg·ha^{-1} of pure nitrogen and one-third nitrogen fertilizer as the base fertilizer, and the rest of the nitrogen fertilizer was applied at the big-flare stage. Field management was carried out by following conventional field cultivation techniques. Because previous studies found that anthocyanins are the main cause of plant coloration [38,39], in order to obtain the maximum range of color variation, we focused on the anthocyanin-rich organs of purple corn (Table 1). In this paper, purple corn plants of different hybrids at vegetative stages (V12–VT) and reproductive stages (R1–R4) in the experimental field were retrieved, and the organs rich in anthocyanins were decomposed, photographed and numbered.

Table 1. Information on various organs containing anthocyanins in 10 hybrids.

Variety	Organ with Anthocyanins	Growth Period
SGHN	Grain, Cob, Husk, Stem, Sheath, Lamina	85 days
ZZN8	Grain, Cob, Husk, Stem, Sheath, Lamina	85 days
JHN3	Grain, Cob, Husk	85 days
HTN168	Grain, Cob, Husk	85 days
SD31	Grain, Cob, Husk	86 days
HTN520	Grain	80–85 days
TNBM508	Grain	85 days
TNHB509	Grain	85 days
JZXN	Grain	80–85 days
HZHN1	Grain	90 days

2.2. Digital Image Acquisition and Preprocessing

The procedure for acquiring and standardizing the digital images is shown in Figure 1. First, we used a Canon EOS M50 Mark II camera (Canon Corporation, Tokyo, Japan) equipped with an EF-M 14–45 mm autofocus lens (transmitting wavelengths of 370–700 nm). This camera has a 22.3 × 14.9 mm CMOS sensor (6000 × 4000 pixels) and shows full regulation of exposure and metering, as recommended for unbiased data acquisition [40]. We manually adjusted these settings for all the samples: a shutter speed of 1/40, a lens aperture of f/3.5, ISO 100, and white balance fixed at 4500 k. The photos were underexposed by +1.7 to prevent color "clipping" or saturation, and we used a uniform illuminance of 500 lx light for illumination [41]. The images were taken in canon RAW format (CR3) because RAW files of unprocessed images can be linearized using specialized software. For the acquisition of images of each organ of the purple corn plants, each sample in this study was photographed using a Calibrite ColorChecker Classic standard 24-color card (X-Rite Inc., Grand Rapids, MI, USA). Due to the significant effect of different lighting on RGB channel color parameters, the light conditions were standardized for different shooting environments [42,43]. First, a profile was created with conversion from RAW into DNG format using ColorChecker Camera Calibration (X-Rite Inc., Grand Rapids, MI, USA). Second, the constructed profile was selected for color calibration using Adobe Lightroom Classic software (v11.5, Adobe, Inc., San Jose, CA, USA). Finally, the non-experimental areas of the digital images were segmented and removed using Abode Photoshop 2020 software (v23.5, Adobe, Inc., San Jose, CA, USA) to eliminate their influence on the extraction of the color parameters. After this series of image processing processes, color-calibrated images were obtained [44].

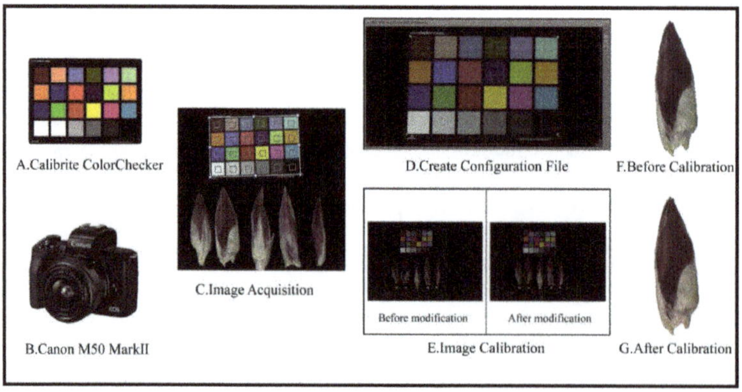

Figure 1. Digital image acquisition and standardization process. (**A**) A picture of the X-Rite ColorChecker classic chart. (**B**) The camera used in the experiment. (**C**) The sample image acquisition. (**D**) Creation of DNG format file in Colorchecker Camera Calibration. (**E**) Image calibration in Lightroom. (**F**) The image before color calibration. (**G**) The image after color calibration.

2.3. Image Analysis and Processing of the Color Data

RGB color channels are a natural color mode that can represent 16 million colors in nature. Numerous color feature indices can be obtained using these channels. However, by referring to the selection of color indices in similar studies, in this study, in addition to the R, G and B parameters in the RGB channels, 11 indices commonly used in previous studies on the relationship between pigment content and RGB were selected as alternatives, and their calculation methods and the related literature are shown in Table 2.

Table 2. Color indices used to estimate anthocyanin content from digital image data.

Color Indices	Formula Used for Digital Images	References
Red:green ratio	$RG_R = N_{red}/N_{green}$	[45]
Red:blue ratio	$RB_R = N_{red}/N_{blue}$	[45]
Green:blue ratio	$GB_R = N_{green}/N_{blue}$	[45]
Strength of red	$S_{red} = N_{green}/(N_{red} + N_{green} + N_{blue})$	[46]
Strength of green	$S_{green} = N_{green}/(N_{red} + N_{green} + N_{blue})$	[46]
Strength of blue	$S_{blue} = N_{green}/(N_{red} + N_{green} + N_{blue})$	[46]
Brightness	$BRT = \sqrt{\left[\left(S_{blue^2} + S_{green^2} + S_{red^2}\right)/3\right]}$	[28]
Chroma	$C = (N_{red} - N_{green})/[(N_{red} + N_{green} + N_{blue})/3]$	[28]
Anthocyanin content, chroma basic	$AC_{CB} = (N_{blue} + N_{red})/N_{green}$	[28]
Anthocyanin content, chroma ratio	$AC_{CR} = N_{green}/[(N_{blue} + N_{red})/2]$	[28]
Anthocyanin content, chroma difference	$AC_{CD} = (N_{blue} + N_{red})/2 - N_{green}$	[28]

2.4. Extraction and Quantification of Anthocyanin

To determine the anthocyanins in the different organs of purple corn, the solvent extraction method mentioned by Tan and Bai et al. [47,48] was adopted and improved. The extraction agent was a mixture of ethanol and hydrochloric acid (95% ethanol and 1.5 mol/L hydrochloric acid, volume ratio of 85:15). The sample was placed in a 10 mL centrifuge tube, heated in a water bath at 80 °C for 30 min and centrifuged at 10,000 $r \cdot min^{-1}$ for 10 min. Then, the supernatant was taken, and this was repeated three times after combining the extraction solution volume to 25 mL. After cooling, the OD value of the extracted solution at 535 nm was determined using an ultraviolet spectrophotometer.

2.5. Establishment and Validation of the Model

Because our primary goal was to test whether the anthocyanin content could be predicted from the values of the indices obtained from the digital images, we used least squares linear regression to test this [49]. Preliminary graphic inspection showed that our data were appropriate for a simple regression model [50]. As for the establishment of a model of the anthocyanin content, this study adopted the isometric sampling method to screen the modeling samples and the validation samples, conducting the isometric sampling with a modeling:validation ratio = 2:1, and compared the coefficient of determination (R^2) of the fitting equation and the root mean square error (RMSE) to determine the optimal image color indices and establish a prediction model. For validation of the prediction model, we used the RMSE and the normalized root mean square error (NRMSE) for the evaluation [51]. In general, an R^2 value higher than 0.7 is considered indicative of a good model that can explain a significant amount of variance, while a higher value indicates a better model fit. A lower RMSE value indicates a better model fit because it measures the deviation between the predicted value and the observed value and is sensitive to outliers in the data [52,53]. The simulation is considered excellent with an NRMSE $\leq 10\%$, good if it is 10–20%, fair if it is 20–30% and poor if it is >30% [54].

$$RMSE = \sqrt{\frac{1}{n} \times \sum_{i=1}^{n} (SIM_i - OBS_i)^2}$$

$$\mathrm{NRMSE} = \sqrt{\frac{1}{n} \times \sum_{i=1}^{n}(SIM_i - OBS_i)^2} \times \frac{1}{\overline{OBS}} \times 100\%$$

where SIM_i and OBS_i represent the simulated and observed values, respectively, $\overline{OBS}$ represents the observed mean value and n is the number of samples.

2.6. Statistical Analysis

Analysis of variance (ANOVA) was performed using SPSS software (v19.0, SPSS, Inc., Chicago, IL, USA). The means were compared using Tukey's LSD (least significant difference) test at $p < 0.05$. Microsoft Excel software (v2021, Microsoft, Inc., Redmond, WA, USA) was used to sort out the test data and produce graphs and tables. Origin 2019 software (v10.1.0.40, OriginLab, Inc., Northampton, MA, USA) and Adobe Illustrator software (v26.5.0, Adobe, Inc., San Jose, CA, USA) were used for drawing.

3. Results

3.1. Anthocyanin Content of Various Organs in Purple Corn

The anthocyanin content of the specific types of organs across various hybrids is shown in Table 3. There were significant differences ($p < 0.05$) in the grain anthocyanin content among different hybrids, of which the highest anthocyanin content was 33.26 mg/100 g in HTN520, while the lowest anthocyanin content was 7.11 mg/100 g in JZXN. Notably, the anthocyanin content in HTN520 is 4.7 times greater than that in JZXN. This difference is caused by hybrid genotypes, and breeding varieties rich in functional phytochemicals such as anthocyanins is considered necessary and will be beneficial to the health of consumers [55,56]. Further analyses uncovered differences in the anthocyanin contents of the other organs. The anthocyanin content of the cob part ranged from 143.84 mg/100 g to 1334.10 mg/100 g. It is worth noting that the anthocyanin content in the cob was 188 times higher than that in the grain. Similarly in the husk part, the anthocyanin content ranged from 91.27 to 862.33 mg/100 g, which was slightly lower than that of the cob part but also significantly higher than that of the grain part, by up to 121 times. In SGHN and ZZN8, there were significant differences in the content of anthocyanins in the sheath parts, and the anthocyanin content of the sheaths was also significantly higher than that of the grain parts, but no significant differences were found for the sheath and lamina parts.

Table 3. Anthocyanin content of different organs in ten purple corn varieties.

Variety	Anthocyanin Content of Specific Organ Type (mg/100 g)					
	Grain	Cob	Husk	Sheath	Lamina	Stem
SGHN	22.22 de	1183.12 d	862.33 a	201.23 a	37.40 a	17.02 a
ZZN8	24.39 cd	1334.10 a	650.48 b	126.10 b	39.45 a	12.25 a
JHN3	27.65 bc	292.74 c	336.46 c			
HTN168	30.84 ab	295.22 c	205.73 d			
SD31	19.94 ef	143.84 d	91.27 e			
HTN520	33.26 a					
TNBM508	16.24 f					
TNHB509	7.29 g					
JZXN	7.11 g					
HZHN1	20.60 de					

Note: Different lowercase letters within a column indicate significant differences ($p < 0.05$) in anthocyanin content between different organs.

At present, the recovery of bioactive compounds from food by-products to obtain higher returns has been widely studied [19,20,57]. According to the above analysis, the cobs, husks and sheaths of purple corn contain a large amount of anthocyanin resources, which can be used as good raw material for the industrial extraction of anthocyanins and should be paid attention to in industrial production.

3.2. Correlation Analysis of Anthocyanin Content and Color Indices in Purple Corn

A heat map of the correlation between the anthocyanin content and common color indices is shown in Figure 2. In the visible light band, the anthocyanin content of specific organ types in purple corn is mostly negatively correlated with their R, G and B values; in particular, the transformed RG_R, RB_R, GB_R, C, BRT, AC_{CB} and AC_{CR} values had a highly significant correlation ($p < 0.01$). This is consistent with previous research results. In general, the darker the color of plant tissue (the lower the RGB value), the higher the pigment content [28,58,59]. In addition, of the 14 color indices, the color index most highly correlation with the anthocyanin content varied according to the organ type. For example, AC_{CR} and RBR were determined for the grain, BRT and R for the cob, AC_{CB} and AC_{CD} for the husk, R for the stem, AC_{CB} for the sheath and BRT for the lamina.

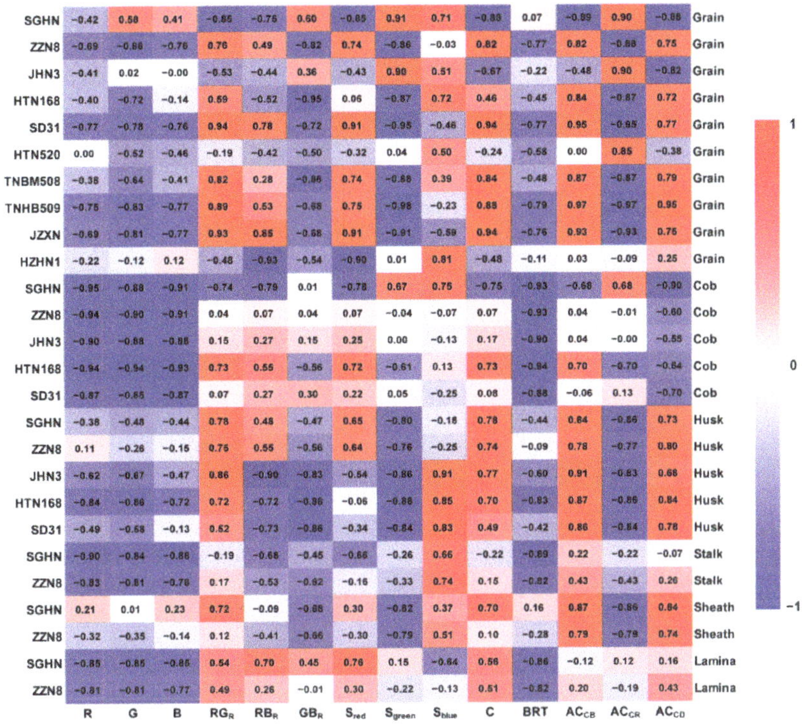

Figure 2. Visual heat map of the correlation between anthocyanin content and color indices in different organs.

3.3. Fitting Robustness of the Relationships between Anthocyanin Content and the Color Indices

Modeling samples were used for linear fitting based on 14 color indices, respectively, and the regression results are shown in Table 4. The color indices with the best goodness of fit were as follows: AC_{CB} (eight studied samples), AC_{CR} (seven studied samples), BRT (five studied samples), R (four studied samples), RB_R (one studied sample) and AC_{CD} (one studied sample). This suggests that such indices can be used in indicating the anthocyanin content. The optimal predictive model for anthocyanin content is shown in Figure 3. The coefficient of determination (R^2) for the fittings on the grain anthocyanin content (Figure 3A) ranged from 0.71 to 0.94. The R^2 of the predictive model for the cob anthocyanin content (Figure 3B) ranged from 0.80 to 0.87. The model error for the grains was smaller than that for the cobs, and the fitting effect for both parts was very good ($R^2 > 0.70$). For the husks (Figure 3C) and sheaths (Figure 3D), with heterogeneous pigmentation patterns, the R^2

ranged from 0.70 to 0.85 and from 0.64 to 0.76. In addition, the R^2 for the stems (Figure 3E) and laminae (Figure 3F) of SGHN and ZZN8 ranged from 0.71 to 0.75 and from 0.68 to 0.75, respectively. As a consequence, the fitting had good accuracy and was thus reliable. Further evaluation and analysis of the regression models for different organs showed that the best modeled color indices varied among different organs, and the high R^2 values (up to 0.94) indicated that the established predictive model had a good fit. Thus, it was feasible to establish a model for the anthocyanin content of purple corn plants by relating the anthocyanin content with the color parameters of visible light images of the purple corn plants.

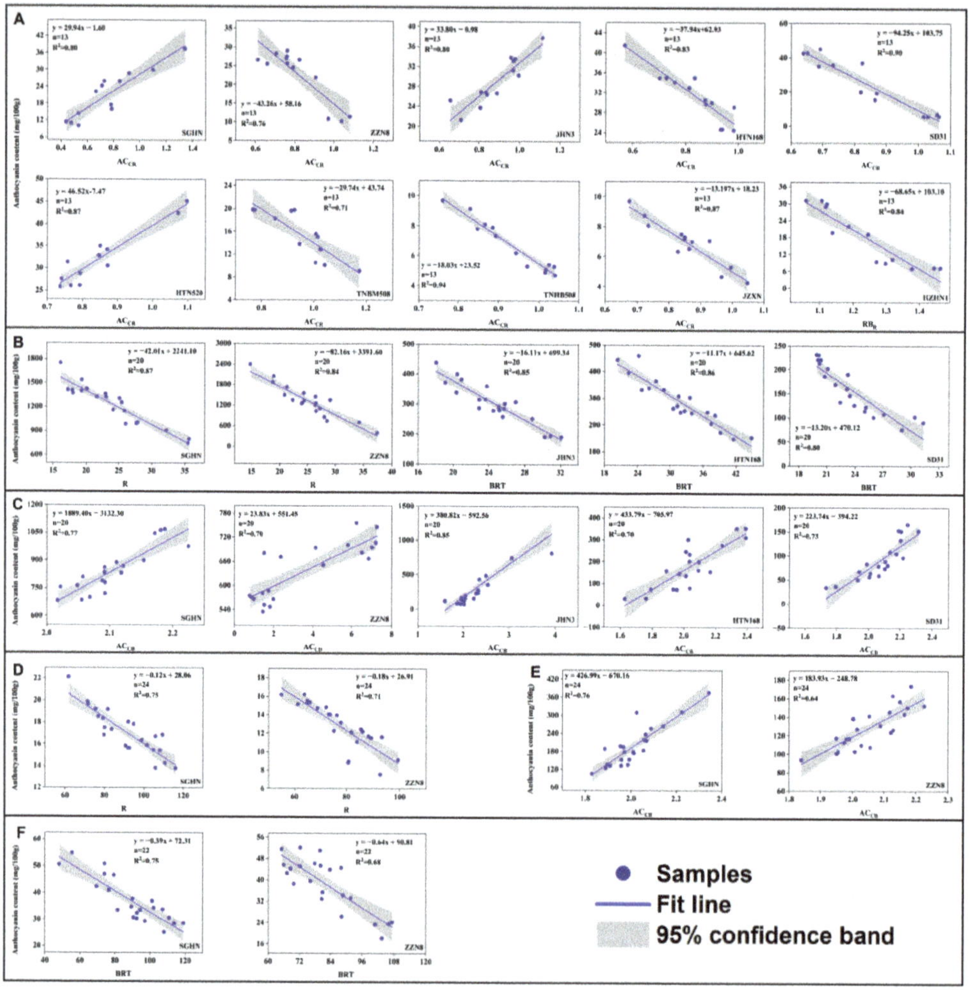

Figure 3. Fitting the relationship between anthocyanin content and the color index. The letters in the figure indicate grains (**A**); cobs (**B**); husks (**C**); stems (**D**); sheaths (**E**) and laminae (**F**).

Table 4. Coefficient of determination (R^2) and statistical significance of the fitting between anthocyanin content and color index.

Indices		R	G	B	RG_R	RB_R	GB_R	S_{red}	S_{green}	S_{blue}	C	BRT	AC_{CB}	AC_{CR}	AC_{CD}
SGHN	Grain	0.10	0.27 *	0.09	0.70 **	0.52 **	0.30 *	0.71 **	0.80 **	0.45 **	0.76 **	<0.01	0.77 **	**0.80** **	0.76 **
	Cob	**0.87** **	0.66 **	0.76 **	0.42 **	0.49 **	<0.01	0.47 **	0.34 **	0.42 **	0.43 **	0.82 **	0.34	0.34	0.73 **
	Husk	0.05	0.15	0.10	0.57 **	0.18	0.30	0.38 *	0.76 **	<0.01	0.56 **	0.10	**0.77** **	0.76 **	0.61 **
	Stem	**0.75** **	0.54 *	0.71 **	0.01	0.24	0.02	0.26	<0.01	0.15	0.02	0.71 **	<0.01	<0.01	<0.01
	Sheath	0.14	<0.01	0.25	0.51 **	<0.01	0.58 **	0.10	0.75 **	0.19	0.48 **	0.10	**0.76** **	0.75 **	0.73 **
	Lamina	0.71 **	0.75 **	0.72 **	0.28	0.47 *	0.16	0.62 **	<0.01	0.31 *	0.27	**0.75** **	<0.01	<0.01	<0.01
ZZN8	Grain	0.43 **	0.72 **	0.54 **	0.55 **	0.18	0.64 **	0.51 **	0.73 **	<0.01	0.64 **	0.55 **	0.63 **	**0.76** **	0.52 **
	Cob	**0.84** **	0.67 **	0.70 **	<0.01	<0.01	<0.01	<0.01	<0.01	<0.01	<0.01	0.79 **	<0.01	<0.01	0.17
	Husk	<0.01	0.10	0.03	0.61 **	0.36 **	0.34 **	0.51 **	0.67 **	0.08	0.60 **	0.00	0.67 **	0.67 **	**0.70** **
	Stem	**0.70** **	0.64 **	0.54 **	<0.01	0.18	0.32 *	<0.01	0.11	0.40 *	<0.01	0.67 **	0.11	0.11	0.03
	Sheath	0.02	0.05	<0.01	0.02	0.22 *	0.48 **	0.06	0.63 **	0.33 **	0.01	0.00	**0.64** **	0.62 **	0.55 **
	Lamina	0.64 **	0.67 **	0.57 **	0.19	0.03	<0.01	0.21	<0.01	<0.01	0.19	**0.68** **	<0.01	<0.01	0.12
JHN3	Grain	0.09	<0.01	<0.01	0.22	0.12	0.05	0.12	0.79 **	0.21	0.40 *	<0.01	0.16	**0.79** **	0.65 **
	Cob	0.84 **	0.69 **	0.47 **	<0.01	<0.01	<0.01	<0.01	<0.01	<0.01	<0.01	**0.85** **	<0.01	<0.01	0.23
	Husk	0.77 **	0.81 **	0.68 **	0.80 **	0.81 **	0.72 **	0.07	0.79 **	0.84 **	0.67 **	0.78 **	0.85 **	0.73 **	0.32 *
HTN168	Grain	0.02	0.36 *	<0.01	0.42 **	0.12	0.82 **	<0.01	0.82 **	0.37 *	0.26	0.06	0.79 **	**0.83** **	0.58 **
	Cob	0.86 **	0.85 **	0.84 **	0.35 **	0.10	0.12	0.29 *	0.32 *	<0.01	0.35 **	**0.86** **	0.32 *	0.31 *	0.30 *
	Husk	0.51 **	0.57 **	0.25 *	0.37 *	0.34 *	0.70 **	<0.01	0.67 **	0.57 **	0.34 *	0.49 **	**0.70** **	0.66 **	0.60 **
SD31	Grain	0.55 **	0.58 **	0.54 **	0.87 **	0.57 **	0.48 **	0.80 **	0.90 **	0.14	0.87 **	0.56 **	0.89 **	**0.90** **	0.55 **
	Cob	0.80 **	0.75 **	0.76 **	<0.01	0.04	<0.01	<0.01	<0.01	0.08	<0.01	**0.80** **	<0.01	<0.01	0.30 *
	Husk	0.20	0.29 *	<0.01	0.23 *	0.51 **	0.73 **	0.10	0.70 **	0.66 **	0.20 *	0.13	**0.73** **	0.69 **	0.58 **
HTN520	Grain	0.14	<0.01	<0.01	0.88 **	0.71 **	<0.01	0.85 **	0.88 **	0.60 **	0.70 **	<0.01	0.86 **	**0.88** **	0.76 **
TNBM508	Grain	0.01	0.35 **	0.02	0.56 **	<0.01	0.70 **	0.34 **	0.70 **	0.34 **	0.58 **	0.11	0.67 **	**0.71** **	0.60 **
TNHB509	Grain	0.65 **	0.71 **	0.56 **	0.69 **	0.08	0.46 **	0.38 **	0.94 **	<0.01	0.68 **	0.65 **	0.94 **	**0.94** **	0.90 **
JZXN	Grain	0.40 **	0.64 **	0.55 **	0.86 **	0.71 **	0.42 **	0.84 **	0.86 **	0.33 **	0.87 **	0.53 **	**0.87** **	0.86 **	0.54 **
HZHN1	Grain	<0.01	<0.01	<0.01	0.15	**0.84** **	0.22	0.77 **	<0.01	0.61 **	0.18	<0.01	<0.01	<0.01	<0.01

Note: The highest R^2 for each species–tissue combination is highlighted in bold. Evaluation using Pearson's correlation coefficients; * $p < 0.05$; ** $p < 0.01$.

3.4. Model Validation with an Independent Dataset

The predicted and measured values for different organs from all the varieties are presented (Figure 4). As a matter of fact, the samples were usually close to the 1:1 line. The RMSE values from the statistical results for model validation are shown in Table 5. The root mean square error (RMSE) was 0.31–6.85 mg/100 g in the grains, 16.55–36.59 mg/100 g in the cobs, 16.08–29.99 mg/100 g in the husks, 10.98–14.96 mg/100 g in the sheaths, 3.33–4.11 mg/100 g in the stems and 6.18–6.46 mg/100 g in the laminae. Meanwhile, the mean NRMSE values for the different organs were 11.68% for the grains, 13.66% for the cobs, 8.90% for the husks, 27.20% for the stems, 7.90% for the sheaths and 15.83% for the laminae. According to the model evaluation criteria mentioned above, it is not difficult to see that the predictive model has excellent accuracy and stability for the sheath and husk parts and also performs well for prediction of the anthocyanin content in the grains, cobs and laminae, but in the stem part, the NRMSE is between 20 and 30%, and the performance is not good.

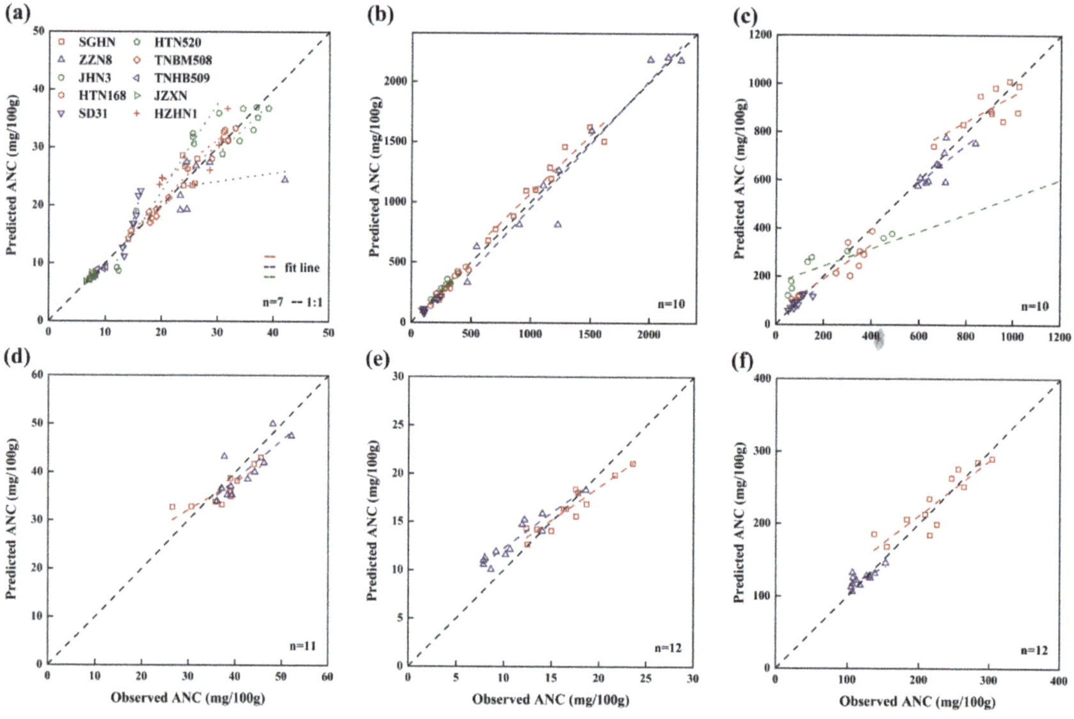

Figure 4. Validation of predictive models for anthocyanin content in different organs of purple corn; (**a**–**f**) are tests of anthocyanin content prediction models for grains, cobs, husks, laminae, stems and sheaths, respectively.

Table 5. Validation of predictive model for anthocyanin content based on color index.

Variety	Organ	Color Index	Validation	
			NRMSE (%)	RMSE (mg/100 g)
SGHN	Grain	AC_{CR}	15.05	3.51
ZZN8	Grain	AC_{CR}	16.19	4.44
JHN3	Grain	AC_{CR}	27.49	5.75

Table 5. *Cont.*

Variety	Organ	Color Index	Validation	
			NRMSE (%)	RMSE (mg/100 g)
HTN168	Grain	AC_{CR}	4.01	1.22
SD31	Grain	AC_{CR}	20.65	6.85
HTN520	Grain	AC_{CR}	6.35	2.25
TNBM508	Grain	AC_{CR}	4.25	0.77
TNHB509	Grain	AC_{CR}	5.04	0.42
JZXN	Grain	AC_{CB}	4.14	0.31
HZHN1	Grain	RB_R	13.60	3.50
SGHN	Cob	R	3.03	33.00
ZZN8	Cob	R	2.73	36.59
JHN3	Cob	BRT	6.04	16.55
HTN168	Cob	BRT	5.64	17.73
SD31	Cob	BRT	23.55	18.68
SGHN	Husk	AC_{CB}	3.33	29.99
ZZN8	Husk	AC_{CD}	3.84	26.02
JHN3	Husk	AC_{CB}	4.48	22.31
HTN168	Husk	AC_{CB}	6.22	16.08
SD31	Husk	AC_{CB}	26.62	24.13
SGHN	Stalk	R	24.35	4.11
ZZN8	Stalk	R	30.06	3.33
SGHN	Sheath	AC_{CB}	6.68	14.96
ZZN8	Sheath	AC_{CB}	9.11	10.98
SGHN	Lamina	BRT	16.18	6.18
ZZN8	Lamina	BRT	15.48	6.46

4. Discussion

4.1. Anthocyanins for Industry Use

Anthocyanins are widely used in cosmetics and in food colorings in industry [60–63]. Numerous studies have shown that anthocyanins have very good medicinal value and significant health effects, such as anti-cancer, anti-inflammation, anti-aging, anti-obesity and protection of vision [64–68]. A a considerable supply of anthocyanins is required for industry use. To date, anthocyanins have primarily been sourced from by-products including the pomace and retentate of dark fruits and vegetables, such as black grapes, blueberries and purple carrots [15,69–71]. Obtaining anthocyanins using this strategy is relatively dear due to the high price of the raw materials, as well as the high costs of processing their residues. In addition, the anthocyanins obtained this way are very limited, as the material is left over after its primary use [15,18]. We found that the hybrids SGHN and ZZN8 had a high anthocyanin content. This provided a rich supply of anthocyanins. In particular, we also identified that the anthocyanin content of the cobs and husks was much higher than that of the other types of organs (Table 3), providing specific target organs for anthocyanin extraction [19,20,72]. Notably, purple corn is increasingly consumed as a fresh vegetable in Asian countries because of the health-promoting properties of the anthocyanin pigments in its aleurone or pericarp [73–76], which means that by-products such as its cobs and husk can be used as premium industrial raw materials for anthocyanin extraction. It can also maximize the economic value of the purple corn industry by utilizing by-product resources.

4.2. Modeling Robustness

AC_{CR} was shown to be the best index for nine varieties of grains but not for HZHN1. This unique abnormality could be due to the presence of white wax on the peel, thus causing obscure images [30,77,78]. It has also been reported that other factors such as the cell shape, cell wall thickness or pigment location may also alter the color perceived by sensors [79], causing errors whist estimating the anthocyanin content from digital images. It is worth noting that using AC_{CB} for the husks of ZZN8 was not the best but it was still chosen since there was only a minor difference in the fitting effect between AC_{CD} (R^2 = 0.70) and AC_{CB} (R^2 = 0.68). Hence, a unique color index that is suitable for a single organ was proposed. A similar situation existed for the predictive model for the cob sections. As such, the indices AC_{CR}, BRT, AC_{CB}, R, AC_{CB} and BRT were recommended for the grains, cobs, husks, stems, sheaths and laminae, respectively. The possible reason for this difference is that the anthocyanin content of different organ types varies greatly, which makes various organ surfaces show inconsistent colors. Despite the fact that digital photography may also fail when the cells of the measured surface are irregular, because visible light images can only capture two-dimensional planes of data [72,80,81]. But it is worth recognizing that numerical images showed better predictive performance than spectral reflectance images [28,82]. For example, digital images with spectrophotometer data were compared to analyze the petal colors of eight species with variable pigmentation patterns [83], which found that spectrophotometers may underestimate the variability in spectral signals when the patterns are complex. This is because the spectrometer probe holder has a relatively small sampling area, which may result in different spectral measurements depending on whether it is incidentally oriented toward light or dark stripes or patches [83]. Though this can be resolved by measuring the reflectance at multiple points, the time required for analysis will undoubtedly add up. Overall, it is undeniable that our proposed method for quantifying the content of anthocyanins in purple corn based on digital image representation has been proven to offer new opportunities to accurately quantify the concentration of anthocyanins in different organs of purple corn [1,84,85]. The main advantages of this method are its high efficiency and that it is completely non-invasive and applicable to plant samples of any size and shape.

4.3. Model Application

Purple corn is regarded as having the darkest grains in the plant kingdom. Anthocyanin is a multifunctional active substance in purple corn, which has potential health-promoting properties [86–88]. It has been widely promoted as a health food and has also attracted the attention of the food and drug industries [56,77,89]. The speed of obtaining a new variety using traditional breeding methods is limited by the acquisition of crop phenotypic data, particularly on tissue inclusions, so it is imperative to develop a high-throughput plant phenotyping analysis. Non-destructive data collected via ground-based and aerial HTP techniques are highly desirable for application in plant breeding since they can be used to assess different traits in large-scale field trials [90–92]. RGB cameras produce digital images, can mimic human visual perception and are available at a low price and a high resolution on the market, and image analysis using free software is simple and easy to learn and requires little training. Therefore, the RGB imaging approach represents a valuable and practical tool for breeders [93,94]. By applying predictive models, breeders and researchers can assess the anthocyanin content of a large number of purple corn varieties more quickly. This method can save time and costs and improve breeding efficiency in the development of more nutritious and commercially valuable varieties of purple corn. Therefore, after the appropriate adjustments, such as obtaining data from multiple locations and years, the model proposed in our study can be extended to ground and UAV platforms, expanding the monitoring range [95–98]. Nowadays, RGB imaging obtained with the rapid development of smartphones has led to the creation of applications with ever-increasing utility, such as the plant phenotyping apps Canopeo (v2.0) [99], Plant Screen Mobile (v1.6) [100] and PhenoApp (v1.0) [101]. As technological innovation advances, a real-time and rapid anthocyanin content estimation platform may be developed. As a consequence, the non-destructive, rapid, high-throughput evaluation of anthocyanin will have good potential to be applied to breeding or cultivation in the anthocyanin industry.

5. Conclusions

Purple corn has potential applications in industry due to its rich anthocyanin content. The anthocyanin content largely varied by organ type. This dissection of plants into specific organs identified the cobs of purple corn as a vital source providing anthocyanins for industry use. Digital image technology based on a RGB camera represents a rapid, non-destructive way to estimate plant tissue inclusions. A linear relationship between the anthocyanin content and the color indices derived from the RGB images was found for various types of organs, which was further used to establish a model for the prediction of the anthocyanin content. The model was then testified to have achieved good accuracy with its NRMSE in the range of 7.90–27.20%. However, considering the power and ability of deep learning, in future work, we will obtain more data through continuous observation to explore the application of deep learning to estimating the anthocyanin content in purple corn. Overall, this study provides a cheap imaging method for rapid assays of anthocyanin content.

Supplementary Materials: The following supporting information can be downloaded at: https://www.mdpi.com/article/10.3390/agriculture14050744/s1, Figure S1: Meteorological data of purple corn planting season (6.12 to 9.09) from 2021 to 2023; Table S1: Meteorological parameters of purple corn growth period from 2021 to 2023.

Author Contributions: Y.S. conceived of and supervised the study. Z.W. carried out the experiment and drafted the paper. Y.L., K.W. and C.X. contributed to drafting and the data analyses. Y.W., X.W. and J.L. helped with the sampling and data analyses. Y.S. and Y.L. improved the manuscript. All authors have read and agreed to the published version of the manuscript.

Funding: The work was supported by Anhui Province Natural Science Foundation (2208085MC59), and Provincial Grant No. 2021H254.

Institutional Review Board Statement: Not applicable.

Informed Consent Statement: Not applicable.

Data Availability Statement: The data presented in this study are available on request from the corresponding author.

Conflicts of Interest: The authors declare no conflicts of interest.

References

1. Custodio-Mendoza, J.A.; Aktaş, H.; Zalewska, M.; Wyrwisz, J.; Kurek, M.A. A Review of Quantitative and Topical Analysis of Anthocyanins in Food. *Molecules* **2024**, *29*, 1735. [CrossRef] [PubMed]
2. Cheaib, A.; Mahmoud, L.M.; Vincent, C.; Killiny, N.; Dutt, M. Influence of Anthocyanin Expression on the Performance of Photosynthesis in Sweet Orange, *Citrus sinensis* (L.) Osbeck. *Plants* **2023**, *12*, 3965. [CrossRef] [PubMed]
3. Landi, M.; Tattini, M.; Gould, K.S. Multiple functional roles of anthocyanins in plant-environment interactions. *Environ. Exp. Bot.* **2015**, *119*, 4–17. [CrossRef]
4. Marone, D.; Mastrangelo, A.M.; Borrelli, G.M.; Mores, A.; Laidò, G.; Russo, M.A.; Ficco, D.B.M. Specialized metabolites: Physiological and biochemical role in stress resistance, strategies to improve their accumulation, and new applications in crop breeding and management. *Plant Physiol. Biochem.* **2022**, *172*, 48–55. [CrossRef] [PubMed]
5. Liu, H.; Liu, Z.; Wu, Y.; Zheng, L.; Zhang, G. Regulatory Mechanisms of Anthocyanin Biosynthesis in Apple and Pear. *Int. J. Mol. Sci.* **2021**, *22*, 8441. [CrossRef] [PubMed]
6. Ma, Y.; Xiang, S.; Cui, Z.; Li, K.; Zhang, Z. Molecular Dynamic Regulation of Na and Mg Ions on Lithium Carbonate Crystallisation in Salt Lakes. *J. Wuhan Univ. Technol.-Mat. Sci. Edit.* **2021**, *36*, 22–28. [CrossRef]
7. Marino, M.; Gardana, C.; Rendine, M.; Klimis-Zacas, D.; Riso, P.; Porrini, M.; Del Bo', C. Nutritional and Phytochemical Characterization of Freeze-Dried Raspberry (*Rubus idaeus*): A Comprehensive Analysis. *Foods* **2024**, *13*, 1051. [CrossRef]
8. Cozzolino, D. Phenolics and spectroscopy: Challenges and successful stories in the grape and wine industry. *J. Sci. Food Agric.* **2023**. [CrossRef]
9. Chachar, Z.; Lai, R.; Ahmed, N.; Lingling, M.; Chachar, S.; Paker, N.P.; Qi, Y. Cloned genes and genetic regulation of anthocyanin biosynthesis in maize, a comparative review. *Front. Plant Sci.* **2024**, *15*, 1310634. [CrossRef]
10. García-Villegas, A.; Fernández-Ochoa, Á.; Alañón, M.E.; Rojas-García, A.; Arráez-Román, D.; Cádiz-Gurrea, M.d.l.L.; Segura-Carretero, A. Bioactive Compounds and Potential Health Benefits through Cosmetic Applications of Cherry Stem Extract. *Int. J. Mol. Sci.* **2024**, *25*, 3723. [CrossRef]

11. Global Flavonoids Market Size & Share Report, 2025. Available online: https://www.grandviewresearch.com/industry-analysis/flavonoids-market (accessed on 13 November 2023).
12. Romani, A.; Campo, M.; Urciuoli, S.; Marrone, G.; Noce, A.; Bernini, R. An Industrial and Sustainable Platform for the Production of Bioactive Micronized Powders and Extracts Enriched in Polyphenols from *Olea europaea* L. and *Vitis vinifera* L. Wastes. *Front. Nutr.* **2020**, *7*, 120. [CrossRef]
13. Leonarski, E.; Kuasnei, M.; Cesca, K.; de Oliveira, D.; Zielinski, A.A.F. Black rice and its by-products: Anthocyanin-rich extracts and their biological potential. *Crit. Rev. Food Sci. Nutr.* **2023**, 1–19. [CrossRef]
14. Silva, S.; Costa, E.M.; Calhau, C.; Morais, R.M.; Pintado, M.E. Anthocyanin extraction from plant tissues: A review. *Crit. Rev. Food Sci. Nutr.* **2017**, *57*, 3072–3083. [CrossRef]
15. Somavat, P.; Kumar, D.; Singh, V. Techno-economic feasibility analysis of blue and purple corn processing for anthocyanin extraction and ethanol production using modified dry grind process. *Ind. Crops Prod.* **2018**, *115*, 78–87. [CrossRef]
16. Jasińska, K.; Fabiszewska, A.; Białecka-Florjańczyk, E.; Zieniuk, B. Mini-Review on the Enzymatic Lipophilization of Phenolics Present in Plant Extracts with the Special Emphasis on Anthocyanins. *Antioxidants* **2022**, *11*, 1528. [CrossRef] [PubMed]
17. Carrillo, C.; Nieto, G.; Martínez-Zamora, L.; Ros, G.; Kamiloglu, S.; Munekata, P.E.S.; Pateiro, M.; Lorenzo, J.M.; Fernández-López, J.; Viuda-Martos, M.; et al. Novel Approaches for the Recovery of Natural Pigments with Potential Health Effects. *J. Agric. Food Chem.* **2022**, *70*, 6864–6883. [CrossRef]
18. Veloso, M.I.; Coelho, E.; Trabulo, O.; Coimbra, M.A. Elderberry Concentrate Juice Industrial By-Products Characterization and Valorisation. *Appl. Sci.* **2022**, *12*, 9463. [CrossRef]
19. Li, C.-Y.; Kim, H.-W.; Won, S.; Min, H.-K.; Park, K.-J.; Park, J.-Y.; Ahn, M.-S.; Rhee, H.-I. Corn Husk as a Potential Source of Anthocyanins. *J. Agric. Food Chem.* **2008**, *56*, 11413–11416. [CrossRef] [PubMed]
20. Fernandez-Aulis, F.; Hernandez-Vazquez, L.; Aguilar-Osorio, G.; Arrieta-Baez, D.; Navarro-Ocana, A. Extraction and Identification of Anthocyanins in Corn Cob and Corn Husk from Cacahuacintle Maize. *J. Food Sci.* **2019**, *84*, 954–962. [CrossRef]
21. Hong, H.T.; Netzel, M.E.; O'Hare, T.J. Optimisation of extraction procedure and development of LC–DAD–MS methodology for anthocyanin analysis in anthocyanin-pigmented corn kernels. *Food Chem.* **2020**, *319*, 126515. [CrossRef]
22. Ata-Ul-Karim, S.T.; Cao, Q.; Zhu, Y.; Tang, L.; Rehmani, M.I.A.; Cao, W. Non-destructive Assessment of Plant Nitrogen Parameters Using Leaf Chlorophyll Measurements in Rice. *Front. Plant Sci.* **2016**, *7*, 1829. [CrossRef] [PubMed]
23. Ji, Y.; Chen, Z.; Cheng, Q.; Liu, R.; Li, M.; Yan, X.; Li, G.; Wang, D.; Fu, L.; Ma, Y.; et al. Estimation of plant height and yield based on UAV imagery in faba bean (*Vicia faba* L.). *Plant Methods* **2022**, *18*, 26. [CrossRef] [PubMed]
24. Huang, H.; Deng, J.; Lan, Y.; Yang, A.; Zhang, L.; Wen, S.; Zhang, H.; Zhang, Y.; Deng, Y. Detection of Helminthosporium Leaf Blotch Disease Based on UAV Imagery. *Appl. Sci.* **2019**, *9*, 558. [CrossRef]
25. Heidarian Dehkordi, R.; El Jarroudi, M.; Kouadio, L.; Meersmans, J.; Beyer, M. Monitoring Wheat Leaf Rust and Stripe Rust in Winter Wheat Using High-Resolution UAV-Based Red-Green-Blue Imagery. *Remote Sens.* **2020**, *12*, 3696. [CrossRef]
26. Wan, L.; Zhang, J.; Dong, X.; Du, X.; Cen, H. Unmanned aerial vehicle-based field phenotyping of crop biomass using growth traits retrieved from PROSAIL model. *Comput. Electron. Agric.* **2021**, *187*, 106304. [CrossRef]
27. Makanza, R.; Zaman-Allah, M.; Cairns, J.E.; Magorokosho, C.; Tarekegne, A.; Olsen, M.; Prasanna, B.M. High-Throughput Phenotyping of Canopy Cover and Senescence in Maize Field Trials Using Aerial Digital Canopy Imaging. *Remote Sens.* **2018**, *10*, 330. [CrossRef] [PubMed]
28. del Valle, J.C.; Gallardo-López, A.; Buide, M.L.; Whittall, J.B.; Narbona, E. Digital photography provides a fast, reliable, and noninvasive method to estimate anthocyanin pigment concentration in reproductive and vegetative plant tissues. *Ecol. Evol.* **2018**, *8*, 3064–3076. [CrossRef] [PubMed]
29. Gong, L.; Zhu, C.; Luo, Y.; Fu, X. Spectral Reflectance Reconstruction from Red-Green-Blue (RGB) Images for Chlorophyll Content Detection. *Appl. Spectrosc.* **2023**, *77*, 200–209. [CrossRef] [PubMed]
30. Riccardi, M.; Mele, G.; Pulvento, C.; Lavini, A.; d'Andria, R.; Jacobsen, S.-E. Non-destructive evaluation of chlorophyll content in quinoa and amaranth leaves by simple and multiple regression analysis of RGB image components. *Photosynth. Res.* **2014**, *120*, 263–272. [CrossRef]
31. Wood, N.J.; Baker, A.; Quinnell, R.J.; Camargo-Valero, M.A. A Simple and Non-destructive Method for Chlorophyll Quantification of Chlamydomonas Cultures Using Digital Image Analysis. *Front. Bioeng. Biotechnol.* **2020**, *8*, 746. [CrossRef]
32. Wang, Y.; Wang, D.; Shi, P.; Omasa, K. Estimating rice chlorophyll content and leaf nitrogen concentration with a digital still color camera under natural light. *Plant Methods* **2014**, *10*, 36. [CrossRef] [PubMed]
33. Faragó, D.; Sass, L.; Valkai, I.; Andrási, N.; Szabados, L. PlantSize Offers an Affordable, Non-destructive Method to Measure Plant Size and Color in Vitro. *Front. Plant Sci.* **2018**, *9*, 219. [CrossRef] [PubMed]
34. Zhang, H.; Ge, Y.; Xie, X.; Atefi, A.; Wijewardane, N.K.; Thapa, S. High throughput analysis of leaf chlorophyll content in sorghum using RGB, hyperspectral, and fluorescence imaging and sensor fusion. *Plant Methods* **2022**, *18*, 60. [CrossRef] [PubMed]
35. Bennett, C.; Sookwong, P.; Jakmunee, J.; Mahatheeranont, S. Smartphone digital image colorimetric determination of the total monomeric anthocyanin content in black rice via the pH differential method. *Anal. Methods* **2021**, *13*, 3348–3358. [CrossRef] [PubMed]
36. Junker, L.V.; Ensminger, I. Relationship between leaf optical properties, chlorophyll fluorescence and pigment changes in senescing Acer saccharum leaves. *Tree Physiol.* **2016**, *36*, 694–711. [CrossRef]

37. Wang, Z.; Sun, W.; Liu, X.; Li, Y.; Collins, B.; Ullah, N.; Song, Y. Analysis on Heat Characteristics for Summer Maize Cropping in a Semi-Arid Region. *Agronomy* **2022**, *12*, 1435. [CrossRef]
38. Andersen, Ø.M.; Jordheim, M. Anthocyanins. In *Encyclopedia of Life Sciences*; John Wiley & Sons, Ltd.: Hoboken, NJ, USA, 2010; ISBN 978-0-470-01590-2.
39. Alappat, B.; Alappat, J. Anthocyanin Pigments: Beyond Aesthetics. *Molecules* **2020**, *25*, 5500. [CrossRef]
40. White, T.E.; Dalrymple, R.L.; Noble, D.W.A.; O'Hanlon, J.C.; Zurek, D.B.; Umbers, K.D.L. Reproducible research in the study of biological coloration. *Anim. Behav.* **2015**, *106*, 51–57. [CrossRef]
41. Stevens, M.; Párraga, C.A.; Cuthill, I.C.; Partridge, J.C.; Troscianko, T.S. Using digital photography to study animal coloration. *Biol. J. Linn. Soc.* **2007**, *90*, 211–237. [CrossRef]
42. Akkaynak, D.; Treibitz, T.; Xiao, B.; Gürkan, U.A.; Allen, J.J.; Demirci, U.; Hanlon, R.T. Use of commercial off-the-shelf digital cameras for scientific data acquisition and scene-specific color calibration. *J. Opt. Soc. Am. A JOSAA* **2014**, *31*, 312–321. [CrossRef]
43. Tedla, S.; Wang, Y.; Patel, M.; Brown, M.S. Analyzing color imaging failure on consumer-grade cameras. *J. Opt. Soc. Am. A JOSAA* **2022**, *39*, B21–B27. [CrossRef] [PubMed]
44. Liang, Y.; Urano, D.; Liao, K.-L.; Hedrick, T.L.; Gao, Y.; Jones, A.M. A nondestructive method to estimate the chlorophyll content of Arabidopsis seedlings. *Plant Methods* **2017**, *13*, 26. [CrossRef] [PubMed]
45. Mathieu, R.; Pouget, M.; Cervelle, B.; Escadafal, R. Relationships between Satellite-Based Radiometric Indices Simulated Using Laboratory Reflectance Data and Typic Soil Color of an Arid Environment. *Remote Sens. Environ.* **1998**, *66*, 17–28. [CrossRef]
46. Mizunuma, T.; Mencuccini, M.; Wingate, L.; Ogee, J.; Nichol, C.; Grace, J. Sensitivity of colour indices for discriminating leaf colours from digital photographs. *Methods Ecol. Evol.* **2014**, *5*, 1078–1085. [CrossRef]
47. Tan, J.; Han, Y.; Han, B.; Qi, X.; Cai, X.; Ge, S.; Xue, H. Extraction and purification of anthocyanins: A review. *J. Agric. Food Res.* **2022**, *8*, 100306. [CrossRef]
48. Bai, X.; Zhou, L.; Zhou, L.; Cang, S.; Liu, Y.; Liu, R.; Liu, J.; Feng, X.; Fan, R. The Research Progress of Extraction, Purification and Analysis Methods of Phenolic Compounds from Blueberry: A Comprehensive Review. *Molecules* **2023**, *28*, 3610. [CrossRef]
49. Warton, D.I.; Wright, I.J.; Falster, D.S.; Westoby, M. Bivariate line-fitting methods for allometry. *Biol. Rev. Camb. Philos. Soc.* **2006**, *81*, 259–291. [CrossRef]
50. Zhang, P.; Wang, X.; Song, P.X.K.; Zhang, J.Y.; So, W.F.K.; Team, T.M.S.; Sugar, C.A.; James, G.M.; Serban, N.; Wasserman, L. *The R Book*; John Wiley & Sons, Ltd.: Hoboken, NJ, USA, 2012; pp. 449–497, ISBN 978-1-118-44890-8.
51. Loague, K.; Green, R.E. Statistical and graphical methods for evaluating solute transport models: Overview and application. *J. Contam. Hydrol.* **1991**, *7*, 51–73. [CrossRef]
52. Qiao, L.; Tang, W.; Gao, D.; Zhao, R.; An, L.; Li, M.; Sun, H.; Song, D. UAV-based chlorophyll content estimation by evaluating vegetation index responses under different crop coverages. *Comput. Electron. Agric.* **2022**, *196*, 106775. [CrossRef]
53. Kim, C.; van Iersel, M.W. Image-based phenotyping to estimate anthocyanin concentrations in lettuce. *Front. Plant Sci.* **2023**, *14*, 1155722. [CrossRef]
54. He, L.; Sun, W.; Chen, X.; Han, L.; Li, J.; Ma, Y.; Song, Y. Modeling Maize Canopy Morphology in Response to Increased Plant Density. *Front. Plant Sci.* **2021**, *11*, 533514. [CrossRef] [PubMed]
55. Cuevas Montilla, E.; Hillebrand, S.; Antezana, A.; Winterhalter, P. Soluble and Bound Phenolic Compounds in Different Bolivian Purple Corn (*Zea mays* L.) Cultivars. *J. Agric. Food Chem.* **2011**, *59*, 7068–7074. [CrossRef] [PubMed]
56. Cai, T.; Ge-Zhang, S.; Song, M. Anthocyanins in metabolites of purple corn. *Front. Plant Sci.* **2023**, *14*, 1154535. [CrossRef] [PubMed]
57. Gullón, P.; Eibes, G.; Lorenzo, J.M.; Pérez-Rodríguez, N.; Lú-Chau, T.A.; Gullón, B. Green sustainable process to revalorize purple corn cobs within a biorefinery frame: Co-production of bioactive extracts. *Sci. Total Environ.* **2020**, *709*, 136236. [CrossRef] [PubMed]
58. Yadav, S.P.; Ibaraki, Y.; Gupta, S.D. Estimation of the chlorophyll content of micropropagated potato plants using RGB based image analysis. *Plant Cell Tissue Organ. Cult.* **2010**, *100*, 183–188. [CrossRef]
59. Lou, H.; Hu, Y.; Zhang, L.; Sun, P.; Lu, H. Nondestructive evaluation of the changes of total flavonoid, total phenols, ABTS and DPPH radical scavenging activities, and sugars during mulberry (*Morus alba* L.) fruits development by chlorophyll fluorescence and RGB intensity values. *LWT-Food Sci. Technol.* **2012**, *47*, 19–24. [CrossRef]
60. Qin, Y.; Liu, Y.; Yong, H.; Liu, J.; Zhang, X.; Liu, J. Preparation and characterization of active and intelligent packaging films based on cassava starch and anthocyanins from Lycium ruthenicum Murr. *Int. J. Biol. Macromol.* **2019**, *134*, 80–90. [CrossRef] [PubMed]
61. Ghareaghajlou, N.; Hallaj-Nezhadi, S.; Ghasempour, Z. Red cabbage anthocyanins: Stability, extraction, biological activities and applications in food systems. *Food Chem.* **2021**, *365*, 130482. [CrossRef]
62. Brudzyńska, P.; Sionkowska, A.; Grisel, M. Plant-Derived Colorants for Food, Cosmetic and Textile Industries: A Review. *Materials* **2021**, *14*, 3484. [CrossRef]
63. Cai, D.; Li, X.; Chen, J.; Jiang, X.; Ma, X.; Sun, J.; Tian, L.; Vidyarthi, S.K.; Xu, J.; Pan, Z.; et al. A comprehensive review on innovative and advanced stabilization approaches of anthocyanin by modifying structure and controlling environmental factors. *Food Chem.* **2022**, *366*, 130611. [CrossRef]
64. Calderón-Reyes, C.; Pezoa, R.S.; Leal, P.; Ribera-Fonseca, A.; Cáceres, C.; Riquelme, I.; Zambrano, T.; Peña, D.; Alberdi, M.; Reyes-Díaz, M. Anthocyanin-Rich Extracts of Calafate (*Berberis microphylla* G. Forst.) Fruits Decrease In Vitro Viability and Migration of Human Gastric and Gallbladder Cancer Cell Lines. *J. Soil. Sci. Plant Nutr.* **2020**, *20*, 1891–1903. [CrossRef]

65. Gašić, U.; Ćirić, I.; Pejčić, T.; Radenković, D.; Djordjević, V.; Radulović, S.; Tešić, Ž. Polyphenols as Possible Agents for Pancreatic Diseases. *Antioxidants* **2020**, *9*, 547. [CrossRef] [PubMed]
66. Matboli, M.; Hasanin, A.H.; Hussein, R.; El-Nakeep, S.; Habib, E.K.; Ellackany, R.; Saleh, L.A. Cyanidin 3-glucoside modulated cell cycle progression in liver precancerous lesion, in vivo study. *World J. Gastroenterol.* **2021**, *27*, 1435–1450. [CrossRef] [PubMed]
67. Park, S.; Choi, M.; Lee, M. Effects of Anthocyanin Supplementation on Reduction of Obesity Criteria: A Systematic Review and Meta-Analysis of Randomized Controlled Trials. *Nutrients* **2021**, *13*, 2121. [CrossRef] [PubMed]
68. Tang, S.; Kan, J.; Sun, R.; Cai, H.; Hong, J.; Jin, C.; Zong, S. Anthocyanins from purple sweet potato alleviate doxorubicin-induced cardiotoxicity in vitro and in vivo. *J. Food Biochem.* **2021**, *45*, e13869. [CrossRef]
69. Bechtold, T.; Mahmud-Ali, A.; Mussak, R. Anthocyanin dyes extracted from grape pomace for the purpose of textile dyeing. *J. Sci. Food Agric.* **2007**, *87*, 2589–2595. [CrossRef] [PubMed]
70. Barnes, J.S.; Nguyen, H.P.; Shen, S.; Schug, K.A. General method for extraction of blueberry anthocyanins and identification using high performance liquid chromatography–electrospray ionization-ion trap-time of flight-mass spectrometry. *J. Chromatogr. A* **2009**, *1216*, 4728–4735. [CrossRef] [PubMed]
71. Assous, M.T.M.; Abdel-Hady, M.M.; Medany, G.M. Evaluation of red pigment extracted from purple carrots and its utilization as antioxidant and natural food colorants. *Ann. Agric. Sci.* **2014**, *59*, 1–7. [CrossRef]
72. Tanner, F.; Tonn, S.; de Wit, J.; Van den Ackerveken, G.; Berger, B.; Plett, D. Sensor-based phenotyping of above-ground plant-pathogen interactions. *Plant Methods* **2022**, *18*, 35. [CrossRef]
73. Choe, E.; Rocheford, T.R. Genetic and QTL analysis of pericarp thickness and ear architecture traits of Korean waxy corn germplasm. *Euphytica* **2012**, *183*, 243–260. [CrossRef]
74. Lim, S.; Yi, G. Investigating seed mineral composition in Korean landrace maize (*Zea mays* L.) and its kernel texture specificity. *J. Integr. Agric.* **2019**, *18*, 1996–2005. [CrossRef]
75. Salvador-Reyes, R.; Clerici, M.T.P.S. Peruvian Andean maize: General characteristics, nutritional properties, bioactive compounds, and culinary uses. *Food Res. Int.* **2020**, *130*, 108934. [CrossRef] [PubMed]
76. Kim, J.-T.; Yi, G.; Chung, I.-M.; Son, B.-Y.; Bae, H.-H.; Go, Y.S.; Ha, J.Y.; Baek, S.-B.; Kim, S.-L. Timing and Pattern of Anthocyanin Accumulation during Grain Filling in Purple Waxy Corn (*Zea mays* L.) Suggest Optimal Harvest Dates. *ACS Omega* **2020**, *5*, 15702–15708. [CrossRef] [PubMed]
77. Chatham, L.A.; Paulsmeyer, M.; Juvik, J.A. Prospects for economical natural colorants: Insights from maize. *Theor. Appl. Genet.* **2019**, *132*, 2927–2946. [CrossRef] [PubMed]
78. Menozzi, C.; Calvini, R.; Nigro, G.; Tessarin, P.; Bossio, D.; Calderisi, M.; Ferrari, V.; Foca, G.; Ulrici, A. Design and application of a smartphone-based device for in vineyard determination of anthocyanins content in red grapes. *Microchem. J.* **2023**, *191*, 108811. [CrossRef]
79. Ingrouille, M. Understanding flowers and flowering: An integrated approach. *Ann. Bot.* **2009**, *103*, vi–vii. [CrossRef]
80. Kay, Q.O.N.; Daoud, H.S.; Stirton, C.H. Pigment distribution, light reflection and cell structure in petals. *Bot. J. Linn. Soc.* **1981**, *83*, 57–83. [CrossRef]
81. van der Kooi, C.J.; Elzenga, J.T.M.; Staal, M.; Stavenga, D.G. How to colour a flower: On the optical principles of flower coloration. *Proc. Biol. Sci.* **2016**, *283*, 20160429. [CrossRef] [PubMed]
82. Gómez, J.; Lián-Cembrano, G. SpotEgg: An image-processing tool for automatised analysis of colouration and spottiness. *J. Avian Biol.* **2017**, *48*, 502–512. [CrossRef]
83. Garcia, J.E.; Greentree, A.D.; Shrestha, M.; Dorin, A.; Dyer, A.G. Flower colours through the lens: Quantitative measurement with visible and ultraviolet digital photography. *PLoS ONE* **2014**, *9*, e96646. [CrossRef]
84. Berger, K.; Machwitz, M.; Kycko, M.; Kefauver, S.C.; Van Wittenberghe, S.; Gerhards, M.; Verrelst, J.; Atzberger, C.; van der Tol, C.; Damm, A.; et al. Multi-sensor spectral synergies for crop stress detection and monitoring in the optical domain: A review. *Remote Sens. Environ.* **2022**, *280*, 113198. [CrossRef] [PubMed]
85. Liu, Y.; Zhang, Y.; Zhou, Y.; Feng, X. Anthocyanins in Different Food Matrices: Recent Updates on Extraction, Purification and Analysis Techniques. *Crit. Rev. Anal. Chem.* **2022**, 1–32. [CrossRef]
86. Petroni, K.; Pilu, R.; Tonelli, C. Anthocyanins in corn: A wealth of genes for human health. *Planta* **2014**, *240*, 901–911. [CrossRef]
87. Lao, F.; Sigurdson, G.T.; Giusti, M.M. Health Benefits of Purple Corn (*Zea mays* L.) Phenolic Compounds. *Compr. Rev. Food Sci. Food Saf.* **2017**, *16*, 234–246. [CrossRef] [PubMed]
88. Elisa, D.-H.; Marcela, G.-M.; Janet Alejandra, G.-U.; Martha Elena, D.-H. The nutraceutical value of maize (*Zea mays* L.) landraces and the determinants of its variability: A review. *J. Cereal Sci.* **2022**, *103*, 103399. [CrossRef]
89. Robles-Plata, V.T.; Serna Saldivar, S.; de Dios Figueroa-Cárdenas, J.; Rooney, W.L.; Dávila-Vega, J.P.; Chuck-Hernández, C.; Escalante-Aburto, A. Biophysical, Nutraceutical, and Technofunctional Features of Specialty Cereals: Pigmented Popcorn and Sorghum. *Foods* **2023**, *12*, 2301. [CrossRef]
90. Loladze, A.; Rodrigues, F.A.; Toledo, F.; San Vicente, F.; Gérard, B.; Boddupalli, M.P. Application of Remote Sensing for Phenotyping Tar Spot Complex Resistance in Maize. *Front. Plant Sci.* **2019**, *10*, 552. [CrossRef]
91. Watt, M.; Fiorani, F.; Usadel, B.; Rascher, U.; Muller, O.; Schurr, U. Phenotyping: New Windows into the Plant for Breeders. *Annu. Rev. Plant Biol.* **2020**, *71*, 689–712. [CrossRef]
92. Lobos, G.A.; Estrada, F.; Del Pozo, A.; Romero-Bravo, S.; Astudillo, C.A.; Mora-Poblete, F. Challenges for a Massive Implementation of Phenomics in Plant Breeding Programs. *Methods Mol. Biol.* **2022**, *2539*, 135–157. [CrossRef]

93. Hu, Y.; Schmidhalter, U. Opportunity and challenges of phenotyping plant salt tolerance. *Trends Plant Sci.* **2023**, *28*, 552–566. [CrossRef]
94. Rößle, D.; Prey, L.; Ramgraber, L.; Hanemann, A.; Cremers, D.; Noack, P.O.; Schön, T. Efficient Noninvasive FHB Estimation using RGB Images from a Novel Multiyear, Multirater Dataset. *Plant Phenomics* **2023**, *5*, 0068. [CrossRef] [PubMed]
95. Jiang, Z.; Tu, H.; Bai, B.; Yang, C.; Zhao, B.; Guo, Z.; Liu, Q.; Zhao, H.; Yang, W.; Xiong, L.; et al. Combining UAV-RGB high-throughput field phenotyping and genome-wide association study to reveal genetic variation of rice germplasms in dynamic response to drought stress. *New Phytol.* **2021**, *232*, 440–455. [CrossRef] [PubMed]
96. Shu, M.; Fei, S.; Zhang, B.; Yang, X.; Guo, Y.; Li, B.; Ma, Y. Application of UAV Multisensor Data and Ensemble Approach for High-Throughput Estimation of Maize Phenotyping Traits. *Plant Phenomics* **2022**, *2022*, 9802585. [CrossRef] [PubMed]
97. Fei, S.; Hassan, M.A.; Xiao, Y.; Su, X.; Chen, Z.; Cheng, Q.; Duan, F.; Chen, R.; Ma, Y. UAV-based multi-sensor data fusion and machine learning algorithm for yield prediction in wheat. *Precis. Agric.* **2023**, *24*, 187–212. [CrossRef] [PubMed]
98. Sarkar, S.; Zhou, J.; Scaboo, A.; Zhou, J.; Aloysius, N.; Lim, T.T. Assessment of Soybean Lodging Using UAV Imagery and Machine Learning. *Plants* **2023**, *12*, 2893. [CrossRef] [PubMed]
99. Patrignani, A.; Ochsner, T.E. Canopeo: A Powerful New Tool for Measuring Fractional Green Canopy Cover. *Agron. J.* **2015**, *107*, 2312–2320. [CrossRef]
100. Müller-Linow, M.; Wilhelm, J.; Briese, C.; Wojciechowski, T.; Schurr, U.; Fiorani, F. Plant Screen Mobile: An open-source mobile device app for plant trait analysis. *Plant Methods* **2019**, *15*, 2. [CrossRef]
101. Röckel, F.; Schreiber, T.; Schüler, D.; Braun, U.; Krukenberg, I.; Schwander, F.; Peil, A.; Brandt, C.; Willner, E.; Gransow, D.; et al. PhenoApp: A mobile tool for plant phenotyping to record field and greenhouse observations. *F1000Research* **2022**, *11*, 12. [CrossRef]

agriculture

MDPI

Article

Estimating Corn Growth Parameters by Integrating Optical and Synthetic Aperture Radar Features into the Water Cloud Model

Yanyan Wang [1,2], Zhaocong Wu [1,*], Shanjun Luo [1,2], Xinyan Liu [1,2], Shuaibing Liu [2] and Xinxin Huang [3]

1 Aerospace Information Research Institute, Henan Academy of Sciences, Zhengzhou 450046, China; yyan@hnas.ac.cn (Y.W.); luoshanjun@hnas.ac.cn (S.L.); lxy_rs@hnas.ac.cn (X.L.)
2 School of Remote Sensing and Information Engineering, Wuhan University, Wuhan 430072, China; liushuaibing@whu.edu.cn
3 School of Economics & Management, Northwest University, Xi'an 710127, China; huangxinxin@stumail.nwu.edu.cn
* Correspondence: zcwoo@hnas.ac.cn

Abstract: Crop growth parameters are the basis for evaluation of crop growth status and crop yield. The aim of this study was to develop a more accurate estimation model for corn growth parameters combined with multispectral vegetation indexes (VI_{opt}) and the differential radar information (DRI) derived from SAR data. Targeting the estimation of corn plant height (H) and the BBCH (Biologische Bundesanstalt, Bundessortenamt and CHemical industry) phenological parameters, this study compared the estimation accuracies of various multispectral vegetation indexes (VI_{opt}) and the corresponding VI_{DRI} (vegetation index corrected by DRI) indexes in inverting the corn growth parameters. (1) When comparing the estimation accuracies of four multispectral vegetation indexes (NDVI, NDVIre1, NDVIre2, and S2REP), NDVI showed the lowest estimation accuracy, with a normalized root mean square error (nRMSE) of 20.84% for the plant height, while S2REP showed the highest estimation accuracy (nRMSE = 16.05%). In addition, NDVIre2 (nRMSE = 16.18%) and S2REP (16.05%) exhibited a higher accuracy than NDVIre1 (nRMSE = 19.27%). Similarly, for BBCH, the nRMSEs of the four indexes were 24.17%, 22.49%, 17.04% and 16.60%, respectively. This confirmed that the multispectral vegetation indexes based on the red-edge bands were more sensitive to the growth parameters, especially for the Sentinel-2 red-edge 2 band. (2) The constructed VI_{DRI} indexes were more beneficial than the VI_{opt} indexes in enhancing the estimation accuracy of corn growth parameters. Specifically, the nRMSEs of the four VI_{DRI} indexes ($NDVI_{DRI}$, $NDVIre1_{DRI}$, $NDVIre2_{DRI}$, and $S2REP_{DRI}$) decreased to 19.64%, 18.11%, 15.00%, and 14.64% for plant height, and to 23.24%, 21.58%, 15.79%, and 15.91% for BBCH, indicating that even in cases of high vegetation coverage, the introduction of SAR DRI features can further improve the estimation accuracy of growth parameters. Our findings also demonstrated that the $NDVIre2_{DRI}$ and $S2REP_{DRI}$ indexes constructed using red-edge 2 band information of Sentinel-2 and SAR DRI features had more advantages in improving the estimation accuracy of corn growth parameters.

Keywords: red-edge vegetation index; DRI; plant height; BBCH

1. Introduction

Optical remote sensing images can obtain rich spectral features of vegetation canopy, especially the red-edge bands sensitive to green vegetation, which have absolute advantages for monitoring crop growth. However, optical remote sensing images are susceptible to weather conditions. It is often difficult to obtain satisfactory optical images during the cloudy and rainy season of crop growth. In view of this, some scholars have studied methods for monitoring crop growth based on time-series Synthetic Aperture Radar (SAR) images [1,2]. However, these methods require SAR images throughout the entire crop growth season, with a large data volume and complex data processing. Moreover, using SAR data alone cannot effectively utilize the rich spectral features of crop canopies reflected by optical data. Therefore, removing the need for time-series SAR data, this study investigated a method for estimating corn growth parameters by combining multispectral and backscatter features based on partially obtainable optical and SAR data during the crop growth season.

Existing research has shown that there is a good correlation between the optical vegetation indexes and crop growth parameters [3,4]. However, when vegetation coverage or aboveground biomass is high, especially for corn crops with a large plant size, the optical vegetation indexes are more prone to saturation in the middle or later growth stages [5,6]. At this time, the optical vegetation indexes are less sensitive to the crop growth parameters. Some studies have found that there is a better correlation between the red-edge bands and the growth parameters of green vegetation. The red-edge vegetation indexes can weaken the saturation phenomenon to a certain extent when the vegetation coverage is high, and they can more effectively monitor the crop growth status and the growth parameters [7,8]. However, even the red-edge vegetation indexes, which are sensitive to crop growth changes, only reflect the spectral reflectance characteristics of the vegetation canopy and cannot reflect the internal structural characteristics of the crop canopy. In comparison, SAR signals are more sensitive to the internal structure and geometric characteristics of the crop due to their penetration ability [9,10], which to some extent compensates for the shortcomings of optical image data [11]. At present, there is still relatively little research on using complementary information from optical and SAR data to estimate crop growth parameters, but some progress has been made [12,13]. Luo et al. proposed a method that combined optical and SAR features to estimate the corn LAI (Leaf Area Index) and biomass parameters, and the results showed that combining spectral and texture features can significantly improve the estimation accuracy of the crop LAI and biomass [14]. Abdikan et al. verified the correlation between variables determined from Synthetic Aperture Radar (SAR) and optical images and the plant height of the sunflower [15]. Yeasin et al., based on machine learning models, examined whether combined Sentinel-1 and Sentinel-2 data are more efficient in predicting the sugarcane phenology than Sentinel-1 and Sentinel-2 data alone [16]. However, the current research based on the combination of these two different types of features is at the data level. There is little analysis of the different responses of optical and SAR features to crop growth parameters from at mechanistic level.

Radar vegetation scattering models describe the scattering mechanism of radar signals on vegetation-covered surfaces, and they accurately characterize the scattering and absorption characteristics of radar waves on these surfaces [17]. Among them, the Michigan Microwave Canopy Scattering (MIMICS) model is currently the most comprehensive vegetation scattering model, which has been used in the study of scattering characteristics of various vegetation types since its establishment [18,19]. However, the MIMICS model has a large number of input parameters, which to some extent affects the accuracy of vegetation scattering model construction and crop growth parameter estimation [20]. The Water Cloud Model (WCM), as one of the typical semi-empirical scattering models, does not require complex geometric mathematical models to describe the interaction between microwaves and vegetation. It is more general than empirical models and easier to use than physical models [21,22]. It has been widely used in the evaluation of vegetation growth parameters in recent years. Yang et al. used three scattering components obtained from polarization decomposition, coupling those with the modified WCM, and they estimated the rice LAI, plant height, and panicle biomass based on time-series RADARSAT-2 fully polarized SAR data throughout the entire growth cycle [23]. Kweon et al. improved the WCM based on corn and soybean crops by introducing the mean and standard deviation of crop canopy leaf inclination distribution, further enhancing the estimation accuracy of crop growth parameters based on the WCM [24]. In addition, Bai et al. proposed a soil moisture estimation method based on the WCM and the Advanced Integral Equation Model (AIEM), and they found that the method has the potential to estimate crop growth parameters [25]. These studies have verified that the scattering mechanism of radar waves over vegetation-covered surfaces described by the WCM can effectively explain the scattering contribution of the vegetation layer and thus achieve growth parameter estimation for different crops.

Therefore, the aim of this study was to explore the combined method of using complementary optical and SAR information at the mechanistic level, and to construct a growth parameter estimation model suitable for the corn crop. Since the WCM is most suitable for describing the microwave scattering mechanism in areas with a relatively uniform vegetation cover [26,27], the optical and SAR satellite images selected in this paper were all in the late jointing or tasseling stages of the corn crop. At this time, the corn already has a large plant body size, and the ground is completely covered by the vegetation, meeting the condition that volume scattering dominates, which is in accordance with the principles of the WCM. In order to obtain a more accurate growth parameter estimation model, this study comprehensively utilized the advantages of optical and SAR data, combined with the principle of the WCM, without the need for other external data or a large volume of data. This approach led us to develop a new method that integrates multispectral vegetation indexes and differential radar information (DRI) features, achieving the high-precision estimation of crop growth parameters. In this paper, estimation models of field corn plant height and phenological stage parameters, respectively, are presented.

2. Materials and Methods

2.1. Experimental Area

The research area is located in Jiaozuo City, Henan Province, with the central coordinates of 113°23′ E and 35°12′ N. Jiaozuo is bordered by the Yellow River in the south and the Taihang Mountains in the north. It is one of the most famous grain-producing areas in China. This area is mainly planted with wheat, corn, soybeans, peanuts, potatoes, etc. The region has a temperate monsoon climate with four distinct seasons. The annual average temperature is 13 °C, with January being the coldest month at an average temperature of 0 °C, while July is the hottest with an average monthly temperature of 28 °C. The annual precipitation in this area is about 600–1200 mm. The main agricultural planting mode is a winter wheat and summer corn rotation. Summer corn is usually sown as soon as possible after the winter wheat harvest in early June and harvested at the end of September, with the entire growth period lasting approximately 110 days. The locations of the experimental area and ground sampling points are shown in Figure 1.

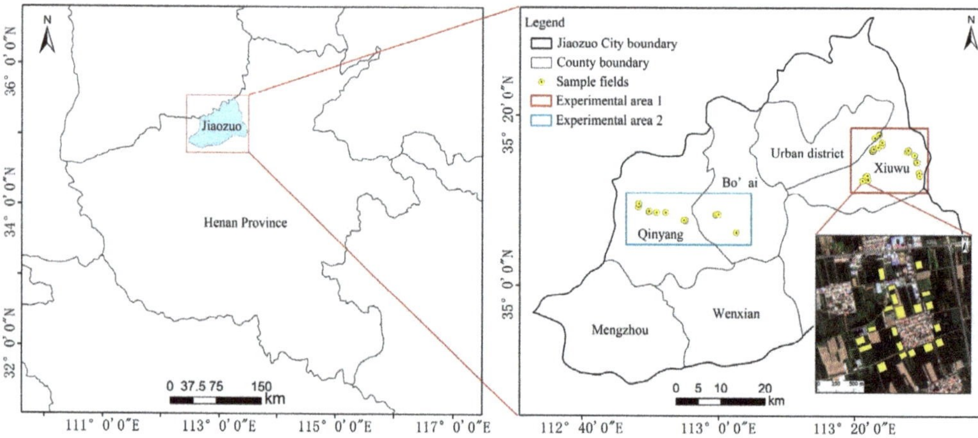

Figure 1. Location of the experimental areas and some ground sampling points (Yellow rectangles show the specific sampling fields).

The experimental area was divided into experimental area 1, located in Xiuwu County to the east of Jiaozuo City, and experimental area 2, located in Qinyang and Bo'ai Counties to the west of Jiaozuo City. In the study area, experimental area 1 was covered by the 113 and 40 orbit data of the Sentinel-1 satellite, while only the 113 orbit data covered experimental area 2. Therefore, the Sentinel-1 SAR satellite data for experimental areas 1 and 2 had different measurement dates and radar incidence angles. Since the SAR data intensity is affected by the incidence angle, and the radar incidence angle varies greatly in different sample fields, especially when the satellite is in different orbits, the effect of the radar incidence angle could not be ignored in this study.

2.2. In Situ Data

The field investigation mainly measured and recorded the plant height and phenological stage information throughout the entire corn growth period in the study area in 2021. In that time, 39 sample fields were observed in experimental area 1, and 20 summer corn fields were observed in experimental area 2. The corn sample fields were planted in a family unit, so the corn plants in the same field had the same cultivated variety and field management level. All the corn fields were sown with a uniform seeder, with a row spacing of 60 cm and a plant spacing of 10–20 cm. The area of each field varied from 0.65 hectares to 1.94 hectares, with an average area of about 1.04 hectares. Before the field investigation, boundary information for each sample field was determined by combining a GPS locator and a Google Images map. The morphological characteristics and corresponding BBCH (Biologische Bundesanstalt, Bundessortenamt and CHemical industry) codes [28] of the corn at different growth stages are shown in Table 1. The BBCH coding is a decimal system based on the well-known code for cereals developed by Zadoks et al., which makes it possible to unify the coding of all crops and weeds at the same physiological growth stage [29].

Table 1. Morphological characteristics and corresponding BBCH codes of corn at different growth stages.

No.	Phonology Stages	Morphological Characteristics	BBCH Code
1	Emergence	Expose the first leaf from the tooth sheath.	10
2	Three Leaves	Expose the third leaf from the second leaf sheath.	13
3	Seven Leaves	Expose the seventh leaf from the sixth leaf sheath.	17
4	Jointing	The round and hard stem nodes can be felt near the ground.	31
5	Tasseling	The top spikelet of the male spike protrudes from the leaf sheath.	51
6	Male florescence	The anthers in the upper part of the male spike are exposed, and pollen is scattered.	55
7	Silking	Floral filaments are exposed in the bracts of female spikes in plants.	61
8	Milk ripening	The shape of the grains has reached normal size, and the lower middle grains of the fruit inflorescence are filled with thick white milk.	79
9	Maturity	More than 80% of plants have yellowed outer bracts, dried filaments, and hardened grains.	89

The field investigation of corn phenological stages was carried out according to the Meteorological Industry Standard of the People's Republic of China [30] and the record specification of the corn crop BBCH [28]. The field investigation of the phenological stages was carried out every other day. The stages of emergence, milky ripening, and maturity phenology were determined by visual discrimination. The other stages were determined by the percentage of the corn plants entering those phenological stages compared to the total number of observed plants. When the percentage was greater than or equal to 50%, this indicated that the field had entered the universal development period, and it was then that it was determined that the corn field had entered this phenological stage. For each sample field, 15–20 corn plants more than 2 m away from the edge of the plot were randomly selected for measurement and judgment.

The plant height was measured with a steel ruler from the root to the highest point of the canopy leaves in the natural state of the corn plant, or to the top of the male tassel after the tasseling stage. The unit of the measured plant height was in centimeters (cm), and the measurement data were rounded to an integer. For each sample field, 8 to 10 corn plants more than 2 m away from the edge of the plot were randomly selected for plant height measurement to obtain the plant height value of the field. In order to better match the ground measurement and satellite image data, and to reduce ground measurement errors, the ground measurement data were filtered and fitted based on logical functions, and they were interpolated with a daily interval. The fitting function is shown in Equation (1).

$$M = \frac{a}{1 + b \cdot \exp(ct)} \quad (1)$$

where M stands for the original field measurement data, natural constants a, b, and c are function fitting parameters, and t is the date of the field investigation, represented here by DOY (day of year).

The original measurement data and corresponding fitted results of the plant height and BBCH for one of the sample fields are shown in Figure 2. The fitting function parameters of a, b, and c for the plant height are 368.732, 7.706 × 109, and −0.116, respectively. For the BBCH, the fitting parameters are 101.430, 5368.613, and −0.040, respectively. In this study, the fitted results were used to represent the surface measurement data synchronized with satellite observations. The date of the surface measurement data was determined by the acquisition times of two optical satellite images. In this paper, the acquisition times of the two optical images were 26 July and 31 July 2021, respectively. Therefore, the fitted ground measurement data on these two days were extracted for estimation model construction and accuracy verification.

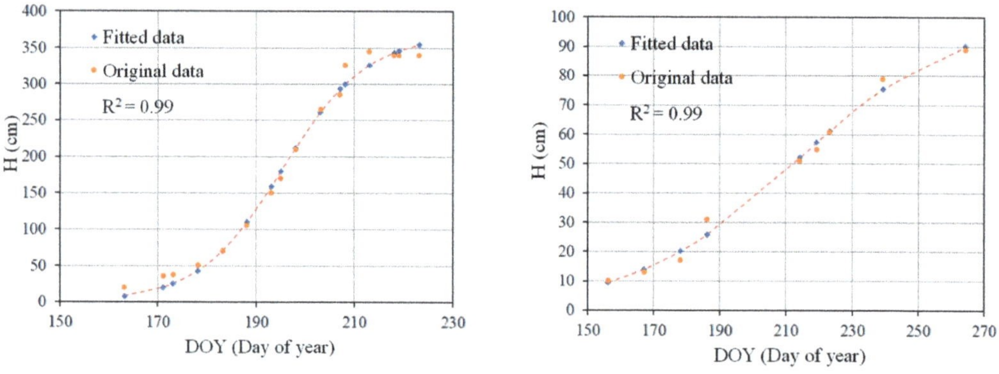

Figure 2. The original measured data (plant height and BBCH) and the corresponding logical fit-ting results (red dashed line represents the logistic fitting curve).

2.3. Image Data Collection

This study obtained synchronous optical and SAR satellite data covering two experimental areas. The detailed image parameters and coverage information are shown in Table 2. Among them, one SAR image acquired on August 1 and two optical images covered experimental area 1 and experimental area 2 at the same time. Due to differences in satellite orbits, the SAR images covering different experimental areas had significant differences in observation intervals and radar incidence angles. Therefore, experimental area 1 and experimental area 2 could be used as two independent experimental measurements for model training and verification, respectively. We trained the model based on the data of experimental area 1, and we used the data of experimental area 2 to further verify the accuracy and stability of the model.

The tasseling stage of the corn is an important turning point in its life. It is the transition period from plant vegetative growth to reproductive growth. At this time, all leaves of the corn have been expanded, the plant height or leaf area index (LAI) has reached the maximum; the plant body essentially stops vegetative growth and enters the stage centered on reproductive growth. The plant is very sensitive to the environmental conditions at this time. A continuous high temperature, drought, or rainy weather will directly affect the yield of the corn. Therefore timely and accurate monitoring of the growth status of corn crop in this phenological stage is necessary for timely guidance of field management and improvement of crop yield. Therefore, the images used in this study were mainly of the tasseling stage of corn.

Table 2. The detailed optical and SAR image parameters and coverage information.

Experimental	Types	Orbits	Platform	Acquisition Date	Phenology
area 1	Optical	/	Sentinel-2A	26 July 2021	Late jointing
		/	Sentinel-2B	31 July 2021	Tasseling
	SAR	40	Sentinel-1A	27 July 2021	Late jointing
		113	Sentinel-1A	1 August 2021	Tasseling
area 2	Optical	/	Sentinel-2A	26 July 2021	Late jointing
		/	Sentinel-2B	31 July 2021	Tasseling
	SAR	113	Sentinel-1A	1 August 2021	Tasseling
		113	Sentinel-1A	13 August 2021	Flowering

2.4. *Image Feature Extraction*

From the Sentinel-1 SAR data, we mainly obtained the parameters of backscatter coefficient ($\sigma^0{}_{VH}$ and $\sigma^0{}_{VV}$) and radar incidence angle (θ). Firstly, in order to ensure that the backscatter coefficient from one image was not affected by the incidence angle, the radar incidence angle effect for each SAR image was normalized and corrected based on cosine normalization theory [31].

From the optical images, we mainly extracted multispectral vegetation indexes. The Sentinel-2 optical data used in this study contain three red-edge bands, which are sensitive to vegetation parameters. Therefore, the multispectral vegetation indexes of each sample field, mainly including the commonly used NDVI index [32], the normalized difference vegetation index NDVIre1 based on the red-edge 1 band [33], the normalized difference vegetation index NDVIre2 based on the red-edge 2 band [33], and the red-edge position index S2REP (Red-Edge Position Index, S2REP) specially designed by the ESA for Sentinel-2 [34], were calculated and extracted in this study.

2.5. *VI_{DRI} Model Construction*

Radar vegetation scattering models can describe a series of complex interactions between radar electromagnetic waves, various components of vegetation, and underlying surfaces. The main impact of vegetation on radar electromagnetic waves is the scattering and absorption of radar signals reaching the vegetation canopy. The scattering intensity of radar electromagnetic waves by vegetation is not only affected by the vegetation itself (the size and direction of scatterers in the vegetation canopy, the dielectric constant of the vegetation) but also by radar system parameters such as electromagnetic wave frequency, incidence angle, and polarization mode. The advantage of the WCM [35] is that the description of the scattering mechanism is relatively simple, and it can be used to describe scattering in areas with a relatively uniform vegetation coverage such as crop fields. However, the model ignores multiple scattering between vegetation and the underlying surface, and the prerequisite for applying this model is that the ground scattering mechanism is dominated by volume scattering. Therefore, when applied to sparse vegetation areas, it may lead to significant errors. However, the corn fields in this study were all in the late jointing or tasseling stages, meeting the condition that volume scattering dominated. Therefore, they were in accordance with the principles of the WCM. This study introduced the application of the widely used Water Cloud Model (WCM) principle to corn growth monitoring.

According to the principle of the WCM [36], the total backscatter received by radar in a crop area is related to vegetation growth status (LAI, biomass, etc.) and underlying surface soil parameters (including the surface soil roughness and moisture). Therefore, directly using the original backscatter coefficient to invert vegetation growth parameters will result in significant errors. Meanwhile, the method of separating canopy and surface scattering terms through radar vegetation scattering models requires a large amount of surface measurement data input, which involves a huge workload for large-scale field crop growth parameters' estimation, and its accuracy is difficult to guarantee. Therefore, based on the WCM theory, combined with optical multispectral vegetation indexes and SAR differential radar information (DRI), the VI_{DRI} (vegetation index corrected by DRI) estimation model was constructed without the need for other external data inputs. The DRI represents the difference value of the backscattering coefficient between two SAR images, and the SAR data need to be synchronized with the optical images. The model establishment process was as follows:

$$\Delta\sigma^0 = \sigma_2^0\left(\frac{\cos\theta_{norm}}{\cos\theta_2}\right) - \sigma_1^0\left(\frac{\cos\theta_{norm}}{\cos\theta_1}\right) = \left(\frac{\sigma_2^0}{\cos\theta_2} - \frac{\sigma_1^0}{\cos\theta_2}\right) \quad (2)$$

θ_1, θ_2 is the radar incidence angle. $\sigma^0{}_1$, $\sigma^0{}_2$ is the radar backscatter coefficient observed at different radar incidence angles in different observation times. θ_{norm} is the parameter used to normalize the incidence angle. Firstly, the backscatter coefficients at different radar incidence angles are projected to a normal vector perpendicular to the ground surface. That is, the value of the θ_{norm} parameter is set to 0 to normalize the effect of the incidence angle and unify the observation angle consistent with the optical remote sensing data. According to the principle of the WCM, $\Delta\sigma^0$ can be expressed as follows:

$$\begin{aligned}\Delta\sigma^0 &= \Delta\sigma^0_{veg} + \left(\tau_2{}^2\sigma^0_{soil_2} - \tau_1{}^2\sigma^0_{soil_1}\right) \\ &= \Delta\sigma^0_{veg} + \left[\tau_2{}^2(C + Dm_2) - \tau_1{}^2(C + Dm_1)\right]\end{aligned} \quad (3)$$

where $\Delta\sigma^0$ describes the total difference value of the backscatter coefficient received by the SAR satellite during two observation intervals, including the VV and VH channels ($\Delta\sigma^0{}_{VV}$, $\Delta\sigma^0{}_{VH}$). $\Delta\sigma^0{}_{veg}$ represents the difference value of the backscatter coefficient from the crop vegetation layer. $\sigma^0{}_{soil1}$ and $\sigma^0{}_{soil2}$ represent the backscatter coefficient from the surface soil layer, and $\tau_1{}^2$ and $\tau_2{}^2$ are the two-way attenuation coefficient caused by the vegetation canopy. $\Delta\sigma^0{}_{veg}$ and $\tau_1{}^2$, $\tau_2{}^2$ are related to the growth status of crop vegetation, and $\Delta\sigma^0{}_{veg}$ is positively correlated with the vegetation growth status, while $\tau_1{}^2$, $\tau_2{}^2$ is negatively correlated with the growth status. Because the observation interval of two SAR images was short, and the corn plants had large body sizes and high vegetation coverage during these two periods, we considered $\tau_1{}^2 \approx \tau_2{}^2 = \tau^2$. $\sigma^0{}_{soil1}$ and $\sigma^0{}_{soil2}$ are related to the surface soil parameters and not the crop growth status. For two different observations of the same corn field, we assume that the soil roughness parameter C remains unchanged. Moreover, for the whole study area, we assume that the soil types and properties are essentially the same, and that the sensitivity parameter D related to the soil moisture content remains consistent. In addition, the changes in surface soil volume moisture contents of different fields within the same observation interval are thought to be similar, making $\Delta mv = m$, at this time:

$$\begin{aligned}\Delta\sigma^0 &= \Delta\sigma^0_{veg} + \tau^2\left(\sigma^0_{soil_2} - \sigma^0_{soil_1}\right) \\ &= \Delta\sigma^0_{veg} + D\tau^2[m_{v2} - m_{v1}] \\ &= \Delta\sigma^0_{veg} + Dm\tau^2\end{aligned} \quad (4)$$

where D and m are constants. $\Delta\sigma^0$ is mainly related to $\Delta\sigma^0{}_{veg}$ and τ^2. Both $\Delta\sigma^0{}_{veg}$ and τ^2 are a function of the parameters related to the vegetation layer in the WCM, and the value of these two parameters is related to the crop growth status. That is, $\Delta\sigma^0$ of different fields calculated by differences weakens the influence of the surface roughness and surface soil moisture content on SAR data, and it can better reflect the growth status of the vegetation layer. Due to the close acquisition dates of the two SAR images, the plant height increment in these two periods was essentially the same. Therefore, $\Delta\sigma^0$ reflects the variation characteristics of the radar backscatter coefficient under the same plant height increment of corn. Moreover, it shows the degree of complexity of the vegetation layer structure in the cross-section. The higher the value of $\Delta\sigma^0$, the more complex the structure of the vegetation layer in the unit cross-section, and the greater the LAI or biomass in the unit volume. Therefore, we introduce the parameter $\Delta\sigma^0$ into the two-way attenuation τ^2 model. It can be expressed as follows:

$$\tau^2 = \exp(-2B \cdot V_2/\cos\theta) = \exp(-2 \cdot \Delta\sigma^0) \tag{5}$$

In the WCM, τ^2 represents two-way attenuation of the radar signal by the vegetation layer. B represents the empirical coefficient, with a value depending on the crop type. Since this study only focused on the corn crop, here, it is defined as 1 to simplify the construction of the VI_{DRI} model. θ is the radar incidence angle, and the incidence angle effect is considered in $\Delta\sigma^0$ in this formula. V_2 is a description of the vegetation canopy related to the crop growth status, which is generally expressed by parameters such as LAI or biomass of the vegetation. In the absence of ground-measured data, some scholars have introduced optical vegetation indexes related to the LAI or the biomass of the vegetation canopy to replace V_2. However, due to the limited penetration ability of optical data, optical vegetation indexes only reflect the spectral reflectance characteristics of the top of the vegetation canopy. For a corn crop with a large plant size, $\Delta\sigma^0$ can better reflect the internal structural characteristics of the vegetation canopy than optical vegetation indexes. Therefore, this study used $\Delta\sigma^0$ to replace V_2. The basic VI_{DRI} estimation model combining optical and SAR parameters was established as follows:

$$VI_{DRI} = \frac{VI_{opt}}{\tau^2_{DRI}} = \frac{VI_{opt}}{\exp(-2 \cdot \Delta\sigma^0)} \tag{6}$$

where VI_{opt} represents a multispectral vegetation index extracted from the optical data, such as the NDVI, NDVIre1, NDVIre2, or S2REP, which was correlated with the crop growth state due to the influence of the chlorophyll content of the vegetation. $\tau^2{}_{DRI}$ represents the two-way attenuation coefficient of the crop and the radar wave described by the DRI, and the value of $\tau^2{}_{DRI}$ ranges from 0 to 1. With the continuous growth of the crop, the attenuation effect of vegetation on the radar wave gradually increases, meaning the value of $\tau^2{}_{DRI}$ gradually decreases. That is, $\tau^2{}_{DRI}$ is negatively correlated with the crop growth state, and the newly established VI_{DRI} parameter is positively correlated with the vegetation growth state of corn. The whole technical process mainly includes data preprocessing, image features construction and growth parameters estimation, as shown in Figure 3.

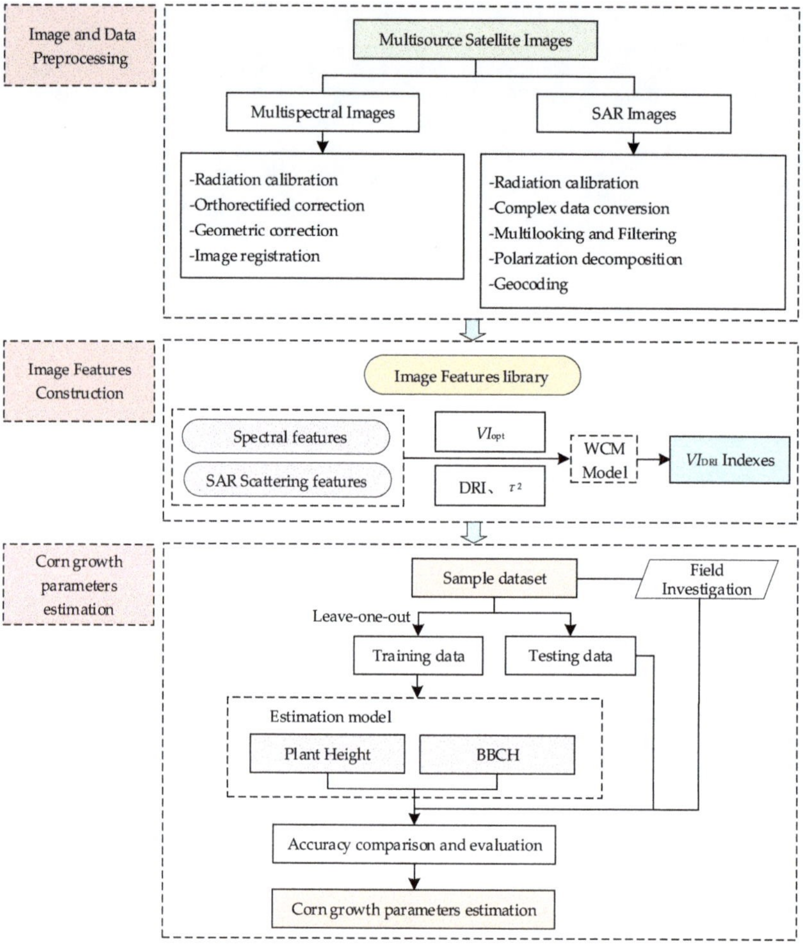

Figure 3. Flow chart of corn growth parameters estimation combined with multispectral and SAR features.

3. Results

3.1. Correlation Analysis

In order to verify the superiority of the constructed VI_{DRI} indexes in estimating corn growth parameters (plant height and BBCH), the Pearson correlation (R) between the vegetation indexes (VI_{opt} and VI_{DRI}) and the plant growth parameters (plant height and BBCH) was analyzed by using the modeling data from experimental area 1, as shown in Table 3 and Figures 4 and 5.

Table 3. Pearson Correlation (*R*) between the vegetation indexes and the growth parameters (plant height and BBCH).

VI_{opt}	Plant Height	BBCH	VI_{DRI}	Plant Height	BBCH
NDVI	0.35	0.08	$NDVI_{DRI}$	0.47	0.28
NDVIre1	0.50	0.37	$NDVIre1_{DRI}$	0.58	0.45
NDVIre2	0.69	0.71	$NDVIre2_{DRI}$	0.74	0.75
S2REP	0.69	0.72	$S2REP_{DRI}$	0.75	0.75

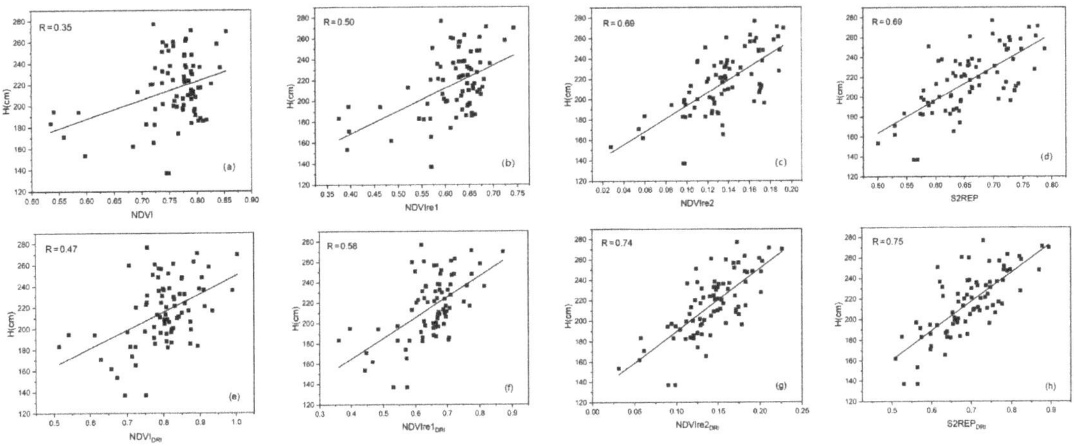

Figure 4. Scatter plot of VI_{opt} and corresponding VI_{DRI} indexes with plant height (NDVI, NDVIre1, NDVIre2 and S2REP are multispectral vegetation indexes. $NDVI_{DRI}$, $NDVIre1_{DRI}$, $NDVIre2_{DRI}$ and $S2REP_{DRI}$ are the corresponding VI_{DRI} indexes. H and R represents the plant height and Pearson Correlation, respectively. (**a–d**) represent the relationship between the plant height and the multispectral vegetation indexes. (**e–h**) represent the relationship between the plant height and the corresponding VI_{DRI} indexes. Black lines represent the linear fitting results).

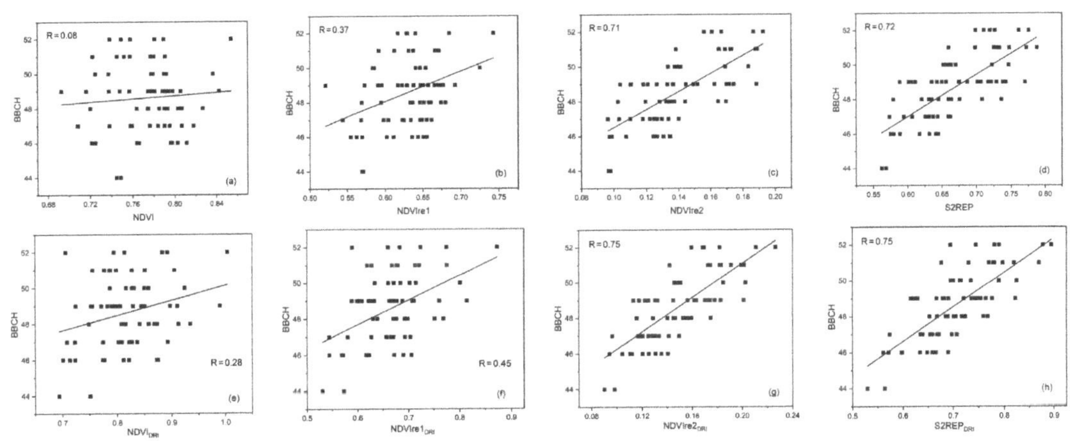

Figure 5. Scatter plot of VI_{opt} and corresponding VI_{DRI} indexes with BBCH (NDVI, NDVIre1, NDVIre2 and S2REP are multispectral vegetation indexes. $NDVI_{DRI}$, $NDVIre1_{DRI}$, $NDVIre2_{DRI}$ and $S2REP_{DRI}$ are the corresponding VI_{DRI} indexes. BBCH and R represents the phenology stage and Pearson Correlation, respectively. (**a–d**) represent the relationship between the BBCH and the multispectral vegetation indexes. (**e–h**) represent the relationship between the BBCH and the corresponding VI_{DRI} indexes. Black lines represent the linear fitting results).

Firstly, for the plant height, the VI_{DRI} constructed by introducing radar DRI could effectively improve the sensitivity of the multispectral vegetation indexes VI_{opt} to the change in the corn plant height. The Pearson correlation coefficients (R) between the measured plant height and the NDVI, NDVIre1, NDVIre2, and S2REP were 0.35, 0.50, 0.69, and 0.69, respectively. Compared with the four VI_{opt} indexes, the correlation between the NDVI and the measured plant height was the lowest (R = 0.35), which indicated that the VI_{opt} based on the red-edge band was more sensitive to the growth change in crops, especially for NDVIre2 and S2REP with the red-edge 2 band, where the correlation coefficient with plant height could reach 0.69. According to the scatter plot in Figure 4, the value of NDVI from the corn canopy in the experimental area was generally above 0.7, and showed a serious saturation phenomenon (R = 0.35) in this situation, while $NDVI_{DRI}$ weakened this saturation phenomenon to some extent (R = 0.47). In addition, NDVIre2 and S2REP calculated by introducing the red-edge 2 band showed better correlations with plant height than NDVIre1 calculated by introducing the red-edge 1 band. This verified the advantages of the Sentinel-2 red-edge 2 band in monitoring vegetation growth. In addition, compared with the four constructed VI_{DRI} indexes, the correlation coefficients between $NDVI_{DRI}$, $NDVIre1_{DRI}$, $NDVIre2_{DRI}$, and $S2REP_{DRI}$ and the measured plant height were 0.47, 0.58, 0.74, and 0.75, respectively. Among them, the correlation between $NDVI_{DRI}$ and the measured plant height was the lowest (R = 0.47), while $S2REP_{DRI}$ calculated by introducing the red-edge 2 band had the highest correlation with plant height (R = 0.75). Essentially, the VI_{DRI} indexes constructed by introducing radar DRI showed higher correlations with plant height than using the multispectral vegetation indexes VI_{opt} alone.

As for the BBCH, according to the scatter plot in Figure 5, the correlation coefficients between the measured BBCH and the NDVI, NDVIre1, NDVIre2, and S2REP were 0.08, 0.37, 0.71, and 0.72, respectively. It can be seen that the high vegetation coverage of the canopy makes it difficult to distinguish different phenological periods of corn just based on NDVI features. Among them, the correlation between the NDVI and the measured BBCH was the lowest (R = 0.08), showing a complete saturation phenomenon. However, the correlation coefficients between the indexes of NDVIre2 and S2REP constructed from the red-edge 2 band and BBCH reached 0.71 and 0.72, respectively. The correlation was much better than NDVIre1 constructed from the red-edge 1 band (R = 0.37), indicating that the multispectral indexes based on the red-edge 2 band are more sensitive to the corn BBCH than those based on the red-edge 1 band. Further comparison of the Pearson correlation coefficients (R) between the measured BBCH and the constructed VI_{DRI} revealed that the correlation coefficients between $NDVI_{DRI}$, $NDVIre1_{DRI}$, $NDVIre2_{DRI}$, and $S2REP_{DRI}$ and the measured BBCH of corn were 0.28, 0.45, 0.75, and 0.75, respectively. Among them, $NDVI_{DRI}$ had the lowest correlation with the measured BBCH (R = 0.28). Essentially, the introduction of red-edge multispectral features or SAR features to some extent improved the sensitivity of the vegetation indexes to the BBCH. In particular, $NDVIre2_{DRI}$ and $S2REP_{DRI}$ constructed by introducing the red-edge 2 band and DRI features showed the best correlations with BBCH (R = 0.75). Similar to the plant height estimation, the introduction of radar DRI when constructing each VI_{DRI} index could effectively enhance the sensitivity of VI_{opt} to the BBCH. The results indicated that the VI_{DRI} indexes combined with optical and SAR data also have certain advantages in improving the accuracy of corn BBCH estimation.

3.2. Estimation Model and Accuracy

In order to compare and analyze the accuracy of VI_{opt} and its corresponding VI_{DRI} indexes in estimating corn plant height and BBCH parameters, a simple linear regression equation determined by least squares combined with the Leave-One-Out cross-validation method was used to establish the estimation models of plant height and BBCH, respectively. We used the coefficient of determination (R^2), root mean square error (RMSE), and normalized root mean square error (nRMSE) to analyze the performance of each regression model. Finally, combined with the field investigation data, a total of 78 iterations were carried out for the two periods of measurement data of 39 sample fields for experimental area 1. Tables 4 and 5 and Figures 6 and 7 show the estimation model and the model accuracy for the plant height and BBCH parameters from experimental area 1.

Table 4 shows the corn plant height estimation model and accuracy based on the multispectral vegetation indexes VI_{opt} and the corresponding VI_{DRI} indexes in experimental area 1. Essentially, the VI_{DRI} indexes show higher estimation accuracy than the VI_{opt} indexes. According to Figure 6a–d, comparing the corn plant heights estimated by four multispectral vegetation indexes NDVI, NDVIre1, NDVIre2, and S2REP, whether for R^2, RMSE, or nRMSE, NDVI shows the lowest estimation accuracy (R^2 = 0.12, RMSE = 29.15, nRMSE = 20.84%), and S2REP shows the highest estimation accuracy (R^2 = 0.48, RMSE = 22.45, nRMSE = 16.05%). NDVIre1 has a limited ability to improve the accuracy of corn plant height estimation based on NDVI, while NDVIre2 and S2REP constructed with the red-edge 2 band have more advantages in improving the accuracy of the NDVI estimation model. This further verifies that the red-edge 2 band of Sentinel-2 data is more sensitive than the red-edge 1 band to crop height variation. In Figure 6e–h, the VI_{DRI} indexes corresponding to each multispectral vegetation index are compared and analyzed. $NDVI_{DRI}$ shows the lowest model estimation accuracy (R^2 = 0.22, RMSE = 27.47, nRMSE = 19.64%), while $S2REP_{DRI}$ shows the highest model estimation accuracy (R^2 = 0.57, RMSE = 20.48, nRMSE = 14.64%). Essentially, the VI_{DRI} indexes uniformly improve the accuracy of using VI_{opt} indexes to estimate the corn plant height. According to the scatter plots of corn plant height estimated by various vegetation indexes (VI_{opt} and VI_{DRI}), as shown in Figure 6, during the tasseling stage of corn, high vegetation coverage leads to a severe saturation phenomenon of corn plant height estimation results based on the NDVI and NDVIre1 indexes. Meanwhile, NDVIre2 and S2REP significantly weaken this phenomenon, especially the $NDVIre2_{DRI}$ and $S2REP_{DRI}$ indexes constructed by further introducing radar DRI. All of these results verify that the combination of an optical red-edge band and radar DRI feature may effectively improve the plant height estimation accuracy for corn even under a high vegetation coverage condition.

Table 4. Plant height estimation model and accuracy based on the data from experimental area 1.

VI Types	*VIs*	Models	R^2	RMSE (cm)	nRMSE
VI_{opt}	NDVI	y = 178.13x + 80.74	0.12	29.15	20.84%
	NDVIre1	y = 219.38x + 80.63	0.25	26.96	19.27%
	NDVIre2	y = 635.14x + 130.06	0.47	22.64	16.18%
	S2REP	y = 331.55x − 2.14	0.48	22.45	16.05%
VI_{DRI}	$NDVI_{DRI}$	y = 171.42x + 78.57	0.22	27.47	19.64%
	$NDVIre1_{DRI}$	y = 203.65x + 83.28	0.34	25.33	18.11%
	$NDVIre2_{DRI}$	y = 616.50x + 127.89	0.55	20.99	15.00%
	$S2REP_{DRI}$	y = 283.30x + 19.20	0.57	20.48	14.64%

Table 5. BBCH estimation model and accuracy based on the data from experimental area 1.

VI Types	*VIs*	Models	R^2	RMSE (cm)	nRMSE
VI_{opt}	NDVI	y = 4.55x + 45.10	0.006	1.93	24.17%
	NDVIre1	y = 17.51x + 37.55	0.14	1.80	22.49%
	NDVIre2	y = 51.64x + 41.35	0.50	1.36	17.04%
	S2REP	y = 24.36x + 32.39	0.53	1.33	16.60%
VI_{DRI}	$NDVI_{DRI}$	y = 8.36x + 41.79	0.08	1.86	23.24%
	$NDVIre1_{DRI}$	y = 13.72x + 39.44	0.20	1.73	21.58%
	$NDVIre2_{DRI}$	y = 48.30x + 41.43	0.56	1.26	15.79%
	$S2REP_{DRI}$	y = 19.24x + 35.07	0.57	1.27	15.91%

Table 5 shows the corn phenological stage (BBCH) estimation models and accuracies based on the multispectral vegetation indexes VI_{opt} and the corresponding VI_{DRI} indexes in experimental area 1. The same as the plant height estimation results, the VI_{DRI} indexes show a higher estimation accuracy than the VI_{opt} indexes. According to Figure 7a–d, when comparing the BBCH estimation results by the four multispectral vegetation indexes NDVI, NDVIre1, NDVIre2, and S2REP with the measured BBCH data on the ground, it can be seen that the NDVI shows the lowest accuracy of BBCH estimation results (R^2 = 0.006, RMSE = 1.93, nRMSE = 24.17%) with a serious saturation phenomenon. Meanwhile, NDVIre2 and S2REP have an obvious effect on weakening the saturation phenomenon, and the improvement effect is far better than with NDVIre1. This indicates that the red-edge 2 band of Sentinel-2 was more sensitive to the variation in the corn BBCH than the red-edge

1 band. According to Figure 7e–h, essentially, the VI_{DRI} indexes show a higher BBCH estimation accuracy than the VI_{opt} indexes. Among them, $NDVI_{DRI}$ shows the lowest BBCH estimation accuracy (R^2 = 0.08, RMSE = 1.86, nRMSE = 23.24%), while the $S2REP_{DRI}$ index constructed by combining the Sentinel-2 red-edge 2 band and radar DRI shows the highest accuracy (R^2 = 0.57, RMSE = 1.27, nRMSE = 15.91%), which further verifies that the combination of an optical red-edge band and radar DRI feature can effectively improve the BBCH estimation accuracy for corn even under a high vegetation coverage condition.

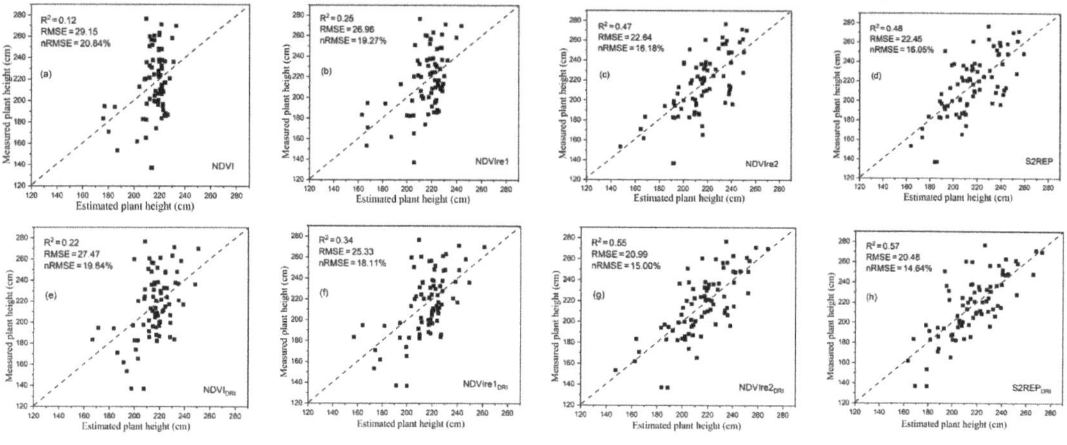

Figure 6. Estimated plant height and measured plant height results based on the data from experimental area 1 ((**a**–**d**) represent the plant height estimation results using the NDVI, NDVIre1, NDVIre2, S2REP. (**e**–**h**) represent the plant height estimation results using the corresponding VI_{DRI} indexes, respectively. Dashed line represents a 1:1 relationship line).

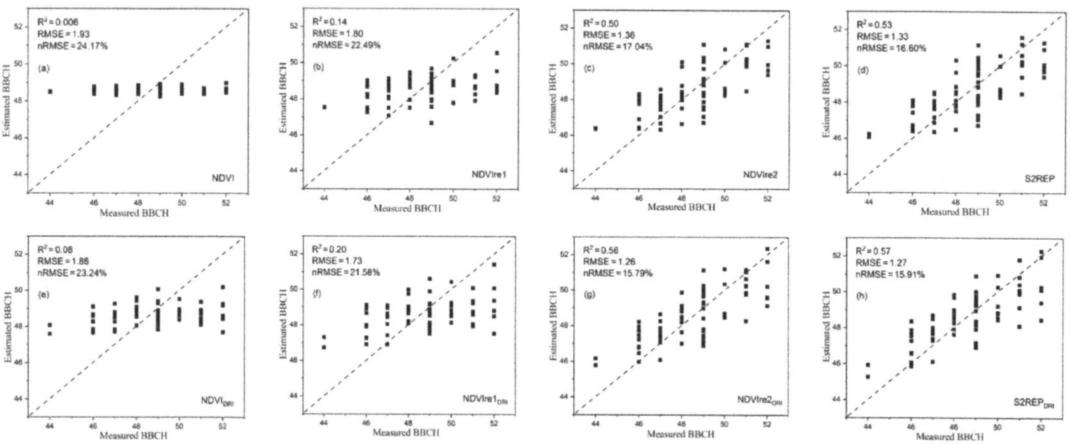

Figure 7. Estimated BBCH and measured BBCH results based on the data from experimental area 1 ((**a**–**d**) represent the BBCH estimation results using the NDVI, NDVIre1, NDVIre2, S2REP. (**e**–**h**) represent the BBCH estimation results using the corresponding VI_{DRI} indexes, respectively. Dashed line represents a 1:1 relationship line).

In addition, we compared and analyzed the accuracy of NDVIre2, S2REP, and the corresponding $NDVIre2_{DRI}$ and $S2REP_{DRI}$ parameters, which were highly correlated with the growth status of corn, in estimating the plant height and the BBCH parameters. For the plant height, the accuracy of R^2 and nRMSE based on $NDVIre2_{DRI}$ increased by 0.08 and

1.18% compared to NDVIre2, and the accuracy (R^2, nRMSE) based on the $S2REP_{DRI}$ indexes increased by 0.09 and 1.41% compared to S2REP. For the estimation of BBCH, the accuracy (R^2, nRMSE) based on $NDVIre2_{DRI}$ increased by 0.06 and 1.25% compared to NDVIre2, and the accuracy (R^2, nRMSE) based on $S2REP_{DRI}$ increased by 0.04 and 0.69% compared to S2REP. This indicated that introducing radar DRI could better improve the accuracy of corn plant height estimation compared to BBCH. Through further analysis, it was found that the plant height reflects the characteristics of the crop in the vertical direction. Meanwhile, the BBCH difference of corn entering the tasseling stage is mainly reflected in the tassel extraction situation in the vegetation canopy, which shows the two-dimensional plane changes at the top of the crop canopy. Meanwhile, due to a certain penetrability, the SAR data can provide vertical structural information for the crop. Therefore, $NDVIre2_{DRI}$ and $S2REP_{DRI}$ are superior in improving the estimation accuracy for the corn plant height parameter compared to the BBCH.

3.3. Accuracy Verification

In order to further verify the superiority of the VI_{DRI} indexes in estimating the corn plant height and BBCH, and to test the accuracy of the estimation model in Tables 4 and 5, the NDVIre2 and S2REP, as well as the corresponding VI_{DRI} indexes, which were sensitive to plant height and BBCH, were directly selected for comparative verification based on experimental area 2. The validation results and the accuracies are shown in Table 6 and Figure 8.

Table 6. Further accuracy verification of the estimation model based on the data from experimental area 2.

Parameters	VI Types	VIs	Models	R^2	RMSE (cm)	nRMSE
Plant height	VI_{opt}	NDVIre2	y = 1078.6x + 62.80	0.52	28.38	15.42%
		S2REP	y = 531.55x − 140.36	0.59	26.31	14.30%
	VI_{DRI}	$NDVIre2_{DRI}$	y = 1072.6x + 64.47	0.55	27.28	14.83%
		$S2REP_{DRI}$	y = 505.89x − 121.17	0.63	25.51	13.86%
BBCH	VI_{opt}	NDVIre2	y = 45.40x + 40.97	0.49	1.29	16.12%
		S2REP	y = 23.23x + 31.84	0.59	1.15	14.37%
	VI_{DRI}	$NDVIre2_{DRI}$	y = 45.44x + 41.00	0.52	1.25	15.62%
		$S2REP_{DRI}$	y = 22.27x + 32.57	0.64	1.09	13.62%

Table 6 and Figure 8 show the plant height and BBCH estimation models and accuracies based on NDVIre2, S2REP, and the corresponding VI_{DRI} indexes, which are sensitive to the corn growth parameters, using the data from experimental area 2. Essentially, the VI_{DRI} indexes constructed by combining optical and SAR data information show higher estimation accuracies than the optical vegetation indexes. However, different from experimental area 1, the constructed VI_{DRI} indexes used in experimental area 2 are relatively poor in improving the VI_{opt} indexes' estimation accuracy. This is because of the long interval between the two SAR images used in experimental area 2 and the poor synchronization with the optical images. Compared with the estimation results in Figures 6 and 8, for experimental area 1, the plant height estimation accuracy of R^2 and nRMSE based on $NDVIre2_{DRI}$ increased by 0.08 and 1.18% compared to NDVIre2, and the plant height estimation accuracy (R^2, nRMSE) based on the $S2REP_{DRI}$ indexes increased by 0.09 and 1.41% compared to S2REP. However, in experimental area 2, the accuracy of R^2 and nRMSE based on $NDVIre2_{DRI}$ increased by 0.03 and 0.55% compared to NDVIre2, and the accuracy (R^2, nRMSE) based on $S2REP_{DRI}$ increased by 0.04 and 0.44% compared to S2REP. As for the BBCH parameter, compared to the results in Figures 7 and 8, for experimental area 1, the BBCH estimation accuracy of R^2 and nRMSE based on $NDVIre2_{DRI}$ increased by 0.06 and 1.25% compared to NDVIre2, and the estimation accuracy (R^2, nRMSE) based on the $S2REP_{DRI}$ indexes increased by 0.04 and 0.69% compared to S2REP. However, in experimental area 2, the accuracy of R^2 and nRMSE based on $NDVIre2_{DRI}$ increased by 0.03 and 0.5% compared to NDVIre2, and the accuracy (R^2, nRMSE) based on the $S2REP_{DRI}$ indexes increased by 0.05 and 0.75% compared to S2REP. That is, the constructed VI_{DRI} indexes used in experimental area 2 are relatively poor in improving the accuracy of using VI_{opt} indexes alone to estimate the crop growth parameter. The findings further indicate that a larger SAR data interval will reduce the VI_{DRI} indexes' ability to improve the estimation accuracy of corn growth parameters using the VI_{opt} indexes alone. In practice, the two SAR datasets used to calculate the DRI should be synchronized with the optical satellite data as much as possible, and the image time interval should not be too large.

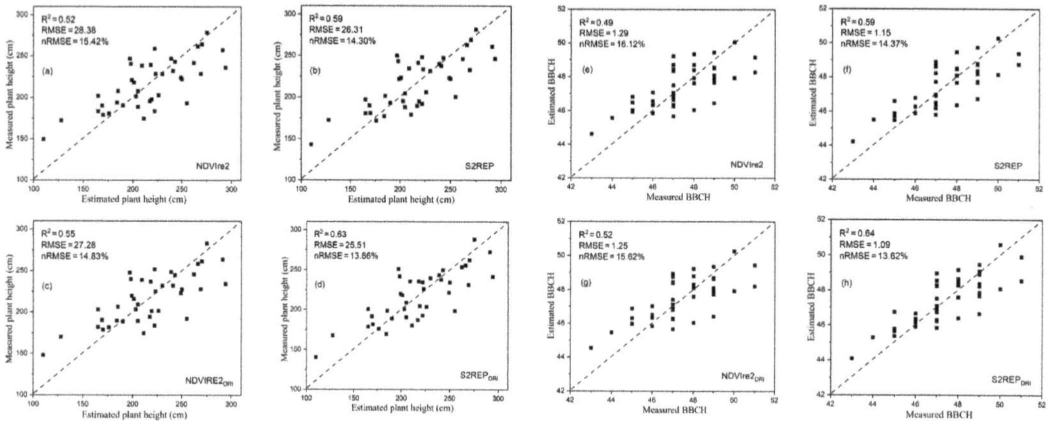

Figure 8. Estimated (plant height and BBCH) and measured (plant height and BBCH) results based on the data from experimental area 2 ((**a–d**) represent the plant height estimation results, (**e–h**) represent the BBCH estimation results using the NDVIre2, S2REP $NDVIre2_{DRI}$ and $S2RE_{DRI}$ indexes, respectively. Dashed line represents a 1:1 relationship line).

4. Discussion

Optical satellite sensors have developed rapidly in recent years, with the advantages of low cost and high accuracy. Multispectral remote sensing data have a unique advantage in crop growth monitoring due to their rich spectral reflectance characteristics. The existing research has shown that the optical vegetation indexes are highly related to the aboveground biomass, LAI, vegetation coverage, etc., of crops [37]. However, the optical vegetation indexes are always sensitive to low vegetation coverage, and there is a serious saturation phenomenon when the vegetation coverage is medium to high [5,6]. In recent years, scholars have discovered important spectral bands, which are highly related to crop growth in the red-edge spectral regions [7]. It has been found that the multispectral vegetation indexes based on the red-edge bands are closely related to the physical and chemical parameters of the vegetation [8]. Based on Sentinel-2 multispectral data, this study compared and analyzed the correlations between the multispectral vegetation indexes NDVI, NDVIre1, NDVIre2, and S2REP and the corn growth parameters (plant height and BBCH). It was found that the NDVI had the lowest correlation with the measured plant height and BBCH when compared with the multispectral vegetation indexes based on the red-edge bands, confirming that the multispectral vegetation indexes based on the red-edge bands are more sensitive to the growth parameters of the corn crop. In addition, the NDVIre2 and S2REP indexes calculated by introducing the red-edge 2 band showed better correlations with plant height and BBCH than the NDVIre1 index calculated by introducing the red-edge 1 band, which verified that the Sentinel-2 red-edge 2 band has great advantages in monitoring vegetation growth parameters. This result is consistent with the research of Dong et al., who found that introducing the red-edge band to multispectral vegetation indices can effectively improve the estimation accuracy of crop biomass [38]. However, even the red-edge band indexes, which are sensitive to crop growth, only display the spectral reflectance characteristics at the top of the vegetation canopy. Especially for a corn crop with a large plant size, the optical-based vegetation indexes cannot reflect the internal structural characteristics of the vegetation layer. Therefore, this study investigated a method of estimating corn growth parameters by combining multispectral and backscatter features based on optical and SAR data during the crop growth season.

Compared with optical satellite sensors, Synthetic Aperture Radar (SAR) can obtain internal information on the crop vegetation layer and even soil layer due to its certain penetration ability. Directly using the original backscatter coefficient to estimate crop growth parameters can cause significant errors. This is similar to the research conducted by Baghdadi et al., where SAR signals could penetrate the crops to obtain vegetation and soil information under the crop cover, while directly using the backscatter coefficient for retrieving the soil moisture was not advantageous in presence of a well-developed vegetation cover [39]. However, a radar vegetation scattering model can accurately describe these scattering mechanisms between the vegetation and soil. Among them, the WCM is the most concise and widely used, and is applicable to explain the microwave scattering mechanism in areas with a relatively uniform vegetation coverage such as crop fields [40]. According to the principle of the WCM, the total backscatter received by the radar is related to the vegetation growth parameters (LAI, biomass, etc.) and the surface soil parameters (including surface roughness and soil moisture) [23–25]. Therefore, in this study, based on the WCM theory, we developed a corn crop growth parameter estimation model that combines optical and SAR data without any other external data input. By calculating the difference value $\Delta\sigma^0$ between the backscatter coefficients of two SAR images synchronized with optical images, it was found that $\Delta\sigma^0$ weakened the influence of the surface layer on SAR data, revealing the internal structural characteristics of the crop vegetation layer. It also described the differences in radar backscatter coefficient characteristics of a corn crop under the same plant height increment, reflecting the complexity of the vegetation layer structure in a cross-section for different fields. The larger the $\Delta\sigma^0$ value, the more complex the structural characteristics of the vegetation layer in a unit cross-section, and the larger the LAI or biomass per unit volume of the crop. As Wang et al. proposed, the scattering intensity of vegetation layers increases with the increase in crop LAI [41]. Therefore, in this study, we introduced the DRI into the attenuation coefficient τ^2 of the WCM to calibrate the optical vegetation indexes VI_{opt}, and we constructed corn growth parameter estimation models VI_{DRI}. Essentially, the introduction of radar DRI when constructing the VI_{DRI} indexes proved to have a better correlation with the corn plant height and BBCH than the use of multispectral indexes VI_{opt}. Among them, the $S2REP_{DRI}$ index calculated based on the red-edge 2 band showed the highest estimation accuracy of corn plant height and BBCH phenology, indicating that the VI_{DRI} indexes constructed based on the WCM principle, combined with the red-edge multispectral vegetation indexes and radar DRI, had certain advantages in improving the estimation accuracy of corn growth parameters. Similarly, based on various regression learning algorithms, David et al. proposed that the combination of optical SAR and optical data can improve the accuracy of vegetation biomass estimation. At the same time, the study found that the Sentinel-2 red-edge 2 band has greater advantages in this regard [42]. However, the existing models were established based on different phenological periods of crops, and the accuracy of the models is difficult to guarantee when the vegetation coverage is high [43,44]. Therefore, this study directly constructed a growth parameter inversion model based on the corn heading phenology, which has important research value for effectively improving the inversion accuracy of a model under a high vegetation coverage.

Additionally, when comparing the estimation results using data from experimental area 1 and experimental area 2, the results showed that the VI_{DRI} indexes had slightly better accuracy in improving the VI_{opt} indexes for estimating corn plant height and BBCH in experimental area 1 than in experimental area 2. This is because the SAR images of experimental area 1 were largely synchronized with the optical images, and there was a small interval between the two SAR images. Meanwhile, the interval between the two

SAR images in experimental area 2 was relatively large, and the synchronization between the SAR and optical images was also relatively poor. This indicates that a larger interval between SAR image data will affect the sensitivity of the DRI feature to estimate the crop growth parameters, thereby affecting the accuracy of the VI_{DRI} model in estimating crop growth parameters. Therefore, in practical applications, the interval between the two SAR images used for calculating DRI should not be too large, and the optical and SAR satellite images should be synchronized as much as possible to ensure that the ground object states observed by the two types of satellites are consistent. In addition, this study found that the VI_{DRI} indexes have a slightly better accuracy in improving the VI_{opt} indexes for estimating corn plant height than estimating the BBCH parameter. This is because the plant height reflects the structural characteristics of crops in the vertical direction. SAR data, due to their certain penetrability, can offer insights into the interior of the corn canopy and vertical structural information on the crop. Meanwhile, the phenotypic differences of the corn plant during the tasseling stage are mainly reflected in the extraction status of male spikes at the top of the vegetation canopy, demonstrating the characteristics of two-dimensional plane changes at the top of the corn canopy. This viewpoint is consistent with Caicoya et al., who proposed that SAR features are beneficial for detecting vertical structural information on the vegetation [45]. As such, it seems that the VI_{DRI} index proposed in this article is more conducive to improving the estimation accuracy of corn plant height compared to the BBCH parameter.

However, the conclusion of this study is mainly based on dual-polarization ($\sigma^0{}_{VH}$, $\sigma^0{}_{VV}$) SAR satellite data in the C-band. Beyond these, there are many full-polarization ($\sigma^0{}_{VV}$, $\sigma^0{}_{VH}$, $\sigma^0{}_{HH}$, $\sigma^0{}_{HV}$) SAR data, and different polarization modes have different abilities in estimating growth parameters of crops. Furthermore, the radar electromagnetic wave scattering characteristics of crop fields vary in different wave bands and polarization modes [2]. Therefore, it is necessary to further verify the applicability of the estimation model in other radar bands and polarization modes. In addition, we mainly studied the corn crops normally planted on the North China Plain. Although we have achieved satisfactory estimation results, due to the limitations of the crop planting region and varieties, additional layout experiments are needed to further verify the universality of the research methods proposed in this paper, by testing them in other corn planting areas such as China's southwest mountainous areas, southern hilly areas, and the Qinghai Tibet Plateau.

5. Conclusions

Based on the theory of the vegetation scattering model, in this study, we developed a corn growth parameter estimation model VI_{DRI} that combines the use of multispectral vegetation indices (VI_{opt}) extracted from partially available optical satellite data covering the research area and the differential radar information (DRI) parameter $\Delta\sigma^0$, which reflects the internal structural characteristics of the vegetation layer and is only related to the growth status of the crop vegetation. After comparing and analyzing the correlation and parameter estimation accuracies of various multispectral vegetation indexes VI_{opt} and their corresponding VI_{DRI} indexes with corn plant height and BBCH phenology, the results indicate that the VI_{DRI} indexes constructed by combining rich multispectral features from the corn vegetation canopy and SAR features related to the vegetation layer structure show a better correlation with growth parameters. Furthermore, we have found that using a combination of red-edge multispectral and SAR DRI features to construct VI_{DRI} indexes is advantageous in improving the accuracy of corn growth parameter estimation. This is especially the case for the $NDVIre2_{DRI}$ and $S2REP_{DRI}$ indexes constructed in conjunction with the Sentinel-2 satellite data red-edge 2 band, which showed the best correlations with growth parameters compared to the other vegetation indexes.

Author Contributions: Conceptualization, Y.W.; methodology, Y.W. and Z.W.; software (MATLAB version R2018a), Y.W.; validation, Y.W., Z.W. and S.L. (Shanjun Luo); formal analysis, Y.W.; investigation, X.H.; resources, X.L.; data curation, S.L. (Shuaibing Liu); writing—original draft preparation, Y.W.; writing—review and editing, Y.W. and Z.W.; visualization, X.L.; supervision, S.L. (Shanjun Luo); project administration, X.H.; funding acquisition, Z.W. All authors have read and agreed to the published version of the manuscript.

Funding: This research was supported by the Scientific Research Foundation of the Henan Academy of Sciences (241825013); the Scientific Research Foundation for High-End Talents of the Henan Academy of Sciences (242025005); the Basic Foundation for Scientific Research of the Henan Academy of Sciences (240625002 and 240625003); and the Key R&D projects in Hubei Province (2020BBB058 "Phenomics Research and New Variety Creation of Hybrid rice Based on UAV Remote Sensing").

Institutional Review Board Statement: Not applicable.

Data Availability Statement: The dataset used in this paper can be found through the European Space Agency Copernicus Data Space Ecosystem: https://dataspace.copernicus.eu/, accessed on 1 September 2021.

Acknowledgments: The authors wish to acknowledge the European Space Agency for provision of datasets.

Conflicts of Interest: The authors declare no conflict of interest.

References

1. Mandal, D.; Kumar, V.; Ratha, D.; Dey, S.; Rao, Y.S. Dual polarimetric radar vegetation index for crop growth monitoring using sentinel-1 SAR data. *Remote Sens. Environ.* **2020**, *247*, 111954. [CrossRef]
2. Wang, H.Q.; Magagi, R.; Goïta, K.; Duguay, Y.; Trudel, M.; Muhuri, A. Retrieval performances of different crop growth descriptors from full- and compact-polarimetric SAR decompositions. *Remote Sens. Environ.* **2023**, *285*, 113381. [CrossRef]
3. Jia, X.Q.; Feng, M.C.; Yang, W.D.; Wang, C.; Zhang, S. Hyperspectral estimation of aboveground dry biomass of winter wheat based on the combination of vegetation indices. *Chin. J. Ecol.* **2018**, *37*, 424–429.
4. Qiao, L.; Tang, W.; Gao, D.; Zhao, R.; An, L.; Li, M.; Sun, H.; Song, D. UAV based chlorophyll content estimation by evaluating vegetation index responses under different crop coverages. *Comput. Electron. Agric.* **2022**, *196*, 106775. [CrossRef]
5. Delegido, J.; Verrelst, J.; Meza, C.M.; Rivera, J.P.; Alonso, L.; Moreno, J. A red-edge spectral index for remote sensing estimation of green LAI over agroecosystems. *Eur. J. Agron.* **2013**, *46*, 42–52. [CrossRef]
6. Rehman, T.H.; Reis, A.; Akbar, N.; Linquist, B.A. Use of Normalized Difference Vegetation Index to Assess N Status and Predict Grain Yield in Rice. *Agron. J.* **2019**, *111*, 2889–2898. [CrossRef]
7. Dong, T.; Liu, J.; Shang, J.; Qian, B.; Ma, B.; Kovacs, J.M.; Walters, D.; Jiao, X.; Geng, X.; Shi, Y. Assessment of red-edge vegetation indices for crop leaf area index estimation. *Remote Sens. Environ.* **2018**, *222*, 133–143. [CrossRef]
8. Bazezew, M.N.; Belay, A.T.; Guda, S.T.; Kleinn, C. Developing Maize Yield Predictive Models from Sentinel-2 MSI Derived Vegetation Indices: An Approach to an Early Warning System on Yield Fluctuation and Food Security. *PFG—J. Photogramm. Remote Sens. Geoinf. Sci.* **2021**, *89*, 535–548. [CrossRef]
9. Liu, C.A.; Chen, Z.X.; Shao, Y.; Chen, J.S.; Hasi, T.; Pan, H.Z. Research advances of SAR remote sensing for agriculture applications: A review. *J. Integr. Agric.* **2019**, *18*, 506–525. [CrossRef]
10. Romero-Puig, N.; Lopez-Sanchez, J.M. Comparing In-SAR Methodologies for the Retrieval of Paddy Rice Height with TanDEM-X Data. In Proceedings of the IGARSS 2020—IEEE International Geoscience and Remote Sensing Symposium (IGARSS), Waikoloa, HI, USA, 26 September–2 October 2020.
11. Yadav, V.P.; Prasad, R.; Bala, R. Leaf area index estimation of wheat crop using modified water cloud model from the time series SAR and optical satellite data. *Geocart. Int.* **2021**, *36*, 791–802. [CrossRef]
12. Castillo, J.; Apan, A.A.; Maraseni, T.N.; Salmo, S.G.I. Estimation and mapping of above-ground biomass of mangrove forests and their replacement land uses in the Philippines using Sentinel imagery. *ISPRS J. Photogramm. Remote Sens.* **2017**, *134*, 70–85. [CrossRef]
13. Xiuliang, J.; Guijun, Y.; Xingang, X.; Hao, Y.; Haikuan, F.; Zhenhai, L.; Jiaxiao, S.; Yubin, L.; Chunjiang, Z. Combined Multi-Temporal Optical and Radar Parameters for Estimating LAI and Biomass in Winter Wheat Using HJ and RADARSAR-2 Data. *Remote Sens.* **2015**, *7*, 13251. [CrossRef]
14. Luo, P.; Liao, J.J.; Shen, G.Z. Combining Spectral and Texture Features for Estimating Leaf Area Index and Biomass of Maize Using Sentinel-1/2, and Landsat-8 Data. *IEEE Access* **2020**, *8*, 53614–53626. [CrossRef]
15. Abdikan, S.; Sekertekin, A.; Narin, O.G.; Delen, A.; Sanli, F.B. A comparative analysis of SLR, MLR, ANN, XGBoost and CNN for crop height estimation of sunflower using Sentinel-1 and Sentinel-2. *Adv. Space Res.* **2023**, *71*, 3045–3059. [CrossRef]

16. Yeasin, M.; Haldar, D.; Kumar, S.; Paul, R.K.; Ghosh, S. Machine Learning Techniques for Phenology Assessment of Sugarcane Using Conjunctive SAR and Optical Data. *Remote Sens.* **2022**, *14*, 3249. [CrossRef]
17. Tao, L.; Li, J.; Jiang, J.; Chen, X. Leaf Area Index Inversion of Winter Wheat Using RADARSAT-2 Data and Modified Water cloud Model. *J. Triticeae Crops* **2016**, *36*, 236–242.
18. Bao, Y.; Zhang, Y.; Wang, J.; Min, J. Surface soil moisture estimation over dense crop using Envisat ASAR and Landsat TM imagery: An approach. *Int. J. Remote Sens.* **2014**, *35*, 6190–6212. [CrossRef]
19. Davitt, A.; Winter, J.M.; Mcdonald, K. Integrated crop growth and radiometric modeling to support Sentinel synthetic aperture radar observations of agricultural fields. *J. Appl. Remote Sens.* **2020**, *14*, 044508. [CrossRef]
20. Ramesh, N.; Heiko, B.; Kevin, T.; Keith, M.; Sarah, J.; France, G.; Charles, G.; Yadvinder, M.; Geoff, B.; Sam, D.; et al. Airborne S-Band SAR for Forest Biophysical Retrieval in Temperate Mixed Forests of the UK. *Remote Sens.* **2016**, *8*, 609. [CrossRef]
21. Zhang, H.B.; Wang, C.C.; Zhu, J.J.; Fu, H.Q.; Han, W.T.; Xie, H.Q. Forest Aboveground Biomass Estimation in Subtropical Mountain Areas Based on Improved Water Cloud Model and PolSAR Decomposition Using L-Band PolSAR Data. *Forests* **2023**, *14*, 2303. [CrossRef]
22. Dave, R.; Saha, K.; Kushwaha, A.; Pandey, D.K.; Vithalpura, M.; Parath, N.; Murugesan, A. Application of sentinel-1 SAR-derived vegetation descriptors for soil moisture retrieval and plant height prediction during the wheat growth cycle. *Int. J. Remote Sens.* **2023**, *44*, 786–801. [CrossRef]
23. Yang, Z.; Li, K.; Shao, Y.; Brisco, B.; Liu, L. Estimation of Paddy Rice Variables with a Modified Water Cloud Model and Improved Polarimetric Decomposition Using Multi-Temporal RADARSAT-2 Images. *Remote Sens.* **2016**, *8*, 878. [CrossRef]
24. Kweon, S.K.; Oh, Y.A. Modified Water-Cloud Model with Leaf Angle Parameters for Microwave Backscattering from Agricultural Fields. *IEEE Trans. Geosci. Remote Sens.* **2015**, *53*, 2802–2809. [CrossRef]
25. Bai, X.; He, B.; Li, X.; Zeng, J.; Wang, X.; Wang, Z.; Zeng, Y.; Su, Z. First Assessment of Sentinel-1A Data for Surface Soil Moisture Estimations Using a Coupled Water Cloud Model and Advanced Integral Equation Model over the Tibetan Plateau. *Remote Sens.* **2017**, *9*, 714. [CrossRef]
26. Ahmadian, N.; Ullmann, T.; Verrelst, J.; Borg, E.; Conrad, C. Biomass Assessment of Agricultural Crops Using Multi-temporal Dual Polarimetric TerraSAR-X Data. *PFG—J. Photogramm. Remote Sens. Geoinf. Sci.* **2019**, *87*, 159–175. [CrossRef] [PubMed]
27. Chauhan, S.; Srivastava, H.S.; Patel, P. Crop Height Estimation Using RISAT-1 Hybrid Polarized Synthetic Aperture Radar Data. *IEEE J. Sel. Top. Appl. Earth Obs. Remote Sens.* **2019**, *12*, 2928–2933. [CrossRef]
28. Bleiholder, H.; Kirfel, H.; Langeluddeke, P.; Stauss, R.; Van, D.B.T. A Uniform Code for the Phenological Stages of Crops and Weeds. *Pesqui. Agropecu. Bras.* **1991**, *26*, 1423–1429.
29. Zadoks, J.C.; Chang, T.T.; Konzak, C.F. A decimal code for the growth stages of cereals. *Weed Res.* **1974**, *14*, 415–421. [CrossRef]
30. *QX/T 361-2016*; Specification for Agricultural Meteorological Observation Maize. China Meteorological Administration: Beijing, China, 2016.
31. Wang, Y.; Fang, S.; Zhao, L.; Huang, X. Estimation of maize plant height in North China by means of backscattering coefficient and depolarization parameters using Sentinel-1 dual-pol SAR data. *Int. J. Remote Sens.* **2022**, *43*, 1960–1982. [CrossRef]
32. Rouse, J.W.; Haas, R.H.; Schell, J.A.; Deering, D.W. Monitoring Vegetation Systems in the Great Plains with Erts. *NASA Spec. Publ.* **1974**, *351*, 309.
33. Fernandez-Manso, A.; Fernandez-Manso, O.; Quintano, C. SENTINEL-2A red-edge spectral indices suitability for discriminating burn severity. *Int. J. Appl. Earth Obs. Geoinf.* **2016**, *50*, 170–175. [CrossRef]
34. Mercier, A.; Betbeder, J.; Baudry, J.; Roux, V.L.; Hubert-Moy, L. Evaluation of Sentinel-1 & 2 time series for predicting wheat and rapeseed phenological stages. *ISPRS J. Photogramm. Remote Sens.* **2020**, *163*, 231–256.
35. Attema, E.; Ulaby, F.T. Vegetation modeled as a water cloud. *Radio Sci.* **1978**, *13*, 357–364. [CrossRef]
36. Lievens, H.; Verhoest, N. On the Retrieval of Soil Moisture in Wheat Fields from L-Band SAR Based on Water Cloud Modeling, the IEM, and Effective Roughness Parameters. *IEEE Geosci. Remote Sens. Lett.* **2011**, *8*, 740–744. [CrossRef]
37. Kokhan, S.; Vostokov, A. Using Vegetative Indices to Quantify Agricultural Crop Characteristics. *J. Ecol. Eng.* **2020**, *21*, 120–127. [CrossRef] [PubMed]
38. Dong, T.; Meng, J.; Shang, J.; Liu, J.; Wu, B. Evaluation of Chlorophyll-Related Vegetation Indices Using Simulated Sentinel-2 Data for Estimation of Crop Fraction of Absorbed Photosynthetically Active Radiation. *IEEE J. Sel. Top. Appl. Earth Obs. Remote Sens.* **2015**, *8*, 4049–4059. [CrossRef]
39. Baghdadi, N.; El Hajj, M.; Zribi, M.; Bousbih, S. Calibration of the water cloud model at C-Band for winter crop fields and grasslands. *Remote Sens.* **2018**, *9*, 13. [CrossRef]
40. Li, J.H.; Wang, S.S. Using SAR-Derived Vegetation Descriptors in a Water Cloud Model to Improve Soil Moisture Retrieval. *Remote Sens.* **2018**, *10*, 1370. [CrossRef]
41. Wang, R.; Chen, J.M.; He, L.M.; Liu, J.E.; Shang, J.L.; Liu, J.G.; Dong, T.F. A novel semi-empirical model for crop leaf area index retrieval using SAR co- and cross-polarizations. *Remote Sens. Environ.* **2023**, *296*, 113727. [CrossRef]
42. David, R.M.; Rosser, N.J.; Donoghue, D.N.M. Improving above ground biomass estimates of Southern Africa dryland forests by combining Sentinel-1 SAR and Sentinel-2 multispectral imagery. *Remote Sens. Environ.* **2022**, *282*, 113232. [CrossRef]
43. Gao, S.; Niu, Z.; Huang, N.; Hou, X. Estimating the Leaf Area Index, height and biomass of maize using HJ-1 and RADARSAT-2—ScienceDirect. *Int. J. Appl. Earth Obs. Geoinf.* **2013**, *24*, 1–8.

44. Hosseini, M.; Mcnairn, H.; Mitchell, S.; Robertson, L.D.; Davidson, A.; Homayouni, S. Integration of synthetic aperture radar and optical satellite data for corn biomass estimation. *Methodsx* **2020**, *7*, 100857. [CrossRef] [PubMed]
45. Caicoya, A.T.; Kugler, F.; Pardini, M.; Hajnsek, I.; Papathanassiou, K. Vertical forest structure characterization for the estimation of Above Ground Biomass: First experimental results using SAR vertical reflectivity profiles. In Proceedings of the IEEE Joint International Geoscience and Remote Sensing Symposium (IGARSS)/35th Canadian Symposium on Remote Sensing, Quebec City, QC, Canada, 13–18 July 2014.

agriculture

MDPI

Article

Winter Wheat Yield Estimation with Color Index Fusion Texture Feature

Fuqin Yang [1], Yang Liu [2,3], Jiayu Yan [1], Lixiao Guo [1], Jianxin Tan [1], Xiangfei Meng [1], Yibo Xiao [1] and Haikuan Feng [2,3,*]

[1] College of Civil Engineering, Henan University of Engineering, Zhengzhou 451191, China; fqyang@haue.edu.cn (F.Y.); yu224409@163.com (J.Y.); kwok@home.hpu.edu.cn (L.G.); tanjianxin0521@163.com (J.T.); 18738500976@163.com (X.M.); 13140576721@163.com (Y.X.)

[2] Key Laboratory of Quantitative Remote Sensing in Agriculture of Ministry of Agriculture and Rural Affairs, Information Technology Research Center, Beijing Academy of Agriculture and Forestry Sciences, Beijing 100097, China; liuyanghe810@cau.edu.cn

[3] National Engineering and Technology Center for Information Agriculture, Nanjing Agricultural University, Nanjing 210095, China

* Correspondence: 2020201097@stu.njau.edu.cn

Abstract: The rapid and accurate estimation of crop yield is of great importance for large-scale agricultural production and national food security. Using winter wheat as the research object, the effects of color indexes, texture feature and fusion index on yield estimation were investigated based on unmanned aerial vehicle (UAV) high-definition digital images, which can provide a reliable technical means for the high-precision yield estimation of winter wheat. In total, 22 visible color indexes were extracted using UAV high-resolution digital images, and a total of 24 texture features in red, green, and blue bands extracted by ENVI 5.3 were correlated with yield, while color indexes and texture features with high correlation and fusion indexes were selected to establish yield estimation models for flagging, flowering and filling stages using partial least squares regression (PLSR) and random forest (RF). The yield estimation model constructed with color indexes at the flagging and flowering stages, along with texture characteristics and fusion indexes at the filling stage, had the best accuracy, with R^2 values of 0.70, 0.71 and 0.76 and RMSE values of 808.95 kg/hm^2, 794.77 kg/hm^2 and 728.85 kg/hm^2, respectively. The accuracy of winter wheat yield estimation using PLSR at the flagging, flowering, and filling stages was better than that of RF winter wheat estimation, and the accuracy of winter wheat yield estimation using the fusion feature index was better than that of color and texture feature indexes; the distribution maps of yield results are in good agreement with those of the actual test fields. Thus, this study can provide a scientific reference for estimating winter wheat yield based on UAV digital images and provide a reference for agricultural farm management.

Keywords: UAV; color index; fusion texture; partial least squares; random forest

1. Introduction

Wheat is one of the most important food rations in China, and its production is directly related to national food security and social stability. The timely, rapid, and accurate forecasting of yields is of great significance to the development of the national economy, early warning of food security, precise fertilization in agriculture, and agricultural insurance [1,2]. Satellite remote sensing provides a new method for estimating crop yields on a large scale because of its large coverage area and short detection period, and in particular, the mobility and flexibility of unmanned aerial remote sensing and its ability to quickly obtain the key growth parameters of a specific growth period of crops are also important [3,4].

In recent years, remote sensing technology has been rapidly applied in crop yield estimation. Currently, there are three main types of methods used for winter wheat yield prediction using remote sensing data: (1) the remote sensing spectral index yield empirical regression method, (2) the potential stress yield model, and (3) the crop dry matter yield model [5].

The empirical statistical regression model directly establishes the relationship between remote sensing and yield [6–8], generally using partial least squares regression, support vector machine regression, neural network regression, random forest regression, and other deep learning methods to establish the relationship between remote sensing and yield, regardless of the complex process of crop yield formation, and it establishes a concise and transparent model that is easy to compute. Still, this yield model has no apparent physical mechanism; it struggles to reflect crops' growth and development process truly. Tao et al. [9] constructed a winter wheat yield estimation model by selecting the vegetation index and red-edge parameters, and the results show that the vegetation index fused with red-edge parameters could significantly improve the estimation effect of the yield model. Zhang et al. [10] used a UAV with a digital camera and a multi-spectral camera to extract different color feature models, vegetation coverage, and vegetation index from images. They constructed a regression model for cotton yield using multiple linear regression methods. The results show that the model established by multiple variables had the best effect. Fei et al. [11] adopted the ensemble Bayesian model averaging (EBMA) method to improve model performance; compared to the best-performing individual model, the EBMA models obtained a weak accuracy improvement by integrating only the linear models or the nonlinear models. Tao et al. [12] constructed a winter wheat yield estimation model based on the uncrewed aerial vehicle (UAV) hyperspectral data using a vegetation index fused with plant height employing partial least squares regression, neural network regression, and random forest regression. The R^2 and RMSE values of the optimal yield model for winter wheat constructed using the partial least squares method were 0.77 and 648.90 kg/ha. The R^2 and RMSE of the optimal yield model for winter wheat constructed using the Random Forest method were 0.44 and 1009.82 kg/ha.

Potential stress yield considers the physiological factors of the crop itself and the growing environmental conditions affecting its growth. It obtains these parameters to estimate the model yield based on remote sensing data [13,14]. This model is reasonable, but how to effectively determine and estimate crop potential stress yield is still a problem that needs further research. The crop dry matter yield model is mainly based on remote sensing information data, used to assess the quality of dry matter on the crop ground, and then based on the relationship between dry matter and fruit, it obtains a more reasonable remote sensing yield estimate model. This method has a certain degree of mechanical rationality, and the model is relatively stable. Although the model is rather complex, it involves agronomic parameters and has recently become a research hotspot [15]. Wang et al. [16] constructed a yield estimation model for winter wheat using a vegetation index fused with meteorological data, soil moisture content, and other multi-source data using a random forest algorithm in a yield prediction model for wheat at different growth stages, constructed by the random forest algorithm. The accuracy of the yield prediction model with the characteristic variables of May in the October sub-annual and April in the October sub-annual was high; the R^2 values were 0.85 and 0.84, and the RMSE values were 821.55 and 832.01 kg/hm^2.

The crop dry matter yield model is mainly based on remote sensing information data, which are used to estimate the quality of the dry matter on the crop ground, and then based on the relationship between dry matter and fruit, it obtains a more reasonable remote sensing yield estimate. This method has a certain degree of mechanical rationality, and the model is relatively stable. Although the model is relatively complex, it involves agronomic parameters, and has become a research hotspot in recent years. Zhang et al. [17] used the dynamic fraction of post-anthesis phase biomass accumulation to estimate the winter wheat harvest index, and then used this to obtain an estimated yield. Huang et al. [18] developed a data assimilation framework coupling remote sensing information with the WOFOST-PROSAIL model to estimate wheat yields in the North China Plain, and the results show that the method improved crop yields at the regional scale. Chen et al. [19]

obtained the critical stages of winter wheat information from remote sensing data, and simulated and adjusted the climatic information in the crop model (MCWLA-Wheat). They assimilated the spatial difference of LAI into the crop model MCWLA-Wheat using the constant gain Kalman filter algorithm.

RGB cameras have become one of the more commonly used sensors on UAVs due to their cheapness, and the ease of their operation and data processing; RGB images represent the color of each pixel by combining the three basic colors of red, green, and blue. Texture features represent another important type of remote sensing information, which can reflect the properties of the object itself and help to distinguish between two different objects [20,21]. Texture features are those that refer to changes in the grey level of the image, which are related to spatial statistics and reflect the properties of the image itself. Datasets such as those regarding the spectra and textures acquired by UAV have successfully been used to predict various plant traits, such as grain yield [20], biomass [21] and so on. Ma et al. [22] extracted the visible vegetation indices and texture features from RGB images for cotton yield monitoring, and the results show that the yield model constructed with the RF_ELM model is optimal the R^2 and RMSE were, respectively, 0.9109 and 0.91277 t/ha. Qu et al. [23] assessed the feasibility of using RF and XGBoost models to predict wild blueberry yields according to the color and texture feature data acquired from drone RGB images.

In terms of model selection, machine learning can establish generalizable models from a large amount of training data, which are increasingly being applied by many scholars in precision agriculture [24–27]. Cui et al. [28] used PLS, support vector machine (SVM), ridge regression (RR) and k-nearest neighbors (KNN) for faba yield estimation based on RGB and multispectral data from drones. The results show that the R^2 value of RF is higher than those of other machine learning algorithms, followed by PLS. Alabi et al. [29] used five machine learning models (Cubist, XGBoost, GBM, SVM and RF) for soybean yield estimation, and the results show that the Cubist and RF estimation models were optimal; their R^2 was 0.89. Cheng et al. [30] used PLSR, SVM and RF for winter wheat yield estimation, and the RF model had the highest estimation accuracy, with R^2 and RMSE values of 0.560 and 1634 kg/hm^2, respectively. Fan et al. [31] used RR, SVM and RF for maize yield modeling. The results show that RF modeling worked best, and its R^2 was 0.88. These results indicate that the RF and PLSR methods are reliable when used in evaluating the relationship between input parameters and yield.

Although remote sensing information combined with agronomic parameters can simulate the physiological growth process of crops, it requires a large amount of agronomic information, hindering the wide application range of the model. However, empirical statistics can establish a quantitative relationship between crop parameters and remote sensing information with fewer data, so it is widely used for the estimation of crop physiological and biochemical parameters. UAV remote sensing is widely used to estimate the physiological and biochemical parameters of crops due to its advantages of high efficiency, high resolution, low operational cost, and flexibility. The above studies used UAV imagery to analyze individual vegetation indexes or multiple vegetation indexes for crop yield estimation. However, there are few methods for winter wheat yield estimation using UAV digital color indexes and texture feature fusion. In this study, the construction of a winter wheat yield model was carried out using color indexes, texture features, and the fusion of color indexes and texture features to explore the different remote sensing information types as the independent variable factors. Empirical statistical regression and machine learning methods were used to improve the accuracy of yield estimation, providing a scientific method for fast and efficient wheat yield prediction.

2. Materials and Methods

2.1. Experimental Design

The experiment was conducted at the National Precision Agriculture Research Demonstration Base in Xiaotangshan Town, Changping District, Beijing, China, which ranges from 116°34′ E to 117°00′ E and 40°00′ N to 40°21′ N, with an average elevation of 36 m. The terrain is flat, and the land is characterized by a warm, temperate continental monsoon climate suitable for wheat growth. Wheat was sown in October 2014 and harvested in June 2015. The two main types of wheat varieties were Jing 9843 (J9843) and ZhongMai 175 (ZM175). These are the main wheat varieties grown in North China. The leaves of the J9843 variety are spread out and have a high protein content; the leaves of Zhongmai 175 variety are upright and have a low protein content. Fertilizers were applied with four nitrogen levels: N1 (0 kg/hm^2), N2 (1/2 normal nitrogen, 195 kg/hm^2), N3 (normal nitrogen, 390 kg/hm^2) and N4 (3/2 normal nitrogen, 585 kg/hm^2). Setting the nitrogen in this way ensures that there are no settings of the same level in any subdivision, whether viewed horizontally or vertically, as well as enabling the use to eliminate differences in land. Water was mainly applied with W1 (rainfall), W2 (normal water), and W3 (2 times normal water). Setting the moisture in this way could enable us to reduce the impacts of neighboring plots and ensure the easy movement of equipment. The plants were planted traditionally. The length of the experimental field was 84 m in the east–west direction and 32 m in the north–south direction, with 16 plots for each treatment, and each treatment was repeated three times. Replicates 2 and 3 were used for modeling, and replicate 1 was used for verification. The detailed statistics are shown in Table 1. There were 48 plots in total, as shown in Figure 1.

Table 1. Descriptive statistics of yield (kg/hm^2) for the calibration and validation datasets.

Dataset	Min	Mean	Max	Standard Deviation	Coefficient of Variation (%)
Calibration	3345	5669	8792	1484	26.60
Validation	3744	6149	8362	1198	20.12

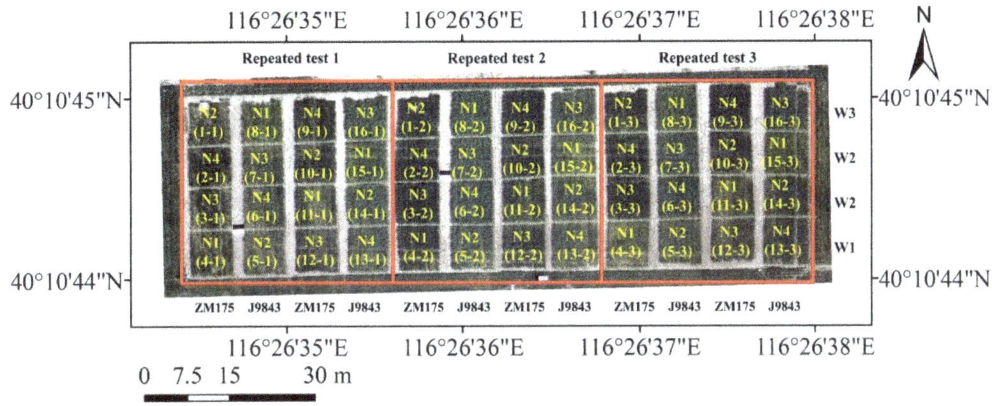

Figure 1. Experimental design: (1) J9843—Jing 9843, ZM175—ZhongMai 175; (2) nitrogen treatments, N1—0 nitrogen, N2—1/2 normal nitrogen, N3—normal nitrogen, N4—3/2 normal nitrogen; (3) water treatments, W1—rainfall, W2—normal water, W3—2 times normal water.

2.2. Data Acquisition

2.2.1. Yield Acquisition

Wheat yield data were measured during the winter wheat harvest. Representative samples were selected from 1 m^2 of each plot, which grew similarly to the whole plot, and the samples obtained were placed in bags and brought back to the laboratory. The wheat was sun-dried to a constant weight, and the yield of each plot was weighed.

2.2.2. Acquisition of Digital Images by UAV

An eight-rotor UAV equipped with a DSC-QX100 digital camera was used to acquire digital images of winter wheat during the flagging (26 April 2015), flowering (13 May

2015) and filling (22 May 2015) stages. The flying height of the UAV was at an altitude of 50 m; it flew at a speed of 4 meters per second, and aerial photographs of the experimental field were taken at noon under a clear and cloudless sky, with a spatial resolution of 0.013 m. The flight time was 15 min, and the heading and lateral overlap were 80%. The digitization footprint of the approach was 10476 Mb/ha. The digital images were stitched with PhotoScan software version 1.1.6 (Agisoft LLC, St. Petersburg, Russia) to obtain a digital elevation model (DEM) and digital orthophoto (DOM) of the experimental field, as described in reference [8,32].

2.3. Color Indexes Selection

Based on the DOM of the winter wheat test field, the average DN (Digital Number) values of the red (red, R), green (green, G), and blue bands (blue, B) of winter wheat in each plot in the DOM image were extracted using ArcGIS software (version 10.7; Esri, Redlands, CA, USA). The DN values of R, G and B were normalized; the values obtained after the normalization of R, G and B are defined as r, g and b. The formula is as follows:

$$r = \mathrm{R}/(\mathrm{R}+\mathrm{G}+\mathrm{B}) \quad (1)$$

$$g = \mathrm{B}/(\mathrm{R}+\mathrm{G}+\mathrm{B}) \quad (2)$$

$$b = \mathrm{B}/(\mathrm{R}+\mathrm{G}+\mathrm{B}) \quad (3)$$

Based on the visible light color index available in the literature, 16 color indexes were selected, as well as the defined R, G, B, r, g, and b, for a total of 22 color indexes, as shown in Table 2.

Table 2. Color index.

Color Feature Index	Formula	References
R	R = R	Red band
G	G = G	Green band
B	B = B	Blue band
r	r = R/(R + G + B)	Normalized red band
g	g = G/(R + G + B)	Normalized green band
b	b = B/(R + G + B)	Normalized blue band
r/b	r/b	[33]
g/b	g/b	[33]
$r-b$	$r-b$	[33]
$r+b$	$r+b$	[33]
$g-b$	$g-b$	[33]
$(r-b)/(r+b)$	$(r-b)/(r+b)$	[33]
$(r-g-b)/(r+g)$	$(r-g-b)/(r+g)$	[21]
EXG	EXG = $2g-b-r$	[34]
GRVI	GRVI = $(g-r)/(g+r)$	[35]
MGRVI	MGRVI = $(g^2-r^2)/(g^2+r^2)$	[25]
RGBVI	RGBVI = $(g^2-br)/(g^2+br)$	[35]
WI	WI = $(g-b)/(r-g)$	[35]
EXR	EXR = $1.4r-g$	[35]
NDI	NDI = $(r-g)/(r+g+0.01)$	[36]
VARI	VARI = $(g-r)/(g+r-b)$	[37]
EXGR	EXGR = $3g-2.4r-b$	[38]

2.4. Texture Feature Acquisition

Image texture features reflect the frequency of hue changes in an image [39,40], which depends not only on surface features, but also on the angle of illumination. In 1973 Haralick et al. proposed the Gray Level Co-occurrence Matrix (GLCM) to describe texture features. The texture calculation was performed in the "Co-occurrence Measures" in ENVI software (version 5.3; Boulder, CO, USA). Eight texture features were extracted in four directions (0°,

45°, 90° and 135°) from the red, green, and blue bands using the GLCM, and the texture features in four directions were averaged to obtain eight texture features for each band. Then, in ArcGIS, the region of interest was delineated for the image of each plot, and the average texture value of each region was extracted and was used as the final texture feature value for this plot. The eight texture feature values were mean (mean), variance (var), homogeneity (hom), contrast (con), dissimilarity (dis), entropy (ent), second moment (sec), and correlation (cor). The corresponding texture features in the red band are, respectively, mean_R, var_R, hom_R, con_R, dis_R, ent_R, sec_R and cor_R. The connected texture features in the green band are, respectively, mean_G, var_G, hom_G, con_G, dis_G, ent_G, sec_G and cor_G. The corresponding texture features in the blue band are, respectively, mean_B, var_B, hom_B, con_B, dis_B, ent_B, sec_B, and cor_B.

2.5. Data Analysis and Accuracy Evaluation

Partial least squares regression (PLSR) [41,42] and random forest (RF) [43,44] were used to construct the estimation model of winter wheat yield. Partial least squares are a mathematical optimization technique that finds the best function match for a data set by minimizing the sum of squared errors. It combines multiple linear regression, typical correlation, and principal component analyses. It simultaneously realizes regression modeling, simplifies the data structure, and analyzes the correlation between independent variables, which brings excellent variables to the statistical analysis of multivariate data and has good robustness in the established model. PLSR model building and charting were done using MATLAB2020a (commercial mathematical software produced by MathWorks, Natick, MA, USA) software and Excel2007 (Microsoft Office Software, Redmond, WA, USA). The random forest algorithm is an integrated learning method proposed by Breiman in 2001. It is a classifier containing many decision trees that can handle classification and regression problems, and is also suitable for problems with dimensionality reduction. RF regression combines multiple decision tree models to solve regression problems. Its basic principle is that each tree randomly extracts a portion of features from a sample, then constructs a decision tree from the training data, and finally combines the results of all the decision trees to produce a final prediction.

2.6. Precision Evaluation

The coefficient of determination (R^2) and root mean square error (RMSE) [45] were used to evaluate the accuracy of the winter wheat yield model. R^2 reflects the stability of the model's establishment and validation; the closer R^2 is to 1, the better the stability of the model is, and the measured value fits the predicted value to a high degree. RMSE is used to test the model's forecasting ability; the smaller the RMSE is, the better the model's estimation ability is.

3. Results and Discussion

3.1. Correlation between Color Indexes and Yield

Table 3 shows the results of the correlation analysis between the color indexes of digital images and yield. From Table 3, we see that there is no correlation between the color indexes g/b and WI and the yield at the flowering stage. In contrast, other color indexes are significantly correlated. During the flagging and flowering stages, $g-b$ was significantly correlated with yield at 0.05, and the rest of the color indexes were considerably associated with yield at 0.01. At the flagging stage, the color index with the highest absolute correlation value with yield was EXR, with a value of 0.6813. The performance metrics EXR, VARI, GRVI, NDI, and MGRVI were selected as independent variables for the winter wheat yield model construction. During the flowering stage, the color index with the highest absolute correlation value with yield was r, with a value of 0.7635. The performance metrics r, VARI, EXR, GRVI, and NDI were selected as the independent variables for yield model construction. During the filling stage, the remaining color index had a highly significant (0.01) correlation with yield. In contrast, the color index with the highest absolute correlation value with yield was r, with a value of 0.7521. r, $(r-g-b)/(r+g)$, EXR, NDI, and GRVI were selected as the independent variables for constructing the yield model.

Table 3. Correlation between color index and yield.

Color Feature Index	Flagging Stage	Flowering Stage	Filling Stage
r	−0.6763 **	−0.7635 **	−0.7521 **
VARI	0.6806 **	0.7609 **	0.7327 **
EXR	−0.6813 **	−0.7604 **	−0.7395 **
GRVI	0.6798 **	0.7579 **	0.7336 **
NDI	−0.6797 **	−0.7579 **	−0.7336 **
MGRVI	0.6796 **	0.7568 **	0.7335 **
$(r-g-b)/(r+g)$	−0.6696 **	−0.7552 **	−0.7484 **
EXGR	0.6485 **	0.7315 **	0.7100 **
$r-b$	−0.6495 **	−0.7161 **	−0.7187 **
r/b	−0.6436 **	−0.7092 **	−0.7034 **
$(r-b)/(r+b)$	−0.6442 **	−0.7082 **	−0.6938 **
g	0.5325 **	0.6841 **	0.6721 **
EXG	0.5325 **	0.6841 **	0.6721 **
$r+b$	−0.5325 **	−0.6841 **	−0.6721 **
RGBVI	0.4580 **	0.6642 **	0.6454 **
b	0.5832 **	0.4528 **	0.3710 **
$g-b$	−0.2965 *	0.3410 *	0.4420 **
g/b	−0.3921 **	0.2056 NS	0.3212 NS
WI	0.4178 **	0.0698 NS	0.0811 NS

Note: * indicates significance at the 0.05 level, ** indicates significance at the 0.01 level, and NS indicates not relevant.

3.2. Correlation between Texture Feature Indexes and Yield

Table 4 shows the results of a correlation analysis of digital image texture feature indices with yield. Table 4 shows that some texture feature indices do not correlate well with yield. During the flag-picking period, the best absolute value of texture feature index correlation with yield was MEAN_R, with a value of 0.5296. The performance metrics MEAN_R, MEAN_G, SEC_G, SEC_R, and ENT_G were selected as the independent variables for yield modeling. During the flowering stage, the best absolute value of correlation between texture character index and yield was MEAN_G, with a value of 0.5136, and the performance metrics MEAN_G, MEAN_R, MEAN_B, COR_B, and COR_G were selected as the independent variables for yield modeling. During the filling period, the best absolute value of texture feature index correlation with yield was MEAN_R, with a value of 0.6263, and the performance metrics MEAN_R, MEAN_B, MEAN_G, SEC_G, and ENT_G were selected as the independent variables for yield modeling.

Table 4. Correlation between texture features and yield.

Texture Features	Flagging Stage	Flowering Stage	Filling Stage
MEAN_R	−0.5296 **	−0.5052 **	−0.6263 **
VAR_R	−0.2586 *	−0.0513 NS	0.2215 NS
HOM_R	0.4229 **	0.0778 NS	−0.2890 *
CON_R	−0.0325 NS	−0.0808 NS	0.0694 NS
DIS_R	−0.3215 *	−0.0759 NS	0.2374 NS
ENT_R	−0.4844 **	−0.0404 NS	0.3418 *
SEC_R	0.4950 **	0.0228 NS	−0.3488 *
COR_R	−0.0650 NS	−0.3299 *	0.1795 NS
MEAN_G	−0.5001 **	−0.5136 **	−0.5169 **
VAR_G	−0.2943 *	−0.0517 NS	0.2152 NS
HOM_G	0.4404 **	0.0541 NS	−0.3058 *
CON_G	−0.0525 NS	−0.0760 NS	0.0702 NS

Table 4. *Cont.*

Texture Features	Flagging Stage	Flowering Stage	Filling Stage
DIS_G	−0.3520 *	−0.0645 NS	0.2417 NS
ENT_G	−0.4878 **	0.0050 NS	0.3595 **
SEC_G	0.4966 **	−0.0270 NS	−0.3676 **
COR_G	−0.0602 NS	−0.3814 **	0.2121 NS
MEAN_B	−0.4145 **	−0.4318 **	−0.5373 **
VARE_B	−0.2831 *	−0.0493 NS	0.1471 NS
HOM_B	0.4265 **	0.0639 NS	−0.2477 NS
CON_B	−0.0500 NS	−0.0764 NS	0.0530 NS
DIS_B	−0.3405 *	−0.0659 NS	0.1776 NS
ENT_B	−0.4718 **	−0.0126 NS	0.3010 *
SEC_B	0.4798 **	−0.0081 NS	−0.3072 *
COR_B	−0.0495 NS	−0.3905 **	0.1893 NS

Note: * indicates significant at the 0.05 level, ** indicates significant at the 0.01 level, and NS indicates not relevant.

3.3. Inversion of Winter Wheat Yield Model

3.3.1. Yield Inversion Based on Color Indexes

A regression model for winter wheat yield was developed based on five color indexes using partial least squares regression and random forest (Table 5 and Figures 2 and 3). The results show that: (1) The PLSR yield estimation model was more accurate than the RF yield estimation model based on visible vegetation index at three stages. (2) The yield estimation model at the filling stage was better than that at the flowering and flag-picking stages when using the PLSR model for yield estimation. Due to the instability of the random forest model, the model used for estimating yield at the filling stage had a lower R^2 (0.01) than the model used for estimating yield at the flowering stage, but it was better than that of the model used for estimating yield at the flag-picking stage.

Table 5. Analysis results of color indexes and yield.

	Flagging Stage				Flowering Stage				Filling Stage			
	Modeling		Testing		Modeling		Testing		Modeling		Testing	
	R^2	RMSE ($kg{\cdot}hm^{-2}$)	R^2	RMSE ($kg{\cdot}hm^{-2}$)	R^2	RMSE ($kg{\cdot}hm^{-2}$)	R^2	RMSE ($kg{\cdot}hm^{-2}$)	R^2	RMSE ($kg{\cdot}hm^{-2}$)	R^2	RMSE ($kg{\cdot}hm^{-2}$)
PLSR	0.68	848.68	0.36	1654.29	0.70	808.95	0.60	905.40	0.75	738.48	0.24	1145.22
RF	0.52	1052.53	0.34	1626.26	0.67	857.28	0.43	1079.48	0.66	936.62	0.37	1150.43

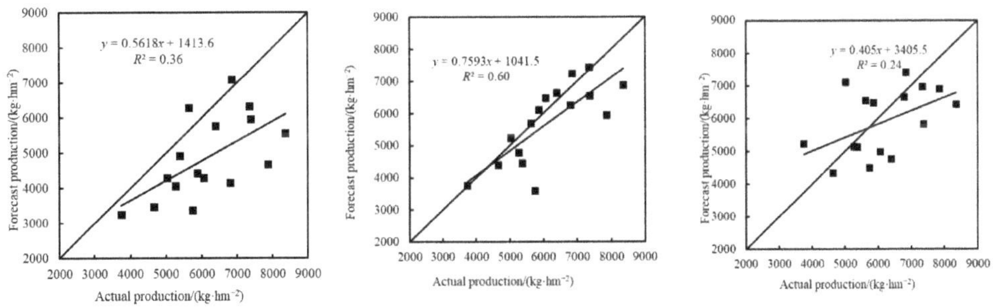

(**a**) flagging stage (**b**) flowering stage (**c**) filling stage

Figure 2. Verification results of different stages' yield prediction model by using the PLSR method based on color indexes.

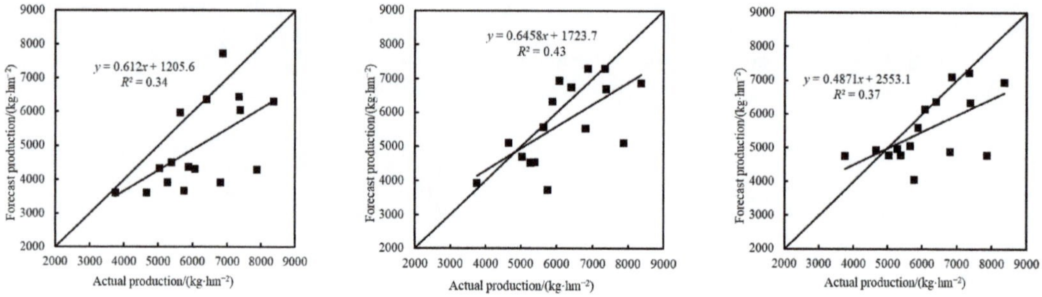

(**a**) flagging stage (**b**) flowering stage (**c**) filling stage

Figure 3. Verification results of different stages' yield prediction using the RF method based on color indexes.

The validation results indicate (Figure 2) that most of the predicted yield values during the flag-picking stage were far away from the 1:1 line, and most of the regions were underestimated in terms of yield; most of the yield values during the flowering stage were near the 1:1 line, and only a few regions were undervalued in terms of yield, whereas the model accuracy during the grouting stage was poor. The predicted yield was underestimated in some regions compared to the actual yield, and some were overestimated and far away from the 1:1 line.

From the verification results in Figure 3, we can see that most of the predicted yield values in the flag-picking period were near the 1:1 line, and most of the expected yield values were underestimated; most of the predicted yield values in the flowering period were near the 1:1 line, but the expected yield values in some regions were underestimated. Many predicted values were underestimated in the filling period, and the predicted yield values In some areas were near the 1:1 line.

In Figure 4, we can see significant differences among replicates 1, 2, and 3 regarding area, with most of replicate 2's area awarding higher yields than replicates 1 and 3, and most of replicate 1's estimated area awarding higher yields than replicates 3. The yields under rainfed level treatments were lower, and were mainly distributed below 5280 kg/hm^2, and the yields under two times water irrigation were better than those under regular water irrigation. The wheat yield under standard N application was around 7500 kg/hm^2, which remained relatively high with excessive N application.

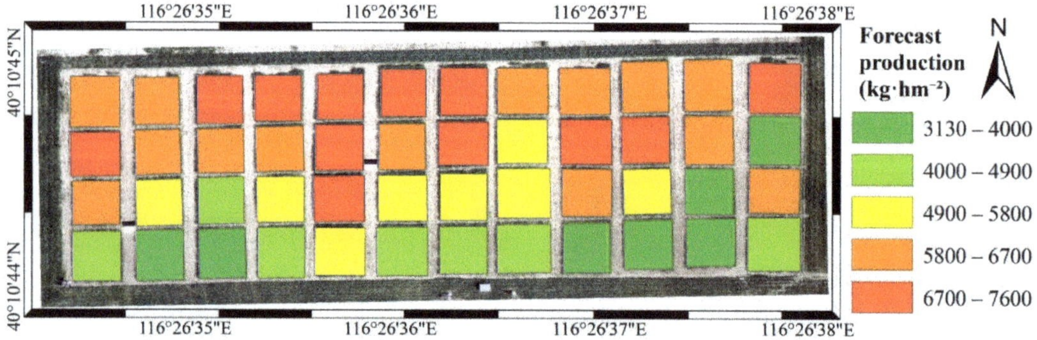

Figure 4. Distribution of optimal model yield based on color feature indexes.

3.3.2. Yield Inversion Based on Texture Feature Indexes

Partial least squares regression and the random forest algorithm were used to establish a regression model for winter wheat yield based on five texture feature indices (Table 6 and Figures 5 and 6). The results show that: (1) the PLSR yield estimation model was more accurate than the RF yield estimation model based on texture feature indexes at three stages. (2) The yield estimation model at the filling stage was superior to the yield estimation model at the flag-picking and flowering stages.

Table 6. Analysis results of texture features and yield.

	Flagging Stage				Flowering Stage				Filling Stage			
	Modeling		Testing		Modeling		Testing		Modeling		Testing	
	R^2	RMSE (kg·hm^{-2})	R^2	RMSE (kg·hm^{-2})	R^2	RMSE (kg·hm^{-2})	R^2	RMSE (kg·hm^{-2})	R^2	RMSE (kg·hm^{-2})	R^2	RMSE (kg·hm^{-2})
PLSR	0.49	1056.4	0.27	1765.35	0.49	1056.20	0.25	1133.59	0.71	794.77	0.40	1241.21
RF	0.16	1396.38	0.16	1390.63	0.43	1125.97	0.36	1115.12	0.45	1110.89	0.30	1192.71

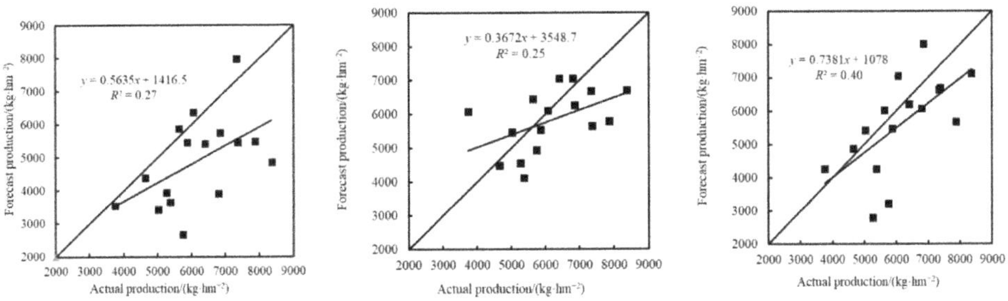

(**a**) flagging stage (**b**) flowering stage (**c**) filling stage

Figure 5. Verification results of different stages' yield prediction model by using the PLSR method based on texture features.

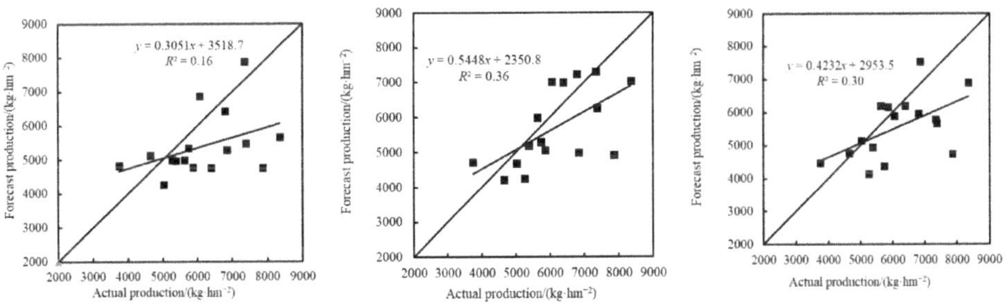

(**a**) flagging stage (**b**) flowering stage (**c**) filling stage

Figure 6. Verification results of different stages' yield prediction using the RF method based on texture features.

Figure 5 shows that most of the yield predictions in the picking stage needed to be underestimated. Aside from the 1:1 line, some yield predictions in the flowering were, and only some areas were overestimated, while others were underestimated. Some yields were around the 1:1 line at the filling stage, and some other areas were minimized.

The results indicate (Figure 6) that most of the predicted yield values in the flag-picking stage were underestimated and far away from the 1:1 line. In contrast, some predicted yield points in the flowering and grouting stages were near the 1:1 line, some points were underestimated, and the underestimated value was more than the overestimated value.

Figure 7 shows that there were significant regional differences among these regions. In the rainfed treatment (W1), winter wheat yield was distributed below 5027 kg/hm^2. In the normal water (W2) and two times normal water (W3) treatments, winter wheat yield was larger, and the yield was concentrated in the range of 5027–8085 kg/hm^2, compared with that in the W3 treatment, which was higher than that in the W2 treatment.

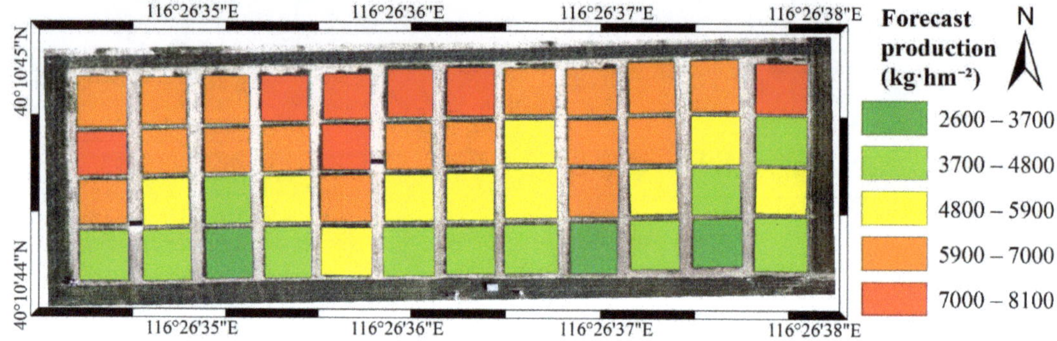

Figure 7. Distribution of optimal model yield based on texture features.

3.3.3. Yield Inversion Based on Fusion of Color Indexes and Texture Feature

In this study we selected the color indexes and texture feature fusion for yield inversion to predict the yield more effectively. The performance metrics EXR, VARI, GRVI, MEAN_R and MEAN_G were selected as independent variables to be used in the model for the estimation of the yield of winter wheat during the flag-picking stage. The performance metrics r, VARI, EXR, MEAN_G and MEAN_R were selected as independent variables to participate in the inversion of the yield model during the flowering stage. The performance metrics r, $(r - g - b)/(r + g)$, EXR, MEAN_R and MEAN_B were selected as independent variables to participate in the inversion of yield model during the filling stage. The results are shown in Table 7 and Figures 8 and 9. The result show that (1) the PLSR yield estimation model was more accurate than the RF yield estimation model based on visible vegetation indexes fused with texture feature indexes at three stages. (2) The yield estimation model at the filling stage was equal or superior to the yield estimation model at the flag-picking and flowering stages.

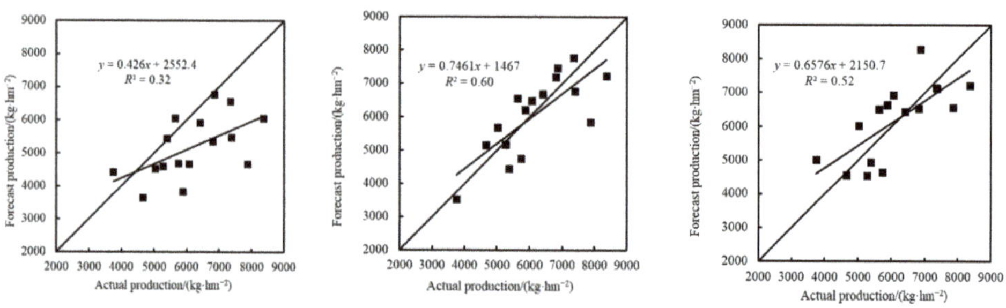

(a) flagging stage (b) flowering stage (c) filling stage

Figure 8. Verification results of different stages' yield prediction model by using the PLSR method based on fusion of color indexes and texture features.

Table 7. Modeling and verification of fusion index and yield.

	Flagging Stage				Flowering Stage				Filling Stage			
	Modeling		Testing		Modeling		Testing		Modeling		Testing	
	R^2	RMSE (kg·hm^{-2})	R^2	RMSE (kg·hm^{-2})	R^2	RMSE (kg·hm^{-2})	R^2	RMSE (kg·hm^{-2})	R^2	RMSE (kg·hm^{-2})	R^2	RMSE (kg·hm^{-2})
PLSR	0.73	775.75	0.32	1406.08	0.72	780.21	0.60	801.95	0.76	728.85	0. 52	859.94
RF	0.57	975.47	0.38	1523.90	0.70	804.74	0.52	928.46	0.70	1163.96	0.41	1081.54

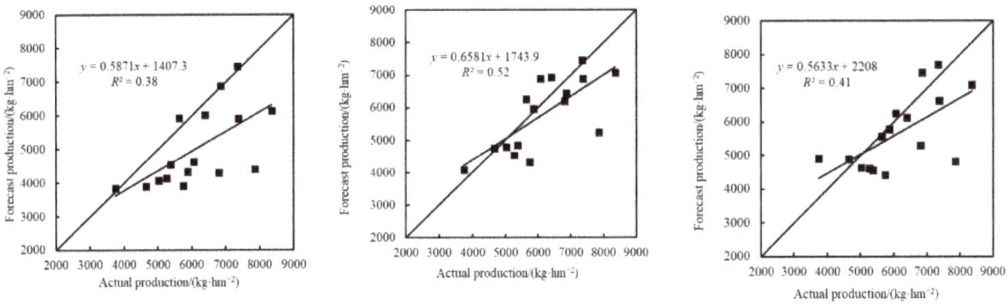

(**a**) flagging stage (**b**) flowering stage (**c**) filling stage

Figure 9. Verification results of different stages' yield prediction using the RF method based on the fusion of color indexes and texture features.

The results indicate (Figure 8) that the yield regions were still underestimated in most regions during the flag-picking period, and the predicted and measured yield values of flowering and grouting stages were distributed near the 1:1 line. The overestimated yield areas of the flowering stage numbered higher than those of the underestimated yield, and the overestimated yield areas of the grouting stage were equal to those of the underestimated yield.

Figure 9 shows that most of the regional yield values were underestimated during the flag-picking stage, and the predicted and measured yield values were near the 1:1 line in the flowering and irrigation stages, with most of the yield values being underestimated and very few points being seriously underestimated.

As shown in Figure 10, the yields of the regions for replicates 1, 2, and 3 were significantly different. Under rainfed treatment, there were significant differences between replicates 1, 2, and 3, but no significant difference in yield between replicates 1 and 2. Under rainfed treatment with no nitrogen application, the yield ranged from 3206 kg/hm^2 to 5427 kg/hm^2, and double water irrigation was shown to increase winter wheat yield.

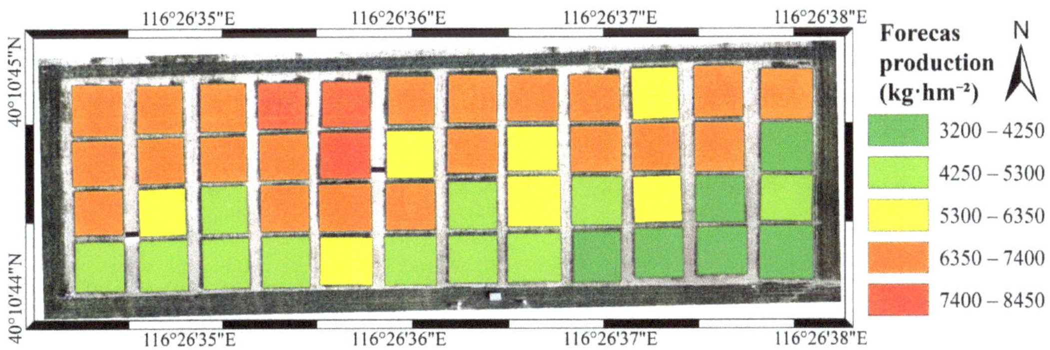

Figure 10. Distribution of optimal model yield based on color index and texture features.

4. Discussion

Accurate early yield estimates are important for food security and the formulation of agricultural policies. In recent years, UAV-based remote sensing data have increasingly been used for the assessment of grain crops such as corn [25] and wheat [31]. Our study extracted color indexes and texture features from UAV digital images, and employed machine learning for winter wheat yield estimation. This method can be used to obtain high accuracy at a relatively low cost.

4.1. The Impact of Growth Period on Yield

Due to the different canopy structures at the flagging, flowering, and irrigating stages of winter wheat, the color features and texture features obtained by a UAV equipped with a digital camera are different, resulting in the greater accuracy of the yield models constructed via other methods in the flagging, flowering, and irrigating stages [46]. The flag-picking and flowering stages are the stages of both vegetative and reproductive growth for wheat. Wheat in the filling stage enters the reproductive growth stage, and its water consumption in the flag-picking stage is large, which is the critical period to determine the number of ears per mu and the number of grains per ear. Wheat in the flowering stage is the most sensitive to fertilizer, light, and temperature. A lack of water or a low temperature will make wheat pollination poor, affecting the seed setting rate and thousand-grain weight. In the filling stage, the leaves and stems of wheat produce starch through photosynthesis, and the transformed proteins are stored in the wheat seeds through assimilation. The filling stage also accelerates the growth of wheat, and many wheat grains are produced at this stage. The remote sensing images collected during these three periods can accurately reflect the yield, consistent with the growth periods selected in the literature [9,30].

4.2. The Impact of Different Algorithms on Yield Estimation

To date, many machine learning models (such as RF and PLSR) have been successfully used for early crop yield estimation. Because the sensitivities of different bands to yield are different, the precision of yield modeling is greater in different growth periods. This study selected five color indexes, five texture feature indexes, and color indexes fused with texture feature indexes to construct yield models in the flagging stage, flowering stage, and filling stage according to the sensitive yield bands in the three growth stages [23]. It was found that the PLSR model achieved better yield estimation accuracy than the RF model in the three growth stages, which may have been caused by inconsistencies between the importance of projection variables used in PLSR and the importance of the out-of-pocket data set used as variables in RF. Whether using RF or PLSR methods, the accuracy of production estimation using color indexes fused with texture feature indexes is greater than the accuracy of production estimation using color indexes or texture feature indexes. The yield model constructed by Ma et al. [22] with color feature indices fused with texture feature indices is optimal; the R^2 was 0.91. The R^2 of the yield modeled by Qu et al. [23] by use of color feature indices fused with texture feature indices was 0.77. The wheat yield prediction model constructed by Liu et al. [47] with color feature indices fused with texture feature indices was verified, and its R^2 was 0.629, which is 16.27% higher than that of the color index model. This study's findings are consistent with those of [22,23,47].

5. Conclusions

Most color indexes in different growth stages significantly correlate with yield ($p < 0.01$). In contrast, only a few texture feature indexes were here significantly associated with yield ($p < 0.01$). The optimal color indexes, texture feature indexes and color indexes combined with texture indexes were used as input factors in the yield model. PLSR and RF were used to establish winter wheat yield estimation models at different growth stages. The results show that:

(1) A model for estimating winter wheat yield using color indexes fused with texture feature indexes outperforms wheat yield models constructed using color indexes or texture feature indexes;
(2) The wheat yield model constructed by PLSR was superior to the yield model constructed by RF for the flagging stage, flowering stage, and filling stage. The R^2 and RMSE values of the optimal yield model modeled with PLSR were 0.75, 0.71 and 0.76 and 738.48 kg/hm^2, 794.77 kg/hm^2 and 728.85 kg/hm^2 when using color indexes, texture indexes and color indexes fused with texture indexes, respectively, as the independent variable in the filling stage;
(3) A winter wheat yield distribution map can be used to more effectively monitor winter wheat yield distribution and provide a more scientific method for guiding fertilization and irrigation, and increasing yield.

Of course, current research and modeling methods also have some limitations. Firstly, this study only used color indexes and texture features extracted from RGB images, which can affect the accuracy of yield prediction. Further research should consider the use of high-spectral-resolution data. The applicability of the model needs to be validated in the future by considering the use of data collected from more years and locations.

Author Contributions: Conceptualization, H.F., F.Y. and Y.L.; methodology, H.F. and F.Y.; software, X.M.; validation, L.G., Y.L. and J.T.; formal analysis, Y.X.; investigation, H.F. and F.Y.; resources, H.F.; data curation, F.Y.; writing—original draft preparation, F.Y. and Y.L.; writing—review and editing, H.F. and F.Y.; visualization, L.G.; supervision, J.Y.; project administration, H.F.; funding acquisition, H.F. All authors have read and agreed to the published version of the manuscript.

Funding: This research was funded by The National Key Research and Development Program of China (No. 2022YFD2001104, 2023YFD2000102); Henan University of Engineering College Student Innovation and Entrepreneurship Training Program Project (No. 202311517028); Key Research Projects of Higher Education Institutions in Henan Province (No. 24B420004).

Institutional Review Board Statement: Not applicable.

Data Availability Statement: The data presented in this paper are part of an ongoing study and the dataset is difficult to access; permission from the corresponding author is required to access the dataset.

Conflicts of Interest: The authors declare no conflicts of interest.

References

1. Liu, Y.; Feng, H.K.; Yue, J.B.; Li, Z.H.; Yang, G.J.; Song, X.Y.; Yang, X.D.; Zhao, Y. Remote-sensing estimation of potato above-ground biomass based on spectral and spatial features extracted from high-definition digital camera images. *Comput. Electron. Agr.* **2022**, *198*, 107089. [CrossRef]
2. Geipel, J.; Link, J.; Claupein, W. Combined spectral and spatial modeling of corn yield based on aerial images and crop surface models acquired with an unmanned aircraft system. *Remote Sens.* **2014**, *6*, 10335–10355. [CrossRef]
3. Wang, L.; Tian, Y.; Yao, X.; Zhu, Y.; Cao, W.X. Predicting grain yield and protein content in wheat by fusing multi-sensor and multi-temporal remote-sensing images. *Field Crop. Res.* **2014**, *164*, 178–188. [CrossRef]
4. Noureldin, N.; Aboelghar, M.; Saudy, H.; Ali, A. Rice yield forecasting models using satellite imagery in Egypt. *Egypt. J. Remote Sens. Space Sci.* **2013**, *16*, 125–131. [CrossRef]
5. Wang, J.H.; Zhao, C.J.; Huang, W.J. *Fundamentals and Applications of Quantitative Remote Sensing in Agriculture*; Science Press: Beijing, China, 2008.
6. Zhu, W.X.; Li, S.J.; Zhang, X.B.; Li, Y.; Sun, Z.G. Estimation of winter wheat yield using optimal vegetation indices from unmanned aerial vehicle remote sensing. *Trans. Chin. Soc. Agric. Eng.* **2018**, *34*, 78–86.
7. Liu, J.M.; Zhou, Z.; He, X.X.; Wang, P.X.; Huang, J.X. Winter Wheat Yield Estimation Method Based on NDWI and Convolutional Neural Network. *Trans. Chin. Soc. Agric. Mach.* **2021**, *52*, 273–280.
8. Zhou, X.; Zheng, H.B.; Xu, X.Q.; He, J.Y.; Ge, X.K.; Yao, X.; Cheng, T.; Zhu, Y.; Cao, W.X.; Tian, Y.C. Predicting grain yield in rice using multi-temporal vegetation indices from UAV-based multispectral and digital imagery. *ISPRS J. Photogramm.* **2017**, *130*, 246–255. [CrossRef]
9. Tao, H.L.; Xu, L.J.; Feng, H.K.; Yang, G.J.; Yang, X.D.; Niu, Y.C. Winter Wheat Yield Estimation Based on UAV Hyperspectral Remote Sensing Data. *Trans. Chin. Soc. Agric. Mach.* **2020**, *51*, 146–155.

10. Zhang, M.N.; Feng, A.J.; Zhou, J.F.; Lv, X.L. Cotton yield prediction using remote visual and spectral images captured by UAV system. *Trans. Chin. Soc. Agric. Eng.* **2019**, *35*, 91–98.
11. Fei, S.; Chen, Z.; Li, L.; Ma, Y.; Xiao, W. Bayesian model averaging to improve the yield prediction in wheat breeding trials. *Agric. For. Meteorol.* **2023**, *328*, 109237. [CrossRef]
12. Tao, H.L.; Feng, H.K.; Xu, L.J.; Miao, M.K.; Yang, G.J.; Yang, X.D.; Fan, L. Estimation of the yield and plant height of winter wheat using UAV-based hyperspectral images. *Sensors* **2020**, *20*, 1231. [CrossRef]
13. Huang, J.X.; Huang, H.; Ma, H.Y.; Zhuo, W.; Huang, R.; Gao, X.R.; Liu, J.M.; Su, W.; Li, L.; Zhang, X.D.; et al. Review on data assimilation of remote sensing and crop growth models. *Trans. Chin. Soc. Agric. Eng.* **2018**, *34*, 144–156.
14. Pantazi, X.E.; Moshou, D.; Alexandridis, T.; Whetton, R.L.; Mouazen, A.M. Wheat yield prediction using machine learning and advanced sensing techniques. *Comput. Electron. Agric.* **2016**, *121*, 57–65. [CrossRef]
15. Huang, J.; Tian, L.; Liang, S.; Ma, H.; Becker-Reshef, I.; Huang, Y.B.; Su, W.; Zhang, X.D.; Zhu, D.H.; Wu, W.B. Improving winter wheat yield estimation by assimilation of the leaf area index from Landsat TM and MODIS data into the WOFOST model. *Agric. For. Meteorol.* **2015**, *204*, 106–121. [CrossRef]
16. Wang, L.G.; Zheng, G.Q.; Guo, Y.; He, J.; Cheng, Y.Z. Prediction of Winter Wheat Yield Based on Fusing Multi-source Spatio-temporal Data. *Trans. Chin. Soc. Agric. Mach.* **2022**, *53*, 198–204.
17. Zhang, N.; Liu, X.; Ren, J.; Wu, S.; Li, F. Estimating the winter wheat harvest index with canopy hyperspectral remote sensing data based on the dynamic fraction of post-anthesis phase biomass accumulation. *Int. J. Remote Sens.* **2022**, *43*, 2029–2058. [CrossRef]
18. Huang, J.; Ma, H.; Sedano, F.; Lewis, P.; Liang, S.; Wu, Q.L.; Su, W.; Zhang, X.D.; Zhu, D.H. Evaluation of regional estimates of winter wheat yield by assimilating three remotely sensed reflectance datasets into the coupled WOFOST–PROSAIL model. *Eur. J. Agron.* **2019**, *102*, 1–13. [CrossRef]
19. Liu, Y.; Feng, H.K.; Yue, J.B.; Fan, Y.G.; Bian, M.B.; Ma, Y.P.; Jin, X.L.; Song, X.Y.; Yang, G.J. Estimating potato above-ground biomass by using integrated unmanned aerial system-based optical, structural, and textural canopy measurements. *Comput. Electron. Agr.* **2023**, *213*, 108229. [CrossRef]
20. Schwalbert, R.A.; Amado, T.; Corassa, G.; Pott, L.P.; Prasad, P.V.; Ciampitti, I.A. Satellite-based soybean yield forecast: Integrating machine learning and weather data for improving crop yield prediction in southern Brazil. *Agric. For. Meteorol.* **2020**, *284*, 107886. [CrossRef]
21. Liu, Y.; Feng, H.K.; Yue, J.B.; Jin, X.L.; Li, Z.H.; Yang, G.J. Estimation of potato above-ground biomass based on unmanned aerial vehicle red-green-blue images with different texture features and crop height. *Front. Plant Sci.* **2022**, *13*, 938216. [CrossRef]
22. Ma, Y.R.; Ma, L.L.; Zhang, Q.; Huang, C.P.; Yi, X.; Chen, X.Y.; Hou, T.Y.; Lv, X.; Zhang, Z. Cotton yield estimation based on vegetation indices and texture features derived from RGB image. *Front. Plant Sci.* **2022**, *13*, 925986. [CrossRef] [PubMed]
23. Qu, H.C.; Zheng, C.F.; Ji, H.; Barai, K.; Zhang, Y.J. A fast and efficient approach to estimate wild blueberry yield using machine learning with drone photography: Flight altitude, sampling method and model effects. *Comput. Electron. Agric.* **2024**, *216*, 108543. [CrossRef]
24. Maimaitijiang, M.; Sagan, V.; Sidike, P.; Hartling, S.; Esposito, F.; Fritschi, F.B. Soybean yield prediction from UAV using multimodal data fusion and deep learning. *Remote Sens. Environ.* **2020**, *237*, 111599. [CrossRef]
25. Wang, Y.M.; Zhang, Z.; Feng, L.W.; Du, Q.Y.; Runge, T. Combining Multi-Source Data and Machine Learning Approaches to Predict Winter Wheat Yield in the Conterminous United States. *Remote Sens.* **2020**, *12*, 1232. [CrossRef]
26. Feng, L.W.; Zhang, Z.; Ma, Y.C.; Du, Q.Y.; Williams, P.; Drewry, J.; Luck, B. Alfalfa yield prediction using UAV-based hyperspectral imagery and ensemble learning. *Remote Sens.* **2020**, *12*, 2028. [CrossRef]
27. Fei, S.P.; Hassan, M.A.; He, Z.H.; Chen, Z.; Shu, M.Y.; Wang, J.K.; Li, C.C.; Xiao, Y.G. Assessment of ensemble learning to predict wheat grain yield based on UAV-multispectral reflectance. *Remote Sens.* **2021**, *13*, 2338. [CrossRef]
28. Cui, Y.X.; Ji, Y.S.; Liu, R.; Li, W.Y.; Liu, Y.J.; Liu, Z.H.; Zong, X.; Yang, T. Faba bean (*Vicia faba* L.) yield estimation based on dual-sensor data. *Drones* **2023**, *7*, 378. [CrossRef]
29. Alabi, T.R.; Abebe, A.T.; Chigeza, G.; Fowobaje, K.R. Estimation of soybean grain yield from multispectral high-resolution UAV data with machine learning models in West Africa. *Remote Sens. Appl. Soc. Environ.* **2022**, *27*, 100782. [CrossRef]
30. Cheng, Q.; Xu, H.; Cao, Y.; Duan, F.; Chen, Z. Grain yield prediction of Winter Wheat using Multi-temporal UAV base on multispectral vegetation index. *Trans. Chin. Soc. Agric. Mach.* **2021**, *52*, 160–167.
31. Fan, J.H.; Zhou, J.; Wang, B.W.; Kaeppler, S.M.; Lima, D.C.; Zhang, Z. Estimation of maize yield and flowering time using multi-temporal UAV-based hyperspectral data. *Remote Sens.* **2022**, *14*, 3052. [CrossRef]
32. Liu, Y.; Feng, H.K.; Yue, J.B.; Jin, X.L.; Fan, Y.G.; Chen, R.Q.; Bian, M.B.; Ma, Y.P.; Song, X.Y.; Yang, G.J. Improved potato AGB estimates based on UAV RGB and hyperspectral images. *Comput. Electron. Agr.* **2023**, *214*, 108260. [CrossRef]
33. Dai, J.G.; Jiang, N.; Xue, J.L.; Zhang, G.S.; He, X.L. Method for predicting cotton yield based on CNN-BiLSTM. *Trans. Chin. Soc. Agric. Eng.* **2021**, *37*, 152–159.
34. Zhang, J.; Qiu, X.; Wu, Y.; Zhu, Y.; Cao, Q.; Liu, X.; Cao, W. Combining texture, color, and vegetation indices from fixed-wing UAS imagery to estimate wheat growth parameters using multivariate regression methods. *Comput. Electron. Agric.* **2021**, *185*, 106138. [CrossRef]
35. He, C.L.; Zheng, S.L.; Wan, N.X.; Zhao, T.; Yuan, J.C.; He, W.; Hu, J. Potato spectrum and the digital image feature parameters on the response of the nitrogen level and its application. *Spectrosc. Spect. Anal.* **2016**, *36*, 2930–2936.

36. Som-ard, J.; Hossain, M.D.; Ninsawat, S.; Veerachitt, V. Pre-harvest sugarcane yield estimation using UAV-based RGB images and ground observation. *Sugar Tech* **2018**, *20*, 645–657. [CrossRef]
37. Bendig, J.; Yu, K.; Aasen, H.; Bolten, A.; Bennertz, S.; Broscheit, J.; Gnyp, M.L.; Bareth, G. Combining UAV-based plant height from crop surface models, visible, and near infrared vegetation indices for biomass monitoring in barley. *Int. J. Appl. Earth Obs. Geoinf.* **2015**, *39*, 79–87. [CrossRef]
38. Pei, H.J.; Feng, H.K.; Li, C.C.; Jin, X.L.; Li, Z.H.; Yang, G.J. Remote sensing monitoring of winter wheat growth with UAV based on comprehensive index. *Trans. Chin. Soc. Agric. Eng.* **2017**, *33*, 74–82.
39. Vol, N. Color indices for weed identification under various soil, residue, and lighting conditions. *Trans. ASAE* **1995**, *38*, 259–269.
40. Gao, C.F.; Ji, X.J.; He, Q.; Gong, Z.; Sun, H.G.; Wen, T.; Guo, W. Monitoring of wheat fusarium head blight on spectral and textural analysis of UAV multispectral imagery. *Agriculture* **2023**, *13*, 293. [CrossRef]
41. Gitelson, A.; Kaufman, Y.J.; Stark, R.; Rundquist, D. Novel algorithms for remote estimation of vegetation fraction. *Remote Sens. Environ.* **2002**, *80*, 76–87. [CrossRef]
42. Wold, S.; Sjöström, M.; Eriksson, L. PLS-regression: A basic tool of chemometrics. *Chemom. Intell. Lab. Syst.* **2001**, *58*, 109–130. [CrossRef]
43. Meyer, G.E.; Neto, J.C. Verification of color vegetation indices for automated crop imaging applications. *Comput. Electron. Agr.* **2008**, *63*, 282–293. [CrossRef]
44. Breiman, L. Random forests. *Mach. Learn.* **2001**, *45*, 5–32. [CrossRef]
45. Wang, J.; Si, H.; Gao, Z.; Shi, L. Winter wheat yield prediction using an LSTM model from MODIS LAI products. *Agriculture* **2022**, *12*, 1707. [CrossRef]
46. Zhao, Y.S. *Principles and Methods of Remote Sensing Applications*; Science Press: Beijing, China, 2013.
47. Liu, X.Y.; Zhong, X.C.; Chen, C.; Liu, T.; Sun, C.M.; Li, D.S.; Liu, E.P.; Wang, J.J.; Ding, D.W.; Huo, Z.Y. Prediction of Wheat Yield Using Color and Texture Feature Data of UAV Image at Early Growth Stage. *J. Triticeae Crops* **2020**, *40*, 1002–1007.

agriculture

MDPI

Article

Estimation of Peanut Southern Blight Severity in Hyperspectral Data Using the Synthetic Minority Oversampling Technique and Fractional-Order Differentiation

Heguang Sun [1,2], Lin Zhou [3], Meiyan Shu [1], Jie Zhang [2], Ziheng Feng [2], Haikuan Feng [2], Xiaoyu Song [2], Jibo Yue [1,*] and Wei Guo [1,*]

[1] College of Information and Management Science, Henan Agricultural University, Zhengzhou 450002, China; sunheguang@henau.edu.cn (H.S.); 13383712711@163.com (M.S.)
[2] Information Technology Research Center, Beijing Academy of Agriculture and Forestry Sciences, Beijing 100094, China; zhangj0216@163.com (J.Z.); fengziheng@stu.henau.edu.cn (Z.F.); 2020201097@stu.njau.edu.cn (H.F.); songxy@nercita.org.cn (X.S.)
[3] College of Plant Protection, Henan Agricultural University, Zhengzhou 450002, China; zhoulinhenau@163.com
* Correspondence: yuejibo@henau.edu.cn (J.Y.); guowei@henau.edu.cn (W.G.)

Abstract: Southern blight significantly impacts peanut yield, and its severity is exacerbated by high-temperature and high-humidity conditions. The mycelium attached to the plant's interior quickly proliferates, contributing to the challenges of early detection and data acquisition. In recent years, the integration of machine learning and remote sensing data has become a common approach for disease monitoring. However, the poor quality and imbalance of data samples can significantly impact the performance of machine learning algorithms. This study employed the Synthetic Minority Oversampling Technique (SMOTE) algorithm to generate samples with varying severity levels. Additionally, it utilized Fractional-Order Differentiation (FOD) to enhance spectral information. The validation and testing of the 1D-CNN, SVM, and KNN models were conducted using experimental data from two different locations. In conclusion, our results indicate that the SMOTE-FOD-1D-CNN model enhances the ability to monitor the severity of peanut white mold disease (validation OA = 88.81%, Kappa = 0.85; testing OA = 82.76%, Kappa = 0.75).

Keywords: peanut southern blight; SMOTE; hyperspectral reflectance; machine learning; FOD

1. Introduction

Peanut southern blight caused by *Agroathelia rolfsii* has caused huge economic losses in peanut production worldwide [1]. Southern blight, a serious soil-borne fungal disease, develops rapidly under hot and humid conditions. In the early stages of infection, the plant leaves are yellowed, and rough white mycelium clings to the lower stems. As the disease intensifies, the mycelium further radiates to the soil surface, the signs of leaf yellowing intensify, and the infected stems and leaves turn a dark brown color, and ultimately the entire plant dies [2]. There are no peanut varieties with high resistance to southern blight, and the control of southern blight is still based on chemical agents [3]. Therefore, timely and effective monitoring of southern blight incidence is important for peanut control.

Unlike stem rot [4] and leaf spot [5], southern blight is very difficult to monitor at an early stage. Affected plants show slight discoloration in the canopy leaves, and this symptom is not easily detectable [2,6]. Further, as the hot and humid weather intensified, the mycelium inside the infected plants started to spread extensively, and this phase was left very short for our investigations [7,8]. Traditional field surveys are time-consuming, labor-intensive, and not easy to monitor over large areas [9]. In recent decades, the emergence of hyperspectral remote sensing technology has provided new technological means for monitoring diseases in a timely and non-destructive manner [10]. Hyperspectral data is composed of a large amount of continuous narrow-band data, which, unlike wide-band multispectral data, provides more detailed information about the target. However, these advantages often come at the cost of high dimensionality and large data volumes, which gives birth to the new problem of the curse of dimensionality [11]. As the noise and sparsity of the feature space increase, the performance of the model gradually decreases [12], Small samples and data imbalances can exacerbate this problem [13]. Spectral feature multiclassification models require large amounts of sample data [14]. For our study, the early onset of southern blight was rapid, the monitoring window was short, and some imbalance in the data was inevitable.

Unbalanced data and small sample sizes can seriously affect the robustness and reliability of the model, and even more so for high-dimensional data such as hyperspectral [15]. Over the past decade or so, a variety of approaches have been developed in various fields to cope with this problem [16,17]. This includes various resampling methods, namely oversampling, undersampling [18], as well as some feature selection and extraction techniques, among others. Often, undersampling is helpful, but it can lead to a loss of information, affecting the performance of the classification model [19]. Unlike undersampling, oversampling methods, while prioritizing the integrity of information, do not remove a significant number of class samples during the synthesis process. This prevents the loss of essential class information that may occur in undersampling [20]. Among the many methods of oversampling, the Synthetic Minority Oversampling Technique (SMOTE) can take into account the samples of the original dataset to generate new data samples and has thus has been widely popularized [21,22]. Özdemir et al. used SMOTE-CNN to classify unbalanced hyperspectral images [23]. Liang et al. used SMOTE combined with XGBoost modeling to detect corn collapse [24]. In this study, to ensure that no information was missing from our study sample set as well as to address the small sample size and data imbalance in the peanut southern blight canopy spectra, we used SMOTE to synthesize new sample data.

The process of plants being subjected to pest and disease stress can be observed through factors such as tissue color, growth density, leaf shape, and more [25,26]. For optical remote sensing, a large number of studies have analyzed the spectral response under stress to diagnose the health status of plants [27,28]. Previous studies indicate that the spectral characteristics of peanut southern blight-affected leaves exhibit significant differences in the red edge and near-infrared regions [29]. Vegetation indices and mathematical transformations can be employed to assess the severity of disease under various growth conditions [30]. For instance, developing new spectral combinations based on the specificity of pests and diseases can be employed for monitoring *Ips typographus* using vegetation indices [31]. However, passive canopy spectral reflectance is susceptible to various factors such as solar angle, lighting conditions, canopy background, and shadows, which can impact the quality of the data [32]. Relying solely on raw spectral data for feature extraction is insufficient for disease detection. To enhance spectral detail and eliminate noise effects caused by factors like soil background, various mathematical transformation methods have been proposed by previous researchers, including CWT [33], SMC [34], SNV [35], differentiation [36], and others. Fractional-Order Differentiation (FOD), in contrast to integer-order, employs a more flexible order, reducing baseline drift and suppressing background noise. It has been widely utilized by many scholars for its advantages in better separating overlapping reflection peaks. Its applications include predicting soil characteristics [37], monitoring diseases [38], and tracking plant biochemical parameters [39]. FOD, built upon a small differential step size, further explores gradient information that is not inherent in integer-order differentiation, maximizing its retention throughout the process. In addition to data preprocessing, the selection of an appropriate model also significantly influences the monitoring of diseases. In the field of remote sensing for disease and pest monitoring, it is primarily divided into two major categories: machine learning and statistical models [40], machine learning models such as SVM, KNN, CNN, etc. have significantly alleviated the constraints of temporal and spatial dimensions, gaining widespread popularity for their excellent training errors and stronger generalization capabilities [41]. In particular, the 1D-CNN model excels at extracting "hidden" features from spectra and has been widely adopted in numerous studies. However, these studies often require large datasets for training [42]. For small datasets, can we overcome the limitations by utilizing synthetic datasets generated through techniques like SMOTE for model training? This approach aims to achieve optimal performance while validating against actual measured data, thereby overcoming data constraints—an aspect that has been seldom reported by scholars.

While ensuring the maximization of spectral information and enhancing the accuracy of the peanut southern blight mold detection model, addressing the challenges of data imbalance and insufficient sample size becomes increasingly intricate. Is it possible to employ SMOTE-FOD to synthesize new sample data, utilizing small differential steps to amplify differences between spectra? To our knowledge, previous studies on disease monitoring have not taken into account the premise of maximizing information, presenting a new challenge for us. The main objective of this study is to assess whether SMOTE-FOD-1D-CNN can enhance the detection performance of different severity levels of peanut southern blight. Specifically, we aim to address the following key questions: (1) Can SMOTE generate new sample data to resolve the issues of data imbalance and insufficient sample size while retaining maximum sample information? (2) Can the small-step FOD enhance spectral information and, in turn, elevate the potential of the constructed peanut southern blight detection model?

2. Materials and Methods

Experiment 1 was conducted in Zhengyang County, Zhumadian City, Henan Province, China, in the year 2022 (32°60′ N, 114°38′ E). The experimental area covered 4560 m^2, with planting initiated on 24 June 2022. During this period, the average temperature was 28 °C. The variety was the southern blight medium-resistant peanut variety Yuhua 37. Plant spacing was set at 35 cm, row spacing at 45 cm, and the experiment concluded on 6 September 2022. A total of 610 peanut canopy spectral data samples were collected, excluding 20 data samples where spectral measurements failed due to improper handling during the measurement process. The distribution of spectral samples for each category is as follows: 150 for healthy, 110 for mild, 120 for moderate, and 210 for severe.

Experiment 2 was conducted in Yanjin County, Xinxiang City, Henan Province, China, in September of the same year (35°15′57″ N, 114°11′8″ E). The climate was mild. Peanuts were a large-scale crop planted in the county with relatively uniform varieties, and standard farmland with a highly intensive planting density was selected. A total of 290 spectral samples representing various severity levels were collected in the experimental area, as illustrated in Figure 1.

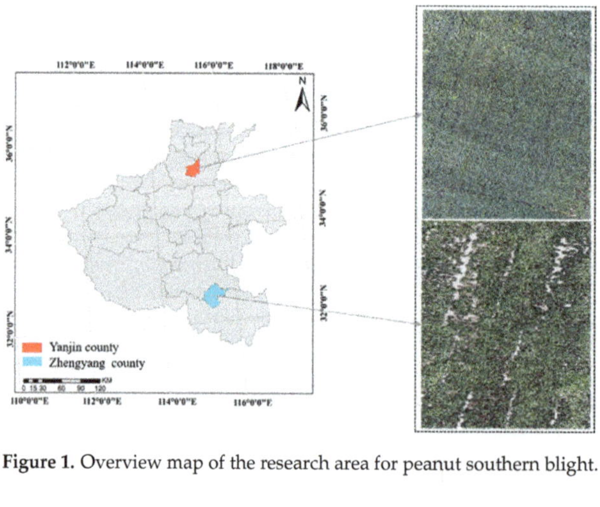

Figure 1. Overview map of the research area for peanut southern blight.

2.1. Canopy-Spectral Data Acquisition

The experiment utilized the ASD Field Spec3 spectrometer, with a spectral range of 350 to 2500 nm and spectral sampling intervals of 1.4 nm (350–1000 nm) and 2 nm (1001–2500 nm). The probe's field of view was approximately 25°, and the probe was positioned approximately 50 cm from the canopy during sampling. Measurements were conducted between 10:00 and 14:00 Beijing time under clear and cloudless weather conditions. Due to the dense planting of peanuts, we selected typical diseased plants for spectral data collection, with a measured area of approximately 0.1 m^2. During the measurement process, the probe collected spectral data from the canopy of peanut plants in a downward, vertical direction. And for each sampled point, radiometric calibration was performed using a BaSo4 standard whiteboard. Furthermore, due to the susceptibility of hyperspectral data to noise from factors such as photonic, atmospheric, and water vapor influences, this study removed the original spectra affected by noise and sidebands. The spectral range retained was from 600 to 1350 nm. Reflectance values were calculated using Formula (1).

$$R = \frac{L_t}{L_b} \times R_b \tag{1}$$

In Formula (1), where R_b is the reflectance of the standard whiteboard, L_t is the canopy radiance, L_b is the whiteboard radiance, and R is the calculated reflectance.

2.2. Data Analysis Methods

2.2.1. Investigation of Peanut Southern Blight Severity

A field investigation was conducted to assess the severity of peanut southern blight. Data acquisition of typical peanut plants in sampled locations based on previous studies on peanut genetic diversity and phenotype was guided by plant protection experts. Plants with a healthy root base, devoid of mycelium, and showing no symptoms on leaves were labeled as "Healthy". Plants with wilting in both leaves and stem bases affecting less than 1/3 of the entire plant were marked as "Mild". Plants with wilting in both leaves and stem bases affecting more than one-third but less than 2/3 of the entire plant were marked as "Moderate". Plants with wilting in both leaves and stem bases affecting more than 2/3 and the appearance of brown fungal sclerotia at the base were marked as "Severe". The four categories, including healthy peanuts and peanuts affected by southern blight, are represented by numerical values 1, 2, 3, and 4, corresponding to mild, moderate, and severe conditions, as illustrated in Figure 2.

Figure 2. Field survey display of peanut southern blight. (**a**) Healthy plants, (**b**) plants with mild disease, (**c**) plants with moderate disease, (**d**) plants with severe disease. (**e**) Mycelium at the base of plants with mild disease, (**f**) leaf symptoms in plants with moderate disease.

2.2.2. Fractional-Order Differential

FOD theory extends the order of differentiation beyond integer values, allowing for arbitrary orders [43]. As a fundamental mathematical operation, FOD enables a more comprehensive analysis of signals [44]. The main forms include Riemann-Liouville (R-L),

Caputo, Weil, Caputo, and Grünwald-Letnikov (G-L). In this study, the discrete Grünwald-Letnikov (G-L) form is employed, which is suitable for small step sizes and computationally efficient. The specific formula is as follows in Equations (2) and (3):

$$D^{\alpha}f(x) = \lim_{h\to 0}\frac{1}{h^{\alpha}}\sum_{j=0}^{(t-\alpha)/h}(-1)^{m}\frac{\Gamma(\alpha+1)}{j!\Gamma(\alpha-j+1)}f(x-jh) \tag{2}$$

where α is the fractional order, h is the step size, t and j are the upper and lower limits of differentiation, and Γ is the gamma function.

$$\Gamma(\beta) = \int_0^{\infty} e^{-t}t^{\beta-1}dt = (\beta-1)! \tag{3}$$

The gamma function, also known as the generalized factorial, is commonly used in the definition of fractional-order differentials.

When $f(x)$ is a one-dimensional spectrum with a sampling interval of $1(h = 1)$, and t and α represent wavelength intervals, $(t-\alpha)/h = t-\alpha = n$. According to the above Equations (2) and (3), the following expression for fractional-order differentiation can be derived (Equation (4)):

$$\begin{aligned}\frac{d^{v}f(\lambda)}{d\lambda^{v}} &\approx f(\lambda)+(-v)f(\lambda-1)+\frac{(-v)(-v-1)}{2}f(\lambda-2)+\cdot\cdot\\ &\cdots+\frac{\Gamma(-v+1)}{(n)!\Gamma(-v+n+1)}f(\lambda-n)\end{aligned} \tag{4}$$

When $v = 0$, the 0th-order differentiation of $f(x)$ is the function itself, and when $v = 1$, it represents the first-order differentiation.

2.2.3. 1D-CNN

The study employed a one-dimensional convolutional neural network (1D-CNN) to build the model [42]. Using peanut canopy spectra of different severity levels as input layer data, the convolutional layer extracts hidden features from the input layer. The feature dimensions are then reduced through a pooling layer. The flattened vector is then input into a fully connected layer using the ReLU activation function. The features extracted are mapped to the required size, representing the four severity levels of peanut southern blight in this study. The Adam gradient descent algorithm was employed with a maximum training iteration of 250, a batch size of 64, and an initial learning rate of 0.01. The 1D-CNN model was implemented using Matlab 2022a and NVIDIA RTX3060. The specific network parameters are detailed in Table 1.

Table 1. Parameters used in the 1D-CNN model.

Stratification	Type	Output Features	Weight
1	Input Layer	37 × 1 × 1	-
2	Convolutional Laye	37 × 1 × 8	2 × 1 × 1 × 8
3	Batch Normalization Layer	37 × 1 × 8	1 × 1 × 8
4	ReLU	37 × 1 × 8	-
5	Max Pooling Layer	18 × 1 × 8	-
6	Convolutional Layer	18 × 1 × 16	2 × 1 × 8 × 16
7	Batch Normalization	18 × 1 × 16	1 × 1 × 16
8	ReLU	18 × 1 × 16	-
9	Fully Connected Layer	1 × 1 × 4	4 × 288
10	Softmax	1 × 1 × 4	-
11	Output Layer	1 × 1 × 4	-

2.2.4. SMOTE Algorithm

SMOTE (Synthetic Minority Oversampling Technique) is a method of data sampling that utilizes existing samples based on linear interpolation to generate new synthetic sample data at random distances from the K-nearest neighbors [45]. The specific process is as follows: First, a minority sample a is selected from the original data. Then, the Euclidean distance between a and the remaining minority samples in the feature space is calculated to find the K-nearest neighbors. Based on the determined K-nearest neighbors, the SMOTE algorithm is used to select a random sample b, and finally, a new synthetic sample $\grave{a}$ is generated according to Equation (5).

$$\grave{a} = a + rand(0,1)|a - b| \quad (5)$$

The SMOTE algorithm has historically been utilized to address imbalances in minority classes within datasets. In recent years, as the efficacy of SMOTE's excellent oversampling strategy has been proven, an increasing amount of research suggests its applicability for synthetic sample generation. In this study, to determine the optimal number of K-neighbors, we set $K = 1, 2, 3$.

2.2.5. ReliefF Arithmetic

High spectral data has a small interval, a large quantity, contains a significant amount of noise and redundant features, and exhibits high multicollinearity among adjacent bands [46]. Blindly using all features will only increase meaningless computational load and decrease the model's generalization [47]. The ReliefF algorithm is one of the most commonly used methods for feature weight selection. Due to its simple calculation and high efficiency, it is widely used for the selection of multidimensional features [48]. In this study, the ReliefF algorithm was employed for rapid selection of features sensitive to peanut southern blight. The specific formula is as follows:

$$W^i(n) = W^{i-1}(n) - \sum_{j=1}^{k} \frac{(X_i(n) - H_j(n))^2}{mk} + \sum_{j=1}^{k} \frac{(X_i(n) - M_j(n))^2}{mk} \quad (6)$$

where m is the number of sampling times, k is the number of nearest neighbors, M is the selected number of features, $W^i(n)$ is the n weight factors updated for the i, $X_i(n)$ is the n feature index of the i random sample, $H_j(n)$ is the n feature of the j class's nearest sample, and $M_j(n)$ is the n feature index of the nearest samples of different classes for $X_i(n)$.

2.2.6. SVM and KNN Models

The Support Vector Machine (SVM) model seeks an optimal classification hyperplane in a high-dimensional space to separate different class samples with minimal error. SVM is commonly used for regression and classification problems. In this study, the kernel function is set to RBF [49]. The K-Nearest Neighbors (KNN) classification is based on the K most similar samples from the training set, using Euclidean distance for measurement. These samples vote on the attributes, and the final values are assigned to the object to be classified [50].

2.3. Model Accuracy Evaluation Metrics

In this study, we used the SMOTE-synthesized sample set for model training, constructed separate 1D-CNN, SVM, and KNN models, and evaluated the models' accuracy using 590 measured samples for validation. Additionally, to demonstrate the good generalization of the models, we tested them using 290 data samples from Yuxian County, Xinxiang City, Henan Province. The overall classification accuracy and Kappa coefficient were calculated based on the confusion matrix of the models, as shown in Equations (7) and (8).

$$\text{OA} = \frac{\left(\sum_{k=1}^{N} akk\right)}{n} \quad (7)$$

where N is the number of classes, n is the total number of classifications, and akk is the number of correct classifications.

$$\text{Kappa} = \frac{N\sum_{i=1}^{m} x_{ii} - \sum_{k=1}^{m}\left(\sum_{i=1}^{m} x_{ij}\sum_{j=1}^{m} x_{ij}\right)}{N^2 - \sum_{k=1}^{m}\left(\sum_{i=1}^{m} x_{ij}\sum_{j=1}^{m} x_{ij}\right)} \tag{8}$$

where N is the total, x_{ii} is the diagonal element of the confusion matrix, and x_{ij} is each element of the confusion matrix.

3. Results

3.1. Synthetic Data Generation

In this study, we used the SMOTE algorithm to synthesize the original data. To further analyze the accuracy of the synthetic data and the optimal number of nearest neighbors (K), we first fixed the generation multiplier at $n = 10$, with a focus on analyzing the similarity between synthetic data and real data for $K = 1$, 2, and 3. To illustrate this situation more intuitively, we used PCA to plot the spatial distribution of the first three principal components, as shown in Figure 3. Compared to the original data, all of the generated synthetic data exhibit excellent spatial similarity.

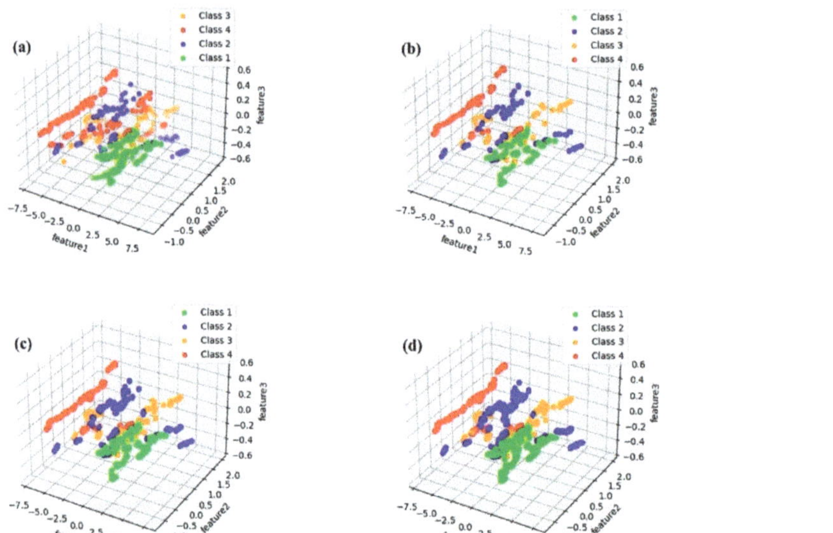

Figure 3. Spatial distribution maps of original data and synthetic samples for different values of K based on PCA. (**a**) Original data. (**b**) Synthetic data for $K = 1$. (**c**) Synthetic data for $K = 2$. (**d**) Synthetic data for $K = 3$. The legend Class 1–4 represents the four categories in this study.

3.2. Features of Spectral Curves under Different Fractional Differentiation Orders

The spectral curves of peanut southern blight at different severities are distinct. After infection with peanut southern blight, the physiological and biochemical parameters of peanuts undergo significant changes, resulting in a decrease in reflectance in the red edge and near-infrared regions, causing a 'blue shift' phenomenon. Monitoring peanut southern blight solely based on the spectral response mechanism still poses challenges, as the canopy environment is always complex and susceptible to various factors. As shown in Figure 4a, spectral curves of different severities intersect and appear similar.

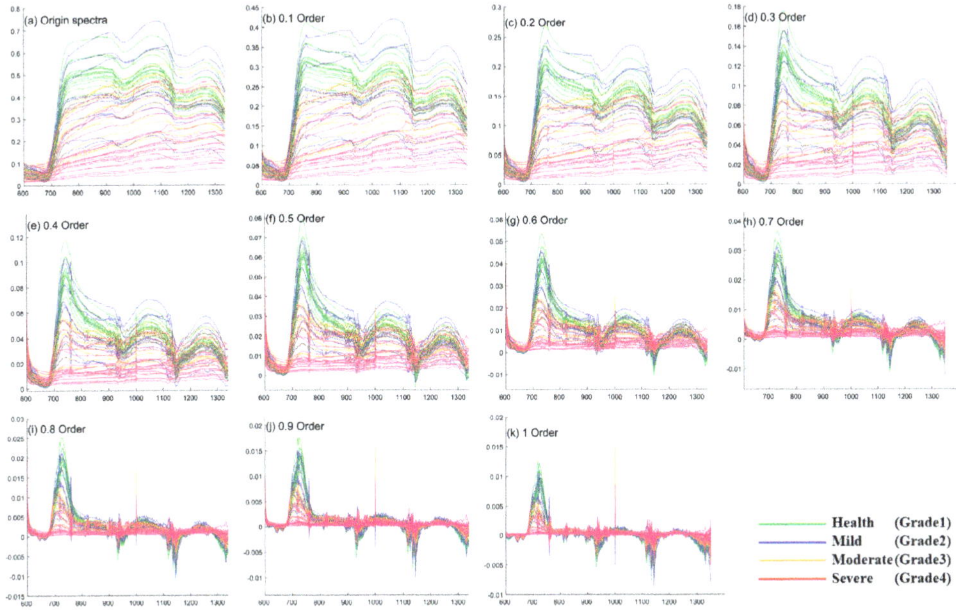

Figure 4. FOD spectral curves in the (0–1.0) fractional-order range.

To investigate the improvement in FOD on peanut southern blight spectra, we applied fractional-order differences to the original spectra with a step size of 0.1, obtaining spectral curves for different severities as shown in Figure 4a–k The original spectra are smooth, with two weak absorption features near 970 nm and 1200 nm influenced by internal leaf structures. Absorption valleys and reflection peaks increase with the FOD order, and at FOD = 0.5, reflectance becomes negative, with significant fluctuations in many curves. As shown in Figure 5a–j, after FOD = 1.1, this fluctuation trend gradually slows down, and after FOD = 1.4, the dimensional differences between various spectral curves gradually decrease, showing signs of overlap. At the same time, the spiky trend of the spectral curves deepens, and the entire spectrum becomes chaotic.

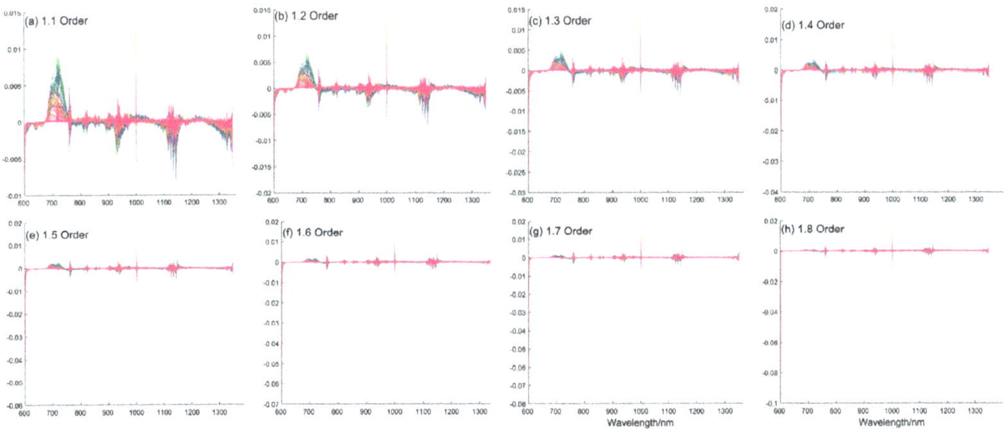

Figure 5. *Cont.*

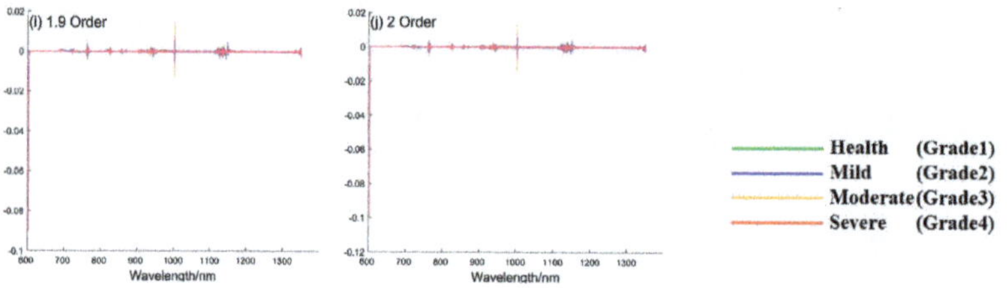

Figure 5. FOD spectral curves in the (1.1–2.0) fractional-order range.

3.3. *Correlation between Disease Severity and Spectra*

To assess whether FOD can improve the correlation between disease severity and spectral reflectance, we compared the correlation information between FOD spectra and disease severity at different orders with a step size of 0.1 (Figure 6). For the original spectra, at FOD = 0, a significant negative correlation was observed in the red edge, with the maximum correlation at 756 nm (R = −0.83). As the FOD order increased, the correlation coefficient changed. For instance, at FOD = 1.1, the correlation gradually became positive around 780 nm. Moreover, the spectra correlations based on FOD were generally better than the original spectra, indicating that using FOD could enhance the spectral details and increase the separability of disease severity.

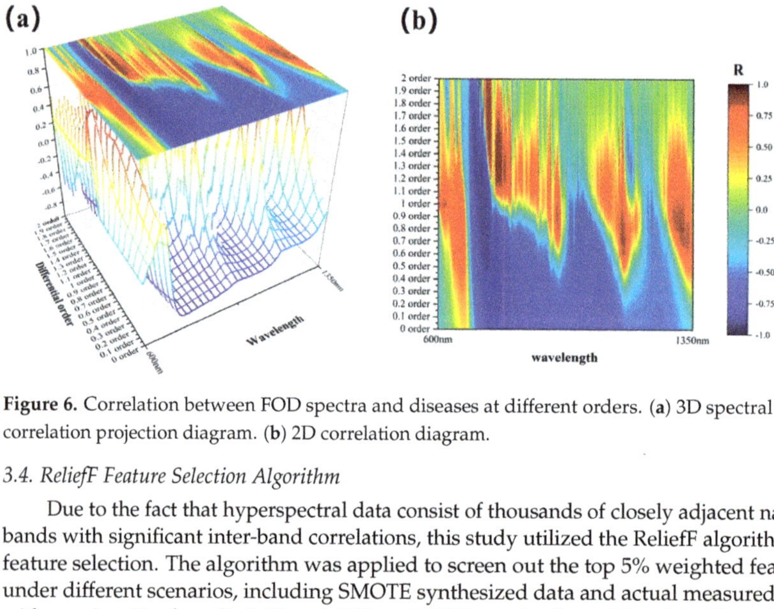

Figure 6. Correlation between FOD spectra and diseases at different orders. (**a**) 3D spectral curve correlation projection diagram. (**b**) 2D correlation diagram.

3.4. *ReliefF Feature Selection Algorithm*

Due to the fact that hyperspectral data consist of thousands of closely adjacent narrow bands with significant inter-band correlations, this study utilized the ReliefF algorithm for feature selection. The algorithm was applied to screen out the top 5% weighted features under different scenarios, including SMOTE synthesized data and actual measured data, with varying *K* values (1, 2, 3) and different FOD ranging from 0.1 to 2.0. The selected features were then employed in the construction of the disease detection model. The process and results are illustrated in Figure 7.

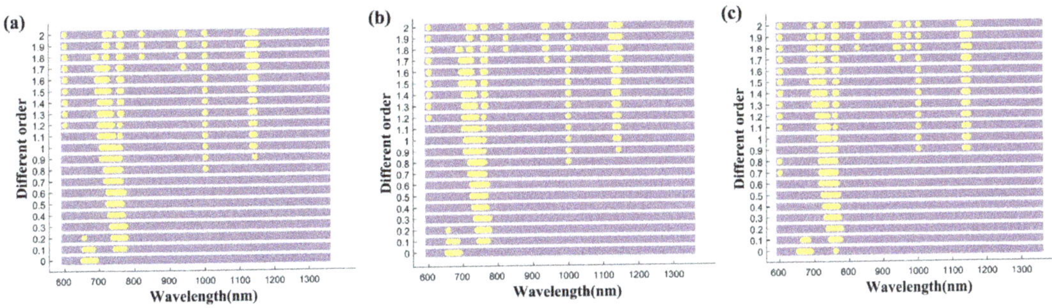

Figure 7. Illustration of feature selection using the ReliefF algorithm for the top 5% weighted features under different scenarios of FOD (0–2). The selected features are highlighted in yellow. Specifically, the features for synthesized data are represented when (**a**) $K = 1$, (**b**) $K = 2$, and (**c**) $K = 3$.

3.5. Construction of Disease Detection Model Based on FOD Spectra

3.5.1. Performance of Multiple Outputs in the 1D-CNN Model

In order to investigate the impact of different FODs on the detection of peanut southern blight and determine the optimal K neighbors for the SMOTE algorithm, we applied the 1D-CNN model to spectra processed with 20 different FOD orders, as shown in Table 2. When $K = 1$ and FOD = 0.2, the overall accuracy (OA) was 88.81%, and the Kappa coefficient was 0.85, which was better than the performance with the original spectra (FOD = 0, OA = 86.78%, Kappa = 0.82). Furthermore, we analyzed the variation of overall accuracy with different values of K for the entire range of FOD, as shown in Figure 8. We observed a decreasing trend in overall accuracy with increasing K values, and the overall accuracy was generally higher when $K = 1$ compared to other values.

Table 2. Based on the 1D-CNN monitoring model of peanut southern blight under various orders of FOD.

	$K = 1$		$K = 2$		$K = 3$	
FOD Order	**OA**	**Kappa**	**OA**	**Kappa**	**OA**	**Kappa**
0	86.78%	0.82	87.29%	0.83	87.12%	0.83
0.1	86.10%	0.81	86.10%	0.81	85.93%	0.81
0.2	88.81%	0.85	85.76%	0.81	87.46%	0.83
0.3	87.46%	0.83	87.12%	0.83	86.44%	0.82
0.4	86.44%	0.82	86.95%	0.82	85.93%	0.81
0.5	86.61%	0.82	86.27%	0.81	86.44%	0.82
0.6	86.78%	0.82	86.44%	0.82	85.93%	0.81
0.7	86.44%	0.82	84.41%	0.79	86.95%	0.82
0.8	85.42%	0.8	84.24%	0.79	82.71%	0.77
0.9	85.25%	0.8	83.05%	0.77	83.56%	0.78
1.0	84.07%	0.79	82.03%	0.76	83.22%	0.77
1.1	83.90%	0.78	85.08%	0.8	83.73%	0.78
1.2	83.22%	0.77	82.37%	0.76	82.71%	0.77
1.3	84.07%	0.79	83.22%	0.77	84.41%	0.79
1.4	83.39%	0.78	81.69%	0.75	81.02%	0.74
1.5	82.54%	0.77	81.36%	0.75	83.56%	0.78
1.6	82.20%	0.76	80.00%	0.73	81.02%	0.74
1.7	79.83%	0.73	80.51%	0.73	80.17%	0.73
1.8	77.29%	0.69	77.29%	0.69	75.25%	0.66
1.9	74.07%	0.65	71.86%	0.61	72.03%	0.62
2	73.73%	0.64	70.85%	0.6	71.69%	0.62

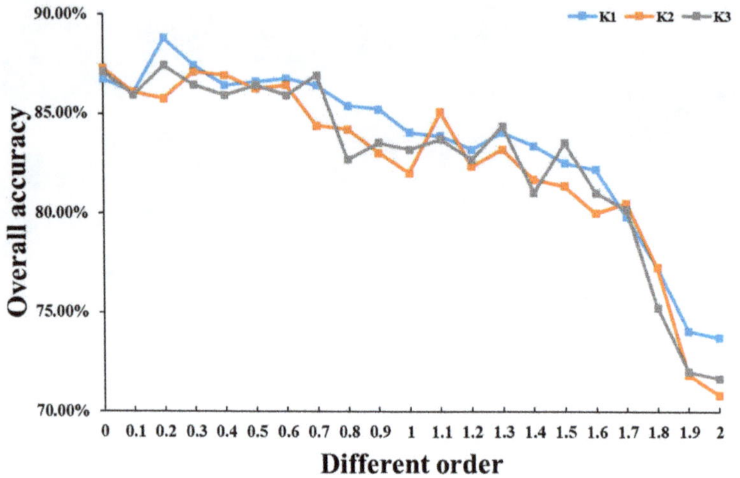

Figure 8. Overall accuracy of the 1D-CNN model under different K-nearest neighbors values.

3.5.2. Performance of Machine Learning Models with Multiple Outputs

To compare the performance of the models and determine the optimal FOD order, we further analyzed the performance of the SVM and KNN models with the best neighbor number $K = 1$ for each FOD. As shown in Table 3, when FOD is in the range of 0.2–0.3, the overall accuracy (OA) is better than other orders, consistent with the results of the 1D-CNN model. The best accuracy of the SVM model was FOD = 0.3 (OA = 86.61%, Kappa = 0.82), and the best accuracy of the KNN model was FOD = 0.2 (OA = 86.95%, Kappa = 0.83).

Table 3. Peanut southern blight monitoring model based on SVM and KNN under FOD.

	Model ($K = 1$)			
FOD Order	SVM		KNN	
	OA (%)	Kappa	OA (%)	Kappa
0	72.20%	0.63	84.75%	0.80
0.1	70.34%	0.60	84.24%	0.79
0.2	84.07%	0.79	86.95%	0.83
0.3	86.61%	0.82	85.76%	0.81
0.4	83.90%	0.78	80.68%	0.74
0.5	79.32%	0.72	75.76%	0.68
0.6	74.41%	0.66	71.53%	0.62
0.7	75.59%	0.68	72.88%	0.64
0.8	75.42%	0.67	72.20%	0.63
0.9	77.29%	0.69	72.54%	0.63
1.0	78.64%	0.71	70.68%	0.60
1.1	77.46%	0.70	73.22%	0.64
1.2	76.10%	0.68	73.73%	0.65
1.3	75.93%	0.68	71.53%	0.61
1.4	74.92%	0.66	67.46%	0.55
1.5	72.37%	0.63	64.24%	0.51
1.6	70.68%	0.60	59.83%	0.46
1.7	67.12%	0.55	54.24%	0.38
1.8	63.22%	0.49	51.53%	0.35
1.9	60.00%	0.45	49.83%	0.33
2	57.80%	0.42	49.83%	0.32

3.5.3. Evaluation of Model Generalization Performance

To assess the robust generalizability of the constructed model, we tested it using 290 spectral samples from various regions with different severity levels in the same year. Additionally, mean processing was conducted prior to utilization. The results are shown in Table 4. It can be observed that under the optimal input parameters, the 1D-CNN model achieved good performance on the validation set, with an accuracy (OA) of 82.76% and a Kappa of 0.75, while the performance of the other machine learning models on the test set was not satisfactory.

Table 4. Accuracy assessment of different models on test data.

Model Input Parameters	Model	Calibration		Validation	
		OA (%)	Kappa	OA (%)	Kappa
$K = 1, n = 10$, FOD = 0.2	1D-CNN	88.81%	0.85	82.76%	0.75
	SVM	84.07%	0.79	48.28%	0.27
	KNN	86.95%	0.83	65.52%	0.49

4. Discussion

In this study, to monitor the severity of peanut southern blight in the canopy, we used the SMOTE algorithm to synthesize canopy spectral data for peanut southern blight. Furthermore, we employed FOD for in-depth analysis. The study is divided into three parts for discussion. Firstly, we analyzed the similarity between the synthesized data using the SMOTE algorithm and real data. We explored the impact of the optimal nearest neighbor number (K) and multiplier (n). Secondly, we compared and analyzed the 1D-CNN model and SVM model, investigating the optimal FOD order for peanut southern blight and further analyzing it with a step size of 0.01. Finally, we summarized the shortcomings of this study and provided future prospects.

4.1. SMOTE Analysis of Synthetic Data

The early stages of peanut southern blight differ from stem rot [51] and leaf spot diseases [52] in that there are no obvious pathogenic features on the plant canopy. Once the fungal hyphae, which have infected the plant internally, are subjected to continuous high-temperature and high-humidity conditions, they will rapidly spread [53]. The monitoring window for this early stage is very short, and our study did not involve continuous monitoring for an extended period, resulting in a limited number of early stage samples obtained.

Although data mining techniques have been widely promoted, we concur with Guo's viewpoint that traditional classification modeling for imbalanced datasets remains a pressing issue [21]. As mentioned by López and Weiss, when dealing with imbalanced sample sets, training machine learning standard classifiers may yield ideal results, but the minority sample set is still neglected. This could potentially lead to poor robustness of the model in the face of rare events and an increased likelihood of misidentifying minority class samples as noise, thereby impacting the overall model accuracy [54,55].

SMOTE does not require training any specific model; it generates new synthetic samples solely based on the spatial characteristics of the original data using the K-nearest neighbor approach [56,57]. The choice of the K value directly influences the reliability of the synthesized data, depending on the density or sparsity of the initial data distribution [58,59]. To illustrate the distribution of the synthetic data compared to the original data more intuitively, as shown in Figure 3, we analyzed the spatial features of the first three PCAs. The spatial features of the synthetic data are extremely similar to those of the original data. However, we do not assert that synthetic data guarantees good performance for such datasets; it merely satisfies visual consistency, as confirmed by Kristian [60]. Further analysis of the subsequent data is still needed.

On this basis, to determine the optimal values for K (number of nearest neighbors) and the synthesis multiplier n, we tested the data results for n = 10 with K1, K2, and K3 separately. As shown in Figure 8, we found that overall FOD differential accuracy is better when using K1 compared to the other values. Using a smaller k can generate a representative dataset for our data, and we agree with Ebrahimy et al., that further experiments are needed to evaluate other crops [61]. In addition, in recent years, the multiplier n for synthetic data has also been widely discussed [62]. In this study, we attempted to analyze the impact of different synthetic multipliers on the model to determine the optimal value for n. We used SVM, the least effective model among the three, for this analysis, and the results are shown in Figure 9. As the synthesis data multiplier n increases, the overall accuracy stabilizes after n = 10. As mentioned by Sun, blindly continuing to increase the synthesis multipliers n and k can undoubtedly increase computational load, which is often undesirable while maintaining optimal accuracy [20].

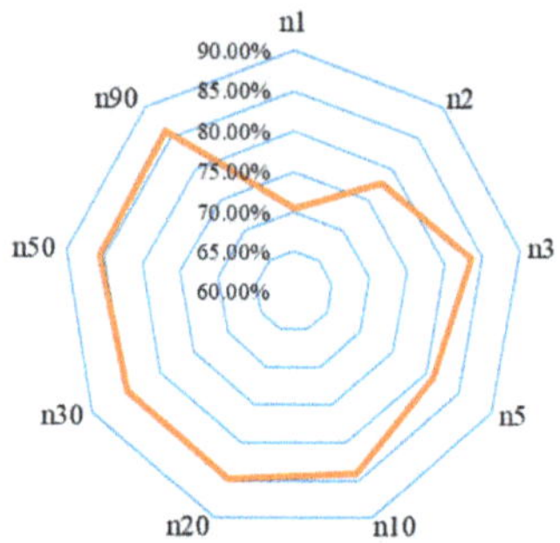

Figure 9. SVM model accuracy with different multiples (n) of synthetic data.

Although SMOTE can synthesize new sample data while ensuring the integrity of information, it is necessary to mention its disadvantage of generating noisy samples [15]. In addressing this drawback, previous researchers have proposed methods to identify and eliminate noise, such as improved SMOTE-IPF [63], SMOTE-Rknn [64], etc. However, in this study, we still aim to retain this noise because we understand that some scholars, in radiative transfer models, add varying degrees of Gaussian noise to simulated datasets to minimize overfitting issues, aligning with their approach [65]. Moreover, the uncertainty of biochemical parameter retrieval can be influenced by the quality of the data, as crown reflectance may vary [66]. Therefore, as shown in Figure 10, we magnified the differences between the synthetic sample dataset and the measured data, allowing for a visual observation of the slight noise issue in the synthetic samples.

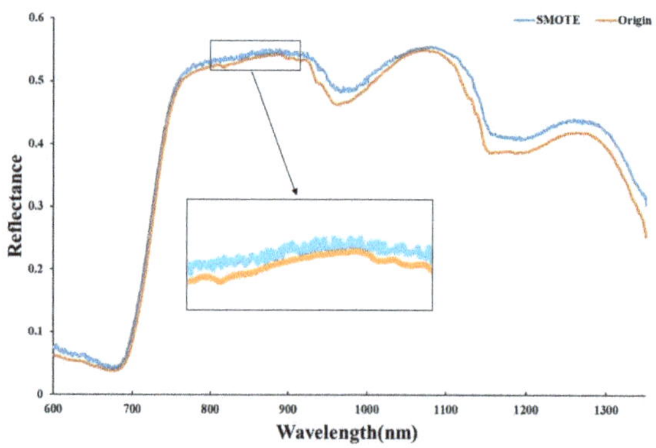

Figure 10. Spectral curves of SMOTE synthetic data and actual measured data.

4.2. Analysis of Various Orders of FOD

Integer-order differentiation is just a special case of fractional-order differentiation. Previous studies have indicated that first-order differentiation is effective in eliminating the influence of background noise, while second-order differentiation can mitigate baseline drift, thereby enhancing analytical accuracy [67]. However, some researchers have proposed that higher-order integer differentiations may introduce noise and compromise the integrity of information [38]. Fractional-order differentiation, while encompassing the meaning of integer-order differentiation, provides a more flexible choice of orders [68,69]. Fractional-order differentials are closely related to full-band reflectance, where the reflectance of each point is influenced by different fractional-order differentials with varying weights. The closer the point, the larger the weight, and hence, the greater the influence of fractional-order differentials. This is what Zhang referred to as the memory and non-locality of fractional-order differentials [70]. For disease spectra, peanut southern blight causes rapid yellowing and wilting of the entire plant, leading to significant changes in the canopy spectra, making the spectral information more complex. Therefore, we attempt to use fractional-order differentials to further amplify subtle spectral differences and explore the capability of this method for monitoring peanut southern blight.

As shown in Figure 4, a fractional-order differential transformation with a step size of 0.1 is applied to the original spectra, and the overall spectral shape exhibits a significant changing trend. Before FOD = 0.9, with the increase in order, the spectral differences are magnified, leading to many distinctive absorption valleys and reflection peaks. However, at higher orders, this unique phenomenon is masked, and the separability of various spectral curves gradually decreases. Zhang suggested that this phenomenon could be explained using the G-L mathematical theory. When the sampling step is smaller than the width of the peaks and valleys, spectral differences are magnified. The noise phenomenon arises because the calculation of FOD introduces high-frequency noise when dealing with short-interval peaks and valleys in the spectrum [38]. This phenomenon can also be observed in Figure 6. Additionally, we observed that while FOD enhances the correlation between the spectrum and peanut southern blight, it also leads to certain originally positive correlations in specific bands becoming negative, and vice versa. The original bands exhibit a significant negative correlation near the red edge, and with the increase in FOD, it gradually turns positive around FOD = 1.1. This conclusion has been supported by various studies; Jiang et al. suggested that it is due to the capture of long-term memory and non-local features in the data by FOD [37], while Kilbas et al. proposed that it might be caused by nonlinear relationships between variables [69].

In order to further investigate the impact of FOD on the monitoring of the severity of peanut southern blight, we used 1D-CNN, SVM, and KNN models for evaluation. As shown in Tables 2 and 4, with the increase in FOD order, the overall accuracy shows an upward and then downward trend. FOD = 0.2 is the optimal order, and all three models have high evaluation metrics. The 1D-CNN model is optimal when $K = 1$ and n = 10 (validation set OA = 88.81%, Kappa = 0.85; test set OA = 82.76%, Kappa = 0.75). Analyzing smaller step sizes on top of limited orders to determine if it can increase model accuracy is an aspect that has not been explored in previous research. Next, we conducted a detailed analysis of the impact of FOD on peanut southern blight detection with a step size of 0.01. The accuracy using SVM and KNN models is shown in Figure 11. There is not a significant improvement in accuracy within the range of FOD from 0.21 to 0.29. The ability to decompose spectral information using FOD with a small step size has reached saturation.

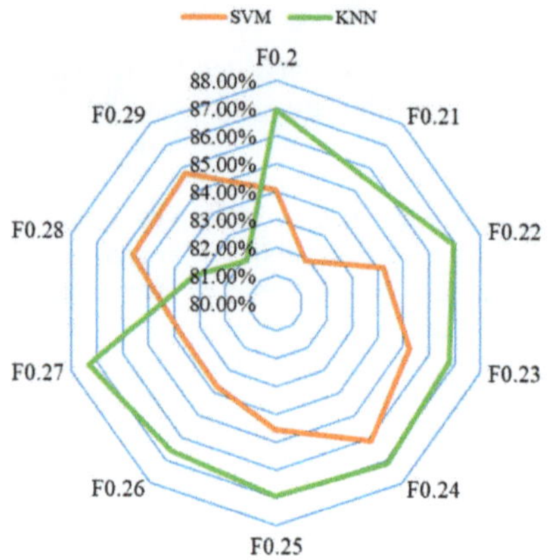

Figure 11. Peanut southern blight severity detection using different models with FOD (0.2–0.29) and a step size of 0.01.

4.3. Limitations and Future Work

On one hand, while our study demonstrates that using SMOTE to generate training samples, further amplifying spectral differences between different severities with FOD, and employing a 1D-CNN model can effectively monitor peanut southern blight, investigations at different stages of peanut southern blight were not conducted. The main reason for this is the transitional continental monsoon climate in Henan Province, transitioning from a northern subtropical zone to a warm temperate zone. The region experiences a high probability of continuous high temperatures and humidity in July and August [71], providing favorable external conditions for the occurrence of peanut southern blight. Early monitoring in the growing season is hindered by the influence of peanut growth density, as the pathogenic hyphae do not erupt extensively in the early stages. On the other hand, due to the highly complex nature of field environments, diseased plants may be subjected to various types of stressors, such as drought, flooding, nutrient deficiencies, and more. Additionally, for the plants themselves, they may be affected by more than one disease during their growth process; the occurrence of multiple diseases concurrently is something that we have not thoroughly considered.

Our future work will extend beyond the scope of Henan Province. We aim to acquire data on peanut southern blight from multiple provinces and varieties to enhance the model. This expansion is crucial for early disease detection, improving prevention and control efficiency, and cultivating disease-resistant varieties. At the same time, we need to further refine our experimental design, make fuller use of experimental resources, systematically control variables, and expand future work to assess the effects of various stressors.

5. Conclusions

This study aimed to enhance the ability to monitor the severity of peanut southern blight by using the SMOTE-FOD-1D-CNN model. A comparison with the SVM and KNN models was conducted, and the optimal model was determined to be 1D-CNN (validation OA = 88.81%, Kappa = 0.85; test OA = 82.76%, Kappa = 0.75). The main conclusions are as follows: (1) SMOTE effectively addresses the issue of imbalanced and insufficient sample data by preserving the maximum amount of sample information and generating new sample data. (2) Small-step FOD shows potential for enhancing spectral information and improving the performance of the constructed peanut southern blight monitoring model.

Author Contributions: H.S.: investigation, methodology, validation, writing—original draft, visualization. L.Z.: investigation, methodology. M.S.: investigation, methodology. J.Z.: methodology, visualization. Z.F.: methodology, visualization. H.F.: methodology, visualization. X.S.: investigation, methodology. J.Y.: investigation, methodology, validation. W.G.: investigation, methodology, validation, writing—review and editing. All authors have read and agreed to the published version of the manuscript.

Funding: This work was supported by the Henan Provincial Science and Technology Major Project (NO.221100110100); National Natural Science Foundation of China, grant number (NO.32271993); The Joint Fund of Science and Technology Research Development program (Cultivation project of preponderant discipline) of Henan Province, China (NO.222301420114).

Institutional Review Board Statement: Not applicable.

Data Availability Statement: The data presented in this paper are part of an ongoing study and the dataset is difficult to access; permission from the corresponding author is required to access the dataset.

Conflicts of Interest: The authors declare that they have no known competing financial interests or personal relationships that could have appeared to influence the research reported in this study.

References

1. Rodriguez-Kabana, R.; Kloepper, J.; Robertson, D.; Wells, L. Velvetbean for the management of root-knot and southern blight in peanut. *Nematropica* **1992**, *22*, 75–80.
2. Xu, M.; Zhang, X.; Yu, J.; Guo, Z.; Wu, J.; Li, X.; Chi, Y.; Wan, S. Biological control of peanut southern blight (*Sclerotium rolfsii*) by the strain *Bacillus pumilus* LX11. *Biocontrol Sci. Technol.* **2020**, *30*, 485–489. [CrossRef]
3. Ryley, M.; Kyei, N.; Tatnell, J. Evaluation of fungicides for the management of sclerotinia blight of peanut. *Aust. J. Agric. Res.* **2000**, *51*, 917–924. [CrossRef]
4. Asuyama, H.; Yamanaka, S. Stem rot of peanut. *Jpn. J. Phytopathol.* **1953**, *18*, 28–32. [CrossRef]
5. Jenkins, W.A. Two fungi causing leaf spot of peanut. *J. Agric. Res.* **1938**, *56*, 317–332.
6. Grichar, W.J.; Woodward, J.E. Fungicides and application timing for control of early leafspot, southern blight, and sclerotinia blight of peanut. *Int. J. Agron.* **2016**, *2016*, 1848723. [CrossRef]
7. Damicone, J.P. *Soilborne Blight Diseases of Peanut*; Oklahoma Cooperative Extension Service: Stillwater, OK, USA, 2014.
8. Melouk, H.; Hunger, R.M.; Mulder, P.G.; Payton, M.E.; Zhang, H. *Characterization of Isolates of Sclerotium rolfsii and Evaluation of Peanut for Reaction to Southern Blight*; Oklahoma State University: Stillwater, OK, USA, 2003.
9. Jia, Z.; Ou, C.; Sun, S.; Wang, J.; Liu, J.; Li, M.; Jia, S.; Mao, P. A novel approach using multispectral imaging for rapid development of seed pellet formulations to mitigate drought stress in alfalfa. *Comput. Electron. Agric.* **2023**, *212*, 108136. [CrossRef]
10. Zhang, M.; Qin, Z.; Liu, X.; Ustin, S.L. Detection of stress in tomatoes induced by late blight disease in California, USA, using hyperspectral remote sensing. *Int. J. Appl. Earth Obs. Geoinf.* **2003**, *4*, 295–310. [CrossRef]
11. Hennessy, A.; Clarke, K.; Lewis, M. Hyperspectral classification of plants: A review of waveband selection generalisability. *Remote Sens.* **2020**, *12*, 113. [CrossRef]
12. Alonso, M.C.; Malpica, J.A.; de Agirre, A.M. Consequences of the Hughes phenomenon on some classification techniques. In Proceedings of the ASPRS 2001 Annual Conference, St. Louis, MO, USA, 23–27 April 2001; pp. 1–5.
13. Virnodkar, S.S.; Pachghare, V.K.; Patil, V.; Jha, S.K. Remote sensing and machine learning for crop water stress determination in various crops: A critical review. *Precis. Agric.* **2020**, *21*, 1121–1155. [CrossRef]
14. Osco, L.P.; Junior, J.M.; Ramos, A.P.M.; de Castro Jorge, L.A.; Fatholahi, S.N.; de Andrade Silva, J.; Matsubara, E.T.; Pistori, H.; Gonçalves, W.N.; Li, J. A review on deep learning in UAV remote sensing. *Int. J. Appl. Earth Obs. Geoinf.* **2021**, *102*, 102456. [CrossRef]
15. Blagus, R.; Lusa, L. SMOTE for high-dimensional class-imbalanced data. *BMC Bioinform.* **2013**, *14*, 106. [CrossRef]
16. Xu, Z.; Shen, D.; Nie, T.; Kou, Y. A hybrid sampling algorithm combining M-SMOTE and ENN based on Random forest for medical imbalanced data. *J. Biomed. Inform.* **2020**, *107*, 103465. [CrossRef] [PubMed]
17. Li, D.; Liu, J.; Liu, J. NNI-SMOTE-XGBoost: A Novel Small Sample Analysis Method for Properties Prediction of Polymer Materials. *Macromol. Theory Simul.* **2021**, *30*, 2100010. [CrossRef]
18. Kumar, N.S.; Rao, K.N.; Govardhan, A.; Reddy, K.S.; Mahmood, A.M. Undersampled K-means approach for handling imbalanced distributed data. *Prog. Artif. Intell.* **2014**, *3*, 29–38. [CrossRef]
19. Van Hulse, J.; Khoshgoftaar, T.M.; Napolitano, A. An empirical comparison of repetitive undersampling techniques. In Proceedings of the 2009 IEEE International Conference on Information Reuse & Integration, Las Vegas, NV, USA, 10–12 August 2009; pp. 29–34.
20. Sun, P.; Wang, Z.; Jia, L.; Xu, Z. SMOTE-kTLNN: A hybrid re-sampling method based on SMOTE and a two-layer nearest neighbor classifier. *Expert Syst. Appl.* **2024**, *238*, 121848. [CrossRef]

21. Deng, M.; Guo, Y.; Wang, C.; Wu, F. An oversampling method for multi-class imbalanced data based on composite weights. *PLoS ONE* **2021**, *16*, e0259227. [CrossRef]
22. Karabulut, E.M.; Ibrikci, T. Effective automated prediction of vertebral column pathologies based on logistic model tree with SMOTE preprocessing. *J. Med. Syst.* **2014**, *38*, 50. [CrossRef]
23. Özdemir, A.; Polat, K.; Alhudhaif, A. Classification of imbalanced hyperspectral images using SMOTE-based deep learning methods. *Expert Syst. Appl.* **2021**, *178*, 114986. [CrossRef]
24. Han, L.; Yang, G.; Yang, X.; Song, X.; Xu, B.; Li, Z.; Wu, J.; Yang, H.; Wu, J. An explainable XGBoost model improved by SMOTE-ENN technique for maize lodging detection based on multi-source unmanned aerial vehicle images. *Comput. Electron. Agric.* **2022**, *194*, 106804. [CrossRef]
25. Lin, Q.; Huang, H.; Wang, J.; Chen, L.; Du, H.; Zhou, G. Early detection of pine shoot beetle attack using vertical profile of plant traits through UAV-based hyperspectral, thermal, and lidar data fusion. *Int. J. Appl. Earth Obs. Geoinf.* **2023**, *125*, 103549. [CrossRef]
26. Hart, S.J.; Veblen, T.T. Detection of spruce beetle-induced tree mortality using high-and medium-resolution remotely sensed imagery. *Remote Sens. Environ.* **2015**, *168*, 134–145. [CrossRef]
27. Tian, L.; Wang, Z.; Xue, B.; Li, D.; Zheng, H.; Yao, X.; Zhu, Y.; Cao, W.; Cheng, T. A disease-specific spectral index tracks *Magnaporthe oryzae* infection in paddy rice from ground to space. *Remote Sens. Environ.* **2023**, *285*, 113384. [CrossRef]
28. Sapes, G.; Lapadat, C.; Schweiger, A.K.; Juzwik, J.; Montgomery, R.; Gholizadeh, H.; Townsend, P.A.; Gamon, J.A.; Cavender-Bares, J. Canopy spectral reflectance detects oak wilt at the landscape scale using phylogenetic discrimination. *Remote Sens. Environ.* **2022**, *273*, 112961. [CrossRef]
29. Guo, W.; Sun, H.; Qiao, H.; Zhang, H.; Zhou, L.; Dong, P.; Song, X. Spectral Detection of Peanut Southern Blight Severity Based on Continuous Wavelet Transform and Machine Learning. *Agriculture* **2023**, *13*, 1504. [CrossRef]
30. Huo, L.; Persson, H.J.; Lindberg, E. Early detection of forest stress from European spruce bark beetle attack, and a new vegetation index: Normalized distance red & SWIR (NDRS). *Remote Sens. Environ.* **2021**, *255*, 112240.
31. Huo, L.; Lindberg, E.; Bohlin, J.; Persson, H.J. Assessing the detectability of European spruce bark beetle green attack in multispectral drone images with high spatial-and temporal resolutions. *Remote Sens. Environ.* **2023**, *287*, 113484. [CrossRef]
32. Stone, C.; Mohammed, C. Application of remote sensing technologies for assessing planted forests damaged by insect pests and fungal pathogens: A review. *Curr. For. Rep.* **2017**, *3*, 75–92. [CrossRef]
33. Moghadam, P.; Ward, D.; Goan, E.; Jayawardena, S.; Sikka, P.; Hernandez, E. Plant disease detection using hyperspectral imaging. In Proceedings of the 2017 International Conference on Digital Image Computing: Techniques and Applications (DICTA), Sydney, Australia, 29 November–1 December 2017; pp. 1–8.
34. Tarafdar, A.; Rani, T.S.; Chandran, U.S.; Ghosh, R.; Chobe, D.R.; Sharma, M. Exploring combined effect of abiotic (soil moisture) and biotic (*Sclerotium rolfsii* Sacc.) stress on collar rot development in chickpea. *Front. Plant Sci.* **2018**, *9*, 1154. [CrossRef] [PubMed]
35. Garhwal, A.S.; Pullanagari, R.R.; Li, M.; Reis, M.M.; Archer, R. Hyperspectral imaging for identification of Zebra Chip disease in potatoes. *Biosyst. Eng.* **2020**, *197*, 306–317. [CrossRef]
36. Zhao, X.; Zhang, J.; Huang, Y.; Tian, Y.; Yuan, L. Detection and discrimination of disease and insect stress of tea plants using hyperspectral imaging combined with wavelet analysis. *Comput. Electron. Agric.* **2022**, *193*, 106717. [CrossRef]
37. Liu, Y.; Lu, Y.; Chen, D.; Zheng, W.; Ma, Y.; Pan, X. Simultaneous estimation of multiple soil properties under moist conditions using fractional-order derivative of vis-NIR spectra and deep learning. *Geoderma* **2023**, *438*, 116653. [CrossRef]
38. Zhang, J.; Jing, X.; Song, X.; Zhang, T.; Duan, W.; Su, J. Hyperspectral estimation of wheat stripe rust using fractional order differential equations and Gaussian process methods. *Comput. Electron. Agric.* **2023**, *206*, 107671. [CrossRef]
39. Song, G.; Wang, Q.; Jin, J. Estimation of leaf photosynthetic capacity parameters using spectral indices developed from fractional-order derivatives. *Comput. Electron. Agric.* **2023**, *212*, 108068. [CrossRef]
40. Ren, K.; Dong, Y.; Huang, W.; Guo, A.; Jing, X. Monitoring of winter wheat stripe rust by collaborating canopy SIF with wavelet energy coefficients. *Comput. Electron. Agric.* **2023**, *215*, 108366. [CrossRef]
41. Zhou, Z.-H. Learnware: On the future of machine learning. *Front. Comput. Sci.* **2016**, *10*, 589–590. [CrossRef]
42. Kiranyaz, S.; Avci, O.; Abdeljaber, O.; Ince, T.; Gabbouj, M.; Inman, D.J. 1D convolutional neural networks and applications: A survey. *Mech. Syst. Signal Process.* **2021**, *151*, 107398. [CrossRef]
43. Peng, Y.; Zhu, X.; Xiong, J.; Yu, R.; Liu, T.; Jiang, Y.; Yang, G. Estimation of nitrogen content on apple tree canopy through red-edge parameters from fractional-order differential operators using hyperspectral reflectance. *J. Indian Soc. Remote Sens.* **2021**, *49*, 377–392. [CrossRef]
44. Li, C.; Wang, Y.; Ma, C.; Ding, F.; Li, Y.; Chen, W.; Li, J.; Xiao, Z. Hyperspectral estimation of winter wheat leaf area index based on continuous wavelet transform and fractional order differentiation. *Sensors* **2021**, *21*, 8497. [CrossRef]
45. Chawla, N.V.; Bowyer, K.W.; Hall, L.O.; Kegelmeyer, W.P. SMOTE: Synthetic minority over-sampling technique. *J. Artif. Intell. Res.* **2002**, *16*, 321–357. [CrossRef]
46. Bioucas-Dias, J.M.; Plaza, A.; Camps-Valls, G.; Scheunders, P.; Nasrabadi, N.; Chanussot, J. Hyperspectral remote sensing data analysis and future challenges. *IEEE Geosci. Remote Sens. Mag.* **2013**, *1*, 6–36. [CrossRef]
47. Chandrashekar, G.; Sahin, F. A survey on feature selection methods. *Comput. Electr. Eng.* **2014**, *40*, 16–28. [CrossRef]
48. Spolaôr, N.; Cherman, E.A.; Monard, M.C.; Lee, H.D. ReliefF for multi-label feature selection. In Proceedings of the 2013 Brazilian Conference on Intelligent Systems, Fortaleza, Brazil, 19–24 October 2013; pp. 6–11.

49. Joachims, T. Making Large-Scale SVM Learning Practical. *Tech. Rep.* **1998**, *8*, 499–526. [CrossRef]
50. Zhang, S.; Li, X.; Zong, M.; Zhu, X.; Wang, R. Efficient kNN classification with different numbers of nearest neighbors. *IEEE Trans. Neural Netw. Learn. Syst.* **2017**, *29*, 1774–1785. [CrossRef]
51. Branch, W.; Brenneman, T. Stem rot disease evaluation of mass-selected peanut populations. *Crop Prot.* **1999**, *18*, 127–130. [CrossRef]
52. Subrahmanyam, P.; Rao, V.R.; McDonald, D.; Moss, J.; Gibbons, R. Origins of resistances to rust and late leaf spot in peanut (*Arachis hypogaea*, Fabaceae). *Econ. Bot.* **1989**, *43*, 444–455. [CrossRef]
53. Flores-Moctezuma, H.; Montes-Belmont, R.; Jimenez-Perez, A.; Nava-Juarez, R. Pathogenic diversity of *Sclerotium rolfsii* isolates from Mexico, and potential control of southern blight through solarization and organic amendments. *Crop Prot.* **2006**, *25*, 195–201. [CrossRef]
54. Lane, P.C.; Clarke, D.; Hender, P. On developing robust models for favourability analysis: Model choice, feature sets and imbalanced data. *Decis. Support Syst.* **2012**, *53*, 712–718. [CrossRef]
55. Weiss, G.M. Mining with rarity: A unifying framework. *ACM Sigkdd Explor. Newsl.* **2004**, *6*, 7–19. [CrossRef]
56. Fernández, A.; Garcia, S.; Herrera, F.; Chawla, N.V. SMOTE for learning from imbalanced data: Progress and challenges, marking the 15-year anniversary. *J. Artif. Intell. Res.* **2018**, *61*, 863–905. [CrossRef]
57. Sivakumar, J.; Ramamurthy, K.; Radhakrishnan, M.; Won, D. Synthetic sampling from small datasets: A modified mega-trend diffusion approach using k-nearest neighbors. *Knowl.-Based Syst.* **2022**, *236*, 107687. [CrossRef]
58. Jiang, Z.; Pan, T.; Zhang, C.; Yang, J. A new oversampling method based on the classification contribution degree. *Symmetry* **2021**, *13*, 194. [CrossRef]
59. Tarawneh, A.S.; Hassanat, A.B.; Altarawneh, G.A.; Almuhaimeed, A. Stop oversampling for class imbalance learning: A review. *IEEE Access* **2022**, *10*, 47643–47660. [CrossRef]
60. Schultz, K.; Bej, S.; Hahn, W.; Wolfien, M.; Srivastava, P.; Wolkenhauer, O. ConvGeN: A convex space learning approach for deep-generative oversampling and imbalanced classification of small tabular datasets. *Pattern Recognit.* **2024**, *147*, 110138. [CrossRef]
61. Ebrahimy, H.; Wang, Y.; Zhang, Z. Utilization of synthetic minority oversampling technique for improving potato yield prediction using remote sensing data and machine learning algorithms with small sample size of yield data. *ISPRS J. Photogramm. Remote Sens.* **2023**, *201*, 12–25. [CrossRef]
62. Peng, J.; Gao, R.; Thng, S.; Huang, W.; Lin, Z. Classification of Non-tumorous Facial Pigmentation Disorders Using Generative Adversarial Networks and Improved SMOTE. In Proceedings of the 2021 43rd Annual International Conference of the IEEE Engineering in Medicine & Biology Society (EMBC), Virtual, 1–5 November 2021; pp. 3770–3773.
63. Sáez, J.A.; Luengo, J.; Stefanowski, J.; Herrera, F. SMOTE–IPF: Addressing the noisy and borderline examples problem in imbalanced classification by a re-sampling method with filtering. *Inf. Sci.* **2015**, *291*, 184–203. [CrossRef]
64. Zhang, A.; Yu, H.; Huan, Z.; Yang, X.; Zheng, S.; Gao, S. SMOTE-RkNN: A hybrid re-sampling method based on SMOTE and reverse k-nearest neighbors. *Inf. Sci.* **2022**, *595*, 70–88. [CrossRef]
65. Zhu, J.; Lu, J.; Li, W.; Wang, Y.; Jiang, J.; Cheng, T.; Zhu, Y.; Cao, W.; Yao, X. Estimation of canopy water content for wheat through combining radiative transfer model and machine learning. *Field Crops Res.* **2023**, *302*, 109077. [CrossRef]
66. Combal, B.; Baret, F.; Weiss, M.; Trubuil, A.; Macé, D.; Pragnere, A.; Myneni, R.; Knyazikhin, Y.; Wang, L. Retrieval of canopy biophysical variables from bidirectional reflectance: Using prior information to solve the ill-posed inverse problem. *Remote Sens. Environ.* **2003**, *84*, 1–15. [CrossRef]
67. Tsai, F.; Philpot, W. Derivative analysis of hyperspectral data. *Remote Sens. Environ.* **1998**, *66*, 41–51. [CrossRef]
68. Podlubny, I. *Fractional Differential Equations: An Introduction to Fractional Derivatives, Fractional Differential Equations, to Methods of Their Solution and Some of Their Applications*; Elsevier: Amsterdam, The Netherlands, 1998.
69. Kilbas, A.A.; Srivastava, H.M.; Trujillo, J.J. *Theory and Applications of Fractional Differential Equations*; Elsevier: Amsterdam, The Netherlands, 2006; Volume 204.
70. Zhang, D.; Zhang, F. Application of fractional differential in preprocessing hyperspectral data of saline soil. *Trans. Chin. Soc. Agric. Eng.* **2014**, *30*, 151–160.
71. Duan, R.; Huang, G.; Zhou, X.; Lu, C.; Tian, C. Record-Breaking heavy rainfall around Henan Province in 2021 and future projection of extreme conditions under climate change. *J. Hydrol.* **2023**, *625*, 130102. [CrossRef]

agriculture

MDPI

Article

Improvement of Winter Wheat Aboveground Biomass Estimation Using Digital Surface Model Information Extracted from Unmanned-Aerial-Vehicle-Based Multispectral Images

Yan Guo [1,2,3], Jia He [1,2], Huifang Zhang [1,2], Zhou Shi [4], Panpan Wei [1,2], Yuhang Jing [1,2], Xiuzhong Yang [1,2,3], Yan Zhang [1,2,3], Laigang Wang [1,5,*] and Guoqing Zheng [1,2,3]

1 Institute of Agricultural Information Technology, Henan Academy of Agricultural Sciences, Zhengzhou 450002, China; 10914063@zju.edu.cn (Y.G.); yzhang1203@hnagri.org.cn (Y.Z.); zgqzx@hnagri.org.cn (G.Z.)
2 Key Laboratory of Huang-Huai-Hai Smart Agricultural Technology, Ministry of Agriculture and Rural Affairs, Zhengzhou 450002, China
3 Henan Engineering Research Center of Crop Planting Monitoring and Warning, Zhengzhou 450002, China
4 Institute of Agricultural Remote Sensing and Information Technology Application, College of Environmental and Resource Sciences, Zhejiang University, Hangzhou 310058, China
5 International School, Huanghe Science & Technology College, Zhengzhou 450016, China
* Correspondence: wanglaigang@hnagri.org.cn

Abstract: Aboveground biomass (AGB) is an important indicator for characterizing crop growth conditions. A rapid and accurate estimation of AGB is critical for guiding the management of farmland and achieving production potential, and it can also provide vital data for ensuring food security. In this study, by applying different water and nitrogen treatments, an unmanned aerial vehicle (UAV) equipped with a multispectral imaging spectrometer was used to acquire images of winter wheat during critical growth stages. Then, the plant height (H_{dsm}) extracted from the digital surface model (DSM) information was used to establish and improve the estimation model of AGB, using the backpropagation (BP) neural network, a machine learning method. The results show that (1) the R^2, root-mean-square error (RMSE), and relative predictive deviation (RPD) of the AGB estimation model, constructed directly using the H_{dsm}, are 0.58, 4528.23 kg/hm^2, and 1.25, respectively. The estimated mean AGB (16,198.27 kg/hm^2) is slightly smaller than the measured mean AGB (16,960.23 kg/hm^2). (2) The R^2, RMSE, and RPD of the improved AGB estimation model, based on AGB/H_{dsm}, are 0.88, 2291.90 kg/hm^2, and 2.75, respectively, and the estimated mean AGB (17,478.21 kg/hm^2) is more similar to the measured mean AGB (17,222.59 kg/hm^2). The improved AGB estimation model boosts the accuracy by 51.72% compared with the AGB directly estimated using the H_{dsm}. Moreover, the improved AGB estimation model shows strong transferability in regard to different water treatments and different year scenarios, but there are differences in the transferability for different N-level scenarios. (3) Differences in the characteristics of the data are the key factors that lead to the different transferability of the AGB estimation model. This study provides an antecedent in regard to model construction and transferability estimation of AGB for winter wheat. We confirm that, when different datasets have similar histogram characteristics, the model is applicable to new scenarios.

Keywords: aboveground biomass; UAV; height; transferability; BP neural network; machine learning

1. Introduction

Aboveground biomass (AGB) has an important impact on light energy utilization and yield formation, and its accurate estimation is one of the key issues in terrestrial ecology research [1,2]. On the one hand, AGB plays an important role in the global carbon cycle [3,4], and an accurate estimation of AGB could help us grasp the feedback between climate change and agroecosystem interactions [5]. On the other hand, AGB is closely related to crop yield and production [1,6–8]. Therefore, a timely and accurate estimation of AGB is extremely important for guiding the scientific management and rational utilization of farmland, protecting and enhancing the carbon sink function, and providing important data on food security issues [8–10].

In recent years, there have been an increasing number of studies that use remote sensing technology to estimate AGB [11–14]. However, satellite remote sensing images, which are usually used as data for AGB estimation and retrieval, suffer from low spatio-temporal resolution and interference from atmospheric conditions [15,16]. Proximal hyperspectral imagery has a high spectral resolution, but the process is time-consuming and labor-intensive, which limits its application in large-spatial-scale surveys [17]. Compared to satellite remote sensing and proximal hyperspectral remote sensing, low-altitude UAVs can carry different types of sensors, such as RGB cameras, hyperspectral imagers, and multispectral imagers, according to the specific purpose of the survey being conducted [10,11,15]. UAVs have various advantages, such as simplicity in regard to their operation, strong maneuverability, and the ability to acquire high-resolution images below the clouds. They are better suited to field-scale monitoring and serve as a crucial technique in modern agriculture's move toward quantitative and refined approaches [11,18–20]. At present, AGB estimation with UAV remote sensing in agriculture mainly utilizes RGB and multispectral digital orthophoto maps (DOMs) to extract spectral parameters, which are then used to calculate vegetation indices for model construction. For example, Ma et al. [21] and Lu et al. [22] estimated wheat AGB using UAV digital imagery and found that a combination of image color index and texture features can improve the accuracy of wheat biomass estimation, with the highest R^2 being 0.91. Previous studies have focused on utilizing spectral, textural, and vegetation indices extracted from UAV images to estimate crop AGB through linear modeling or machine learning methods [7,12,23,24]. However, due to the interaction of various factors, such as the crop planting area, crop type, and crop growth stages, during the acquisition of canopy information by UAVs, a saturation phenomenon occurs in the vegetation index, which negatively affects the accuracy of the biomass estimation model, as well as the transferability of the model.

In parallel to DOMs, a digital surface model (DSM) is another key piece of information involving ultra-high-resolution UAV images, which is directly related to crop height [25–27]. For example, Chang et al. [28], Watanabe et al. [29], and Luo et al. [30] used UAVs to acquire digital remote sensing images of maize, sorghum, and other crops, and then adopted a digital terrain model (DTM) and a DSM to estimate the plant height of these crops. Their results indicated that the estimated plant height and the measured plant height had an RMSE that varied between 0.33 and 0.88 m. The rise of real-time kinematic (RTK) and post-processing kinematic (PPK) technologies, in particular, provide UAVs with a more prominent advantage in obtaining plant heights quickly and accurately. Wang et al. [31] showed that their crop surface model (CSM), obtained by correcting the DSM using PPK and RTK technologies, can essentially improve plant height estimation accuracy. Therefore, an increasing number of scholars are utilizing UAV images to extract plant heights for biomass estimation [31–33]. For example, Niu et al. [32] extracted the height of maize directly from point cloud data using the Phantom 4 wizard; the R^2 was 0.90 and 0.82 for the plant height estimation and maize biomass estimation, respectively. Bendig et al. [15], Bareth et al. [34], and Wang et al. [31] reported that combining DSM-extracted plant height information with the vegetation index could improve the estimation accuracy of AGB.

However, the extent of the contribution of DSM information to biomass estimation models and the transferability of such models remain largely unclear. Therefore, in this study, we employed a UAV equipped with a multispectral camera, coupled with RTK technology and ground control points, to obtain remote sensing images and elevation information at different key growth stages of winter wheat. Then, we extracted wheat heights from the data obtained by the UAV during these key growth stages and constructed an AGB estimation model using machine learning regression methods. After that, we analyzed the transferability of the model under different water treatments, across different years, and at various N levels. Our results are expected to provide critical technical support and a theoretical basis for rapid AGB estimation of winter wheat and phenotype research, as well as crop water and fertilizer decision making.

2. Materials and Methods

2.1. Study Area and Experimental Design

The experiments were conducted on a state-owned farm in Shangshui County, Zhoukou City, Henan Province, central China (33°33′ N, 114°37′ E), from 2020 to 2022, with a plot area of approximately 42 m^2. The region is located in the southern part of a warm temperate zone, with a monsoon semi-humid climate and suitable temperatures for crop growth throughout the year. The test soil is sand ginger black soil. Before sowing, the pH is 7.3 in the surface (0–20 cm) layer, and the soil organic matter, total nitrogen content, available phosphorus content, and available potassium content are 25.0 g/kg, 1.69 g/kg, 22.6 mg/kg, and 139.6 mg/kg, respectively. Using a randomized block experimental design, 5 nitrogen application levels (N0 (0 kg/hm^2), N6 (90 kg/hm^2), N12 (180 kg/hm^2), N18 (270 kg/hm^2), and N24 (360 kg/hm^2)) and 2 water treatments (rainfed and irrigated) were set. Each N treatment was repeated 3 times, and the two water treatments were named W0 (rainfed) and W1 (irrigated); the total number of plots was 30 (Figure 1). About 50% of each fertilizer was applied as a base fertilizer, and the remaining 50% of the fertilizer was applied as top-dressing during the jointing stage; the amount of the phosphorus fertilizer was 120 kg/hm^2 and the amount of the potassium fertilizer was 90 kg/hm^2, both of which were applied at once before sowing.

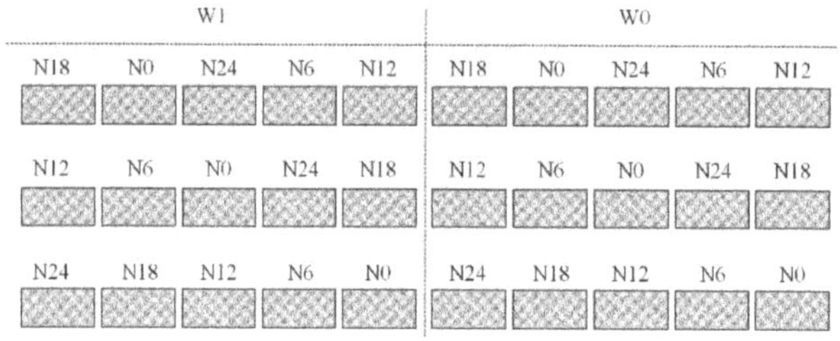

Figure 1. Design of the experiment.

2.2. Study Framework of AGB Estimation

A general framework of our study is presented in Figure 2. Firstly, a DJ M600 pro UAV was used to acquire UAV remote sensing images during the jointing, flowering, and filling stages of winter wheat, and the images were preprocessed using the Agisoft PhotoScan Professional 12.0 software. During the process of establishing a 3D point cloud, DSM data of the study area were obtained. Then, the height of winter wheat plants in each plot was extracted based on the DSM data. Through an analysis of the relationship between the extracted plant height (H_{dsm}), the measured plant height (H), and aboveground biomass (AGB), a winter wheat AGB estimation model was established using the BP neural network method. To improve the estimation accuracy, the ratio of AGB to H_{dsm} was determined to establish the AGB model, and the transferability of the improved model was analyzed across different water treatments, years, and nitrogen treatment scenarios.

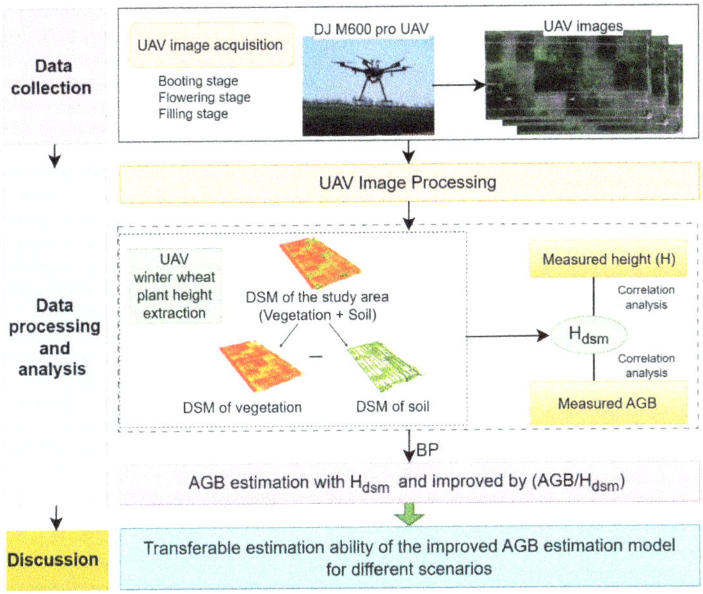

Figure 2. Flowchart of the study framework.

2.3. *Data Acquisition*

2.3.1. UAV Platform and Image Acquisition

From 2020 to 2022, during the key growth periods of two winter wheat growth cycles, images were obtained using a DJI M600 Pro UAV equipped with an Anzhou Technology K6 multispectral imager during clear weather from 10:00 to 14:00. The sensor mainly included five bands: a blue band (center wavelength of 450 nm, B), a green band (center wavelength of 550 nm, G), a red band (center wavelength of 685 nm, R), a red-edge band (center wavelength of 725 nm, Rededge), and a near-infrared band (center wavelength of 780 nm, Nir). Four radiometric calibration plates with standard reflectance of 5%, 20%, 40%, and 70% were laid on the ground before the flight. The ground control points (GCPs) of the four vertices and the middle points in the experimental area were measured using a real-time kinematic (RTK) receiver for precise correction of flight position and altitude. The flight altitude was 50 m, and the obtained images had a spatial resolution of 0.02 m.

2.3.2. UAV Image Processing

The preprocessing of UAV data mainly included five steps, namely image format conversion, image filtering, image stitching, orthophoto correction, and radiometric calibration. The details were as follows: (1) The raw MAPIR-format data acquired by K6 was batch converted into TIFF-format data that could be recognized by the Agisoft PhotoScan Professional 12.0 software through the MAPIR Camera Control software. (2) To save time during image stitching, images outside the study area were deleted according to the geographic coordinate information before image stitching. (3) The Agisoft PhotoScan Professional 12.0 software was used for image stitching based on the 3D model mode, which simultaneously obtained orthophoto images and a digital surface model (DSM) of the study area. (4) Based on the RTK geographic information coordinates, the geographic position of the UAV images was accurately corrected. This step could eliminate the positional deviation caused by the fast flight speed. (5) Using the Digital Number (DN) values of the radiometric calibration plates, linear conversion formulas were established to convert the DN values to reflectance values (Table 1). This was performed by assuming that there is a linear relationship between a reflectance value and a DN value: $y = \text{gain} \times \text{DN} + \text{bias}$, where

y is the surface reflectance of a particular band, and gain and bias are the corresponding gain and offset values, respectively. Based on the standard reflectance of the radiometric calibration plates used to establish the relationship with the corresponding pixel DN value, the gain and bias of each band were obtained, and then the DN value was converted to reflectance.

Table 1. Reflectance conversion formulas.

Center Wavelength (nm)	Conversion Formulas	R^2
450	$y = 6.683 \times 10^{-6}DN - 0.0433$	0.995
550	$y = 7.207 \times 10^{-6}DN - 0.0728$	0.995
685	$y = 7.261 \times 10^{-6}DN - 0.0263$	0.999
725	$y = 8.511 \times 10^{-6}DN - 0.0384$	0.999
780	$y = 8.812 \times 10^{-6}DN - 0.0506$	0.999

2.3.3. UAV Winter Wheat Plant Height Extraction

The steps of extracting winter wheat plant height (H_{dsm}) from UAV images are shown in Figure 3. The process included the following steps: (1) generating point-cloud and aligned photos based on the UAV images; (2) importing ground control points for geometric correction; (3) reconstructing height and output of the crop surface model (CSM); and (4) performing raster calculation to output the winter wheat plant height. Steps (1) to (3) were completed using the Agisoft PhotoScan Professional 12.0 software, and step (4) was completed using the ArcGIS software (version 10.6.1, ESRI). Specifically, bare-ground images were collected on 5 October 2020 for the establishment of a Digital Elevation Model (DEM) of the topography of the study area. During the image stitching process, which aimed to establish the CSM (steps 1 to 4), if the elevation of the ortho-rectified CSM at the control points deviated greatly from the elevation of the measured control points, it was necessary to re-adjust the parameters and re-locate the projection point of the control points on each image before modeling. Therefore, the maximum deviation of the CSM from the measured elevation at the control points was set to be less than 0.01 m, and the CSM could be outputted after achieving this accuracy. The DSM was imported into ArcGIS 10.6 in step (4), and the raster images of the DSM in each growth stage were subtracted from the raster images of the study area's DEM to obtain a standardized winter wheat CSM. Meanwhile, according to the plot range, a rectangular region of interest (ROI) was drawn. When drawing the ROI, each edge was reserved 1 m from the plot edge to exclude boundary interference. Finally, the plant height of each plot of winter wheat was obtained by partitioning and calculating the statistics of the standardized CSM.

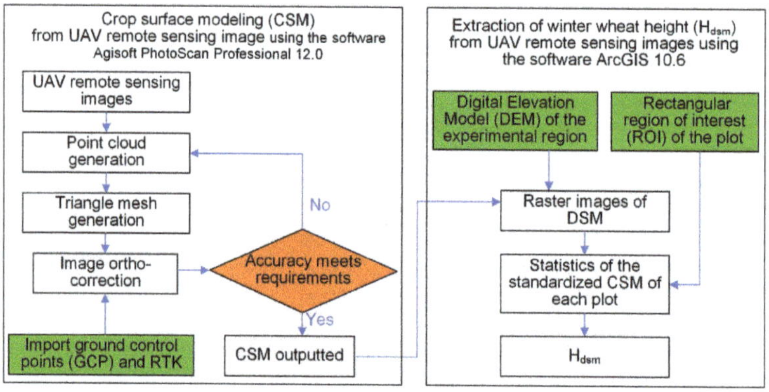

Figure 3. Flowchart of the extraction of plant height of winter wheat.

2.3.4. Measurement of AGB and Height of Winter Wheat

The acquisition of ground data was synchronized with the acquisition of UAV images. The field samples were collected using a Beidou intelligent handheld terminal (UG908) to obtain the geographic location information of the sampling points. Ten plants with a uniform growth were selected from each plot to measure plant height (H), and the stem samples were packed into sealed bags. The samples were heated for 30 min at 105 °C to halt the metabolic processes, dried at 80 °C in a forced-draft oven, and then weighed to obtain the AGB. A total of 180 samples were obtained.

2.4. Methodology

2.4.1. AGB Estimation with Backpropagation Neural Network Method

A backpropagation (BP) neural network is a multi-layer feed-forward network that uses error backpropagation for algorithm training; it is one of the most widely used neural network models [35–37]. Currently, there are more than 20 commonly used activation functions for BP neural networks, including identity, sigmoid, and ReLU. When the function identity is active, the input of the node is equal to the output, and it is most suitable for tasks in which the potential behavior is linear [38]. For this reason, we used identity as the activation function of the training model for the nitrogen content of plants. Meanwhile, to prevent overfitting, parameters such as learning rate and regularization were introduced to optimize the model [39]. In this study, a three-layer network structure was designed using a quasi-Newton method family optimizer (lbfgs) to improve the operation speed. Assuming that the output of the hidden layer is set as F_j, the m-quantity of the output layer is set as O_k, the excitation function of the system is set as G, and the learning rate is set as β, the following mathematical relationships can be obtained:

$$\begin{cases} F_j = G\left(\sum_{i=1}^{m} \omega_{ij} x_i + a_j\right) \\ O_k = \sum_{j=1}^{l} F_j \omega_{jk} + b_k \end{cases} \tag{1}$$

If the expected output of the system is set to T_k, the error E of the system can be expressed by the variance between the actual output value and the expected target value, and the specific relationship is as follows:

$$E = \frac{1}{2} \sum_{k=1}^{n} (T_k - O_k)^2 \tag{2}$$

Let $e_k = T_k - O_k$; using the principle of gradient descent, the updated formulas of system weights and bias are as follows:

$$\begin{cases} \omega_{ij} = \omega_{ij} + \beta F_j (1 - F_j) x_i \sum_{k=1}^{n} w_{jk} e_k \\ \omega_{jk} = \omega_{jk} + \beta F_j e_k \end{cases} \tag{3}$$

$$\begin{cases} a_j = a_j + \beta F_j (1 - F_j) x_i \sum_{k=1}^{n} w_{jk} e_k \\ b_k = b_k + \beta e_k \end{cases} \tag{4}$$

2.4.2. Model Metric Evaluation

In this study, three widely used indices—the coefficient of determination (R^2), the root-mean-square error (RMSE), and the relative predictive deviation (RPD)—were used to evaluate the model performance. The larger the values of R^2 and PRD and the smaller the RMSE, the better the model performs. When the estimated value matches the measured value perfectly, $R^2 = 1$ and RMSE = 0, which indicates strong estimation and transferability of the constructed model. When RPD ≥ 2, it indicates that the model has excellent robustness; when 1.4 ≤ RPD < 2, it indicates that the model has moderate robustness; and when RPD < 1.4, it indicates that the robustness of the model is slightly weak [20,40,41]. The formulas are as follows:

$$R^2 = \frac{\sum_{i=1}^{n} (\hat{y}_i - \overline{y})^2}{\sum_{i=1}^{n} (y_i - \overline{y})^2} \quad (5)$$

$$RMSE = \sqrt{\frac{1}{n}\sum_{i=1}^{n} (\hat{y}_i - y_i)^2} \quad (6)$$

$$RPD = \sqrt{\frac{\sum_{i=1}^{n} (y_i - \overline{y})^2}{\sum_{i=1}^{n} (y_i - \hat{y}_i)^2}} \quad (7)$$

where y_i and $\hat{y}_i$ are the measured and predicted biomass of the *i*th sample, respectively; $\overline{y}$ denotes the mean AGB; and n is the number of samples.

3. Results

3.1. Statistical Analysis of Plant Height (H) and Aboveground Biomass (AGB) of Winter Wheat

The changes in H and AGB of winter wheat at different water–N treatments are shown in Figure 4. The W0 and W1 treatments show a gradual increase in both H and AGB with an increase in the N level, but there are variations in the magnitude of the increase. H increases rapidly with an increase in the N level from N0 to N12, while the increase in H from N12 to N24 is smaller. AGB increases quickly with an increase in the N level from N0 to N18; however, a clear difference was detected for the increase in AGB with an increase in the N level from N18 and N24 under different water treatments. Specifically, the AGB of the W0 treatment remains unchanged, while the AGB of the W1 treatment still increases rapidly.

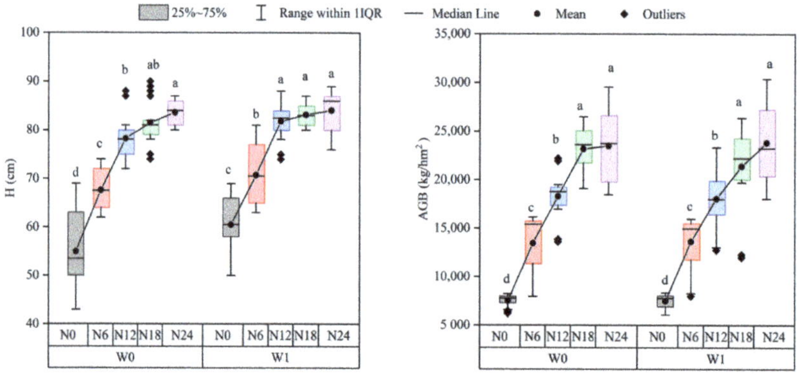

Figure 4. H (the **left** plot) and AGB (the **right** plot) of winter wheat at different water and nitrogen levels (note: the lowercase letters a, b, c, and d in the figure indicate significant differences at the 0.05 level).

In addition, N treatments can largely affect H and AGB (Figure 1). With an increase in N application, H and AGB increase significantly, but the magnitude of the increase is different. H increases sharply at N levels below N12 and then tends to be stabilized in both W0 and W1 treatments, while AGB continues to sharply increase at N levels above N12 in the W1 treatment. The one-way ANOVA reveals significant differences ($p < 0.05$) for H and AGB with different N levels. The *t*-test results also reveal that there are significant differences ($p < 0.05$) for H and AGB under different water treatments. In conclusion, this study shows that the effect of stress induced by water on H during water–nitrogen coupling is greater than the effect on AGB.

3.2. Relationship between H_{dsm} and H under Different Water–N Treatments

The relationship between H estimated by means of DSM (H_{dsm}) and the measured H of winter wheat is shown in Figure 5. The correlation between the H_{dsm} and measured H values declines from 0.59 to 0.07 with an increase in the N level. This is mainly because the change in H tends to become stabilized after N has been applied to a study plot to a certain extent under the same irrigation condition, after which H no longer increases with a further increase in N. Moreover, as presented in Figure 5, the distribution of the H_{dsm} values is more consistent when the N level increases from N12 to N24, whereas the distribution of H at the N levels of N0 and N6 is relatively dispersed. As the canopy cover of winter wheat increases, winter wheat plants become luxuriant, and three-dimensional structural spatial information of winter wheat may be lacking. Therefore, the errors of the lower boundary and upper boundary of plants caused by the advancement of the growth stage lead to the increase in estimation errors of plant height.

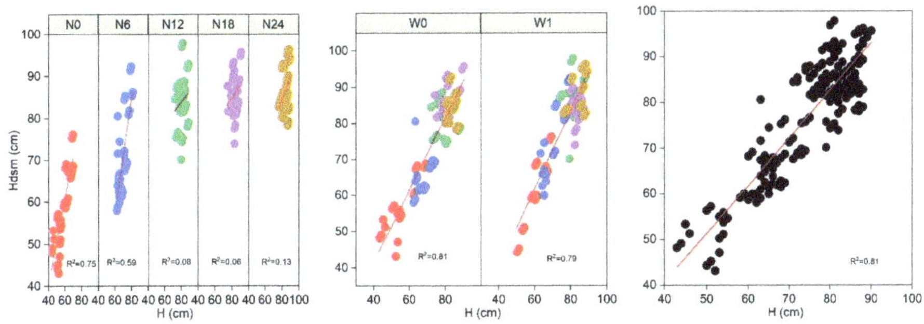

Figure 5. Relationship between H_{dsm} and H under different water–N treatments.

The relationship between H_{dsm} and H under different water treatments shows that the W0 treatment is superior to the W1 treatment, with R^2 of 0.81 and 0.79, respectively. Combined with Figure 4, this indicates that under the rainfed condition of water–N coupling, the change in H of winter wheat is small, while under the condition of sufficient N, irrigation can increase H. Overall, the linear relationship between H_{dsm} and H has an R^2 of 0.81, which means that H_{dsm} can explain more than 80% of the variation in plant height.

3.3. Relationship between H_{dsm} and AGB under Different Water–N Treatments

The relationship between the H_{dsm} and measured AGB values is shown in Figure 6. The correlation between the H_{dsm} and measured AGB values is not significant as the N level increases. The correlation efficient between the H_{dsm} and measured AGB values in the W0 treatment (R^2 = 0.69) is higher than in the W1 treatment (R^2 = 0.50). Combined with Figure 1, it can be concluded that there are differences in the effects of water on AGB and H of winter wheat. This is mainly because when the changes in plant height become stabilized, irrigation causes the increase in biomass to be more likely to manifest as an increase in leaf and stem biomass. Overall, the simple linear relationship model established between H_{dsm} and AGB has an R^2 of 0.57, which means that H_{dsm} can explain 57% of the variation in AGB.

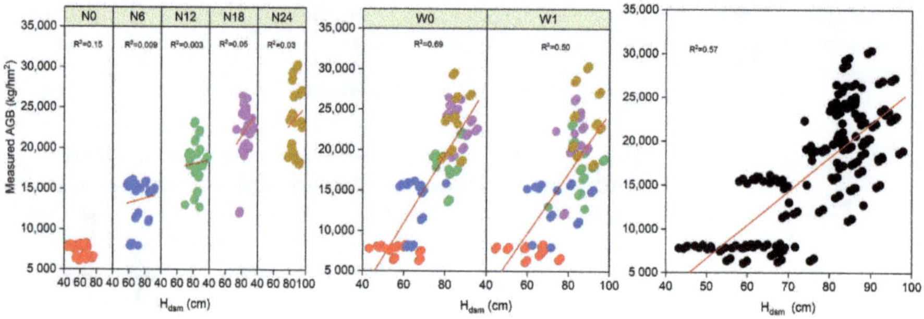

Figure 6. Relationship between H_{dsm} and measured AGB under different water–N treatments.

3.4. AGB Estimation Model Construction and Improvement

In the present study, we used the BP method to estimate AGB based on the H_{dsm} values. The R^2, RMSE, and RPD of the constructed BP model are 0.58, 4528.23 kg/hm^2, and 1.25, respectively (Figure 7). The estimated average value of AGB (16,198.27 kg/hm^2) is smaller than the measured average value (16,960.23 kg/hm^2), and the estimated values are more dispersed. Generally speaking, the predicted values of AGB are dispersed, with large 95% confidence intervals. The values of R^2, RMSE, and RPD indicate that the robustness of the model is slightly weak.

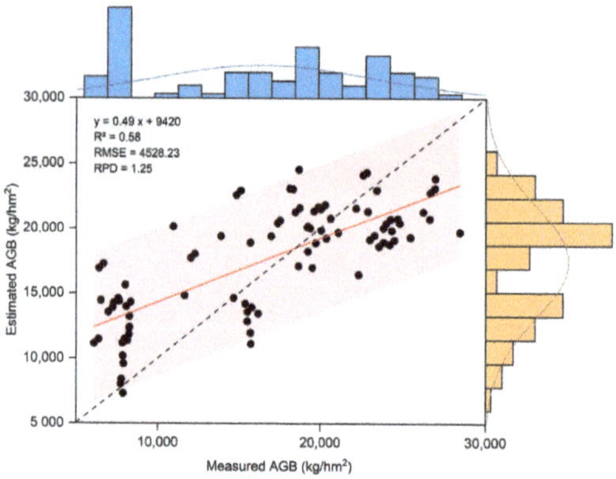

Figure 7. Relationship between the measured and estimated AGB based on H_{dsm}.

Can the estimation ability and robustness of the model be improved by means of data transformation? In this study, we found that the AGB per unit plant height of winter wheat shows an approximately parallel increasing trend with increasing N levels (Figure 8). Based on this relationship, we propose a rapid estimation method of AGB based on the ratio of AGB to H_{dsm} (AGB/H_{dsm}) to improve the estimation accuracy (Figure 9). The AGB was estimated by constructing a model using the same method as described above. The R^2, RMSE, and RPD of the model based on AGB/H_{dsm} are 0.88, 2291.90 kg/hm^2, and 2.75, respectively. The improved model based on AGB/H_{dsm} could estimate the AGB well, and the estimated mean AGB (17,478.21 kg/hm^2) is very close to the measured mean AGB (17,222.59 kg/hm^2). The improved model based on AGB/H_{dsm} (Figure 9) outperforms the model described in Section 3.4 (Figure 7), with a higher R^2, a higher RPD, and a lower RMSE. Specifically, the R^2 is improved by 51.72%.

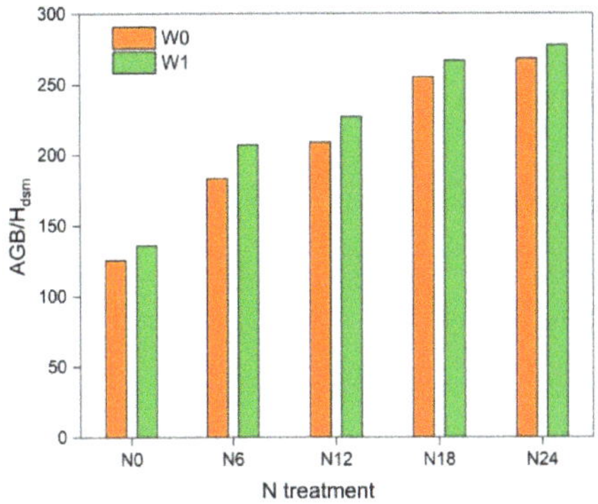

Figure 8. Changing pattern of the ratio AGB to H_{dsm} under different water–N treatments.

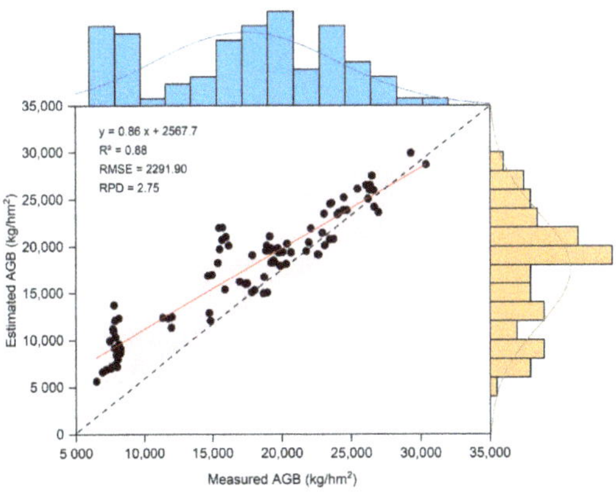

Figure 9. Relationship between measured AGB and estimated AGB according to the model-based ratio.

The improved model assuming a relationship between AGB (y) and ratio (x) is denoted as $y = f(x)$. After the data were substituted into the formula, the model was obtained as $y = kx - 4004.8$. Considering the gradually increased AGB across the jointing, flowering, and filling stages, the AGB dataset was intercepted several times to form 10 datasets. The BP method was used for the construction of the AGB estimation model. The relationship between k and H_{dsm} is denoted as $k \approx H_{max}$, with H_{max} being the maximum value of H_{dsm} for each dataset. So, the improved model was transformed for AGB estimation, and the final AGB estimation model can be expressed by the following formula: $AGB = (4004.80 \times H_{dsm})/(H_{max} - H_{dsm})$.

4. Discussion

4.1. Transferability Estimation Ability of the Improved AGB Estimation Model under Different Water Treatments

Based on the W0 and W1 treatment datasets, an AGB estimation model was constructed to validate the transferability estimation of AGB under the W1 treatment and W0 treatment scenarios. The relationships between the measured and estimated AGB under the W1 treatment and the W0 treatment are shown in Figure 10. The model constructed from the W0 treatment dataset was transformed to fit the W1 treatment dataset, with R^2, RMSE, and RPD of 0.90, 2407.44 kg/hm^2, and 2.72, respectively. Similarly, the model constructed from the W1 treatment dataset was transformed to fit the W0 treatment dataset, with R^2, RMSE, and RPD of 0.88, 2496.97 kg/hm^2, and 2.54, respectively. Overall, the AGB estimation model proposed in this study has high accuracy and robustness, and the models show improved transferability under different water treatment scenarios in the same study area, which can achieve an accurate and fast estimation of AGB.

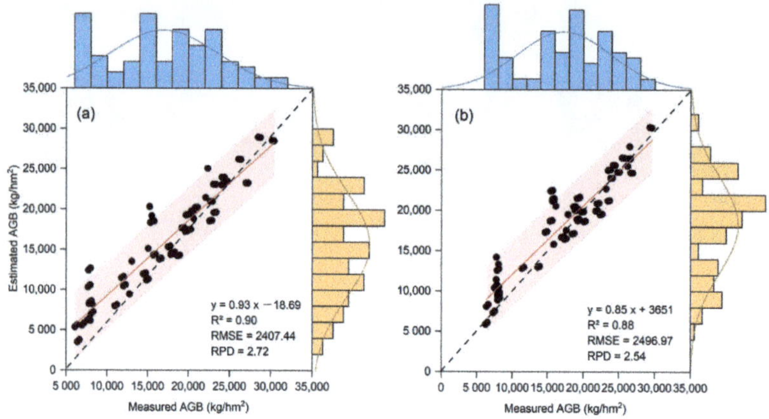

Figure 10. The transferability estimation ability of the improved AGB estimation model under different water treatments: (**a**) the transferability estimation of the W0 model for the W1 treatment, and (**b**) the transferability estimation of the W1 model for the W0 treatment.

4.2. Transferability Estimation Ability of the Improved AGB Estimation Model across Different Years

In this study, the growing season of winter wheat in 2020–2021 was set as n, and that of 2021–2022 was set as n + 1. An AGB estimation model was constructed based on the datasets of year n and n + 1 to validate the transferability estimation of AGB in the context of year n + 1 and year n. The estimation accuracy of the model for AGB is shown in Figure 11. The model constructed on the data of year n was transformed to estimate the AGB in year n + 1, with R^2, RMSE, and RPD of 0.88, 2257.36 kg/hm^2 and 2.75, respectively. The model constructed from the year n + 1 dataset was transformed to estimate the AGB in year n, with R^2, RMSE, and RPD of 0.86, 2239.37 kg/hm^2 and 2.93, respectively. Generally speaking, the AGB estimation model shows good transferability estimation performance between years.

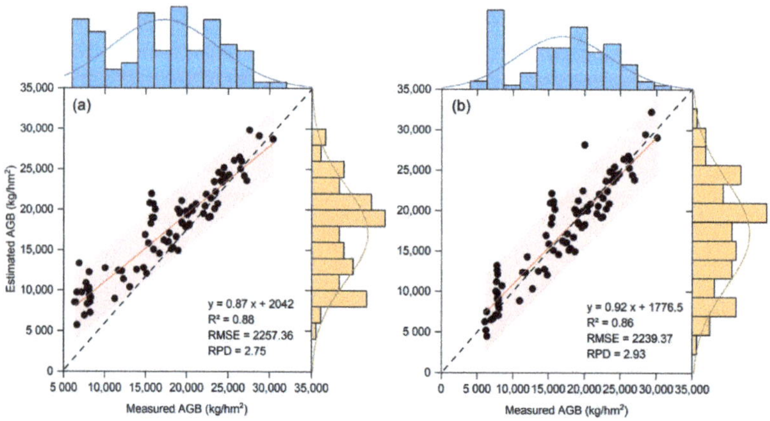

Figure 11. The transferability estimation ability of the improved AGB estimation model across different year scenarios: (**a**) the transferability ability of the nth-year model to estimate AGB for the (n + 1)th year, and (**b**) the transferability ability of the (n + 1)th-year model to estimate AGB for the nth year.

4.3. Transferability Estimation Ability of the Improved AGB Estimation Model across Different N Levels

In this part of the study, an AGB estimation model was first constructed based on the N0 dataset, and then it was used to validate the transferability estimation of AGB in the N6, N12, N18, and N24 scenarios. The R^2, RMSE, and RPD of the model, which was trained using the N0 dataset, are 0.49, 466.91 kg/hm^2, and 1.49, respectively. When the model was transformed to fit the N6, N12, N18, and N24 scenarios, the model showed bad performance with a large RMSE and a low RPD (Table 2). But the model trained on the N24 dataset had a good performance, with R^2, RMSE, and RPD of 0.88, 1304.16 kg/hm^2, and 3.04, respectively. Moreover, the model trained on the N24 dataset also performed well when it was transformed to fit the N12 and N18 scenarios, with a high R^2, a high RPD, and a low RMSE, which means it has great predictive transferability (Table 2).

Table 2. Transferability of the AGB model at different N levels.

Model Dataset	R^2	RMSE	RPD	Model Datasheet	R^2	RMSE	RPD
N0_Traning dataset	0.49	466.91	1.95	N24_Traning dataset	0.88	1304.16	3.04
N6_Test dataset	/	5339.59	0.61	N0_test dataset	/	4922.29	0.57
N12_Test dataset	/	9370.43	0.53	N6_Test dataset	/	4400.67	0.92
N18_Test dataset	/	12,755.63	0.53	N12_Tset dataset	0.70	1402.77	1.97
N24_Test dataset	/	13,917.14	0.53	N18_Test dataset	0.90	1053.85	3.06

4.4. Factors Affecting the Transferability of Models

In summary, a clear difference was detected regarding the transferability of models trained on datasets for different water treatments, years, and N levels. The models show better transferability across different water treatment and year scenarios, while the transferability of the AGB estimation model across different N levels is not satisfactory. The statistical characteristics of the datasets may play an important role in the transferability of the AGB estimation model. As shown in Figures 12 and 13, the statistical characteristics of the measured AGB and AGB/H_{dsm} data are more similar under different water treatments and across different years, with similar values of the means, standard deviations, and other indicators, and the fitted curves basically overlap. But the statistical characteristics of the measured AGB and AGB/H_{dsm} are significantly different at different N levels (Figure 14). The datasets of the measured AGB and AGB/H_{dsm} at different N levels present different mean values, standard deviations, and other indicators. Combined with Table 2, we can conclude that the statistical characteristics of the employed dataset play an important role in affecting the model's transferability. In this regard, Wang et al. [42] reported that marginal and conditional distributions usually have different contributions to the domain discrepancy. Zhou [39] and Li et al. [43] also argued that transferability is the application of knowledge from one environment to another, and to obtain an ideal transferable prediction model, it requires that the original training dataset not only has a larger amount of data but also a higher data quality so that the model would contain more feature information when transformed to the target model.

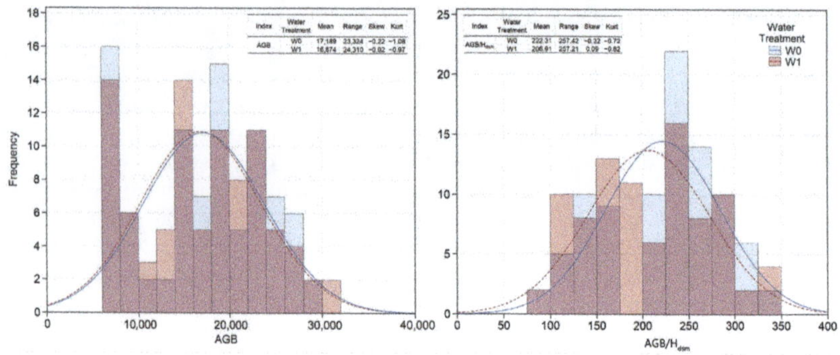

Figure 12. Data characteristics of measured AGB and AGB/H_{dsm} under different water treatments.

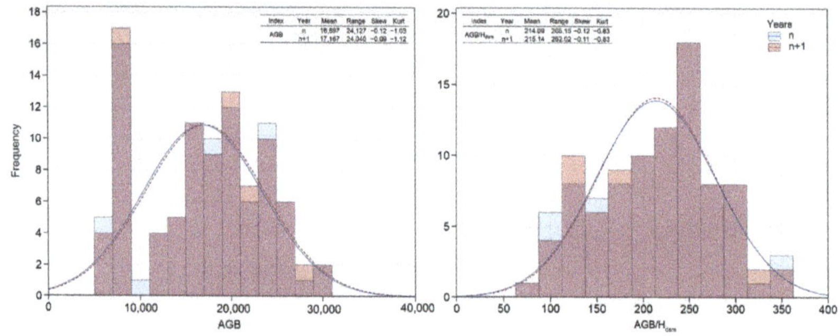

Figure 13. Data characteristics of measured AGB and AGB/H_{dsm} across different years.

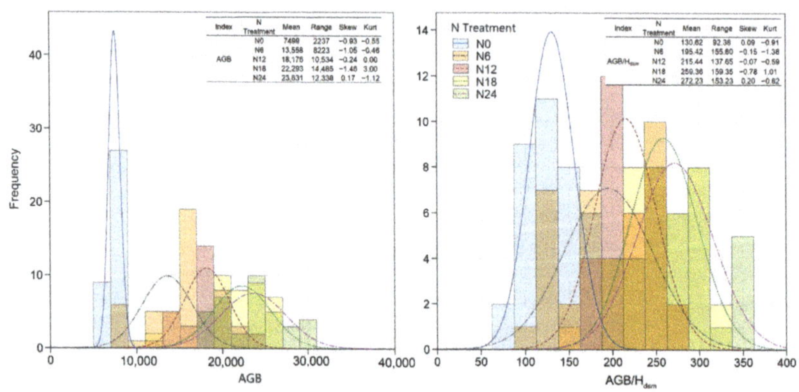

Figure 14. Data characteristics of measured AGB and AGB/H_{dsm} at different N levels.

In this study, the transferability of the proposed AGB estimation model was validated under different water treatments, across different years, and at different N levels. The training dataset synthesized information on winter wheat biomass in the study area during several key growth periods. And the results of the statistical analysis of the training dataset and the test dataset were well fitted. Thus, the AGB estimation model has high accuracy and robustness. Our model also shows better transferability across different water treatments and different year scenarios than across different N levels. In practical applications, a targeted selection of pre-trained models for transferability based on the basic characteristics of the data is more helpful in improving model estimation [44].

4.5. Factors Affecting the Accuracy of Models

In this study, the improved winter wheat AGB estimation model based on plant height has an R^2 of 0.88; although its accuracy is lower than the model accuracy of AGB estimation in cases using a combination of vegetation indices, texture features, and other data [23], this model only requires H_{dsm} information from UAV remote sensing images, which saves index calculation, texture feature extraction, and other steps, thus presenting the characteristics of simplicity and speed. In addition, Steduto et al. [45] and Han et al. [46] concluded that crop water and other resource utilization is constant during most of the growth period of field crops, and the extraction of a single index based on UAV remote sensing images can be used to estimate AGB; in this regard, this study promotes the efficiency and accuracy of crop biomass estimation based on UAV remote sensing images. However, the use of different methods also has some effects on the estimation results of a model [47]. In this study, the BP neural network method was used to construct the AGB estimation model, and the time taken to train the model was 0.044 s. The parameter settings of the model are shown in Table A1. The R^2 and RMSE of the model for the training dataset are 0.89 and 2099.19 kg/hm^2, respectively, while the R^2 and RMSE of the model for the test dataset are 0.88 and 2291.90 kg/hm^2, respectively. Compared with the models developed by Wang et al. [31], the accuracy of the proposed model is better than that of the linear model and the PLSR model, but lower than that of the RF model. This is mainly due to the fact that RF is an ensemble machine learning algorithm wherein multiple indicators are involved and constantly selected when performing model construction, resulting in the improved accuracy of the constructed AGB estimation model, but this method takes more time and increases the complexity of the process when performing the extraction of multiple indicators.

5. Conclusions

In this study, the AGB estimation model of winter wheat was improved by applying different water–N treatments and utilizing plant height information extracted from UAV images. The prediction model for AGB was enhanced by introducing data transformation, and the improved AGB model's R^2, RMSE, and RPD were 0.88, 2291.90 kg/hm^2, and 2.75, respectively. Specifically, R^2 was improved by 51.72% compared to that for the model constructed with H_{dsm}. Our model shows strong estimation and transferability across different nitrogen levels and different year scenarios, but there are variations in transferability under different nitrogen level scenarios. Differences in the statistical characteristics of the employed datasets are the key factor that leads to different transferability of AGB estimation models. This study provides an antecedent for model construction and transferability estimation, and we found that when different datasets have similar histogram characteristics, the constructed model is applicable to new scenarios. However, we should also note that the AGB is affected by many factors and, thus, the accuracy of its estimation model is also related to many factors such as the representativeness of the samples, the vegetation coverage, and the planting density. In this study, we analyzed the effects of factors such as water, year, and N levels on the accuracy of the AGB estimation model, but when building the estimation model, the methods used also influenced the estimation results of the model. Therefore, expanding the training dataset and considering the influencing factors of the constructed AGB model from multiple perspectives will help to further improve the generalization ability and robustness of the AGB model and increase the practical value of the model.

Author Contributions: All authors have made significant contributions to this research. Conceptualization, Y.G., P.W. and Y.J.; writing—original draft preparation, Y.G., J.H., X.Y. and L.W.; experimental design and data curation, Y.J., H.Z., Y.Z. and G.Z.; funding acquisition, Y.G. and L.W.; discussion of results and manuscript revision, Y.G., Z.S. and G.Z. All authors have read and agreed to the published version of the manuscript.

Funding: This research was funded by the National Key R&D Special Projects (Grant no. 2022YFD2001 105), the Outstanding Youth Program of Henan Academy of Agricultural Sciences (Grant no. 2021JQ02), and the Science and Technology Innovation Leading Talent Cultivation Program of the Institute of Agricultural Information Technology, Henan Academy of Agricultural Sciences (Grant no. 2022KJCX01), the Independent innovation projects of Henan Academy of Agricultural Sciences (Grant no. 2023ZC062), and the Agricultural Remote Sensing Innovation Team, Henan Academy of Agricultural Sciences (Grant no. 2024TD28).

Institutional Review Board Statement: Not applicable.

Data Availability Statement: The datasets for this manuscript are not publicly available because our team is working on other publications with them and they are not yet ready for sharing. Requests to access the datasets should be directed to Y.G. at 10914063@zju.edu.cn.

Acknowledgments: We would like to thank Yongzheng Cheng, Hongli Zhang, and Ting Liu for their help in data collection. The authors also thank the editors and the anonymous reviewers for their suggestions on improving the manuscript.

Conflicts of Interest: The authors declare no conflicts of interest.

Appendix A

In this study, BP was performed using a computer with an Intel Core i7-9700K CPU and 64 GB RAM, and the parameter settings are shown in Table A1.

Table A1. Parameters for BP neural network.

Parameters	Parameter Value
Training time	0.044 s
Data slicing	0.5
Data shuffling	No
Cross-validation	30% of dataset
Activation function	identity
Solver	lbfgs
Learning rate	0.1
L2 regular term	1
Number of iterations	1000
Number of neurons in 1st hidden layer	100

References

1. Wang, D.; Li, R.; Zhu, B.; Liu, T.; Sun, C.; Guo, W. Estimation of wheat plant height and biomass by combining UAV imagery and elevation data. *Agriculture* **2023**, *13*, 9. [CrossRef]
2. Zeng, L.; Liu, X.; Li, W.; Ou, J.; Cai, Y.; Chen, G.; Li, M.; Li, G.; Zhang, H.; Xu, X. Global simulation of fine resolution land use/cover change and estimation of aboveground biomass carbon under the shared socioeconomic pathways. *J. Environ. Manag.* **2022**, *312*, 114943. [CrossRef] [PubMed]
3. Piao, S.; Fang, J.; Ciais, P.; Peylin, P.; Huang, Y.; Sitch, S.A.; Wang, T. The carbon balance of terrestrial ecosystems in China. *Nature* **2009**, *458*, 1009–1013. [CrossRef]
4. Bar-On, Y.M.; Phillips, R.; Milo, R. The biomass distribution on Earth. *Proc. Natl. Acad. Sci. USA* **2018**, *115*, 6506–6511. [CrossRef] [PubMed]
5. Wei, M.; Ma, T.; Cao, M.; Wei, B.; Li, C.; Li, C.; Zhang, K.; Fang, Y.; Sun, X. Biomass estimation and characterization of the nutrient components of thinned unripe grapes in China and the global grape industries. *Food Chem. X* **2022**, *15*, 100363. [CrossRef] [PubMed]
6. Zheng, Y.; Zhang, M.; Zhang, X.; Zeng, H.; Wu, B. Mapping winter wheat biomass and yield using time series data blended from PROBA-V 100- and 300-m S1 products. *Remote Sens.* **2016**, *8*, 824. [CrossRef]
7. Alabi, T.R.; Abebe, A.T.; Chigeza, G.; Fowobaje, K.R. Estimation of soybean grain yield from multispectral high-resolution UAV data with machine learning models in West Africa. *Remote Sens. Appl.* **2022**, *27*, 100782. [CrossRef]
8. Zhang, J.; Zhao, Y.; Hu, Z.; Xiao, W. Unmanned aerial system-based wheat biomass estimation using multispectral, structural and meteorological data. *Agriculture* **2023**, *13*, 1621. [CrossRef]
9. Delécolle, R.; Maas, S.J.; Guérif, M.; Baret, F. Remote sensing and crop production models: Present trends. *ISPRS J. Photogr.* **1992**, *47*, 145–161. [CrossRef]

10. Chen, Z.; Wang, J.; Jin, J. Fully automated proximal hyperspectral imaging system for high-resolution and high-quality in vivo soybean phenotyping. *Precis. Agric.* **2023**, *24*, 2395–2415. [CrossRef]
11. Zhu, W.; Sun, Z.; Peng, J.; Huang, Y.; Li, J.; Zhang, J.; Yang, B.; Liao, X. Estimating maize above-ground biomass using 3D point clouds of multi-source unmanned aerial vehicle data at multi-spatial scales. *Remote Sens.* **2019**, *11*, 2678. [CrossRef]
12. Imran, A.B.; Khan, K.; Ali, N.; Ahmad, N.; Ali, A.M.; Shah, K. Narrow band based and broadband derived vegetation indices using Sentinel-2 Imagery to estimate vegetation biomass. *Glob. J. Environ. Sci. Manag.* **2020**, *6*, 97–108.
13. Adar, S.; Sternberg, M.; Paz-Kagan, T.; Henkin, Z.; Dovrat, G.; Zaady, E.; Argaman, E. Estimation of aboveground biomass production using an unmanned aerial vehicle (UAV) and VENμS satellite imagery in Mediterranean and semiarid rangelands. *Remote Sens. Appl.* **2022**, *26*, 100753. [CrossRef]
14. Falcioni, R.; Santos, G.L.A.A.d.; Crusiol, L.G.T.; Antunes, W.C.; Chicati, M.L.; Oliveira, R.B.d.; Demattê, J.A.M.; Nanni, M.R. Non−invasive assessment, classification, and prediction of biophysical parameters using reflectance hyperspectroscopy. *Plants* **2023**, *12*, 2526. [CrossRef]
15. Bendig, J.; Yu, K.; Aasen, H.; Bolten, A.; Bennertz, S.; Broscheit, J.; Gnyp, M.L.; Bareth, G. Combining UAV-based plant height from crop surface models, visible, and near infrared vegetation indices for biomass monitoring in barley. *Int. J. Appl. Earth Obs. Geoinf.* **2015**, *39*, 79–87. [CrossRef]
16. Zhou, Y.; Liu, T.; Batelaan, O.; Duan, L.; Wang, Y.; Li, X.; Li, M. Spatiotemporal fusion of multi-source remote sensing data for estimating aboveground biomass of grassland. *Ecol. Indic.* **2023**, *146*, 109892. [CrossRef]
17. Thomson, A.; Jacobs, J.; Morse-McNabb, E. Comparing the predictive ability of Sentinel-2 multispectral imagery and a proximal hyperspectral sensor for the estimation of pasture nutritive characteristics in an intensive rotational grazing system. *Comput. Electron. Agric.* **2023**, *214*, 108275. [CrossRef]
18. Zou, M.; Liu, Y.; Fu, M.; Li, C.; Zhou, Z.; Meng, H.; Xing, E.; Ren, Y. Combining spectral and texture feature of UAV image with plant height to improve LAI estimation of winter wheat at jointing stage. *Front. Plant Sci.* **2024**, *14*, 1272049. [CrossRef]
19. Fu, Y.; Yang, G.; Song, X.; Li, Z.; Xu, X.; Feng, H.; Zhao, C. Improved estimation of winter wheat aboveground biomass using multiscale textures extracted from UAV-based digital images and hyperspectral feature analysis. *Remote Sens.* **2021**, *13*, 581. [CrossRef]
20. Guo, Y.; He, J.; Huang, J.; Jing, Y.; Xu, S.; Wang, L.; Li, S.; Zheng, G. Effects of the spatial resolution of UAV images on the prediction and transferability of nitrogen content model for winter wheat. *Drones* **2022**, *6*, 299. [CrossRef]
21. Ma, J.; Li, Y.; Chen, Y.; Du, K.; Zheng, F.; Zhang, L.; Sun, Z. Estimating above ground biomass of winter wheat at early growth stages using digital images and deep convolutional neural network. *Eur. J. Agron.* **2019**, *103*, 117–129. [CrossRef]
22. Lu, N.; Zhou, J.; Han, Z.; Li, D.H.; Cao, Q.; Yao, X.; Tian, Y.; Zhu, Y.; Cao, W.; Cheng, T. Improved estimation of aboveground biomass in wheat from RGB imagery and point cloud data acquired with a low-cost unmanned aerial vehicle system. *Plant Methods* **2019**, *15*, 17. [CrossRef] [PubMed]
23. Luo, S.; Jiang, X.; He, Y.; Li, J.; Jiao, W.; Zhang, S.; Xu, F.; Han, Z.; Sun, J.; Yang, J.; et al. Multi-dimensional variables and feature parameter selection for aboveground biomass estimation of potato based on UAV multispectral imagery. *Front. Plant Sci.* **2022**, *13*, 948249. [CrossRef] [PubMed]
24. Singh, R.; Biradar, C.; Behera, M.; Prakash, A.; Das, P.; Mohanta, M.; Krishna, G.; Dogra, A.; Dhyani, S.; Rizvi, J. Optimising carbon fixation through agroforestry: Estimation of aboveground biomass using multi-sensor data synergy and machine learning. *Ecol. Inform.* **2024**, *79*, 102408. [CrossRef]
25. Xie, T.; Li, J.; Yang, C.; Jiang, Z.; Chen, Y.; Guo, L.; Zhang, J. Crop height estimation based on UAV images: Methods, errors, and strategies. *Comput. Electron. Agric.* **2021**, *185*, 106155. [CrossRef]
26. Qiu, R.; Zhang, M.; He, Y. Field estimation of maize plant height at jointing stage using an RGB-D camera. *Crop J.* **2022**, *10*, 1274–1283. [CrossRef]
27. Yang, K.; Mo, J.; Luo, S.; Peng, Y.; Fang, S.; Wu, X.; Zhu, R.; Li, Y.; Yuan, N.; Zhou, C.; et al. Estimation of rice aboveground biomass by UAV imagery with photosynthetic accumulation models. *Plant Phenomics* **2023**, *5*, 0056. [CrossRef]
28. Chang, A.; Jung, J.; Maeda, M.; Landivar, J. Crop height monitoring with digital imagery from Unmanned Aerial System (UAS). *Comput. Electron. Agric.* **2017**, *141*, 232–237. [CrossRef]
29. Watanabe, K.; Guo, W.; Arai, K.; Takanashi, H.; Kajiya-Kanegae, H.; Kobayashi, M.; Yano, K.; Tokunaga, T.; Fujiwara, T.; Tsutsumi, N.; et al. High-throughput phenotyping of sorghum plant height using an unmanned aerial vehicle and its application to genomic prediction modeling. *Front. Plant Sci.* **2017**, *8*, 421. [CrossRef]
30. Luo, S.; Liu, W.; Zhang, Y.; Wang, C.; Xi, X.; Nie, S.; Ma, D.; Lin, Y.; Zhou, G. Maize and soybean heights estimation from unmanned aerial vehicle (UAV) LiDAR data. *Comput Electron Agric.* **2021**, *182*, 106005. [CrossRef]
31. Wang, F.; Yang, M.; Ma, L.; Zhang, T.; Qin, W.; Li, W.; Zhang, Y.; Sun, Z.; Wang, Z.; Li, F.; et al. Estimation of Above-Ground Biomass of Winter Wheat Based on Consumer-Grade Multi-Spectral UAV. *Remote Sens.* **2022**, *14*, 1251. [CrossRef]
32. Niu, Y.X.; Zhang, L.Y.; Zhang, H.H.; Han, W.T.; Peng, X.S. Estimating above-ground biomass of maize using features derived from UAV-based RGB imagery. *Remote Sens.* **2019**, *11*, 1261. [CrossRef]
33. Shu, M.Y.; Li, Q.; Ghafoor, A.; Zhu, J.; Li, B.; Ma, Y. Using the plant height and canopy coverage to estimation maize aboveground biomass with UAV digital images. *Eur. J. Agron.* **2023**, *151*, 126957. [CrossRef]

34. Bareth, G.; Bendig, J.; Tilly, N.; Hoffmeister, D.; Aasen, H.; Bolten, A. A comparison of UAV- and TLS-derived plant height for crop monitoring: Using polygon grids for the analysis of crop surface models (CSMs). *Photogramm. Fernerkun.* **2016**, *2016*, 85–94. [CrossRef]
35. Du, B.; Lund, P.D.; Wang, J.; Kolhe, M.L.; Hu, E. Comparative study of modelling the thermal efficiency of a novel straight through evacuated tube collector with MLR, SVR, BP and RBF methods. *Sustain. Energy Technol.* **2021**, *44*, 101029. [CrossRef]
36. Lan, W.Q.; Yang, X.; Gong, T.S.; Xie, J. Predicting the shelf life of Trachinotus ovatus during frozen storage using a back propagation (BP) neural network model. *Aquac. Fish.* **2023**, *8*, 544–550. [CrossRef]
37. Tang, X.; Liu, H.; Feng, D.; Zhang, W.; Chang, J.; Li, L.; Yang, L. Prediction of field winter wheat yield using fewer parameters at middle growth stage by linear regression and the BP neural network method. *Eur. J. Agron.* **2022**, *141*, 126621. [CrossRef]
38. Li, H. *Machine Learning Method*; Tsinghua University Press: Beijing, China, 2022. (In Chinese)
39. Zhou, Z.H. *Machine Learning*; Tsinghua University Press: Beijing, China, 2022. (In Chinese)
40. Chang, C.; Laird, D.A.; Mausbach, M.J.; Hurburgh, C.R. Near-infrared reflectance spectroscopy–principal components regression analyses of soil properties. *Soil Sci. Soc. Am. J.* **2001**, *65*, 480–490. [CrossRef]
41. Mireei, S.A.; Mohtasebi, S.S.; Massudi, R.; Rafiee, S.; Arabanian, A.S.; Berardinelli, A. Non-destructive measurement of moisture and soluble solids content of mazafati date fruit by NIR spectroscopy. *Aust. J. Crop Sci.* **2010**, *4*, 175–179.
42. Wang, J.; Chen, Y.; Feng, W.; Yu, H.; Huang, M.; Yang, Q. Transfer learning with dynamic distribution adaptation. *ACM Trans. Intell. Syst. Technol.* **2019**, *11*, 1–25. [CrossRef]
43. Li, C.G.; Zhang, B.; Zhao, Q.; Cheng, X.P.; WANG, X.F. Empathy prediction from texts based on transfer learning. *J. Comput. Appl.* **2022**, *42*, 3603–3609. (In Chinese)
44. Zhu, W.; Braun, B.; Chiang, L.H.; Romagnoli, J.A. Investigation of transfer learning for image classification and impact on training sample size. *Chemom. Intell. Lab.* **2021**, *211*, 104269. [CrossRef]
45. Steduto, P.; Albrizio, R. Resource use efficiency of field-grown sunflower, sorghum, wheat and chickpea: II. Water use efficiency and comparison with radiation use efficiency. *Agric. For. Meteorol.* **2005**, *130*, 269–281. [CrossRef]
46. Han, W.T.; Tang, J.D.; Zhang, L.Y.; Niu, Y.X.; Wang, T.H. Maize water use efficiency and biomass estimation based on unmanned aerial vehicle remote sensing. *Trans. CSAM* **2021**, *52*, 129–141. (In Chinese)
47. Xu, W.K.; Zhao, L.G.; Li, J.; Shang, X.P.; Ding, X.P.; Wang, T.W. Detection and classification of tea buds based on deep learning. *Comput. Electron. Agric.* **2022**, *192*, 106547. [CrossRef]

MDPI AG
Grosspeteranlage 5
4052 Basel
Switzerland
Tel.: +41 61 683 77 34

Agriculture Editorial Office
E-mail: agriculture@mdpi.com
www.mdpi.com/journal/agriculture

www.ingramcontent.com/pod-product-compliance
Lightning Source LLC
Chambersburg PA
CBHW061616220926
51850CB00005B/524
* 9 7 8 3 7 2 5 8 6 8 1 4 8 *